European Distance and E-Learning Network Annual Conference (EDEN 2019)

Connecting through Educational Technology to Produce Effective Learning Environments

Bruges, Belgium
16 – 19 June 2019

Editors:

Airina Volungeviciene
Andras Szucs

ISBN: 978-1-7138-2382-7

Printed from e-media with permission by:

Curran Associates, Inc.
57 Morehouse Lane
Red Hook, NY 12571

Some format issues inherent in the e-media version may also appear in this print version.

European Distance and E-Learning Network (EDEN)
Budapest University of Technology & Economics
H-1111 Budapest, Egry J. u.1.
Hungary

secretariat@eden-online.org

Additional copies of this publication are available from:

Curran Associates, Inc.
57 Morehouse Lane
Red Hook, NY 12571 USA
Phone: 845-758-0400
Fax: 845-758-2633
Email: curran@proceedings.com
Web: www.proceedings.com

EDEN 2019 ANNUAL Conference

Connecting through Educational Technology

to produce effective learning environments

EDEN 2019 Annual Conference

Bruges, Belgium

16-19 June 2019

CONFERENCE PROCEEDINGS

Edited by

Airina Volungeviciene, András Szűcs
on behalf of the European Distance and E-Learning Network

European Distance and E-Learning Network, 2019

EDEN 2019 Annual Conference
Bruges, Belgium

Published by the European Distance and E-Learning Network

Editors:
Airina Volungeviciene
András Szűcs

Editorial co-ordination:
Judit Kőműves

Conference organised in collaboration with

Principal Sponsor

Conference Publication Sponsor

Conference Sponsors

Supported by the Erasmus+ Programme of the European Union
The publication reflects the authors' view, the EACEA and the European Commission are not responsible for any use that may be made of the information it contains.

Introduction

Connecting through Educational Technology – to produce Effective Learning Environments

Technology is with us everywhere which validates the horizontal-holistic approach for imperative questions of the period. For the transforming education landscape, challenges come increasingly from the socio-cultural-economic, structural and policy fields. Education has to be visionary to reach efficiency gains, new sources – and to offer sustainable services, reflecting the complexity of modern societies.

Market realities put similar pressures on the corporate and University worlds. Stakeholders expect academia to respond to needs beyond teaching and research, better promote innovation and the knowledge economy, manage the new student populations. Universities are expected to detect and attract talents, be magnet of inputs from practitioners, resulting cooperative surplus.

Vocationalisation of education also means the emergence of new skill sets. The progress in industrial automation and ICTs opens possibilities for lifelong learning resources, for work based learning and integration of human-machine intelligence models.

Educational technologies are about connections among information, knowledge, action, emotion and value: knowledge construction, learning activities by sharing and thinking, interactivity, aggregative mechanisms, cooperation and integration – to meet the requirements of the knowledge age, to satisfy the needs of social transformation and learning innovation.

New generation of learning technologies and networks are ubiquitous, embedded and mobile which reshape access to and delivery of learning. Cutting edge fields are artificial intelligence, learning analytics, micro-learning, new credentialing, revolution of assessment, massive open online courses (MOOCs), personalized learning, game-based learning, flipped classroom, Digital Makerspaces and alike.

> *The questions remain: Which one(s) of these will have significant and sustained impact in the future? Can the network society become an enhanced learning society? How can information and communication technology in the age of Industry 4.0 create and enhance synergies between online learning programmes, the increased diversity of stakeholders, the workplace experience, socio-cultural influences and students' work-life balance?*

EDEN is pleased to welcome again at its 2019 Annual Conference the scholars, practitioners, experts from Europe and all around the world in Bruges to discuss the issues of Connecting through Educational Technology.

Major themes of the Conference included:

- *Global connections*: How to organise online study programmes that enhance the students' competences, provide connections with international partners and promote virtual mobility?
- *Connections with workplace*: How can innovative study programmes be developed to involve the workplace impact and experience (virtual dual learning, (distance/digital) internships)?
- *Connections with the community*: How to organise study programmes that focus on relations of curriculum, delivery and the socio-economic environment?
- *Connection with learners*: Caring about the work-life balance of the students, attentive to learners' needs, expectations and the changing behaviour of diverse student populations.

Andras Szucs	Sylke Vandercruysse	Airina Volungeviciene
Secretary General	VIVES University of Applied Sciences	President, EDEN

Acknowledgement and thanks are given to the Programme and Evaluation Committee

Airina Volungeviciene, EDEN President, Vytautas Magnus University, Lithuania
Isabel Vanslembrouck, Director of the Research Unit, VIVES University of Applied Sciences, Belgium

Diana Andone, Politehnica University of Timisoara, Romania

Ulrich Bernath, Ulrich Bernath Foundation for Research in ODL, Germany

Lisa Marie Blaschke, Carl von Ossietzky University of Oldenburg, Germany

Mark Brown, National Institute for Digital Learning, Dublin City University, Ireland

Elena Caldirola, University of Pavia, Italy

Helga Dorner, Central European University, Hungary

Josep Maria Duart, Universitat Oberta de Catalunya (UOC), Spain

Ulf-Daniel Ehlers, Co-Operative State University Baden-Wurttemberg (DHBW), Germany

Kurt Galle, VIVES University of Applied Sciences, Belgium

Rebecca Galley, The Open University, United Kingdom

Sandra Kucina Softic, University of Zagreb, Croatia

Mark Nichols, The Open University, United Kingdom

Don Olcott Jr., Carl von Ossietzky University of Oldenburg, Germany

Ebba Ossiannilsson, Swedish Association of Distance Education, Sweden

Wim Van Petegem, Katholieke Universiteit Leuven, Belgium

Antonella Poce, University Roma III, Italy

Timothy Read, National University of Distance Education (UNED), Spain

Alfredo Soeiro, University of Porto, Portugal

Andras Szucs, Secretary General, EDEN, United Kingdom

Ferenc Tatrai, EDEN, United Kingdom

Leen Thys, VIVES University of Applied Sciences, Belgium

Sylke Vandercruysse, VIVES University of Applied Sciences, Belgium

Delphine Wante, VIVES University of Applied Sciences, Belgium

TABLE OF CONTENTS

INSTITUTIONAL INNOVATION: STRATEGY AND PRACTICE

LEARNING AND TRAINING FOR WORK: CONCEPT AND IMPLEMENTATION

DIGITAL LEARNING THEORY AND GOVERNANCE

SOCIO-CULTURAL FEATURES OF ICT ENHANCED LEARNING

COLLABORATIVE LEARNING IN ONLINE ENVIRONMENTS

QUALITY, ASSESSMENT AND EVALUATION

LEARNER PERCEPTIONS, CHARACTERISTICS AND ATTITUDES

POLICY DEVELOPMENT IN ORGANIZATIONS

MOOCS: ENRICHING AND CONSOLIDATING THE EXPERIENCE

SELECTED LEADING RESEARCH AND INNOVATION CASES

INTERNATIONAL AND NATIONAL LEARNING DEVELOPMENT CASES

OPEN EDUCATION RESOURCES – STRATEGY AND PRACTICE

TEACHERS PROFESSIONAL EDUCATION AND ICTS

APPLICATIONS OF GAMES AND NEW ICT TOOLS IN EDUCATION

POSTERS

Connecting through Educational Technology
Proceedings of the European Distance and E-Learning Network 2019 Annual Conference
Bruges, 16-19 June, 2019

IMPLEMENTATION OF A FLEXIBLE LEARNING STUDY PROGRAMME IN A BLENDED-LEARNING DESIGN: RESULTS FROM THE FIRST TWO COHORTS

Claude Müller, Reinhild Fengler, Zurich University of Applied Sciences, Switzerland

Abstract

Zurich University of Applied Sciences (ZHAW) launched the flexible learning study format FLEX, a blended learning design allowing students increased flexibility as to when and where they study. FLEX reduces classroom time by about half, while adding an e-learning environment for self-study that includes instructional videos. An analysis of the first two cohorts in the assessment level showed that the new study format was broadly accepted and that students using the FLEX format achieved exam results equivalent to students in the conventional learning format.

Introduction

Our society is subject to a constant process of transformation, and flexibility plays an increasingly important role in various areas of life. Examples of this include flexible working hours and high availability at work, new family models, and, particularly in the tertiary sector, highly mobile and globalized learners. In this context, more flexibility is expected from universities, and in recent years, flexible learning has come into the focus of pedagogical quality development. Initially established in the USA in the 1970s, interest in flexible learning has steadily developed, which is reflected in an increasing number of publications in this field (Li & Wong, 2018). Current discussions about the digitalization of education are also strongly influenced by the concept of flexible learning, hence the expressions *flexible learning, digital learning, blended learning*, and *distance learning* are often used synonymously.

Flexible learning is a broad term with different interpretations (Boer & Collis, 2005; Li & Wong, 2018). In general, flexible learning is intended to meet the diverse needs of learners and enable them to take more responsibility for the learning process (Wade, 1994). Learners and their needs are at the heart of flexible learning, and study programmes should give them the opportunity to make their own decisions regarding how they learn. The British Higher Education Academy describes this concept as "flexible learning is about empowering students by offering them choices in how, what, when and where they learn: the pace, place and mode of delivery" (HEA, 2015; p.1).

From a pedagogical point of view, different dimensions of flexible learning can be identified. According to the frequently quoted article by Chen (2003), flexible learning requires flexibility in at least one of the following learning dimensions: time, place, pace, learning style, content, assessment, or learning path. Li and Wong (2018) analysed previous publications and found similar components of flexible learning: time, content, entry requirement, delivery, instructional approach, assessment, resource and support, and orientation and goal. These dimensions provide a framework for orientation with respect to the aspects of flexible learning and offer an opportunity to assess the degree of flexibility of a study program. Nowadays, flexible learning is mainly realized through the use of new technologies (Tucker & Morris, 2012). However, the dimensions mentioned above show that flexible learning is much more than just the use of new technologies (Li & Wong, 2018). New technologies, however, serve as important enablers with which flexible learning environments can be designed.

Whether flexible learning leads to equivalent learning outcomes compared with traditional learning approaches has received little attention so far. The current meta-analyses on blended learning (Bernard, Borokhovski, Schmid, Tamim, & Abrami, 2014; Means, Toyama, Murphy, & Baki, 2013; Vo, Zhu, & Diep, 2017) are the best indicators. They find a moderate but significant positive effect of blended learning compared with face-to-face instruction. The problem is that these studies usually do not indicate whether traditional teaching is supplemented by e-learning or replaced. Confounding factors such as additional learning resources, additional learning time, or more/different interactions with the instructor could thus contribute to positive outcomes for blended learning. The authors of the meta-analysis mentioned above concluded that further controlled experimental research is needed to investigate the outcomes of blended learning (Bernard et al., 2014), and that tested design principles must be developed for blended learning (Means et al., 2013).

This paper analyses these issues from a learner's perspective. The following research questions are addressed:

- What are student perceptions of the blended learning format FLEX?
- Does a blended learning design with reduced face-to-face time by half influence the effectiveness of learning?

First, the flexible learning programme FLEX is used as an example to illustrate objectives and considerations when implementing flexible learning in a blended learning design. Then, the research design of the FLEX study program is introduced. Finally, the results are presented and discussed.

Implementation of the FLEX Study Program

The ZHAW School of Management and Law (SML) launched a new study format for flexible learning (FLEX) in 2015 as part of its comprehensive e-learning strategy. The Bachelor's in Business Administration with a Specialization in Banking and Finance (BSc BA BF), a successful and established programme, was selected as the first to be offered in the FLEX study format. The BSc BA BF is already taught in a full-time (FT) and part-time (PT) format. Accordingly, the FLEX format was the third study format for this degree program. The programs have two levels: In the first, the assessment level (first-year studies for full-time students, first three semesters for part-time and FLEX students) worth 60 ECTS (European Credit Transfer System), basic knowledge for the programme is taught. Then in the second section of the programme, 66 ECTS are awarded for the specialization in banking & finance and 54 ECTS for general business management topics. In the part-time programme, classroom sessions are held on one weekday and a maximum of two evenings and/or Saturday mornings every week during the 14-week semester, while the FLEX format schedules classroom lessons for two days approximately every three weeks during the semester. Full-time programmes are normally conducted in six semesters, while part-time and FLEX programmes take eight semesters to complete. For part-time studies (including FLEX), a maximum vocational employment level of 60% is recommended. The concept of the new FLEX study format was developed in 2014 and tested in a business administration course. After a positive evaluation of the pilot module (Müller, Stahl, Alder, & Müller, 2018), the transformation of a total of 34 courses for the BSc BA BF study programme was conducted. The first cohort of the FLEX study programme will graduate in 2019.

The primary objective of the newly introduced FLEX format is to offer students the best possible opportunity to combine a study program with professional and personal responsibilities. Regarding the number and distribution of face-to-face lessons over the 14-week semester, compatibility with a distant place of residence was the guiding principle, e.g., how many overnight stays away from home would be acceptable for potential students. At the same time, regular face-to-face sessions encourage reflection on the course content developed during the online phases. As a result of these considerations, on-site classroom teaching for FLEX was reduced by about half compared with the part-time programme and replaced with online sessions every three weeks. This means that FLEX students attend the campus every three weeks for two days and the interjacent self-study phase allows them to learn flexibly concerning time and place, and to follow their preferred learning path. The selected 49% face-to-face time corresponds with the current state of empirical knowledge regarding blended learning, namely that with an online ratio of between one third and one half, learning success is higher than for blended learning with a smaller online proportion (Owston & York, 2018).

After the time structure for the new course of study had been determined, the transition to the flexible learning format was carried out at course level. In so-called *scripting workshops*, the courses were redesigned according to a defined process using a specially developed didactic visualization language. In the online self-study phase, web-based technologies such as LMS Moodle and other tools are used, and the information is provided in digital form, mainly using learning videos produced in-house. Lecturers create videos for their courses because it is crucial that the content is presented at the appropriate student skill level to enable an exact fit of the self-study phase and the face-to-face phase. A new studio was set up to produce high-quality educational videos, and lecturers receive technical and didactical support. So as not to leave the students alone with an abundance of online learning resources, they are provided with a task plan as guidance for each self-study phase, especially for the assessment level of the curriculum. With regard to the dimensions of flexible learning according to Chen (2003), the FLEX format offers greater flexibility in terms of time, place, pace, learning style, and learning path than the conventional study format, but not in terms of assessment and content, which are identical in the FLEX and conventional study formats. As a result, FLEX students take the same examinations at the same time as students in both the full-time and part-time programmes, which allows for a comparison of the exam results with high empirical significance.

Research Design and Methodology

The research design consists of the first two cohorts of the experimental group FLEX (cohort 15, $N = 28$; cohort 16, $N = 28$) with students attending all courses in the new FLEX format and the corresponding cohorts of the control group PT (cohort 15, $N = 100$; cohort 16, $N = 117$). All the students were from the first-year intake, and eligibility requirements, lecture content, exam questions, and grading scale were identical for all students in all courses. For the assessment level (the first three semesters), an analysis was conducted to determine how the students evaluated the learning environment and to what extent the results of the end-of-semester examinations of the experimental and control groups differed from one another. An initial survey was conducted to determine student profiles in order to assess whether deviations in the examination results were primarily due to the learning format or because a cohort was different in some other way. The research design was tightly controlled for a field study in an educational area, firstly because the framework conditions were comparable owing to the same learning objectives and identical assessment and, secondly, because the presence of a control group ensured a quasi-experimental design (see also Fraenkel, Wallen, & Hyun, 2015).

Analysis of the student profiles in the initial survey showed that most students in the FLEX programme came from the greater Zurich area, with the proportion of students coming from outside being higher in the FLEX programme than in the part-time format. As far as professional employment was concerned, almost all part-time students and all FLEX students were employed, with a high average level of employment of 70% (PT) and 79% (FLEX) respectively. Employers tended to support FLEX students by providing a high degree of flexibility in working hours. For example, students were allowed to reduce their working hours during the semester for exam preparation and to work more during the semester breaks. However, no working time could be used for studying. The results concerning the affinity to teamwork were also interesting. FLEX students saw fewer opportunities to learn from others than part-time students and preferred to spend more time learning alone. FLEX students differed significantly from part-time students in terms of teamwork affinity ($p = 0.01$). Regarding ICT literacy, the results showed that both part-time and FLEX students felt secure or very secure when using computers, software, or the Internet. However, FLEX students rated their ICT competence across all items significantly better ($p = 0.00$) than part-time students.

Results

Student Perceptions

At the SML, standardized student evaluations at course level are carried out at the end of each semester, when indicators such as course structure, teaching, or content quality are assessed. With an average of 3.18 across all FLEX fall semester 2015 and 2016 courses (on a 4-level scale, with 4 being the highest value), the global indicator, in which all factors are combined, showed very similar values to PT (3.20). However, at course level, there were considerable variations between the years and study formats. It is, therefore, difficult to assess the acceptance of the new study format based on the results of the student evaluation since year-specific characteristics (e.g., changes in lecturers) may have a strong influence. Together with the qualitative feedback from FLEX students in both years, however, it can be concluded that students generally accepted the FLEX format.

The survey also proved that the investment in setting up a video studio for the production of short learning videos was perceived as very positive. "Watching learning videos" was described by all students in all FLEX cohorts as the most beneficial activity for learning (see Cohort 15 in Figure 1).

Of course, there are also difficulties in learning in the FLEX format, reflecting problems described in the literature (Samarawickrema, 2005). These lie mainly in self-motivation and also time management: "time management and finding time for self-study" (22_160115), or in the combination of both: "in the beginning, I learned more, and now I postpone it more and more" (18_160215). One student emphasizes the difficulties of the FLEX format with comprehension problems: "Very complex topics are difficult; you can't ask the questions face to face" (17_160216). It seems that offering regular asynchronous and synchronous discussions in forums and online meetings cannot completely replace face-to-face sessions.

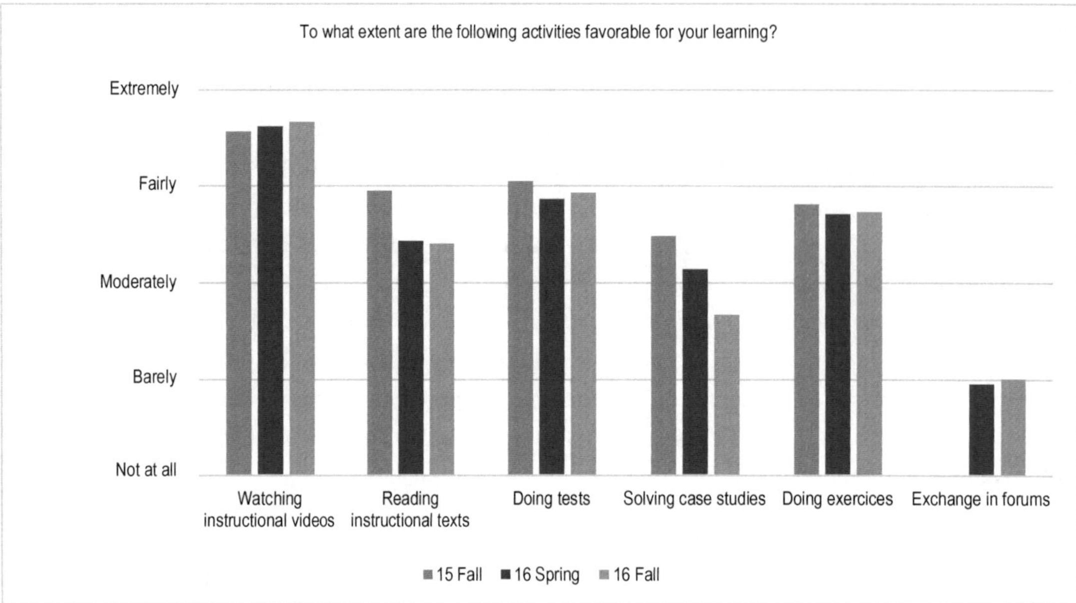

Figure 1. Effectiveness of different learning activities assessed by cohort FLEX 15 (n=16).

Learning Effectiveness

The following Tables 1 and 2 list the exam results of Cohort 15 (beginning in Fall Semester 2015) and Cohort 16 (beginning in Fall Semester 2016) for the assessment level (Semesters 1-3). The exam results of the FLEX students (FLEX) are compared with those of the BF students from the part-time programme (PT). Assessment is identical in all courses and the exams are not corrected by the lecturer of the respective class but by an independent pool of lecturers. In "Business Management Skills" a group project paper is graded by the class teacher. Due to the lower reliability of the assessment, this course is not included in the comparison. The FLEX and PT samples are independent, and the sample size and histograms of the test results do not indicate a violation of the requirements of normal distribution and uniformity of variance.

Table 1: Statistical Analysis of Course Grades FLEX and PT Assessment Level, Cohort 15

	FLEX format (FLEX)			Part-time format (PT)				
Courses (Semester)	*N*	*M*	*SD*	*N*	*M*	*SD*	*d*	*p*
Business Administration (1)	27	4.24	0.53	93	4.17	0.67	0.12	0.60
Mathematics 1 (1)	27	4.19	0.90	92	4.11	0.76	0.10	0.66
Business Law (1)	28	4.23	0.88	92	4.15	0.90	0.10	0.66
Marketing (1)	28	4.18	0.56	94	4.29	0.50	-0.22	0.31
Mathematics 2 (2)	21	4.31	0.73	81	4.23	0.83	0.09	0.71
Business English 1 (2)	18	4.50	0.64	83	4.33	0.73	0.24	0.35
Financial Accounting (2)	20	4.08	0.78	79	4.25	0.79	-0.22	0.39
Strategy (3)	21	4.83	0.53	78	4.82	0.68	0.02	0.94
Communication (3)	20	4.20	0.66	76	4.11	0.65	0.15	0.56
Microeconomics (3)	21	3.71	0.73	74	3.74	0.76	-0.04	0.88
Business English 2 (3)	19	4.58	0.51	75	4.43	0.60	0.26	0.31

Note: * $\alpha = 0.05$ (two-tailed)

The results for Cohort 15 (see Table 1) show that the mean values differ only slightly. The direction is indicated by the effect size (Cohen's *d*); in 8 of the 11 courses examined, the mean values of the FLEX cohort are higher than those of the PT students (positive sign, range of marks from 1-6, where 6 is the best performance, and all grades below 4 are unsatisfactory). The results of the t-test do not show any significant differences in the exam results between FLEX and PT students. At this point, it should be mentioned that this outcome is not a proof of equivalence. In general, a non-significant result cannot be clear proof of the correctness of a null hypothesis (Schmidt & Hunter, 1997).

To consider a possible bias at the entry competence level of the first FLEX cohort, the exam results of the second year (Cohort 16) were also analysed (see Table 2). Cohort 16 of the FLEX format also has higher mean values than the control group of PT students (in 8 out of 11 courses). For the three courses "Business Law" ($t(139) = 2.23$, $p = 0.028$, with effect size Cohen's $d = 0.47$), "Business English 1" ($t(117) = 2.04$, $p = 0.044$, $d = 0.47$), and "Business English 2" ($t(110) = 2.07$, $p = 0.041$, $d = 0.48$) significant differences can be observed. FLEX students achieved significantly better exam results in these courses compared with PT students.

In summary, it can be concluded that students in the assessment level of the FLEX format achieve exam results equivalent to students in the part-time format.

Table 2: Statistical Analysis of Course Grades FLEX and PT Assessment Level, Cohort 16

	FLEX format (FLEX)			Part-time format (PT)				
Courses (Semester)	*N*	*M*	*SD*	*N*	*M*	*SD*	*d*	*p*
Business Administration (1)	28	4.23	0.74	117	4.25	0.70	-0.03	0.89
Mathematics 1 (1)	28	4.04	0.82	108	3.79	0.79	0.31	0.14
Business Law (1)	28	4.34	0.72	113	3.98	0.78	0.47	0.03*
Marketing (1)	28	4.14	0.54	110	4.20	0.67	-0.09	0.68
Mathematics 2 (2)	23	3.98	0.70	96	3.68	1.02	0.31	0.18
Business English 1 (2)	24	4.71	0.78	95	4.31	0.87	0.47	0.04*
Financial Accounting (2)	22	4.50	0.67	91	4.26	0.92	0.28	0.25
Strategy (3)	23	4.70	0.42	90	4.41	0.67	0.45	0.06
Communication (3)	22	4.14	0.47	90	4.01	0.67	0.21	0.39
Microeconomics (3)	22	4.07	0.54	87	4.08	0.97	-0.01	0.95
Business English 2 (3)	23	4.59	0.56	89	4.24	0.76	0.48	0.04*

Note: * $\alpha = 0.05$ (two-tailed)

Discussion

The ZHAW School of Management and Law is currently transforming an entire study programme into a flexible learning format with the aim of providing more flexibility in terms of time and location. In the blended learning study programme Banking & Finance FLEX, on-site teaching has been reduced by about half and replaced by three-week online phases. The FLEX results confirm previous findings regarding blended learning (see, e.g., Bernard et al., 2014; Means et al., 2013; Vo et al., 2017) which show that students in blended learning courses produce at least equivalent or even slightly better exam results compared with students in face-to-face courses. However, a selection bias in the selection of the study format, i.e., that systematically high-performing students opt for the FLEX programme, cannot be ruled out and must be examined more closely in future research.

Since, in addition to student performance, student satisfaction is also high, it can be concluded that the implementation of the FLEX programme has succeeded in creating an effective learning environment and a satisfactory learning mode for students. This is almost certainly due to the relatively high investment made to meet the requirements of a successful change. Initially, a strategy and vision were formulated, and the transformation was materially and technically supported, including substantial investment in the technical infrastructure.

The FLEX format makes it easier to combine work and study. This is demonstrated by very high employment levels among FLEX students. According to feedback from lecturers and students, this means that learning time and thus the learning activities are concentrated in the time immediately before examinations. FLEX students say they want even more time flexibility in their learning process, i.e., they are provided with as many learning resources as possible without time restrictions or formal conditions and that they can freely decide when they want to learn and with what for optimal exam preparation. Lecturers, on the other hand, have difficulty with this "learning-to-the-test behaviour" and sometimes criticize a lack of commitment to learning and insufficient attendance. Some lecturers would like to have more control, such as being able to set compulsory assignments or tests. Other lecturers view their courses more as a learning opportunity and would like to let students decide how to use it. Therefore, in the future, the presence of students in the face-to-face and online phases should be examined more closely. It needs to be clarified what significance this has for the learning success (Schulmeister, 2017) and how students can be best supported with appropriate incentives and measures (or their combination) to activate learning processes in a flexible study programme.

References

Bernard, R. M., Borokhovski, E., Schmid, R. F., Tamim, R. M., & Abrami, P. C. (2014). A meta-analysis of blended learning and technology use in higher education: from the general to the applied. *Journal of Computing in Higher Education, 26*(1), 87-122. doi:10.1007/s12528-013-9077-3

Boer, W. d., & Collis, B. (2005). Becoming more systematic about flexible learning: beyond time and distance. *ALT-J, 13*(1), 33-48. doi:10.1080/0968776042000339781

Chen, D.-T. (2003). Uncovering the provisos behind flexible learning. *Educational Technology & Society, 6*(2), 25-30.

Fraenkel, J. R., Wallen, N. E., & Hyun, H. H. (2015). *How to design and evaluate research in education* (9th ed.). New York: McGraw-Hill.

HEA (2015). *Framework for flexible learning in higher education.* Retrieved from https://www.heacademy.ac.uk/system/files/downloads/flexible-learning-in-HE.pdf

Li, K. C., & Wong, B. Y. Y. (2018). Revisiting the Definitions and Implementation of Flexible Learning. In K. C. Li, K. S. Yuen, & B. T. M. Wong (Eds.), *Innovations in Open and Flexible Education* (pp. 3-13). Singapore: Springer Singapore.

Means, B., Toyama, Y., Murphy, R., & Baki, M. (2013). The Effectiveness of Online and Blended Learning: A Meta-Analysis of the Empirical Literature. *Teachers College Record, 115*(3), 1-47. Retrieved from http://www.tcrecord.org/Content.asp?ContentId=16882

Müller, C., Stahl, M., Alder, M., & Müller, M. (2018). Learning Effectiveness and Students' Perceptions in a Flexible Learning Course. *European Journal of Open, Distance and E-learning, 21*(2), 44-53.

Owston, R., & York, D. N. (2018). The nagging question when designing blended courses: Does the proportion of time devoted to online activities matter? *The Internet and Higher Education, 36*(Supplement C), 22-32. https://doi.org/10.1016/j.iheduc.2017.09.001

Samarawickrema, R. G. (2005). Determinants of student readiness for flexible learning: Some preliminary findings. *Distance Education, 26*(1), 49-66.

Schmidt, F. L., & Hunter, J. E. (1997). Eight Common but False Objections to Discontinuation of Significance Testing in the Analysis of Research Data. In L. L. Harlow, S. A. Mulaik, & J. H. Steiger (Eds.), *What if there were no significance tests?* (pp. 37-64). Mahwah, N.J.: Lawrence Erlbaum Associates Publishers.

Schulmeister, R. (2017). Presence and Self-Study in Blended Learning. *eleed, 12*(1).

Tucker, R., & Morris, G. (2012). By Design: Negotiating Flexible Learning in the Built Environment Discipline. *Research in Learning Technology, 20*(1), n1.

Vo, H. M., Zhu, C., & Diep, N. A. (2017). The effect of blended learning on student performance at course-level in higher education: A meta-analysis. *Studies in Educational Evaluation, 53*(Supplement C), 17-28. https://doi.org/10.1016/j.stueduc.2017.01.002

Wade, W. (1994). Introduction. In W. Wade, K. Hodgkinson, A. Smith, & J. Arfield (Eds.), *Flexible Learning in Higher Education* (pp. 12-17). Abdington: Routledge.

EXPLORING STUDENTS CULTURAL EXPERIENCES IN AN INTERNATIONAL LEARNING PROJECT USING DIGITAL REALITY – TALKTECH

Diana Andone, Politehnica University of Timisoara, Romania, Mark Frydenberg, Bentley University, United States of America

Introduction

Digital reality (augmented and virtual reality and other immersive multimedia experiences) have brought about new forms of engagement in a variety of industries in recent years as advances in mobile technologies have raised awareness and usage of these technologies. VR provides a computer-generated simulation of a three-dimensional environment, which seems very real to the person experiencing it. By wearing a special headset or goggles, the user achieves a state of awareness of being present in that virtual environment. Some headsets such as those manufactured by Microsoft, HTC and Oculus offer high-resolution displays to provide immersive experiences for their users. Inexpensive VR viewers require users to insert their smartphones into the viewers to experience VR content.

In an immersive learning environment, "the learner is promoted from an observer of the synthetic world to one of its inhabitants. Immersion promises learners new access to experience." (Jacobson, 2018). The use of augmented and virtual reality technologies has increased the popularity and accessibility of immersive learning environments across the curriculum.

Stewart and Dansie conclude that "immersive media is the future of teaching" (Stewart & Dansie, 2018) including AR and VR among other new media technologies. Immersive technologies enable students to experience effective intercultural collaboration. Computer-based video and serious games have been found to help learners acquire cultural proficiency. (Fulmore, 2015; Johnson, 2009) As universities continue to incorporate themes of globalization in their curricula, the ability to collaborate and communicate internationally becomes increasingly relevant.

This paper describes the results of TalkTech 2018(TalkTech: An Exploration of Technology, Digital Media, and Culture across Continents, 2019), a learning collaborative study, which since 2008, has paired students at universities in the United State and in Romania, to research and discuss current technologies. The earliest TalkTech projects required students to use what then, were new online tools for collaboration and communication; recordings of those conversations were the deliverables for the project. As student familiarity with online collaboration and communication tools (and the tools, themselves, evolved) the project became more complex. Now the tools (often Skype, Facebook Messenger, Google docs and email) that facilitate and enable collaboration and communication in the global economy enable students today to complete projects and create deliverables that are much more complex than what their peers might have produced in earlier years of the TalkTech project. Since 2017, the students have applied their knowledge and digital skills to create and share digital reality content (Andone & Frydenberg, 2019; Frydenberg & Andone, 2018b; 2018a) that conveys cultural landmarks in each other's home countries. Students must choose appropriate tools to communicate with their partners and manage the project.

TalkTech 2018

Globalization means that we will be increasingly connecting with diverse individuals even if we stay at home (Yook & Turner, 2018; p.380). The TalkTech project adds a global perspective to the digital and information literacy curriculum by pairing students Bentley University enrolled in IT 101, introduction to information technology, with fourth-year students at University Politehnica of Timisoara (UPT) enrolled in a Technology of Multimedia course to explore uses of virtual reality. Each team determines how to communicate using web-based collaboration and communication tools, as they create VR experiences for their partners that present locations of cultural interest in their home cities. Locations for TalkTech 2018 included bus or train stations, places of worship, coffee shops, museum exhibits, historic buildings, outdoor markets, public squares, historical statues, sporting venues, and retail establishments. Students navigate the challenges of no in-person meetings and significant time differences as they. work together for 8 weeks during the Fall 2018 semester to complete the project. At the end of the semester, students share their VR scenes with their partners, and then discuss cultural similarities and differences during a video call.

Rather than using readily available VR content, students create their own immersive learning environments for their international partners, developing their own VR scenes using called CoSpaces EDU (cospaces.edu). The process of researching a cultural landmark, creating and communicating that experience in a VR scene, consuming similar content created by international partners, discussing similarities and differences requires students to interact globally as they them to interact with and fuse digital content, images, and information into a tangible product that provides evidence of their learning and proclivity with digital reality technologies Team members write blog posts in which they reflect on their own experiences as members of an international team, and how they and their group worked through problems and challenges. Students also created Augmented Reality (AR) content to share information about their landmarks and locations using a variety of AR apps such as ROAR, Blippar, and HP Reveal. The TalkTech project requires students to apply their digital skills as they become creators of deeply engaging digital reality content.

To evaluate the students' work for a course grade, both instructors graded each group's project separately. They considered technologies used, evidence of documentation of the group's process, and creativity and complexity of the VR scenes created. The instructors shared their evaluations with each other, and then determined final grades for their own students. Each instructor made a virtual appearance by Skype to introduce the project at the beginning, and to debrief with students at the end of the project. Due to a coincidence in class meeting times and the time zone difference, two groups were able to present their projects together over Skype to a joined classroom of both American and Romanian students.

Students from both universities had previous experience using the web, collaboration tools, and mobile devices. The Romanian students were mostly in the age group of 21-23, while the American students were all aged 17-20. Recognizing differences in age, academic interests and backgrounds, and technical abilities, the authors created a project that would be accessible and meaningful to this diverse student population and see these differences as representative of those found in today's global workforce.

The authors studied how collaboratively creating and sharing VR artefacts enables students to better appreciate the possibilities for VR in many settings and encourages the development of new digital and computational thinking skills. Students, in the process, have a glimpse of the culture of their international partners.

The CoSpaces EDU Platform

When designing a VR immersive experience with CoSpaces EDU, students incorporate three-dimensional objects from the platform's library, such as avatars, everyday objects (such as trees, animals, tables and chairs), and background scenes. They personalize the environment by uploading a 360-degree photo created with a 360-degree camera or smartphone app. Students turn their digital images into digital stories by adding animations and interactivity using a visual programming language called CoBlocks. After designing, developing, and coding their virtual worlds with the CoSpaces web application, students can explore their virtual worlds on their mobile devices using the CoSpaces EDU mobile app, available for Android and iOS devices. Through the mobile app, students can visit their virtual worlds by placing their smartphones into a Google Cardboard headset or similar VR viewer, creating a fully immersive experience. They share their VR worlds in blogposts or webpages by providing a link or a QR code.

As an example, one group created a VR experience comparing Starbucks coffee shops in Boston and Timisoara. Clicking an animated avatar in a 360-degree photo outside of the store (Figure 1a) transports the visitor inside the shop, where they can witness a dialogue between two customers discussing their beverage choices and spin the scene around to see the décor and environment of the shop. Clicking the Christmas Tree avatar in the Boston shop (Figure 1b) teleports the viewer to the Timisoara shop, and clicking the Starbucks logo in the Timisoara shop returns the visitor to Boston, creating an almost seamless experience. Figure 1 shows how the VR experience appears in a browser, and on a mobile device to be inserted into a Google Cardboard VR viewer.

(a)
(b)
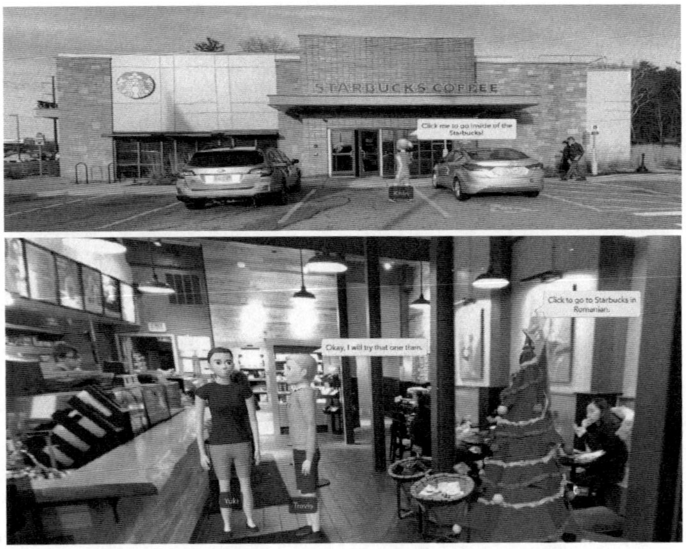

Figure 1. Virtual visit to Starbucks in Boston

Figure 2. Virtual Visit to Starbucks in Timisoara

Students use the CoBlocks visual programming tool (Figure 3) within the CoSpaces app to give realistic actions such as walking, turning, or gesturing to their avatars, and display conversation bubbles to create a dialogue between them. Simple Turtle Geometry commands carry out the animations. Advanced students can use JavaScript to interact with the avatars and create their scenes.

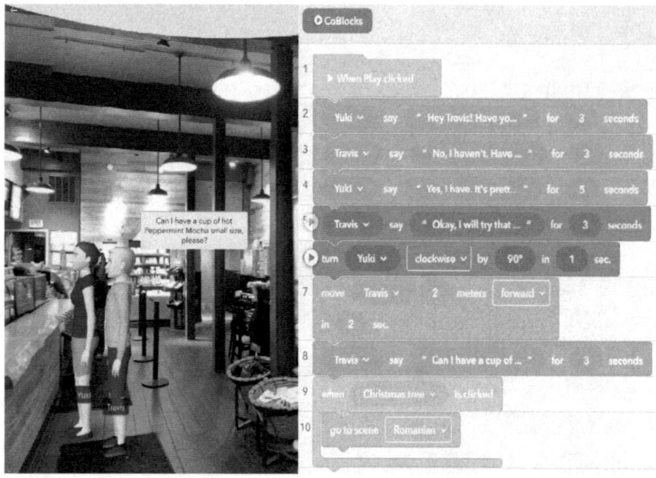

Figure 3. Creating and Animating a VR Scene using CoBlocks

TalkTech 2018 Survey Results

During the fall 2018 semester, 30 Bentley and 31 UPT students participated in the project. All had prior experience with using mobile phones, text messages, search engines, and online chat tools. Students from both countries cited Facebook messenger as the most popular tool of choice for their group communications, with email the second most popular method of communication. Most groups spoke live at least twice during the project, relying on email, text, and mobile communications to arrange next steps of the project.

Even though students were challenged by using new apps and tools and did not always have the tech skills needed to apply them, all students completed the project successfully. They relied on their team members, the Internet, and their instructors for additional information and guidance when necessary.

Familiarity with VR

Figure 4 shows that most students were not familiar with tools for creating or consuming immersive content prior to this project. None had used CoSpaces EDU prior to this project. Bentley students, most of whom had no prior coding experience, were offered a one-hour optional training session by a former TalkTech project participant, to learn basic techniques to set up animations using CoBlocks. The UPT students, most of whom had prior coding experience, learned to use CoSpaces on their own.

Several students, when asked about the most important skill learned from a technology perspective, commented, that they "learned how to create" digital reality environments. The experience showed the importance of coding

> *"I learned that it is crucial to understand basic coding languages and functions in order to be able to apply it to create a VR experience."*

and that tools for developing such experiences are evolving.

> *"From a technology point of view, I learned more about AR and VR and that it really isn't terrible to create either platform. I also learned that the technology is still in development, and the viewers can be very touchy and unresponsive."*

Students also shared sentiments that

> *"it is simple nowadays to create AR or VR using the appropriate tools."*

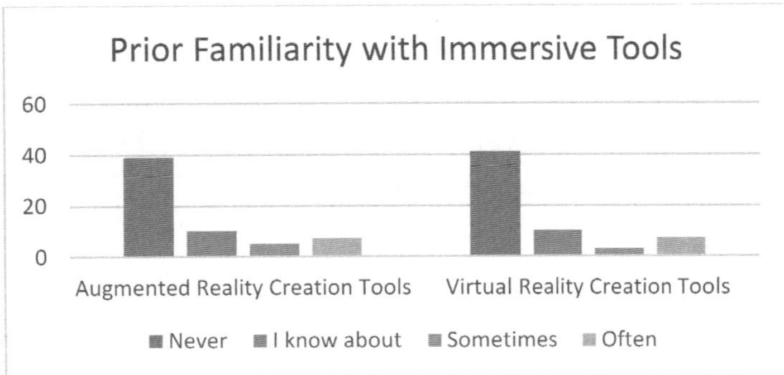

Figure 4. Prior Familiarity with Immersive Media Creation Tools

Said one student,

> *"This project was really eye opening to the power and convenience behind the rising technologies of virtual reality and augmented reality. It was, to an extent, a learning curve to do some of the aspects of this project. Personally, I never really used AR or VR except for Pokémon Go when it was popular and never would have thought that I would need to create anything similar. Creating the VR was interesting because on the CoSpaces application it was unlike an interface I have used before. It was not difficult nor confusing, it was just different in that it was a three-dimensional space we had to interact with and manipulate. This shows using VR is more suitable for creating more of an experience of an entire space to be more interactive and more exploratory."*

Cultural Awareness through Shared VR Experiences

When asked, "how did this project help you experience the culture of your international partners, and did AR or VR have an impact on this?" American students said:

> *"This project allowed us to talk with others from completely different cultures. The VR made us feel like would it would be like it was in Romania."*

> *"The AR and VR helped reveal the architecture of Romania and how it is less commercial in layout."*

> *"The VR definitely impacted my experience of the culture of my international partners because it showed me the similarities and differences that existed as well as how their history impacted the creation of their chosen place".*

> *"The VR allowed us to see an important public square in Romania as though we were actually there."*

Romanian students remarked:

> *"I got an idea about the way they live there. The VR helped a lot in this sense."*

> *"The VR gave us a snapshot of their culture and had a bigger impact for me. We were able to see what a local marketplace looks like for them and were able to see that things are not extremely different between the US and Romania."*

Students from both universities cited difficulties in communication as a reason for not learning about each other's culture. One remarked,

> *"The VR certainly helped me [see places in Romania], but I didn't think I truly experienced their culture."*

Another said,

> *"We just got to see some places from their place through AR and VR. There was not an impact about their culture."*

Many students noted the similarities between cultural landmarks in both countries as a result of viewing each other's immersive experiences.

Of the 30 responses from students at each school, the majority from Romanian students (23/30) were positive about the use of VR on understanding culture of their American partners, and 16/30 responses from American students expressed positive sentiments about using VR to experience the culture of their Romanian partners.

Another student reflected,

> *"From watching the VR experience we created, I learned that we honestly have everything at our fingertips when it comes to technology. I was able to experience the sights of Timisoara from 4,000 miles away. This added to my learning experience because it felt like what I was doing would be applicable. It wasn't just memorizing data, it was interacting with people across the world, building a space that captured both of our perspectives, and learning how people can think about the same concept in many ways."*

Effective Tools

Students from both universities considered the tools that were most effective for them to learn about the culture of their partners. They evaluated their learning through real time voice or video conversations, and by viewing or watching a video of the augmented and virtual reality scenes their partners created (see Figure 5.).

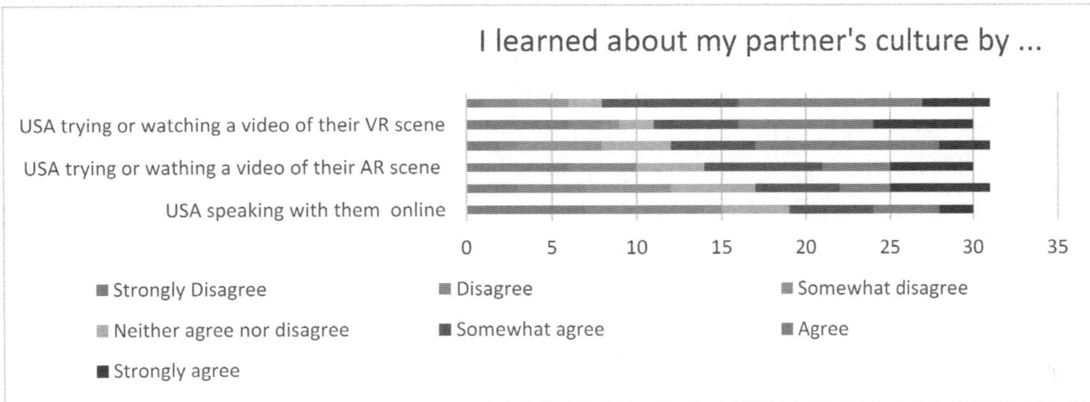

Figure 5. How Students Learned Most About Their International Partner's Culture

Results show that for both the American and Romanian students, both groups agreed or strongly agreed that viewing their partners' VR scenes on their laptops or in a cardboard headset was, the most effective way for them to experience their partner's culture. AR was next, and real time conversations scored the least favourable. This could be because most real time conversations were spent planning the project rather than discussing cultural differences or similarities.

Summary and Conclusions

The TalkTech 2018 project presents a learning scenario where students interact as members of international teams to create and exchange VR scenes that share aspects of local culture and landmarks. Most students agree that their participation in the TalkTech project taught them about culture, collaboration, working on international teams, and the tools to carry out these tasks. They saw the promise of digital reality technologies in education and in business.

Students also learned that creating, sharing, and exploring VR scenes can change how they experience virtual worlds, as well as how they apply their knowledge gained in those virtual worlds, to the real world. By creating, sharing, and experiencing immersive VR scenes, results suggest that student's use of VR has a favourable impact on their understanding and appreciation of the culture of their international partners.

References

Andone, D., & Frydenberg, M. (2019). Creating Virtual reality in a Business and Technology Educational Context. In T. M. tom Dieck, & T. Jung (Eds.), *Augmented Reality and Virtual Reality* (pp. 147-159). Switzerland: Springer International Publishing.

Frydenberg, M., & Andone, D. (2018a, June 25). Creating Virtual Reality Artefacts to Enhance and Transform Digital Learning. *Proceedings of the EdMedia + Innovate Learning, Jun 25, 2018 in Amsterdam, Netherlands*, 1543–1552. Retrieved from https://www.learntechlib.org/primary/p/184376/

Frydenberg, M., & Andone, D. (2018b). Enhancing and Transforming Global Learning Communities with Augmented Reality. *Journal of Information Systems Education, 29*(1), 37.

Fulmore, Y. (2015). Video Games and the Customization of Learning: Interactive Narratives as a Promising Design Framework for Crafting Inclusive Educational Environments. *Proceedings of the Third Conference on GenderIT – GenderIT '15*, 32–39. https://doi.org/10.1145/2807565.2807710

Jacobson, D. (2018, April). 12 Steps Toward Immersive Learning. eLearn Magazine. Retrieved February 15, 2019, from http://elearnmag.acm.org/archive.cfm?aid=3152720

Johnson, W. L. (2009). Developing intercultural competence through videogames. *Proceeding of the 2009 International Workshop on Intercultural Collaboration – IWIC '09*, 99–100. https://doi.org/10.1145/1499224.1499226

Stewart, D., & Dansie, T. (2018). VFX to teach religion??: learning from immersive media. *Proceedings of the ACM SIGGRAPH 2018 Educator's Forum on – SIGGRAPH '18*, Article 7. https://doi.org/10.1145/3215641.3215644

TalkTech (2019). An Exploration of Technology, Digital Media, and Culture across Continents. Retrieved from http://talktechproject.net

Yook, E. L., & Turner, P. K. (2018). Bringing International Perspectives to the Communication Curriculum in the Age of Globalization. *Journal of Intercultural Communication Research, 47*(5), 375–381. https://doi.org/10.1080/17475759.2018.1480517

HUMAN CAPITAL IN ONLINE HIGHER EDUCATION SETTINGS: A SOCIO-EDUCATIVE PERSPECTIVE APPLIED TO GRADUATES OF AN ONLINE UNIVERSITY

Riccardo Valente, Albert Sánchez Gelabert, Josep Ma Duart, Universitat Oberta de Catalunya, Spain

Introduction

In recent decades, a series of changes has shaped a model for universities backing new ways of understanding education and educational institutions in our societies. The appearance of completely online universities and traditional university departments offering online programmes, openly and *en masse*, bear witness to this. All these changes are an opportunity to rethink the role and function of universities in our increasingly interconnected and global societies. In what follows, we propose our contribution to this debate by focusing on the specific case of the "Universitat Oberta de Catalunya" (UOC), an online university of the Spanish educational system.

The use of technology – particularly the internet – has led to a process of expansion in education and fostered access to higher education for groups historically underrepresented: the working class, older people, ethnic minorities, women with family responsibilities, people with disabilities, etc. The importance of this process of expansion lies in the impacts and benefits of the university and of the increased educational level of the population feeding back to a broad raft of dimensions, at both individual and social levels, and transcending purely economic impacts (Brennan, Durazzi, & Tanguy, 2013; McMahon, 2010). As noted in a recent study published by Valero and Van Reenen (2016), the economic impact of higher education is not restricted to the investment in personnel and students, but must also be interpreted on the basis of the increase in human capital and a greater propensity for pro-democratic attitudes. More generally, in recent decades, the need to broaden the scope of economic analyses by including elements can help define (and potentially quantify) the social benefits of higher education has received increasing acceptance. In 2017, for example, a report published by the 22 institutions comprising the "League of European Research Universities" (LERU, 2017; p.7) highlighted "the rising demand for universities to explicitly demonstrate (consideration of) societal impact". Against this backdrop, new challenges are being added to universities' classic functions. According to Zgaga (2009), for example, the contemporary model of the university as an institution is characterised by its social dimension: in other words, by its links with the community and the notion of citizenship as core elements. This model involves the incorporation of a broader vision of the benefits of higher education for both students and society at large. Accordingly, this framework requires a wider-ranging analysis to evaluate the impact of education beyond the development of knowledge and strictly professional skills.

The Concept of Human Capital

As Teixeira (2014) notes in his review of Becker's work (1964), the idea that education provides social and economic benefits is not new. Nevertheless, it was only from the 1950s that this supposition became consolidated within the framework of a consistent line of research. In a period of post-war reconstruction, education began to be interpreted as a key resource with a view to the need to boost economic recovery, as can be seen from the proliferation of studies on the matter (Fisher, 1946; Harrod, 1943). It was Becker (1964), in his book "Human Capital", who systematised these prior works and gave structure to one of the first theories on education's impact upon society. According to this author's definition, human capital can be defined as "activities that influence future monetary and psychic income by increasing resources in people" (Becker, 1993; p.11). According to this standpoint, the chief role of educational institutions is associated with their contribution to increasing the level of learning, which, in turn, creates an (economic) impact that affects society as a whole.

Since the publication of "Human Capital" in 1964, most studies on education's impact on society have focused on its ability to create benefits for the economy in terms of productive knowledge-based resources. With regard to higher education, the conclusions of previous literature indicate that the combination of education and training offered by universities fosters a series of benefits in terms of students' greater employability and the quality of their jobs (Blundell, Dearden, Goodman, & Reed, 1997), or higher salaries (Carnoy et al., 2012), which, in the end, has an impact upon the economy as a whole via final consumption expenditure.

Turning to the specific case of this study and the specific features of online universities, impact studies note, firstly, the flexibility of the courses offered and the benefits in terms of accessibility for certain groups (adults with family responsibilities, full-time workers, the disabled, etc.) (UNESCO, 2002). Additionally, given their characteristics, these students' profiles differ from those of their fellow-students at face-to-face universities with regard to their motivations. As shown by the results of the IDEAL project (2013-2015), carried out across five European counties (Germany, Finland, Greece, Hungary and the United Kingdom), the main factors influencing the choice of online university are associated with the aspiration to improve theoretical knowledge, career consolidation and improving future employment prospects.

On the other hand, with his concept of "externalities", McMahon (2009) is regarded as making the first attempt to formulate a theory specifically designed to estimate the spillover effects of (higher) education on society as a whole. Externalities are social benefits spilling over into society and future generations, as the result of the mediating role of the human capital transmitted by universities to their students. Additionally, this author's work points to a difference between private benefits, in terms of the monetisation of the skills acquired when studying, and the social benefits, such as the fostering of democratic attitudes, and greater awareness of civic engagement which, although indirect, have a substantial impact on a social level. From this author's perspective, then, higher education is a "public asset" in that it contributes to a better quality of life. Other research has provided evidence regarding the role of education in developing active citizenship, i.e., the learning of participatory attitudes, social justice values, citizenship values, and cognition about democratic institutions (Hoskins, D'Hombres, & Campbell, 2008). Within the context of Catalonia, studies show the same patterns, with the population with higher education levels showing greater participation, political engagement and volunteering, as well as individual electoral participation and likelihood of voting (Soler-í-Martí, 2011). In this same regard, Anduiza, Cantijoch, and Gallego (2009) note the importance of the level of education with regard to new forms of participation in online contexts and to the differences in forms of participation, be they institutional or extra-institutional (protests, political consumption or expressive participation). Nevertheless, it should be noted that although these *democratic externalities* are associated with a higher level of education, the relationship is not linear. In the exclusive case of university students and their participation in the institution's bodies, there are differences depending upon the type of university. Specifically, online university students place less importance on the different forms of participation than their peers in face-to-face ones (Laker, Naval, & Mrnjaus, 2014).

Objectives

The analysis that follows is based upon a multidimensional definition of *human capital* that is not limited to the creation of added value or increased salaries arising from a boost in skills prized on the job market. Instead, the objective consists in testing a construct oriented towards an updated definition of human capital (Becker, 1964) that could encompass the spill over effects upon society as a whole (McMahon, 2009). Additionally, given the specificities of the case study (an online university), particular emphasis has been placed on the role of higher education in fostering an improvement in digital skills and a consolidation of career prospects. To empirically test the proposed theoretical model, confirmatory factor analysis was performed. Based on the outputs of the factor structure, a series of *ad hoc* nonparametric tests were implemented to check for the existence of potential differences based on the characteristics of the graduates.

Methodological Approach

The data collection method (a questionnaire) is the result of a process of updating an earlier version used in a study published in 2009 by Carnoy et al. (2012) and designed to identify potential salary increases and/or improvements in job quality for former students. This updated version includes a series of items for which students assess the benefits on digital skill levels and in the social sphere (greater social responsibility, greater participation, etc.) derived from their enrolment at the UOC. The construct labelled *human capital* involved four latent factors:

1. Firstly, *learning*, which represents a classic dimension of a university's role in society. To measure the impact in terms of learning, we included a raft of questions by means of which respondents could score on a scale from 1 (*no impact*) to 5 (*maximum impact*) the UOC's role in the transference of new concepts, personal development (self-affirmation, self-discipline, etc.) and the incorporation of an interdisciplinary and crosscutting vision.
2. Secondly, *socio-political awareness*: defined as the development of pro-social attitudes promoting participation in society. Respondents were asked to specify their degree of agreement with three statements of the role of their studies at the UOC in establishing a greater social engagement, civic and social responsibility and political participation. The measurement scale consisted of five points, with low values indicating positions of disagreement and higher values, greater agreement.
3. Thirdly, *digital skills*, which constitute a particular aspect of academic contexts in which activities are performed in virtual and online environments. Account was taken of a list of five online skills: the search for and access to information on the Internet, task planning in virtual environments, the creation of digital content in different formats, the ability to guarantee one's own online security and personal data protection, and the identification and resolution of technical problems. The question included in the survey was as follows: "Thinking of before and after your entry into the UOC, we would ask you to rate from 1 to 5, where 1 is a *novice level* and 5 an *expert level*, your user level with regard to the digital skills listed below". Formulated in this way, the question permitted the *quantification* of potential improvements in digital skills by calculating the difference between the initial level and that after obtaining the qualification.
4. Lastly, we included a focus on *career consolidation* and the impact upon employment. Respondents were asked to self-assess the impact of their studies at the UOC in terms of the incorporation of new concepts that were useful in the workplace and of improvements in working conditions, on a scale from 1 to 5 (*no impact* vs. *maximum impact*).

Table 1: Description of data

Dimensions	Variables	Mean	SD
Learning	Incorporation of new concepts	3.92	1.047
	Self-affirmation and self-discipline	3.76	1.164
	Interdisciplinary and crosscutting vision	3.53	1.189
Socio-political awareness	Social engagement	2.37	1.224
	Political participation	2.42	1.214
	Civic and social responsibility	2.62	1.229
Digital skills	Search for and access to information on the internet	1.15	1.138
	Task planning in virtual environments	1.42	1.190
	Digital content creation	1.07	1.054
	Online security	.72	.991
	Problem solving	.80	.955
Career consolidation	Improving my working conditions	2.32	1.365
	Practical job-related knowledge	3.12	1.330

Instrument Validation and Survey Administration

After conclusion of the design phase, the questionnaire was subjected to expert validation. Subsequently, a pilot test was implemented for nine days between 25 September and 3 October 2018, involving a sample of 150 subjects. The final version of the survey was administered online. Potential participants were contacted in advance by email, informing them of the study's nature and objectives. The email included a link to access the consent form for processing personal data. Respondents' explicit consent was *sine qua non* for their participation in the survey. The web platform used to administer the survey was Qualtrics (www.qualtrics.com). Emails were sent on 22 October, 2018, at 12:00, and the survey was closed at the same time on 9 November, 2018. A reminder was sent on 29 October.

Statistical Processing of the Data

Initially, we analysed the basic characteristics of the available data (frequency distribution, contingency tables and percentages). Subsequently, we opted for confirmatory factor analysis, as it was regarded as the most suitable technique for proposing a statistically validated conceptualisation of the possible increases in human capital among the UOC's graduates. To examine the reliability and internal consistency of the components, the coefficients of the composite reliability index were calculated, as was the average variance extracted. Based on the results of the confirmatory factor analysis, a "self-estimated human capital index" was calculated on the basis of the weighted sum of the factor scores making up the factor structure. The factor scores were used to implement the nonparametric tests Kruskal-Wallis and Mann-Whitney U, depending upon the type of variable to be analysed (ordinal or dichotomous, respectively). Interpretation of the tests' p values permitted verification of the potential existence of statistically significant differences based on demographic features (sex and age), the state of psycho-physical health, the number of years since graduation and the level of the studies completed (undergraduate or postgraduate) by alumni.

Results

Description of the Sample

The 18 days of data collection meant it was possible to reach a sample size of 2,869 subjects, 55% of whom were women and 45% men. The average age of respondents was 44. With regard to nationality, 93% were Spanish. 70% of the sample was resident in Catalonia, 22% in another Spanish Autonomous Community and 8% from outside Spain. Two-thirds of respondents lived with a partner at the time of entering the UOC, whether with children (32%) or without (31%). The third-most common family situation, in decreasing order, was childless singles, at 29%, as well as 1.4% single parents. Less frequent were those separated (5.6%) or widowed (0.5%), or with a status other than the aforementioned (1.5%). In terms of family background, 8% of fathers and 10% of mothers of UOC graduates have no qualifications, and 30% and 36%, respectively, only received primary education. These figures coincide with previous surveys conducted by other bodies (see for example, AQU Catalunya,

2017) whose conclusions indicate that, in comparison with graduates of other Catalan universities, those of the UOC come from families with a lower educational level (in terms of formal education). 91% of respondents were working when they entered the UOC. The remaining 9% stated they were unemployed (5.3%), retired (0.7%) or in another unspecified situation (3%). Additionally, 54% stated that the studies they followed at the UOC were associated with their job, against the 46% who declared that they were not. With regard to the level of the studies, 70% followed an undergraduate course, while the remaining 30% enrolled for a master's or a doctorate. On average, respondents had ceased studying at the UOC 2.4 years previously (around 29 months). The graduates making up the sample were characterised by a certain degree of job stability, as, at the time of the survey, 89% were working, predominantly in public administration or in the field of information and communication technology.

Validation of an Updated Construct of Human Capital applied to HE in online settings

To estimate the factor structure, we chose the weighted least square mean and variance adjusted (WLSMV) model, which is regarded as the most suitable with categorical variables. According to the goodness of fit statistics, the model shows a highly satisfactory fit. The x^2/df ratio is 4.9, the comparative fit (CFI) and Tucker-Lewis (TLI) indices showed values above the cut-off ($\geq .95$), while the root mean square error of approximation (RMSEA) stood at .039. Interpretation of the factor loading values confirms the existence of strong and statistically significant relations between the variables and factors. Also, the calculations of the internal reliability index (CR $\geq .60$) and the average variance extracted (AVE $\geq .50$) support results pointing to a solid factor structure with good internal consistency. Interpretation of the model's standardised coefficients suggests that all the factors make a significant contribution to the model. Both learning ($\beta = .87$; $p < .001$) and socio-political awareness ($\beta = .67$; $p < .001$) contribute significantly. Moreover, the factor associated with skills fostering career consolidation ($\beta = .69$; $p < .001$) identifies one of the dimensions peculiar to the UOC as a *professionalising* university that attracts the profile of a student/worker whose motivations for studying are related to the need to improve their working conditions. Lastly, the results indicate that progress in terms of digital skills ($\beta = .51$; $p < .001$) has significant weight in the self-estimation of human capital on the grouping analysed.

Differences Between Profiles

Given the promising results obtained through the implementation of confirmatory factor analysis, we decided to explore the likelihood of the existence of differences in terms of perceived impact depending upon the respondents' characteristics and life conditions. A preliminary step was to calculate a value that could summarise the proportional contribution of each factor to the factor structure. To do this, after obtaining the factor scores using the regression method (regression scores), their proportional value was calculated on the basis of the β value emerging from the outputs of the previous factor analysis. The sum of the proportional β factors for each latent factor provides a final value we have called the "self-estimated human capital index". Two nonparametric tests (Kruskal-Wallis and Mann-Whitney's U) were then applied using the following grouping variables: sex, age ranges, presence or absence of health problems during studies, years since obtaining qualification (as an ordinal variable), and level of studies completed at the UOC (undergraduate or postgraduate). Additionally, the variables to be compared were the first-order latent factors (learning, socio-political awareness, career consolidation and digital skills).

Initially, it is worth highlighting that no statistically significant differences were found between men and women, with the sole exception of the latent factor identifying the benefits in terms of career consolidation. In this particular case, the difference is significant ($p < .05$) and the mean rank value is greater among men, which points to a greater propensity for this grouping to consider that their studies have had a positive impact upon their careers. The same tendency is seen when it comes to comparing respondents stating that they had experienced health problems during their studies with those that did not. Again, in this case, the significant difference ($p < .01$) and the mean rank are greater among those who did not experience any health problems. In both cases, one could make the hypothesis that the emphasis on career consolidation depends, to a great extent, on a better and more consolidated position on the job market for men and for those not suffering from health problems, compared with women and graduates whose academic performance was negatively affected by health problems.

Age differences are significant for all analysis levels taken into account. At a first level, it was noted that self-estimation of impact increased among respondents in the age ranges *36-50* and *over 51* (i.e., that adult graduates perceive the greatest benefits). Looking in detail at each of the first-order latent factors, this tendency is consolidated if one considers, for example, that the average range values associated with improvements in digital skills and socio-political awareness are higher in these two age ranges. On the other hand, it is the young who perceive more benefits in terms of learning (in its more traditional definition as the acquisition and consolidation of knowledge), and career consolidation, which takes on especial importance considering that they are at a stage of their lives in which career consolidation is a key factor.

Significant differences also emerge if we consider the number of years that have passed since obtaining the qualification. In this case, the tendency is unmistakable and in the expected direction: the more years that have passed since graduation, the more the perception of benefits diminishes. However, one significant exception was recorded, with regard to the factor associated with learning. The results indicate that the benefits in this sense become more tangible with the passing of time (from three years and more after completing the studies).

Lastly, we explored the differences arising from the level of studies followed. Although no differences were found in terms of learning, the Mann-Whitney U test shows that the perceived benefits in digital skills and career consolidation are more evident with master's and

PhD students. Additionally, the levels of socio-political awareness are proportionally greater among postgraduate students.

Conclusions

This paper contributes to literature presenting a statistically validated definition of *human capital* including factors associated with learning, civic education, digital skills and career consolidation. Additionally, it found that the principle means of differentiating between graduates' profiles was time-based, in the dual sense of their age and the number of years since they had obtained their qualification. Specifically, the (perceived) benefits are greater in age ranges from 36 years and up, backing the intuition regarding the UOC's contribution to lifelong learning processes. However, the perceived benefits progressively diminish with an increase in the number of years that have passed since leaving the university. Lastly, the impacts in terms of theoretical and/or practical skills valued on the job market are clearer among respondents who are at a time of their lives in which they have just entered the job market and need to consolidate their position there.

References

AQU Catalunya (2017). *Enquesta d'inserció laboral.* Barcelona: Agencia per a la Qualitat del Sistema Universitari de Catalunya.

Becker, G. (1964). *Human Capital.* New York: Columbia University Press.

Becker, G. (1993). The economic way of looking at behavior. *Journal of Political Economy, 101*(3), 385–409.

Blundell, R., Dearden, L., Goodman, A., & Reed, H. (1997). *Higher Education, Employment and Earnings in Britain.* London: Institute for Fiscal Studies.

Brennan, J., Durazzi, N., & Tanguy, S. (2013). Things we know and don't know about the Wider Benefits of Higher Education: A review of the recent literature.

Carnoy, M., Rabling, B., Castano-Munoz, J., Duart Montoliu, J. M., & Sancho-Vinuesa, T. (2012). Does Online Distance Higher Education Pay Off for Adult Learners? The Case of the Open University of Catalonia. *Higher Education Quarterly, 66*(3), 248-271.

Fisher, A. (1946). *Education and Economic Change.* South Australia: W.E.A. Press.

Harrod, R. (1943). Full employment and security of livelihood. *The Economic Journal, 53*(212), 321–342.

Hoskins, B., D'Hombres, B., & Campbell, J. (2008). Does Formal Education Have an Impact on Active Citizenship Behaviour? *European Educational Research Journal, 7*(3), 386–402.

IDEAL (2013-2015). *Impact of Distance Education on Adult Learning.* Project number: 539668-LLP-1-2013-1-NO-ERASMUS-ESIN.

Laker, J., Naval, C., & Mrnjaus, K. (2014). Citizenship, Democracy and Higher Education in Europe, Canada and the USA. London: Palgrave Macmillan.

LERU (2017). *Productive interactions: societal impact of academic research in the knowledge society.* Retrieved from https://www.leru.org/files/Productive-Interactions-Societal-Impact-of-Academic-Research-in-the-Knowledge-Society-Full-paper.pdf

McMahon, W. (2009). Higher Learning, Greater Good. The Private and Social Benefits of Higher Education. Baltimore: The Johns Hopkins University Press.

McMahon, W. (2010). The private and social benefits of Higher Education: the evidence, their value, and policy implications. TIAA-CREF Institute.

Soler-i-Martí, R. (2011). *Democràcia, participació i joventut.* Barcelona: Departament de Benestar Social i Família.

Teixeira, P. (2014). Gary Becker's early work on human capital – collaborations and distinctiveness. *IZA Journal of Labor Economics, 3*(12), 1-20.

UNESCO (2002). *Open and Distance Learning. Trends Policy and Strategy Considerations.* Retrieved from http://unesdoc.unesco.org/images/0012/001284/128463e.pdf

Valero, A., & Van Reenen, J. (2016). *The Economic Impact of Universities: Evidence from Across the Globe.* Retrieved from https://www.nber.org/papers/w22501

Zgaga, P. (2009). Higher education and citizenship: "The full range of purposes." *European Educational Research Journal, 8*(2), 175–188. https://doi.org/10.2304/eerj.2009.8.2.175

VALIDATION OF THE COMMUNITY OF INQUIRY SURVEY (SPANISH VERSION) AT UNED COURSES

Inés Gil-Jaurena, Daniel Domínguez Figaredo, Belen Ballesteros Velázquez, Javier Morentin Encina, Universidad Nacional de Educación a Distancia (UNED), Spain

Abstract

The paper covers the validation process of the Community of Inquiry (CoI) survey in its Spanish version. This task was undertaken by a group of researchers – the CO-Lab teaching innovation group – at the Universidad Nacional de Educación a Distancia (UNED) in 2018, as a first step in the process of analysing the educational practices in the online courses we teach. The paper explains the CoI model, some studies that have validated the survey in different languages, and the validation we have developed at UNED. We conclude with a discussion and future studies we aim to undertake as a follow-up of this project.

Introduction

Between March and December 2018, within the frame of the CO-Lab Teaching Innovation Group at the Universidad Nacional de Educación a Distancia (UNED), we undertook a research and teaching innovation project, funded by the Vice-Rectorate for Methodology and Innovation. The project was focused on the analysis, using the *Community of Inquiry* (CoI) theoretical model, of the educational practices developed in 25 Bachelor and Master distance courses in the Faculties of Education and Philosophy, with the aim of making proposals for improvement based on the analysis. We used the CoI survey (Arbaugh et al., 2008), originally developed in English. Its application in our case required a translation into Spanish and adaptation to the UNED context. Hence, one of our objectives was to undertake this task and validate the internal consistency of the CoI survey in the Spanish version.

The Community of Inquiry (CoI) model

The Community of Inquiry model (CoI), based on socio-constructivism, has been widely used in online education. An educational community of inquiry is a group of individuals who collaboratively engage in purposeful critical discourse and reflection to construct personal meaning and confirm mutual understanding (The Community of Inquiry, 2017). Thus, an online higher education course, a MOOC, etc. can be considered communities of inquiry.

The Community of Inquiry conceptual framework represents a process of creating a deep and meaningful (collaborative-constructivist) learning experience through the development of three interdependent elements: social, cognitive and teaching presence (The Community of Inquiry, 2017), as shown in Figure 1.

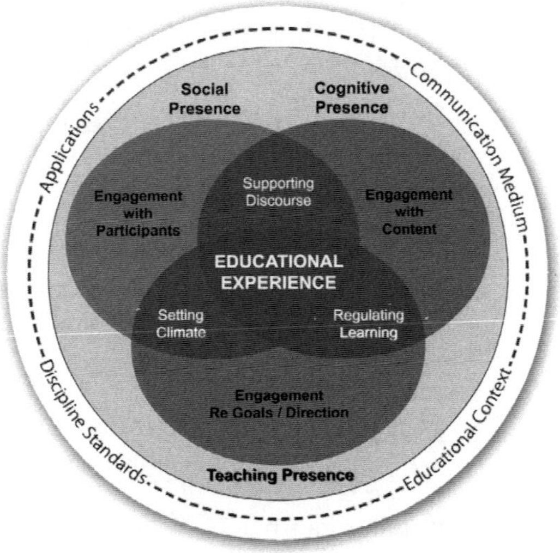

Figure 1: The Community of Inquiry model
(http://www.thecommunityofinquiry.org/content/images/diagram.coi.jpg)

The CoI model is composed by 3 interrelated presences:

- Social presence: the ability of learners to project their personal characteristics into the community of inquiry, thereby presenting themselves as "real people". It refers to interaction with peers.
- Cognitive presence: the extent to which the participants are able to construct meaning through sustained communication. It refers to interaction with content.
- Teaching presence: the design, facilitation, and direction of cognitive and social processes for the purpose of realising personally meaningful and educational worthwhile learning outcomes. It refers to interaction with the teachers and/or their directions.

The key to the model, as one of its authors emphasises (Anderson, 2016), is its simplicity (since it includes only three large dimensions, but which interact, as shown in Figure 1) and its ease of use by teachers and researchers.

Validation of the Community of Inquiry (CoI) survey

The CoI survey is 34-items questionnaire which sought to reflect to what extent the three dimensions or interdependent presences (teacher, social and cognitive) were perceived by students in their learning experiences on digital platforms, based on constructivist and collaborative approaches of the CoI model. The survey uses a Likert-type scale.

Previous validation studies

The validation of the CoI survey in different contexts of distance learning offers, as a general result, the verification of the theoretical structure of the instrument, as well as a high reliability from the point of view of its internal consistency. In table 1 we synthesise the contributions of the five validation studies we have analysed.

Table 1: CoI survey validation studies

Reference	Country and language	Method	Sample	Results
Arbaugh et al. (2008)	USA & Canada /English	Construct: analysis of main components	287 postgraduate students in 4 universities	Verification of the 3 theoretical factors but identification of a 4th factor
Swan et al. (2008)	USA & Canada /English	Construct: analysis of main components Reliability: internal consistency	287 postgraduate distance students in 4 universities	Verification of the theoretical structure High reliability
Yu & Richardson (2015)	South Korea / Korean	Construct: exploratory factor analysis Reliability: internal consistency	995 students in a distance university	Verification of the theoretical structure High reliability
Kovanović et al. (2018)	USA, India, UK & The Netherlands / English	Construct: exploratory factor analysis Reliability: internal consistency	1487 MOOC learners	Verification of the theoretical structure High reliability
Olpak & Kiliç (2018)	Turkey / Turkish	Construct: exploratory and confirmatory factor analysis Reliability: internal consistency	1150 students in online courses in 3 universities	Verification of the theoretical structure High reliability

Validation of the Spanish version of the CoI survey

The original CoI survey is an open resource with a Creative Commons license (CC-BY-SA), available on the CoI website (Garrison, 2011). In accordance with the terms of the license, we have adapted the questionnaire and, published and distributed the Spanish version with a similar license, CC-BY-SA, in a journal article (Ballesteros, Gil-Jaurena, & Morentin, 2019).

The Spanish version of the survey we have adapted consists of 34 questions with a Likert rating scale of 1 to 5 points. Thirteen questions correspond to the teaching presence, nine to the social presence and twelve to the cognitive presence (similarly to the original survey in English).

We converted the survey into an online form using Google forms, and distributed it through 25 online courses (Undergraduate and Master level). We collected 162 students' replies, 75% of them female students (in accordance with the profile of the students in the Faculty of Education). The average age was 37 years old. The majority (76.5%) were studying a Bachelor programme. The validation process is shown in Table 2.

Table 2: CoI survey validation study at UNED

Reference	Country and language	Method	Sample	Results
Ballesteros, Gil-Jaurena, & Morentin (2019)	Spain / Spanish	Construct: exploratory factor analysis Reliability: internal consistency	162 students	Verification of the theoretical structure High reliability

Construct validity was analysed through exploratory factor analysis. The results of the matrix of rotated factor structure (Table 3) show the achievement of a discrepancy between the saturations in the first two factors above .50/.20 or .60/.20, that is, a difference of .30-.40, which indicates the adjustment of the dimensions to the theoretical structure.

In Table 3, we keep the items in Spanish. The English version can be found in the CoI website: https://coi.athabascau.ca/coi-model/coi-survey/

Table 3: Factor structure matrix, CoI survey Spanish version

	Teaching presence	Social presence	Cognitive presence
El profesorado ha comunicado con claridad los contenidos de la asignatura	.864	.215	.617
El profesorado ha comunicado con claridad los objetivos de la asignatura	.820	.225	.670
El profesorado ha facilitado instrucciones claras acerca de cómo realizar las actividades de aprendizaje	.798	.246	.626
El profesorado ha informado claramente de los plazos de realización y las fechas de entrega de las actividades	.516	.236	.455
El profesorado ha facilitado la identificación de aspectos polémicos y diferentes perspectivas en los contenidos	.859	.342	.665
El profesorado ha orientado la actividad del grupo facilitando la comprensión de los temas de forma tal que me ayudó a aclarar mis ideas	.873	.337	.690
El profesorado ha propiciado la implicación y la participación de los/las estudiantes en debates productivos	.865	.365	.518
El profesorado ha mantenido a los/las estudiantes centrados en las tareas de forma tal que facilitó el aprendizaje	.921	.361	.651
El profesorado ha animado a los/las estudiantes a explorar nuevos conceptos	.878	.275	.607
Las aportaciones del profesorado han promovido el sentido de pertenencia al grupo	.857	.392	.537
El profesorado ha facilitado que los debates se enfoquen hacia cuestiones relevantes	.897	.317	.579
El profesorado ha respondido con comentarios que me ayudaron a entender mis puntos fuertes y débiles en relación con los objetivos de la asignatura	.860	.293	.667
El profesorado ha ofrecido respuestas adecuadas (feedback) en los momentos oportunos	.867	.255	.609

Conocer a otros/as compañeros/as hizo que me sintiera parte del grupo	.095	.655	.276
He podido conocer un poco más a fondo a algunos/as de los/las compañeros/as del curso	.105	.642	.346
La comunicación digital (online) es un medio excelente para la interacción social	.137	.635	.317
Me he sentido cómodo/a conversando a través de la plataforma digital	.489	.763	.391
Me he sentido cómodo/a participando en los debates de la asignatura	.558	.794	.481
Me he sentido cómodo/a interactuando con los/las compañeros/as de la asignatura	.277	.888	.321
Me he sentido cómodo/a manifestando mi desacuerdo con otros/as compañeros/as en un clima de confianza	.349	.874	.389
He sentido que mi punto de vista era reconocido por otros/as compañeros/as	.279	.825	.304
Los debates en la plataforma me han ayudado a desarrollar un espíritu colaborativo	.528	.800	.453
Las problemáticas que se han planteado han aumentado mi interés en los temas tratados	.775	.368	.834
Las actividades del curso han despertado mi curiosidad	.678	.315	.885
Me he sentido motivado/a para explorar cuestiones relacionadas con los contenidos	.720	.355	.867
He utilizado diversas fuentes de información para explorar las cuestiones que se plantean en la asignatura	.411	.300	.697
La búsqueda de información relevante y las ideas compartidas durante el curso me han ayudado a responder cuestiones relacionadas con los contenidos	.586	.375	.869
Los debates en la plataforma me han ayudado a valorar perspectivas diversas	.579	.603	.626
La integración de nueva información me ha ayudado a responder a las actividades de la asignatura	.630	.417	.802
Las actividades de aprendizaje me han ayudado a construir explicaciones y soluciones	.665	.302	.891
La reflexión sobre los contenidos y los debates me han ayudado a comprender los conceptos fundamentales de la asignatura	.671	.415	.844
Soy capaz de describir formas de contrastar y aplicar los conocimientos generados en la asignatura	.586	.325	.761
He encontrado soluciones a problemas propios de la asignatura que pueden aplicarse en la práctica	.520	.449	.837
Soy capaz de aplicar el conocimiento generado en la asignatura en mi trabajo o en otras actividades ajenas a la asignatura	.482	.389	.806

Source: Ballesteros, Gil-Jaurena, and Morentin, 2019

Reliability was analysed from the internal consistency approach, using the Cronbach alpha statistic. The results show values of 0.921, 0.926 and 0.938 in the teaching, social and cognitive dimensions, respectively, so we can justify that the CoI survey in its Spanish version has a high level of reliability and can be used as a measuring instrument in other studies.

Discussion and conclusions

The study of the technical characteristics of the CoI survey (Spanish version) supports its use as an instrument of measurement in educational research. The construct validity through the exploratory factor analysis allows to identify the teaching, social and cognitive presences, according to the theoretical basis that sustains the instrument. On the other hand, the results of the analysis of the internal consistency show a high reliability.

Further analyses are explained in Ballesteros, Gil-Jaurena, and Morentin (2019). Among them, we highlight the correlation between the 3 factors, which suggests a remarkable correlation between the teaching and cognitive presences, while the social factor shows a low correlation with the other two components. These results contrast with the theory on which the CoI survey is based (Figure 1); the CoI model indicates an interdependence between the three factors. This has led us to review the way in which the items are formulated within each factor in the survey, particularly the social dimension, which additionally is the one that shows the lowest scores in the courses we have analysed (Gil-Jaurena et al., 2018). The way the social presence items are stated in the survey poses a self-assessment of the students on feelings arising in the process of learning, without clearly visualising the role of the teacher. That is, these social presences related items are closer to an emotional perspective, centred on the student, than to the social approach promoted by the teacher.

In future studies, we aim to further explore the social dimension, either it happens within or beyond the virtual platform we use in the courses. Social connection and interactions between learners and its role in the learning process will be the focus of our next study in the CO-Lab teaching innovation group at UNED.

References

Anderson, T. (2016, January 4). A Fourth Presence for the Community of Inquiry Model? Virtual Canuck [Blog post]. Retrieved from http://virtualcanuck.ca/2016/01/04/a-fourth-presence-for-the-community-of-inquiry-model

Arbaugh, J. B., Cleveland-Innes, M., Diaz, S. R., Garrison, D. R., Ice, P., Richardson, & Swan, K. P. (2008). Developing a community of inquiry instrument: Testing a measure of the Community of Inquiry framework using a multi-institutional sample. *The Internet and Higher Education, 11*(3-4), 133-136. https://doi.org/10.1016/j.iheduc.2008.06.003

Ballesteros, B., Gil-Jaurena, I., & Morentin, J. (2019). Validación de la versión en castellano del cuestionario 'Community of Inquiry'. *Revista de Educación a Distancia – RED, 59.*

Garrison, D. R. (2011). About the Framework. An introduction to the Community of Inquiry. The Community of Inquiry. Retrieved from http://www.thecommunityofinquiry.org/coi

Gil-Jaurena, I., Domínguez, D., Izquierdo, A., & Morentin, J. (2018). Análisis de cursos online y a distancia desde el modelo "Community of Inquiry". In J. Valverde-Berrocoso (Ed.), *Campus Digitales en la Educación Superior. Experiencias e investigaciones* (pp. 346–356), Cáceres, Spain: Universidad de Extremadura.

Kovanović, V., Joksimović, S., Poquet, O., Hennis, T., Čukić, I., Vries, P., Hatalae, M., Dawson, S., Siemens, G., & Gašević, D. (2018). Exploring communities of inquiry in Massive Open Online Courses. *Computer & Education, 119*, 44-58. https://doi.org/10.1016/j.compedu.2017.11.010

Olpak, Y. Z., & Kiliç Çakmak, E. (2018). Examining the Reliability and Validity of a Turkish Version of the Community of Inquiry Survey. *Online Learning, 22*(1). http://dx.doi.org/10.24059/olj.v22i1.990

Swan, K. P., Richardson, J. C., Ice, P., Garrison, D. R, Cleveland-Innes, M., & Arbaugh, J. B. (2008). Validating a Measurement Tool of Presence in Online Communities of Inquiry. *E-mentor, 2*(24). Retrieved from http://www.e-mentor.edu.pl/_xml/wydania/24/543.pdf

The Community of Inquiry (2017). About the model. Athabasca University. Retrieved from http://www.thecommunityofinquiry.org/coi

Yu, T., & Richardson, J. (2015). Examining reliability and validity of a Korean version of the Community of Inquiry instrument using exploratory and confirmatory factor analysis. *The Internet and Higher Education, 25*, 45-52. https://doi.org/10.1016/j.iheduc.2014.12.004

Acknowledgments

This work was supported by the educational innovation project "Use of the Community of Inquiry (CoI) model in the analysis and evaluation of courses at UNED (Spain)", Ref. GID2016-30, funded by the UNED Vice-Rectorate for Methodology and Innovation (2018).

Connecting through Educational Technology
Proceedings of the European Distance and E-Learning Network 2019 Annual Conference
Bruges, 16-19 June, 2019

EXPANDING THE BOUNDARIES OF SERVICE-LEARNING AT HIGHER EDUCATION THROUGH E-LEARNING SCENARIOS: LESSONS FROM TEACHING INNOVATION PROJECTS

Amalia Creus, Mirela Fiori, Inés Cambra, Nadja Gmelch, Universitat Oberta de Catalunya, Spain

Introduction

Service-learning can be defined as a pedagogical approach that attempts to integrate community service in the academic curriculum. Through service-learning, students engage in organised activities designed to meet community needs and, at the same time, enhance their intellectual, social, and ethical development (Porter Honnet & Poulsen, 1989). The synergy between learning and civic engagement distinguishes service-learning as an educational approach that, beyond forming students for particular professional skills, has the goal to prepare them for practical community-based problem solving. From a methodological point of view, it places community-improvement and social-engagement in the centre of the learning process, while reinforcing students' cross-disciplinary skills, as critical thinking, co-creation or community building (Billig, Root, & Jesse, 2005).

Previous research suggests that participation in service-learning is associated with positive outcomes in different areas, among others attitudes toward self, attitudes toward learning, civic engagement, social skills, and also academic achievement (Blank, 1997; Billig, 2009; Conway et al., 2009; White, 2001). Studies on the topic also demonstrate significant increases in students' interest and commitment to their communities, and significant growing in leadership and problem solving (Creus & Lalueza, 2011; Giles & Eyler, 1994; Harwood & Radoff, 2009).

But even though service-learning has been deeply studied and is well recognized as a rich learning tool in face-to-face higher education, less is known about the challenges related to its implementation in an e-Learning context. Following this idea, this paper reports on the process and discusses the preliminary findings of two in-progress innovation projects that explore service-learning as a pedagogical approach in distance education.

Conceptual background

e-Learning pedagogical models are usually characterised by high flexibility, as a context where students can self-manage time and places of study, generally following an asynchronous and previously defined calendar of tasks and assignments. These aspects, which represent an important asset of e-learning models based on the personalisation of learning itineraries, can become problematic when – as happens at service-learning approaches – the learning experience of students is affected by the unpredictability and the complexity implicit in connecting the learning process with the times and needs of external agents.

Nevertheless, e-learning can also provide an opportunity to explore new approaches to service-learning. Approaches that can be distinguished, for instance, by major numbers of collaborative scenarios or by a potentially widespread interaction between a greater diversity of actors. In short, an opportunity to break the boundaries of traditional learning settings by taking advantage of the wide range of possibilities offered by virtual learning environments based on digital and interactive technologies.

Indeed, several authors have drawn attention to the fact that new digital technologies are promoting radical changes in learning (Seely Brown & Alder, 2008; Cobo & Moravec, 2011). This is related to the fact that in our network societies the abundance and dispersion of information exists alongside the proliferation of personal devices, spaces, and strategies for the production and dissemination of knowledge that goes beyond educational institutions (Lalueza & Creus, 2013). From the perspective of professional training, universities face the challenge of preparing students to succeed in a social and labour environment that is constantly changing, where employees are becoming increasingly mobile (Sullivan, 1999; Eby et al., 2003; Baruch, 2003; Briscoe et al., 2006) and where professional success is strongly linked to the ability to pass through different scenarios, learn continuously, and enhance professional networks.

Another remarkable aspect is the role that Internet and social media have nowadays as a space for personal and professional development. As Benson and others remark, graduates who are starting their professional career are expected to be comfortable with interactions using social networks and to be proficient in handling electronic media to work in a team, build social capital and share knowledge (Benson et al., 2010). In fact, looking to the emergence of digital technologies from this broader perspective, Luther and others state that online creative collaboration may be one of the most remarkable consequences of the increased access to information technology. As the same authors argue, examples such as Wikipedia and open-source software projects are turning online creative collaboration into an evolving phenomenon that needs to be studied in depth (Luther et al., 2009).

However, beyond the impact that the aforementioned social and cultural changes have on professional training, it is also important to pay attention to how this very same scenario is affecting the third mission of universities, which includes the aim to prepare new generations to impact on the quality of life of their community (Coffield, 1994). A commonly-used concept in this context is Education for Sustainable Development (ESD) that, following the definition of UNESCO, aims to empower and equip current and future generations to meet their needs using a balanced and integrated approach to the economic, social and environmental dimensions of sustainable development (Leitch et al., 2018).

Following this aim, the two innovation projects presented in this paper explore different ways to enhance social production of knowledge through e-learning. Based on former collaboration between university degree courses and non-profit organisations, both innovation projects have as an ultimate aim to enhance the contribution of universities to society and sustainable development, while providing students with a meaningful and professional significant learning experience.

Project context

The Universitat Oberta de Catalunya (UOC) is an online university whose mission is to provide people with lifelong learning and education by designing learning activities using advanced technological and communication resources, some of which include: social tools that facilitate collaborative work, multimedia content, advanced communication systems (both synchronous and asynchronous) and access to learning through mobile devices. Furthermore, a distinctive trait of UOC's educational model is the promotion of collective knowledge-building through an interdisciplinary and open approach to students' educational, social, and working experience (Gros, 2009). This is achieved by incorporating collaborative learning methodologies that involve problem-solving, collective development of projects, joint creation of products (Lalueza & Creus, 2013) and cooperative research.

In this framework, we highlight the development of two specific teaching innovation projects, both designed from a service-learning perspective: "L'Agència", an online communication agency managed by students, and a more recent initiative named "Participatory Final Degree Projects" (P-FDP) implemented in different bachelor's and master's degrees at UOC.

Project 1

"L'Agència" is a virtual platform in which students have the opportunity to develop communication projects, experiencing authentic professional dynamics and issues. Moreover, they do so from a perspective of social commitment based on voluntary participation, as the projects are developed for free to non-profit organisations. This virtual agency was created in 2012 and since then more than 100 students have taken part in its activities. This teaching innovation project is being carried out in the context of a Communication Degree course that prepares students with the necessary skills to design, plan, implement, and evaluate communication projects.

Project 2

Through "Participatory Final Degree Projects" students have the opportunity of developing their degree or master final dissertation focusing on a specific social need of their community, and working in collaboration with a non-profit organisation or a social entrepreneurship. Departing from needs and challenges identified by different organisations, students are invited to develop research questions through a participatory research.

Topics for discussion

The specific objective of this paper is to share the preliminary results of a study focused on the above-mentioned teaching innovation projects, both of them based on a service-learning approach. Our main aim is the comprehension of participants' experience, paying special attention to the patterns of interaction generated among students and non-profit organisations. Interactions here can be understood as the set of cognitive and social actions that takes place among the actors in the educational process.

Another question that we will explore in our presentation is how participants' experience is supported and/or constrained by the e-Learning technological environment. Among others, some of the preliminary results that will be discussed in that respect are the followings.

The selection of social tools that adequately support collaboration between students and non-profit organisations

The relationship that our students have with technology is "natural", pragmatic, and social-oriented. Universities are now welcoming the first generations of students who were born and raised in the digital age. It is a new generation of learners who have grown up along with the development of the Internet and who see digital technologies and social networks as a "naturalised" dimension of their professional and social life. To engage this profile of students in any activity where they are expected to take the lead requires a usable, accessible and non-hierarchical virtual environment (by non-hierarchical we mean an environment where users have high levels of administration permissions). In fact, it is noteworthy that students often tend to resolve questions and problems of a technical nature among their peers, rather than resorting to formal tutorials or technical support services. It is also significant that the diversity of media that students know and use every day makes it easier for them not to remain restricted to established resources and to embrace technological alternatives "outside the system", especially in regard to mobile communication. In that respect, the design of a successful collaboration must consider the inclusion of a decentralised selection of media and technologies, leaving room to incorporate developments in the learning process that occur outside the domain of the formal e-Learning environment.

The importance of rethinking the nature of "presence" and leadership in virtual collaboration

Several authors stress the idea that virtual groups afford a great opportunity to redefine leadership. According to the traditional model, leaders are supposed to offer encouragement, reward and motivation, and reinforce the development of relations inside the group (Ruggieri et al., 2013). Where in face-to-face situations the physical presence is a significant strategy for leaders, virtual collaboration makes it necessary to rethink some aspects of leadership. One of the more remarkable characteristics of this new context is the recognisability of the leader's status. As Ruggieri and others maintain, in face-to-face interactions leadership indicators involve body language, vocal inflection, eye contact, clothing, etc. However, virtual media forces the leader to adopt other indicators to let followers know that they are in charge. These indicators, as we can observe, include, among others, frequency of interventions, short delays between request and response, and availability to answer questions and help colleagues. The analysis of the projects also showed that effective leadership has much to do with the leader's ability to influence the emotional climate of the group. Messages of motivation, the capacity to express empathy or interest in the work of others as well as the ability to post messages that drive colleagues to action without generating conflict are almost always more effective than just having knowledge of the subject. In that sense, while the role assumed by teachers and non-profit organisations tends to be recognised as the "established authority" which is in charge of validating and assessing the quality of the work developed, students who emerge as natural leaders among their peers tend to make a substantial difference to the formation and sustainability of a successful team collaboration.

Final remarks

This study enables us to understand in depth the role that technology plays in shaping collaboration among the participants (students, teachers and non-profit organisations). Emergent results call our attention to the importance of moving the focus of the environment's design from the technology itself to the interactions generated by the users, who usually appropriate it in unexpected ways.

The study also addresses the importance of constant and progressive feedback as a key factor to ensure shared objectives and evaluation of results. This leads us to the need to further analyse the impact of the service-learning approach focusing on students' motivation and learning and also in its benefits from the participant organisations' point of view.

Finally, the study allows us to identify the need to develop more flexible assessment tools and better methodologies to evaluate virtual collaboration in service-learning, taking into account the different levels of participation, social roles, individual expertise, and the ability of students to take cooperative decisions and manage conflict. These are some of the questions we want to address in further developments of our research.

References

Benson, V., Filippaios, F., & Morgan, S. (2010). Online Social Networks: Changing the Face of Business Education and Career Planning. *International Journal of e-Business Management, 4*(1).

Billig, S. H. (2009). Does quality really matter: Testing the new K–12 service- learning standards for quality practice. In B. E. Moely, S. H. Billig, & B. A. Holland (Eds.), *Advances in service-learning research: Vol. 9. Creating our identities in service-learning and community engagement* (pp. 131–158). Greenwich, CT: Information Age.

Billig, S. H., Root, S., & Jesse, D. (2005). Impact of Participation in Service-Learning on High School Students' Civic and Academic Engagement. Report to the Carnegie Corporation of New York. Denver: RMC Research Corporation.

Blank, W. (1997). Authentic Instruction. In W. E. Blank & S. Harwell (Eds.), *Promising Practices for Connecting High School to the Real World* (pp. 15–21). Tampa: University of South Florida.

Briscoe, J., Hall, D., & Frautschy DeMuth, R. (2006). Protean and Boundaryless Careers: An Empirical Exploration. *Journal of Vocational Behaviour, 69*(2006), 30–47.

Cobo, C., & Moravec, J. (2011). Aprendizaje Invisible. Hacia una Nueva Ecología de la Educación. Barcelona: UBe.

Coffield, F. (1994). Research specification for the ESRC Learning Society Research Programme. Swindon: ESRC.

Conway, J. M., Amel, E. L., & Gerwien, D. P. (2009). Teaching and learning in the social context: A meta-analysis of service learning's effects on academic, personal, social, and citizenship outcomes. *Teaching of Psychology, 36*, 233–245.

Creus, A., & Lalueza, F. (2011). Learning through Professional Environments: The ComCity Project. *eLearn Center Research Paper Series, 5*, 32-40.

Eby, L. T., Butts, M., & Lockwood, A. (2003). Predictors of Success in the Era of the Boundaryless Career. *Journal of Organizational Behavior, 24*, 689-708.

Eyler, J., Giles, D. E., Stenson, C. M., & Gray, C. J. (2001). *At-a-glance: What we know about the effects of service-learning on students, faculty, institutions, and communities, 1993–2001.* Retrieved June 15, 2009, from the National Service-Learning Clearinghouse website: http://www.servicelearning.org/pubs/materials/L054

Harwood, A. M., & Radoff, S. A. (2009). Reciprocal benefits of mentoring: Results of a middle school–university collaboration. In B. E. Moely, S. H. Billig, & B. A. Holland (Eds.), *Advances in service-learning research: Vol 9. Creating our identities in service-learning and community engagement* (pp. 131–158). Greenwich, CT: Information Age.

Lalueza, F., & Creus, A. (2013). Prácticas Reales en Entornos no Presenciales: La Agencia Virtual de Comunicación como Herramienta de Aprendizaje Profesionalizador. *Historia y Comunicación Social, 18*(spec. 2013), 199-211.

Leicht, A., Heiss, J., & Byun, W. J. (2018). *Issues and trends in Education for Sustainable Development.* Paris: UNESCO Publishing. Retrieved from https://unesdoc.unesco.org/ark:/48223/pf0000261445

Luther, K., Counts, S., Stecher, K. B., Hoff, A., & Johns, P. (2009). *Pathfinder: an online collaboration environment for citizen scientists.* CHI 2009.

Porter Honnet, E., & Poulsen, S. (1989). Principles of good practice for combining service and learning. Wingspread Special Report. Racine, WI: The Johnson Foundation.

Ruggieri, S., Boca, S., & Garro, M. (2013). Leadership Styles in Synchronous and Asynchronous Virtual Learning Environments. *The Turkish Online Journal of Education Technology, 12*(4), 96-102.

Seely Brown, J., & Alder, R. (2008). Minds of Fire. Open Education, The Long Tail and Learning 2.0. *Educause*, 17-32.

Sullivan, S. E. (1999). The Changing Nature of Careers: A Review and Research Agenda. *Journal of Management, 25*(3), 457-484.

Sutherland, R., Eagle, S., & Joubert, M. (2012). A Vision and Strategy for Technology Enhanced Learning: Report from the Stellar Network of Excellence. Bristol, UK, 60.

White, A. (2001). *Meta-analysis of service-learning research in middle and high schools* (Unpublished doctoral dissertation). University of North Texas, Denton.

Connecting through Educational Technology
Proceedings of the European Distance and E-Learning Network 2019 Annual Conference
Bruges, 16-19 June, 2019

HIGH IMPACT PRACTICES – ADDRESSING WORKPLACE NEEDS

Maureen Snow Andrade, Ronald M. Miller, Utah Valley University, United States of America

Introduction

For at least three decades, employers have observed a gap between the skills they look for in recent college graduates and the skills these graduates possess. This has been noted in multiple studies involving both direct employer input and curricular reviews to determine alignment with professional standards (Association of American Colleges & Universities [AAC&U], 2013, Azevedo, Apfelthaler, & Hurst, 2012; Bayerlein & Timpson, 2017; Hart Research Associates, 2006a; 2006b; 2008; 2010; 2013; 2015; 2018; Pratt, Keys, & Wirkus, 2014; Ray, Stallard, & Hunt, 1994; Ullah, Kimani, Bai, & Ahmed, 2018). These studies have also indicated consistency in the specific skills that employers value, typically written and oral communication, teamwork, ethical decision-making, critical thinking, and the ability to apply knowledge in real-life situations (Hart Research Associates, 2015). These are prioritized by most employers over technical or discipline-specific knowledge and abilities (Hart Research Associates, 2015).

Possession of these skills, referred to as cross-cutting skills in that they are important across academic disciplines and professions, prepare individuals for lifelong learning as those who possess them have greater ability to re-skill or up-skill as needed throughout their working lives. This study examined the effectiveness of high impact practices (HIPs), or activities that require a "worthwhile investment of student time and effort" (Kuh, O'Donnell, & Schneider, 2017; p.9). HIPs are designed to help learners develop the cross-cutting skills needed for the workplace. Selected HIPs were implemented in a required course for business students at a large, regional, open admission university. The course is taught in multiple modalities (face-to-face, blended, and online). In particular, students in the online version of the course are required to navigate multiple forms of technology to collaborate as virtual teams as they learn together. The objective of the study was to determine the impact of four high impact practices – writing intensive courses, collaborative assignments and projects, community-based learning, and ePortfolio – in preparing students for their future professions.

Literature Review

High impact practices were first identified as such in 2006 (Kuh et al., 2017). Derived from what were called engaging educational practices based on both data and anecdote reflecting "accumulated wisdom" (Kuh et al., 2017; p.9), they were included in the National Survey of Student Engagement (NSSE), a standardized self-report instrument that explores students' learning experiences in higher education. These engaging practices demonstrated strong relationships with other NSSE scales such as academic challenge, active and collaborative learning, student-faculty interaction, and supportive campus environment; they were also highly correlated with the following NSSE learning outcomes: critical thinking, writing competence, and quantitative reasoning (Kuh et al., 2017).

The practices that have been identified as high impact include common intellectual experiences, learning communities, writing and inquiry intensive courses, first-year seminars and experiences, collaborative assignments, undergraduate research; diversity/study away/global learning; service learning, community-based learning; internships and field experiences; capstone courses and projects; and ePortfolio. In addition to data from instruments such as the NSSE, each of these practices has independent lines of research pointing to its effectiveness in a range of contexts. This review briefly examines the four HIPs that are the focus of this study.

Many universities, particularly in the United States, have a required writing course which students typically take in the first year of university; sometimes this is a two-course sequence in the first and second semesters. Although some institutions also require an advanced level writing course in the third or fourth year of study, which may focus on writing in the discipline, in other cases, a certain number of writing intensive courses are required. The purpose of these is to help students continue to develop their skills after the first-year writing course and provide a discipline-based writing experience. These courses typically meet certain requirements in order to be designated as writing intensive: writing skills are explicitly taught, students receive feedback on their writing and the opportunity revise, a certain number of papers or words is designated, writing constitutes a certain percentage of the final grade, support services such as writing centre student tutors are utilized, classes are small in size (e.g., 15-25 students), and classes are taught by a faculty member rather than a teaching assistant (Farris & Smith, 1992). The focus is on writing to learn and learning to write. Writing intensive courses help fill the gap between what students view as their level of preparation and the views of their employers. In one study, while 65% of recent college graduates felt well-prepared in this area, only 27% of employers concurred (Hart Research Associates, 2015).

Collaborative learning, or teamwork, has been used extensively in business education as it deepens learning, develops critical thinking skills, improves motivation, aids knowledge retention, and establishes professional competencies (Biggs & Tang, 2011; Hall, Ramsay, & Raven, 2004; Ohl & Cates, 2006; Scott-Ladd & Chan, 2008; Volkov & Volkov, 2015; Wageman & Gordon, 2005). However, students may object to it on the basis of previous negative experiences, preferences for working alone, problems with social loafing, scheduling issues, and lack of skill for doing it well (Pfaff & Huddleson, 2003; Schultz, Wilson, & Hess, 2010). As such, it needs to be carefully structured and explicitly taught.

Online teams may have difficulty establishing communication protocols, in part due to the inability to see facial expressions (if video conferencing is not used); however, online teams have also observed an increased task-focus in that they avoid casual chatter and get straight to the point (Saghafian & O'Neill, 2017). Developing the skill to work in virtual teams is increasingly relevant and may require somewhat different skills than communicating in a face-to-face context. Few business schools accredited by the Association to Advance Collegiate Business Schools (AACSB) are actively assessing teamwork, however, in spite of its emphasis by employers (Hart Research Associates, 2015). In 2007, 42% of business school deans reported assessing teamwork (Martell, 2007) compared to 26.5% in 2010 (Kelley et al., 2010) and none in 2015 (Wheeling et al., 2015).

Research on service and community-engaged learning demonstrates the following types of outcomes: personal (increasing self-efficacy, forming one's identity, growing spiritually, developing morally, learning to work with others, exploring leadership potential, and communicating effectively); social (addressing stereotypes, improving cultural and racial understanding, becoming more socially responsible, engaging in good citizenship behaviours, and establishing commitment to service); learning (increasing capability to apply and deepen knowledge, think critically, and problem-solve); and career development (exploring career choices, establishing connections, and increasing employability) (Eyler, Giles, Stenson, & Gray, 2001). Such projects help students form connections to their communities in a reciprocal relationship in which they contribute their developing knowledge of academic concepts to address real-life problems and community partners share actual experience and insights.

ePortfolios, which entail students creating artifacts that represent their learning (Cambridge, 2010; Miller & Morgaine, 2009; Watson et al., 2016), may involve the demonstration of content mastery as well as the integration of learning across courses. They are a sort of personal learning space characterized by reflection on one's strengths and weaknesses as a learner and related goal-setting (Dalziel, 2012). They can be shared with employers to provide evidence of learning and used for on-going professional development in the workplace (Dalziel, 2012; Moretti & Giovannini, 2011; Smith & Tillema; 2003). They also serve as an alternative form of assessment, offering insights into how students apply their learning and progress over time; overall, the goal of an ePortfolio is to create "stories of deep learning" (Finger & Jamieson-Proctor, 2009; p.69). ePortfolio outcomes include competencies such as "active learning; goal setting; autonomous learning; collaborative learning; cross-curricular competencies; interpersonal communication; self-assessment; digital literacy; work-readiness; lifelong learning; self-management; higher order thinking; and self-awareness" (Watty & McKay, 2015; p.199; Zinger & Sinclair, 2014).

Any practice that has the goal of engaging students' time and effort to achieve desired learning outcomes can be high impact. The list of eleven HIPs is not meant to be all inclusive. HIPs have been referred to as "a demonstrably powerful set of interventions to foster student success," with success defined as "an undergraduate experience marked by academic achievement, engagement in educationally purposeful activities, satisfaction, persistence, attainment of educational objectives, and acquisition of desired learning outcomes that prepare one to live an economically self-sufficient, civically responsible, and rewarding life" (Kuh et al., 2017; p.9). The eight key elements of HIPs provide a helpful framework for developing and implementing HIPs, which could be course- or institution-specific. These elements consist of high performance expectations; a significant investment of concentrated effort over time; interactions with faculty and peers over important matters; experiences with diversity where students work with individuals unfamiliar to them; regular, timely, and helpful feedback; real-life application of learning; public demonstration of expertise; and structured reflection and integration (Kuh & O'Donnell, 2013).

Methods

Students in three sections of an introduction to organizational behaviour course at a large, open admission regional university participated in this study. The total number of participants was 153. The course is required for all business majors and covers topics such as diversity, personality, job satisfaction, emotions, organizational change, leadership, motivation, power and politics, conflict, and communication. The course is taught across delivery modes – face-to-face, blended, and online, and is structured to help students develop and apply what they are learning through two key tasks: a team ePortfolio and a community engaged project. The former involves students working in teams to identify a key concept or theme, explore it in depth, and demonstrate their learning in an ePortfolio artifact. They need to show how the concept applies in real-life, reflect on what they learned, and evaluate their performance as a team. A rubric outlines expectations for the assignment. This assignment also sets the foundation for a community consulting project in which the teams work with an organization in the community, identify a problem, collect and analyse data, and make recommendations based on organizational behaviour theory. Students report on their community projects in the format of an ePortfolio artifact.

For each artifact submitted, teams evaluate what is working and what is not in terms of their norms and behaviours as a team. At midterm, they complete an additional reflection on their work as teams, determine needed changes to their team charters, and set goals for improvement as needed. This is submitted to the instructor in a brief report. At the end of the semester, students respond individually to key questions to reflect on their teamwork in the course. For this study, all of these documents were examined to determine learning outcomes using the framework of high impact practices and their elements as a guide. Having multiple measures, both team and individual, allows for triangulation of the data (Creswell, 2013; Trochim, 2006; Yilmaz, 2013). In all cases, the assignments required students to connect with each other through technology, specifically the ePortfolio platform (Google Sites), a discussion forum in the learning management system in which students reviewed and reflected on the work of other teams, and various methods of virtual communication such as Google hangouts or other forms of video conferencing, text messaging, or email. Individual teams determined what worked best for them. Course design was consistent across delivery modes.

The study used qualitative methodology to explore the phenomena of learning outcomes in the form of cross-cutting skills for the workplace. The goal was to understand students' learning experiences through their own stories and deep, rich reflections rather than to test theory, the focus of quantitative research (Baker & Edwards, 2012). The course assignments noted earlier were reviewed using the constant comparative method to identify commonalities across responses and integrate these into themes. The analysis utilized dependability, or finding repeated outcomes that could be confirmed across study participants. Qualitative research focuses on the context of the phenomena rather than transferability to other situations; however, others can learn from the findings and determine their applicability to new contexts (Trochim, 2006). The transcribed interviews were analysed using NVivo software, which assisted in the process of coding and categorizing the data into themes (Saldana, 2013).

Findings

A key finding from documents across delivery modes was workplace application of the concepts they studied, which were the focus of their artifacts and the foundation for their recommendations in their community consulting project.

> *"I haven't done anything like our eportfolios in any of my classes. It was a fun and interesting way to present our understanding of each concept. We were able to learn each concept really clearly because . . . it required us to look more in depth."*

> *"Most of all, the ePortfolio helped me combine what I was learning through the trainings with the business issues I saw at [name of company]. The ePortfolio was a place to display the thoughts of our team in a clear and organized way. It deepened my learning because I revisited the training modules and reinforced what I learned in them by applying them to real-life situations and writing about it."*

> *"As our group studied purpose and its relation to motivation, we realized that this is very important in helping members of a company work towards a common goal. If the executives of a company can create a culture of a common vision and purpose, the members will work towards that purpose."*

> *"Understanding diversity is critical as it allows employees from all backgrounds to communicate and form an effect team. Our challenge to our fellow classmates is to identify an aspect of diversity that is difficult to understand--then study it. Learn all that you can about those from different backgrounds."*

Teams also developed leadership and teamwork skills, specifically being open to different ideas and acting on feedback from peers and the instructor in order to set goals for improvement.

> *"Each team member has taken on leadership in a different part of this semester-long project. Although we have a mix of formal and informal leadership styles, our dedication to lead by example has given us great success.*

> *". . . Having a group project to accomplish via the internet has been new to many of us, and we have all done a great job opening up to new ideas and being willing to try something that might fail. We try to take the constructive criticism from the previous weeks' discussion and implement the ideas in hopes of bettering our score from our previous artifact. We have found leadership to be key in growing our knowledge and teamwork skills."*

As teams evaluated their performance midway through the course, they determined changes they wanted to make and set goals. These included items such as changing roles, creating new roles (e.g., a polisher to revise the final artifact draft), assigning tasks differently, starting tasks earlier, meeting earlier in the week, responding more promptly to communications, and adhering to deadlines. They also identified ways to improve accountability.

> *"If a member of the group doesn't have their piece of the artifact completed by the group-proposed deadline, then it won't be included. Tough. "(We need to be proactive in working together. Guidelines need to be enforced.)*

Teams also demonstrated that they were progressing through the stages of team formation to achieve the performing stage (Tuckman, 1965; Tuckman & Jensen, 1977).

> *"Our team comradery has come a long way since the beginning. Every time we meet as a group, we get more comfortable with each other. This helps with sharing ideas because no one is afraid that if they say something it will get shut down."*

In other cases, teams demonstrated effective communication skills.

> *"We all agreed that our biggest strength has been communication. Communication was the first topic of our team charter which was created the first week. We made it our goal to keep a constant open line of communication through group text messaging. Multiple times throughout each week team members update their status via text. This keeps everyone up to date on the progression of group projects. Each team member is then responsible to respond back to the texts or emails within 24 hours. Because the team meets every week during class, we have also done a great job at informing each other when one of us will be absent from class. This allows us to assign each other tasks even though the whole team isn't present. So far, we are all happy with our communication efforts as a team."*

From their projects, teams noted additional learning outcomes.

> *"What we learned is that even a big, well-known company isn't perfect. . . . However, with proper research and a desire to improve, companies can continue to become better and better. We've also learned that no matter what job you end up choosing for a career, you will always need people skills.*

Learning how to work as a team and lead people to achieve business goals is an invaluable skill."

Conclusions

Overall, the analysis indicated that students were gaining the cross-cutting skills desired by employees through the high impact practices implemented in the course. In particular, application of the content studied to the real-world, particularly to students' own teamwork and to their consulting projects, communication, and teamwork skills were evident. In sum, this study demonstrated that writing intensive courses, collaborative assignments and projects, community-based learning, and ePortfolio are effective in preparing students with the skills needed for their future professions.

References

Association of American Colleges & Universities (2013, April 10). *It takes more than a major: Employer priorities for college learning and student success.* Washington, DC: Hart Research Associates. Retrieved from https://www.aacu.org/sites/default/files/files/LEAP/2013_EmployerSurvey.pdf

Association of American Colleges & Universities (2019a). *LEAP states initiative.* Retrieved from https://www.aacu.org/leap/states

Association of American Colleges & Universities (2019b). *Multi-state collaborative to advance quality student learning and SHEEO.* Retrieved from https://www.aacu.org/value/msc

Azevedo, A., Apfelthaler, G., & Hurst, D. (2012). Competency development in business graduates: An industry-driven approach for examining the alignment of undergraduate business education with industry requirements. *The International Journal of Management Education, 10*(1), 12–28. Retrieved from http://dx.doi.org/10.1016/j.ijme.2012.02.002

Bayerlein, L., & Timpson, M. (2016). Do accredited undergraduate accounting programmes in Australia meet the needs and expectations of the accounting profession? *Education + Training, 59*(3), 305-322.

Biggs, J. B., & Tang, C. (2011). *Teaching for quality learning at university* (94th ed.). Open University Press, Buckingham.

Cambridge, D. (2010). *Eportfolios for lifelong learning and assessment.* San Francisco, CA: Jossey-Bass.

Eyler, J. S., Giles, D. E., Stenson, C. M., & Gray, C. J. (2001). At a glance: What we know about the effects of service-learning on college students, faculty, institutions, and communities, 1993-2000 (3rd ed.). Corporation for National and Community Service. Retrieved from http://www.compact.org/wp-content/uploads/resources/downloads/aag.pdf

Farris, C., & Smith, R. (1992). Writing-intensive courses: Tools for curricular change. In S. H. McLeod & M. Soven (Eds.), *Writing Across the Curriculum: A Guide to Developing*

Programs (pp. 52-62). Retrieved from https://wac.colostate.edu/books/mcleod_soven/chapter6.pdf

Hall, M., Ramsay, A., & Raven, J. (2004). Changing the learning environment to promote deep learning approaches in first year accounting students. *Accounting Education: An International Journal, 13*(4), 489-505.

Hart Research Associates (2006a, December 28). *How should colleges prepare students to succeed in today's global economy?* Washington, DC: Hart Research Associates. Retrieved from https://www.aacu.org/sites/default/files/files/LEAP/2007_full_report_leap.pdf

Hart Research Associates (2006b, January 31). *Report of findings based on focus groups among business executives.* Washington, DC: Hart Research Associates. Retrieved from https://www.aacu.org/sites/default/files/files/LEAP/PrivateEmployersFindings.pdf

Hart Research Associates (2008, January 22). *How should colleges assess and improve student learning? Employer views on the accountability challenge.* Washington, DC: Hart Research Associates. Retrieved from https://www.aacu.org/sites/default/files/files/LEAP/2008_Business_Leader_Poll.pdf

Hart Research Associates (2010, January 20). *Raising the bar. Employers' views on college learning in the wake of the economic downturn.* Washington, DC: Hart Research Associates. https://www.aacu.org/sites/default/files/files/LEAP/2009_EmployerSurvey.pdf

Hart Research Associates (2015, January 20). *Falling short? College learning and career success.* Washington, DC: Hart Research Associates. Retrieved from https://www.aacu.org/sites/default/files/files/LEAP/2015employerstudentsurvey.pdf

Hart Research Associates (2018, July). *Fulfilling the American dream: Liberal education and the future of work.* Washington, DC: Hart Research Associates Retrieved from https://www.aacu.org/sites/default/files/files/LEAP/2018EmployerResearchReport.pdf

Kuh, G. D., & O'Donnell, K. (2013*). Ensuring quality & taking high-impact practices to scale.* Washington, DC: Association of American Colleges & Universities. Retrieved from http://ts3.nashonline.org/wp-content/uploads/2018/04/AACU-LEAP-High-Impact-Practice-Characteristics.pdf

Kuh, G. D., O'Donnell, K., & Schneider, C. G. (2017). HIPs at ten. *Change: The Magazine of Higher Learning, 49*(5), 8-16. doi: 10.1080/00091383.2017.1366805

Miller, R, & Morgaine, W. (2009). The benefits of e-portfolios for students and faculty in their own words. *Peer Review, 11*(1), 8-12. Retrieved from https://www.aacu.org/publications-research/periodicals/benefits-e-portfolios-students-and-faculty-their-own-words

Ohl, T., & Cates, W. (2006). The nature of groups: Implications for learning design. *Journal of Interactive Learning Research, 17*(1), 71-89.

Pfaff, E., & Huddleston, P. (2003). Does it matter if I hate teamwork? What impacts student attitudes toward teamwork. *Journal of Marketing Education, 25*, 37–45.

Pratt, J. A., Keys, A., & Wirkus, T. (2014). Preparing information systems graduates for a complex society: Aligning IS curricula with liberal education learning outcomes. *Journal of Information Systems Education, 25*(1), 35-44.

Ray, C. M., Stallard, J. J., & Hunt, S. C. (1994). Criteria for business graduates' employment: Human resource managers' perceptions. *Journal of Education for Business, 69*(3), 140–144.

Schultz, J. L., Wilson, J. R., & Hess, K. C. (2010). Team-based classroom pedagogy reframed: the student perspective. *American Journal of Business Education, 3*(7), 17–24.

Scott-Ladd, B., & Chan, C. C. A. (2008). Using action research to teach students to manage team learning and improve teamwork satisfaction. *Active Learning in Higher Education, 9*(3), 231-248.

Tuckman, B. W. (1965). Developmental sequence in small groups. *Psychological Bulletin, 63*(6), 384-399.

Tuckman, B. W., & Jensen, M.A. C. (1977). Stages of small group development revisited. *Group and Organization Studies, 2*(4), 419-427.

Ullah, S., Kimani, D., Bai, Y., & Ahmed, R. (2018). Assessing the design of accounting modules across UK higher education institutions. *Cogent Business & Management, 5*(1), 1-12. https://doi.org/10.1080/23311975.2018.1510717

Volkov, A., & Volkov, M. (2015). Teamwork benefits in tertiary education. *Education + Training, 57*(3), 262-278.

Wageman, R., & Gordon, F.M. (2005). As the twig is bent: how group values shape emergent task interdependence in groups. *Organization Science, 16*(6), 687-722.

Watson, C. E., Kuh, G. D., Rhodes, T., Light, T. P., & Chen, H. L. (2016). Editorial: ePortfolios—The eleventh high impact practice. *International Journal of ePortfolio, 6*(2), 65-69.

Watty, K., & McKay, J. (2015). Pedagogy and ePortfolios: Purpose aligned to design (or the why and how). *International Journal of Pedagogies and Learning, 10*(3), 194-207. Retrieved from http://dx.doi.org/10.1080/22040552.2015.1135498

SENDING ONLINE TRAINING CONCEPT – COMPETENCY-BASED, ADAPTIVE LEARNING IN DATA SCIENCE FOR ICT PROFESSIONALS

Teemu Patala, ChangeLearning Alliance, Finland, Alan Bruce, ChangeLearning Alliance, Ireland

Overview

The European Union has noted over many years the existence of rapidly changing skills and persistent skills mismatches in the EU labour market. In the ICT sector, gaps have been regularly reported between the skills required and the skills actually attained by graduates of European Higher Education Institutes. The focus therefore has been to adopt a more proactive learning policy that can develop and test mechanisms that will help ICT graduates and workers to acquire the key relevant skills that will make them employable and adaptable to future market trends. In addition, such mechanisms will be designed to enhance worker mobility and flexibility.

The key steps proposed need to centre on engagement with employers to clarify their needs and with Higher Education Institutes to assess the nature of the skills, attributes and competences with which they are seeking to equip graduates. Further issues identified in this process include; the development of flexible modules of learning to address identified gaps, piloting of learning modules in several countries, and the evaluation of the impact of such learning modules from the point of view of ICT employers and workers. Making available learning modules in an OLE (together with systems such as a learning badge and an e-portfolio which will allow potential workers to record their relevant non-academic achievements in a structured way) would facilitate the dissemination and exploitation of such outputs in a sustainable and dynamic way.

A result of this endeavour is the SENDING project (KA2: Cooperation for innovation and the exchange of good practices – Sector Skills Alliances) which started in early 2018 with aims to address the skills' gap of Data Scientists and Internet of Things engineers that had been identified in the ICT and other sectors (e.g. banking and energy) in which Data Science and Internet of Things have broad applications.

To achieve this goal, SENDING is developing two learning outcome-oriented modular VET programmes using innovative teaching and training delivery methodologies for the two identified occupational profiles (data scientists and IoT engineers). Each VET program is being provided to employed ICT professionals into three phases that include: (a) 100 hours of on-line asynchronous training, (b) 20 hours of face-to-face training and (c) 4 months of work-based learning. A certification mechanism has been designed and will be used for the certification of the skills provided to trainees of the two vocational programs, while further recommendations will be outlined for validation, certification & accreditation of provided VET programs. Furthermore, SENDING has defined a reference model for the vocational skills, e-competences and qualifications of the targeted occupational profiles that are compliant with the European eCompetence Framework (eCF) and the ESCO IT occupations, ensuring transparency, comparability and transferability between European countries. Finally, a set of exploitation tools will be developed, giving guides to stakeholders and especially companies and VET providers, on how they can exploit project's results.

In this paper, we will focus specifically on the development of the SENDING online training concept – how the project team was able to identify what kind of approach would fit this specific purpose of training, what the key design principles were and how technology solutions will be used to implement the concept in practice.

Skill gaps identified among ICT professionals

Competitiveness, innovation and job creation in European industry are increasingly being driven by the use of new Information and Communication Technologies (ICTs) and the availability of high skilled and qualified workers in line with rapidly evolving market trends. ICT is an economic sector that is rapidly changing, has a strong momentum and an important contribution to the growth of almost every economy. According to EC, during 2010, the ICT contribution to Europe's growth represents 5% of GDP and ICTs drive 20% of Europe's overall productivity growth. Furthermore, despite the uncertainty seen on global labour markets during and after the economic crisis, the employment of ICT specialists has been largely unaffected, as at European level the employment growth rate for ICT specialists has remained on an upwards path averaging 3% growth per annum since 2006, i.e. it was more than eight times higher than the average growth rate of total employment over the same period (Eurostat, 2019).

As ICT is a general-purpose technology, changes and disruptions in the economy can have significant influence on the future skill demands for ICT professionals. Data Science (DS) and Internet of Things (IoT) have been recognized as the technologies among the key drivers of change with regards to the skills required by ICT professionals (Skills Panorama, 2016). Furthermore, Big Data and Data Science in general have the potential to directly contribute €206 billion to the EU economy by 2020. However, one of the main barriers to achieving this potential is the forecast skills gap associated with Big Data given that, according to estimations, there will be a 160% increase in demand for Data Scientists from 2013 to 2020 for 346.000 new jobs (European Commission, 2019).

This forecast, together with the rapid and continuous evolution of Data Science and IoT technologies and their broad application at other industry's sectors than ICT sector (e.g. banking, energy, assurance) make the skills required by related occupational profiles (e.g. Data Scientists, Internet of Things Engineers) increasingly sophisticated, and the need to be constantly updated is now imperative. In the aforementioned landscape, the specific needs and challenges that the SENDING project intends to address can be outlined as follows:

- Challenge 1: Addressing the skills' gap of Data Scientists and IoT engineers, by developing curricula for the provision of learning outcome-oriented modular VET programmes using innovative teaching and training delivery methodologies.
- Challenge 2: Providing the Data Scientists and IoT engineers skills and competences, that are transferable and recognized among European countries according to European established frameworks and standards.
- Challenge 3: Contributing to the increased demand of industry sectors other than ICT sector (e.g. banking, energy, logistics) for high-qualified Data Scientists and IoT Engineers occupied with e-skills and competences that meet their expectations.
- Challenge 4: Making the trainings provided more relevant to the actual needs of labour market, by focusing on learning outcome-oriented programs that include strong work-based learning components and combine knowledge and skills with personal and sociocultural competences.

Education and Training 2020 (ET 2020) strategic framework (European Commission, 2018) is the main framework established by EC for the European cooperation in the fields of education and training. It is a forum for exchanges of best practices, mutual learning, gathering and dissemination of information and evidence of what works, as well as advice and support for policy reforms. SENDING contributes to achieving the objectives set by ET 2020 by the following means:

1. Eliminating skills deficits in the ICT workforce, and further development of skills, through the design, delivery and assessment of VET programs that include effective learner tracking systems and feedback loops and are more relevant to the ICT labour market.
2. Improving the quality and efficiency of vocational education and training, through the design of learning-outcome oriented VET curricula, as the trend is moving away from learning objectives set for teachers, to designing curricula based on learning outcomes, defined as a set of knowledge, skills and competences.

Furthermore, SENDING contributes to the Bruges Communiqué on enhanced European Cooperation in VET (European Commission, 2010) for the period 2011-2020 which reinforces the main VET development directions established within the Copenhagen Process. Its contributions lie in (a) delivering VET programs that include high quality courses which provide the right skills for specific jobs and give to learners more opportunities for transnational mobility and (b) increasing the cooperation between the major players responsible for ICT professionals' enhancement, namely employers, professional associations, VET providers, higher education institutes, research centres, and SMEs, across Europe.

ICT skill gaps in the European context

The skills gap in the ICT sector and especially that of Data Scientists and IoT engineers is a European wide problem which can potentially affect the ICT sector and other sectors at which ICTs are widely used, together with the European economy growth, innovation, competitiveness and sustainability. Furthermore, enterprises and organizations need to know the core areas of expertise required for each role and maintain appropriate levels of competences; they must be able to recruit and train suitable and high qualified employees in a European and global competitive and continuously changing technological environment. Handling this problem in an efficiently and effectively manner at European level, ensuring the transferability, transparency and applicability of the proposed solutions, requires the transnational cooperation between all the relevant stakeholders: higher education institutes, VET providers, associations representing IT companies, associations representing IT scientists, enterprises and accreditation organizations.

The fact that the stakeholders and beneficiaries of the project originate from four EU countries (Greece, Bulgaria, Cyprus, Ireland) that are characterized by diverse socioeconomic characteristics, VET systems and institutional environments is intended to result in project outcomes of broader European relevance and applicability. Furthermore, the European cooperation among main stakeholders will enable the definition of a skills' certification mechanism according to European standards, thus increasing the recognition of qualifications at European and national level within a sector, facilitating cross-border certification and building mutual trust.

Furthermore, EU labour-market mobility is particularly important in the ICT sector (and other economy's sectors) both from enterprises' point of view within the sector and the countries that either have or are seeking to have a developed ICT sector. Significant numbers of jobs in the EU ICT sector are filled from outside the EU. In Ireland, for example, over 25% of foreign nationals employed in the information and communication sector in 2012, and 30% of those in professional, scientific and technical activities came from outside the EU. SENDING will contribute to the increased professionals' mobility in the economic sectors at which Data Science and Internet of Things have broad applications (e.g. ICT, banking, assurance, energy) due to its European approach and relevance.

Finally, as the main outcomes of the project will be implemented according to European standards and policies, (e.g. the common reference scheme of competences, skills, knowledge and proficiency levels for Data Scientists and IoT engineers, that will be designed taking into account the eCF and ESCO), they will benefit the whole European ICT sector and additionally the VET system.

The profound changes in technology in recent years have touched all aspects of human life. These of course are also related to profound changes in society in general and the structured world of work in particular. There is a general acceptance that traditional schooling, the "front-end loading" approach for preparation for the world of work, is no longer appropriate. This is so for a number of reasons including:

- Rapid changes in the world of work.
- The changing nature of goals for education and training.
- The realization that most people will have a number of occupations and job changes during the period of their working life.

Emphasis has altered form a concentration on instrumental conceptions of vocational education as a preparation for work during the years of formal schooling towards a concept of lifelong learning that is work related. The old dichotomies between general and vocational education, between liberal education and specific job training, are dying away. There is a growing realization that – as well as highly specific job-related technical skills, the demands of the workplace make it imperative that social and interpersonal knowledge, skills and competencies be incorporated in any program of learning both for and in the world of work.

Traditional companies often saw training as being all that was required – enough to learn to do the job. This stratified and minimalist approach fits badly with the realities of rapidly changing external environments where all employees have to work together in anticipating change and challenge.

In this context employees are no longer seen as merely selling their labour. They are also seen as producers who have the capacity and, some would say, obligation to learn. Many companies increasingly see on-job learning as essential to growth and enhanced competitiveness. This is because new skills are continually being acquired by staff. New ways of using old skills are also being learned. The learning organization produces employees who are: adaptable, flexible, innovative, pro-active, responsible and highly motivated through critical thinking.

Methodology

The main principles of the strategy adopted by the consortium to address the needs identified are:

1. Design of modular learning-outcome oriented curricula. This is critical in order to ensure that the knowledge, skills and competences provided to trainees are in line with the needs of labour market.
2. Participatory design with the involvement of companies in the development of curricula and training material. This is also a critical aspect to ensure that the vocational curricula and the training content meet the needs of labour market.
3. Developing a training framework that incorporates a strong work-based learning component. Work based learning will be a major component of vocational trainings to provide opportunities to apply knowledge in practical real-life workplace situations, and embedding transnational learning experience.

4. Structuring the training framework in a modular format to ensure that it can be adapted with minimum effort to the training needs of interested companies after the end of the project.
5. Developing a training framework that includes effective learner tracking systems and feedback loops. This is critical in order to be able to track the progress of the trainees during the implementation of vocational trainings and after their completion and evaluate their impact.

Expected outcomes

The expected outcomes of the project are:

- A report of the desired learning outcomes of the vocational trainings in terms of knowledge, skills and competences for the occupational profiles of Data Scientists and Internet of Things engineers.
- A common reference scheme of competences, skills, knowledge, and proficiency levels of Data Scientists and IoT engineers.
- Two modular learning outcome oriented vocational curricula, one targeting Data Scientists and another targeting IoT engineers. Its curricula will include at least five educational modules. In the case of Data Science vocational trainings an indicative list of educational modules is the following: (a) Python for Data Science, (b) Statistics for Data Science, (c) Storing and retrieving data, (d) applied machine learning and (e) Data Visualization. In the case of Internet of Things vocational trainings an indicative list of educational modules is the following: (a) smart cities and homes, (b) wearables, (c) location tracking, (d) security and (e) communication technologies.
- Training material for the implementation of the two VET programs. This training material will cover 200 hours of on-line asynchronous training (100 hours of Data Science and 100 hours for Internet of Things) and 20 hours of face to face training (soft and transversal skills).
- A training methodology (online, face to face and work based learning) for the delivery of the VET programs to the learners.
- A methodology for the assessment of the learners during the delivery of the VET programs.
- A mechanism for the certification of the skills and competences provided to the beneficiaries.
- Three workshops organized at Greece, Cyprus and Bulgaria to promote project's activities and services to stakeholders and main target groups.
- Exploitation toolkits for higher education institutes, VET providers and companies.
- One final conference organized at Greece, to present to all stakeholders the main outcomes of the project, its sustainability plan, and how its outcomes can be further exploited by higher education institutes, VET providers and companies.

Development of SENDING adaptive training concept

During the first year of the project, the main focus has been in reviewing existing research on e-skills, e-competences and qualifications required by Data Scientists and IoT engineers. Based on this an analysis has been carried out about the specific demands of learners, and the curriculum to meet these demands has been established. The next steps of the project focused on outlining the pedagogical concept for training and identifying technological enablers to implement the concept in practice.

Pedagogical design principles

It's become evident that most learners participating the training would be employed full time when taking the training. Secondly, there's a lot of variety and diversity in the skills background and competences of participants. These issues set some specific demands for how the training should be delivered, particularly with regard to efficiency and effectivity of the training. When outlining the concept for training, three key design principles were considered critical:

1. Competence-basis – the training should appreciate and value the existing competences of participants.
2. Adaptivity – there should be mechanisms that shape the training content based on individual need and existing competences. This
3. Continuous assessment – to keep track of learning progress and to ensure learners are motivated in each stage of the training, assessment against learners' competences should be continuous and results of assessment should be fed back to learners. Self-assessment is considered essential as well.

The SENDING training concept applies principles from competency-based learning, where the focus of learning is in concrete skills rather than abstract learning (Gervais, 2016). "Adaptive learning" (Ravindra, 2017) has gained popularity in corporate learning over the recent years. It refers to learning systems that adapt to learner-specific needs using automation and artificial intelligence (AI). Adaptation can make learning for workplace learners more targeted and can provide a better learning environment since learners perceive and process information in very different ways (Verdú et al., 2008).

In the context of SENDING training adaptation is made possible by using assessment before each learning module. The learning environment then recommends topics to be studied based on how the learner performed in the assessment. It is, however, yet to explore how much intelligence can be built into the system to make this process as precise, efficient and automated as possible.

To help understand the idea of SENDING training concept, a workflow chart was created defining the steps of course completion in the course platform (Figure 1.)

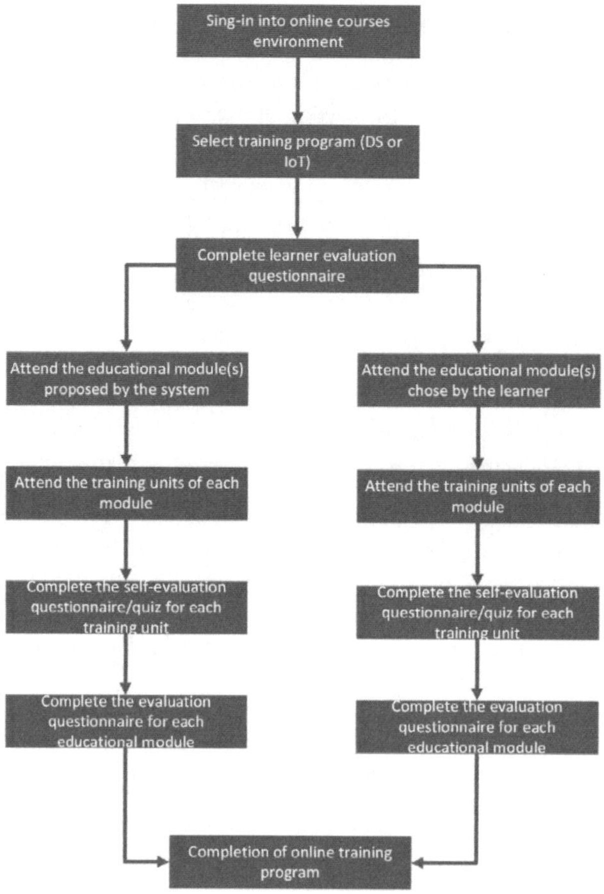

Figure 1. SENDING course completion workflow

Implementation and identification of technological enablers

Once the concept was outlined, it was time to look at the issue from the functional and technical perspective to understand what concrete mechanisms are needed to implement the concept in practice. This phase included expert interviews and a review of online sources covering most popular learning management systems and their applicability to demands identified by the project team. Using these sources an initial list of features was compiled including brief description of each feature in an easy-to-understand, practical manner. This list was shared with project partners and interest groups in the form of survey to allow them to assess the validity/applicability of each feature for the project purpose. A summary of survey results with total average weights assigned per each feature/functionality was compiled. The SENDING training concept will be implemented later in 2019 according to the concept definitions and the functional and technical specifications mentioned earlier.

Conclusions

The findings related to training concept development put strong emphasis on features that allow a flexible, modular and personalized learning experience for course participants. Noting the high volume of participants and plans to extend the training to larger audiences (particularly in companies) after the project much weight was put on user management, how easy and effortless it is and how course progress could be followed efficiently. Content development features are among the most valued features as well.

Thanks to the emergence of advanced learning data collection mechanisms and artificial intelligence (AI) there are new possibilities to develop online learning systems that enable more personalized and demand-driven provision of training. This will be highly important in workplace learning environments where time-efficiency and return on training investment are always considered critical.

References

European Commission (2010). Press Release Database. Bruges Communiqué: Education Ministers back Commission strategy for vocational training. Brussels, December 7, 2010.

European Commission (2018). European Policy Cooperation (ET2020) framework. Retrieved January 4, 2018, from https://ec.europa.eu/education/policies/european-policy-cooperation/et2020-framework_en

European Commission (2019). Digital Single Market Strategy. Retrieved February 5, 2019, from https://ec.europa.eu/digital-single-market/en

Eurostat (2019). ICT specialists in employment. Retrieved February 3, 2019, from https://ec.europa.eu/eurostat/statistics-explained/index.php/ICT_specialists_in_employment

Gervais, J. (2016). The operational definition of competency-based education. *The Journal of Competency-Based Education, 1*(2), 98–106. doi:10.1002/cbe2.1011.

Ravindra, S. (2017, September 5). Using Adaptive Learning in Corporate Training. Training Industry [Blog post]. Retrieved September 5, 2017 from https://trainingindustry.com/blog/learning-technologies/using-adaptive-learning-in-corporate-training/

Skills Panorama (2016). ICT professionals: skills opportunities and challenges. Retrieved December 1, 2016, from https://skillspanorama.cedefop.europa.eu/en/analytical_highlights/ict-professionals-skills-opportunities-and-challenges

Verdú, E., Regueras, L. M., Verdú, M. J., De Castro, J. P., & Péres, M. A. (2008). *Is Adaptive Learning Effective? A Review of the Research.* Paper presented at the 7th WSEAS International Conference on Applied Computer & Applied Computational Science (ACACOS '08), Hangzhou, China, April 6-8, 2008. Retrieved from https://www.researchgate.net/publication/228689326_Is_Adaptive_Learning_Effective_A_Review_of_the_Research

Connecting through Educational Technology
Proceedings of the European Distance and E-Learning Network 2019 Annual Conference
Bruges, 16-19 June, 2019

TOWARDS A PROTOTYPICAL CATEGORIZATION OF DISTANCE EDUCATION IN TEACHER EDUCATION

Andy Thys, Luc Vandeput, Jan Elen, University of Leuven, Belgium

Abstract

Higher Education is in constant transition. In the Flemish context this is illustrated by a gigantic transformation in teacher education (TE). In the context of this transformation Educational master-level programs (EQF 7 – VKS 7) are designed and will be implemented in 2019-2020. The main factor that has to be taken into account is the a priori choice to offer the master programs at different locations throughout the Flemish region. This demands from the new educational masters in TE a radical focus on multi-campus education. This article stresses the need to establish a strong vision on distance education (DE) in TE. To do so a typology of distance education in teacher education is developed. Elen et al. (2014) can be seen as a prime inspiration for the different approaches (of distance education in teacher education).

At the core of this article are the three outlined approaches as a basis for discussion. A methodology is presented to systematically sketch this process and its future aspirations. It has to be noted that this search for prototypes can never be seen as a fixed description but as a constant search and debate.

Context

At the core of this contribution are the descriptions of three prototypes of distance education (in teacher education). As an introduction, we first outline the background of this proposal by pointing at elements on three different levels.

Macro-level

At a Macro-level diverse challenges are arousing in the field of teacher education. Without being exhaustive four interrelated factors can be laid out. These are globalization and its impact on (higher) education, the rise of MOOCs (in higher education), the regional/national (and global) teacher shortage and probably the most pertinent, the decision of the Flemish government to launch educational masters at universities.

Meso-level

At the meso-level or program level there is a clear need to make well-informed choices regarding educational practices and, more specifically, about the use of distance education. Designing new courses within the new educational master programs (but also educational bachelors and graduates) can benefit from a typology of distance education in TE. Regarding the quality of DE, Wheeler (2012; p.1019) states that "distance education, when managed effectively, can provide remote learners with an equivalent quality of experience to leaners studying in more traditional setting". This statement clearly shows the possibility of distance education to provide quality education. The prototypes may help institutions in making adequate decisions with respect to distance education and to provide quality in distance education.

Micor-level

The micro-level covers the interactions between the student and different aspects of the learning environment (e.g. interaction within a digital learning environment between teacher and student). The assumption is made that a typology can guide teacher educators and designers in making informed choices about the learning environment. Future research can show to what extent the presented typology is experienced as a scaffold for teacher educators in their day-to-day job.

Nonetheless, the key point is to stimulate TE programs to position themselves in one of the approaches, so they can think differently about teacher education at remote locations, university colleges and universities. As a spill-over this article can support the establishment of a research agenda towards distance education in teacher education.

Method

Three consecutive steps can be distinguished in this paper: First the construction of the prototypes was strongly inspired by Elen et al. (2014). This conceptual article shows the necessity to think about different approaches to ICT-integration in Flemish education based on large scale surveys (see MICTIVO). The idea of working with prototypes to increase the quality in programs was adopted. Second the use of roundtable discussions is described. Third and last the proposed activity at EDEN 2019 is expressed. These steps are an attempt to validate the prototypes and dimensions through an iterative process with an extensive group of (educational) stakeholders.

Constructing the prototypes

To make a connection between the two central concepts in this contribution (DE and TE), the authors present three prototypes/approaches. The approaches are constructed as a basis for debate and discussion with other teacher education institutions. This is represented in the method used. To distinguish these types of approaches different source materials were used. After selection based on an exploratory literature study (see e.g. Ossiannilsson & Landgren, 2012; Ehlers, 2006) five dimensions were distracted on which the prototypes might differ. These are: (a) integration of research and practice, (b) possibilities towards innovation, (c) designing of learning environments, (d) policy and support and (e) the role of the teacher trainer. Each of these five dimension will be discussed in the presentation of the three approaches.

Roundtable

Once the prototypes have a stable (qualitative) description roundtable discussions with different stakeholders will be organized (the roundtables are still on-going). During these roundtable discussions two central questions are put forward: Can these prototypes be a first step towards a vision on DE in TE? Second, can these prototypes act as scaffolds for designing and implementing distance education in teacher education? Answers to these questions are rather complex and can't be given in one session. In order to get in-depth discussions different rounds of roundtables are organized with a semi-structured set of questions. The five previously mentioned dimensions will be used to structure the discussion. Input from different roundtables will be summarized in a plenary session, in order to get a full and comprehensive view on the above-mentioned questions.

EDEN 2019

Prototypes (as they stand) will be presented during the EDEN 2019 session. Second the participants will be integrated in the methodology by participating in a concluding roundtable. This will result in a final version of the prototypes.

Participants

A diversified group of participants will be invited to the roundtable discussions. Without being exhaustive these are: teacher educators, heads of programs, institutional experts of supportive services, researchers, learning path counsellors and students from universities and university colleges. These participants will be grouped in alternate sessions to get a diverse image of the presented issue.

Three approaches towards distance education in teacher education: a first proposal

The literature and a first analysis indicate that three prototypes can be identified based on the question on the central role of 'distance education': a leaner-centred approach, a modelling approach and a anticipating approach. The approaches also evoke speaking images about DE in TE, these will be added at the end of each approach.

Approach 1: A learner-centred approach toward distance teacher education

In this first approach, institutions for teacher education take a stance towards distance education that appeals to requests of the learner: more specifically, requests from students concerning for a teacher education program that is ubiquitous and hence, independent from time and place.

Research and follow-up aren't core values of the institution (and/or program) but can nonetheless be present mostly based on ad hoc initiatives.

Innovation is mainly directed at serving the student, making the TE program as flexible and ergonomic as possible.

With respect to the learning environment mainly teachers and sometimes designers use an ad hoc approach. In most cases the learning environment is implemented by one person with maximal adoption towards learners' requests. In other words, this approach tends to focus on adaptive learning environments for the students. Technology in this first approach is more used to distribute teaching materials and to stimulate learning by means of one-way or two-way communication (Albright et al., 2009; p.37).

The policy is primarily related to "marketing" and so the student is regarded to be a consumer who needs to be pleased. This for example manifests itself in large scale (student-centred) satisfaction surveys.

In this first approach the role of the teacher trainer is limited to instructor and evaluator, thus an individual teacher educator is responsible for testing and supporting the learning goals. In some cases, he/she can also be described as an ad hoc designer of learning environments.

In a metaphor, this approach can be labelled as *the servant* or *the waiter*, always very keen on servicing his clients.

Approach 2: A modelling approach toward distance teacher education

The exemplary approach confronts future teachers with the possibilities (and limitations) of distance learning in practice. By doing this, students experience distance education in an exemplary manner. This approach models so called *good practices* of distance education in preparation of future teachers.

Research and projects aim at optimizing the support of learning processes through the use of evidence-based teaching practices. The research and projects reflect the current understanding of distance education and are in line with on-going developments (e.g., how to organize co-teaching, how to use tablets in the classrooms).

Innovations in this approach tends to be focused on including more diverse student populations, becoming more elaborated for a broader range of learning goals and signal new developments in education.

In order to design learning environments that can be characterized as *modelling*, the design and implementation process are carried out by colleagues/teams using a systematic design and development.

To constantly be seen as a modelling teacher education program oriented towards offering high quality distance education, resources are made available to support the development of high-quality learning environments. Consequently, the teacher program can be seen as an 'example' of good practices and so this implies study visits and training from other teacher training institutions.

In this second approach the teacher educator aims to be an example and thus is a mentor, a coach and a designer in distance education (also see "guide on the side teacher").

For this second approach the image of the "proud sport champion" comes to mind. A person who, through many effort, creates a buzz around him and his sport and by doing so attracts others.

Approach 3: An anticipating approach towards distance teacher education

Distance education is not a means for an end but the starting point for designing and developing TE. By taking distance education as a constituent, the approach questions leading practices. Or in other words, this approach shows a vision on distance education that is a catalyst to seriously question existing teaching practices (e.g. Why use fixed class groups? What's the role of physical presence in TE? What's the place of ad hoc constructed learning materials? etc.). This approach also includes diverse approaches to Blended Learning. Therefore, alignment throughout different dimensions of the program is a necessity in this anticipating approach (Biggs, 2003).

Research in this approach dares to question leading practices and generally assumed activities with emphasis on learning, teaching, teacher training and the societal role of education. As a logical consequence innovation in different educational settings is always at the forefront of research. In this dimension the 'pro-active' aspect is prominent on the agenda.

The innovations are closely linked with the research being done. Innovations start from the question on how regular problems can be solved by assuming that distant education is at the core, in other words that teachers' presence is only essential in very specific circumstances. From that radical starting point it is wondered how teacher education can be effective (resulting in excellent student learning outcomes) and sustainable. Examples can be seen in the use, make and share of Open Educational Resources (OER), the attention towards developing a disposition towards critical thinking stimulation, close relationships with partner(schools) in order to test and research educational innovations.

The dimension "designing of learning environments" can be characterized in this approach by four notions. First the design is always planned, thus never a so-called ad hoc design. This is particularly seen in the timing of the design process. The design is made long in advance to make sure there is the ability to get feedback from different stakeholders on the design. Linked with this, second, the designing of learning environments is always a team endeavour. Or in other words, it's well recognized that achieving high-quality materials and experiences and more satisfactory teaching and learning experiences, requires (or it's at least desirable to apply) a team-based approach (see e.g. Hirumi, 2002). Third, in order to get a qualitative and well-balanced learning environment the team responsible for the course maximizes the use of the present support (local, regional, national and international) at hand. A forth characteristic that is at stake here is what Hannafin et al. (1997) define as *grounded design*: "the systematic implementation of processes and procedures that are rooted in established theory and research in human learning" (p.102). This can be seen in the design that is neither teacher-centred or student-centred, but always learning-centred with an emphasis on technology integration.

As to policy and support, this third (challenging) approach represents a policy that takes distance education as self-evident, is integrated and widespread in order to establish these challenging practices. This can be seen in policies and practices towards special needs education (e.g. UDL), assessment policy that is aligned with policies on distance education, HR-policy, etc.

It's noteworthy to mention that the role of the teacher educator in this third approach is complex and multi-layered. Teacher educators are facilitators of learning, innovators in education; they are researchers, (co-)designers, and so on and in addition they are fundamental change agents that are oriented not only towards innovation but towards transformation.

In this third approach the question rises, who is the student? It is not so farfetched that the recruitment of students is no longer a regional aspect but has an international order of magnitude.

Institutions applying this approach try to anticipate to evolutions and societal challenges (e.g. teacher shortage, rise of educational technologies). In this sense these programs can't be seen as teacher training programs but are always teacher education (see e.g. Masschelein & Simons 2012).

This last approach can be depicted as a *surrealist painter*. Surrealism is many times seen as a revolutionary movement, a questioning of existing practices and ideas, affecting various fields (visual arts, philosophy, politics, literature, etc.). About his painting "The Son of Man" René Magritte pointed out that: "Everything we see hides another thing. We always want to see what is hidden by what we see. There is an interest in that which is hidden and which the visible does not show us. This interest can take the form of a quite intense feeling, a sort of conflict, one might say, between the visible that is hidden and the visible that is present.".

Discussion

This proposal attempted to describe, through three prototypical approaches, how distance education and teacher education can be connected or in the last approach even fused together. All programs benefit from additional educational research with regard to distance learning and advanced curriculum development.

As mentioned earlier this proposal aims to start a constructive and well-informed debate about the status of distance education in teacher education. The presented methodology is a first step in giving articulation to this goal. Future revision and re-examination are prerequisites for the development of the approaches. This puts the authors in a vulnerable position. The methodology, where different stakeholders are implemented, tries (at least to a certain extend) to overcome this.

References

Albright, M., Simonson, M., Smaldino, S., & Zvacek, S. (2009). *Teaching and learning at a distance: Foundations of distance education* (4th ed.). Boston: Pearson.

Biggs, J. B. (2003). *Teaching for quality learning at university* (2nd ed.). Buckingham: Open University Press/Society for Research into Higher Education.

Ehlers, J. (2006). Handbook on quality and standardisation in e-learning. Berlin: Springer.

Elen, J., Pynoo, B., Goeman, K., & Van Braak, J. (2014). Betrokken, voorbeeldig, proactief: ICT-integratie in de lerarenopleiding. *VELON Tijdschrift Voor Lerarenopleiders, 35*(4), 19-23.

Hannafin, M., Hannafin, K., Land, S., & Oliver, K. (1997). Grounded practice and the design of constructivist learning environments. *Educational Technology Research and Development, 45*(3), 101-117.

Hirumi, A. (2002). The design and sequencing of e-Learning interactions: A grounded approach. *International Journal on E-Learning, 1*(1), 19.

Masschelein, J., & Simons, M. (2012). *Apologie van de school: Een publieke zaak* (Educatieve ideeën: wereldse gebaren 5). Leuven: Acco.

Ossiannilsson, E., & Landgren, L. (2012). Quality in e-learning - a conceptual framework based on experiences from three international benchmarking projects. *Journal of Computer Assisted Learning, 28*(1), 42–51. https://doi.org/10.1111/J.1365-2729.2011.00439.X

Wheeler, S. (2012). Distance Learning. In N. M. Seel (Ed.), *Encyclopedia of the Sciences of Learning.* Boston, MA: Springer.

Acknowledgement

All participant to the round table discussion are thanked for their constructive and rigorous feedback during the entire process of this article.

EMBEDDING BLENDED LEARNING ENVIRONMENTS IN HIGHER EDUCATION: TOWARDS A EUROPEAN MATURITY MODEL

Katie Goeman, Stephan Poelmans, Veerle Van Rompaey, KU Leuven, Belgium, Wiebe Dijkstra, Willem Van Valkenburg, TU Delft, The Netherlands

The EMBED Project: A Quest for a European Maturity Model

A Partnership in Higher Education

The "European Maturity Model for Blended Education" (EMBED) is a higher education (HE) project (2017-2020) led by a consortium of universities across Europe: KU Leuven, TU Delft, the University of Edinburgh, the University of Aarhus, Dublin City University and Tampere University of Applied Sciences. It is coordinated by The European Association of Distance Teaching Universities (EADTU) and funded by the European Commission.

Aim is to support institutions when introducing, developing and implementing blended learning (BL) in HE. A reference model is created that encompasses all levels of an institution: the design of a course, organisational aspects such as policy making, staff support, training and leadership, while guarding the institution's quality culture. Internal stakeholders include learners, teaching staff, support services, technology departments and university leaders, while external stakeholders are key persons responsible for policy making such as governments, European university networks and the EU.

Basic Assumptions of the Maturity Model

The European maturity model or EMM includes criteria and instruments to assess the degree of maturity of BL in a HE institution. It is conceived as a staged maturity model; it includes a framework for change, based on progress markers related to stakeholder-focused outcomes. To this end, the aim is to look at the tangible practices at the micro level (courses and programme) and the meso-level (strategies and conditions) in place at a particular institution. It focuses on practices and conditions in-place, not processes nor input-output procedures. In accordance with its logic, maturity of a practice indicates a more holistic approach in terms of design, informed by evidence or experience. Maturity does not equal better practice, maturity equals in this view being "more comprehensive". In each of the maturity levels QA standards and indicators can assess the quality of a particular practice. However, this is not the aim of the EMM. The EMM is designed to assess blended teaching and blended education in terms of different levels of maturity, and to propose follow-up actions. These actions are embedded in the particular context institutions operate in.

The Project Phases

The project partners embrace a multilevel framework in order to tackle conceptual and implementation issues at the course level (micro), at the strategic level (meso) and with the intent to give relevant input to governmental policy (macro). Figure 1 depicts the different phases of the EMBED project:

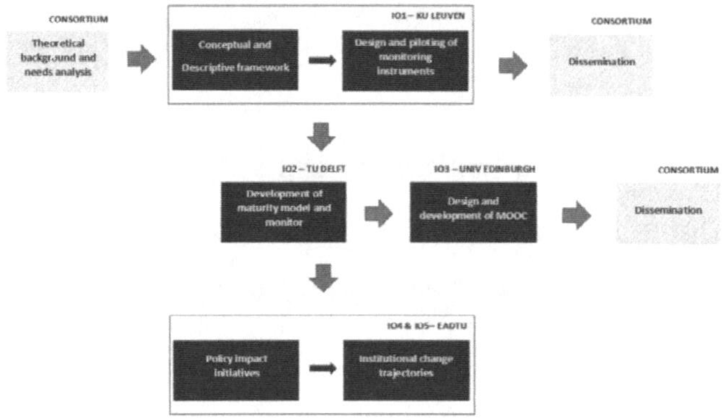

Figure 1. Phases of the EMBED Project

The EMBED Project: Status of Affairs

Between November and December 2018, TU Delft and KU Leuven have guided the transition from iO1 to iO2, and currently (February 2019) the design and development of a MOOC is being prepared. In the following paragraph the prominent past activities are described.

Conceptual and Descriptive Framework

During iO1 a thorough literature review was carried out to get an overview on current conceptions, theories and models. The desk research resulted in a general conceptual and operational framework, the blueprint of EMBED. It includes the outline of key terminology principles on blended learning, teaching and education (see also Goeman, Poelmans, & Van Rompaey, 2018). It allows researchers, practitioners and policymakers to talk common language and design, develop and assess current practices, strategical and implementation conditions in a systematic manner.

BL was defined as "learning as a result of a deliberate, integrated combination of online and face-to-face learning activities", while blended teaching (BT) was described as "designing and facilitating blended learning activities". The term *deliberate* refers to the explicit role of a design which specifies the proportion and sequencing of online and offline learning activities (course) or courses (program). The term 'integrated combination' refers to the logic for using a particular "blend" of virtual and physical spaces. Finally, blended education (BE) refers to "the formal context of BL (practices) that is determined by policies and conditions with regard to the organization and support of blended learning". It impacts hybrid (re)designs of courses and programs by the nature of their policies and conditions for organizing and supporting BL and BT. The complete process encompasses 4 iterative phases with particular ground(s) of decision guiding these phases (Table 1):

Table 1: The ground(s) of decisions and design of BL practices

	Design ground	Design phase
1	Context and curriculum specifications	Set up the blended learning environment What is to be learned? – define learning objectives and contents at course and program level Who is involved? (learner and instructor characteristics) – define the attributes of the LE What resources are available? – assess the implementation and change conditions that shape the teaching and learning context
2	Learner, program and instructor profile	Determine flexibility at course and program level: To what extent is flexibility offered? – determine one or more categories and dimensions of flexibility
3	Learning theory / Instructional design model	Define learning activities and their sequencing in line with learning objectives: Which learning tasks are offered, composed by the didactical components content, communication and construction and what is their grouping (individual vs group)? What learning activities will take place online, which onsite, in what order?
4	Learning activities and media affordances	Choose tools for delivery and organization of the learning activities: Which tools are employed? – determine interactivity and synchronicity as a function of media affordances

Design and Piloting of Monitoring Instruments

In parallel to the desk research, instrumentation for multilevel monitoring purposes was designed and piloted. Objective was to understand in detail which BL environments are in place staff, which designs for BL designers and teaching staff in higher education adhere to (and why), and the way these practices are reinforced by the university context, i.e. the strategical measures and operational conditions. Moreover, it tries to explain which factors promote or hamper maturity transition, at the course, programme and/or institutional level.

A mixed-method field study was set up across the different partner universities. This encompassed an online questionnaire and semi-structured interviews. A range of knowledge domains were covered, such as ICT, Nursing, Teacher Education, History, Economics. Detailed quantitative data was collected regarding the number and nature of both online and offline learning activities, next to tools for delivery and organisation of blended courses. The findings show that the flipped classroom approach is very popular as a BL design. The most frequently used resources, media and tools are not sophisticated. Detailed qualitative data was collected during in-depth interviews with policy makers, support and teaching staff. To this end, a protocol was developed which was translated in different languages. Many cases are driven by the lecturers' personal interest, their wish to improve the quality of in-class time, and to encourage deeper learning. The respondents' perceived advantages of BT include: active learning, strengthening of learning experiences, enhanced interactivity, and more contemporary education. Difficulties and crucial success factors were also identified. The analysis of the qualitative data suggests the following core themes: added value and constraints of BL approaches, drivers for BL implementation, course interaction, course design, course sustainability, institutional view on BL and institutional support, propagation of practices.

Development and Review of the Maturity Model

With the overarching themes and critical issues being identified, the next step involved the definition of different levels, dimensions and indicators of maturity. For this purpose, a pre-Delphi study and an expert panel were conducted between December 2018 and January 2019. The pre-Delphi study's objective was to assess the wording (labelling, clear understanding) of the dimensions of the EMM, and its completeness (definitions, demarcations of dimensions and levels of maturity). During the MID2018 conference in Maastricht, subgroups of participants generated feedback on the interim model. Their input, along with the outcomes of the pre-Delphi study has led to an enhanced version of the EMM.

The current maturity model consists of three maturity levels, subdivided in dimensions and indicators considered crucial for discerning course and programme practices, next to institutional conditions and strategies. These were deducted from literature and the series of research, development and review activities as previously described.

Dissemination Activities

Throughout the whole project dissemination activities, including multiplier events and training initiatives, are organised on a regular basis. The purpose is to create awareness about the EMBED project, its progress and results (see https://embed.eadtu.eu). It gives different (local) stakeholders (students, teaching and support staff, course designers and programme coordinators, university leaders) the opportunity to learn about the core insights of the project, and benefit from the project instruments for practice and policy making. In September 2018, for example, a 3-day training was organized at the Tampere University of Applied Sciences. Training activities were clustered around the following topics: (a) General framework – Blended learning, teaching and education, (bc Blended learning design, (c) Embedding existing materials in a BL environment, (d) Embedding interactivity and tools in a BL environment and (e) Embedding video and screencast in a BL environment.

The EMBED Project: An Outlook and a Critical Retrospect

TU Delft will establish the final version of the EMM based on the outcomes of a 3-round Delphi study. The Delphi method allows to collect and interpret a collective point of view of expert-participants in order to generate empirical validation. An international panel of experts is invited to critically review in a grounded way the complete EMM. Throughout three rounds they will receive questionnaires which constitute Likert-scale assessments of each indicator per action level, ranked and described in detail per maturity level. The expert feedback, including convergent and divergent views, is analysed statistically and incorporated after each round (between round 1 and 2, between round 2 and 3). The results give impetus to shape the questionnaire in the subsequent round.

The strength of the EMBED project is at the same time its Achille's heel. Even though a profound literature review was carried out which allowed to assess recent evidence on BL and related topics and terms, it is still difficult to reach consensus within the project consortium on the terminology and, consequently, operational procedures and instruments. In this regard, using the Delphi method to define each of the general EMBED parts, as well as assess the completeness and appropriateness of the specific dimensions, indicators and criteria is an asset. The diversified composition of the expert panel allows to consider different perspectives and experiences, and to work towards an agreed multilevel, multidimensional model.

References

Goeman, K., Poelmans, S., & Van Rompaey, V. (2018). Framing Blended Learning, Teaching and Education. *ICERI2018 Proceedings, Sevilla*, 1676–1680.

EMBED (2017). European Maturity model for Blended Education. Retrieved from https://embed.eadtu.eu/en

PROMOTING PERSONALIZED LEARNING DESIGN: THE ROLE OF ONLINE PEDAGOGICAL INTERVENTION

Hamdy A. Abdelaziz, Hamdan Bin Mohammed Smart University, United Arab Emirates

Abstract

Online learning technology and design has maximized and optimized the potential chances of personalized, customized, and adaptive learning. This theoretical paper is proposing a new dynamic pedagogical intervention model for effective personalized learning design. The author is trying to share a personal and practical answer to the following two questions: (a) What are the disruptive learning principles of the third renaissance learning paradigm that impact pedagogical engineering and intervention for personalized learning design? (b) What is the suggested model for effective online pedagogical intervention to promote personalized learning design? This perspective was guided by ten emergent disruptive learning principles of the third renaissance learning paradigm that impact online pedagogical engineering, management and intervention for personalized learning design. Effective online pedagogical intervention has four major dimensions that are grounded/interacted and focused on four metaphoric lenses: (a) types of learners (4Cs): Casual, Committed, Concentrated and Continuing; (b) pedagogical levels (4Ps): Intelligent, Agile, Distributed and Situated Pedagogy; (c) intervention levels (4Es): Enriching, Enhancing, Engaging and Empowering; and (d) online assessment frames (4As): Assessment of learning, Assessment for learning, Assessment as learning, and Assessment in learning.

Introduction

Online educational systems and programs worldwide are facing many challenges and issues such as: retention rate, reduce time-to-degree, non-formal and open-personalize learning, freeload and overload learners, pedagogical distance (isolation), organizational analytics and quality matter – to mention few. These challenges are pushing to reshape and re-engineering online pedagogical design models and practices to promote the competencies of personalized learning design.

Since the beginning of the 21st century, there are major shifts in educational paradigm. These shifts are applied on both conventional and online learning contexts. Of these shifts: (a) from standardization to personalization, (b) from content engagement to knowledge engagement and creation, (c) from judgmental assessment to developmental and dynamic assessment, (d) from dominant culture of testing to dominant culture of value and learnability, (e) from instructional systems design (ISD) to personalized learning design (PLD), and f) from problem solving to design thinking and design authoring (Abdelaziz, 2015).

In the third renaissance-learning paradigm, new advances in the science of learning and emerging education goals emphasize the importance of helping people control, mediate and regulate their own personalized learning. Therefore, the roles of online pedagogy should be expanded beyond the traditional concepts of delivering and testing to help learners build their own personalized values and illustrate their deep cognition to themselves, peers, teachers, their macro and micro community and professional networks (Abdelaziz, 2014a). The ultimate goal of any pedagogical and educational system is to prepare learners to become knowledge generators and life-long learners (Ally, 2008). Without a plan for transformative pedagogical design, smart technology often remains ancillary to personalized learning.

In online learning contexts, the role of pedagogical design became an integral part of effective personalized learning, especially with increased demand on MOOCs, cMOOCs, and on online learning certificates, degrees, and programs. As such, pedagogical design models are also changed to play a multi-dimension role. According to Gustafson & Branch (2002), the role of models in instructional development is to provide us with conceptual and communication tools that we can use to: (a) visualize, direct, and manage processes for generating episodes of guided learning; (b) view both the linear and concurrent aspects of instructional development; and (c) select appropriate operational tools to maximize learning paradigms.

With the increasing demand of online courses, higher education institutions started to offer open and online courses and programs. Massive Open Online Courses (MOOCS) are example of unlimited participation and open access course via the Web. Although, these courses have varieties of electronic content, e.g. videos, lectures, and readings, but still have an issue regarding the pedagogical design and management. To activate online learners and increase their potential learning abilities and personalized and professional outcomes, there should be online pedagogical intervention initiatives and practical models and approaches.

This theoretical paper is proposing a new dynamic pedagogical intervention model for effective personalized learning design. The researcher is trying to share a personal and practical answer to the following two questions:

- What are the disruptive learning principles of the third renaissance learning paradigm that impact pedagogical engineering for personalized learning design?
- What is the suggested model for effective online pedagogical intervention to promote personalized learning design?

Pedagogical Intervention (PI)

In online learning context, pedagogical intervention (PI) emphasizes on coaching, facilitating, and promoting learners' current and potential intellectual capabilities, dispositions and attributes. The purposes of PI are to know how and when online learners learn, unlearn, re-learn and help others to learn collaboratively. The core idea and concern of pedagogical intervention is that it exceeds the teaching and social presence dimensions. Teaching and social presence are important but are not enough to reflect or promote online learners' cognitive tempo, epistemological belief and ontological identity or pattern.

Pedagogical intervention is also a tetrad process to help both online facilitators and learners to visualize, personalize, manage and capitalize online teaching and learning activities and feedback. The ultimate goal of pedagogical intervention is to re-engineer online learning context to be customized and dynamic to fit with each individual learner's needs and online groups' collective minds. It gives a great chance and support for online facilitators to transform their foci from content benchmarks to mental benchmarks. It is a dynamic process to re-engineering online learning context to achieve smart technologies integration in the delivery and production of knowledge, skills and competencies.

Online pedagogical intervention has four major lenses that reflect levels of learners, pedagogical levels, levels of intervention, and assessment frames. Pedagogical intervention in online teaching and learning context is a cubic and grounded/interacted perspective and focuses on four metaphoric lenses: (a) types of learners (4Cs): Casual, Committed, Concentrated and Continuing (Al-Awar, 2009); (b) pedagogical levels (4Ps): Intelligent, Agile, Distributed and Situated Pedagogy (Guardia et al., 2016); (c) intervention levels (4Es): Enriching, Enhancing, Engaging and Empowering (Abdelaziz, 2015), and (d) online assessment frames (4As): Assessment of learning, Assessment for learning, Assessment as learning, and Assessment in learning. These four dimensions are interacting vertically and horizontally to produce 256 techniques for effective personalized learning design. Figure 1 presents the pedagogical intervention dimensions/lenses.

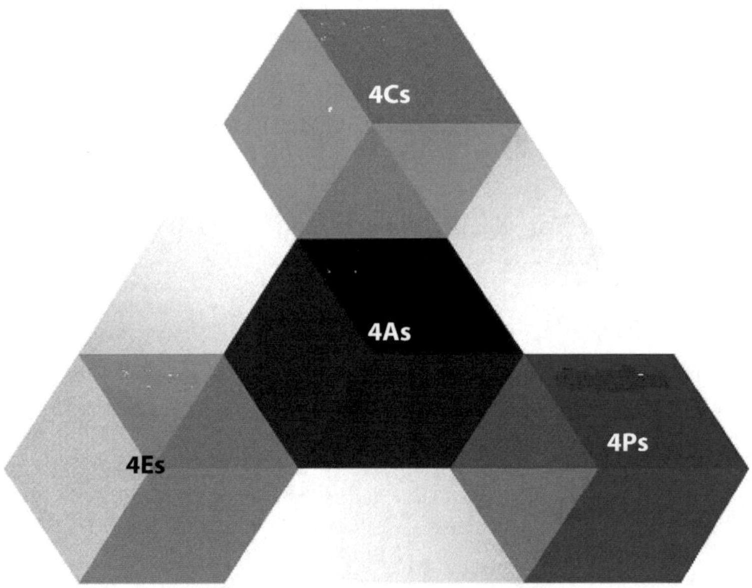

Figure 1. Pedagogical Intervention Dimensions/Lenses

Pedagogical Engineering (PE)

Pedagogical engineering refers to all efforts that online facilitator takes into account to innovate, disrupt, customize, personalize and manage online teaching and learning smart solutions and applications that reflect online learners' level, epistemological bases of the content knowledge, and core values of learning. Pedagogical engineering is a paradigm of mental and psychological practice to activate and empower online learning programs and courses. The ultimate goal of pedagogical engineering is to manage and lead effective online courses delivery and assessment process by supporting online learners to explore, discover, generate and capitalize new academic and professional content knowledge and competencies. PE could also be used as transformative mindtool to design thinking, modelling, re-modelling and design authoring of online learning practices and experience.

Grounded Goals of PI and PE

PI and PE of online teaching and learning are guided by the following grounded/emergent goals:

- Build models and patterns of learning in the third renaissance age.
- Empower design thinking and design authoring among online learners.
- Create a culture of creativity and innovation in online learning context.
- Activate personalization and self-organized learning competencies among online learners.
- Activate knowledge synergy and economy.
- Activate ontological conceptions and pedagogical analytics in online learning context.

What are the disruptive learning principles of the third renaissance learning paradigm that impact pedagogical intervention and engineering for personalized learning design?

To answer previously stated question, the authors reviewed some of recently published models of online pedagogical design and its related issues, variables and applications (e.g. Abdelaziz, 2012; 2013a; 2013b; 2014a; 2014b; Anderson, 2008; Burke, & Crozier, 2013; Chonody, 2015; Guardia, Witthaus, Rodriguez, & Campillo, 2016; Lockyer, Heathcote, & Dawson, 2013; Mekala, Shantha, & Ponmani, 2017; Ramdass & Masithulela, 2016; Robinson, 2011; Tegos, Demetriadis, Papadopoulos, & Weinberger, 2016; Saville, Zinn, & Elliott, 2005; Shum & Ferguson, 2015; Silva, 2013; Westberry & Fanken, 2015; Wise, 2014; Wright & Collins, 2007; Zhu, Yu, & Riezebos, 2016).

Pedagogical intervention and engineering paradigm is guided disruptive learning principles to suits online learning context (people, place and purpose). These principles are:

- Strong and profound online knowledge is gained through a networking process of collective mind and collective efficacy.
- Online cognition is an engineering process that needs immersive, interactive, active and reflective online mediator.
- The wisdom of practice in online teaching and learning context is a continuous process of reflection-on-action not just reflection-in-action.

- Online teaching is a productive and developmental dialogue to reduce alternative conception and free-load achievement through well-design cognitive and affective scaffolds.
- Delivering effective online courses needs a transformative pedagogical design to empower online learners through tetrad-like and loop-like learning activates and feedback.
- Online cognition catalyst is enhanced through effective integration of communication tools.
- Effective pedagogical intervention emphasizes problem analysis and design thinking.
- Early vision of pedagogical intervention comes from analysing learners' cognitive and affective tempo.
- In online learning context, when and who have the same importance like what, why, how and where.
- Effective pedagogical design gives a considerable attention to learners' disposition. Current generation of learners are divers, dynamic and differentiated by nature.

Pedagogical Intervention Techniques

Most of online teaching programs and courses are delivering online materials and content in a linear manner such as online lecturers, video segments, readings, asynchronous and synchronous activities, and online assignments. This linearity may improve the quality control of online course delivery, but it does not improve and assure the quality and the impact of online learning (Abdelaziz, 2012). Online pedagogical intervention exceeds the traditional techniques of delivering online courses. It emphasizes multimodality techniques that increase the level interaction and interactivities in online learning context for any type of learners (regular and special needs learners). PI depends on techniques that decrease the level of isolation and free-load learning. PI techniques increase the level of engaging of online learner to produce, generate, and innovate new knowledge or solution. Pi techniques are new windows of immersive learning design that support design thinking and design authoring tools and skills. Of these techniques:

- Cognitive scaffolding.
- Ongoing feedback and feedforward (360-Degree).
- Productive dialogues (error – reduction techniques).
- Cognitive Guided Instruction (accuracy mirrors).
- PSI attributes (Triangulation Practices: TP, SP and CP).
- Loop Learning Activities (Tetrad-Like Activities).
- DA (Dynamic Assessment Techniques).
- Interteaching (Mutually Probing Conversation).

The authors believe that these grounded online pedagogical intervention techniques may help in increasing retention rate and reduce-time to degree. They may also close the gap between pedagogical distance (Isolation) and pedagogical presence; and the gap between free-load and over load learner in online learning context. In addition, these techniques may increase the level of learning and organizational analytics.

What is the suggested model for effective online pedagogical intervention?

To design this PI model, the researcher reviewed some of recently published models of online pedagogical design and its related applications in online learning context. PI is a cubic and grounded perspective and focuses on four integrated dimensions: (a) types of online learners (Al-Awar, 2009), (b) pedagogical patterns (Guardia et al., 2016), and (c) intervention levels (Abdelaziz, 2015), (d) online assessment frames. These four lenses are generally articulated in Figure 1. These four dimensions are integrated and dynamic in a specific manner in which it produces 256 techniques for effective online personalized learning design. Figures 2, 3, 4, and 5 represent each dimension and its related concepts.

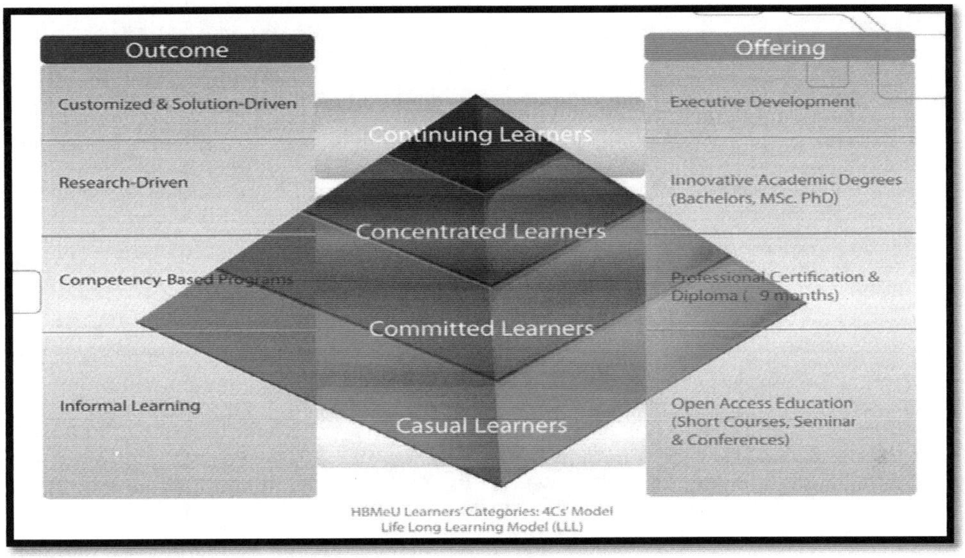

Figure 2. Types of Life Long (Online) Learners

Figure 3. Pedagogical Patterns

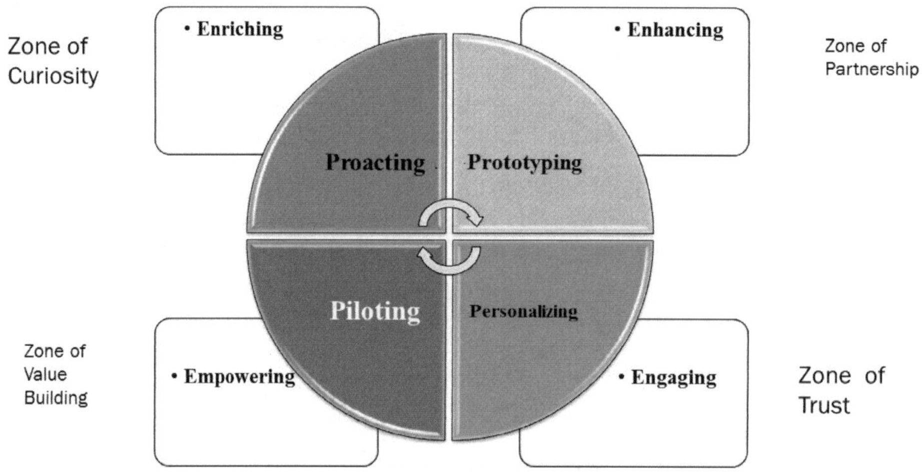

Figure 4. PI Intervention Levels

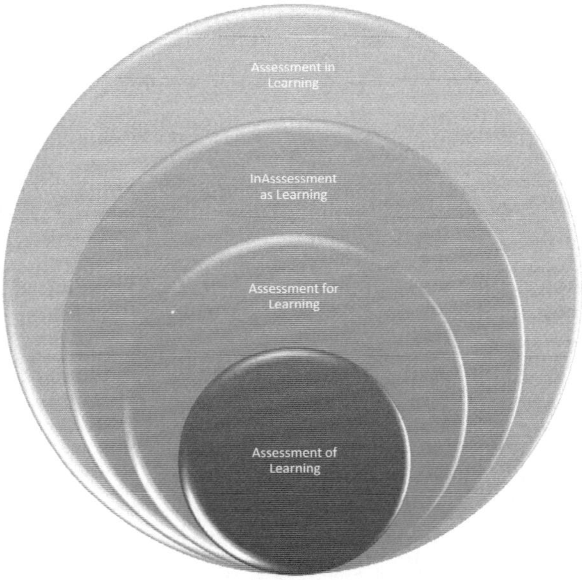

Figure 5. Assessment Frames

Mapping Learning Principles with PI Model

The following is an example to link one of the ten previously mentioned learning principles. "Strong and profound knowledge is gained through a networking process of collective mind and collective efficacy." To engineer the pedagogical intervention of this principle, online instructor should support his leaners (any level of learners) to interact with factual, conceptual, procedural and metacognitive knowledge by creating personal and group or collective learning spaces. These e-spaces are supported by Intelligent Pedagogy (e.g. creative utilization of emerging technologies), or by Agile pedagogy (e.g. facilitating personalization and flexibility of learning pathways), or by Distributed pedagogy (e.g. increase the focus on learning task and problem design and analysis), or by Situated pedagogy (e.g. increase the focus on context – big ideas or work-related issues/examples). Applying these four pedagogical levels needs sequential and parallel treatment from online mediator to enrich, enhance, engage and empower online learners' collective efficacy.

To validate this model, the researcher applied it on a sample of concentrated leaners (n = 23) studying a blended master degree in education registered in fall 2016 at Hamdan Bin Mohammed Smart University. The following are four samples of leaners' reflection about this model (Learners' reflection space (Sawti), HBMSU, 2016-17).

Search results

I'm writing here to express my deep interest to continue my study in this UNI that considered as advanced and prestigious educational edifice with various study disciplines and quality of learn; aiming also to expand knowledge and gain meaningful taste in my work, study as well as obtaining a gratifying social role in the future. For the class of Research Methods with Professor Dr Hamdy Abdulaziz I began my study and would like to point out some significant benefits I myself acquired. First of all, I found his work delivered properly certainly when it comes to th research's importance, role, value and consideration. Secondly, his GREAT patience with our different level of understandings as well as constant cooperation to clarifying any misconception information. Thirdly, many and many and many terminologies, concepts, aspects regarding research methods have eventually clarified! These outcomes from this class made me very happy since I really was so enthusiastic to seek research tools and techniques' comprehend . On the other hand, I just have one tiny criticism about the tasks given to us weekly, very intensive and long where most of us do not have the time to complete them, so kindly please minimize them in order to provide comfort for all students Thank you Professor for your efforts in this semester ... Kindest regards, Maneh Alahbabi

Take me there →

sawti Maneh Hababi 12/28/2016 - 16:04

Search results

The scale of measurement is very interesting topic as it assists the reasercher during the data collection, there are four types of S.M which are nominal, ordinal, interval and ratio to make it more easy to remember call it NOIR. Last semester i was enrolled in a course called "Research method in E-education LEAD600" with Prof. @habdelaziz , we learned step by step how to conduct and write a good research paper. He guided, instruct and taught us many important and useful steps that i refer to whenever i start writing my assignment papers. Its really very important to take RESEARCH METHOD training prog or courses before you enrol in any other courses, as it important for the masters degree students' to know step by step how to write and submit a high quality paper. Thank you

Take me there →

sawti Hind Al Maazmi 02/13/2017 - 23:07

My learning moments (Week 1)

1. The first L.M i learned is to write down a learning moments in any kind of field. Whether if i am attending a ecture, reading a book, talking to my mother, watching a tv show. I will start to write down anything new i earn and collect all the information in one notebook and by the end of each week i will go through my notes share and discuss it with my friends, family... etc.

2. It was so useful to know about the DIKW Hierarchy which stands for Data, information, knowledge and wisdom . On the same day, i went back home ad read a lot about DIKW pyramid and the relation between each element in the pyramid.

Thank you Professor Hamdy Abdullaziz

Hind Almazmi 20010221

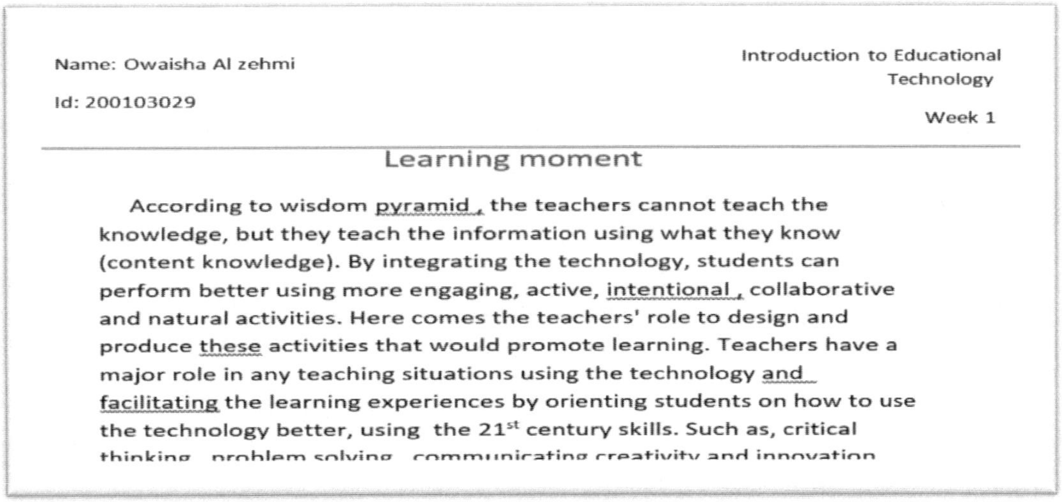

Name: Owaisha Al zehmi

Id: 200103029

Introduction to Educational Technology

Week 1

Learning moment

According to wisdom pyramid , the teachers cannot teach the knowledge, but they teach the information using what they know (content knowledge). By integrating the technology, students can perform better using more engaging, active, intentional , collaborative and natural activities. Here comes the teachers' role to design and produce these activities that would promote learning. Teachers have a major role in any teaching situations using the technology and facilitating the learning experiences by orienting students on how to use the technology better, using the 21st century skills. Such as, critical thinking, problem solving, communicating creativity and innovation

Conclusion and Recommendations

Online education in the fourth industrial revolution is facing a paradigm shift. This shift is very impacted by the advancement of learning technologies and learners' emergent attributes. Online learning technology, design and delivery modes are maximizing and optimizing the potential chances of personalized, customized, and adaptive learning. In the near future, online education and training models, programs, strategies and platforms will focus on developing human capital and learners' disposition and attribute to foster an innovation-driven culture of learning for impact. Without a plan for transformative pedagogical design, smart technology often remains ancillary to personalized learning. In the current theoretical paper, the author presented a grounded perspective that could be used to increase the level and quality of online pedagogical design and intervention to promote penalized learning. This perspective was guided by ten emergent disruptive learning principles of the third renaissance learning paradigm that impact online pedagogical engineering, management and intervention for personalized learning design.

Online pedagogical intervention has four major lenses that reflect types of learners, pedagogical approaches, levels of intervention, and assessment frames. Pedagogical intervention in online learning context is a cubic and grounded/interacted perspective and focuses on four metaphoric lenses: (a) types of learners (4Cs): Casual, Committed, Concentrated and Continuing; (b) pedagogical levels (4Ps): Intelligent, Agile, Distributed and Situated Pedagogy; (c) intervention levels (4Es): Enriching, Enhancing, Engaging and Empowering; and (d) online assessment frames (4As): assessment of learning, assessment for learning, assessment as learning, and assessment in learning.

As per the theoretical perspective presented in this paper, and as per the indicators that were collected from a piloting process, the author recommends the following highlights to be considered from online learning providers, instructors and practitioners:

- A shift from the concept of online teaching to online pedagogical engineer and intervention is highly demanded to promote personalized learning design and assessment.
- Assuring the quality of online learning needs a focus on humans' capital (online instructors, facilitators or pedagogists) and their role to apply and evaluate effective pedagogical practices, not only best practices.
- Online learning programs' providers need to invest on the concept of "Online Pedagogist" to make a transformation toward online pedagogical design, engineering, management, and intervention. The outcome of this paper could be used as a focal and starting point to mobilize this recommendation.

References

Abdelaziz, H. A. (2012). D4 S4: A Four Dimensions Instructional Strategy for Web-based Learning. *Turkish Online Journal of Distance Education, 13*(4), 220-235.

Abdelaziz, H. A. (2013a). Bridges of Trust: Towards a Constructive Model for Assessing Web-based and Electronic Learning. *International Journal of Technology Diffusion, 4*(2), 53-70.

Abdelaziz, H. A. (2013b). STEPP: A Grounded Model to Assure the Quality of Instructional Activities in e-learning Environments. *Turkish Online Journal of Distance Education (TOJDE), 14*(3), 56-77.

Abdelaziz, H. A. (2014a). Creative Design of Interactive eLearning Activities and Materials (IEAM): A Psycho-Pedagogical Model. *International Journal of Technology Diffusion, 5*(4), 14-34.

Abdelaziz, H. A. (2014b). Immersive learning design (ILD): A new model to assure the quality of learning through flipped classrooms. *Open Journal of Social Sciences, 2*, 212-223. http://dx.doi.org/10.4236/jss.2014.211027

Abdelaziz, H. A. (2015, November). *The Echo of Value: A Suggested Model to Build a Culture of Personalized Learning through Digital Media.* Paper presented at The D4Learning 2015, International Conference on Innovations with Digital Learning for Inclusion (d4l) in Aalborg, Denmark, November 17-20, 2015.

Al-Aawar, M. (2009). 4Cs model for smart learning in higher education. Retrieved from http://www.hbmsu.ac.ae

Ally, M. (2008). Foundations of educational theory for online learning. In T. Anderson (Ed.), *The Theory and Practice of Online Learning* (2nd ed., pp. 15-44). AU Press.

Anderson, T. (2008). Teaching in an online learning context. In T. Anderson (Ed.), *The Theory and Practice of Online Learning* (2nd ed., pp. 273-294). AU Press.

Burke, P. J., & Crozier, G. (2013). *Teaching inclusively: Changing pedagogical spaces* (2nd ed.). University of Roehampton. Retrieved from https://www.newcastle.edu.au/__data/assets/pdf_file/0004/305968/UN001_Teaching_Inclusively_Resource_Pack_Online.pdf

Chonody, J. M. (2015). Addressing ageism in students: a systematic review of the pedagogical intervention literature. *Educational Gerontology, 41*, 859–887. doi: 10.1080/03601277.2015.1059139

Guardia, L., Witthaus, G., Rodriguez, B., & Campillo, C. (2016). *Next generation pedagogy: IDEAS for online and blended higher education.* University of Oberta de Catalunya. Retrieved from http://openaccess.uoc.edu/webapps/o2/bitstream/10609/51441/1/Next_Generation_Pedagogy.pdf

Gustafson, K. L., & Branch, R. M. (2002). *Survey of instructional development models* (4th ed.). New York: Syracuse University. ERIC Clearinghouse on Information & Technology.

Lockyer, L., Heathcote, E., & Dawson, S. (2013). Informing pedagogical action: Aligning learning analytics with learning design. *American Behavioural Scientist, 57*(10), 1439-1459. https://doi.org/10.1177/0002764213479367

Mekala, S., Shantha, S., & Ponmani, M. (2017). The role of pedagogical intervention in improving the oral proficiency of engineering students. *The IUP Journal of Soft Skills, 11*(3), 7-28.

Ramdass, K., & Masithulela, F. (2016). Comparative analysis of pedagogical strategies across disciplines in open distance learning at Unisia. *International Review of Research in Open and Distributed Learning, 17*(2), 1-18. http://dx.doi.org/10.19173/irrodl.v17i2.2402

Robinson, K. (2011). *Out of our minds: Learning to be creative* (2nd ed.). UK: Capstone Publishing Ltd.

Saville, B., Zinn, T., & Elliott, M. (2005). Interteaching versus traditional methods of instruction: A preliminary analysis. *Teaching of Psychology, 32*(3), 161-163.

Shum, S. B., & Ferguson, R. (2012). Social learning analytics. *Educational Technology & Society, 15*(3), 3-26.

Silva, J. (2013). Understanding the construction of the teaching discourse in an on-line environment. *International Education Studies, 6*(3), 143-155. http://dx.doi.org/10.5539/ies.v6n3p143

Tegos, S., Demetriadis, S., Papadopoulos, P., & Weinberger, A. (2016). Conversational agents for academically productive talk: A comparison of directed and undirected agent interventions. *International Journal of Computer-Supported Collaborative Learning, 11*(4), 417–440. http://dx.doi.org/10.1007/s11412-016-9246-2

Westberry, N., & Fanken, M. (2015). Pedagogical distance: Explaining misalignment in student-driven online learning activities using Activity Theory. *Teaching in Higher Education, 20*(3), 300-312. http://dx.doi.org/10.1080/13562517.2014.1002393

Wise, A. F. (2014). *Designing pedagogical interventions to support student use of learning analytics.* Indianapolis, IN, USA: ACM. http://dx.doi.org/10.1145/2567574.2567588

Wright, R., & Collins, D. (2007). Developing pedagogical tools for intervention: Approach, methodology, and an experimental framework. *Proceedings of the 30th Annual Conference of the Mathematics Education Research Group of Australasia, J. Watson & K. Beswick (Eds)*, 843-852. MERGA Inc.

Zhu, Z. T., Yu, M. H., & Riezebos, P. (2016). A research framework of smart education. *Smart Learning Environments, 3*(4), March 2016. http://dx.doi.org/10.1186/s40561-016-0026-2

Connecting through Educational Technology
Proceedings of the European Distance and E-Learning Network 2019 Annual Conference
Bruges, 16-19 June, 2019

FUTURE SKILLS AND HIGHER EDUCATION "FUTURE SKILL READINESS"

Ulf-Daniel Ehlers, Baden-Wurttemberg Cooperative State University, Germany

Introduction

The discourse on the future of higher education is already an old one. Higher education Institutions are used to it and are slow in turning around which makes them stable and enduring organisations. In a way institutions and society are benefitting from their internal protection mechanisms which goes along with the status of autonomy and independence they are granted in democratic societies. However, in recent times it becomes clear that we are approaching a peak point in the "race between technology and education" as the Dutch Nobel Prize winner Jan Tinbergen called it about four decades ago (Tinbergen, 1975). One popular theory to explain the rising trend in inequality was first put forward by the Dutch Nobel Prize winner in Economics Jan Tinbergen over four decades ago. He characterised wage inequality as being the outcome of a "race between education and technology". In this theory, technology increases the relative demands for more skilled labour while education increases the relative supplies of such labour. Thus, rising inequality implies that technology is winning this race. It is characterized by technology, global and globally networked societies, institutions and individuals and education systems as a whole will have to make the next move in this race – and evolve in the light of to these developments, change their mode of working and evaluate their objectives. This is especially true for higher education amongst educational institutions, as the last autonomous and self-governed institutions in the education sphere. One important piece in this puzzle is the question of direction – change in which direction? What are the new skills which are needed for our societies to be sustainable and our organisations to be fit for the changed environments?

In this article we are presenting parts of a 2019 international Delphi survey about future skills in higher education (more in Ehlers, 2019, in print). The research is based on a multi-part research project called "Next Skills" in which we have been conducting research to shed light on the demand for specific skills which we refer to as "future skills" (more on www.nextskills.org). As has been demonstrated by other studies, too (see for instance Deming, 2017; Noweski, Scheer, Büttner, von Thienen, Erdmann, & Meinel, 2012; OECD, 2017), research in this area is of vital importance as future graduates need to adapt to an increasingly changing and complexity-gaining world that demands agility and "innovation in action". To address this field systematically, we pursued the question which skills are necessary for future employees and which skills are perceived as necessary to shape the future of society in a sustainable way. Other questions which we focus on in the project but will not present in this paper are how learning will look like on the future and how higher education institutions will have to change.

We approached these questions from a systems-ecological understanding of changing systems in society and their interconnectedness (Woodside et al., 2006), as well as from an education science point of view on competences (following the action oriented competence concept defined by Erpenbeck, 2010). Two studies have been conducted prior to the Delphi survey. The first project started in June 2015. In this we identified and analysed competence concepts in more than 120 German organizations. These had been identified on basis of submissions to an award scheme rewarding advanced concepts of skill, learning and competence frameworks within organizations. To take part in this award, organizations were asked to share their competence models and trainings offered to promote their employees' skill formation. Winners were then invited to participate in a qualitative interview study. Through an expert screening and analysis, we were able to identify main dimensions of action competence within the overall concepts submitted by the participating organizations. According to the expert's opinion, about 20 organizations in the sample proved to have very advanced, developed, and elaborated conceptions and documented approaches for competence development with their employees and advanced learning architectures. Within these documents, experts also found evidence of skill and competence descriptions, which are seen as important and essential for individuals' and organizations' performances in future markets and activities. For the second research project, the research team chose 17 organizations from this group of advanced, future organizations in order to conduct further research into finding dimensions and structures of future skills. To gain further insights into the specific skill set, organizational approaches to promote them as well as for the purpose of identifying drivers leading to the changed skill demand, we took a qualitative approach and conducted 17 in-depth interviews with representatives from a sample of those organizations, resulting in more than 700 minutes of interview material addressing the above questions. Based on the material, two researchers coded all interviews independently using the inductive coding technique (Thomas, 2006) and the software MAX QDA (VERBI Software, 2017). After coding, passages lacking unanimity were discussed among the researchers to gain inter-operator reliability in coding. As a result, we have obtained a set of future skills, insights into dimensions of change in organizations through digital and networked global collaboration processes and have specified a number of scenarios of future higher education. These results were taken as the basis for the international Delphi survey on future skill – future learning and future higher education. The international Delphi study focused on validating and elaborating the qualitative constructs gained through the interview study. In this paper we are presenting the result on one particular part of the study, the 16 future skills derived from our analysis, validated and elaborated through the international Delphi experts, as well as their opinion about higher education "future skill-readiness".

Methodology

The survey design has been carefully crafted on basis of previous experiences: Firstly, the international expert panel is described below (their professional as well as national backgrounds, and their fields of interest). Secondly, an overview on the themes, questions and survey logic of the two rounds of the Delphi survey will be provided.

The panel

We invited 53 international experts from different organizations and institutions. They worked within higher education institutions, as researchers in the field of pedagogy, networks concerned with learning and skill formation topics, the digitalization of higher education or within NGOs (more details in Ehlers & Kellermann, 2019). It was important to us, to consider the perspectives of both, representatives from higher education institutions as well as from consultants and practitioners from the economy. Further, we paid close attention to the fact that within the two sub-samples, people occupying different positions were included in order to allow for a maximum of differentiation and plurality of opinions on the topics surrounding the future of learning, skills and higher education, and avoid blind spots. 49 international experts participated in round 1, 46 experts in round 2, representing about 17 different countries (Australia, Austria, Belgium, Canada, France, Germany, China, Italy, Lithuania, Netherlands, New Zealand, Norway, Portugal, Spain, Sweden, Switzerland, and the United Kingdom).

Delphi method

The Delphi survey had two rounds, the second administered four weeks after the first. Both rounds were mainly focusing on asking experts to clarify concepts, definitions, terminology and rating importance (round 1) and of time to adoption in the field of future skills (round 2). The question logic can be seen in the figure representing the different thematic parts and showing how the two rounds build on each other. An important focus was put on participants' views of the abilities, the processes, the strategies, skills and competences which employees needed and will need in the future in order to cope and productively deal, as well as further develop the increasingly faster changing organizational reality. The experts provided ratings and opinions through qualitative comments which were analysed and resulted into improved and enhanced formulation of statements.

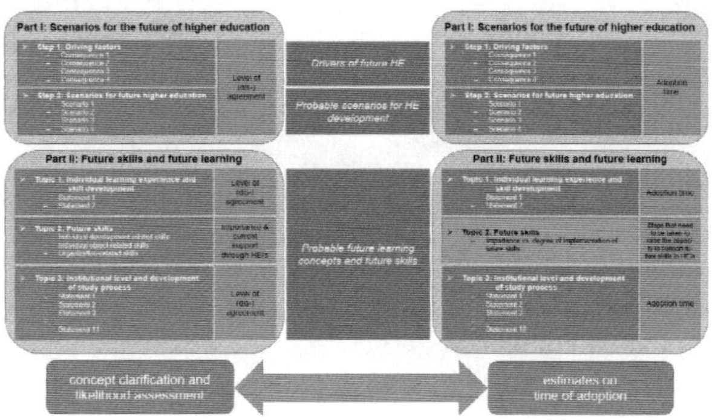

Figure 1. Delphi survey structure

Future Skills – and Higher Education Institutions'"Future Skill Readiness"

The Future Skills Approach – A Theoretical Model

Data for the future skill model were triangulated regarding methodology, data sources and theories used to reconstruct skills. The analysis of data resulted in a reconstruction of factors which are underlying future skill demands and reveals insights into the form and importance of learning in todays and future professional work environments of advanced "future" organizations. It allows a reconstruction of those specific individual abilities and skills which will – in the future – will be necessary to deal with challenges in professional future work environments.

A first important issue is to note that "skill" is a term which is always expressing a relation. Only in a relation, a skill becomes meaningful. A communication skill for example as such is not meaningful but communication in a skillful way *of* somebody *in relation* to something is. Using this insight, we were able to identify an inherent structure within the list of future skills, allowing for classification of such "future skill relations" into field of skill profiles which each has distinct relations. They can be classified according to the target of their relation – weather it is related to a subject (individual to itself) – object (individual to a certain task) – or environment (individual to social environment). Thus three dimensions allow to allocate skills according to their relation to subject – object – world. Important: All three dimensions are interrelated, and influence each other. We are introducing this threefold distinction (see Figure 2) because any kind of skill, ability or action can either be an expression to shape (a) an individual's relation to itself in past present or future (time dimension), (b) an individuals' relation to a certain thing or object (object dimension), or (c) an individuals' relation to somebody else or a group in the word (social dimension).

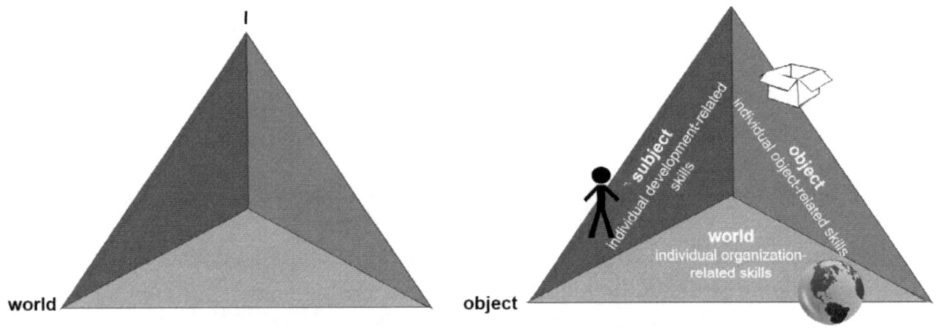

Figure 2. Three-fold distinction of future skills

This threefold distinction is rooted deep into philosophy of education (e.g. Dewey in his essay Knowing the Known) but recently goes back to Meder (2007, also Roth 1971), who is presenting a foundational, constitutive structure for education as a threefold relation. Our future skill concept is based on three different moments of theoretical reflection:

- skills are understood as "competences" as defined by Erpenbeck (2010), emphasizing that competences are dispositions to act in complex unknown future contexts;

- skills are viewed as relational concepts which can be described within the three dimensions of the structural view of education;
- future skills are viewed as a reaction to shifts which take place within the different parts of the theoretical framework, and can be described through the set of 16 future skill profiles.

The threefold concept which we suggest in our research as a theoretical basis allows to root the future skill discourse in education theory. This gives more direction and precision to skill terminology and allow to describe more precisely what we refer to as future skills instead of just listing terms in an additive fashion. In all of the three dimensions' shifts are going on. The interview data reveal a clear change in nature of what is demanded in the future in comparison to the past and in parts the present.

- Shift 1 – Subject related individual skills: Whereas in the past individuals could rely on following requirements, the future will demand more self-organization instead.
- Shift 2 – Object related individual skills: Whereas in the past individuals could rely on applying knowledge, methods and tools, the future will demand original creative development of new knowledge, methods and tools.
- Shift 3 – World/ organizational related skills: Whereas in the past organisations were organized and management according to clear structures, the future will demand fluid, enabling, agile cultures.

Figure 3 shows that shifts take place in all three dimensions (called "areas of action" in Figure 3). In addition, data reveal shifts in different fields as well by emphasizing the greater importance of individuals' responsibility for their own development, as well as competence management and autonomous navigation through an ever faster changing environment. Whereas in the past external (organizational) structures were a scaffold which provided guidance and orientation to individuals, such external structure and scaffolding will be decreasing in the future. Thus, individuals will have a stronger role to be navigators of themselves (in Figure 2 referred to as "relational structure"). And, finally, the components which skills are made up through (e.g. knowledge, skills and attitudes) are subject to shift as well. In our concept of skills, a skill is made up of four dimensions: knowledge, an (instrumental) application ability, a design-ability, and critical reflection-ability. Within these four parts of a skill, a greater emphasis will be on design-ability and critical reflection-ability can be perceived for future skills. Figure 2 shows that knowledge and application of knowledge will be such foundational elements which will, in the future, not be sufficient for successful performance. Much more importance was given to the two elements "design-ability" and "criticism/ reflection-ability" for future performance (called "skills dimensions" in Figure 2).

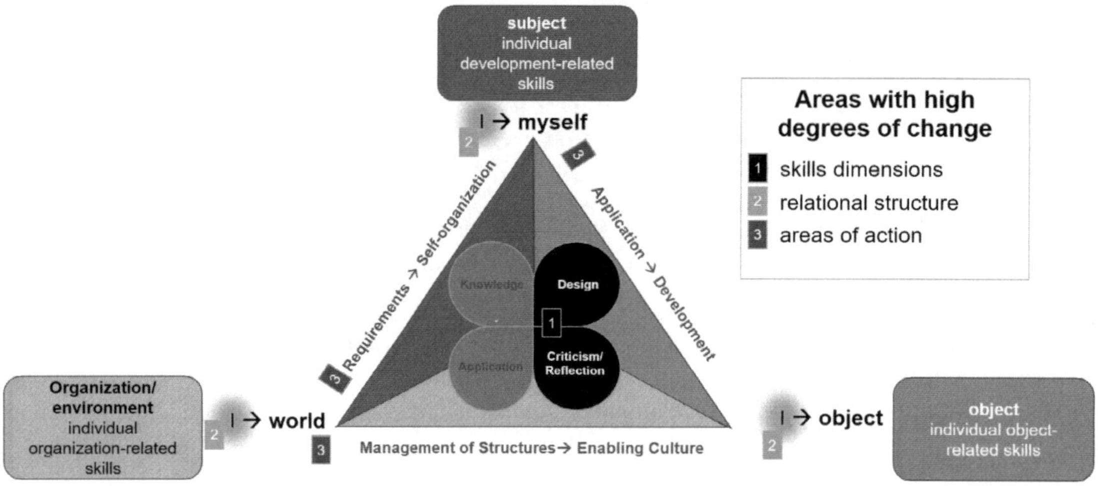

Figure 3. Combing the structural education model with the competency model to explain future skills

All three dimensions interact with each other and are not sole expressions of isolated skill domains. Subjective aspects influence outlook on objective aspects as well as social aspects impact subjective and objective aspects. The presented future skill model is thus going beyond a static model of listing a set of defined skills. It is secondly going far beyond digital or technical skills which will no doubt be important but represent just one ingredient for future skills. Their true values lie in the *personal development of dispositions to act self-organized* in a defined domain.

In summary, the future skill model is capable of describing the wide array of future skills in a clearly structured and well-described set of dimensions:

- The first future skill dimension is the subjective dimension of futures skills profiles. It is relating to an individuals' subjective, personal abilities to learn, adapt and develop in order to improve their opportunities to productively participate in the workforce of tomorrow, actively shape the future working environment and involve themselves into forming societies to cope with future challenges. It contains seven future skill profiles.
- The second future skill dimension is relating to an individual's ability to act self-organized in relation to an object, a task or a certain subject matter related issue. It is emphasizing a new approach which is rooted into the current understanding of knowledge but is suggestion to take knowledge several steps up the ladder, connect it to motivation, values and purpose and impregnate it with the disposition to act self-organized in the knowledge domain in question. It is not just a quest for more knowledge but for dealing with knowledge in a different way which is resulting into professionalism and not into knowledge expertise.
- The third future skill dimension is relating to an individual's ability to act self-organized in relation to its social environment, the society and organizational environment. It is emphasizing the individuals' dual role as the curator of its social portfolio of membership in several organizational spheres and at the same time having

the role of rethinking organizational spaces and creating organizational structures anew to make it future proof. It contains an array of five skill profiles.

The 16 Future Skills Profiles

Two main orientations for future skills have been defined through the study and the experts' judgement, they represent the main foundation for the future skill concept. They point to the essence of the future skills context: (a) constant adoption through learning and (b) uncertainty as inherent trait of professional contexts of the future. Specifically, the second aspect is constitutional for skills, as skill is defined as *dispositions to act in future unknown contexts* – rather than as *reproduceable knowledge*. In the Delphi survey, both statements received high levels of agreement, supported through qualitative commenting of experts, and are also seen as relevant today or within the next 5 years by the majority of experts. 89.2% of the respondents indicated agreement with our first proposition that the greatest challenge students would need to be prepared for through HEIs would be the constant need for "adaption through learning" in constantly changing future work environments ($M = 4.17$, $SD = 0.81$, $A_{Adaption(strongly\ agree)} = 37.0\%$, $A_{Adaption(agree)} = 52.2\%$). $A_{Adaption(strongly\ agree)}$ indexes the percentage of respondents, who strongly agreed with the statement, whereas $A_{Adaption(agree)}$ shows the percentage of the sample that expressed agreement.

Table 1: List of future skills

Subject	Object	Social
Autonomy: capacity to make an informed, uncoerced decision and act accordingly	Agility: ability to orient oneself in fast changing contexts, constantly changing objects	Sense making: ability to identify with and make sense of given organizational rules and values for one's own life and work
Self-initiative: individual ability to take an active and self-starting approach to work goals and tasks	Creativity: to be able to deal with task in a new, unforeseen way	Future mindset: ability to productively develop an organizations' context, continuously learn and develop one's skills and to be open for new and unknown challenges within a given organizational context
Self-management: ability to lead and regulate oneself to decide in a self-responsible way	Tolerance for ambiguity: ability to deal with uncertainty and in different roles	Cooperation skills: ability to cooperate in teams and have social and intercultural skills
Need/ motivation for achievement: individual's desire for significant accomplishment, mastering of skills, control, or high standards	Digital literacy: ability to utilize digital technology in a creative way for learning, working, collaboration	Communication competence: ability to actively create dialogue, achieve consensus and criticize
Personal agility: positive attitude, resilience and openness to changes, being comfortable in ambiguous and changing situations	Ability to reflect: ability to critically analyse made experiences and learn for future contexts	

Autonomous learning competence: ability to continuously adapt through learning, know learning methods, evaluate own progress, ability to learn motivated
Self-efficacy: one's own conviction to be able to act successfully on a given task

Figure 4 shows the skill profiles which are described in Table 1. As mentioned above it is important to note that each 'skill profile' contains a number of subskills which are viewed by the participants of the interview study as important within this skill profile (Ehlers, 2019, in print). The second statement suggested that the ability to successfully deal with uncertainty would become the most important skill in future work environments. The experts' opinion was largely overall in agreement with this position ($M = 3.73$, $SD = 1.10$, $A_{Uncertainty(strongly\ agree)} = 26.7\%$, $A_{Uncertainty(agree)} = 40.0\%$). $A_{Uncertainty(strongly\ agree)}$ indexes the percentage of respondents, who strongly agreed with the statement, whereas $A_{Uncertainty\ (agree)}$ shows the percentage of the sample that expressed agreement. The majority of elaborative comments stressed that experts perceived this skill to be or to become increasingly important, accompanying other future skills in their rise to importance.

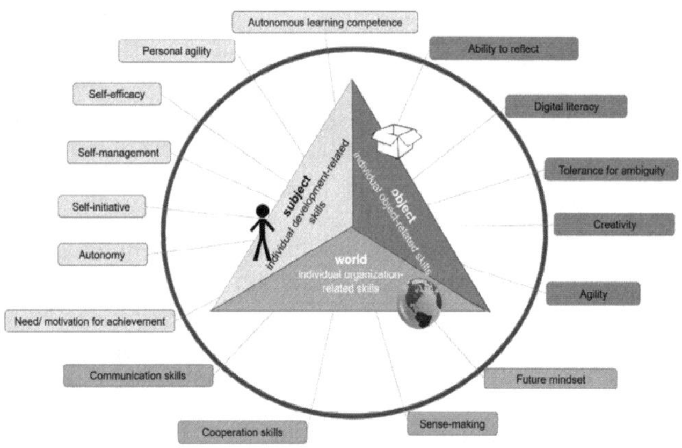

Figure 4. Delphi survey structure

The future skill profiles were validated and rated through Delphi experts – both on their importance, as well as on experts' opinion about higher education readiness to adopt those future skills into their mission. Both variables were assessed on a five-point Likert-scale, whereby importance ranged from 5 – *very important* to 1 – *not important* and support from 5 – *very good* to 1 – *very poor*. To gain an overview on the discrepancy between skill's importance and its respective level of support in higher education, we calculated the delta, subtracting the *mean support* from the *mean importance*.

All individual development-related Future Skills are perceived as important, with autonomy being rated as very important ($M = 4.53$, $SD = 0.62$). Autonomous learning competence ($M = 4.48$, $SD = 0.69$) and self-management ($M = 4.46$, $SD = 0.72$) occupied the second and third most important positions. Contrary to that the degree of implementation in higher education, expressing the evaluation of exerts how well HEI are equipped to support the development of these skills is rated. The delta between both values has been calculated. It shows that the largest discrepancy is perceived for the autonomous learning competence (Δ = 1.83) and autonomy (Δ = 1.81) – two of the skills that earlier had been rated among the most important.

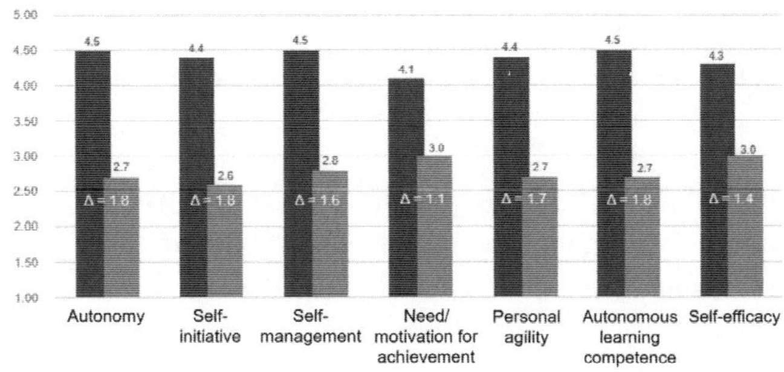

Figure 5. Subject and individual development related skills:
Importance (dark blue bars) versus current degree of higher education support (light blue bars) (N = 46)

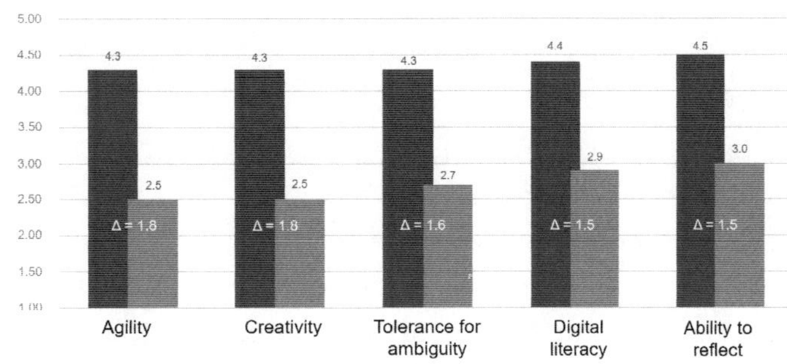

Figure 6. Object-related skills (Instrumental skills):
Importance (dark blue bars) versus current degree of higher education support (light blue bars) (NImportance = 44, NSupport = 45)

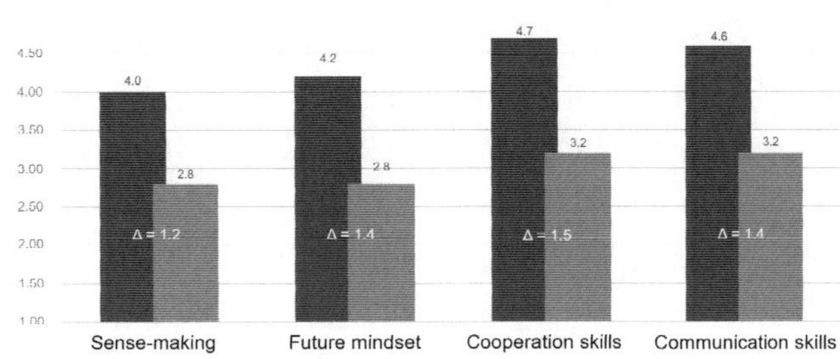

Figure 7. Organization-related skills:
Importance (dark blue bars) versus current degree of higher education support (light blue bars) (N = 45)

Object related skills are skills which are relying on individual dispositions to act in unknown future environments but where the object of action is not the individual itself but a certain object which needs to be acted upon – e.g. a certain task.

The expert sample rated all skills to be important, except for the ability to reflect, which was even voted to be very important ($M = 4.50$, $SD = 0.67$). Furthermore, the data reveals that the ability to reflect is one of the currently best-supported skills in HEIs compared to the other object-related skills. Least support apparently exists for agility and creativity skills ($M = 2.53$, $SD = 0.87$; $M = 2.52$, $SD = 0.85$), leading to the highest perceived discrepancy between agility skills' importance and their current support through HEIs.

Individual organization related skills are those skills which are needed to act in organizational and social environments. Action is self-organized and understood as disposition. In this section all skills are perceived of as important, whereby cooperation and communication skills are even rated to be very important ($M = 4.59$ $SD = 0.67$; $M = 4.67$, $SD = 0.67$). Moreover, all skills were rated to be acceptably support within HEIs, whereby the two most important skills (cooperation and communication skills) were deemed to be the best supported across all Future Skills ($M = 4.59$ $SD = 0.67$; $M = 4.67$, $SD = 0.67$)

Conclusion

With regards to future skills we can conclude:

- Future skills can be analysed and described as a set of profiles, each containing an array of skill definitions covering future skill demands.
- These skills can be referred to as future skills and can generally be described through two cornerstone characteristics: a strong, transversal and well-developed ability of self-organization, which is mutually supported through a high-articulated supposition to act under conditions of uncertainty. Proficiency in any profession in the future will entail these two traits.
- Future skills can be described within a model, which is structured into three dimensions: subjective – individual development-related, objective – task and subject matter-oriented, social – organizational and environment-related. All three dimensions interact with each other and are not sole expressions of isolated skill domains. Subjective aspects influence the outlook on objective aspects as well as social aspects impact subjective and objective aspects.
- The future skill approach presented here is going beyond a static model of listing a set of defined skills. It is going beyond digital or technical skills which will – no doubt – carry high importance for the future workforce but represent just one ingredient. The specific value of the presented future skill approach lies within the combination of focusing on the development of dispositions to act in a self-organized manner in the respectively described domain with a defined array of skills.

References

Bronfenbrenner, U. (1977). Toward an experimental ecology of human development. *American Psychologist, 32*(7), 513–531.

Brown, B. B. (1968). Delphi process: A methodology used for the elicitation of opinions of experts. (No. RAND-P-3925). Santa Monica, CA.: RAND Corp.

Deloitte (2018). Reconstructing Jobs: Creating good jobs in the age of artificial intelligence. Retrieved from https://www2.deloitte.com/content/dam/insights/us/articles/AU308_Reconstructing-jobs/DI_Reconstructing-jobs.pdf

Ehlers, U. D. (2019, in print). Future Skills – Zukunft des Lernens, Zukunft der Hochschule. Gütersloh.

Ellebracht, H., Lenz, G., Osterhold, G., & Schäfer, H. (2009). *Systemische Organisations-und Unternehmensberatung.* Springer Fachmedien.

Erpenbeck, J. (2010). Kompetenzen. Eine begriffliche Klärung. In H. Volker (Ed.), Grundstrukturen menschlicher Kompetenzen. Praxiserprobte Konzepte und Instrumente. Münster.

Helmer, O. (1967). *Analysis of the future: The Delphi method* (No. RAND-P-3558). Santa Monica, CA.: RAND Corp.

Linstone, H. A., & Turoff, M. (1975). The Delphi method: Techniques and applications. London: Addison-Wesley.

Meder, N. (2007). Der Lernprozess als performante Korrelation von Einzelnem und kultureller Welt. Eine bildungstheoretische Explikation des Begriffs. *Spektrum Freizeit, 07*(I&II), 119-135.

OECD (2017). *Future of Work and Skills. 2nd Meeting of the G20 Employment Working Group.* Hamburg. Retrieved from https://www.oecd.org/els/emp/wcms_556984.pdf

OECD (2017). *OECD Digital Economy Outlook 2017.* Paris: OECD Publishing. https://doi.org/10.1787/9789264276284-en

OECD (2017). *OECD Employment Outlook 2017.* Paris: OECD Publishing. https://doi.org/10.1787/empl_outlook-2017-en

OECD (2018). *"A Brave New World: Technology and Education". Trends Shaping Education Spotlights, No. 15.* Retrieved from http://www.oecd.org/education/ceri/Spotlight-15-A-Brave- New-WorldTechnology-and-Education.pdf

OECD (2018). *The Future of Education and Skills. Education 2030.* Position Paper. Retrieved online from https://www.oecd.org/education/2030/E2030%20Position%20Paper%20(05.04.2018).pdf

OECD (2019). *Trends Shaping Education 2019. OECD Publishing.* Paris. https://doi.org/10.1787/trends_edu-2019-en

Roth, H. (1971). Pädagogische Anthropologie. Band II. Entwicklung und Erziehung. Grundlagen einer Entwicklungspädagogik. Hannover: Schroedel.

Thomas, D. R. (2006). A general inductive approach for analyzing qualitative evaluation data. *American Journal of Evaluation, 27*(2), 237–246.

Tinbergen, J. (1975). *Income Distribution: Analysis and Policies.* Amsterdam: North-Holland.

VERBI Software (2017). MAXQDA 2018 [computer software]. Berlin, Germany: VERBI Software. Retrieved from https://www.maxqda.com

Woodside, A. G., Caldwell, M., & Spurr, R. (2006). Advancing Ecological Systems Theory in Lifestyle, Leisure, and Travel Research. *Journal of Travel Research, 44*(3), 259–272. doi:10.1177/0047287505282945

World Economic Forum (2018). Towards a Reskilling Revolution: A Future of Jobs for All.

HEARABLES: ELEARNING IN THE WORKPLACE

Rory McGreal, Athabasca University, Canada

Introduction

Hearables, a term first coined by Hunn (2014), are wireless smart micro-computers with artificial intelligence that incorporate both speakers and microphones. They fit in the ears and can connect to the internet and to other devices; they are designed to be worn daily. These devices, such as the Bragi Dash, Vinci and Bose Hearphone are now appearing on the market, which is expected to exceed $40 billion in the USA by 2020 (Omnicom, 2018). Hearables are not headphones, nor hearing aids, nor ear plugs, although they could take on the affordances of any of these devices (Banks, 2018). Headphones are designed for listening to music. Hearing aids are designed as an aid for the hearing impaired. Ear plugs reduce unwanted sounds by cancelling noise. Hearables offer comparable features and additionally provide users with a microphone and connectivity to the internet supporting telephony and personal digital assistant (PDA) services (Computational Thinkers, n.d.). Prior to 2017, in the USA, such devices required the approval of the Food and Drug Administration. This approval is no longer required for hearables, as they are no longer considered to be medical hearing aids (Over the Counter Hearing Aid Act, 2017). This paves the way for the expansion in the market of significantly lower-priced hearables, undercutting the expensively-priced hearing aid market.

Hearables for Workplace eLearning

Hearables stream music or audio content wirelessly using Bluetooth. Phone calls can be taken hands-free. Noises can be filtered out and speech amplified and filtered. And, with augmented audio, hearables can transform the user experience with sound controls and special effects (Traynor, 2017).

Hearables can be also used to simply enhance the listening experience. Hunn (2014) refers to them as the "new wearables". As such, they represent a subset of wearable computers, which now includes wrist bands like *Fitbit*, eye wear like *Google Glass*, intelligent garments like *CruchWear*, or shoes like *Nike+*. Hearables must be distinguished from audibles like Amazon's *Alexa*, Apple's *Siri*, Microsoft's *Cortana* and *Google Assistant*. The difference is that of mobility – hearables can go anywhere with the user, whereas audibles are place-based.

To date, hearable companies have focused on either music, because of its wide popularity or the health and sports markets because of their devices' ability to monitor and track body performance such as the heart-rate, energy, oxygen saturation, etc. or physical activity such as, speed, time, counting steps, etc. The ear is one of the best places to accurately measure biometrics and physical activities. In addition, the newest hearables can now provide as-needed advice on request by users. A PDA can instantly access various web applications, such as news and weather reports or route planning. Another form of specialised hearables are the earphone language translators such as *Google Pixel Buds* and *Waverly Labs Pilot*. This feature and others open up the possibility of taking full advantage of these devices to support mobile learning and other forms of both traditional and distance education.

Distance learning has been evolving at a rapid pace since the arrival of the ubiquitous internet at the end of the last century. The old correspondence school model based on the postal system was ported to the Internet, increasing response times. Then the affordances of the internet allowed for greater interactivity, at the beginning through simple email, then with social networking, audio and video conferencing and Voice-Over-IP using desktop computers. Mobile devices including smart phones, tablets and laptops are now ubiquitous. They allow users to access the internet from wherever they are. More people today access the Internet using these mobile devices than by any other means (ITU, 2017). Students are taking full advantage by accessing their lessons online. Both formal and informal learners are also accessing instructional videos, audio books and manuals, podcasts, personal recordings, and other training, explaining, and skill enhancing websites.

More recently, place-based audible technologies have demonstrated the convenience of using these PDAs in the home and office. Their capability for intelligent voice recognition (IVR) and natural language understanding (NLU) enables these devices to serve as powerful interactive digital advisers. In fact, these interactions could become the principal means for spontaneous queries (Burrows, 2018). This has opened the possibilities for using IVR and NLU to support learning.

Place-based audibles can be used in the administration of education. Ellis (2018), reported on a campus-wide distribution of *Echo Dot* audible devices with *Alexa* to all the students. She noted how the devices are being used to relay information from the institution to students, alerting them to deadlines or dates on the academic calendar, as well as faculty office hours or even the cafeteria menus. She also noted that students were using their devices as PDAs advising them on a wide range of campus and other activities. Hearables could be used in a similar manner, while allowing students more flexibility, because they can remain connected wherever they are, and so not be confined to their residences in accessing *Alexa* and the broader internet.

Now, with the availability of hearable devices, one can begin to explore in what ways, they can be advantageous. Hearing is a private and personal activity. This should be kept in mind when designing applications and tasks. Perhaps the most significant advantage for hearables comes with their ability to provide features that exceed the capabilities of the basic hearing aid. Hearables can augment the ability of the user to hear and discriminate sounds, helping the users to focus on those sounds that are the most important – super hearing. For example, an emergency respondent could be alerted to the slightest sound in a burning building. Hearables also facilitate switching from one function to another seamlessly, while providing useful advice as needed. With the growth of augmented reality and other forms of multimedia, users will need to have audio input, so hearables could become essential in these alternative environments. As we know from the user experience with home-based audible devices, the voice interactions can be natural and personal. In a mobile environment, perhaps the most important application will be the ability of users to instantly access the information they need in real time; in the workplace, the added advantage of being hands-free cannot be underestimated.

Brown (2016) noted several advantages of hearables. Notably, they can be used for most, if not all, of the traditional sound-related applications, such as listening to music, and mitigating hearing loss. In addition, hearables can augment sounds; this improves hearing above the norm by empowering users to apply selective noise cancellation (removing extraneous noise) and focus on specific sounds, such as a baby crying. Instant replay and recording of words is also possible, so users can check for understanding or file a recording as a record of an agreement. Another important feature is the ability to instantly translate between languages. The biometric capabilities allow for measuring health and fitness variables, providing users with a health record and even sound an alert for a sudden medical emergency. Biometrics can also be used for security authentication.

For educators, the information/communications functions can be effectively exploited. These features support the delivery of lectures, educational podcasts, notifications, and reminders through a wide variety of applications, while supporting interactivity. Intelligent hearables can determine the context and choose the right time and place to deliver the best content. These PDAs can become one of the principal ways we interact in learning.

There are significant challenges in using hearable devices. There are major concerns related to the social acceptability of people talking out loud in a public space or office. There has also been a stigma attached to hearing aids, with many people considering them to be unfashionable and only for the elderly. Manufacturers are addressing the stigma by designing devices that are unobtrusive, sitting securely inside the ear. Hunn (2015) suggests that the comfort of these new lightweight devices will help to destigmatise their use. Of course, another approach is to create more fashionable devices – the earrings of the future (Lumen, 2018).

Just-in-time learning/Context-based learning

With ubiquitous access to the internet and its plethora of educational/training content, hearables are well-placed to play a significant, if not the most important role in supporting Just-in-Time Learning. Using hearables, learners can now access important training whenever and wherever it is needed. In the mobile workplace, using hearables, continuous training can be integrated into every workday. For example, when faced with faulty new machinery, a machinist can access instructions on how to fix the problem or even contact the manufacturer directly using hearables, while leaving his hands-free to follow instructions in real time. Sales people, while driving on their way to meet clients can use their hearables to brush up their knowledge of the customer, of their product line or even their presentation skills. To facilitate these training opportunities, designers should organize the content into bite-sized chunks as there are few workers who can spend an hour or even a half hour away from the job. People learn faster when the learning is immediately needed and in a meaningful context.

Self-directed learning

Hearables can play a key role in independent study. They can serve to detach learners from formal institutional education, expanding the variety of places, times and ways their learning can be supported. They can serve as an important tool, helping a learner to become more directed, autonomous, motivated, organized and disciplined. A PDA can help with identifying the learning resources needed, providing constructive feedback, monitoring progress, and aiding in the process of self-assessment and setting personal goals. In addition, hearables can be used to help structure study plans and create reasonable timelines. Having an advisor available with relevant information whenever needed also helps to instil in the learners the confidence to succeed.

Personal learning/Connectivism

Hearables are well-placed to support context-aware, adaptive personal learning tailored to each individual learner's personal characteristics and situation. In this way, they can help learners to make their own decisions about what, where, when and how to learn. Learners can take maximum advantage of the continuous connectivity afforded via hearables to achieve their learning objectives, and in the creation of a personal learning network. Immediate access, filtering knowledge domains for the most relevant information distributed on the internet can be facilitated with the help of a PLA.

Conclusion

So, hearables are coming here to stay both in the wider society and the educational community. Piers Fawkes has commented on one negative effect from using hearables. "Maybe instead of people staring at their screens, they are going to be staring off into the distance. What's it called? The thousand-yard stare" (Glazer, 2014). On a more positive note, perhaps hearables will be helpful in bringing users down to earth, like the slave of Augustus Caesar, who rode with him in his chariot, reminding him that he was not a god, repeatedly whispering in his ear "Memento homo" (Remember you are a man).

References

Banks, L. (2018, June 13). The complete guide to hearable technology in 2018. Everyday hearing [Blog post]. Retrieved from https://www.everydayhearing.com/hearing-technology/articles/hearables/

Bragi – https://bragi.com/

Bose Hearphones – https://www.bose.com/en_us/products/wellness/conversation_enhancing_headphones/hearphones.html

Brown, S. (2016, November 3). Hearables: The next big wearable platform. Bald Futurist [Blog post]. Retrieved from http://www.baldfuturist.com/blog/2016/11/1/hearables-the-next-big-platform

Burrows, P. (2018, August 2). The future is ear: Why "hearables" are finally tech's next big thing. Fast Company [Blog post]. Retrieved from https://www.fastcompany.com/90212065/the-future-is-ear-why-hearables-are-finally-techs-next-big-thing

Computational Thinkers (no date). Hearables No Longer Whispering Wearables. Retrieved from https://www.computationalthinkers.com/hearables-no-longer-whispering-wearables/

Ellis, L. (2018, August 2). Hey, Alexa, Should we bring assistants to campus? These colleges gave them a shot. The Chronicle of Higher Education [Blog post]. Retrieved from https://www.chronicle.com/article/Hey-Alexa-Should-We-Bring/244129

Glazer, J. (2014, April 29). Psst! Wearable devices could make big tech leaps, into your ear. Npr [Blog post]. Retrieved from https://www.npr.org/sections/alltechconsidered/2014/04/23/306171641/psst-wearable-devices-could-make-big-tech-leaps-into-your-ear

Hunn, N. (2014, April 4). Hearables – the new Wearables. Wearable technologies [Blog post]. Retrieved from http://www.wearable-technologies.com/2014/04/hearables-the-new-wearables/

Hunn, N. (2015, February). *The Market for Smart Wearable Technology: A Consumer Centric Approach.* Retrieved from http://www.nickhunn.com/wp-content/uploads/downloads/2014/08/The-Market-for-Smart-Wearables.pdf

ITU (2017). *ICT Facts and figures 2017.* Retrieved from https://www.itu.int/en/ITU-D/Statistics/Documents/facts/ICTFactsFigures2017.pdf

Jones, A., Issroff, K., & Scanlon, E. (2007). Affective factors in learning with mobile devices. In M. Sharples (Ed.), *Big issues in mobile learning. Report of a workshop* (pp. 15-20.): Nottingham: Learning Sciences Research Institute, University of Nottingham. Retrieved from https://telearn.archives-ouvertes.fr/hal-00190254/document

Lumen Couture (2018, July 9). Hearables: Wearable Tech for your ears. Retrieved from https://www.youtube.com/watch?v=GsBRKr1jQG8

Mehdipour, Y., & Zerehkafi, H. (2013, June). Mobile learning for education: Benefits and challenges. *International Journal of Computational Engineering Research, 03*(6). Retrieved from http://www.ijceronline.com/papers/Vol3_issue6/part%203/P03630930100.pdf

Mims, C. (2013, August 15). Google is preparing for screenless computers. Quartz [Blog post]. Retrieved from https://qz.com/115304/google-is-preparing-for-screenless-computers/

Omnicom Health Group (2017, March). *SXSW Interactive Trends.* Retrieved from http://www.omnicomhealthgroup.com/pdfs/SXSW 2017 Interactive Trends Paper_FINAL_041717.pdf

Over the Counter Hearing Aid Act, S.670 Stat. (2017). Retrieved from https://www.congress.gov/bill/115th-congress/senate-bill/670?s=7&r=670

Traynor, R. (2017). Headphones: They have come a long way, baby. *Canadian Audiologist, 4*(1). Retrieved from http://www.canadianaudiologist.ca/issue/volume-4-issue-1-2017/column/stories-from-our-past/

Vandergrift, L. (2007). Recent developments in second and foreign language listening comprehension research. *Language Teaching, 40*(30), 191-210. https://doi.org/10.1017/S0261444807004338

VinciLanguage Teaching, 40(3), pp. 101 - 210. Retrieved from https://doi.org/10.1017/S0261444807004338

Vinci – https://shop.vinci.im/

ASSESSMENT OF WHAT? FROM MEASURING MEMORIZED CONTENT KNOWLEDGE TOWARDS A MULTILEVEL ASSESSMENT OF COMPETENCIES – THE JOURNEY'S STARTING POINT

Sarah A. Kellermann, Baden-Wurttemberg Cooperative State University, Germany

Abstract

The present paper draws on recent calls from the industry to support students' development of "Future Skills" (Ehlers, forthcoming), thereby highlighting the corresponding need for new assessment methods that can be applied in both contexts: organizations as well as higher education institutions (HEIs). To date, identification of such skill sets makes up the lion's share of publications, dedicating little attention to the important question of how to assess them. The present paper seeks to provide an attempt to fill this gap thereby linking Hackman's conceptualization of effective outcomes (organizational perspective) and Bloom's Learning Taxonomy (educational perspective). The key point the present paper aims to make is that to assess future skills, pure performance evaluation is not sufficient; instead, viability and learning are introduced as two additional types of outcomes suited for the future skills context.

Introduction

This article investigates the nature of competencies and how they can be assessed, placing a special focus on future requirements for organizations as well as for higher education. Daniel Pink described these special requirements for future graduates and employees as follows: "The future belongs to a very different kind of person with a very different kind of mind—creators and emphathizers, pattern recognizers, and meaning makers. These people—artists, inventors, designers, storytellers, caregivers, consolers, big picture thinkers—will now reap society's richest rewards and share its greatest joys" (2008; p.1). Pink's vision of the future worker is now already more than ten years old, and recent research evidence supports what Pink saw evolving in his crystal bowl. Ehlers (forthcoming) inquiring advanced German organizations identified seventeen "Future Skills" – skills organizations deemed to be key for the future worker. This umbrella term houses skills such as communication competence, creativity or innovation competence as well as sense-making, for instance – skills related to the types of minds described by Pink. By communication competence we understand "the ability of an interactant to choose among available communicative behaviours in order that he (she) may successfully accomplish his (her) own interpersonal goals during an encounter while maintaining the face and line of his (her) fellow interactants within the constraints of the situation" (Wiemann, 1977; p.198). Innovation competence is understood „as the disposition of an individual to act and react in an innovative manner in order to deal with different critical incidents, problems or tasks that demand innovative thinking and reactions, and which can occur in a certain context" (Cerinšek & Dolinšek, 2009; p.170). With sensemaking competence, we refer to "a motivated, continuous effort to understand connections (which can be among people, places, and events) in order to anticipate their trajectories and act effectively" (Klein, Moon, & Hoffmann, 2006; p.71). Rieckman (2011), Noweski et al. (2012), Deming (2017), the Organization for Economic Cooperation and Development (OECD, 2017; 2018), or Loshkareva, Luksha, Ninenko, Smagin, and Sudakov (2018) identified similar skill sets. These studies stress that students and employees need to not only possess the necessary knowledge within a certain field or domain, but further, and with increasing vehemence, need to be equipped with future skills, too. This trend has its roots within shifting labour market demands – a result of our changing work-world reality – affected by digitalization, demographic change and globalization (OECD, 2017). Within Industry 4.0, companies have realized that in order to stay competitive, they need to become much more flexible and agile, and so need their employees (OECD, 2017). A focus on future skills thus emphasizes the importance of "learning for life" instead of "learning to the test" (Cliath et al., 2000; Jones & Egley, 2007), which becomes explicit in such future skills as "(self-) study skills" (Loshkareva et al., 2018) "self-guided learning skills" (Luksha et al., 2018), or "learning skills" (Ehlers, forthcoming).

Although working formats like group work have manifested within classrooms acknowledging the fact that social skills are important (Magnesio & Davis, 2012; Zhang, 2012), outcomes are still measured mainly in terms of performance (Johnston & Miles, 2004), that is, focusing on assessing the "product" as opposed to the "process" (Centre for Teaching Excellence, 2017; Luksha, Cubista, Laszlo, Popovich, & Ninenko, 2018), which goes contrary to the "learning for life approach" education is aiming at (Jones & Egley, 2007). Hence, one may assume that cooperation and communication competencies are being developed through engaging in a group task, but usually no major focus is on measuring whether competency-levels have increased indeed. However, as indicated by the research cited above, there is a strong need for the development of future skills. With this shift of what students should be equipped with, assessment methods need to be adapted accordingly (Ang & Slaughter, 2000), or as Andreas Schleicher (Director for Education and Skills, OECD) recently stated: "We need to transform assessment to address transformation of our society. Assessment instruments haven't really evolved since 1950s, it is the area of education where the least progress has been made" (as cited in Luksha et al., 2018; p.36). The present paper positions itself within this problem area, acknowledging that although there are many definition attempts to what a future skill is, the concept of preparing students and professionals for tomorrow's challenges follow often naïve approaches. It appears to us that it is not enough to focus on a number of new soft skills and enrich the current education approaches in this way but that a fundamental rethinking of the assessment of learning outcomes is needed. For a similar line of thought, see Loshkareva, Luksha, Ninenko, Smagin, and Sudakov (2018). This is not only a major challenge for HEIs; for organizations (companies, firms, enterprises), determining whether an individual has successfully completed a certain training program, or whether the outcome of a group can be considered a success, for instance, are but two sides of the same coin. Adopting a complexity theories view calls for realizing phenomena not just as states (learning outcomes), but also as processes (Arrow, McGrath, & Berdahl, 2000). Thus, in addition to performance, the present paper aims at broadening our understanding, drawing on a multilevel conceptualization of outcomes from organizational research as performance, viability, and learning (Hackman, 1987) that accounts for the circular effects of achieved outcomes for future activities.

The current paper aims at providing a fruitful approach for both, higher education and professionals that shall serve to kick-off paving the way for future assessment models, thereby linking organizational research with learning theories. Specifically, we ask: "How can successful learning outcome(s) within the context of changing skill demands be defined?"

To answer this question, we will investigate and relate to different approaches of 'success', 'outcomes', and competency levels: (a) we investigate how to define "success" vs. "effectiveness", (b) we will describe Hackman and Morris's "Input-Process-Outcome-Framework" (1975), (c) use Hackman's (1987) three-fold typology of performance, viability, and learning, and (d) draw on "Bloom's Taxonomy" to provide a first approach for potential measurement of the identified outcomes. We will finish the paper by drawing a conclusion.

Defining success and outcome

To understand what is meant by "successful outcomes", we need to understand a) what is meant by *successful,* and b) what *outcomes* refer to in this context. The next two sub-chapters aim at shedding some light onto these concepts.

Differentiating "Success" from "Effectiveness"

Success and *effectiveness* have a long and problematic tradition of interchangeable use (Belout, 1998). Although the concepts are related to each other, there are some differences to be noted. Effectiveness approaches outcomes from a mechanistic point of view (Murdick & Shuster, 1976), generally pursuing objectives such as attaining target dates, achieving financial plans and controlling the quality of the final product (Belout, 1998; p.22). Thus, effectiveness usually can be measured numerically; for example, whether a certain target date coincides with the actual date the task was completed, or whether the calculated budget was exceeded, met, or remained below the calculation. On the other hand, whether a task has been completed *successfully*, is a question of perspective. Thus, we can refer to effectiveness as an objective criterion for achieved outcomes, whereas a successful outcome inherently exhibits a subjective evaluation.

A following question would then be: *Who* is evaluating? We can assume that a certain outcome may not only adopt various forms but that it will also depend on the evaluator whether this outcome is considered as successful or not. According to Mohammed and Ringseis (2001), an outcome of a group task can be valued by the team or by the organization the team is working for. Approaching the question of potential beneficiaries more systematically, we adopt an ecological systems perspective (Bronfenbrenner, 1977). This perspective allows for a multi-level inspection of the interrelated systems that represent the different parties. Being surrounded by a variety of microsystems, such as his/ her family members or group members in a work context, the individual forms the nucleus in Bronfenbrenner's framework. The sum of micro-systems together comprises the individual's mesosystem, e.g. this individual's organization (s)he is working for. The norms, laws, economic structures and culture of the individual's society characterize the macro-system. According to Bronfenbrenner, these systems are interrelated, and thus changes on one layer induce changes on other layers (1977). Moreover, the direction is bidirectional, meaning that not only macro-level changes will level down to effect the individual, but also that changes on the individual level can lead to changes on the higher levels (Bronfenbrenner, 1977). This is important in so far as it underlines the fact that (group) outcomes are not only beneficial for one of the systems, but usually have positive effects for other systems as well. For instance, from an organizational point of view, the success of an individual actor may lead to this individual being committed to the organization and his/ her work. This, in turn, will be positive for an organization as well, because commitment has been found to be positively related to e.g. job performance (see e.g. Becker, Billings, Eveleth, & Gilbert, 1996). The same holds true for the group's outcome. If the group meets its performance goals, the organization benefits, too, as it contributes to the achievement of overall organizational objectives. Using this framework, we are able to identify relevant parties for our question about who may evaluate an outcome as successful: the work world, an employee's and/ or group's organization, as well as the group an employee is affiliated with, and the employee him-/ herself.

So far, we have clarified what we mean by "successful", thereby also taking into consideration that the evaluation of an outcome may depend on the respective perspectives of different, yet interrelated parties. In a second step, we can now approach the concept of "outcomes".

Understanding "Outcome"

The term "outcome" is used adopting the Input-Process-Outcome framework (Hackman & Morris, 1975). This framework is considered the dominant theoretical approach for group and team work (Martins et al., 2004; Mohammed & Ringseis, 2001), but as we will see, it is also suitable to describe outcomes for and of individuals. According to the framework, inputs refer to the starting conditions for group work such as material or human resources (Martins et al., 2004). Processes then describe how these inputs are transferred into outcomes, thus representing "the dynamic interactions among group members as they work on a group's task" (Martins et al., 2004; p.809). However, we can also speak of processes within the context of individuals. Processes may then refer to an individual's activities of transforming certain inputs into outcomes. Finally, outcome is understood as the result of the (group's) activity that represents the consequences of these activities; these may be task- and non-task related (Martins et al., 2004). Adopting the ecological system's perspective again, we have seen that the systems – here, the parties – are interconnected; thus, we would expect outcomes in one system to be beneficial for other systems as well. Additionally, an individual is not "only" an employee, but moreover a private person, maybe a basketball player, a member of a certain religious orientation, and the like. Introducing axes to Bronfenbrenner's framework serves to illustrate this line of thought: One axis in the n-dimensional space (where all systems are located) represents the individual as an employee, whereas on another axis, the systems making up an individual's space as a basketball player may reside. Depending on the respective axis, different outcomes are to be expected – some outcomes may be relevant for an individual as a person and as an employee, whereas others might only be relevant to the individual as a basketball player. Thus, not only systems, but also the spaces made up by the introduced axes are interrelated.

Still, we currently only have a basic understanding of the outcome itself. To investigate the nature of potential outcomes in a more detailed way, we draw on Hackman's three-dimensional conceptualization as *performance*, *viability*, and *learning* (1987). *Performance* thereby refers to meeting the quality standards assigned with the activity. Hackman and Wageman (2005; p.272) further specify that the outcome may be a product, a service, or a decision, for instance. Although the performance outcome dimension seems to be easily assessable applying objective criteria, (e.g. Was a certain deadline met? Have certain skills been acquired?), Suskie reminds us that every assessment is inherently subjective (2009; p.19). Thus, whether a certain performance is deemed successful or not is again dependent on the perspective of the evaluator. Whereas one student may be frustrated with a "B" in an exam, another could be delighted achieving a "B". Both receive the same grade representing the student's performance, but the perceptions differ from one another. Moreover, the measurement of performance as either subjectively evaluated by the team (subjective measurement), or in terms of objective performance data (measures of team decision quality) has been shown to lead to different patterns in an analysis of shared mental models within student teams (van den Bossche, 2006). Drawing on the previous students grading example again, the "happy B student" would rate his outcome as successful, whereas the "sad B student" would probably not claim it a success. The teacher however, would rate the success of both students as equally good, as they both obtained the same grade. Only if all actors (in a group context) or the individual (in the context of an individual engaging in a certain task) define certain performance measures before they engage in the task (e.g. a certain grade), will it be possible to objectively assess the performance afterwards. Otherwise, multiple heterogeneous interpretations might exist that probably cause variability in the perceptions of an outcome as (un-)successful.

Instead, *viability* – acknowledging the circular learning effects of outcomes – refers to the group's ability to work together in the future as "the social processes used in carrying out the work should maintain or enhance the capability of members to work together on subsequent team tasks" (Hackman, 1987; p.323). Exploring viability beyond the group context, we find that it primarily means an individual's "ability to live, grow, and develop" (viability, 2019). Hence, we infer that viability may also refer to an individual's grown abilities to solve a given task. Thus, where a group's increased viability denotes the actor's ability to maintain to work together again in the future (individual-group-relationship), an individual's *self-viability* may characterize his/ her improved ability to find successful ways for future task solving (individual-self-relationship). Note that whereas group viability is a potential outcome solely possible in situations of group members interacting with each other, we find the more individual-oriented self-viability to occur as an outcome of both, group and individual task solving situations. Thus, we classify viability into group and self-viability.

Ultimately, *learning* denotes the actors' professional growth (Hackman, 1987). Thus, we do not see learning as a mere process here that leads to a certain outcome, e.g. some behaviour because of an individual having learnt something, but rather as an outcome itself. To understand what is meant by professional growth, we draw on the "Interconnected Model of Professional Growth" by Clarke and Hollingsworth (2002). For them, professional growth as an outcome means changes within an individual's personal domain and his/ her domain of practice. The domains are part of the individual's growth environment as represented in Figure 1. Within the personal domain, an individual's knowledge, beliefs and attitudes are located, whereas the domain of practice houses (professional) experimentation. Change processes (learning) in one of the domains are transferred via reflection and enactment into change processes in the other domain. By enactment Clarke and Hollingsworth (2002) refer to the translation of a belief or model into action. When these changes occur, learning takes place and the individual grows professionally. Note that in the original model, four domains are present that influence each other. However, we stick to the personal and the domain of practice for the purposes of this paper as they represent the two main learning objectives.

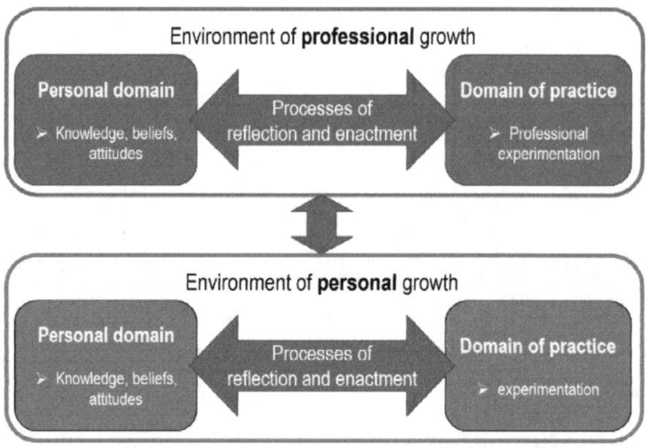

Figure 1. Learning as professional and/ or personal growth (own representation based on Clarke and Hollingsworth (2002))

Although Hackman's typology accounts for important outcomes, it seems plausible to extend his understanding of learning not only considering it as professional growth, but also in terms of *personal growth.* As work and private life become increasingly more intertwined (Ehlers, forthcoming), personal growth is likely to be an important outcome, too, and should therefore be added to the typology. Our adapted framework building on Bronfenbrenner's ecosystems framework elaborated on earlier, accounts for this fact as the integrated axes concept acknowledges that individuals may act out different roles – a professional one as an employee as well as a private one as for instance a mother. Although the interconnected model of professional growth as it is exemplified by Clarke/Hollingsworth was intended to describe a person's professional growth only, no apparent reason argues against applicability to the personal context, too. Here, as for the professional context, changes in knowledge, beliefs and attitudes (personal domain) can spur behavioural experimentation (domain of practice), as well as the other way round, trying out a new activity (domain of practice) can change the way one feels, believes or thinks about a certain topic (personal domain). To sum up, learning as an outcome refers to developments in the personal domain (knowledge, beliefs, attitudes) and the domain of practice (behaviour) leading to professional and/ or personal growth.

Having gained a clear understanding of the outcome types relevant within an organizational context, we can now move on to propose ways of how to assess them in both contexts, the organizational and the educational.

The three outcome types within a future assessment scenario

As has been stated in the introduction part, the performance outcome type is probably the most prevalent and assessed outcome type within the current educational and professional context. When employers consider hiring a graduate, one of the key criteria assessed are the grades that are deemed to represent a student's performance. Of course, it is handy for recruiters to have grades as they serve to discriminate between individuals, suggesting that the students having obtained better grades in relevant subjects might be better suited for a certain position. In the context of (group) performance, we have seen that performance is commonly measured in terms of reaching a certain target, such as designing a product until a certain deadline for instance. To evaluate the success of this, usually a supervisor assesses then, whether the prescribed objective was reached or not (Hackman & Wageman, 2005). Performance as an outcome type will definitely maintain its right to exist as it serves to evaluate the degree to which quality standards have been met for the activity or task carried out. However, performance mainly provides a snapshot, usually not acknowledging that the processes during the task can yield benefits for future activities. Therefore, our emphasis in this chapter will be on the two types of outcomes that we believe are able to capture these circular effects, and thus are suitable for measuring the development of future skills: viability and learning.

We want to dedicate the remainder of this paper to suggest potential ways for assessment building based on what is commonly known as "Bloom's Taxonomy" (Bloom et al., 1964). We chose Bloom's taxonomy, as it is one of the most cited and discussed taxonomies in the field (Forehand, 2010), but will use it in its most recent version rethought by Anderson and Krathwohl in 2001. We do so because the newer version was developed taking into consideration many of Bloom's own concerns surrounding his original taxonomy (Krathwohl, 2002; Wilson, 2016). This taxonomy arranges cognitive learning outcomes in a hierarchical fashion sorting them from the least complex (at the bottom) to the most complex outcome (at the top) ranging from remembering and understanding over applying and analysing up to evaluating and creating. However, and as Piaget noted: "[A]t no level, at no state […] can we find a behaviour or a state which is purely cognitive without affect nor a purely affective state without a cognitive element involved" (as cited in Clark & Fiske, 1982; p.130). Thus, it is somewhat alarming that Shephard (2008) upon analysing educational endeavours in affective learning found that most teaching and assessment focused on cognitive skills only – leaving aside affective outcomes. The present paper seeks to acknowledge this by means of considering potential affective elements within the identified outcome types, too. Consider for instance the group viability outcome type: Here, it was argued that the social processes within the group should lead to improved abilities to work together again in the future. Within a group context, values and attitudes of the group members will play a key role because they affect the "ability to listen, to respond in interactions with others, to demonstrate attitudes or values appropriate to particular situations, to demonstrate balance and consideration, and […] to display a commitment to principled practice on a day-to-day basis, alongside a willingness to revise judgement and change behaviour in the light of new evidence" (Shephard, 2008; p.88). In Krathwohl's taxonomy the affective learning outcomes (enumerated from the least complex to the most complex) are: Receiving, responding, valuing, organization, and characterization (Krathwohl et al., 1964). Thus, a potential way to assess group viability, and individuals' different levels of this type of outcome, could be to draw on Krathwohl's taxonomy of the affective domain. For an overview on particular assessment methods based on the Krathwohl taxonomy, see for instance Buissinik-Smith, Mann, and Shephard (2011). The same holds true for self-viability. Yet, in this situation no other individuals are involved. Thus, the individual rather grows affectively in terms of getting to know him-/ herself better instead of developing affectively as a result of working together with others. For instance, Shephard (2008) states that an individual needs to be willing to revise judgements in the light of new evidence; this accounts for revising a judgement about a colleague within a group work context (group viability), as well as for reconsidering whether a certain way of handling a given task is beneficial (self-viability).

However, and acknowledging Piaget's interjection, the other outcome types should also possess elements of affective development, as well as cognitive outcome properties.

In addition to cognitive and affective learning, Dave (1975) formulated a third taxonomy that focuses on the psychomotor domain. As the two taxonomies discussed before, Dave's taxonomy also arranges the five outcomes in a hierarchical fashion. The psychomotor learning outcomes (enumerated from the least complex to the most complex) are: Imitation, manipulation, precision, articulation, and naturalization (Dave, 1975). Taking a look at the learning outcome types of personal and professional growth for instance, we can assume that psychomotor skills will play a role here. According to the Clarke and Hollingsworth's model (see previous chapter), growth is triggered by changes on both, the personal domain (in terms of knowledge, beliefs, and attitude changes), and/ or the domain of practice (experimentation). The latter can be associated with the psychomotor domain of learning, whereas the personal domain is related to cognitive and affective development. Along the development of manual tasks and physical movement, the psychomotor domain is also concerned with communication skills for example in terms of public speaking, or the operation of IT equipment, such as telephone and keyboard skills (Chapman, 2006; Rovai, Wighting, Baker, & Grooms, 2009). Thus, in a situation where an employee is asked to represent some data in a graph for instance, this will stimulate the psychomotor domain. If it is a new task for the employee, (s)he might try to recall other charts (s)he has seen and replicate them using the new data ("manipulation"). A more experienced employee (concerning graphical data representation) might instead analyse what kind of chart would be best suited, to design a new graph, which would fall under the "articulation" level. Bringing this back to the Clarke/Hollingsworth model we would assume that the skill of drafting a graph (domain of practice) would stimulate reflection processes, which serve to transfer the behavioural experimentation into knowledge, maybe beliefs and/ or attitude changes, resulting in professional growth. This in turn points back to Piaget (see above), who argued that the affective and the cognitive domain cannot be viewed separately; from the preceding explanation follows that this holds true considering the Clarke/Hollingsworth model, and, moreover, that a third domain, the psychomotor domain, also needs to be taken into account.

One additional note on the assessment of outcomes: Shephard emphasizes that it is of vital importance to specifically evaluate affective outcomes, as otherwise they would easily be missed (2008). Though we generally agree with him, we argue to extend this view to be valid for all three domains, thereby pointing towards Burch's "Four Stages of Competence Learning Model" (1970 as cited in Spool, 2011). Although Burch relabelled the model thinking the steps from a learner's perspective, the original version was developed by Broadwell as "the four levels of teaching" in 1969. According to the model, learners start their learning process in the stage of "unconscious incompetency". When they realize that they lack a certain competency, they enter the stage of "conscious incompetency". Through learning efforts directed at improving the respective competency, they may then progress towards the stage of "conscious competency", where they become aware of the fact that their learning efforts pay off, as they are able to display the competency. Within the last stage, the awareness of being competent has become so natural that it disappears from an individual's consciousness, making the competency unconscious. This should not only hold true for the affective domain, but also for the cognitive and the psychomotor as individuals generally need to develop an awareness for their current level of competency to be able to take meaningful next steps in accordance with this level.

The next chapter will briefly summarize the previous discussion, highlighting the main points and providing some food for thought on potential next steps.

Conclusion – Where do we go from here?

We started our discussion asking what we would need to measure in the light of changing skill demands towards an emphasis on future skills. We have contrasted the concepts of success and effectiveness, yielding that effectiveness describes objectively whether an outcome fulfilled certain predefined criteria, whereas a successful outcome is linked to the perspective of an evaluator. To gain a more precise overview on potential beneficiaries, who may assess outcomes as (un-)successful, we drew on an ecosystem's perspective, incorporating an axes concept that allows to acknowledge that individuals act out different roles within different contexts (e.g. professional vs. private) and that development in one space can also leverage change in another. Moving on to gain a clearer understanding of outcomes, we generally defined them in an IPO-framework fashion as the valuable result of transformed inputs. However, when assessing, it was claimed that we should focus on assessing more than just the performance. To support a fit between what HEIs equip their graduates with and the employees' organizations are looking for, HEIs will need to shift their focus on developing graduates' future skills (Ehlers, forthcoming). As the demand shift is fuelled by organizational changes, it seems reasonable to also take a look at what organizations deem to be important outcomes. Therefore, we drew on Hackman's (1987) conceptualization expanding it to be applicable beyond the group context, i.e. for individuals.

As we have argued, performance, viability, and learning can also be assessed within a higher education context drawing on the taxonomies of learning outcomes elaborated on in the preceding chapter. They enable us to assess the different outcome types in terms of their complexity level and the respective domain. Using the already developed methods to assess the different levels in the cognitive, affective, and psychomotor domain (see for instance Rovai, Wighting, Baker, & Grooms, 2009), will help to evaluate students' and employees' performance, viability, and learning, and could also serve them to accurately self-assess their current competency levels. The authors developed a short self-assessment instrument to evaluate students' cognitive, affective, and psychomotor learning. Moreover, future research may compile an instrument following the approach of Sipos, Battisti, and Grimm (2008) for the purpose of curricula design, following a constructive alignment approach (Biggs, 1996). Yet, before we engage in such endeavours, a systematic segmentation of the outcome types identified is required in order to be able to understand which cognitive, affective, and psychomotor components they are based upon. The examples provided above only mark the journey's starting point towards assessing the key competencies of the future.

References

Anderson, L. W., & Krathwohl, D. R. (Eds.). (2001). *A taxonomy for learning, teaching and assessing: A revision of Bloom's Taxonomy of educational objectives*. New York: Longman.

Ang, S., & Slaughter, S. (2000). The missing context of information technology personnel: a review and future directions for research. In R. W. Zmud (Ed.), *Framing the domains of IT management: Projecting the future … through the past* (pp. 305–327). Cincinnati, OH: Pinnaflex Education Resources, Inc. Retrieved from http://soonang.com/wp-content/uploads/2011/04/2000-Ang-Zmud-PINNAFLEX.pdf

Arrow, H., McGrath, J. E., & Berdahl, J. L. (2000). *Small groups as complex systems: Formation, coordination, development, and adaptation*. Thousand Oaks, London, New Delhi: Sage Publications.

Becker, T. E., Billings, R. S., Eveleth, D. M., & Gilbert, N. L. (1996). Foci and bases of employee commitment: Implications for job performance. *Academy of Management Journal, 39*(2), 464-482.

Belout, A. (1998). Effects of human resource management on project effectiveness and success: Toward a new conceptual framework. *International Journal of Project Management, 16*, 21–26.

Biggs, J. (1996). Enhancing teaching through constructive alignment. *Higher Education, 32*(3), 347-364.

Blass, E., & Hayward, P. (2014). Innovation in higher education. Will there be a role for "the academe/university" in 2025? *European Journal of Futures Research, 2*(41), 1-9.

Bloom, B. S., Masia, B. B., & Krathwohl, D. R. (1964). *Taxonomy of Educational Objectives* (Two Volumes: The Affective Domain & The Cognitive Domain). New York, NY: David McKay & Co.

van den Bossche, P. (2006). *Minds in teams: The influence of social and cognitive factors on team learning* (Doctoral Dissertation). Universeit Maastricht, Maastricht. Retrieved from https://cris.maastrichtuniversity.nl/portal/files/1720718/guid-5a2de486-5040-4523-a84d-5da96cc190d3-ASSET1.0

Broadwell, M. M. (February 1969). Teaching for learning (XVI). *The Gospel Guardian, 20*(41), 1-3a. Retrieved from http://www.wordsfitlyspoken.org/gospel_guardian/v20/v20n41p1-3a.html

Bronfenbrenner, U. (1977). Toward an experimental ecology of human development. *American Psychologist, 32*(7), 513–531.

Buissink-Smith, N., Mann, S., & Shephard, K. (2011). How do we measure affective learning in higher education? *Journal of Education for Sustainable Development, 5*, 101–114. doi:10.1177/097340821000500113.

Centre for Teaching Excellence, University of Waterloo (2017, June 27). Methods for Assessing Group Work. Retrieved from https://uwaterloo.ca/centre-for-teaching-excellence/teaching-resources/teaching-tips/developing-assignments/group-work/methods-assessing-group-work

Chapman, A. (December 2006). An Explanation of Bloom's Taxonomy of Learning Domains. Retrieved from https://www.businessballs.com/self-awareness/blooms-taxonomy

Clark, M. S., & Fiske, S. T. (1982). *Affect and cognition*. Hillsdale, NJ: Erlbaum.

Clarke, D., & Hollingsworth, H. (2002). Elaborating a model of teacher professional growth. *Teaching and teacher education, 18*(8), 947-967.

Cliath, B. A., Rialtais, O. D. F., Alliance, T. S., Laighean, S. T., Rialtais, F., & Post-tráchta, A. R. (2000). Learning for life: White paper on adult education. *Dublin: Stationery Office*. Retrieved from https://files.eric.ed.gov/fulltext/ED471201.pdf

Deming, D. J. (2017). The growing importance of social skills in the labor market. *The Quarterly Journal of Economics, 132*(4), 1593–1640.

Ehlers, U.-D. (forthcoming). *Future Skills - Zukunft des Lernens, Zukunft der Hochschule.* Karlsruhe

Forehand, M. (2010). Bloom's taxonomy. In Orey, M. (Ed.), *Emerging Perspectives on Learning, Teaching and Technology* (39-47). North Charleston: CreateSpace. Retrieved from http://www.palieducationsociety.org/images/ebooks%20(13).pdf

Hackman, J. R. (1987). The design of work teams. In J. W. Lorsch (Ed.), *Handbook of organizational behavior* (315–342). Englewood Cliffs, NJ: Prentice-Hall.

Hackman, J. R., & Morris, C. G. (1975). Group tasks, group interaction process, and group performance effectiveness: A review and proposed integration. *Advances in Experimental Social Psychology, 8*, 45-99.

Hackman, J. R. & Wageman, R. (2005). A theory of team coaching. *Academy of Management Review, 30*(2), 269-287.

Johnston, L., & Miles, L. (2004). Assessing contributions to group assignments. *Assessment & Evaluation in Higher Education, 29*(6), 751-768.

Jones, B. D., & Egley, R. J. (2007). Learning to take tests or learning for understanding? Teachers' beliefs about test-based accountability. *The Educational Forum, 71*, 232–248. Retrieved from https://files.eric.ed.gov/fulltext/EJ763214.pdf

Krathwohl, D. R. (2002). A revision of Bloom's taxonomy: An overview. *Theory into practice, 41*(4), 212-218.

Krathwohl, D. R., Bloom, B. S., & Masia, B. B. (1964). *Taxonomy of educational objectives, the classification of educational goals.* Handbook II: Affective domain. New York: David McKay Co., Inc.

Loshkareva, E., Luksha, P., Ninenko, I., Smagin, I., & Sudakov, D. (2018). *Skills of the future. How to trive in the complex new world.* Retrieved from http://www.globaledufutures.org/images/people/WSdoklad_12_okt_eng-ilovepdf-compressed.pdf

Luksha, P., Cubista, J., Laszlo, A., Popovich, M., & Ninenko, I. (2018). *Global education futures report. Educational ecosystems for societal transformation.* Global Education Futures 2018. Retrieved from http://www.globaledufutures.org/images/people/GEF_april26-min.pdf

Magnesio, S. & Davis, B. H. (2010). A novice teacher fosters social competence with cooperative learning. *Childhood Education, 86*(4), 216-221, doi:10.1080/00094056.2010.10523152

Martins, L. L., Gilson, L. L., & Maynard, M. T. (2004). Virtual teams: What do we know and where do we go from here? *Journal of Management, 30*, 805–835. https://doi.org/10.1016/j.jm.2004.05.002

Mohammed, S., & Ringseis, E. (2001). Cognitive diversity and consensus in group decision making: The role of inputs, processes, and outcomes. *Organizational Behavior and Human Decision Processes, 85*, 310–335. https://doi.org/10.1006/obhd.2000.2943

Murdick, R. G., & Shuster, F. E. (1976). Managing human resources in project management. *Project Management Quarterly, 7*, 21–25.

Noweski, C., Scheer, A., Büttner, N., Thienen, J. P. A. von, Erdmann, J., & Meinel, C. (2012). Towards a paradigm shift in education practice: Developing twenty-first century skills with design thinking. In H. Plattner, C. Meinel, & L. Leifer (Eds.), *Design thinking research. Measuring performance in context* (71-94). Berlin: Springer.

OECD (2017). *Future of work and skills. 2nd Meeting of the G20 Employment Working Group.* Hamburg. Retrieved on 03.09.2018, from https://www.oecd.org/els/emp/wcms_556984.pdf

OECD (2018). *The future of education and skills. Education 2030.* Paris. Retrieved from https://www.oecd.org/education/2030/E2030%20Position%20Paper%20(05.04.2018).pdf

Pink, D. (2008). *A whole new mind: Why right-brainers will rule the world.* Nova Iorque: Penguin Group.

Rieckman, M. (2011). Future-oriented higher education: Which key competencies should be fostered through university teaching and learning? *Futures, 44*(2), 127-135.

Rovai, A. P., Wighting, M. J., Baker, J. D., & Grooms, L. D. (2009). Development of an instrument to measure perceived cognitive, affective, and psychomotor learning in traditional and virtual classroom higher education settings. *The Internet and Higher Education, 12*(1), 7-13.

Shephard, K. (2008). Higher education for sustainability: seeking affective learning outcomes. *International Journal of Sustainability in Higher Education, 9*(1), 87-98. https://doi.org/10.1108/14676370810842201

Sipos, Y., Battisti, B., & Grimm, K. (2008). Achieving transformative sustainability learning: engaging head, hands and heart. *International Journal of Sustainability in Higher Education, 9*(1), 68-86. https://doi.org/10.1108/14676370810842193

Spool, J. M. (2011, December 07). Die Flexibilität des Modells der vier Kompetenzstufen. Seibert Media [Blog post]. Retrived from https://blog.seibert-media.net/blog/2011/12/07/modell-der-vier-kompetenzstufen/

Suskie, L. A. (2009). *Assessing student learning: A common sense guide* (2nd ed.). The Jossey-Bass higher and adult education series. San Francisco, CA: Jossey-Bass. Retrieved from http://site.ebrary.com/lib/alltitles/docDetail.action?docID=10412696

Viability (2019). In *Merriam-Webster's collegiate dictionary*. Retrieved from https://www.merriam-webster.com/dictionary/viability

Wilson, L. O. (2016). *Anderson and Krathwohl–Bloom's taxonomy revised. Understanding the New Version of Bloom's Taxonomy*. Retrieved from https://quincycollege.edu/content/uploads/Anderson-and-Krathwohl_Revised-Blooms-Taxonomy.pdf

Zhang, A. (2012). Peer assessment of soft skills and hard skills. *Journal of Information Technology Education Research, 11*, 155-168.

CONNECTING STAKEHOLDERS THROUGH EDUCATIONAL TECHNOLOGY FOR EFFECTIVE AND DIGITALISED HIGHER EDUCATION ENVIRONMENTS

Christian-Andreas Schumann, Claudia Tittmann, Kevin Reuther, Helge Gerischer, West Saxon University of Zwickau, Germany, Feng Xiao, Oliver Schirmer, Tongji University Shanghai, China

Introduction

The idea of "Education for All" is already explained in detail in the corresponding UNESCO World Declaration in the form of a "Framework for Action to Meet Basic Learning Needs" in 1990. Interestingly, challenges for global access to education are being worked out that are still relevant today: Universalising access and promoting equity, focusing on leaning acquisition, broadening the means and scope of basic education, enhancing the environment of learning, strengthening partnerships. Since then, many things have been turned to good, much remains to be done. However, today's omnipresent digitization offers completely new opportunities to live up to this vision. Serious changes and disruptive innovations are pushed by digital transformations. (UNESCO, 1990)

Leveraging ICT for Achieving Education 2030 was the focus of further development in education in the UNESCO Qingdao Declaration in 2015. The connection between ICT as part of general digitization and challenges for education is illustrated by the chosen priorities: Access and inclusion, open educational resources and open solutions, quality learning, lifelong learning pathways, online learning innovations, recognition of online learning, accountability and partnership, international cooperation, etc. (UNESCO, 2015).

The consistent continuation of this approach is being pursued in the European Digital Education Action Plan in 2018, which focuses in particular on challenges and opportunities for digital transformation for education. Priorities are: Making better use of digital technology for teaching and learning, developing relevant digital competences and skills for the digital transformation and improving education through better data analysis and foresight, while still referring to educational policy goals such as support for high-quality education, developing Europeans' digital skills and making them more visible, boosting innovation and digital competences in all education institutions, opening up education systems, etc. (European Commission, 2018)

Planning, implementation and control of teaching and learning processes are now linked to a digitized environment. The use of efficient methods, educational materials and modern technical media are expanded by the dimensions of digitization. International connections, relations to the future world of work places as well as community and individual social relationships are increasingly being intertwined in a digitized world and interlinked with the classic aspects of didactics, methodology and content. As a result, education systems are becoming increasingly complex and are characterized by a growing degree of networking. The interaction of stakeholders in educational technology has a significant impact on the generation of effective learning environments in the digitalised education. This particular view on a holistic development problem in education leads to new insights and concepts that are constantly being developed and which are currently being used more and more in practice.

Theoretical approach

Technology and computer-based working and learning worlds are complex systems whose design can only be successful through a holistic approach. Holisticness always means looking at complete systems, implying a systemic approach. A system is a set of ordered elements with properties that are linked by relations. The set of relations between the elements of a system is its structure. An element is a component of a system that cannot be further broken down within this totality. The order and/or the structure of the elements of a system is its organization in the sense of the system theory. A system is a holistic connection of units (elements) whose relationships with each other differ quantitatively (higher number of interactions) and qualitatively (higher productivity of interactions) from their relationships with other entities. This difference in relationships constitutes a system boundary by which the system differentiates itself from its environment (Feess, 2019).

Learning environments in the context of connecting, equivalent educational technologies form special learning systems that can be understood as a connection between a community of learners or teachers and learners, for example, including connections to future workplaces and global partners beyond their system boundaries. If several such systems are brought together in a global cooperation, this results in mega-systems that are already known from information system theories. Learning systems are combined systems with artificial (human-made), logical, informal, organisational and social impacts. The interplay between learning system and learning environment is based on sociological system theory, in which a connection is established between the terms system, complexity, communication and meaning (Stichweh, 2011).

The sociological impact on learning systems and their learning environments implies the combination of different theories to understand the processes and the effects of technology-based learning. The investigation of the technology-based interaction of stakeholders in digitized learning worlds is based on a multitude of theories, of which the stakeholder theory and connectivism as learning theory are particularly important. The Triple Helix and the Transparent Knowledge Graphs are helpful in describing the knowledge gained from selected theories as models.

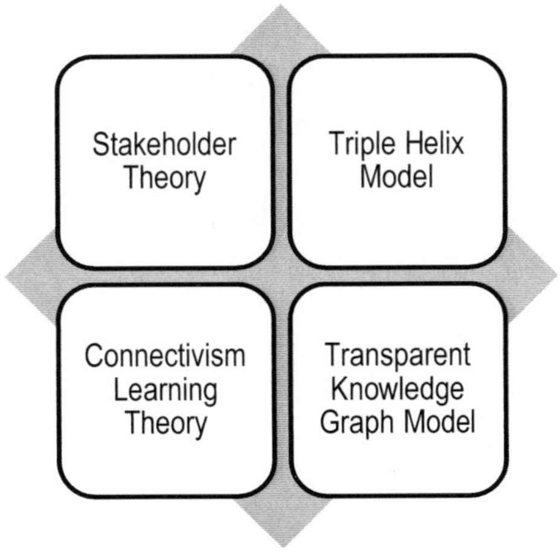

Figure 1. Key theories and models for connecting stakeholders in digital learning environments

Stakeholder theory means that organisations have obligations not only to shareholders but to other interest groups such as customers, employees, providers and the wider community, amongst many others. It is related to system theory, corporate social responsibility, and organisation theory concerning the role of cooperation in social systems and explanation of the behaviour in organisations and their environments. Stakeholders can be defined as any group of people that is affected by or is able to influence the achievement of organisation's objectives (Freeman, 2010).

The Triple Helix concept describes the growing role of the social effects of universities in a hybrid system of university, industrial and governmental processes as well as their interdependencies and interactions in the knowledge society. The aim is to enhance the potential for innovation and business development through new institutional and social formats for the production, transfer and application of knowledge. Thus the model of the interaction of several stakeholders in a new organisational context can be used for case study analysis. In particular, complex institutional processes and relationships and their permanent change can be recognized and influenced in a multi-dimensional social context (Leydesdorff, 2012).

Connectivism describes how an individual brings his networked knowledge to the organizations or institutions that reflect the network knowledge, thereby enabling the individual to continue learning. It brings together elements of chaos, network, complexity and organizational theories. The permanent further learning is more important than the reference to existing knowledge, whereby a suitable mixture between human-centred and technology-based knowledge acquisition is to be found (Siemens, 2005).

Transparent Knowledge Graph Model is based on graph theory, which is used to describe relations between objects using edges and nodes. Knowledge objects are mapped as knowledge nodes and can be used to represent complex, multidimensional relationships in knowledge management. If several links between knowledge objects are grouped together, they can be used to describe knowledge paths. The special feature of this model is the increased transparency, which is created by opening the knots and edges by cutting, so that the inner structure and inner processes are revealed. Such knowledge networks based on knowledge graphs can be used to describe networked and technology-driven learning in social environments up to deep learning, thereby building a bridge to connectivism (Tittmann & Schumann, 2010).

Connecting stakeholders to large networks is a complex challenge in itself, and its complexity is further increased by technology-based digitization in a learning environments. Therefore, more specific theories and concepts based on the system theory are used to derive a conceptual approach.

Conceptual framework

However, the holistic approach that can be achieved through the application of system theory and related concepts and models should not only be considered technologically and organizationally, but also in terms of behavioural orientation, since the actors in technology-based learning environments enter into cooperations that are influenced by human behavioural patterns combined with technological applications and in the future more and more with artificial intelligence. Behavioural learning theory influences the creation of learning environments (Schunk, 2014; pp.21-25.).

The behaviour is initiated by respective stimuli coming from the environment. It could be strengthened or weakened. In this context, each stakeholder displays a certain behaviour that is characterised by the environment in general and, in concrete terms, by a digitised and technologized learning environment. Therefore, the change in the learning environment caused by the new changes will influence the behaviour positively or negatively. Related to the goal theory, it can still be assumed that the stakeholders pursue goals dependent on the respective environment and shaped not only by cognitive and emotional characteristics, but also by behaviour. (Anderman & Patrick, 2012)

Following the achievement theory, the motivation of all stakeholders depends on their own condition as well as on the impact of the environment, whereby various dimensions, such as psychological, physical, social, etc., have to be taken into account (Kirikkanat, 2014). This complex structure is positively or negatively influenced by the technologization of learning through additional influences, which is expressed in a further dimension of "digitisation". If the behavioural approaches are now linked to the stakeholder theory, then not only classical relationships to organizations, management and leadership should be in focus, but also the aspects of the positive motivation based on corporate social responsibility and ethical behaviour under the conditions of digitization and technologization.

Stakeholders should be provided with a framework in which motivating conditions for the joint, successful development of educational technologies exist in a digitized learning and cooperation environment. The main issues are skills gaps, low return on investment (ROI), and the need for innovation, entrepreneurship, and job creation. That means strengthening the skills, increasing education's ROI, and enabling all groups to be more innovative. The key aspects for the digital education are integrated digital education ecosystems, integrated learning life cycle, integrated technology solutions, as well as an effective and motivating environment (Banerjee & Belson, 2015).

All relevant stakeholders must be involved in these processes. The stakeholder groups that are interested, affected or have influence should be identified. The stakeholder analysis is conducted in two phases. First, the stakeholder groups are determined. Second, the role of each stakeholder group is defined (Hanschke, Giesinger, & Goetze, 2013; p.42).

If the Triple Helix Model is assumed, there are three main roles that remain even under the conditions of technology-based, digital learning worlds: University, Business and Government. Due to the omnipresence of digitisation and the transformations induced by it, each group and each stakeholder must have their own digital literacy capabilities. However, the highly specialised enablers ensuring that each stakeholder group has access to educational technologies and that the group is perceived as competent in the field of digitised learning environments form a subgroup in each group and beyond a cross-group community.

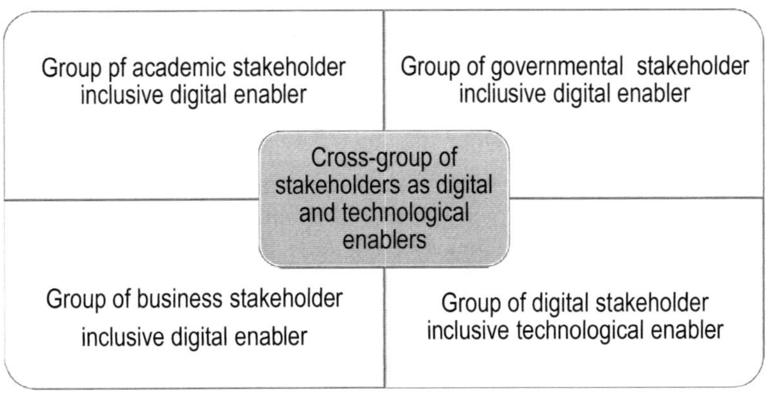

Figure 2. Extended connection of stakeholder groups by digitisation and educational technology

The existing and necessary degree of interdependence and connections between stakeholders and their groups is drastically increased by digitisation in general and educational technologies in particular. Digitised education systems therefore require fundamentally new strategic decisions, in particular the move towards organisationally and digitally networked education systems and the associated stakeholder groups. New educational technologies lead to a dynamization of these processes because they constantly generate new organisational and methodological possibilities and thus imply new behavioural patterns and challenges.

Special connecting model

The framework for technology-based, digitised education is based on social, ethical and behavioural aspects, as in classical education systems. The new thing is that every view is additionally penetrated by digitalization. Stakeholders and their groups form communities for special target groups and application areas, which use the new technological and media possibilities to come together in connected education systems. In order to be able to successfully carry out their diverse and variously interests and motivations as an association or as a network, both individually and in cooperation, they need technology-based and service-oriented connecting subsystems, especially with regard to the new learning environments. These sub-areas are complemented by digital infrastructures and tools for technologized learning and teaching.

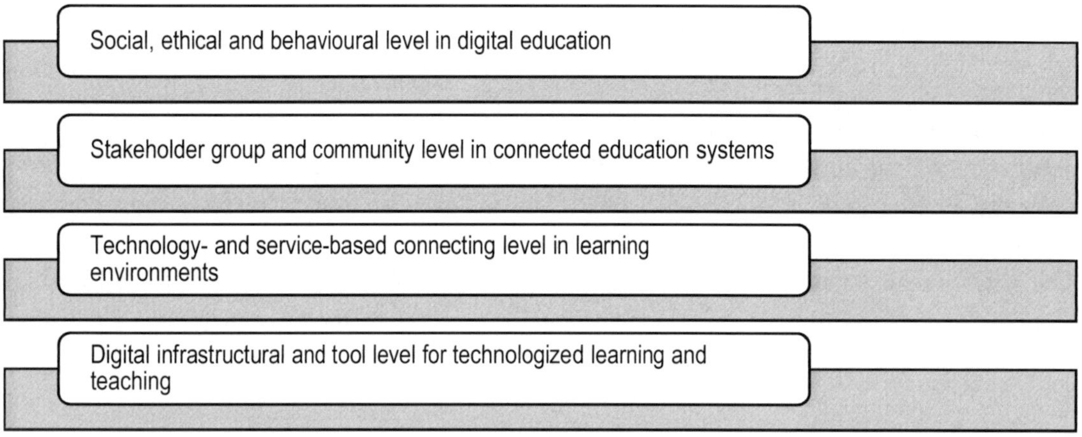

Figure 3. Multilevel connecting model for stakeholders based on educational technology

In organisational-structural terms, this results in a four-level architecture whose individual levels can be specifically designed and modified, but which is all interconnected by cooperative, behaviour-oriented and digital cross-sectional tasks. Connections are the "putty" in such a typical networked system, in which both internal networking at the individual levels and external networking between the levels via connectors and interfaces are established and guarantee the functionality of technology-based learning environments.

Case of application

Nowadays, stakeholders and their groups work together in networked learning worlds in order to be able to operate national and international successful for joint study offers with several partners. As state of the art, stakeholder networks based on the Triple Helix Model are linked by a service-oriented, technology based architecture to create productive and efficient education systems. Rational education systems based on a process- and function-oriented approach are currently being created. The educational technologies in interaction with the information systems and tools promote the connections by providing services for the control and operation of the educational networks and learning environments as well as for related applications with their help. The connections to the social, ethical and behavioural aspects of digital education should be further developed by means of suitable services in order to further increase the learning effectiveness.

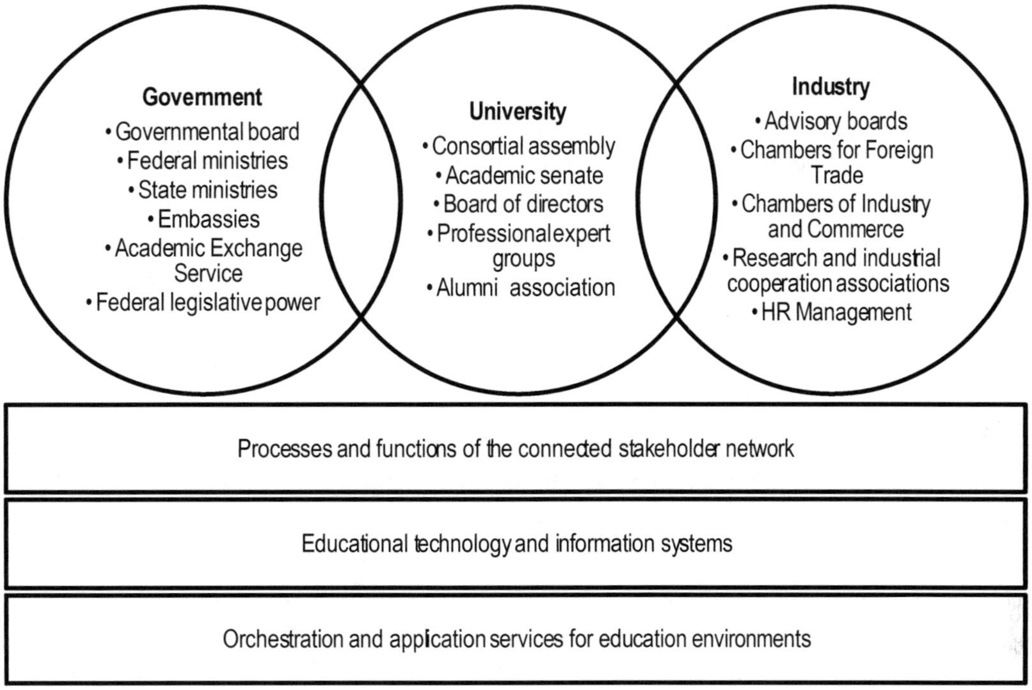

Figure 4. Educational technology connecting stakeholders in a service-based environment

The interaction of stakeholders in digitised education systems implies connecting through educational technologies according to a holistic approach, which results in a multidimensional model for the connections in different dimensions.

International double degree programs and exchange semester programs were supplemented by online components and are offered in perspective online in parity to classroom teaching with the participation and support of all stakeholders. This makes it possible for students to acquire international skills in a variety of ways, including online, and promotes virtual mobility. The prerequisite for this path was the extensive expansion of the connections with international partners.

The existing workplace impact and experience through stakeholder connectivity is complemented by online learning forms and educational technologies such as distance internship. On the other hand, new educational offers in the field of digital transformation and industry 4.0 act as catalysts for the dissemination of new technologies with a corresponding influence on the increased use of new educational technologies and their connecting effect.

Existing and developing study programmes will be further profiled in terms of education policy and society in line with the Ecosystem approach. Existing models, which include non-profit learning, social partnerships, interdisciplinary and intercultural projects, are further qualified by educational technologies. A better connectivity of the individual forms in the sense of a digital ecosystem in unity of social, ecological and economic aspects will be established.

New educational technologies are used, among other things, to further improve connectivity among learners and with stakeholders. Social media plays a central role. Digital learning worlds based on further developing educational technologies influence the further development of study concepts with regard to work-life-balance, target group and application orientation, professional qualification as well as the compatibility of family, study and career. Integrated study programmes with different forms of study are better suited to the use of modern educational technologies and to implementation of lifelong learning systems.

Summary

In the course of further digitization and automation based on new educational technologies, new possibilities of better connections for the purpose of improving effectiveness in learning and educational environments arise. However, the human-centred approach has a higher priority because it is always about human potential. Therefore, the technology driven view must be linked to the behavioural view of stakeholders in educational environments through appropriate services. Such very complex educational systems and learning environments have been successively built up in iterative stages for several years. The consistent further connecting of stakeholders from different interest groups in the education sector is the prerequisite for using the advantages of new educational technologies to make teaching and learning processes more effective. Ultimately, it is a strategic decision that will only lead to success in tactically and operational terms as a holistic solution.

References

Anderman, E. M., & Patrick, H. (2012). Achievement goal theory, conceptualization of ability/intelligence, and classroom climate. In S. L. Christenson, L. Reschly, & C. Wylie (Eds.), *The handbook of research on students engagement* (pp. 173-191). Springer Science.

Banerjee, P. M., & Belson, G. (2015). Digital education 2.0: From content to connections. *Deloitte Review, 16.*

European Commission (2018). *Digital Education Action Plan.* Communication from the Commission to the European Parliament, the Council, the European Economic and Social Committee and the Committee of the Regions. COM/2018/022 final. Brussels.

Feess, E. (2019) System. Gabler Wirtschaftslexikon, Wiesbaden. Retrieved January 27, 2019, from https://wirtschaftslexikon.gabler.de/definition/system-50117/version-273342

Freeman, R. E. (2010). *Stakeholder Theory.* The State of the Art. Cambridge University Press.

Hanschke, I., Giesinger, G., & Goetze, D. (2013). *Business Analyse.* München.

Kirikkanat, B. (2014). Achievement motivation: Its structure and relation with learning environments. *Journal of Psychological Counseling and Education, 1*(1), 77-90.

Leydesdorff, L. (2012). The Triple Helix of University-Industry-Government Relations. In E. Carayannis & D. Campbell (Eds.), *Encyclopedia of Creativity, Innovation, and Entrepreneurship*. New York: Springer.

Schunk, D. H. (2014). *Learning Theories: An Educational Perspective* (6th ed.). Harlow.

Siemens, G. (2005). Connectivism: A Learning Theory for the Digital Age. *International Journal of Instructional Technology & Distance Learning, 2*(1).

Stichweh, R. (2011). *System theory.* International Encyclopedia of Political Science. Bonn. Retrieved January 27, 2019, from https://www.fiw.uni-bonn.de/demokratieforschung/personen/stichweh/pdfs/80_stw_systems-theory-international-encyclopedia-of-political-science_2.pdf

Tittmann, C., & Schumann, Chr.-A. (2010). Potentials for Externalizing and Measuring of Tacit Knowledge within Knowledge Nodes in the Context of Knowledge Networks. In D. Harorimana (Ed.), *Cultural Implications of Knowledge Sharing, Management and Transfer. Identifying Competitive Advantage. Information Science Reference* (pp. 84-107). Hershey New York.

UNESCO (1990). *World Declaration on Education for All, Working Documents of the World Conference on Education for All.* Jomtien. 5-7.

UNESCO Institute for Information Technologies in Education (2015). *Qingdao Declaration. Seize digital opportunities, lead education transformation.* PDF Version. 1-3.

YESTERDAY, TODAY AND TOMORROW: THE BLOSSOMING ART OF TEACHING AND LEARNING REQUIRED TO PREPARE STUDENTS FOR THE 4TH INDUSTRIAL REVOLUTION

Ignatius G. P. Gous, University of South Africa, South Africa

Abstract

The future is not what it used to be. It is more complex than ever, and it changes faster than ever. Traditional educational institutions do not teach the skills sets students need to be future ready. Most of them still follow the industrial model that focuses on content and testing answers about known questions. Research reports point to ways in which higher education needs to change to meet the challenges, such as teaching abilities instead of content, becoming network universities, my-universities, or life-long universities. The time frame expected to change the current systems and structures are between 5 and 10 years. That is too long. The future is now. Distance Education, though, can make an immediate difference. Departing from the premise that "I learn for a reason", grounded in the Golden Spiral for Life-Long Learning model, the way Distance Education teaches may become sufficient to engender future readiness. The future requires students with specific personal characteristics and abilities, linked to effective mastery strategies, and being open to the future and change. A lesson structure and flow is suggested, based on a combination of tried-and-tested teaching and current mind, brain, and education research. Using the *Brunfelsia Pauciflora* "Floribunda" plant as metaphor, also called the Yesterday-today-and-tomorrow plant, the past, the present and the future are juxtaposed in an organic whole. In this way, a balanced approach is reached, that still attends to indispensable past knowledge and current application, but adding a required future ready perspective.

Introduction

"The future is not what it used to be!" This is an old saying, probably true since time immemorial, pronouncing several shades of feelings of uncertainty about what is to happen in the future, and especially how we are to prepare for it (see a well-researched history of the saying by Garson, 2012). Fact is, the future is looming large, and we are on the cusp of a new era and at the start of the 4th Industrial Revolution. Artificial Intelligence and automation, for one, is already changing our worlds and the workplace. Many reports about expected changes are seeing the light, as well as contemplations about future ready schools and curricula.

Aligned to this is the question whether Education, and Online Education in particular, is preparing our students for the futures they are being faced with. Are we delivering future ready students? Are our courses and curricula imparting the kinds of knowledge and skills our students need to cope in years to come?

This paper is a concise literature review about the kinds of skills, knowledge and attitudes students need to manage the future. A brief overview of reports and books on future expectations is presented, followed by a focus on students' skills in terms of identity, mastery and legacy. The latter classification stems from my research on effective learning strategies, which was translated into a program called the Golden Spiral of Lifelong Learning, presented in schools, universities and the workplace (Gous, 2018), and is worded in the mantra "I learn for a reason".

The conclusion is that our teaching and learning should cultivate something akin to the plant *Brunfelsia Pauciflora* "Floribunda". It is a plant with sweet-smelling flowers in three shades carried simultaneously, which changes from one day to the next. It starts off being deep purple, then change to pale lavender blue, and finally becomes pale white – hence the name "yesterday-today-and-tomorrow". Each subject that we teach, has a disciplinary history and growth – in German it is called the "Forschungsgeschichte". It also has a focus on current applicability and relevance, requiring answers to known questions and preparing learners for their worlds of work. These two aspects are getting ample attention in present-day teaching and learning. The aspect of "tomorrow", however, is not always part of the curriculum, probably because there is so much to learn from yesterday and a lot to apply today, that there is not enough time to focus on tomorrow. It may also be that tomorrow is too vague and unknown to receive a lot of attention. The changing world and the half-life of knowledge, however, is forcing us to reconsider these practices.

Learners also comes with a yesterday, a today and a tomorrow. They have yesterdays in terms of personal histories and situatedness. They too have a today to get through in terms of mastery and application of knowledge. They will have to manage all their tomorrows, which will dawn onto them earlier than they might think.

With Distance and Online learning set to become all the more important, the question is whether it will be able to juxtapose all three aspects, especially to add a focus on the future. With distance education students coming from often radically diverse yesterdays, and with widely differing challenges facing them today, it is very perplexing to decide which of the unknown tomorrows to cater for. The spectrum of colours to blossom into will have to be more than just three – but the question is how to do it when your students are at a transactional distance?

"The Future is not what is used to be"

We are on the cusp of a new era and at the start of the 4th Industrial Revolution. According to a report on the World Economic Forum, changes in the workplace is going to create in twelve years' time – the time it takes a child to complete school – between 400 to 800 million people who will need to be retrained and reskilled because their jobs have become obsolete. Research on the half-life of qualifications have shown that people who complete their degrees now, will have a half-life of their knowledge that necessitates 5 to 6 hours per week of dedicated and serious learning just to keep abreast of new developments in their fields.

Several reports and publications have been generated on expected disruptive changes in the workplace over the next 3 to 32 years. In the World Economic Forum report published in 2018 called "Eight Futures of Work: Scenarios and their Implications" the changing world of work is mentioned.

Several factors contribute to the expected changes. Technology is the most important. Automation, robotics and artificial intelligence are bound to make some jobs obsolete, change some others, and create some jobs that do not exist yet. The world, which has become a global village, creates mobile and migratory labour and brings about demographic changes. Education changes in the sense that face-to-face institutions do not have monolithic student populations any more, which has been a characteristic for distance education and online education for a long time. All of this brings about that the talent needs of workers are changing and expanding.

As a result of this, a 2018 report on "The Future of Jobs" the World Economic Forum (WEF) points to the need of re- and up-skilling of workers, brought about by changes in the workplace. According to the report, by 2022, a mere 3 years from now, 54% of all workers will need significant reskilling and upskilling. These will range from additional education and training of up to 6 months (35% of workers), up to 12 months (9% of workers), or more than a year (10% of workers). The kind of knowledge and skills that the will need additional skilling in, will be basic mastery of new developments in their fields, but also aspects such as innovation, analytical thinking, as well as active learning and learning strategies.

In terms of what is being expected to happen in Africa, a 2017 report by the WEF "The Future of Jobs and skills in Africa – Preparing the region for the Fourth Industrial Revolution" points to the influence of automation on work. The predict that more than 40% of all work activities in Africa are vulnerable to automation – 41% in South Africa, 44% in Ethiopia, 46% in Nigeria and 52% in Kenya, even though it may be toned-down by low labour costs and counterbalanced by the creation of new jobs. Even so, the report underscores the need of skilling and re-skilling in Africa. In South Africa, by 2020 39% of core skills required across occupations will be entirely different. 41% of firms in Tanzania, 30% in Kenya, 9% in South Africa and 6% in Nigeria are inadequately skilled, and this pattern is set to continue or may even get worse in the future.

Yuval Noah Harari (author of Sapiens, Homo Deus, and 21 Lessons for the 21st century) predicts the emergence of a new class of people by 2050. He calls them "the useless class" – people who are not just unemployed, but unemployable. According to him,

> *"... the big danger of the appearance of a useless class is not because of the absolute loss of jobs, it's because of the difficulty in retraining and reinventing yourself."*

From this and other reports, it is clear that radical change in the world of work is not only inevitable, it is already happening. It is therefore important for educational institutions to take this into account in their teaching offerings, their curricula as well as the kind of skills they teach their students. The challenge for distance and online educational institutions is even bigger, in the light of their diverse student populations. What needs to be taught?

The need for a different set of skills, added to content knowledge

Curricula needs to include content that is up to date in terms of their discipline, relevant to their contexts and meaningful in terms of application. In addition to this, it needs to include the teaching of skills needed not only to master the prescribed content, but skills to become "future ready".

According to reports, "future readiness" entails aspects such as lifelong learning skills, cognitive flexibility, creativity, critical thinking, and emotional intelligence, and not merely mastering content by means of rote learning. According to the 2017 White Paper by the World Economic Forum titled "Realizing Human Potential in the Fourth Industrial Revolution: An Agenda for Leaders to Shape the Future of Education, Gender and Work", education should be thoroughly reimagined to include the following:

- expanded access to early-childhood education;
- ensuring the 'future-readiness' of curricula;
- investing in developing and maintaining a professionalized teaching workforce;
- early exposure to the workplace and career guidance;
- investing in digital fluency and ICT literacy skills;
- providing robust and respected technical and vocational education and training (TVET);
- creating a culture of lifelong learning; and
- openness to education innovation.

It is clear that current curricular content and educational offerings need to be expanded and augmented. It calls for a balancing act between the past and current disciplinary content, but also a future oriented openness, and readiness for content that is developing or not even developed. The only way to prepare for something that is still unknown, is to empower students with skills, habits, attitudes and abilities to master new knowledge as it emerges.

Research on the half-life of qualifications have shown that people who complete their degrees now, will have a half-life of their knowledge that necessitates 5 to 6 hours per week of dedicated and serious learning just to keep abreast of new developments in their fields.

In 2017 Deloitte brought out a report called "The 2017 Deloitte Global Human Capital Trends: Rewriting the rules for the digital age". They surveyed more than 10,000 business and HR leaders from all over the world, focussing on the challenges ahead in an intensely changing demographic, social, digital and economic landscape. In the chapter "Careers and learning: Real time, all the time", they wrote:

> *"What does it mean to have a career today? More specifically, what does it mean in a world where careers span 60 years, even as the half-life of learned skills continues to fall to only about five years? In the past, employees learned to gain skills for a career; now, the career itself is a journey of learning."*
>
> *"As companies build the organization of the future, continuous learning is critical for business success. For today's digital organizations, the new rules call for a learning and development organization that can deliver learning that is always on and always available over a range of mobile platforms."*

Thomas and Brown (2011, CreateSpace) wrote in their book "A New Culture of Learning: Cultivating the Imagination for a World of Constant Change" that

> *"learning requires*
> *content – which can be taught,*
> *skill – which can be mentored, and*
> *disposition – which can be cultivated."*

Ehlers and Kellerman (2019) published a report on "Future Skills – Future Learning and Future Higher Education", a Delphi survey of an international panel of 50 experts from academia and business. The survey evaluated the readiness of higher education institutions within the next 5 years to teach their students the kind of skills needed to be future ready. According to the experts, these institutions are not ready to teach in ways and develop curricula and systems to engender future skills that are becoming increasingly relevant and important.

Ehlers and Kellerman (2019; p.3) define future skills as "the ability to act successful on a complex problem in a future unknown context of action". It refers to an individual's disposition to act in a self-organised way, visible to the outside as performance.

They divided the future skills into three interrelated dimensions, namely a subjective dimension, an object dimension and a social dimension. The subjective dimension relates to an individual's subjective, personal abilities to learn, adapt and develop to be able to productively participate in the workforce of tomorrow, actively shape the future working environment and involve themselves into forming societies to cope with future challenges. The future skills linked to this are (2019; p.3):

- autonomy;

- self-initiative;
- self-management;
- need / motivation for achievement;
- personal agility;
- autonomous learning competence; and
- self-efficacy.

The object dimension relates to an individual's ability to act self-organized in relation to an object, a task or a certain subject matter related issue. It is about mastering knowledge, but additionally to connect it to motivation, values and purpose, as well as using it in an organised way. The skills related to this are (2019; p.3):

- agility;
- creativity;
- tolerance for ambiguity;
- digital literacy; and
- ability to reflect.

The social dimension relates to an individual's ability to act self-organized in relation to its social environment, the society and organizational environment. The skill profiles are:

- sense-making;
- future mindset;
- cooperation skills; and
- communication competence.

The report also reflects about whether higher educational institutions are structurally ready and pedagogically able to teach and support the learning of these. They identify four aspects that need to change in institutions to be so.

The first is the future skill university, which redefines graduate attributes. The current "reduced / narrow focus on academic and valid knowledge acquisition as a means to provide correct answers for known questions based on a curriculum which is focused on defined skills for fixed professions" is to be replaced with a "next mode" of studying, with the focus on future skills, such as autonomous learning, self-organization, applying and reflecting knowledge, creativity and innovation (Ehlers & Kellermann, 2019; pp.4-5).

The second is the networked multi-institutional study scenario, where higher education moves from a "one institution" model to a multi-institution one, providing qualifications through alliances of several institutions (2019; pp.4-5).

The third is the "my-university" scenario where students have the choice to build their own personalized curriculum. It is no longer a fully predefined and 'upfront' given structure, but rather a more flexible, personalized and participatory model in which students actively cooperate with professors / teachers / advisors in curriculum building of higher education programs (2019; pp.4-5).

The fourth model is the lifelong higher learning scenario, where higher education institutions no longer focus on preparing students up front for future a profession, but compliment it with lifelong learning offerings (2019; pp.4-5).

The period for the adoption and implementation of these scenarios, are more than 10 years from now for the first three, and within the next 5 years for the fourth (Ehlers & Kellermann, 2019; p.4).

To summarise, it is clear that traditional education focussed on the acquisition of past and current knowledge and skills. Existing knowledge and skills were taught to students, who had to learn and master them. The goal was to be able to apply them in present settings such as known jobs or careers. The new knowledge economy of the 21st century questions the ability of this to deal with its complexities and rapidly changing nature. For this reason, the need to teach and learn other kinds of competencies emerged in order to help students become future ready. Because technologies are responsible for the rapid changes and complexities, the focus is often on teaching technological skills, as well as skills related to use technology to teach and learn. However, the realisation has dawned that personal attributes, characteristics and skills are equally important, and should also be taught and mastered.

The future is now. The future calls for different skills sets to be taught and acquired. Higher education institutions are not ready to provide it. Will Distance Education be able to do it sooner than 5 or 10 years?

Future Ready Distance Education, Teaching and Learning

Macro systems of Higher Education, such as accreditation of qualifications and curricula, are cumbersome to change. That is why any of the above suggestions will take as many as 10 years to put in place. It is clear and crucial that these changes should be attempted, and that it should be done as quickly as it is feasible. What is within reach to change immediately, though, is how we teach our subjects. It is right now within our locus of control to attend to the aspects of Identity, Mastery and Legacy in a single lecture, and by doing it, attend to the learners', the subject's and discipline's yesterdays, todays and tomorrows.

There are even some aspects of online and distance education that will make it easier to do than is the case at contact tuition institutions.

As has been pointed out, traditional teaching focuses on mastery of current knowledge, and assessing the mastery of known understanding. The development of the identity of the student, in other words their personality attributes and characteristics were seen as falling outside of the scope of practice of the institution and the lecturer. In similar vein, a focus on how the subject and discipline is going to change was also not a major concern. This was the case where students were present in face-to-face classes and often part of a homogenous group from similar contexts, aiming to apply their gained knowledge in comparable circumstances.

Being at a distance, made it even more difficult or even impossible to personalise teaching and learning to all students.

The diverse student population hailing from dissimilar backgrounds and studying asynchronously is actually a positive aspect in terms of engendering future readiness. Lecturers who take it seriously that their students are from different contexts, will make sure that their content takes this into account, and that it has to be made relevant in meaningful in more contexts than the one from which the lecturer or the establishment hails.

With this reality clearly in mind, the way each lesson is taught can be planned, according to a scaffolding framework to make sure all relevant and important aspects are attended to. This framework is called The Golden Spiral for Life-Long Learning, and is based on aspects of learning as identified and practiced by age-old pedagogical wisdom, as well as current mind, brain, and education science.

Six broad aspects of learning are placed on a spiralling trajectory through a learning landscape. These six are (a) future perspective (dream), (b) planning, (c) the learning curve, (d) productive mistakes, (e) help and support, and (f) assessment of progression. A seventh aspect is present at each of these six, namely a metacognitive reflection on each of them on its own and all of them working together (Gous, 2018).

The point of departure is always the endpoint of the spiral, namely the future perspective. This is supported by the work of Wiggins and McTighe on backward planning. They compared two kinds of planning performed by students. Backward planning starts at the envisioned goals and outcomes and then formulates actions from a current point of departure. Forward planning starts at the point of departure, and plans actions steps towards the envisioned goal. While the action steps of the two groups of students were similar, the motivational value of backward planning outperformed the forward planners (McTighe & Thomas, 2003; Wiggins, Wiggins, & McTighe, 2005; Jones, Vermette, & Jones, 2009; Wiggens & McTighe, 2011).

Starting each lecture with the future in mind in terms of meaning and relevance is important for motivation to learn. Adding to this a focus on envisaged future developments in the discipline, field or subject, and how the current knowledge may contribute towards future change, is crucial to make students aware that they are responsible and able to create the future they want to see. In this way, the future blossoms concurrently become part of the past and present in an organic whole like the yesterday-today-and-tomorrow flowers.

Future studies in disciplines are just as important as the histories thereof. It is, however, just as specialised an area of research that needs to be mastered than becoming an expert in the subject, its history and applications itself. For this reason, it will be necessary for subject societies and professional bodies to devote special attention to envisaged future developments. This knowledge should be made available to educators to include in their lectures.

Becoming future ready and future fit is the combined responsibility of all involved in the discipline – from the lecturers who should be at the forefront of knowledge mastery, to the students who have to make it part of their identity, to the professional discipline leaders who should keep an eye on the legacy.

An example in case is the teaching of economics. Tieleman (2019) shared some thoughts in The Conversation, arguing the case Why the world is due a revolution in economics education. Tieleman is a co-founder of Rethinking Economics in the Netherlands, and he does part-time work for a charity dedicated to a fairer, more sustainable economic system Our New Economy. According to him,

> *"Economic thinking governs much of our world. But the discipline's teaching is stuck in the past. Centred around antiquated 19th-century models built on Newtonian physics, economics treats humans as atomic particles, rather than as social beings."*

Real world issues were not addressed, for example in the Netherlands, real-world problems, from climate change to inequality, were seriously treated in only 6% of all modules and that only 2% of methods courses were not focused on statistical work. He concludes:

> *"Let's hope that we don't have to wait for the present generation of economists to retire before this can happen. By that time, it might be too late."*

This example show how people involved the field and knowledgeable about the discipline become future-oriented, advocating the teaching of their discipline in a way to get their students future-fit.

Conclusion

Like the *Brunfelsia Pauciflora* "Floribunda", also called the Yesterday-today-and-tomorrow plant, the past, the present and the future needs to be taught juxtaposed in an organic whole. In this way, a balanced approach is reached, that still attends to indispensable past knowledge and current application, but adding a required future ready perspective.

References

Ehlers, U.-D., & Kellermann, S. A. (2019). *Future Skills – The Future of Learning and Higher education. Results of the International Future Skills Delphi Survey.* Karlsruhe. Retrieved from https://nextskills.org/future-skills-report-2019/

Garson (2012, December 6). The Future Is Not What It Used to Be. Quote Investigator [Blog post]. Retrieved from https://quoteinvestigator.com/2012/12/06/future-not-used/

Gous, I. G. P. (2018). Learning Explained: A schema-building scaffolding framework to make sense of personalized guidance and support for learning. In J. M. Duart, & A. Szűcs (Eds.), *Towards personalized guidance and support for learning* (pp. 289-311).

Harari, Y. N. (2014). *Sapiens: A brief history of humankind.* Random House.

Harari, Y. N. (2016). *Homo Deus: A brief history of tomorrow.* Random House.

Harari, Y. N. (2018). *21 Lessons for the 21st Century.* Random House.

Jones, K. A., Vermette, P. J., & Jones, J. L. (2009). An integration of "backwards planning" unit design with the "two-step" lesson planning framework. *Education, 130*(2), 357-361.

McTighe, J., & Thomas, R. S. (2003). Backward design for forward action. *Educational Leadership, 60*(5), 52-55.

Tieleman, J. (2019, April 15). Why the world is due a revolution in economics education. The Conversation [Blog post]. Retrieved from https://theconversation.com/why-the-world-is-due-a-revolution-in-economics-education-112785

WEF (2017). *Deloitte Global Human Capital Trends: Rewriting the rules for the digital age.* White Paper. World Economic Forum.

WEF (2017). *Realizing Human Potential in the Fourth Industrial Revolution: An Agenda for Leaders to Shape the Future of Education, Gender and Work.* White Paper. World Economic Forum.

WEF (2017). *The Future of Jobs and skills in Africa – Preparing the region for the Fourth Industrial Revolution.* White Paper. World Economic Forum.

WEF (2018). *Eight Futures of Work: Scenarios and their Implications.* White Paper. World Economic Forum.

WEF (2018). *The Future of Jobs.* White Paper. World Economic Forum.

Wiggins, G., Wiggins, G. P., & McTighe, J. (2005). *Understanding by design.* ASCD (Association for Supervision and Curriculum Development).

MAAM PROJECT – HOW DIGITAL LEARNING CAN BRING LIFE INTO THE WORKPLACE

Elisa Vimercati, Francesca Cirianni, MAAM Research & Development team, Italy

Abstract

Moving from conflicted situation between one's own roles and life experiences to the synergy allows people to have greater awareness of their personal resources and to apply them in all areas of their lives. But how does this happen, in what way? How do people experience it?

This is the question and objective behind the MAAM project. The research uncovers how digital innovation can build new bridges between people's life experiences and the workplace. The research starts from the experience of motherhood, which is paradoxical in its nature – on one hand unleashes energy, strength and competencies in the woman, on the other hand it is often perceived as a condition of fragility (physical, psychological) and is not recognized as a bearer of skills at the workplace.

The MAAM project is scientifically based on theories such as role accumulation, *positive spillover*, generativity, experiential learning and enriches them with two original views: life-based learning, that postulates that life is in itself one of the richest learning sources, and *transilience*, a meta-competence that identifies people's ability to actively bring resources and skills from one life domain to another and vice versa. This is an *action-research* project, with the aim to investigate and simultaneously activate the development of personal resources and soft skills in people.

This objective is achieved through an innovative digital platform that guides the woman in a process of self-reflection and awareness on different topics: the relationship with her identity and her own desires; the caretaking experience with the child and other people; the ways of listening, observing and empathizing and the consequences towards herself, others and the environment; the dynamics of delegation and decision making; the discovery of own "superpowers" and the reflection on the changes taking place.

The research summarizes the results of the digital platform for the first 19 months and has been focused on mothers' experience. It has the aim of investigating the impact of motherhood on the personal development and the soft skills of the women, highlighting which resources are active, which behaviours are adopted, how women perceive their roles and deal with the changes that comes with maternity. This is part of a broader framework, which has been starting to investigate / activate personal development and soft skills in fathers and whose aim is to investigate how caretaking activities trigger people's personal development and embed them with soft skills that can be used in every area of life, including workplace.

Current setting and theory

Current setting

The relevance of the research derives from two factors: maternity being considered as a period of crisis at the workplace and a national dramatic scenario: female employment in Italy is among the lowest in Europe (48.9% in 2017 against an EU average 62.4% – Istat data, Annual Report 2018); the socio-economic participation of women in 2017 remains dramatically low and ranks 118 out of 149 countries (Global Gender Gap Report 2018); over one woman in 5 does not return to work after maternity leave (22.4%, a value that rises to 30% if all mothers are considered – (Istat, Chamber Hearing, 8 October 2015); the fertility rate continues to be among the lowest in Europe: 1.34 children per woman in 2016 (EU average 1.6) (Eurostat, 2017).

This scenario clearly shows how there is a large part of the population that is left out of the labour market, or on the contrary – in order to remain, sometimes decides to renounce having more children due to evident difficulties in reconciling family and work commitments.

For this reason, women, often responsible for caring for people, represent a large part of underused human capital, both in terms of non-full participation in the labour market and lack of full appreciation of their potential for the benefit of society.

The MAAM project is part of this big picture of cultural change: a path that enhances the educational potential of motherhood and transforms this period into an occasion for the development of new skills and a stronger and more complex identity, becoming a driving force for personal and professional growth.

Theory and MAAM method

The theory behind MAAM starts from the studies on family and work interactions, theories studying the impact of covering multiple roles on the individual and has its theoretical basis mainly in the following topics: Role Theory (Barker, 1999), Role Conflict (Goode, 1960) and Role Facilitation (Sieber, 1974; Marks, 1977).

The theories of the role accumulation demonstrate how covering several roles leads to personal strength, development and enrichment instead of struggling to balance the different areas of life the person is involved in (Ruderman et al., 2002). MAAM vision is based on it – this is a way of understanding life and work that is relevant and involves both men and women after becoming parents. For MAAM the aim is not to reach conciliation or even balance, but to have synergy between the different areas of life. Resources only "overflow" between the different roles only if we recognize the synergy between the parts of our life holding them together and strengthening them mutually.

As role accumulation theory states that the whole person is more than the sum of the parts and that participation in some roles can generate resources for use in others. The MAAM method stimulates, makes people aware and triggers this positive spillover ("positive overflow") from maternal caretaking (but not only) to work and vice versa. MAAM is enhancing the educational potential of parenting experience and transforming the experience of parenting in a tool for professional development. It is achieved by concept of transilience, coined as a combination of two words – transition and resilience (Vitullo & Zezza, 2014). Transilience is a meta-competence that is exercised when your skills, energies, emotional resources flow from one role to another. "What we call resources, involvement and emotional gratification emerge from every role. If it is true that these three elements can be a useful way to create alliances between work and family, it must be kept in mind that they work for this purpose only if they are used with intelligence" (Friedman & Greenhaus, 2000). For the transilience to be activated, the individual should be aware of two things- his/her agency to act and the positive impact transilience can have on the soft skills at his/her disposal.

Development of these skills is achieved through *life-based learning* (Staron, Jasinski, & Weatherley, 2006), a model of learning that starts from experiential learning (Kolb, 1984) and brings the awareness that the complexity of today's work requires new paradigms for professional development. Thus, life becomes a training ground after it is recognized so by an adult who learns, accepts and internalizes this experience.

With MAAM this activation happens through a digital platform rich in multimedia contents, structured as a pathway guiding person before, during and after childbirth. This way, the platform links the experience of parenthood to the specific soft skills, making parents aware and supporting them in the discovery and use of transilience.

At the digital level, MAAM is an environment consisting of three areas: the *community* (for networking and peer-coaching), the *personal area* (for self-assessment) and the *training ground* for the competencies, where through positive examples, open-ended questions designed to trigger reflection and practical exercises parents are guided to discover the extraordinary life experience they are living; they discover their own resources, making them visible to themselves, available to be used and transferred to other contexts of their lives, specifically - to the workplace.

Method and sampling

Object of survey, approach and methodology

In this study we have analysed a series of speeches starting from a key message, which is summarized in the name of the product itself – MAAM, whose name originally came out of the acronym "Maternity As A Master". This key message (maternity seen as a master) is refrained throughout the digital pathway and stimulates the self-reflection of women.

Speeches that can be used as arguments to define points of view, narratives to build the Self-identity, reflections that explore their emotions, relationships and behaviours (cfr. Mantovani, 2008; pp.15-16; pp.41-47; pp.51-55).

Which methodology proves to be best for this particular text that triggers reactions and thoughts? Our resolution was the adoption of an empirical approach that combines two methodologies and perspectives of qualitative analysis: *grounded theory* and *speech analysis.* Following the grounded theory, the textual corpus was subjected to theoretical sampling and followed by codification.

Phases of Analysis:

- *Theoretical sampling and choice of exercises*, with consecutive adjustments as the analysis proceeds.
- *Reconstruction of textual context* by collecting the following information for each analysed exercise:
  - Starting content;
  - Stimuli in the form of questions;
  - Set of answers.
- *Codification*: splitting the speech, identification of recurrent "patterns" and key elements, clustering and analysis based on the frequency (how often they appear in the speech) and intensity (with what force they appear in the speech).
- *First categorization* – constructing categories based on the answers and words coming from women themselves.
- *Second categorization and re-elaboration of the categories* – definition of an overall "grounded" design based on the data and comparison of the primary theory.

In the coding phase the categories borrowed from the speech analysis will be used in correspondence with Halliday's systemic-functional grammar (SFG): particularly the concepts of: *density* and *frequency* corresponding to the "weight" of the individual items in the speech (see Halliday, Spoken language and written language, 1992; pp.117-127); the concepts of *positive* and *negative polarity* (see Halliday, Halliday's Introduction to Functional Grammar, 2014; pp.22-23); the concepts of the field, tenor and mode pertaining to three levels of analysis: "what happens" (field), "who takes part in the situation" (tenor), "what role does the language have" (mode) (cf. Halliday, Spoken language and written language, 1992; p.84).

Sampling

The period under review includes a period of 19 months, from 30 July 2015 to 26 April 2017. The analysis has covered 20 exercises of a textual corpus that counts in total 152 focused questions, 2800 answers, 70.000 words (69.143). The exercises with the most answers have an average of 100-150 up to 200-290 responses; those with the least number of answers have an average of 25-40 answers. The average response rate - the ratio between those who read the content and those who answered the questions – exceeds 50%, with peaks of 70 to 90%. The people who responded to the exercises were 745 women from all over Italy, working at 10 different companies.

Analysis and results

Analysis shows that motherhood is an experience that empowers and frees personal development and soft skills and in order to trigger this experience it is needed to have:

- an initial positive message (imprinting);
- a guidance to self-reflection.

This lead to two things: skills enablement and the activation of transilience, the meta-competence that is exercised when skills, energies, emotional resources flow from one role to another.

Skill enablement

The most extensive series of exercises are related to soft skill identification and their practice. Women are triggered to understand their own peculiar strategies, and the particular role that caretaking plays in them. Caretaking helps woman to develop skills such as empathy, observation and listening as the basis for all of them is a strong desire to understand the child and satisfy his/her needs.

The result? A better environment, both in relationships and in one's own experience and emotions.

Experience the delegation (example)

Some behaviours are hard to acquire: being able to laugh at one's own mistakes and delegating are among those "hard to get" behaviours. But, especially with delegation, after one's own experience with delegation, and even though women do not always have positive experiences with delegation, the result is of great relief.

> *"My daughter forced me to delegate; the needs forced me to delegate".*

Motherhood breaks known patterns and habits and, in doing so, it obliges the woman to leave certain things for others. It therefore enhances a predisposition to change.

Here is how the woman experiences the delegation. The reflection exercise is guided by four questions, each describing the delegation mechanism:

> *"Try to do an experiment. Think of an activity that you struggle to delegate and write it below:"*
>
> *"Now choose a person who, by virtue of his/her characteristics, could carry out this activity for you and write his/her name:"*

"Try to overcome your fear and ask for help from this person. Then he/she will tell you how things went. Did he/she do the same things you would have done? "

"Are there any things that surprised you positively? Do you feel more relieved knowing you can count on him/her? "

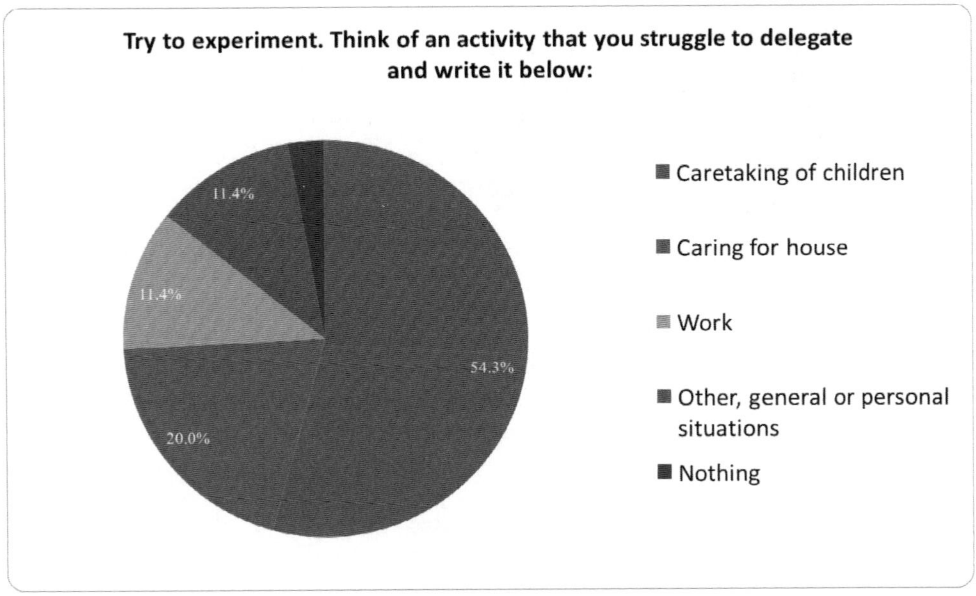

Figure 1. Tasks to be delegated
"Try to experiment. Think of an activity that you struggle to delegate and write it below:"

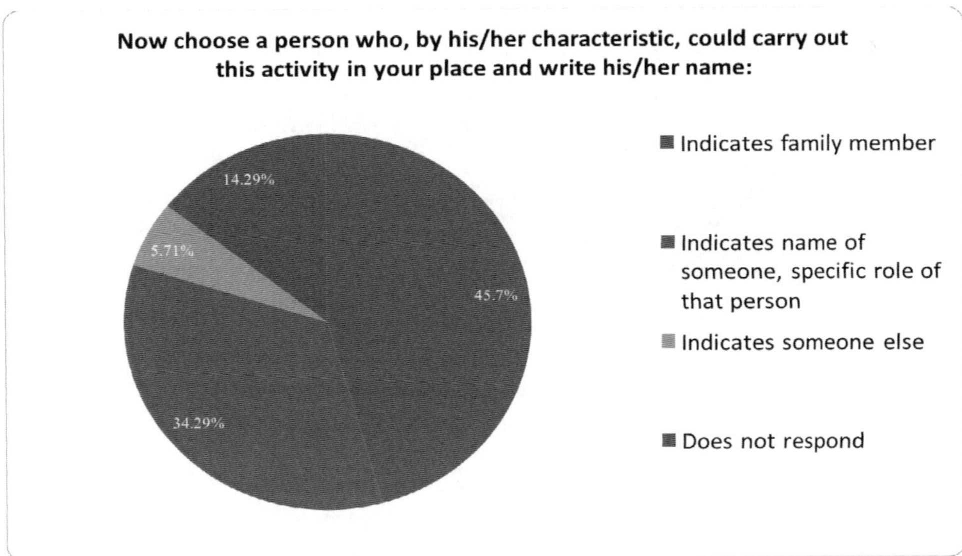

Figure 2. Person to whom to delegate
"Now choose a person who, by his/her characteristic, could carry out this activity in your place and write his/her name:"

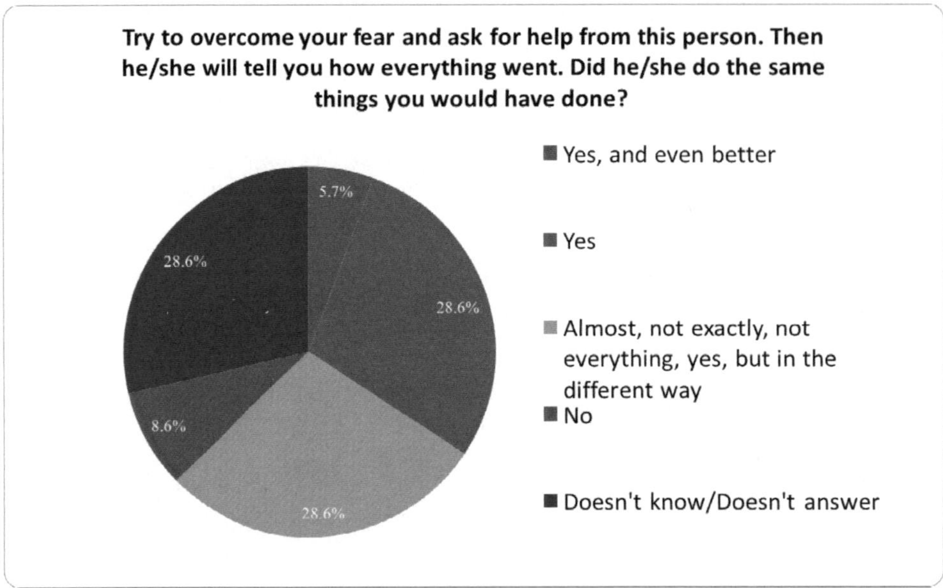

Figure 3. Wait
"Try to overcome your fear and ask for help from this person. Then he/she will tell you how everything went. Did he/she do the same things you would have done?"

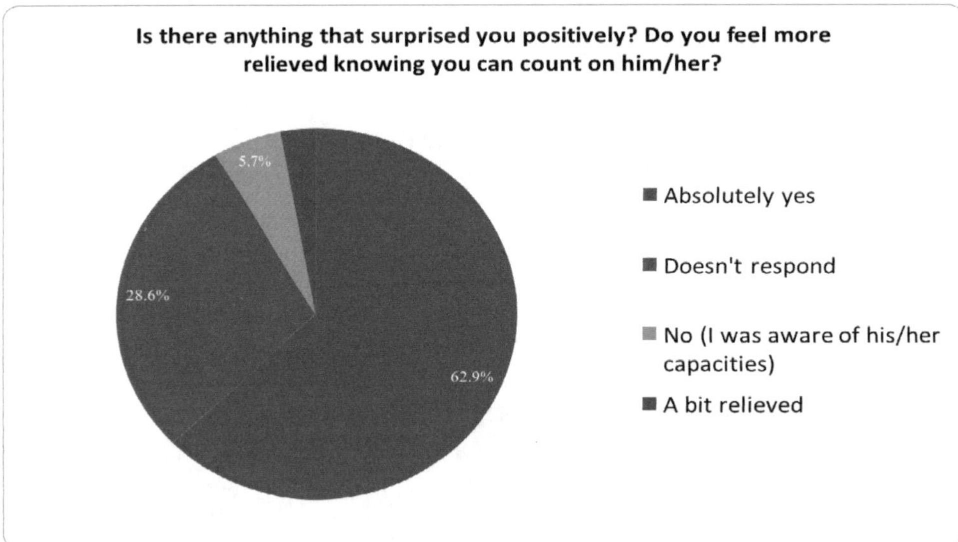

Figure 4. Final realization
"Is there anything that surprised you positively? Do you feel more relieved knowing you can count on him/her? "

How does the delegation work?

- The most important and vital activities for women are delegated: childcare, care for the home, work tasks.
- The person to whom to delegate is chosen carefully and it's a trusted person: a partner, one of the parents, a colleague or a friend.

- Reflecting on how the delegated activity is performed, women discover new strategies and solutions - In half of the cases the person "does the same things", in others – performs "even better".
- In terms of attitude and emotions there is a certain difficulty in delegating and leaving someone else in charge. But in almost all of the cases, the result is relief.

Transfer of skills and transilience

What is transilience? It is the "meta-competence" that allows skills and energies to flow naturally from one area of life to another.

If we look back over the exercises just analysed, we will see how the woman is, and wants to be, present to herself in all areas of her life. She wants to live all her roles, every nuance of her identity and every power of her skills.

Welcome Transilience (example)

Which soft skills do mothers train the most? Relational and organizational soft skills appear to be the most trained and transferred from one area to another.

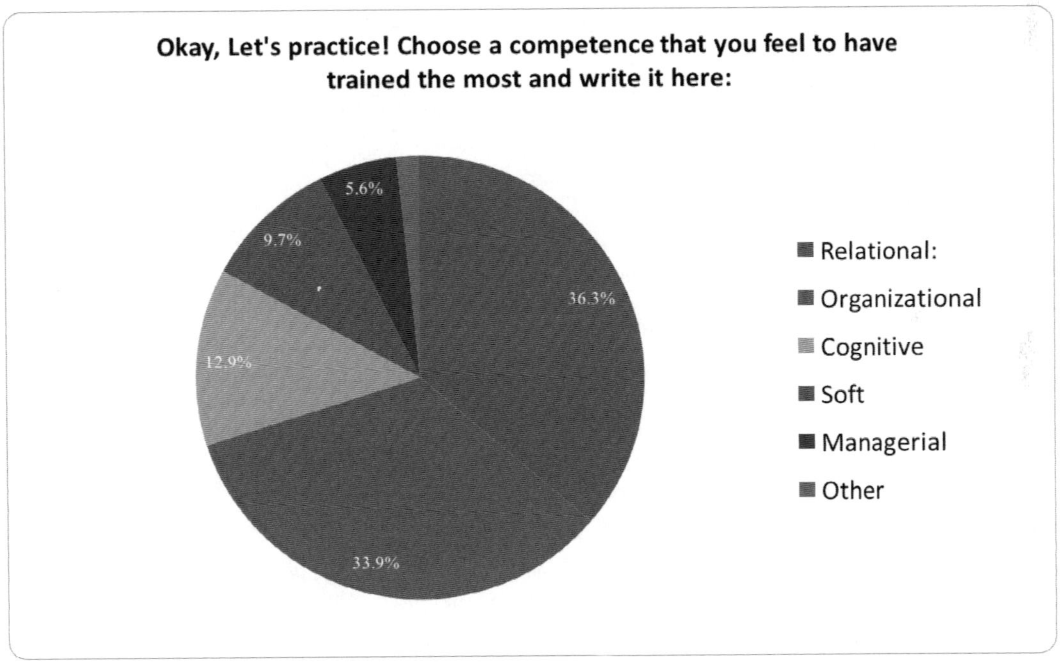

Figure 4.

In fact, if we divide soft skills mostly picked up by mothers into macro categories, the order is as follows:

- Relational: 36%;
- Organizational: 34%;
- Cognitive: 13%;
- Soft: 10%;

- Managerial: 6%.

Going into detail, the most trained skills are organization and planning, management of interpersonal relationships, problem solving; followed by listening, time and priority management and flexibility.

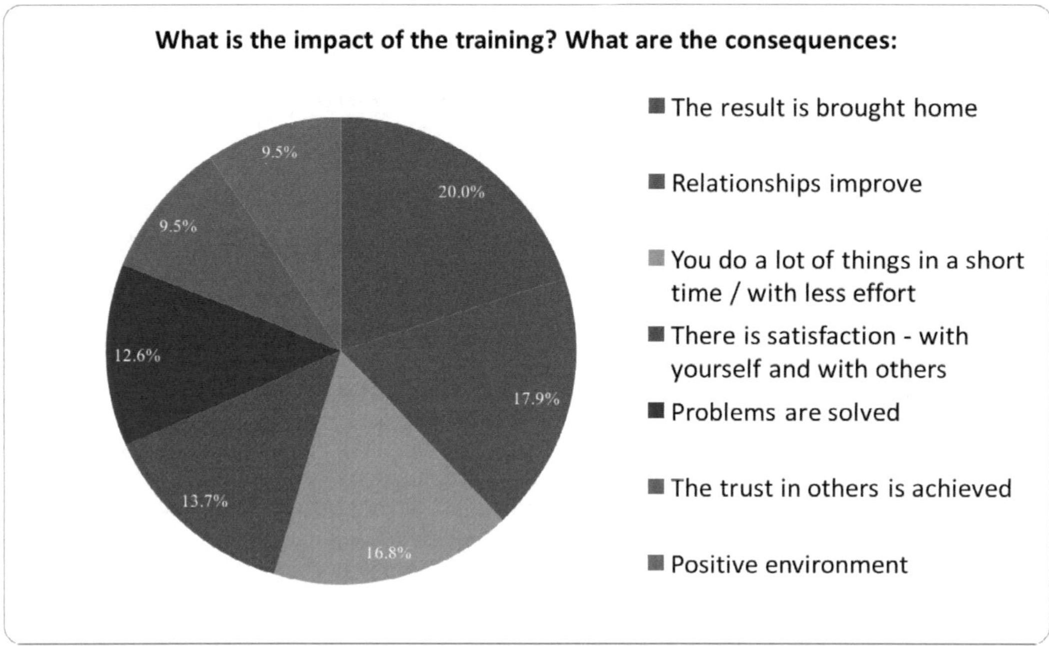

Figure 5.

What happens when women train skills?

- The result is brought home (20%);
- Relationships improve (17.9%);
- You do a lot of things in a short time / with less effort (16.8%);
- There is satisfaction – towards yourself and towards others (13.7%);
- Problems are solved (12.6%);
- The trust in others is achieved (9.5%);
- Positive environment (9.5%).

Conclusion

The following results emerge from the analysis:

- Questions influence answers, and it's like the mirror shapes what is seen inside it. Thus, in this analysis we see that using a positive message generates positivity: women experience positive emotions, are positively surprised by reversing the prospect of their motherhood from a "problem" to a "professional resource".
- Women enrich the way they live their roles, have aspirations and the desire to be "present" in all areas of their lives.

- If women become aware of their resources and behaviours, they strengthen their soft skills.

As a proof of this, we did a survey and asked the women to assess how much they used the 12 soft skills before and after maternity: the result of the survey shows an average 11% improvement in soft skills before and after maternity.

Motherhood is a life experience that liberates strength, resources and skills in women. It happens because this experience fully involves woman – her will, identity and desires.

It involves her will: many of the positive changes, such as listening, empathy, the management of unexpected events, complex situations and emergencies are carried out because there a great will in the woman to listen, understand, manage situations and solve problems.

It involves her identity: an identity which, in the transition to the maternal-generative phase becomes both unitary and complex, more rich and multifaceted. Woman remains a woman, a set of desires for personal and professional fulfilment but at the same time she is a mother. The woman-mother is a duality which despite the moments of conflict (expressed in fear, fatigue, tiredness), is mostly experienced and perceived as ONE, and progressively enriched by all the experiences and areas of both private life and work: to prove that the accumulation and synergy between the roles is not an abstraction but a natural condition of the human being.

The effects are multiple.

The force gives the woman more security, courage and positivity.

In turn, the woman becomes more capable of making good use of time and resources available, of optimizing time and priorities and finding unexpected solutions.

There's more trust where this relationship goes both ways – from the woman towards herself and towards others, and from others towards the woman (she becomes a point of reference for those around her).

Care softens the sometimes "stiffened" mechanisms of relationships. The will to understand the child and to satisfy his/her needs is the engine that enhances the *skills of listening*, *attention*, and *empathy*. All of these is reflected on the woman, on the people around her and the way she acts, both at home and at work.

The *caretaking*, while being the main source to activate the will, is also the element that guides *decision-making*: women's decisions of wanting good for herself and for others (to avoid negative consequences for herself and other people around her), her desire to make right decision, look for the solution.

Finally, caretaking is what makes women more "powerful". A power made of the ability to simplify, decide, manage people and situations. A power made of strength, commitment, tenacity. A power made of intuition, listening, presence, attention. A power made of calm, patience, sweetness, empathy.

This happens in all the contexts that the woman lives and in which she wants to "be", to affirm her own identity, her own desires and her abilities.

References

Allen, T. D. (2012). The work and family interface (review of work-family literature). In S. W. J. Kozlowski (Ed.), *The Oxford Handbook of Organizational Psychology* (pp.1163-1198). Oxford University Press.

Barker, R. L. (1999). *The social work dictionary* (4th ed.). Washington, DC: NASW Press.

Donadio, A. (2017). *HRevolution. HR nell'epoca della social e digital transformation.* Franco Angeli.

Eurostat (2017). *Fertility Statistics.* Retrieved from http://ec.europa.eu/eurostat/statistics-explained/index.php/Fertility_statistics

Friedman, S. D., & Greenhaus, J. H. (2000). *Work and Family: Allies or Enemies?* Oxford University Press.

Goode, W. J. (1960). A theory of role strain. *American Sociological Review, 25*, 483-496.

Halliday, M. A. K. (1992). *Lingua parlata e lingua scritta.* La Nuova Italia.

Halliday, M. A. K. (2014). *Halliday's Introduction to Functional Grammar* (4th ed.). Revised by Christian M.I.M. Matthiessen. Routledge.

Istat (2015). *Indagine conoscitiva sull'impatto in termini di genere della normativa previdenziale e sulle disparità esistenti in materia di trattamenti pensionistici tra uomini e donne, Audizione presso l'XI Commissione Lavoro Pubblico e privato della Camera dei Deputati.* Retrieved from http://www.istat.it/it/files/2015/10/A-Audizione-commissione-lavoro-camera_8-ottobre.pdf?title=Normativa+previdenziale+e+disparit%C3%A0+di+genere+-+09%2Fott%2F2015+-+Testo+integrale.pdf

Istat (2018). *Annual Report 2017.* Retrieved from https://www.istat.it/it/files//2018/06/AnnualReport2018.pdf

Istat (2019). *Employed and unemployed – December 2018.* Retrieved from https://www.istat.it/it/files//2019/01/Employment-and-unemployment_201812.pdf

Kolb, D. A. (1984). *Experiential learning. Experience as the Source of Learning and Development.* Prentice Hall

Marks, S. R. (1977). Multiple role and strain: Some notes on human energy, time and commitment. *American Sociological Review, 42*, 921-936.

Mantovani, G. (2008). *Analisi del discorso e contesto sociale.* Il Mulino.

Rosina, A., & Zezza, R. (2016). *Generare futuro – Cultura e politiche per tornare ad essere un paese vitale.* Retrieved from https://voltaitalia.org/wp-content/uploads/2016/05/Volta-Paper-03-natalita.pdf

Ruderman, M. N., Ohlott, P. J., Panzer, K., & King, S. N. (2002). Benefits of multiple roles for managerial women. *The Academy of Management Journal.*

Save the Children (2017). *Le equilibriste. La maternità tra ostacoli e visioni di futuro – Rapporto mamme 2017.* Retrieved from https://www.savethechildren.it/sites/default/files/files/uploads/pubblicazioni/le-equilibriste-la-maternita-tra-ostacoli-e-visioni-di-futuro.pdf

Sieber, S. D. (1974). Toward a theory of role accumulation. *American Sociological Review, 39,* 567-578.

Staron, M., Jasinski, M., & Weatherley, R. (2006). *Life Based Learning. A strength based approach for capability development in vocational and technical education.* Research Project 'Designing Professional Development for the Knowledge Era', TAFE NSW ICVET with Department of Education, Science and Training (DEST).

Tarozzi, M. (2008. *Che cos'è la grounded theory.* Carocci.

Vitullo, A., & Zezza, R. (2014). *MAAM. La maternità è un master che rende più forti uomini e donne.* BUR.

FREE DIGITAL DISTANCE LEARNING FOR EMPLOYABILITY AND SOCIAL INCLUSION: THE PERCEPTIONS OF MIGRANTS LIVING ON THE MALTESE ISLANDS

Joseph Vancell, University of Hull, United Kingdom, Teemu Patala, ChangeLearning Alliance, Finland, Alan Bruce, ChangeLearning Alliance, Ireland

Introduction

Asylum seekers are still moving, in great numbers, from Sub-Sahara Africa (SSA) and the Middle East to the European Union (EU) to seek protection from political oppression, war and poverty, as well as to reunite with family, and benefit from entrepreneurship and education (EC, 2017; EU, 2018). The UNHCR (2019) notes that 68.5 million people were forcibly displaced from their native countries. Mediterranean EU Member States are seeing an ever-growing influx of illegal migrants, through land and sea routes. During the first month of 2019, 6,727 migrants arrived in Europe, of which 5,685 were sea arrivals through Malta, Spain, Greece and Italy – the strategic entry points to the EU. In the previous year, Malta took 1,445 arrivals.

The issue of mass migration and population movement has dominated European discourse for at least 40 years. Since the invasion of Iraq and the various destabilization efforts against countries like Libya, Syria and Afghanistan, however, an entirely new phenomenon has erupted onto the centre stage – millions of people fleeing failed States, violence, terrorism and despair. Especially in the case of Syria (now in its fifth year of war) the problem of millions seeking to depart from the chaos has become huge. We are now entering a period of real transition however. Far from the malicious impact of war and violence, new problems arise around family fragmentation, emotional trauma, and the need to rebuild lives.

Maltese researchers indicate that these migrants stay in Malta for many months before being forcibly deported or given refugee status. Pisani (2012) also notes that there are also many migrants whose request for asylum is rejected and but cannot be deported because the countries they claim to come from (e.g. Somalia, Eritrea, Côte d'Ivoire, DRC) either pose a threat to migrants' safety or have no diplomatic relations with Malta. This renders enforcement of diplomatic relations very difficult (Pisani & Giustiniani, 2009) and the "end result is experienced as a state of limbo: no chance of leaving the carceral archipelago of Malta and travelling to mainland Europe, and no real opportunity of return".

During their stay in Malta, asylum seekers, refugees and illegal migrants experience many difficulties, most notably "exploitation by unscrupulous employers who capitalize on the migrants' lack of choice in having to work" (English & Mayo, 2019). They receive a pittance for their work, and do not enjoy the same rights as local or legal immigrant workers. They also have the threat of deportation constantly hanging over them. This precariousness is made more acute by immigrants' lack of basic education and employability skills, as well as social exclusion created mainly by lack of command of the local language and instances of racism, increased xenophobia and Islamophobia (Pisani, 2012) which run high in the Maltese islands. Indeed, although Malta's economy currently needs 35,000 new foreign workers to maintain its welfare state, owners of Maltese Small and Medium-Sized Enterprises (SMEs) prefer and employ Europeans and TCNs from India and Asian countries (including the Philippines) rather than the already available or incoming asylum seekers from African or Middle Eastern countries.

These desperate people have often survived traffickers, criminal gangs, corrupt police and other exploiters in their journey. The human cost of drowning, disruption, injury and deaths on land has only underlined the legal obligations of international law and treaties – the requirement for States to provide sanctuary and succour. This has not been done consistently. Although the warning signs were there, the scale and intensity of the refugee problem seemed to catch the European Union by surprise. The responses were uncoordinated, fragmented and often counter-productive. While many Member States were unprepared, others became actively antagonistic. Driven by a rising tide of xenophobia, they began to erect barriers not seen for decades in an effort to repulse often-desperate populations. Only one EU country articulated an initial policy of acceptance and welcome – Germany. For other countries in the front line the social and economic impact was significant with the burden falling particularly intensely on Greece, Italy and Malta.

Similar problems exist in the wider European context, where, as the official statistics show, more than 82% of asylum seekers are younger than 35 (Eurostat, 2018). This clearly indicates a demand for educational programmes for this group before they journey to Europe. This paper, based on the findings of a small qualitative research project, argues for free digital distance learning (FDDL) with the objective of enhancing employability, social inclusion and empowerment of potential adult refugees in European countries and, particularly, immigrants living in Malta, the smallest EU state but the country with the highest per capita number of illegal immigrants.

The case for free digital distance learning for inclusion and employment

The literature indicates that immigrants, travelling by land or sea, or both, to reach Europe, typically use smart technology and the Internet, in particular, smartphones and social media. They also use smart technology when in the host countries for seeking work and staying in contact with their families (Mason & Buchmann, 2017). Despite this, various commentators agree that existing research offers limited insights into the process by which digital learning provision can contribute to the social inclusion of asylum seekers and refugees (Lewis & Thacker, 2016; Castaño Muñoz, Colucci, & Smith, 2018). Moreover, research shows that the use of digital learning, including MOOCs, by migrants and refugees is still very low (Liyanagunawardena, Adams, & Williams, 2013; Glass, Shiokawa-Baklan, & Saltarelli, 2016).

Colucci et al. (2017), in their review of available free digital learning (FDL) initiatives for migrants and refugees in Europe, note that the field of FDL for migrant/refugee learning and inclusion was developing rapidly and argued that, the scant research that exists indicates that

> *"MOOCs and other FDL offers (including free mobile learning) are effective and efficient ways of developing the skills needed by migrants and refugees for inclusion, civic integration, re-engagement in formal or non-formal education and employment."*

However, the availability of cost-free dimension of these educational resources does not guarantee the migrants' participation in this type of learning. This is particularly true for potential migrants who are still living in their country of origin and those who are on their way to Europe. A number of papers and reports addressing migrants and their education indicate a number of pedagogic principles that must be integrated into an FDDL programme to ensure success.

English and Mayo (2019), banking on the work of many critical pedagogists, including Freire (1970), insist that Lifelong Learning (LLL) initiatives for migrants should not only prioritise skills and employability. The authors argue that

> *"Although the work factor weighs heavily on migrants' minds, the notion of citizenship ascribed to them would extend beyond that of being producers/consumers; hence, the education to be provided needs to help migrants obtain secure employment. This should be commensurate with their qualifications and life experiences, albeit more holistic to enable them to become critically active citizens with basic human rights."*

English and Mayo (2019) also insist that any educational programme should treat migrants as assets to their current or potential host country instead of a burden. They argue that, in practice

> *"this would entail providing learning environments that treat migrants as active beings and not simply as passive consumers of knowledge being fed from above. It would engage their own strengths and cultures and build on them, taking into account their perspectives on things. It would allow them co-ownership of the programme through democratic participation and a dialogical approach through which all knowledge is at the centre of epistemological co-investigation. It would entail praxis or the means for all participants in the group setting, including the official educator, to be able to step back from their past and present environments to perceive them in a critical light."*

This would valorise the migrants' role of their labour in the smooth functioning of some of their host country's essential services, including the health and transport services and child and elderly care. This type of education can also "foster an understanding of the richness of the cultures that migrants bring with them" (English & Mayo, 2019).

Other key pedagogical features for successful FDDL

In various studies about distance digital education (as, for example, compared to blended learning), self-directed learning and digital skills are considered to be very important for effective and meaningful participation. However, migrants and refugees may lack these skills. Moreover, their stressful situation might impede their learning (Castaño Muñoz, Colucci, & Smidt, 2018). Mason & Buchmann (2016) also make a case for an outreach plan with a strong support structures. Colucci et al. (2017) also indicate that migrants and refugees prefer approaches which are tailored to their specific needs and characteristics. These approaches are also in line with the UNHCR's recommendations for delivering education in crisis and conflict situations (UNHCR, 2019).

Another key pedagogical characteristic is the student-centred learning approach which is also personalised to the students' learning needs and preferences (Pane et al., 2017). Studies show that migrants and refugees are a more heterogeneous learning group than traditional adult learners. These studies indicate the importance of understanding the participants' learning demands and abilities (De Waard et al., 2014; Lewis & Thacker, 2016). Obviously, migrants and refugees have unique needs and qualities that might affect their participation in any learning programme. This is true for face-to-face programmes and also digital learning initiatives which also come with their specific problems, including the lack of physical interaction that usually works against social presence.

Mason & Buchmann (2016) identify many of the migrants' particular needs. These include their different backgrounds, their previous education, their location, their literacy level and language skills, whether their studies were interrupted, and any traumatic experiences they may have had. Moser-Mercer, Hayba, and Goldsmith (2016) and English and Mayo (2019) agree that human-centred initiatives are essential in fragile contexts and, ideally, learning must be designed following a bottom-up approach that involves the learners "as subjects and not objects" of the learning process (ibid.).

Moreover, Knowles (1973; p.45), through his andragogy model, argues that an adult has a "reservoir of knowledge that causes him (sic) to become an increasingly rich resource for learning, and at the same time provides him with a broadening base to which to relate new learning". It is therefore important for Knowles (1973) that FDDL initiatives are designed to engage migrants and refugees in collaborative learning activities in which every adult's experience is never devalued or ignored, otherwise the adult would not only perceive this as a rejection of his or her experience, but a rejection of him or her as a person.

For the concept of digital learning that would be applied for FDDL a couple of case studies were identified. In 2009, Context Learning Finland (Finland's leading developer of digital learning content solutions) – and Amiedu (Finland's leading vocational adult education centre with 22,000 students) implemented a series of online training modules as part of the Immigrant Integration training program for immigrants to familiarize them with the Finnish employment system and working life (Amiedu, 2019). Organizations that have a central role in the Finnish employment system contributed to the project (e.g. Confederation of Finnish Construction Industries RT and The Federation of Finnish Enterprises) which was funded by The Ministry of Education. The online training was provided free of charge to immigrants who were either looking for employment in Finland or who had recently been employed in Finland. The training provided a highly practical and realistic approach to learning about working in Finland by using digital storytelling, case examples and video-based interactive exercises that let the learners engage with situations they are likely to face at work. Many of the challenges for immigrants when entering the Finnish working life deal with issues of language (in 2009 most employees still demand their employees to speak Finnish), Finnish culture, habits, legislation and "Finnishness" which is often related to introversion and other culture-specific communicational characteristics. Another aim of the program was to prepare students for a final test to achieve the "Working Life Certificate". It's an award to prove potential employers that the candidate has basic understanding about Finnish working life and knows the basic procedures regarding employment and working under contract.

Cultural Awareness in Technical and Industrial Vocational Training (CATIT) project, funded by the European Union's Leonardo da Vinci program in 2005-2007, developed an online program specializing in employment challenges in technical subject professions (training focused on the specific challenges identified with immigrants in technical and industrial professions of which many have to do with safety culture in work). The online program addressed these challenges by using animated case-based exercises which allow learners to experience working in the European context (Redecker et al., 2010).

Methodology

This qualitative study was based on a sample of 16 migrants who were either seeking asylum, whose request for asylum was rejected but could not be deported and were living in Malta for over a year, and refugees. To ensure that these participants are not harmed (in terms of the risk of job loss, discrimination and problems with government authorities), the anonymity of the participants was maintained throughout the whole project. Other ethical measures were taken, including ensuring that their right to interrupt their participation in the research was communicated to the participants. The average age of interviewed workers was 26 (14 male, 2 female).

Findings

The participants all came from Sub-Saharan African countries and were resident in Malta from 6 months to 4 years. They moved away from their country of origin to seek better economic opportunities, safety from war or both. Their intended final destination was a European country, but not Malta. They ended up in Malta by accident, not by choice. They all lived outside the detention centres in rented apartments with other migrants or refugees and paid their part of the rent from the money they gained through their job. They were all unskilled, had no educational qualifications, received only education comparable to Malta's primary education level, but all were literate and could speak English (although their proficiency in the language was weak yet comprehensible).

The migrants and refugees were all familiar with smart technology and the Internet. They all knew how to use their mobile phones for local and international calls as well for communicating with family and friends, in Malta, and in their native country, through social media. They were also using their smartphones, and in 2 cases, their laptops (which they bought in Malta and paid using money gained through their employment), for informal online learning through, for example, YouTube. Some used Facebook and/or WhatsApp so that they could discuss and learn, in collaboration with others, about such things as dealing with government officers, how to submit their asylum applications and clarify other formalities, including getting their residence permit, health insurance and accommodation. This also required the immigrants to communicate with different groups including local authorities, governmental offices, locals and volunteers.

Their preferred settlement was mainland Europe, and therefore, they preferred, if offered the opportunity, to learn more English, French, Italian or German, but not Maltese (the language of the Maltese Islands). Since English is Malta's other official language, during their stay in Malta, immigrants have various opportunities to learn the language. These include basic language courses offered by the Directorate of Lifelong Learning, and "ntegration courses" offered by various education agencies as part of the "Migrant Integration Strategy and Action Plan" (Ministry for European Affairs and Equality, 2017). Despite these opportunities none of the participants were, at the time of the interviews, following any of the courses on offer. They were also not participating in any training programmes, despite they had very low skills. They argued that they did not have the time to join face-to-face classes because their primary concerns were finding and keeping a good job (or jobs), and taking care of their family. Thus, the participants perceived e-learning through online means as a preferred option, even though none of the immigrants had participated in an online course.

A common thread in the interviews was that, as one participant put it, "countries of Europe know that there are (a) lot of problems in Africa" and should help people living in poverty or in dangerous environments by offering learning initiatives through the Internet. They argued that if given the opportunity, while still in their country of origin, to learn to enhance their employability, language proficiency and knowledge of a potential host country's traditions and customs, they would have participated eagerly in it. Some explained that deciding to move away from one's country, and saving enough money for the journey, took many months. For some it took years. During this period, they believed that they could have improved their knowledge of a specific European language, or mastered a skill through courses that were accessible in their country via online means. However, none of the participants knew of MOOCs (see for example, Colucci, Castaño Muñoz, & Devaux, 2017) and learning resources that were already available, and were specifically designed to help prospective asylum seekers.

The participants also indicated that, given their low level of education and their weak foreign language skills, any digital learning initiative should present information in a simple and intuitive way, "just like phone apps" (participant 4). Preferably, it should also come with a strong support structure.

Conclusion

In general terms, education systems in Europe often do a poor job in providing opportunities for existing disadvantaged students, let alone vast numbers of new (and often traumatized) populations. The evidence of PISA research, for example, demonstrates a gap between rich and poor students in Europe which is significant and already growing before the refugee crisis emerged. The socio-economic crisis since 2008 exacerbated this. The reality is that education systems in most EU countries are not inclusive. Segregation is often seen by school type: students from disadvantaged backgrounds tend to be disproportionally in vocational secondary schools. In these the quality of schooling appears poorer and the resulting reading and mathematics skills are weaker. Immigrant children end up in poorer schools, usually vocational, and problems multiply into a systemic crisis of low expectations and inadequate outcomes.

Refugee children and youth need targeted support as they enter these already challenged school systems (such as intensive language and general induction programs to allow them to participate in mainstream classes as soon as possible). Some also present with war trauma, suggesting that schools need to offer psychological support. But beyond that, refugees will benefit from measures that make education systems more inclusive.

This study showed that FDDL can be a means of empowerment through knowledge and skills for employability – including language proficiency – and social inclusion. Many asylum seekers and refugees already learn informally through YouTube, Facebook and WhatsApp. FDDL initiatives give migrants more flexibility and accessibility to learning initiatives. However, despite the potential of e-learning for asylum seekers and refugees, the study identified significant challenges for the development and implementation of FDDL. This includes a lack of awareness of online educational offerings, particularly in the country of origin of the asylum seekers.

References

Amiedu (2019). Have you moved to Finland? Training and guidance for immigrants looking for employment in Finland. Retrieved 14 February, 2019, from https://www.amiedu.fi/in-english/individual-customers/moved-to-finland/

Castaño Muñoz, J., Colucci, E., & Smidt, H. (2018). Free Digital Learning for Inclusion of Migrants and Refugees in Europe: A Qualitative Analysis of Three Types of Learning Purposes. *International Review of Research in Open and Distance Learning, 19*(2), 1-21.

Colucci, E., Castaño Muñoz, J., & Devaux, A. (2017). MOOCs and Free Digital Learning for the Inclusion of migrants and refugees: A European policy study. *Proceedings of EMOOCs 2017: Work in Progress Papers of the Experience and Research Tracks and Position Papers of the Policy Track*, 96-103. Retrieved from http://ceur-ws.org/Vol-1841/P02_114.pdf

Colucci, E., Smidt, H., Devaux, A., Vrasidas, C., Safarjalani, M., & Castaño Muñoz, J (2017). *Free Digital Learning Opportunities for Migrants and Refugees. An Analysis of Current Initiatives and Recommendations for their Further Use.*

De Waard, I., Gallagher, M., Zelezny-Green, R., Czerniewicz, L., Downes, S., Kukulska-Hulme, A., & Willems, J. (2014). Challenges for conceptualising EU MOOC for vulnerable learner groups. In U. Cress & C. Delgado Kloos (Eds.), *Proceedings of the second European MOOC Stakeholder Summit* (pp. 33 – 42). Lausanne, Switzerland: EMOOCs.

Díaz Andrade, A., & Doolin, B. (2016). Information and Communication Technology and the Social Inclusion of Refugees. *MIS Quarterly, 40*(2), 405-416.

English, L., & Mayo, P. (2019). Lifelong learning challenges: Responding to migration and the Sustainable Development Goals. *International Review of Education, 1.*

Eurostat (2018). Asylum Statistics. Retrieved from https://ec.europa.eu/eurostat/statistics-explained/index.php/Asylum_statistics#Age_and_gender_of_first-time_applicants

Freire, P. (1970). *Pedagogy of the Oppressed.* New York: Continuum.

Gillespie, M., Ampofo, L., Cheesman, M., Faith, B., Iliadou, E., Issa, A., Osseiran, S., & Skleparis, D. (2016). *Towards effective digital provision for refugees.* The Open University and France Medias Monde.

Glass, C. R., Shiokawa-Baklan, M. S., & Saltarelli, A. J. (2016). Who takes MOOCs? *New directions for Institutional Research, 167*, 41-55.

Lewis, K., & Thacker, S. (2016). ICT and the Education of Refugees: A Stocktaking of Innovative Approaches in the MENA Region. *SABER-ICT Technical Paper Series; No. 17.* World Bank, Washington, DC.

Liyanagunawardena, T. R., Adams, A. A., & Williams, S. A. (2013). MOOCs: A systematic study of the published literature 2008–2012. *The International Review of Research in Open and Distributed Learning, 14*(3), 202–227.

Mason, B., & Buchmann, D. (2017). *ICT 4 Refugees.* Deutsche Gesellschaft für Internationale Zusammenarbeit (GIZ) GmbH.

Ministry for European Affairs and Equality (2017). *Integration = Belonging: Migrant Integration Strategy and Action Plan, Vision 2020.* Malta. Retrieved from https://meae.gov.mt/en/Documents/migrant%20integration-EN.pdf

Moser-Mercer, B., Hayba, E. & Goldsmith, J. (2016, May). *Higher education spaces and protracted displacement: How learner-centered pedagogies and human-centered design can unleash refugee innovation.* Paper presented at the UNESCO Chair Conference on Technologies for Development: From Innovation to Social Impact (Tech4Dev Conference). Lausanne, Switzerland 2-4 May 2016.

Pisani, M. (2012). Addressing the 'Citizenship Assumption' in Critical Pedagogy: Exploring the Case of Rejected Female Sub-Saharan African Asylum Seekers in Malta. *Power and Education, 4(*2), 185-195.

Pisani, M., & Giustiniani, A (2009). *Programmes and Strategies in Malta Fostering Assisted Return to and Reintegration in Third Countries.* Valletta: EMN.

Redecker, C., Haché, A., & Centeno, C. (2010). *Using Information and Communication Technologies to promote Education and Employment Opportunities for Immigrants and Ethnic Minorities – POLICY BRIEF.*

UNCHR (2019). Operational Portal: Refugees – Mediterranean Situation. Retrieved from https://data2.unhcr.org/en/situations/mediterranean

Connecting through Educational Technology
Proceedings of the European Distance and E-Learning Network 2019 Annual Conference
Bruges, 16-19 June, 2019

DIGITAL LEARNING TECHNOLOGIES IN PROCESSES OF INNOVATION AND DEMOCRATIC CHANGE? – REFLECTIONS AND QUESTIONS

Elsebeth Wejse Korsgaard Sorensen, Aalborg University, Denmark

"Nothing influences our abilities to cope with the difficulties of existence, so much as the context in which we view them" (Zeldin, 1994)

Introduction

Innovation with digital technologies in formal teaching and learning processes with the purpose of educating learners to become global citizens suffers from inertia. In particular, when it comes to innovation with digital technologies within processes of collaboration and dialogue. It seems that digital dialogue in education utilized for democratic change appears a complex challenge to address. However, historically, new technological innovations have often been rejected. It takes a long time to become accustomed to new technology and to realise its advantages, let alone to be actively utilized (Castells, 1998). Regardless of attitudes towards technology in general, the arguments have been strong for preparing learners for a future in a society permeated with digital technologies.

On the collaborative and dialogic fronts, however, the challenges seemed more complex. While digital technologies seem to have led to enhanced collaboration between teachers (in terms of use and re-use of resources), the promotion of student collaboration has not been enhanced notably. This corresponds to the observation pointed out by the teachers that the integration of digital technologies has not led to a real change in practice and innovation in teaching and learning methodology or alterations of teacher authority, teacher-student roles and power relationships within the learning processes.

Why does it take so long for educational communities to assert the digital perils and potential and implement the digital communicative and pedagogic potential of education of technologies in ways that cultivate, support and enhance the quality of education in general – and lifelong learning (LL) in particular?

Well, on the one hand, innovative development is hampered by tradition. On the other hand, innovation does not primarily generate from research directed towards technologies and their virtues, but more often it appears as a result of the bottom-up processes of educators in their own practices – in other words, from the use context.

In the present context, while reflecting on the contradiction, several issues and questions come to mind:

- The first issue (Q1) concerns the weight, impact and assumptions of traditions and the resulting general inertia with respect to implementing digital educational technology in innovative ways (e.g. for the cultivation of learning communities of practice) in the educational system.
- The second issue (Q2) concerns the ethical issue of "building" (general education) in a global educational perspective including: (a) the fostering of democratic citizens ("building" or socialization), (b) the promotion of ethical values, (c) the empowerment of the learners – with a focus on meta-learning.
- The third issue (Q3) concerns the pedagogical design of online learning architectures for the promotion of shared dialogue and knowledge construction.
- The forth issue (Q4) concerns teacher roles, innovation and learner-centeredness
- The fifth (Q5) issue concerns the role of technology in processes of innovation and change.

This paper reflects on these issues, and discusses the various aspects involved. The structure of the paper and the discussions evolves around identified themes, and reflections on the issues and on their contextual premises are provided. The themes are: (a) The weight of traditions, (b) Educating ethically responsible and democratically empowered learners/citizens?, (c) The impact of pedagogic design decisions and meta-learning?, (d) Technology as vehicle in processes of innovation and change, and (e) Technology as vehicle in processes for innovation and change?

The weight of traditions?

In a research perspective we may talk about at least 3 types of research traditions, that – to a smaller or larger extent – impact on the inertia of digital innovation within teacher education (in terms of digital collaboration and dialogue.

The tradition of Distance Education (DE)

As early as in 1989, Søren Nipper coined and described the concepts of "3 generations of DE" (Nipper, 1989):

1. Correspondence education (more than a hundred years of tradition).
2. Enhanced material concept/distribution (a focus on developing materials).
3. A "virtual" organization, using virtual learning environments (VLEs), allowing collaboration/interaction between students and between students and teachers, requiring competencies on behalf of teachers in pedagogical "organization"/ "design" of an entire virtual world/context for collaborative learning and dialogue (a qualitative shift in the evolvement of DE generations).

Therefore, within the context of DE (especially in Norway), technology/VLE's, carrying the load of tradition, were initially implemented as add-on phenomena. Unfortunately, in a way that did not really utilize the collaborative and dialogic potential of VLEs.

The tradition of Computer Supported Collaborative Learning (CSCL)

Historically, within the tradition of CSCL, the collaborative potential of "virtuality" and the challenge of utilizing this in collaborative learning processes enjoyed a higher degree of awareness in the tradition. Nevertheless, as noted by Kreijns and Kirchner, as early as in 2001:

> *"Support of social interaction has received little attention in the design of CSCL environment, due to the generally accepted assumption that social interaction (also in virtuality) can be taken for granted ...it is not surprising that numerous field observations report disappointing results..." (Kreijns & Kirchner, 2001)*

Admittedly, within the last decade, the CSCL community has with high priority addressed the social interaction issue CSCL (Woodruff, 2002; Stahl, 2006; Roschelle & Teasley, 1995). Not only analytically in terms of the nature of collaborative knowledge building in itself, but also the challenge of designing virtual learning architectures that are holistically integrated for the promotion of online COP's.

Throughout the years, CSCL has also been widely known for struggling with some more "traditional" problems (Stahl, 2006):

- Group formation: How do we form groups in pedagogically sound ways?
- Social awareness: How can the learning environment provide awareness of peer learners – even if they participate remotely in the learning process? Alternatively: How can pedagogical designs provide awareness?
- Moderation/guidance/scaffolding/teacher role: How can collaborative learning processes in virtual COP's be effectively moderated/guided by a tutor/by the learning environment?
- Different interpretations of the role of dialogue in collaborative learning (Koschmann, Dillenbourg....) and what it means to collaborate virtually – and share knowledge?
- The vision of today's CSCL challenges, as identified by Gerry Stahl (2006): Opening new worlds of collaboration, where Groupware systems may create meta-structure to (a) help to create and structure communities, (b) define and generate educational realms of knowledge, give form to intentions and meaning, (c) helping users to come to an understanding of the system's designed affordances, (d) imposes new tasks and transform existing social practices, and (e) make life more rewarding, if also more complex.

The tradition of teacher education (TE)

TE practice suffers from more conflictive issues:

- The separation between theory and practice of the education?
- The pendling shift in focus from "teaching" to "learning" from legislation?
- The minds of teacher trainees? The minds of teacher trainers? The ultimate goal of teaching is learning…..?

Is it a question of understanding the challenge of "integrated pedagogical design" for the establishment of collaboration or for the formation of communities of practice (COPs) (Wenger, 1998) in a technology-enhanced setting, or is it may be a question of understanding the didactical challenge of designing FOR collaboration in a technology-enhanced setting? To what extent – and in what sense – do these three heavy traditions and practices (DE, CSCL and TE) possibly enhance or hamper understanding and didactical innovation in relation to the challenge of forming "integrated pedagogical designs" that are conducive to the creation of innovative collaborative digital COPs (e-COPs)? Do the 3 heavy traditions (DE, CSCL and TE) enhance or hamper understanding and digital innovation in relation to the challenge of forming "integrated pedagogical designs" that are conducive to innovation of formation of collaborative e-COPs?

Educating ethically responsible and democratically empowered learners/citizens?

This issue concerns ethical values. It includes utilizing the digital potential in ways that support the "production" of democratically-oriented empowered learners in a global educational perspective, including: (a) fostering democratic citizens ("building"/upbringing), (b) promoting ethical values, (c) empowering learners – with a focus on meta-learning. It denotes teachers' pedagogical promotion of ethical values and choice of non-authoritarian methodologies (learning for all, global prosperity, empowering the learner etc.). It includes teaching learners a democratic attitude through a pedagogical method that practices digital collaboration, dialogue and negotiation, with a value of co-existence and a global perspective on prosperity.

This may be done through a pedagogical focus on applying online negotiation and meta-learning methodology as pedagogical method. In relation to the need for an educational Ethos of democratic dialogue and collaboration, other current international trends in learning – e.g. like lifelong learning (LL) and learning-to-learn (L2L) – could potentially be of inspiration.

A look back at the field of CSCL, the literature (ex. Crawley, 2014) states that "CSCL …. fulfills some sound educational principles, not least of which being the promotion of an educational Ethos of cooperation" (Crawley, 2014).

How to "educate" globally and multi-culturally oriented learners in becoming democratic citizens is a strong concern. As educational designers facing the challenges of our global society it is essential, to adapt an explicit democratic standpoint when we design. But it may not be sufficient to barely incorporate and keep transparent the ethical values of "building"/education when designing for online COP's. We also need to design and practice online pedagogical methods that "train" pedagogical values (i.e. features of becoming a global democratic citizens), and on how important it is to focus in research on pedagogical design on online learning architectures that promote collaboration and dialogue among learners.

Dialogue is the essential medium for this, but nothing – not even dialogue (in my experience) – appears out of the blue. Rather, it must be designed/induced through online designs that are conducive to dialogue and stimulate authenticity and motivation in learners). Thus, the goal and rationale behind evaluation criteria used to evaluate the dialogic process, which evolves, are based on the following rationale, when it comes to characteristics of a democratic world citizen:

The expectation to learners of what characterizes a democratic dialogue (Sorensen, 2005; Sorensen & Brooks, 2018), could be disseminated to – and practiced with – students:

- knows how to be tolerant and supportive of a fellow human being;
- is open to new ideas and alternative solutions;
- is able to listen to others and incorporate the opinion of others in their views;
- wants to learn from each other's and share knowledge for the course of shared goals;
- does not strive or take initiatives to control others;
- does not submit to authoritarian methodology in any area, but respects the quality of the argument.

An example of a tested model of evaluation criteria for dialogue, which fits and train the democratic dialogue (Sorensen, 2005):

Quantitative evaluation:

- at least 5 contributions;
- 3 of them should be responses to contributions of other students.

Qualitative evaluation (examples of contents which enhances knowledge building):

- questions that ask for clarity;
- adding new knowledge to the discussion;
- etc.

Rationale behind criteria:

- The goal is to support digital human interaction, which contributes to the development of a democratic collaborative knowledge building negotiation and discussion:
  - Participation in discussion (that learners are driving towards a shared goal);
  - Response on others' contributions (the one are listening to what is said);

- Elicit response from others (that you are contributing with relevant interesting views).

Now, one could raise the question if it is possible to implement democratic dialogic meta-learning methodology (with changed teacher-learner roles), not only in in teacher training programs "locally", but also in diverse global intercultural contexts for the purpose of enhancing co-existence, promotion of dialogue and shared intercultural knowledge construction, and the building of global ecological online learning communities? Which types of problems may arise? May an overall methodology of meta-learning/double loop learning strategies, coupled by digital techniques, work for ethical change, transcendence and innovation?

The impact of pedagogic design decisions and meta-learning?

In other words, from the above discussion we may arrive at a need for issues, knowledge and advices of pedagogical design of online learning architectures for the promotion of shared dialogue and knowledge. The important thing here is the predicted interaction (the planned) and what actually emerges. In other words, the ability of teaching and learning to interact in ways, in which they become structuring resources for each other. Thus, Sorensen and Ó Murchú (2004) argue that important considerations are:

- How to minimize teaching (the predicted) in order to maximize learning?
- How to maximize processes of negotiation of meaning enabled by interaction?

Therefore, from a Wengerian perspective (Wenger, 1998), design is about creating a proper balance of participatory and reificatory elements in the instructional design:

- Which elements to structure and make procedures for on the basis of prediction?
- To what extent the design should depend on de-contextualized knowledge?
- How to balance student initiative/ownership and pedagogical authority?

Meta-learning (ML) is the most significant and powerful aspect of the learning-to-learn (L2L) phenomenon. It implies learning of meta-knowledge about learned knowledge (i.e. learning about how one learns) and learning about one's own learning, thinking and acting. L2L is part of that learning, and knowing how to learn is an important knowledge (Knowles, 1975; Garrison, 1997).

It is also important to understand how people learn in social contexts. Wenger explains the negotiation of meaning as involving two constituent processes: participation and reification. These two processes exist in duality, affecting each other and being the source of development to each other. But since production of meaning is distributed inseparably across reification and participation in a shared practice, a dynamic relationship between the two must be established in our design and facilitation of learning. If not, the negotiation and construction of meaning may become problematic:

> *"If participation prevails – if most of what matters is left un-reified then there may not be enough material to anchor the specificities of coordination and to uncover diverging assumptions.(...) If reification prevails – if everything is reified, but with little opportunity for shared experience and interactive negotiation – then there may not be enough overlap in participation to recover a coordinated, relevant, or generative meaning" (Wenger, 1998; p.65)*

It is a widely accepted view within pedagogical enhancement of technology, that nothing happens without a fixed shared structure - determining what, why, how, where, when. Even processes of improvisation and creativity are often happening as challenged deviations from organizations, structures, etc.

> *"...teachers and instructional materials becomes resources for learning in much more complex ways than through their pedagogical intentions. Teaching must be opportunistic, because it cannot control its own effects." (Wenger, 1998; p.267)*

Which problems, which possibilities and what degree of importance as a catalyst for change should we anticipate would be resting on the shoulders of the teacher/designer?

Technology as vehicle in processes for innovation and change?

In different aspects or areas of society, we find different positive and negative views on the question of technology. While technology optimism is widespread, more pessimistic voices on the role of technology have also been heard over time.

One of these voices were the voice of Martin Heidegger (Heidegger, 1996). While the optimistic view perceived technology as entailing the powers of seduction/persuasion/fascination, Martin Heidegger's view was a very pessimistic one (Heidegger, 1977).

- Our fundamental relation to the world is through "the use". With modern technology man is made alien to "the use" and, therefore, to the world.
- Through our use-relationship to the world, we must accept the products of technology, although they do not commit us epistemologically.
- Technology dangerous: humans are exposed to the danger from the structure, which lies behind technology as an instrumental-economical complex.

But (Heidegger's optimism), if we seek/find the nature of technology through (a) poiesis (creation on terms which transcend the creation itself), and (b) techne (an art serving religion and philosophy), things may be different.

Now, in contrast, if we follow Heidegger's advice and focus on "use" (which may be viewed as quit in line with an emphasis on bottom-up processes and practice) and take a look at what happens today, mostly in informal learning communities, then we face quit a different and, from a formal educational perspective, intriguing technology scenery and practice.

It is however indisputable that Web 2.0 either works empowering on the individual and/or provides an outlet for what could be called the voice of the voiceless. In other words, social software makes possible (e.g. Anderson, 2016):

- democratization of knowledge and content (from centrally defined to user-driven content);
- moving focus from communities to networked structures;
- moving focus from consumers to producers, distributing news (participant agency).

Social software also supports the creation and maintenance of different types of networks:

- networks between people working collaboratively;
- empowering networks between people sharing a context (students and teachers within a course, use each other as resources);
- networks between people sharing a field of interest.

Consequently, this leaves us with the following pedagogical/didactical tasks:

- facilitating networks between students within the same course;
- facilitating networks between students and other people working with the field.

It is claimed that the social fabric of Web 2.0 technologies is tightly closed to the local, the place, the location and the creation of a personal, but relational identity. In a perspective of globalization, we do become more global, but not less local or grounded (Wellman, 2012):

- How might the social software transform learning culture and individual behaviours?
- What are the pedagogical changes? What are the new organizational and learning strategies with the new learning tools?
- What impact has social software had on institutionalized learning and training?
- How can best practices be identified regarding what works in e-learning, in which environments, and what does not?
- What will be the impact of open educational content and resources?

Conclusion

What may then be, in essence, the latent potential of social software, if any – for acting as catalysts for innovating TE? How does one evaluate the potential of social software and its sustainability? And what is the need for organizational and pedagogical "legitimization" (perhaps a premise for IT to play a genuine role in TE)?

> *"We do at times engage in conscious reflection and systematic thought, but these are secondary to the pre-reflective experience of being thrown in a situation in which we are always already acting. We are always engaged in acting within a situation, without the opportunity to fully disengage ourselves*

> *and function as detached observers. Even what we call "disengagement" occurs within thrownness: we do not escape our thrownness, but shift our domain of concern. Our acts always happen within thrownness and cannot be understood as the results of a process (conscious or non-conscious) of representing, planning, and reasoning." (Winograd & Flores, 1986; p.70)*

With this final statement in relation to the complexity of research perspectives, I would like to again point to Heidegger, who in my opinion – through his notion of "thrownness" – has something rather important to say about our inescapable embodiment in context.

We should remind ourselves Virtual Learning Environments provide possibilities for a different type of human interaction than that of the physical world. The virtual interaction is susceptible to a dynamic principle related to time and space (i.e. context), and has general characteristics that resemble the features of both spoken and written interaction. Although the interaction may appear as if it was spoken and share a high degree of features of spoken dialogue (due to an often high interactivity), the interaction also contains certain permanent properties, typical of traditional written interaction, which are not subject to the same dynamic time/space principle (Mason, 1993).

This paper has presented some reflections on the various aspects of the development and design of digital architectures in an international perspective. The SLAF model below is an example of such an architecture (Sorensen, 2018):

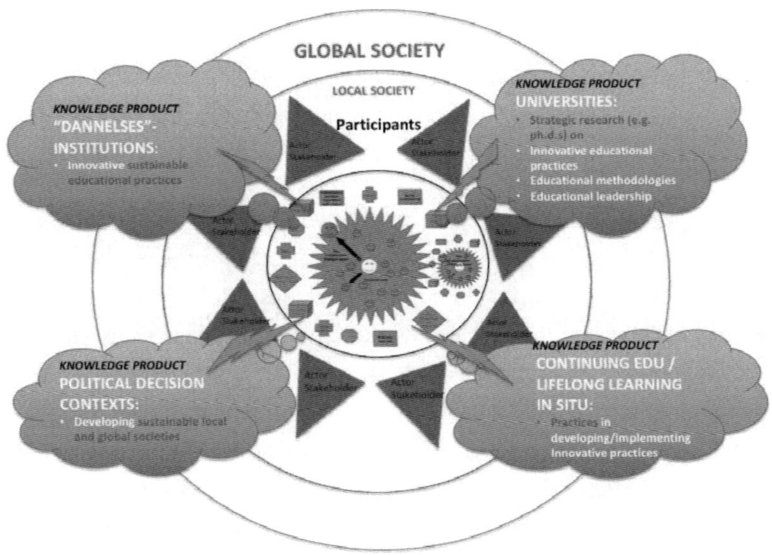

Figure 1. The SLAF model. Innovative learning and collaborative knowledge building across positions and disciplines. Innovation and data generation in situ.

SLAF serves as an inclusive and sustainable model for establishing global intercultural educational program, drawing on existing knowledge in different layers of society.

The paper has argued for a necessity of constructing educational design models based on ethical values in terms of participation and inclusion. It makes a plea for the use of design models that enculture a fundamental dialogic/participatory approach across types of participants. It promotes non-authoritarian principles and liberating and empowering ethical values at the same time. In addition, the models have to be based in a realistic and strategic context experiencing the needs of the networked society and the knowledge economy. Key issues have been identified, described and discussed that are envisioned to promote sound sustainability and global educational growth.

SLAF (Figure 1) integrates a net-based dialogical model for collaborative knowledge building. It becomes a communicative melting pot, in which all stakeholders – across hierarchical positions and disciplines – in a "modus 2" setting participate, create and innovate in a collaborative knowledge building process in a digital learning architecture. All participants (i.e. members of society, researchers etc.) are contributors (provide input) as well as learners (gaining output). Everyone involved may be characterized as "prosumers" (Helms & Agerbaek, 2010). All stakeholders from the four main areas of society contribute as input their insights and expertise to the collaborative work and negotiated identification/learning process, and likewise every stakeholder takes away, as output from the collaborative learning and negotiation process, exactly that which makes sense to him/her and is useful from his/her individual position and perspective. In the wording of Edwards (2007):

> *"(…) boundaries as spaces where the resources from different practices are brought together to expand interpretations of multifaceted tasks, and not as barriers between the knowledge and motives that characterize specialist practices. Importantly, the learning that occurs in these spaces is not a matter of learning how to do the work of others, but involves gaining sufficient insight into purposes and practices of others to enable collaboration" (2007; p.27)*

This paper set out to assert to what extent – and it which sense pedagogical foundations offer a potential for serving as an inclusive and sustainable model for establishing global intercultural educational program. The paper argues for a necessity of constructing educational design models based on ethical values in terms of participation and inclusion. It makes a plea for the use of design models that enculture a fundamental dialogic/participatory approach across types of participants. It promotes non-authoritarian principles and liberating and empowering ethical values at the same time. In addition, the models have to be based in a realistic and strategic context experiencing the needs of the networked society and the knowledge economy. Key issues have been identified, described and discussed that are envisioned to promote sound sustainability and global educational growth.

References

Anderson, T. (2016). *The theory and Practice of Online Learning* (2nd ed.). CA: AU Press.

Bates, A. W. (2015). *Teaching and learning in a digital age. Guidelines for designing teaching and learning.* Creative Commons CC.

Crawley, R. L. (2014). Favor. An autoethnography of survival. In R. M. Boylorn & M. P. Orbe (Eds.), *Critical Autoethnography – Intersecting Cultural Identities in Everyday Life.* Walnut Creek, CA: Left Coast Press, Inc.

Edwards, A. (2007). Relational Agency in Professional Practice: A CHAT Analysis. *An International Journal of Human Activity Theory, 1*, 1-17.

Garrison, R. (1997). Self-Directed Learning: Toward a Comprehensive Model. *Adult Education Quarterly, 48*(1), 18-33.

Heidegger, M. (1977). The Question Concerning Technology. In D. F. Krell (Ed.), *Basic Writings* (p. 287). Harper & Row.

Heidegger, M. (1996). *Being and Time. A Translation of "Sein und Zeit".* Translated by Joan Stambaugh (7th ed.). Albany, New York: SUNY Press.

Helms, N. H., & Agerbæk, L. (2010). *Nettets læringstopografi. Et anslag til didaktisk kortlægning af metaverse, i Onedge 2_10.* Knowledge Lab, University of Southern Denmark.

Knowles, M. (1975). *Self-Directed Learning: A Guide for Learners and Teachers.* Chicago, IL: Follett Publishing Company.

Kreins, K., & Kirchner, P. A. (2001). Designing sociable CSCL Environments. In J. W. Strijbos, P. A. Kirchner, & R. L. Martens (Eds.), *What We Know About CSCL and Implementing It in Higher Education.* Boston, USA: Klüver Academic Publishers.

Mason, R. D. (Ed.) (1993). *Computer Conferencing: The Last Word.* Victoria, Canada: Beach Holme Publishers.

Miyake, N. & Koschmann, T. D. (2002). Realizations of CSCL Conversations: Technology Transfer and the CSILE Project. In T. Koschmann, R. Hall, & N. Miyake (Eds.), *CSCL 2: Carrying forward the conversation.* Mahwah, NJ: Lawrence Erlbaum.

Ó Murchú, D., & Sorensen, E. K. (2004). Online Master Communities of Practice: Collaborative Learning in an Intercultural Perspective. *European Journal of Open and Distance Learning, 2004*/I. Retrieved from http://www.eurodl.org/?p=archives&year=2004&halfyear=1&abstract=96

Roschelle, J., & Teasley, S. (1995). The construction of shared knowledge in collaborative problem solving. In C. E. O'Malley (Ed.), *Computer Supported Collaborative Learning* (pp. 69–97). Heidelberg: Springer-Verlag.

Sorensen, E. K. (1993). Dialogues in networks. In P. B. Andersen, B. Holmqvist, & J. F. Jensen (Eds.), *The Computer as Medium* (pp. 389-421). Cambridge, UK.

Sorensen, E. W. K. (2005). Networked elearning and collaborative knowledge building: design and facilitation. *Contemporary Issues in Technology and Teacher Education (CITE), 4*(4).

Sorensen, E., & Brooks, E. I. (2018). Designing Inclusive Reflective Learning with Digital Democratic Dialogue Across Boundaries and Diversities. In E. I. Brooks & A. Brooks (Eds.), *Interactivity, Game Creation, Design, Learning, and Innovation: 6th International Conference, ArtsIT 2017, and Second International Conference, DLI 2017, Heraklion, Crete, Greece, October 30–31, 2017* (pp. 251-261).

Stahl, G. (2006). *Group Cognition. Computer Support for Building Collaborative Knowledge.* Cambridge, Massachusetts, USA: The MIT Press.

Winograd, T., & Flores, F. (1986). *Understanding Computers and Cognition: A New Foundation for Design.* NY, USA: Addison-Wesley Publishing Company.

Zeldin, T. (1994). *An Intimate History of Humanity.* London: Minerva.

YESTERDAY-TODAY-TOMORROW: AN E-LEARNING PROGRAM ON MIGRATION

Bryan McCormack, YTT Association, France, Paola Perucchini, Maria Gaetana Catalano, Fridanna Maricchiolo, Roma Tre University, Italy

Background

The present study presents an e-learning platform based on the educational programs carried out by Yesterday-Today-Tomorrow Association (YTT) and Roma Tre University. YTT is an independent Paris-based Educational & Humanitarian Non-Profit which combines visual language with learning tools to facilitate migrants' and refugees' inclusive processes, promote human-rights, the prevention of violent extremism, freedom, diverse, multi-ethnic and multi religious societies. YTT is also aimed at positively affecting national and international migration policy-making. Since 2016, YTT has been collaborating with thousands of refugees/migrants (from more than 50 nationalities, aged from 3 to 70 years old) in over 35 camps and squats across Europe/North Africa. They receive 3 sheets of paper and coloured pens and are invited to draw 3 sketches: one of their life before: Yesterday; one of their current life: Today; and one of their life imagined in the future: Tomorrow. These drawings define the YTT visual language, a raw, emotional and explicative language that speaks logically and directly to the audience. Figure 1 shows the YTT drawings by a 9 years old Iraqi girl, living in the Miksaliste Refugee Camp (Belgrade, Serbia), who represented in her Yesterday (the first on the left) which is what she saw when on a Sunday morning, coming back from church, she found both her parents and brother killed. In the Today, she drew her hands and arms with the cuts she self-inflicts on her body. In the Tomorrow, she drew her dream to be a doctor, so that she can help others.

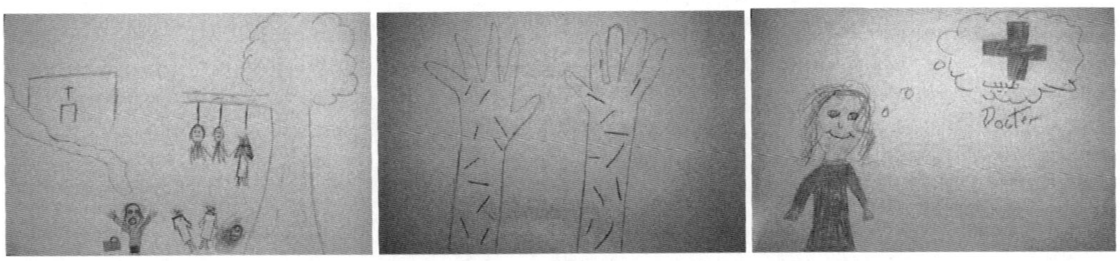

Figure 1. The Yesterday, Today, Tomorrow drawings by a 9 years old Iraqi girl currently living in Miksaliste Refugee Camp, Belgrade, Serbia.

As it is well known, through drawing, people can express clearly their thoughts and feelings independently of dialect, nationality or education (Arizpe, Colomer, & Martínez-Roldán, 2014). Thus, migrants can leave their own trace, creating their own contemporary culture and voice, whereas simultaneously losing all traceability of their inherited culture.

All of these drawings, along with some basic information (age, gender, nationality and current location, etc.) have been collected, filed, scanned and now makeup a digital database of thousands of voices, which is constantly updated with new drawings.

Each drawing has been also analysed and coded, considering different elements regarding the author of the drawing, the content, and the graphical features. With respect to the author, gender, age, nationality, camp (name/city/nation) are analysed. With respect to the content, we code the presence of elements representing human figures, emotions, war, blood, boat, tears, family, school, constructions, barbed-wire fences, animals, vegetables, sky elements, writing, flags, symbols, etc. For the graphic features, tools (pen or pencil) and colours, specifying the precise colour present, are considered. This YTT electronic visual catalogue of drawings allows selecting specific drawings for specific educational programs.

The YTT educational program

The educational program has the aim to stimulate awareness of the living conditions of migrants and refugees, promote deconstruction of prejudice and reduction of discrimination practices, raising awareness among students to fundamental human rights and cultural differences.

Since the early years of life, children show social discrimination and preference for persons and toys similar to their own ethnic (Kinzler et al., 2007; Kelly et al., 2007), which are influenced by adult and peer socialization processes (Aboud & Doyle, 1996). School results to be of optimal context to contrast the development of ethnic prejudice (Hello et al., 2004; Baron, 2015; Bigler & Liben, 2006). The intergroup contact theory by Allport (1954) has been demonstrated to be effective in the reduction of prejudice; and more specifically, educational strategies that promote real or imaginary contact results are successful (Batson et al, 2002; Birtel & Crisp, 2012). Thus, we created an educational program for pupils in schools using the YTT visual language to produce an imaginary contact with a migrant/refugee of the same age.

The educational program was carried out with around 200 5th-grade children from five primary schools in Rome. It used student-centred strategies, which activate empathy and perspective taking, creating a contrasting effect between their own experiences and migrants'/refugees' experiences. The goal of these activities was to stimulate a deep emotional understanding of the migration experience.

The fundamental part of the program concerns activities in which children were asked to draw their YTT drawings, i.e. their past, present and future; then, to draw an imaginary migrant age-mate's YTT drawings; and finally, to look, describe and reflect on migrant children's YTT drawings (see Figure 2).

Pupils and teachers involved in the program showed great appreciation and interest, and schools' principals have asked to include other classes and continue next year. During the lessons, children expressed emotional engagement, non-verbally and verbally, and understood the migrants' condition. They seem also to change their attitudes towards migrants; as a child told, at the end of the program,

> *"Now, when I go into a cafe and I see a refugee in front of it, I ask my father to buy an extra croissant and I give it to him" (Marco, 10y).*

To verify the effects of the educational program on pupils' prejudice, a pilot study was conducted. Participants were 99 children (a subgroup of the pupils involved in the program) distributed in experimental ($n = 56$) and control ($n = 43$) groups. Explicit and implicit prejudice were evaluated with standardized tests (Pirchio et al., 2018). Preliminary results show a statistically tendency to reduction in implicit prejudice in the experimental group ($t(38) = 1.73$, $p = .09$) but not in the control group, and a reduction of explicit prejudice for both groups (experimental group $t(43) = 2.45$, $p = .019$ and control group $t(16) = 3.27$; $p = .005$).

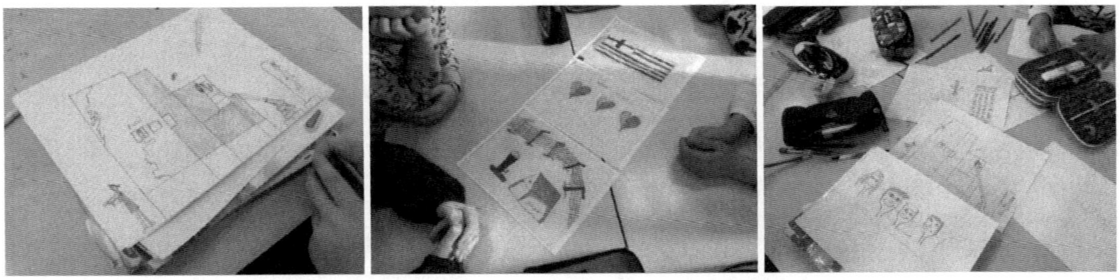

Figure 2. Pupils during the drawing activities

"Exploring the world around us": YTT e-learning Italian version

Based on the research experience described, the e-learning program was created to provide a tool and a guide for teachers to utilize the YTT educational program presented above. A learning platform is implemented which contains a teacher tool-kit, a YTT drawing database and other materials such as suggested activities, information, additional tools that could be combined with the drawings in the educational activities.

Currently, two programs are available: a two hours lesson and a five lessons program. For both versions, the e-learning program defines learning objectives, activities and strategies to realize them. The tool-kit is organized in an easy format so that teachers can download, print and use it to help realize the lessons. The YTT drawing visual database, organized as a catalogue, allows teachers to choose the refugees' drawings more suitable for their educational, social, cultural, ethnic context.

Future directions

The aim is to use the YTT e-learning platform at a global level to contribute to the refugee/migrant crisis. To reach that aim, the "Exploring the world around us" – Italian platform will be adapted for different strategic or at-risk regions, such as, Bosnia & Herzegovina, Turkey, Morocco, Lebanon and Bangladesh, countries where the YTT Association has established contacts with local authorities, universities and NGO's.

Moreover, the program will be addressed to three different topics: "Global Warming", "Women's Rights" and "Children's Rights". For each of them, specific drawings will be selected. The program on "Global Warming" will include drawings coming from climate migrants and in the same way, the programs "Women's Rights" and "Children's Rights" will adopt drawings realized respectively by female and children refugees/migrants. The reasons for having multiple programs are numerous, i.e. proposing different approaches to the refugee/migrant crisis; addressing such vital issues as Global Warming/Women's/Children's Rights from a completely unique and powerful angle; giving more options to teachers/schools/authorities in certain regions and countries where for different political and/or ideological reasons it can be complicated and/or dangerous to address directly head-on the refugee/migrant issue

References

Aboud, F. E., & Doyle, A. (1996). Does talk of race foster prejudice or tolerance in children? *Canadian Journal of Behavioral Science, 28*, 161–170.

Allport, G. W. (1954). *The nature of prejudice.* New York, NY: Addison-Wesley.

Arizpe, E., Colomer, T., & Martínez-Roldán, C. (2014). *Visual journeys through wordless narratives: An international inquiry with immigrant children and the arrival.* A&C Black.

Baron, A. S. (2015). Constraints on the development of implicit intergroup attitudes. *Child Development Perspective, 9*, 50–54.

Batson, C. D., Chang, J., Orr, R., & Rowland, J. (2002). Empathy, Attitudes, and Action: Can Feeling for a Member of a Stigmatized Group Motivate One to Help the Group? *Personality and Social Psychology Bulletin, 28*(12), 1656–1666.

Bigler, R. S., & Liben, L. S. (2007). Developmental intergroup theory: Explaining and reducing children's social stereotypes and prejudice. *Current Direction in Psychological Science, 16*(3), 162-166.

Birtel, M. D., & Crisp, R. J. (2012). "Treating" prejudice: An exposure-therapy approach to reducing negative reactions toward stigmatized groups. *Psychological Science, 23*, 1379-1386.

Hello, E., Scheepers, P., Vermulst, A., & Gerris, J. R. M. (2004). Association between educational attainment and ethnic distance in young adults: socialization by schools or parents? *Acta Sociological, 47*, 253–275.

Kelly, D. J., Liu, S., Ge, L., Quinn, P. C., Slater, A. M., Lee, K., et al. (2007). Cross-race preferences for same-race faces extend beyond the African versus Caucasian contrast in 3-month-old infants. *Infancy, 11*, 87–95.

Kinzler, K. D., Dupoux, E., & Spelke, E. S. (2007). The native language of social cognition. *Proceeding of The National Academy of Sciences, U.S.A. 104*, 12577–12580.

Pirchio S., Passiatore Y., Panno A., Maricchiolo F., & Carrus G. (2018). A Chip Off the Old Block: Parents' Subtle Ethnic Prejudice Predicts Children's Implicit Prejudice. *Frontiers of Psychology, 9*, 110.

Connecting through Educational Technology
Proceedings of the European Distance and E-Learning Network 2019 Annual Conference
Bruges, 16-19 June, 2019

THE INSTRUCTIONAL DESIGN OF AN ONLINE LEARNING ENVIRONMENT (RISSC) FOR UPPER SECONDARY SCHOOL STUDENTS' RESEARCH SKILLS

Louise Maddens[123], Fien Depaepe[123], Annelies Raes[123], Jan Elen[12], KU Leuven & KU Leuven Campus KULAK Kortrijk[1], Centre for Instructional Psychology and Technology[2], ITEC, KU Leuven, also at imec[3], Belgium

Summary

In today's complex world, the acquisition of research skills is considered an important goal in (upper secondary) education. Consequently, there is a growing body of literature that recognises the value of well-designed (online) learning environments for effectively supporting the development of this complex set of skills. However, a clear consensus on how these research skills can be facilitated is currently lacking. Furthermore, interventions aiming to foster these skills are often implemented in specific domains, mostly in physics, biology and chemistry. In addition, current approaches to facilitation often refer to only a few epistemic activities related to research skills. Because of the broad and (mainly) domain-specific character of research skills, the purpose of this paper is to articulate the instructional design considerations for an online learning environment for upper secondary school students' (broad set of) research skills in a(n) (underrepresented) behavioural sciences context.

Introduction

Defining research skills

In recent decades, the importance of the acquisition of research skills has been reflected in numerous curriculum and policy documents (Departement onderwijs en vorming, 2017; OECD, 2006; Opitz et al., 2017). These research skills should enable students to address problems in research, professional practice, and daily life (Opitz et al., 2017). Because of its broad (Fischer et al., 2014) character, it is necessary here to clarify exactly what is meant by research skills in this paper. While a variety of conceptualizations have been suggested in (recent) literature (Kestens, Elen, & Verburgh, 2016), such as *scientific reasoning skills* (Engelmann et al., 2016; Fischer et al., 2014; Opitz et al., 2017); *scientific literacy* (Norris, Phillips, & Burns, 2014) or *research methods skills* (Earley, 2014), in the present study the term *research skills* is used, as it adequately reflects the target concept as a broad set of skills (not merely referring to reasoning, literacy or research methods skills). Throughout this paper, the term will be used to refer to the definition suggested by Fischer and colleagues (2014), labelling research skills as a set of "skills and abilities to understand how scientific knowledge is generated in different scientific disciplines, to evaluate the validity of science-related claims, to assess the relevance of new scientific concepts, methods, and findings, and to generate new knowledge using these concepts and methods" (Fischer et al., 2014; p.29). Fischer and colleagues (2014) refer to this definition using the term scientific reasoning skills as a 21st century skill. In short, research skills include the knowledge and skills involved in eight scientific activities, namely: (a) problem identification, (b) questioning, (c) hypothesis generation, (d) construction and redesign of artefacts, (e) evidence generation, (f) evidence evaluation, (g) drawing conclusions and (h) communicating and scrutinizing (Fischer et al., 2014).

Domain-specificity of research skills

Recent literature highlights the importance of domain-specific knowledge when it comes to apply higher-order cognitive skills (such as skills for problem-solving, critical thinking and/or research) (Kirschner, 2017). The (mainly) domain-specific character of research skills is also underlined by Fischer and colleagues (2014) (see also Engelmann et al., 2018), arguing that the relative weights of the eight activities involved in preparing, performing and evaluating research will differ across disciplines. Fischer and colleagues (2014) argue that some aspects of research skills may be similar across domains (such as the identification of dependent and independent variables), but stress that many aspects of research skills are domain-specific (such as, for example, evidence generation). Approaches to facilitation of research skills typically focus on one specific domain (Engelmann et al., 2018; Fischer et al., 2014). In addition, it is clear that a vast majority of studies on supporting research skills focuses on specific natural sciences disciplines (OECD, 2006; Gess, Wessels, & Blömeke, 2017; Opitz et al., 2017), while very little attention has been paid to behavioural sciences disciplines (Gess et al., 2017). Furthermore, studies on the differences of research skills between disciplines have been rare (Fischer et al., 2014).

Two main questions arising from the literature

In order to deepen our understanding of research skills, the current research project builds on two existing categories of research questions. First, questions related to the assessment (and assessment instruments) of research skills are central. Second, we take a closer look at approaches aiming to answer questions related to the support of research skills in educational contexts. Although the first type of questions is receiving considerable attention in this research project (see, for example, Maddens, Depaepe, Janssen, Raes, & Elen, in press), this paper focusses on the latter group of questions. In this paper, the instructional design considerations for an online learning environment aiming to foster upper secondary school students' research skills (in a behavioural sciences context) are outlined. The online learning environment is called RISSC (Research In Social SCiences).

Designing the online learning environment

Preliminary remarks

Definition and relevance of instructional design

According to the definition of Elen and Clarebout (2006 p. 1), "instructional design aims at contributing to the development of learning environments by describing the basic components of a learning environment, their interrelations and their interaction with learner characteristics". The notion learning environment encompasses both the learning *task* (what the learner needs to learn), as the *support* (elements integrated into the learning task in order to foster learning) (Elen & Clarebout, 2006). It is argued by Elen and Clark (2006) that various elements and interactions between these elements influence learning from instruction.

As learners do not *automatically* engage in epistemic activities (Weinberger et al., 2005), there seems to be an agreement on the importance of well-designed (online) learning environments for effectively supporting the development of complex skills. It is argued that, if designed with caution (Seel, 2006), and if adequately used by the learners (Elen & Clarebout, 2006), the process of complex problem solving can be substantially supported by means of multimedia programs (Elen & Clarebout, 2006; Engelmann et al., 2016; Seel, 2006).

(Online) learning environments

As stated by Merrill, "principles of instruction can be implemented in any delivery system or using any instructional architecture" (Merrill, 2002; p.44). In addition, according to Clark (1983; p.445), "there are no learning benefits to be gained from employing any specific medium to deliver instruction". As such, citing Cook and McDonald (2008; p.7), we believe "the argument of superiority, inferiority, or equivalence is moot. It is a far better investment of resources to investigate "what works?" in e-learning, rather than trying to justify its existence". Following this rationale, the technology versus non-technology question does not seem to be the most important one to be raised. The question does remain *how* to design (technology-enhanced) learning environments.

In what follows, first, the structure, the goal and the target group of the instructional design of the RISSC-environment are outlined. Second, some important theoretical principles underpinning the design decisions are described and illustrated. To conclude, some further areas in research on research skills are suggested in the concluding section.

Structure, goal and target group of the RISCC learning environment

The goal of the online learning environment (further on referred to as RISSC) is to support upper secondary school students' research skills (as defined in the conceptualization section), relying on theoretical instructional design principles (as defined in the following sections). In doing so, we focus on the support and the design of learning tasks for students in a specific behavioural sciences context, because (a) the reliance of research skills on domain-specific knowledge has been emphasized several times in research (Fischer et al., 2014; Engelmann et al., 2016; Kirschner, 2017; Opitz et al., 2017), and (b) a majority of (intervention) studies on the support of research skills limits the focus to scientific disciplines almost exclusively situated in the field of natural sciences. In Flanders, four different types of education are offered from the second stage of secondary education onwards. In general, secondary education (one of the four types), students can choose to enrol in a program called *behavioural sciences*. As a result, research into supporting research skills in a behavioural sciences context is particularly scarce. In RISSC, content is available related to each of the eight epistemic activities (Fischer et al., 2014).

RISSC: theoretical considerations

Five principles

Merrill (2002) identified five *first principles* that can be found in instructional design models. According to these five principles, learning is promoted (a) when learners are engaged in solving real-world problems, (b) when existing knowledge is activated as a foundation for new knowledge, (c) when new knowledge is demonstrated to the learner (ideally by means of a demonstration of the whole task, rather than by means of a list of abstract objective statements); (d) when new knowledge is applied by the learner, and (e) when new knowledge is integrated into the learner's world (Merrill, 2002; p.43). Although not all of the five principles are addressed in an equally explicit way, all five principles are (in some way) implemented in the 4C/ID model (van Merriënboer & Kirschner, 2018). The differences between programs and principles are discussed in Merrill (2002). This model (and its relation to the first principles) is described in the next section. In addition, the implementation of the instructional design principles is illustrated by means of the RISSC-environment.

Four components

It is recommended not to base instructional design decisions on one instructional design model, but rather to evaluate and to compile elements from a variety of models (Elen & Clarebout, 2006). A model generally known because of its aim to integrate elements from different models and theories, focusing in the first place on training domain-specific complex skills, is the 4C/ID model (van Merriënboer & Kirschner, 2018). Roughly sketched, the 4C/ID model is built upon four crucial components: learning tasks, supportive information, part-task practice, and just-in-time information. Central assumptions related to these four components are that (a) a high variability in authentic learning tasks is needed in order to deal with the complexity of the task; (b) supportive information is provided to the students in order to help them build mental models and strategies for solving the task under study (Cook & McDonald, 2008); (c) just-in-time (procedural) information (related to steps, procedures, facts, concepts and principles) is provided for recurrent skills, and (d) part-task practice is provided for recurrent skills that need to be automated. The "Ten steps" – related to the 4C/ID model described by van Merriënboer and Kirschner (2018) – were used as a prescriptive guideline in designing the online learning environment for the present study. The sections below discuss how the four main steps (the design of learning tasks, the design of supportive information, the design of procedural information and the design of part-task practice) are addressed in the RISSC.

1. Design learning tasks

A problem-centred approach (indicating that learning is promoted when learners are engaged in solving real-world problems), the importance of student's application of new knowledge, and the integration of this new knowledge into the learner's world by means of creation and reflection tasks are prescribed in principle 1, 4 and 5 of Merrill's (2002) first principles of instruction. This whole-task approach is also key in the 4C/ID model, where the design of (a variety of) simple-to-complex real-life based whole tasks, aiming at integrating knowledge, skills and attitudes is the core design activity of the training blueprint (van Merriënboer & Kirschner, 2018). As such, the identification of these real-life tasks for the domain under study (research skills in behavioural sciences) appeared crucial in designing the RISSC. In RISSC, cases, (modelling) examples and tasks were selected from research in the domains of psychology, educational sciences and sociology. The complexity of the learning tasks increases with each task class, and the support decreases within each task class (Merrill, 2002; van Merriënboer & Kirschner, 2018). By means of emphasis manipulation (van Merriënboer & Kirschner, 2018), different sets of constituent skills are stressed in different task classes, without losing sight of the whole task. The first task class, for example, focusses on problem identification, questioning and hypothesis generation, but the tasks are integrated in several cases involving real (whole) research projects.

2. Design supportive information

Supportive information helps learners to carry out the non-recurrent aspects of the learning tasks related to research skills (van Merriënboer & Kirschner, 2018). In the first principles, Merrill (2002; p.47) states that "learning is promoted if the instruction provides a structure that the learner can use to build the required organizational schema for the new knowledge". In the 4C/ID model, structural, conceptual and causal domain models are provided to the learners in order to help them reasoning in the task domain. Concerning research skills, the supportive information can differ for different epistemic activities (de Jong & van Joolingen, 1998; Fischer et al., 2014). For the epistemic activity *evidence generation*, for example, experimentation hints (or SAPs (van Merriënboer & Kirschner, 2018)) and reflection prompts can be provided, while in the epistemic activity *drawing conclusions*, visualizing tools and knowledge integration environments (or conceptual domain models (van Merriënboer & Kirschner, 2018)) might be helpful (de Jong & van Joolingen, 1998). In RISCC, the transferability of the effectivity of these support tools was always evaluated based on the domain under study (behavioural sciences). Supportive information is provided in RISSC for complex tasks such as formulating a research question, where students can consult general *information* on characteristics of a good research question in behavioural sciences, can consult *examples or demonstrations* (see principle 3, Merrill, 2002) of this general information (for example a typical research question in behavioural sciences) and can receive *cognitive feedback* on their own research questions (Merrill, 2002; van Merriënboer & Kirschner, 2018). In doing so, learners are for example asked to critically compare and contrast their own research question with an example. The supportive information is offered by means of multimedia such as pictures, texts, and information videos, and is directly accessible during the whole learning task (de Jong & van Joolingen, 1998). An example of supportive information can be found in Figure 1. When students click on the link "criteria for a good research question", they are guided towards an in instruction video (conceptual model).

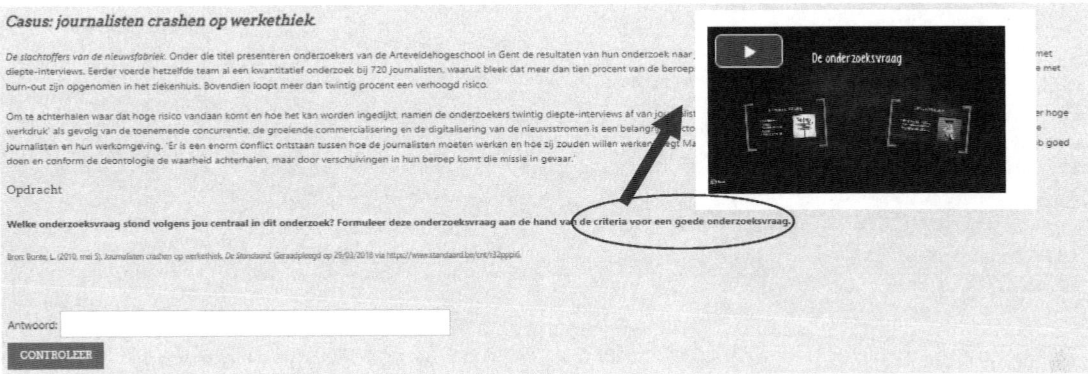

Figure 1. Example of supportive information for the non-recurrent skill "formulating a research question" in RISSC

3. Design procedural information

Procedural information is necessary for carrying out recurrent aspects of learning tasks (van Merriënboer & Kirschner, 2018). As such, in RISSC, procedural information is provided for tasks such as the use of Boolean operators in a literature search, or the identification of dependent and independent variables. This information is presented just-in-time: students can consult information displays on a specific rule, procedure, fact, concept or principle (for example on the effect of the word "AND" in a search query). An example of procedural information (with procedural directions for formulating a search query) in RISSC can be found in Figure 2.

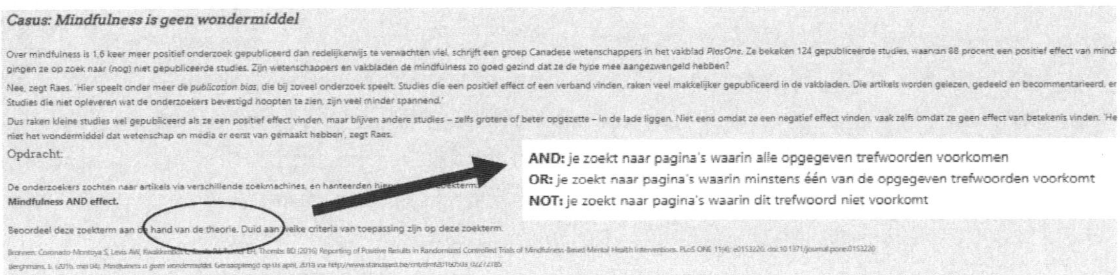

Figure 2. Example of procedural information for the Boolean operators (rules)

4. Design part-task practice

Part-task practice involves practice items promoting rule automation for recurrent aspects of the whole complex skill. Because an overreliance on part-task practice is not helpful for complex learning (van Merriënboer & Kirschner, 2018), in RISSC, additional part-task practice is available for some (but not all) of these recurrent routine aspects of skills (for example for the formulation of a search query or the identification of dependent and independent variables). In addition, students receive corrective feedback, pointing the students to an error, and giving a hint for applying the correct rule (van Merriënboer & Kirschner, 2018). An example of part-task practice and related corrective feedback in RISSC (for the recurrent aspect "formulating a search query") can be found in Figure 3.

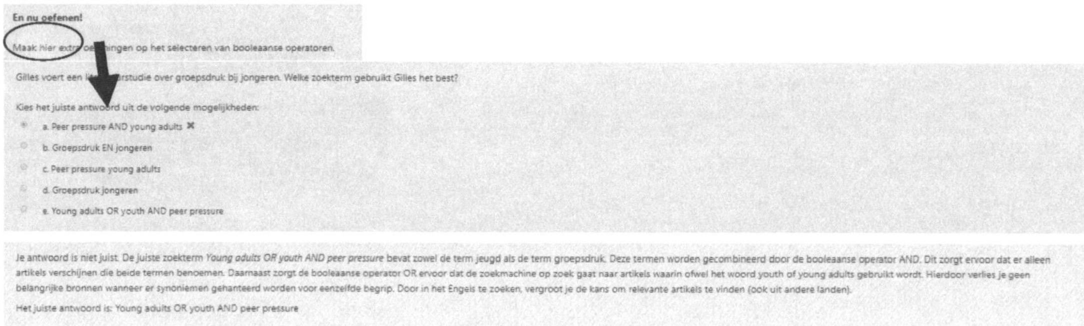

Figure 3. Example of part-task practice for the recurrent aspect "formulating a search query"

Conclusion and further research

RISSC's systematic design is based on the aforementioned insights from instructional theory, with a main focus on the 4C/ID model (van Merriënboer & Kirschner, 2018) and the first principles of instruction (Merrill, 2002), and is unique because of its domain-specific focus on research in behavioural sciences, and its attention to eight distinct epistemic activities (Fischer et al., 2014). Although the models mentioned offer very specific guidelines, it is up to the designer to concretely operationalize these guidelines taking into account the domain under study. As such, more research is needed (and planned) into the validation of these instructional guidelines for the context of research skills in a behavioural sciences domain.

In a first planned study, the impact of two different approaches to present the learning goals in the beginning of the RISSC-environment on students' affective, behavioural and cognitive outcomes is investigated. In the first approach (also called the *topic-centred approach*), an abstract clarification of learning objectives is presented to the learners, while in the second approach (also called the *problem-centred approach*), a concrete discussion of the learning objectives is provided to the students with a concrete link to the application and integration phase. More concrete, the second approach contains a specific explication of the particular whole task the learners will perform following instruction. As such, the central question in this study is to what extent a problem-centred online learning environment influences students' affective, behavioural and cognitive learner characteristics, compared to a topic-centred online learning environment.

References

Clark, R. E. (1983). Reconsidering research on learning from media. *Review of Educational Research, 53*(4), 445-459.

Cook, D. A., & McDonald, F. S. (2008). E-learning: Is there anything special about the "e"? *Perspectives in Biology and Medicine, 51*(1), 5-21.

Departement Onderwijs en Vorming (2017). Secundair onderwijs - Derde graad ASO – Humane wetenschappen – Specifieke eindtermen. Retrieved June 6, 2018, from http://eindtermen.vlaanderen.be

Earley, M. A. (2014). A synthesis of the literature on research methods education. *Teaching in Higher Education, 19*(3), 242–253. https://doi.org/10.1080/13562517.2013.860105

Elen, J., &, Clarebout, G. (2006). The use of instructional interventons: lean learning evironments as a solution for a design problem. In J. Elen & R. E. Clark (Eds.), *Handling complexity in learning environments: Theory and Research.* Oxford, G.B.: Elsevier Science Ltd.

Elen, J., & Clark, R. E. (Eds.) (2006). *Handling Complexity in Learning Environments. Theory and Research.* Oxford, G.B.: Elsevier Science Ltd.

Engelmann, K., Neuhaus, B. J., & Fischer, F. (2016). Fostering scientific reasoning in education – meta-analytic evidence from intervention studies. *Educational Research and Evaluation, 22*(5–6), 333–349.

Engelmann, K., Chinn, C.A., Osborne, J., & Fischer, F. (2018). The roles of domain-specific and domain-general knowledge in scientific reasoning and argumentation. An introduction. In F. Fischer, C. A. Chinn, K. Engelmann, & J. Osborne (Eds.), *Scientific reasoning and argumentation. The roles of domain-specific and domain-general knowledge* (1st ed.) (pp. 1-19). London & New York: Routledge.

Fischer, F., Chinn, C. A., Engelmann, K., & Osborne, J. (2018). *Scientific reasoning and argumentation. The roles of domain-specific and domain-general knowledge.* London & New York: Routledge.

Fischer, F., Kollar, I., Ufer, S., Sodian, B., Hussmann, H., Pekrun, R., Neuhaus, B., Dorner, B., Pankofer, S., Fischer, M., Strijbos, J-W., Heene, M., & Eberle, J. (2014). Scientific reasoning and argumentation: Advancing an interdisciplinary research agenda in education. *Frontline Learning Research, 4*, 28–45.

Gess, C., Wessels, I., & Blömeke, S. (2017). Domain-specificity of research competencies in the social sciences: Evidence from differential item functioning. *Journal for Educational Research Online/Journal für Bildungsforschung Online, 9*(2), 11-36.

de Jong, T., & Van Joolingen, W. R. (1998). Scientific discovery learning with computer simulations of conceptual domains. *Review of Educational Research, 68*(2), 179-201.

Kestens, J., Elen, J., & Verburgh, A. (2016). *Kritisch denken en onderzoekscompetenties: de nexus.* (Unpublished master's thesis). KU Leuven.

Kirschner, P. (2017, December 21). De Holle Retoriek van '21st-Century Skills' – Hoezo is Kennis Minder Belangrijk? Blogcollectief Onderzoek Onderwijs [Blogpost]. Retrieved from https://onderzoekonderwijs.net/2017/12/21/de-holle-retoriek-van-21st-century-skills-hoezo-is-kennis-minder-belangrijk/

Maddens, L., Depaepe, F., Janssen, R., Raes, A., & Elen, J. (in press). *Evaluating the Leuven Research Skills Test for 11th and 12th grade.* Manuscript accepted for publication.

van Merriënboer, J. J. G., & Kirschner, P. A. (2018). *Ten steps to complex learning.* New York: Routledge.

Merrill, M. D. (2002). First principles of instruction. *Educational Technology Research and Development, 50*(3), 43-59.

Norris, S. P., Phillips, L. M., & Burns, D. P. (2014). Conceptions of Scientific Literacy: Identifying and Evaluating Their Programmatic Elements. In M. Matthews (Eds.), *International Handbook of Research in History, Philosophy and Science Teaching* (pp. 1317–1344). Dordrecht: Springer Netherlands. https://doi.org/10.1007/978-94-007-7654-8_40

Opitz, A., Heene, M., & Fischer, F. (2017). Measuring scientific reasoning – a review of test instruments. *Educational Research and Evaluation, 23*(3–4), 78–101. https://doi.org/10.1080/13803611.2017.1338586

Organisation for Economic Co-operation and Development – OECD (2006). Assessing Scientic, Reading and Mathematical Literacy: A framework for PISA 2006. In *Programme for International Student Assessment* (pp. 3–125).

Seel, N. M. (2006). Mental Models and Complex Problem Solving: Instructional Effects. In J. Elen & R. E. Clark (Eds.), *Handling complexity in learning environments: Theory and Research.* Oxford, G.B.: Elsevier Science Ltd.

Weinberger, A., Ertl, B., Fischer, F., & Mandl, H. (2005). Epistemic and social scripts in computer–supported collaborative learning. *Instructional Science, 33*(1), 1-30.

Acknowledgements

This study was carried out within imec's Smart Education research programme, with support from the Flemish government.

Connecting through Educational Technology
Proceedings of the European Distance and E-Learning Network 2019 Annual Conference
Bruges, 16-19 June, 2019

EDUCATIONAL TECHNOLOGY FOR ACTIVE CONNECTIONS IN BLENDED LEARNING ENVIRONMENTS

Philip Uys, Charles Sturt University, Australia

Introduction

This conference focuses on employing educational technology for connections. It assumes that these connections will be *active*, and not latent – otherwise these will be meaningless and ineffective. The emphasis is thus on creating effective learning environments. Such learning environments are not just online or digital, but can also be physical learning spaces in which educational technology can play a key role.

A key strategy to ensure that educational technology connections are indeed active is to employ educational technology within an active learning framework for both online and on-campus learning i.e. blended learning. Educational technology on its own does not lead to active learning – only when it is used within well-founded learning designs – of which constructive alignment is highlighted below. I am thus agreeing with Veletsianos and Moe (2017) that educational technology by itself is not "education's silver bullet" but should be located within "the essentials of teaching and learning: theory, pedagogy and emergent trends in the research." Such active learning will lead to learner engagement, leading to effective learning and learner success.

The vision for instance for educational technologies at Charles Sturt University is to "support educational practices focussed on student success by providing cutting edge, stable learning environments".

Literature review

This cursory literature review explores the concepts of learning spaces, learning environments, blended learning, constructive alignment, and active learning – all within the context of educational technology enabling active connections for effective learning.

Learning spaces and learning environments

Learning spaces in the context of higher education refer to physical, digital and cognitive learning environments (Oblinger, 2006). The terms *learning spaces* and *learning environments* are thus used interchangeably in this paper. Learning spaces are further not just the traditional *classrooms* but all "spaces" where formal and informal learning occurs – for instance in libraries (Bridgland & Blanchard, 2001; Keating & Gabb, 2005, Lonsdale, 2003), laboratories, workplaces, green spaces (Massey, 2004), and a variety of other locations – both offline and online.

Blended learning

The concept of *blended learning* acknowledges the above: learning, if not fully online, in many cases now occurs as a thoughtful (Stacey & Gerbic, 2008) blend or convergence of face-to-face interactions and online learning activities (Garrison & Vaughan, 2008; Graham, 2006). The challenge is thus to ensure effective blended learning environments – not merely in purely online or purely face-to-face environments.

Constructive alignment

Biggs (2003; p.27) similarly focuses the attention on the active involvement of the learner, and defines constructive alignment as "the 'constructive' aspect refers to what the learner does, which is to construct meaning through relevant learning activities. The 'alignment' aspect refers to what the teacher does, which is to set up a learning environment that supports the learning activities appropriate to achieving the desired learning outcomes". In consulting assignments of the writer in various settings, constructive alignment has been used to guide workshop participants to define learning activities based on learning outcomes and assessment, and only thereafter consider content delivery or content creation – the focus being on actions by the learner.

Active learning

It is proposed that active learning, which well aligns with the tenets of constructive alignment, leads to effective blended learning environments that is supported by educational technology.

What is active learning?

Active learning is "students doing things and thinking about what they are doing" (Bonwell & Eison, 1991). It involves and engages learners in the learning processes which is opposed to a transmission approach (Freire, 1970) and provides greater agency to learners but also require thought and reflection about the learning taking place (Horton & Freire, 1990). Michael (2006) describes active learning as "the process of keeping students mentally, and often physically, active in their learning through activities that involve them in gathering information, thinking, and problem solving".

Why active learning?

It is clear from the literature that learner engagement leads to learning and learner success (Kahu & Nelson, 2018; Nelson, Readman, & Stoodley, 2018). Kahu and Nelson (2018) depict it as follows in Figure 1.

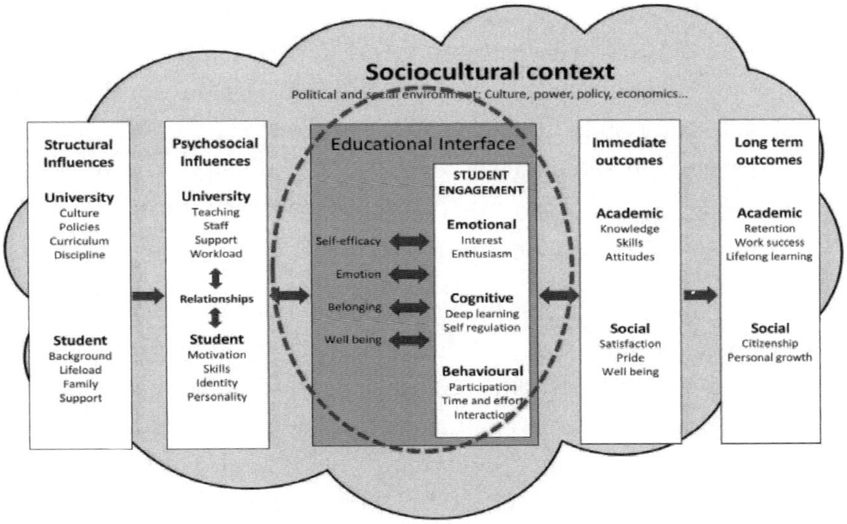

Figure 1. Refined conceptual framework of student engagement

Active learning, fully supported by educational technology, is a key strategy to ensure learning engagement, thus leading to effective learning and learner success. It can be depicted as follows in Figure 2.

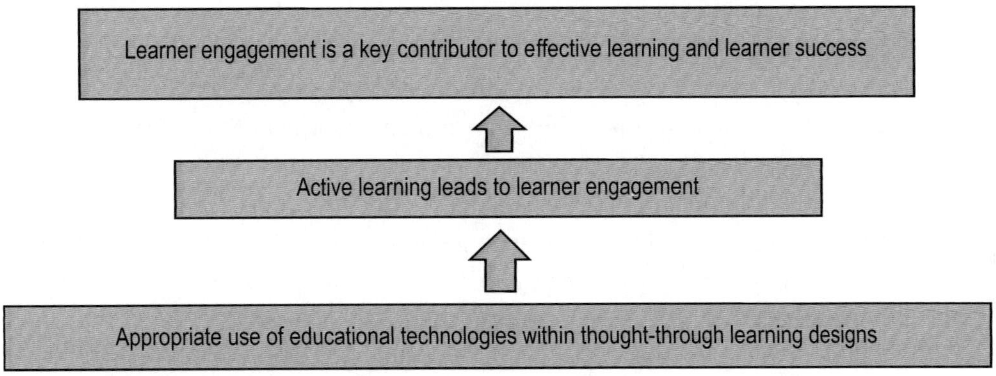

Figure 2. Relationship between learner engagement, learner success, active learning and educational technologies

Michael (2006) furthermore reviewed the evidence from a large volume of literature and various fields (exceeding 100 sources) indicating that "active learning works" and is more effective than more passive approaches.

Using educational technologies for active learning in blended learning environments

In the online dimension of blended learning, a myriad of educational technologies is available to support active learning. Learning management systems (LMSs) in themselves provide a variety of technologies. Moodle, the largest open source LMS internationally, provides facilities for collaboration on online and mobile devices (groups, forums, wikis, glossaries); for interaction (games, forums, chat, messaging, online-conferencing); for communication (messaging, announcements, calendar); for assessment (assignments, quizzes, grading/marking, feedback, assignment submission); for managing resources (pages, book, bookmarking), and for learner management. The Moodle Plugin directory now has more than 1,500 listed plugins. In addition to LMSs there are further a vast array of (often free) external educational technologies and social media tools available to support active learning. These educational technologies connect the learner to the teacher, the learners to each other, and learners to learning activities and resources.

Many of these technologies are accessible by mobile devices that can be used offline, and further support other off-line use – thus supporting active learning in face-to-face environments. In face-to-face environments there are educational technologies available to conduct polls in classrooms, group-work through online participation in class, the use of smartboards, augmented reality, virtual reality, movable computer displays, flexible furniture, shared writing surfaces, and simulations like intelligent paramedic patient dummies. Using such educational technologies creates blended environments where face-to-face and online activities are integrated. The *flipped classroom* is similarly an approach that was designed for face-to-face learning (introduced as the Thayer Method in 1835) often using educational technologies such as web searches, online exercises, and reviewing online resources before class. At the University of Technology, Sydney (date unknown) "online pre-labs were introduced, requiring students to complete a series of questions based on material presented in lectures before coming to class." EDUCAUSE (2012; p.1) describes the flipped classroom as a "pedagogical model in which the typical lecture and homework elements of a course are reversed". This definition blurs in the online environment as it is not possible to easily define what is "before class" and what is "during class". Honeycutt and Glova (2014) posit thus that "at its core, the flip means shifting the focus from the instructor to the students" indicating that the flipped classroom in the blended learning environment, be it integrated, face-to-face or online, is about focussing on activities by the learners "to construct knowledge, connect with others, and engage in higher levels of critical thinking and analysis". Jenkins et al. (2017) acknowledges though the continued role of the teacher and the role of "content" in their "Flipped Learning Matrix model".

The writer proposes that physical learning spaces (for formal and informal learning) itself can be seen as *educational technology* potentially supporting, or inhibiting, active learning in blended learning environments. Its impact is so significant on learning that it has been described as the "third teacher" (Pigozzi et al., 2010). Examples of active learning enabled by physical spaces range from group work and mind mapping to project work. Figure 3 depicts a blended, collaborative arrangement at Charles Sturt University linking online and face-to-face technologies and encouraging active learning.

Figure 3.

At Case Western Reserve University an active learning project occurred in two rooms with blended technologies, "optimized for collaboration both within the classroom and through telecommunication with others off campus" and reported very positive outcomes (Juergensen et al., 2015). These rooms used "large displays that let students collaborate on projects and flexible furniture that can be easily reconfigured to suit various learning activities. The classes also featured bright colours and shared writing surfaces, including multiple white boards and writable walls". The project report included the following quotes from two students:

> *"I am so engaged that I didn't clock watch at all. Is there a clock in here? I didn't even notice that."*

> *"Doing a class like this in just one format may get boring. Having so many different methodologies using these different technologies made it more interesting and informative. I need more going on than just PowerPoint. Using these different ways to learn is much more engaging."*

At Charles Sturt University a 2019-initiative is the development of a learning spaces portal (following a successful pilot last year), to encourage active learning by displaying on mobile devices or online, the layout of each teaching room, technology and furniture available, and active learning strategies that can be used in the room.

Figure 4. Learning spaces portal under development at Charles Sturt University: accessing information on a mobile device

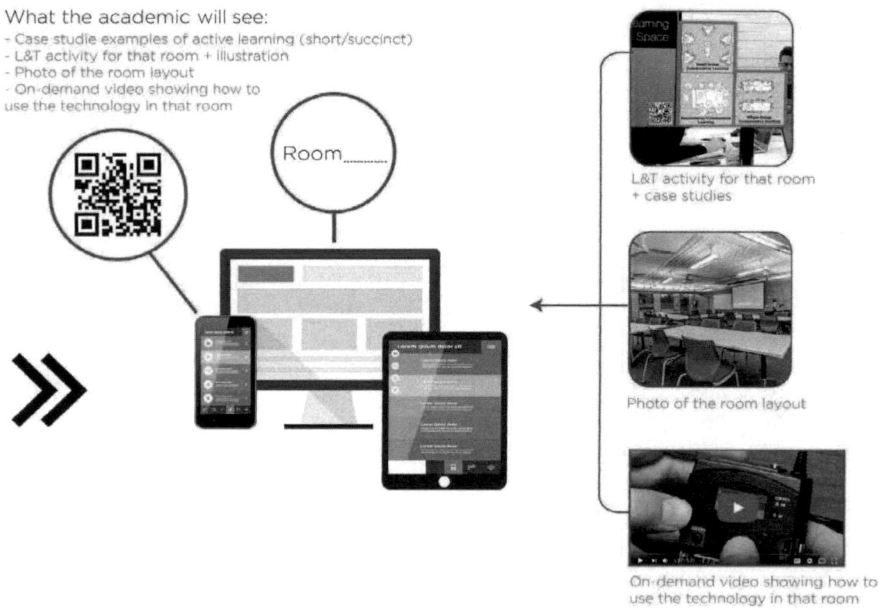

Figure 5. Earning spaces portal under development at Charles Sturt University: what the teacher sees

Conclusion

Educational technology can indeed be used to create active connections for blended learning by supporting and enabling active learning. Educational technology can thus play a key role in creating effective blended, online, face-to-face, digital or physical learning environments. The fundamental precondition is that educational technology is employed within an active learning framework, based on the tenets of constructive alignment, thus leading to student engagement and ultimately effective learning and learner success.

References

ACODE (2018). Introduction to Learning Spaces. Retrieved from https://www.acode.edu.au/course/view.php?id=28&section=1

Biggs, J. B. (2003). *Teaching for quality learning at university* (2nd ed.). Buckingham: Open University Press/Society for Research into Higher Education.

Bonwell, C., & Eison, J. (1991). *Active learning: Creating excitement in the classroom* (ASHE-ERIC Higher Education Report No. 1). Washington, DC: George Washington University.

Bridgland, A., & Blanchard, P. (2001). Flexible delivery/flexible learning ... does it make a difference? *Australian Academic & Research Libraries, September*, 177-191.

EDUCAUSE Learning Initiative (2012). *7 Things You Should Know About Flipped Classrooms.* EDUCAUSE Learning Initiative (ELI).

Freire, P. (1970). *Pedagogy of the Oppressed.* New York: Herder and Herder.

Garrison, R., & Vaughan, H. (2008). *Blended learning in higher education: Framework, principles and guidelines.* San Francisco: Jossey-Bass.

Graham, C. (2006). Blended learning systems. Definitions, current trends and future directions. In C. Bonk & C. Graham (Eds.), *The handbook of blended learning: Global perspectives, local designs.* San Francisco: John Wiley and Sons.

Honeycutt, B., & Glova, S. (2014, March 31). Can You Flip an Online Class? Faculty Focus. Faculty Focus [Blog post]. Retrieved from https://www.facultyfocus.com/articles/blended-flipped-learning/can-flip-online-class/

Horton, M., &Freire, P. (1990). *We Make the Road by Walking.* Philadelphia, PA: Temple University Press.

Hua, P., Uys, P. M., & Eeles, P. (2017). *Adapting to new learning spaces: resistance and remedies.* Paper presented at the CSU Digital Showcase. 2018 IUT Conference, Port Macquarie, Australia.

Jenkins, M., Bokosmaty, R., Brown, M., Browne, C., Gao, Q., Hanson, J., & Kupatadze, K. (2017). Enhancing the design and analysis of flipped learning strategies. *Teaching & Learning Inquiry, 5*(1). Retrieved from http://dx.doi.org/10.20343/teachlearninqu.5.1.6

Juergensen, J., Oestreich, T., Yuhnke, B., Kenney, M., Skapin, K., & Shapiro, W. (2015, January 26). Active Learning at Case Western University. EDUCAUSE Review [Blog post]. Retrieved from https://er.educause.edu/articles/2015/1/active-learning-at-case-western-university

Kahu, E. R., & Nelson, K. (2018). Student engagement in the educational interface: understanding the mechanisms of student success. *Higher Education Research & Development, 37*(1), 58-71. Retrieved from http://www.tandfonline.com/doi/full/10.1080/07294360.2017.1344197

Keating, S., & Gabb, R. (2005). *Putting learning into the learning commons: A literature review.* Postcompulsory Education Centre, Victoria University.

Lonsdale, M. (2003). *Impact of School Libraries on Student Achievement.* A review of the research. Melbourne: Australian Council for Educational Research.

Massey, S. (2004). *The benefits of a Forest School experience for children in their early years.* Forest school in Worcestershirelea, 10.

Michael, J. (2006). Where's the evidence that active learning works? *Advances in Physiology Education, 30*, 159-167.

Nelson, K., Readman, K., & Stoodley, I. (2018). *Shaping the 21st century student experience at regional universities. Final report: 2018.* Canberra: ACT. Retrieved from http://shapingtheregionalstudentexperience.com.au/wp-content/uploads/2018/06/SP14-4602_NelsonandReadman_Report_2018.pdf

Oblinger, D. (2006). *Learning Spaces.* EDUCAUSE Review.

Pigozzi, O. W., Peterson & Mau, B. (2010). *The Third Teacher.* Retrieved from http://thethirdteacherplus.com/resources/

Stacey, E., & Gerbic, P. (2008). Success factors for blended learning. *Hello! Where are you in the landscape of educational technology? Proceedings of the ASCILITE Conference, Melbourne 2008*, 964-968. Retrieved from http://www.ascilite.org/conferences/melbourne08/procs/stacey.pdf

University of Technology Sydney (n.d.). learning.futures in the classroom. Retrieved from https://www.uts.edu.au/research-and-teaching/learning-and-teaching/learningfutures/learningfutures-classroom

Veletsianos, G., & Moe, R. (2017, April 10). The Rise of Educational Technology as a Sociocultural and Ideological Phenomenon. EDUCAUSE Review [Blog post]. Retrieved from https://er.educause.edu/articles/2017/4/the-rise-of-educational-technology-as-a-sociocultural-and-ideological-phenomenon?lipi=urn%3Ali%3Apage%3Ad_flagship3_feed%3BgTGfmuchTny2kpDc2AjtlA%3D%3D

Connecting through Educational Technology
Proceedings of the European Distance and E-Learning Network 2019 Annual Conference
Bruges, 16-19 June, 2019

TOWARDS MATCHING ACCESS WITH SUCCESS: USING TECHNOLOGY TO CREATE AN EFFECTIVE LEARNING ENVIRONMENT FOR POSTGRADUATE DISTANCE LEARNING STUDENTS

Karin Müller, Marilize Putter, Milpark Education, South Africa

Introduction

Distance learning has been identified as a key enabler in providing greater access to education. Yet, in order to provide meaningful access and constitute a productive application of both the student and country's resources, such access must include a reasonable chance of success (Department of Higher Education and Training – DHET, 2014). In the South African higher education environment, success – if measured by dropout and throughput rates– has been considerably lower on undergraduate distance learning programmes than on contact learning programmes (DHET, 2018b). On a postgraduate level, the graduation benchmark rate set by government similarly shows a significant disparity between contact and distance learning. For postgraduate qualifications (up to honours level), it is earmarked at 60% for contact learning; but for distance learning, the target is halved, and set at only 30% (Ministry of Education – MOE, 2001). These low rates indicate that for many distance learning students, they may have gained access to education, but have a small chance of converting such access into success.

There are many and varied factors that impact on distance learning students' ability to be successful in their studies, ranging from an individual to institutional level. Students who opt for distance learning, often do so at an older age, when they may be mid-career or have families (DHET, 2014), and there is thus a balancing act to be achieved between the competing pressures of work, family life and studies. In a South African context, the political past has left indelible marks on all aspects of society, giving rise to inequality, disadvantage and socio-economic challenges which are further factors to take into account (Subotzky & Prinsloo, 2011). The diverse profile of the students of the School of Financial Planning and Insurance reflects and is impacted by these factors. The School forms part of Milpark Education, a private higher education institution in South Africa. It offers undergraduate and postgraduate programmes in financial planning and insurance, on a distance learning basis. On the National List of Occupations in High Demand, the roles these students are able to fill or render with greater competence upon completion of their studies are categorised as "highest" and "higher" – descriptions that indicate the level of shortages in the current employment market, and that reflect the historical and anticipated growth rates for these occupations (DHET, 2018a). It is therefore critical that as many as possible students are successful at their studies and enter the market equipped with the necessary skills.

In this article, the focus is on the School's Postgraduate Diploma in Financial Planning, which is offered on an honours' level (NQF8). It has been offered as a distance learning programme since inception in 2010. In 2016, the programme was reviewed, and the guiding question was how the qualification could be restructured in order to give effect to the DHET's call for meaningful access, and also to address the factors that challenge distance learning students in their studies. This article is a reflection on the progress made since the introduction of the new model, and how the use of technology has facilitated the successes achieved thus far. For purposes of this article, we have accepted the two-part description of educational technologies of Cleveland-Innes & Wilton, being firstly, the tools or systems that can be used in education; and secondly, the relationship to its purpose: to solve problems in teaching and learning - as they aptly state, "a tool becomes a technology when it is applied with some intention to meet some human need" (Cleveland-Innes & Wilton, 2018).

Establishing the context

Aim of the qualification

Students study this qualification to obtain specialist knowledge in the various fields of financial planning. A principal aim of the qualification is therefore to equip students with the necessary expertise to work in the financial planning sector, and capably render services to individual and corporate clients (Milpark Education, 2019).

Financial planning is also an interdisciplinary field; sectors as diverse as retirement, health, estates and wealth, asset management, insurance, employee benefits, law and tax are intersected. The qualification therefore serves a second purpose: to enhance the professional expertise and skills of persons employed in related roles in the financial services industry or associated sectors, including investment managers, insurance agents, legal advisers, corporate benefits consultants, pension fund trustees, actuaries, lawyers and accountants whose work environment or interests include financial planning.

Importantly, obtaining the qualification also renders students eligible to write the professional competency exam (CFP® PCE) of the Financial Planning Institute of Southern Africa (FPI). The FPI is recognised by the South African Qualifications Authority as the professional body for financial planners and is the only institution in Southern Africa who may award the Certified Financial Planner® (CFP®) designation. The FPI is affiliated to the international Financial Planning Standards Board (FPSB), the body responsible for the certification and promoting of financial planning professional standards in the global community. The CFP® designation is an international accreditation, and is regarded as the highest standard for financial planning professionals. For many, this is the most important drawcard to the qualification: it is a pathway to be recognised as and practice as a Certified Financial Planner® Professional.

Relevance of the qualification

The qualification's target student population are therefore those who work or wish to enter the financial services industry. The industry is vast and includes different institutions – however, central to the function of all role-players, is that financial transactions and financial products are involved, and therefore, individuals, corporates, society in general and the economy of the country are all directly affected and impacted by the financial services industry (Botha et al., 2019). It stands to reason that upskilling those who work in the industry not only produces a better equipped workforce and professionalises the industry, but also improves consumer protection and trust, and leads to the stability of the economy.

In South Africa, financial literacy levels are low (Botha et al., 2019) and the financial education of students addresses these backlogs, which in turn has a ripple effect on the clients and industry they serve. Financial planning, in particular, is described as the process of developing strategies to assist clients in managing their financial affairs, in order to meet their life and financial goals, and become financially independent. (FPI, 2012). Ensuring that clients are financially independent, in the sense of providing adequately for their retirement, health needs and other contingencies, and do not need rely on their families, the state or welfare institutions for support, reveals the important public interest role that financial planning fulfils (Botha et al., 2019).

It was pointed out above that many students seek to ultimately achieve the CFP® designation, for which this qualification meets the education component. Obtaining this designation, may on a personal level, lead to individual growth and better career prospects for students. This is illustrated by a recent study, which found that 80% of firms in South Africa viewed the designation as favourable when considering candidates for employment; the majority also indicated that they plan to increase the number of CFP® professionals within their firm, whilst 80% of CFP® professionals indicated that they achieve higher rates of career advancement and hold longer terms of employment than their counterparts who do not hold the certification (FPSB, 2013). On a business level, the same study found that CFP® professionals are able to generate higher levels of profit, with 60% indicating that, as a result of their employment, legal risks and compliance costs were reduced and fewer complaints resulted, with 80% noting increased client satisfaction and retention (FPSB, 2013). Currently, only 4,744 CFP® professionals have been awarded the designation in South Africa (FPSB, 2018), and there is therefore ample room for growth in these numbers in order to efficiently serve the South African population.

Only six higher education institutions have been recognised by the FPI in South Africa as approved education providers. All other institutions other than the School are public universities; and of these, only one offers the qualification via distance learning. The access provided by the School via distance learning to this qualification is therefore crucial in, firstly, ensuring that students are not excluded simply by reason of the fact that they cannot attend contact-based learning at universities; and secondly, to increase in the number of candidates eligible to become CFP® professionals.

Profile of students enrolled for the qualification

The student profile on the qualification is becoming more gender balanced, with the number of females enrolled for the qualification currently at 45% (Figure 1 below). This is promising, as on a previous count, only 30% of CFP® professionals were women (FPI, 2016). As the demographic distribution reveals, the student profile is also diverse. Particularly encouraging are the student numbers of racial groups regarded as previously disadvantaged (due to racial discrimination policies under the political regime pre-1994), whose entry to education and employment opportunities are critical to address historical imbalances (Figure 2 below).

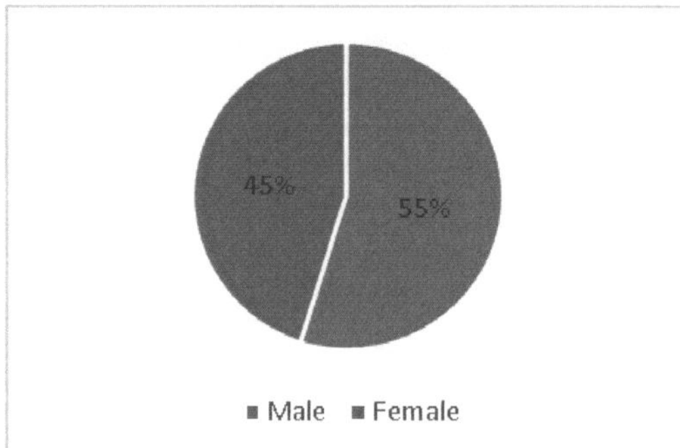

Figure 1. Gender distribution – DLO period: 2017–2018

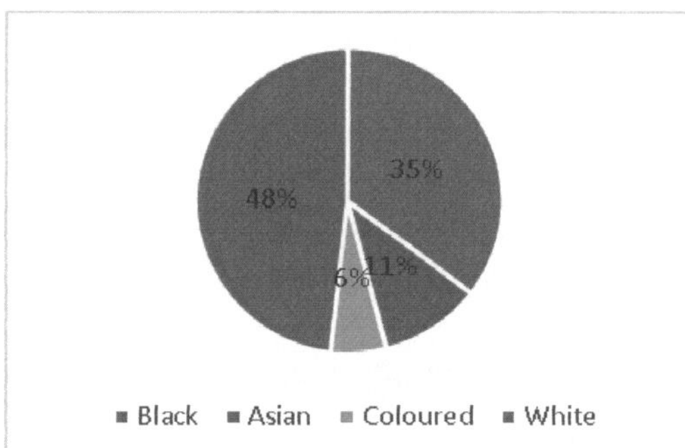

Figure 2. Race Distribution – DLO period 2017–2018

In distance learning, students are typically older, work and study part-time (DHET, 2014), and can be seen as non-traditional students (Stöter et al., 2014; Subotzky & Prinsloo, 2011). An analysis of the School's student profile correlates with this description. Over the period the postgraduate diploma in its new format has been applicable (this is referred to as the Distance Learning Online period; i.e. the "DLO period"), the biggest group of students fell within the age range of 31–40 years (44%), followed by 41–50 years (26%). Only 23% of students were younger than 30 years, with 7% in the highest age group of 51–60 years. The median age of students was 37.62 for 2017, and 35.78 for 2018. Turning to their employment status, the vast majority are employed, with 54% of students in managerial, supervisory or non-client-facing roles; 39% in client-facing roles; and the remaining 8% represent those who are not employed, did not indicate their employment status, or are not active in the financial services industry.

Another factor affecting the profile of the students is the fact that the School subscribes and applies a "recognition of prior learning" policy, so as to promote access to education. Adapting the definition for the School's context, Recognition of Prior Learning (RPL) can be described as the principles and processes through which the prior knowledge and skills of a person are made visible and assessed for the purposes of alternative access and admission (SAQA, 2013). In short, it seeks to address those who may not have had access to formal learning, but have knowledge and skills obtained through life, personal improvement and work experience, and allows for such knowledge and skills to be recognised for the purposes of obtaining access. The School aims to allow at least 10% of the cohort of students admitted to the qualification as RPL candidates. These candidates are often older and have varied backgrounds, thereby adding to the diversity of the student population. However, as they have not had the formal training up to the required level, support should be embedded, in order to ensure that these candidates can perform on par with other students.

Factors affecting student success

In its academic policies, the School acknowledges that the following factors can influence a learner's success: academic preparation (i.e. the effectiveness of prior education/learning), adequate financial support, traditional study age, external support system, positive self-concept, realistic short- and long-term goals, and leadership experience (Milpark Education, 2018).

Taking into account the particular profile of students on the qualification (i.e. as older, working and non-traditional students), it must be recognised that these types of students fall amongst those who are more likely to be faced by barriers to success that arise from non-academic factors, such as work-related and domestic obligations, than traditional contact learners, and even more so, when there are also socio-economic challenges present (Subotzky & Prinsloo, 2011). The latter is prevalent in South Africa, given its historical past, and the inequity still remaining holds further challenges for previously disadvantaged groups. Persisting disadvantage in the form of constrained financial resources, geographic distance, literacy (i.e. language and previous schooling), as well as other sociocultural factors, detract from effective and successful studies (Jones et al., 2008).

The various factors specific to studying an online learning environment should also be noted; these include the requirement for a more proactive self-directed approach by the leaner, technical difficulties that may arise, perceived isolation, challenges balancing study, work and family commitments, content misunderstanding, poor academic performance, or a lack of motivation (Amiet et al., 2017). In a South African context, access to technology resources (i.e. devices, data, bandwidth) is also challenging – the cost of communication is high, internet penetration, although the highest on the continent, lags far behind other developing countries for similar income levels, with only half of the population connected, and connectivity is also problematic (Gent & Meyer, 2016; Gillwald et al., 2018). Cognisance should also be taken of digital literacy levels and the divide "not only between the connected and unconnected, but between those who have the skills and financial resources to use the Internet optimally and those barely online" (Gillwald et al., 2018). The DHET refers to this as the "uneven readiness of staff and students", and acknowledges it as a factor to be addressed, when programmes that are internet and technology dependent are submitted for accreditation (DHET, 2014).

Changing for success

It is against this background that the qualification was reviewed. The changes, as discussed below, were then implemented, so as to transform the offering of the qualification on a distance learning basis (hereafter, referred to as "DL") to a distance learning online (hereafter referred to as "DLO") basis from 2017 onwards.

Time, timing and timetables

Time, or the lack thereof, is often cited as an important factor in the success and/or dropout rates of a distance learning students (Hachey, Wladis, & Conway, 2018). It also implicitly points to the competing demands and socio-economic factors that influence distance learning students (Aboo, 2017). Having perceived this to be a factor, it was found that the first semester was over-weighted in comparison to the second, as the modules taken in the first semester had far greater knowledge components. The qualification was initially structured as consisting out of four modules, and a student could elect to take up to two modules per semester. Where students did elect to take two, there was often an overlap of assignments and exams at the same/adjacent intervals. The course structure was therefore not conducive to the effective application of students' available time or their work-life-study balance.

On restructuring the course, the module contents were revised and aligned to the Financial Planning Institute's professional competency profile, which identifies six core financial planning components (FPI, 2012). The result was six credit-bearing compulsory modules, with each module now dedicated to covering a particular practice area, before culminating in the case study module, which synthesises the knowledge and skills of the preceding modules. In addition, one non-credit-bearing induction module was also introduced. Students complete one module at a time, over a period of eights week, and are therefore able to focus all their efforts onto one subject area. (Milpark, 2019). Six cycles are scheduled per year and students therefore have the flexibility to plan their studies around these intakes. This has been made possible by an online admissions program and learning management system.

As part of their studies, students are also required to prepare a proposed study plan (i.e. a timetable), indicating how they plan to approach their studies per week; taking into account their personal and work demands. This connects their studies to their lives in a practical manner. They then receive feedback from the programme manager on their proposed study plan, and have the option to make use of student counselling for further guidance and support.

Interaction, Communication and Connection

Perceived isolation is cited as another factor that impedes successful studies (Amiet et al., 2017). In order to overcome feelings of isolation, a dedicated online lecturer is assigned to each module, who is an expert in that field of study. The online lecturer is tasked to lead discussions; prompt conversation and debate; and manage the atmosphere of the course. Students are monitored on a weekly basis as to whether they have accessed the course page and have participated in the weekly activity – for students who have not done so, the programme manager establishes contact with them. This in turn ensures a higher hand-in rate, and lessens the chances of students dropping out. The online lecturer's role is aimed at pro-active engagement, not only between students and the institution, and students and their learning material, but also between students themselves.

Such high engagement has been made possible by technology that allows for discussions forums, tutor emails, voice notes, video meetings (via the School's online resources) and even WhatsApp groups (the latter at the initiative of the students), whereby participation is facilitated. The study guide and all related support materials are available online at all times; and this, together with a live classroom (periodically) and recorded video sessions, allows students to be stimulated by different mediums. Moreover, it provides flexibility, as they are able to access and interact with the material, or the online lecturer from any place, and at any time (Milpark, 2018); in addition, the asynchronous structure addresses erratic internet connectivity.

The course is focused on structured learning and each week now has a formative assessment (i.e. an assignment/online test). This ensure that students remain committed. Similarly, assignments are scaffolded so that as students become more competent in their abilities and their knowledge of the material over time, they require less scaffolding or support from their lecturer (Northern Illinois University, 2015). Feedback is critical in order for students to learn from their assessments; however, it must also be provided timeously (Cleveland-Innes & Wilton, 2018; Conole, 2009). Feedback also bears a correlation to student motivation (Hoskins & Newstead, 2009). Individualized feedback on formative assessments is provided on a weekly basis. Again, technology has been an enabler: assignments are submitted as well as marked electronically, allowing for flexibility and ease of use on both the students' and lecturers' side. Feedback can now be provided much quicker, as the time delay, costs and logistics of managing manual scripts via postal services has been removed. This promotes the assessment for learning experience.

To address the uneven readiness amongst lecturers, an online training certification course in online lecturing was developed by Milpark Education; and must be completed in order to lecture on distance learning online programmes. For students, an induction programme, which precedes the formal study programme, was introduced. It is offered at no cost to the students, so to allow for increased access and the uniform treatment of all students. The induction programme comprises eight weeks, with the first two weeks aimed at familiarising students with the online course environment, the technology to be used, the study programme and the soft skills required to complete their studies (i.e. time management, professional writing, report planning). It also looks at the financial planner and the professional competency framework so to enable students to link their studies to the industry. Students who may not be as digitally literate, are encouraged through continued interaction with the course platform to build their confidence and abilities. Some students may have numeracy and literacy backlogs, some RPL students may not have formal learning in undergraduate tax; other students may not have industry experience and therefore do not have product knowledge. The next six weeks attempt to address these deficiencies, with two weeks dedicated to the development of the maths skills and basic economic theory required; a further two weeks on aspects of taxation within the financial planning environment; and the final two weeks on a products overview. Students who complete the course are able to enrol for the compulsory credit-bearing courses of the qualification.

Integration

The curriculum of the qualification has been developed taking into account the prescribed knowledge components, abilities and skills for a postgraduate degree level set by the South African Qualifications Authority, and also to align with the competencies of a Certified Financial Planner® professional as required by the FPI. Students however need to be able to relate their learning to the workplace environment. The online lecturer is therefore tasked, in a weekly communication, to explain the purpose of the week's work and link it back to practice, so that students understand why it is important and how it fits into the framework of what can be expected of a financial planner. Aside from technology facilitating such communication, it has also allowed the study material to be updated, amended or expanded quickly and relayed to students. As financial planning is affected by various laws, including financial services regulation and tax laws that change frequently, it is imperative that students study the correct and up-to-date material. Moreover, developments in the field (for example, cryptocurrencies as an asset class, robo-advice, or the impact of fintech) can now be swiftly incorporated.

Initial results and feedback

With the exception of one compulsory module (the final case study module), all modules on the qualification have, over the past two years, been offered four times; i.e. twice per academic year. Throughput on a module level has been monitored. The graph below indicates an improvement on the throughput rate during the period the new DLO model has been applicable, when compared to the previous DL rates:

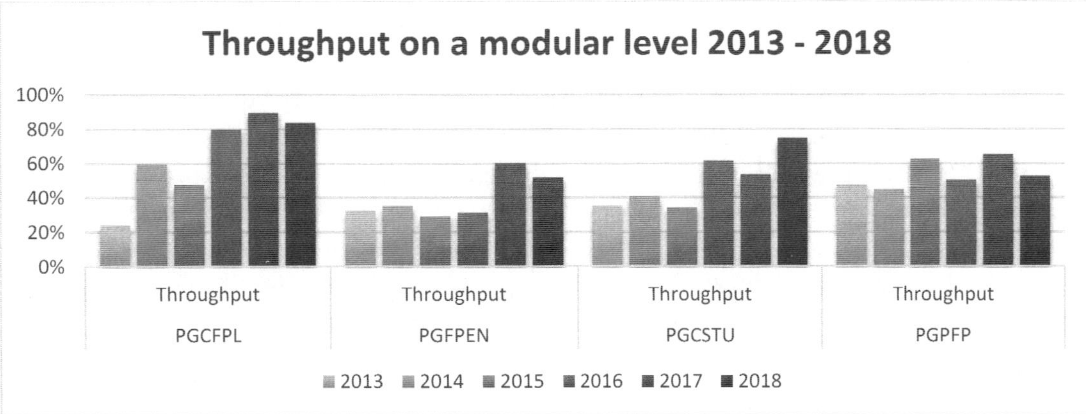

Figure 3. Throughput rates on module level – DL period (2013–2016) and DLO period (2017–2018)

Feedback on recent student surveys are positive about the course model and platform, as these quotes illustrate:

> *"Compared to the Milpark National Certificate in Financial planning course, I did 7 years ago, this new learning model is light years ahead and I feel I'm am getting much more value and substance in the way of learning and interaction."*

> *"So far the course has been incredible. It is great how all the material is available online and electronically. The way the website and interface are structured is brilliant, it is easy to follow and know what is required for each week."*

These two further quotes indicate the importance of interaction and feedback:

> *"I've thoroughly enjoyed studying this course, and although I'm looking forward to getting the final exam finished I'm going to miss the stimulation of it all."*

> *"The speed at which the lecturers get back to students are admirable. The amount of study material is a lot though. The course has taught me a lot."*

In addition, the course structure's positive effect on student motivation becomes evident from the following learner quotes:

> *"I like the weekly structure of this module. It forces me to do my part every week and every day. Thank you for an excellent program."*

> *"Dividing the work into weekly parts is working nicely. It forces you to do a small bit every day, instead of 500 pages at the end of the 8 weeks."*

Another important indicator has been the learners' performance on the independent professional competency exams for certified financial planners (CFP®). As these exams only take place in February and August, students who complete their postgraduate diploma via the new DLO model would, depending on their date of completion, have been able to sit for the past three CFP® exam sessions. The results for the last CFP® exam held in February 2019 is at date of writing not yet available. The results for the February 2018 and August 2018 exams have been encouraging: on each occasion, the School's pass rate has surpassed all other educational providers, including public universities and those who offer the qualification via contact learning. For the February 2018 exam, the School's pass rate was double the national pass rate. For the August 2018 exam, the school's pass rate was 73% on its candidates who sat for the exam, which was well above the national pass rate of 57%.

Conclusion

In this article, we have reflected on the need to turn access into success for distance learning students, particularly on a postgraduate level and as it relates to financial planning students in a South African context. More closely, some of the factors inhibiting success were identified, and it was considered how these were addressed when the postgraduate diploma in financial planning was restructured and presented in a distance learning online format. There are indications that technology has indeed served as a tool to alleviate these problems, as indicated by the improved throughput rate, positive student survey feedback and the above-average performance of our students on the external professional competency exams. The latter shows that technology has, to a certain extent, levelled the playing field, in that distance learning students are able to perform as well as (or better than) contact learning students.

The new model has, however, only been in force for the past two years, and thus some aspects can therefore not be fully assessed – for example, the throughput rate on a qualification level can only be assessed after three years and there is still limited comparative professional competency exam results available for the DLO period. It is also still an adaptive process: student surveys and polls raise aspects that require further intervention. To name but a few: ad hoc connectivity problems to the online portal; online lecturers that become passive; some modules being experienced as heavier than others; inadequate assessment feedback and negative interaction amongst students. These require further consideration and study.

It is submitted that the definition of educational technologies by Cleveland-Innes and Wilton, as discussed in the introduction above (Cleveland-Innes & Wilton, 2018), implicitly contains a third part: that technology *is used*; thus denoting an ongoing and continuous process. Our future plans therefore include to continue monitoring the performance of our students, to reflect on the issues the various groups of our student population may experience as detractors to success, to continue reviewing the qualification to ensure it leads to optimal workplace integration, and to seek how and where technology can be applied to further the connection between our students, their learning experience, and ultimately their success.

References

Aboo, F. (2017). *Non-academic factors contributing towards performance of postgraduate open distance learning accounting students.* UNISA, South Africa. Retrieved from http://uir.unisa.ac.za/handle/10500/23393

Amiet, D. L., Holt, C., Lodge, J. M., Shaw, L., McKenzie, S., Roddy, C. & Garivaldis, F. (2017). Applying best practice online learning, teaching, and support to intensive online environments: an integrative review. *Frontiers in Education, 2*(November), 1–10.

Botha, M., Rossini, L., Geach, W., Goodall, B., du Preez, L., Rabenowitz, P. (2019). *The South African Financial Planning Handbook 2019.* Durban: LexisNexis.

Cleveland-Innes, M., & Wilton, D. (2018). *Guide to blended learning. Canada*: Commonwealth of Learning.

Conole, G. (2009). Introduction: the 7Cs of learning design framework, 1–33. Retrieved from https://www.slideshare.net/GrainneConole/the-7-cs-of-learning-design

Department of Higher Education and Training (2014). *Policy for the provision of distance education in South African universities in the context of an integrated post-school system* (Vol. 535). Pretoria: Government Gazette.

Department Higher Education and Training (2018a). *National list of occupations in high demand.* Pretoria: Government Gazette.

Department of Higher Education and Training (2018b). *2000 to 2015 First time entering undergraduate cohort studies for public higher education institutions.* Pretoria: Department of Higher Education and Training. Retrieved from http://www.dhet.gov.za/SitePages/UniversityEducation.aspx

Financial Planning Institute of Southern Africa (2012). *Financial Planner Competency Profile.* Johannesburg: FPI. Retrieved from https://www.fpi.co.za/documents/Competency_Profile.pdf

Financial Planning Standards Board (2013). *FPSB's global value of certification survey* (insights into how firms value CFP® certification- South Africa). Denver, CO: FPSB Ltd.

Financial Planning Standards Board (2018). *Infographic.* Retrieved from https://www.fpsb.org/wp-content/uploads/2019/02/R2-FPSB-0365-2018-Growth-Infographic-GLOBAL-1.pdf

Gent, P., & Meyer, I. (2016). *The status of ICT in education in South Africa and the way forward.* Centurion, South Africa: NECT. Retrieved from http://nect.org.za/publications/technical-reports/the-state-of-ict-in-education-in-south-africa/view

Gillwald, A., Mothobi, O., & Rademan, B. (2018). *Policy paper no. 5, Series 5: The state of ICT in South Africa.* Cape Town: Research ICT Africa. Retrieved from https://researchictafrica.net/research/research-papers-and-publications/

Hachey, A. C., Wladis, C., & Conway, K. M. (2018). What factors influence student decisions to drop online courses? Comparing online and face-to-face sections. In A. Volungeviciene & A. Szűcs (Eds.), *Exploring the micro, meso and macro. Proceedings of the European Distance and E-learning Network 2018 Annual Conference* (pp. 99–107). Genoa, Italy: European Distance and E-Learning Network.

Hoskins, S. L., & Newstead, S. E. (2009). Encouraging student motivation. In H. Fry, S. Ketteridge, & S. Marshall (Eds.), *A handbook for teaching and learning in higher education: enhancing academic practice | University of Portsmouth* (pp. 27-39). New York: Routledge Taylor & Francis Group.

Jones, B., Coetzee, G., Bailey, T., & Wickham, S. (2008). *Factors that facilitate success for disadvantaged higher education students.* Athlone, South Africa: Rural Education Access Programme. Retrieved from http://www.reap.org.za/pieces/reports/pdf/tracking_reports/2008_June_factors_that_facilitate_success.pdf

Milpark Education (2018). *Academic Policies.* Claremont: Milpark Education.

Milpark Education (2019). Postgraduate diploma in financial planning factsheet. Claremont: Milpark Education. Retrieved from https://www.milpark.ac.za/-/postgraduate-diploma-in-financial-planning

Ministry of Education (2001). *Draft national plan for higher education in South Africa.* Pretoria: Ministry of Education. Retrieved from http://www.dhet.gov.za/HED Policies/National Plan on Higher Education.pdf

Northern Illinois University (2015). Instructional scaffolding to improve learning. Retrieved from https://www.niu.edu/spectrum/archives/scaffolding.shtml

South African Qualifications Authority – SAQA (2013). *National policy for the Implementation of the recognition of prior learning.* Waterkloof: SAQA. Retrieved from http://www.saqa.org.za/docs/pol/2013/natpol_irpl.pdf

Stöter, J., Bullen, M., Zawacki-Richter, O., & von Prummer, C. (2014). From the back door into the mainstream. In O. Zawacki-Richter & T. Anderson (Eds.), *Online distance education. Towards a research agenda* (pp. 421–458). Edmonton, Canada: AU Press, Athabasca University.

Subotzky, G., & Prinsloo, P. (2011). Turning the tide: a socio-critical model and framework for improving student success in open distance learning at the University of South Africa. *Distance Education, 32*(2), 177–193.

DIGITAL VERSUS MANUAL. TWO SIDES OF THE SAME COIN

Ingrid le Roux, University of Pretoria, South Africa

Introduction

In their preparation to educate future professionals, higher education institutions often employ innovating teaching methods, including games and simulations (Vlachopoulos & Makri, 2017). Digital games and simulations have been used in entrepreneurship and business disciplines for many years and are designed to increase knowledge, improve skills and enable a positive learning environment in a realistic setting (Fox, Pittaway, & Uzuegbunam, 2018). These simulations typically highlight the integration of business know-how such as strategy, marketing, positioning and finance to help students understand how a business works (Caruso, 2018). Furthermore, the need for entrepreneurs to obtain and acquire certain skills for them to be successful cannot be over emphasised (Costin, O'Brain, & Slattery, 2018). Digital game-based learning is recognised as creating effective learning environments, engaging learners cognitively, emotionally as well as socially (Huang, Johnson, & Han, 2014).

It is important to acknowledge the rapid expansion in technology such as online learning but there is unfortunately also another reality. This other side of the coin often lies outside of higher education and normally in poor communities who are in dire need of attention. Disadvantaged learners in third world countries are in desperate need of acquiring business knowledge to enable them to better their situation and alleviate poverty. In many of these environments, the internet is not always available or, if available, data is too expensive for the ordinary citizen to afford and therefor digital game-based learning is not a reasonable option. The community of learners affected by the lack of resources are also in need of business knowledge and information to help them navigate the negative environment and equip them with hands-on learning by doing. In an attempt to address their specific needs, educators need to include such communities in their thinking, encourage innovation around business start-ups and provide a collaborative atmosphere for obtaining business know-how and develop human capital. A gap exists to develop new innovative and effective learning environment to create the same value for these learners. BDS, a board game simulation with a proven track record to transfer knowledge, involve learners and create an efficient learning environment (Le Roux, 2018) may be one solution to the existing gap.

The main aim of this study is to better understand, from a design perspective, how game features such as game structure, game involvement as well as game appeal are perceived and experienced when the simulation game is played manually. The three groups taking part in the study consist of post graduate (Honnours) students, full time third year entrepreneurship students as well as school exit level students. The study is based on Huang et al (2014) who used a digital game to determine the game features, motivational support and cognitive investment of learners. A board game simulation (BDS) was administered after which the participants reflected on their experience.

The contribution is to better understand if the BDS design caters for the different game features such as the game structure, game involvements as well as game appeal compared to that of a digital game-based simulation. Without the visual stimulation and features that characterise digital games, learners may lose interest in playing a manual game. BDS board game simulation can increase business and entrepreneurial know-how in an environment where youth unemployment is 47% through equipping youth and disadvantaged people in general with know-how to break out of the poverty cycle and create a business of their own.

Literature Review

Simulations Games in Education and Training

Simulations and educational games have a long history in management and other educational settings (Hodkiewicz, 2015). Business simulations as a pedagogy tool is an innovative and active learning experience with tremendous potential to enhance a student's comprehension of the fundamentals of business (Nugent, & Brook, 2018). Simulation games are interactive experience-based learning environments as well as educational tools, valued because they combine input, application, reflection and feedback (Geithner & Menzel, 2016). It creates a scenario-based environment, where participants interact to apply previous knowledge and practical skills to a real world problem (Vlachopoulus & Makri, 2017). Simulations allow for a shift away from lecture-based education to an active learning method, theoretically grounded on Kolb's experiential learning theory (Kolb, 1984; Kolb & Kolb, 2010). Simulations can be defined as a dynamic, simplified and accurate model of reality (Saive, Renaud, Kaufman, & Marquis, 2007) where users learn *about* through interaction with the simulation (Alessi & Trollip, 2001). Furthermore, simulations create a scenario-based environment where students interact as well as apply prior knowledge and practical skills to real-world problems. It allows participants to become active members and drivers of their own learning process. One of the differences between a manual and digital game is that the game is faster when played on a computer (Antonietti & Mellone, 2003), but the players still acquire the same important skills such as teamwork, interpersonal communication, teamwork, leadership, decision-making, and stress management (Vlachopoulus & Makri, 2017). However, the development of skills that enable students to face and meet the challenges of tomorrow is often undervalued (Geithner & Menzel, 2016; p.229).

The other side of the coin

In South Africa, where the study was undertaken, unemployment is currently at its highest level since 1994 reported at 27% and increasing. Youth unemployment is at a staggering figure of more than 45% and in some areas is as high as 60%. Companies are currently shedding jobs with the government sector as the only job creator. Creating a critical mass of entrepreneurs requires a long-term investment in human capital development, linking entrepreneurial training to enterprise development (Herrington, Kew, & Mwanga, 2017). Introducing BDS, a start-up to growth board game simulation, could equip young people with the skills and experience to operate their own businesses successfully. This has potential positive effects in terms of profitability, survival of enterprises and long-term employment creation. Starting a new business is complex and requires a wide range of competencies and knowledge (Kriz & Auchter, 2016). Board game simulations played around a table is of immense value where electricity, internet facilities and financial resources are limited. Using BDS, a start-up board game simulation to support the understanding of start-up activities through the venture life cycle business activities, this study aimed to better understand which game features were perceived by participants when playing the manual BDS game and if these features were perceived as positive or negative.

The main research question is: Can a non-digital board game simulation create the same perceived motivational impact/drive as a digital simulation? The sub questions are:

- How is the BDS game perceived in relation to digital game simulation features?
- How is the game structure perceived?
- How is the game involvement perceived?
- How is collaboration perceived?
- How is the feedback perceived?
- How is the experience of real business perceived?

Thus, the BDS used in this study is a simulation and not a game based on the following attributes: it is a simplified, dynamic and accurate model of a real start-up and growth experience and allows for decision-making in a secure, practical learning environment. Simulations have many benefits. Students are more involved, the simulation offers a space of freedom where mistakes can be made without negative consequences; it is a hands-on approach which allows for problem-solving, decision-making, critical thinking and taking personal responsibility for the outcome (Palmunen, Pelto, Paalumaki, & Lainema, 2013; Geithner & Menzel, 2016).

Context and Data

Over the past years' attempts were made to accredited the BDS board game as an educational tool for the transfer of business know-how in higher education to support learning and gaining practical business experience (Le Roux & Steyn, 2007; Le Roux, 2017; 2018). With the rise in youth unemployment the game is now also used outside of formal educational settings and is perceived as a training tool for start-ups and small business owners. However, with the rapid development in digital games and simulations, the question arises if the board game without animation, soundtrack and other digital game features is still perceived as a valuable support tool in teaching and learning. The study was done with three different groups: two student groups and a group of school leavers. The student groups were from the University of Pretoria, South Africa. The first group consisted of Honours students who have done digital simulations as part of support learning in some of their courses. The second group was an undergraduate group specialising in entrepreneurship with an understanding of business but experience only of video games and gaming for fun. The final group consisted of a group of school leavers without the marks or means to enter a higher education institution potentially exposed only to video and gaming for fun experiences. The participants reflected on their experience after playing the BDS game using a questionnaire. The analysis comprised of depicting the data related to a Likert scale in pie charts as well as mean scores in Table 1. Each pie chart (1 being *strongly disagree*, 5 being *agree strongly*) represents the frequency to which each sample group scored questions on the Lickert scale (1 being *strongly disagree*, 5 being *agree strongly*).

Findings

The findings report on how participants perceived the game features of a manual board-game simulation. The design of an instructional game needs to enhance the learning process while the game features engage, motivate and allow for cognitive processing (Huang et al., 2012).

Table 1: Game Features and other variables

Groups	Structure	Involvement	Collaboration	Knowledge Information	Feedback	Reality
Hons (4th)	3.55*	3.97	4.43	3.82	3.80	3.64
Undergrads	3.8	4,32	4.58	3.81	3.87	3.84
School leavers	3.97	4.22	4.18	4.25	3.95	4.15

* Scale of 1 to 5 where 1 – *disagree strongly*, 2 – *disagree*, 3 – *unsure*, 4 – *agreed* and 5 – *agree strongly*.

Table 1 shows a difference in perception on collaboration, knowledge information as well as reality. To give insight in Table 1, we use the following section shows pies charts for the following features namely structure, involvement, collaboration, knowledge Information, feedback and reality.

Figure 1 depicts the perceived level of *structure* experienced while playing the game. Game structure refers to several components such as rules, instructions, explanation and game tasks (Huang, Johnson, & Han, 2012).

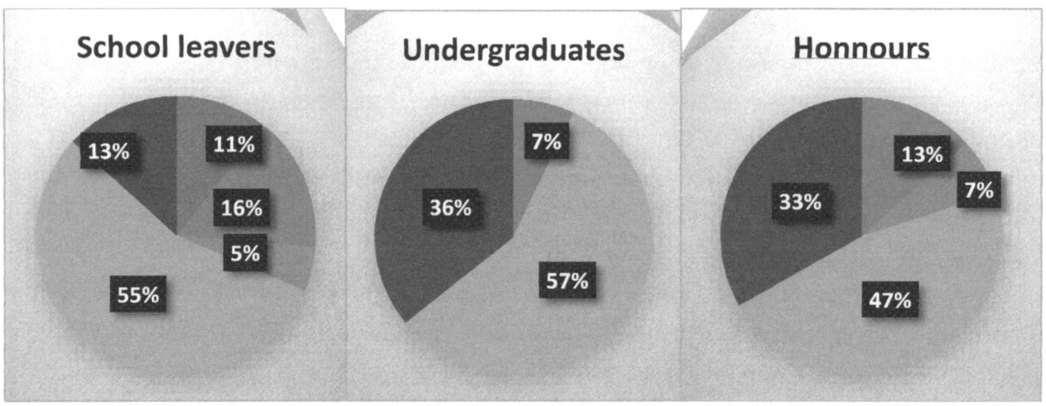

Figure 1. Perceived level of structure
(Dark blue – *agree strongly*; yellow – *agree*; grey – *unsure*; red – *disagree*; light blue – *disagree strongly*)

Eighty-two percent (82%) of the school leavers perceived the tasks as clearly presented. The facilitators spent more time explaining the game to this group because they did not have the subject content and knowledge of the student groups. The undergraduate and post-graduate students received instruction sheets with the information, rules and guidelines to read with less time explaining the game at the beginning. However, that posed a problem because they did not want to spend time reading and just started to play. There appears support that the BDS as a manual game can provide the structure necessary for a motivated, conducive and effective learning environment.

Figure 2 depicts the level of *involvement* perceived by the different groups. Involvement refers to involvement features such as fun, fantasy and role-play (Huang, Johnson, & Han, 2012) as well as motivation and engagement (Vlachopoulus & Makri, 2017).

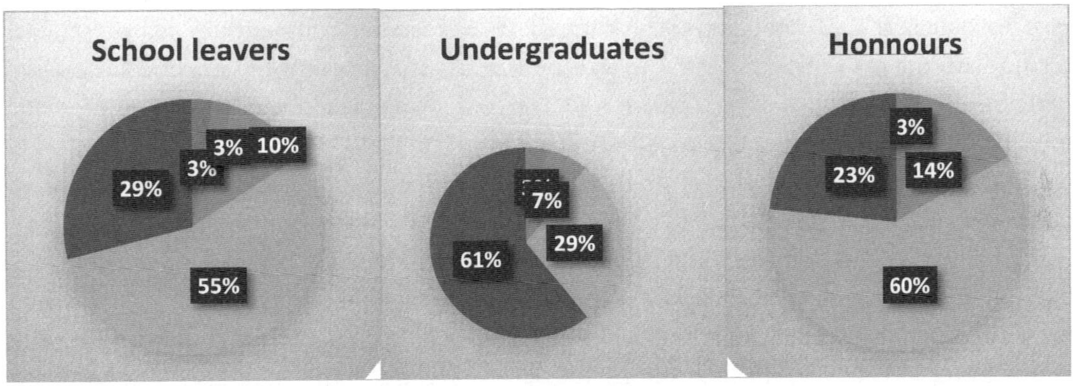

Figure 2. Perceived level of involvement
(Dark blue – *agree strongly*; yellow – *agree*; grey – *unsure*; red – *disagree*; light blue – *disagree strongly*)

Although there is no fantasy, animated features or audio graphics involved, merely replication of reality, the involvement level was still high. All three group scored their involvement as 80% and above. The participants appeared fully occupied by the learning tasks and engaged on a cognitive, emotional as well as social level (Huang, Johnson, & Han, 2012).

Figure 3 depicts the level of *collaboration* perceived by the different groups. Collaboration refers to interpersonal skills, communication, teamwork and leadership, decision making and stress management (Vlachopoulus & Makri, 2017).

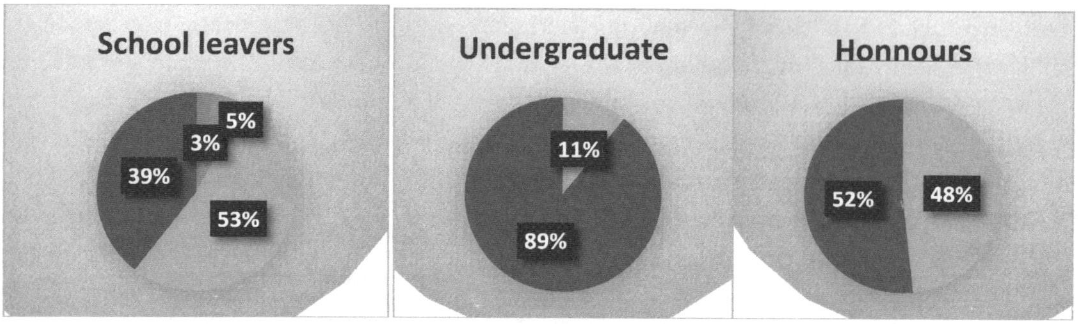

Figure 3. Perceived level of collaboration
(Dark blue – *agree strongly*; yellow – *agree*; grey – *unsure*; red – *disagree*; light blue – *disagree strongly*)

The participants were cognitively and emotionally involved, formed partnerships, but also tried to outsmart the other players. Although an element of competition was present (the person with the highest net asset value was the winner), participants understood the business principle of cooperation and participation to overcome working alone. The level of interaction and collaboration were high across all groups. However, the 89% of undergraduate students specialising in Entrepreneurship strongly agreed that collaboration was very high, 52% of post graduates and only 39% of school leavers perceived the collaboration as high. This could be explained by the fact that the students studied at the same university for 3–4 years and knew each other, compared to the school leavers who came from different communities, schools and environments and did not know each other that well. It seems that that may be the reason for the lower level of perceived collaboration. This is an important finding and the facilitators should keep that in mind when starting a new training session. Facilitators and trainers of BDS need to allow adequate time for a get-to-know session before the actual training commences.

Figure 4 depicts the level of *feedback* received as perceived by the different groups. Meaningful feedback is seen as a key factor in participants achieving their objectives by reflecting on misunderstandings and mistakes to help them transfer learning to a new educational context (Vlachopolous & Makri, 2017)

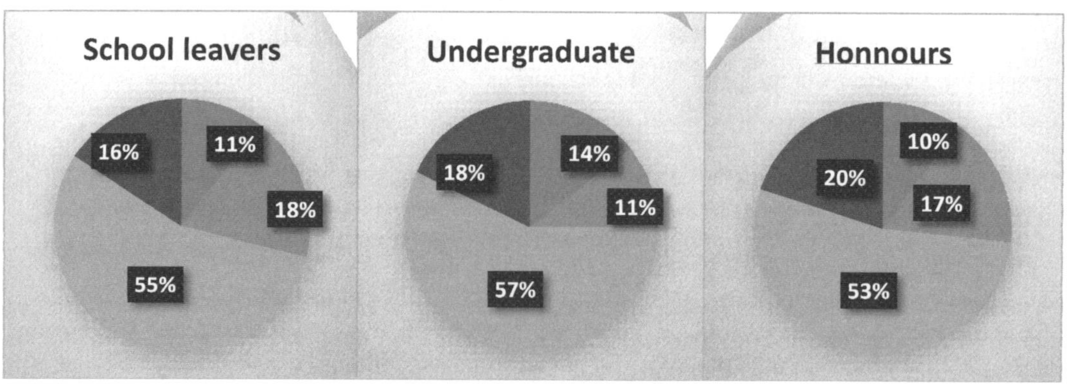

Figure 4. The perceived level of Feedback received
(Dark blue – *agree strongly*; yellow – *agree*; grey – *unsure*; red – *disagree*; light blue – *disagree strongly*)

The strongly agree and agree categories varied very little between the groups and consists of 70% and more. From the data it can be deducted that all three groups perceived the feedback as beneficial and necessary for their understanding and learning. Two facilitators administered the BDS game to make sure that participants received feedback on a continuous basis.

Figure 5 depicts the level of *reality* perceived by the different groups. Reality refers to the ability to represent real-world systems and enable participants to practice concepts relevant to the context. It represents a replica of reality, actual events, decisions making within a given context (Costin et al., 2018).

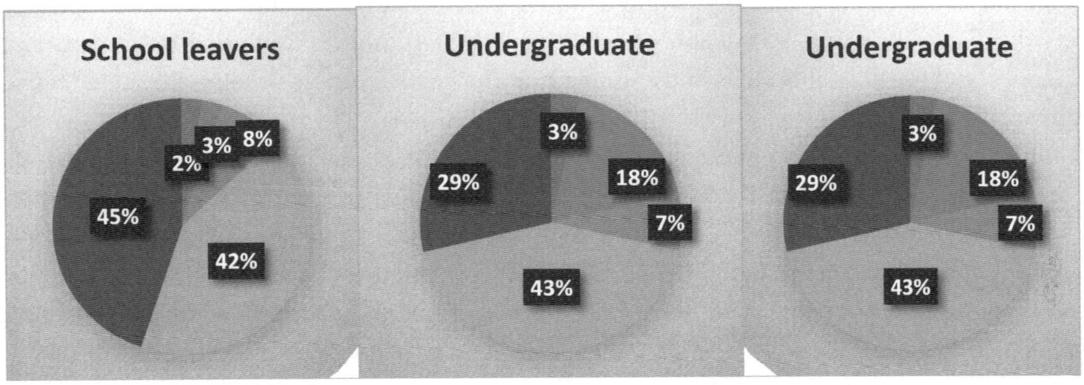

Figure 5: The perceived level of reality
(Dark blue – *agree strongly*; yellow – *agree*; grey – *unsure*; red – i; light blue – *disagree strongly*)

The school leaver group with no work experience and no additional business knowledge perceived the BDS games as high in representing a business start-up – much higher than the other two groups. As with the perceived levels of information and knowledge, this is possibly due to the fact that the two student groups, through their tertiary studies, have gained knowledge and experience through theory and case studies before participating in the BDS.

Figure 4 depicts the level of *information and knowledge* perceived by the different groups.

Eighty-four percent (84%) of school leavers perceived the *information and knowledge* gain as very high, 72% of undergraduates and 70% of the post-graduate students agreed. This could be explained by the fact that both student groups were students of entrepreneurship and thus had previous knowledge of the elements contained in the board game, whereas the school leavers had no previous knowledge of entrepreneurship and most of the information in the board game was brand new.

Although all the features as discussed in the above findings were present in the manual game, it is important to note that all three groups found the manual game challenging. Sixteen present of school leavers said that they did not find the game challenging which direct one to question their lack of business know-how and knowledge accumulated in their school years. In a written evaluation after the game one student reported: "I have learned more about doing business in this session than all my years at varsity (university)". Again a confirmation that learning by doing is perceived as more valuable than learning by listening.

Conclusion

The research question responds to the call for education to be effective, progressive but also serve the community. We implemented BDS, a non-digital board game simulation to determine if the participants perceived the same game features as favourably compared to a digital game-based simulation. It is of importance to determine if a manual game can create an effective learning environment, motivate participants and hold their attention.

From the data gathered, we made some tentative generalisations. It appeared evident that the board game simulation is valuable in creating a better understanding of how a start-up operates and grows. All three groups agreed that the game features presented were adequate and all felt that the game was challenging, the tasks were clearly defined, they received feedback on their performance, gained insight in a "real start-up" and it provided the opportunity to collaborate. It is interesting to see that the post-graduate group, with more experience than the other two groups, strongly agreed that the game provided them insight into a real start-up. Furthermore, the perceived opportunity for collaboration with others and the interaction around the table were high in all groups, but the highest in the third-year group.

The BDS manual game provides a solution in a setting where the environment is not conducive due to the lack of resources. It provides the same game features and may serve as a training solution for learners, small business as well as community members who are unemployed. BDS board game simulation provides the same game features as a digital game and therefore motivate and keep participants interested. It serves as a training tool to understand business start-up and growth which may serve as a solution to unemployment and poverty alleviation. Educators, trainers and other service providers need to relook the plight of people in a social setting that is not conducive for digital learning and allow manual games to fill the gap.

Limitations and recommendations

All studies have limitations and the main limitation of this study is the small sample limited to South Africa.

A quantitative longitudinal study needs to be done to provide information if the game knowledge transferred relate to sustainable small businesses.

References

Alessi, S. M., & Trollip, S. R. (2001). *Multimedia for learning: methods and Development* (3rd ed.). Boston: Allyn and Bacon.

Antonietti, A., & Mellone, R. (2003). The difference between playing games with and without the computer: A preliminary view. *Journal of Psychology, 137*, 133-144.

Caruso, J. V. (2018). Integrating Acumen and analytics: A simulation based approach. *Development in Business Simulation and Experiential learning, 45*, 231-233

Costin, Y., O'Brien, P., & Slattery, D.M. (2018). Using simulation to develop entrepreneurial skills and mind-set: An exploratory case study. *International Journal of teaching and learning in Higher Education, 30*(1), 136-145.

Fox, J., Pittaway, L., & Uzuegbunam, I. (2018). Simulations in Entrepreneurship Education: Serious Games and Learning Through Play. *Entrepreneurship Education and Pedagogy, 1*(1), 61–89.

Geithner, S., & Menzel, D. (2016). Effectiveness of learning through experience and reflection in a project management simulation. Simulation & Gaming, 47(2), 228-256.

Herrington, M., Kew, P., & Mwanga, A. (2017). *South African Global Entrepreneurship report.* Retrieved from https://www.gemconsortium.org/report/49833

Huang, W. D., Johnson, T. T., & Han, S-H. C. (2012). Impact of online instructional game features on college students' perceived motivational support and cognitive investment: A structural equation modelling study. *Internet and Higher Education, 17*, 58-68.

Kolb, D. A. (1984). *Experiential learning: experience as the source of learning and development.* Englewood Cliffs, NJ: Prentice-Hall.

Kolb, Y. A., & Kolb, D. A. (2010). Learning to play, playing to learn. A case study of a ludic learning space. *Journal of Organisational Change Management, 23*(1), 26-50.

Kriz, W. C., & Auchter, E. (2016). 10 Years of Evaluation research into gaming simulation for German entrepreneurship and a new study on its long-term effect. *Simulation & Gaming, 47*(2), 179-205.

Le Roux, I. (2018, June). *Using a Blended Business Simulation (BDS) to gain practical business experience.* Paper Presented at the Eden Annual Conference, 2018, Genoa.

Le Roux, I. & Steyn, B. (2007). Experiential learning and critical reflection as a tool for transfer of business knowledge: An empirical case study of a start-up simulation intervention for nascent entrepreneurs. *South African Journal of Economic and Management Science, 10*(3), 330-347.

Nugent, M., & Brook M. (2018). Business simulation performance after completing a reflective observation module. *Development in Business Simulation and Experimental Learning, 45*, 31-41.

Palmunen, L. M., Pelto, E., Paalumaki, A., & Lainema, T. (2013). Formation of novice business students' mental models through simulation gaming. *Simulation & Gaming, 44*(6), 846-868.

Saive, L., Renaud, L., Kaufman, D., & Marquis, J-S. (2007). Distinguishing between games and simulations: A systemic review. *Educational Technology & Society, 10*(3), 247-256.

Vlachopoulus, D., & Makri, A. (2017). The effect of games and simulations on higher education: a systematic literature review. *International journal of Educational Technology in Higher Education, 14*, 22.

Connecting through Educational Technology
Proceedings of the European Distance and E-Learning Network 2019 Annual Conference
Bruges, 16-19 June, 2019

SELF-EVALUATION MANDALAS – AN INNOVATIVE AND MOTIVATING TOOL IN DISTANCE LEARNING COURSES (RESULTS FROM THE VTT-PROJECT)

Peter Mazohl, University of Technology Vienna, Harald Makl, Pedagogical University College, Austria

Introduction

This paper refers to the ERASMUS+ Project 2017-1-ES01-KA201-038199 (School Education). The project aims to develop a toolbox to assist teachers to develop and create high quality distance learning courses.

The innovation in the project is the self-evaluation mandala. This is a newly developed tool used in distance learning courses and in blended learning.

Competence as course requirements

Competence-based learning is an approach to education that focuses on mastery (Lassnigg, 2017). Students must demonstrate the desired learning outcomes as central to the learning process. Competence-based uses a keyword: "I can". Learning and teaching is geared on competences in Europe. To define the taught competences is an initial and crucial step for teachers and should always be done before the teaching process. The students should be informed about the competences they have to develop during the learning before they start to learn.

Self-evaluation as a motivation for learners

Self-assessment involves students in evaluating their own work and learning progress. They can identify their skills gaps and missing knowledge as well as they can track their progress. McMillan and Hearn (2008) mentioned as early as in 2008 that self-assessment and self-evaluation are useful processes to motivate students. Self-evaluation is an element of active learning.

Likert scale to measure the competence level

Self-evaluation means "Looking at your progress, development and learning to determine what has improved and what areas still need improvement. Usually involves comparing a 'before' situation with a "current situation" (BusinessDictionary, 2018). Likert scales (McLeod, 2008) are used to measure attitudes, opinions, perceptions, and behaviours. The used levels do not represent equal intervals and do not represent absolute values. A Likert scale for self-evaluation (of competences) can be designed by several levels of agreement to a given question, like "I can explain something". The selected revel reflects a personal level of estimation, like "strongly agree". In the developed self-evaluation the process of self-judgement is based more on "feelings" than on absolute values.

Learning success evaluation by mandala comparison

Self-evaluation is a promising method also for the evaluation of learning processes, especially in Livelong Learning. The comparison of the competences at the beginning of the learning with the current competences after finishing the learning process provides a valuable picture of the learning success. Evaluation of learning success can easily be done with different types of assessments, which normally is expressed in grades. But – learning success is more than grades – to find out how much you have learned is a motivation for learners to learn and strengthen their self-confidence. It must be taken into account that self-evaluation can be influenced by the maturity of the learners.

Research questions

The issues mentioned created the impact to the research questions and are widely answered in this paper. It focuses on the following two research questions:

- Is there a method to motivate educators to define the taught competences before the course creation?
- Does there exist a simple self-evaluation method to compare the competence before and after the course?

Methodology

To find answers to the research questions special courses (using active learning methods) have been developed, implemented, and evaluated. The courses were distance learning based and lasted for a period of four to six weeks. The expected learning outcomes were defined using the competency that should be developed by the learners during the learning process. The defined competencies followed the guideline of the European Commission and were expressed in terms of knowledge, skills, and behaviour.

The development of the mandala – from the idea to the tool

To express the competencies a depiction based on a half circle was developed and labelled with the three competence items. The heading defines the description of the competence.

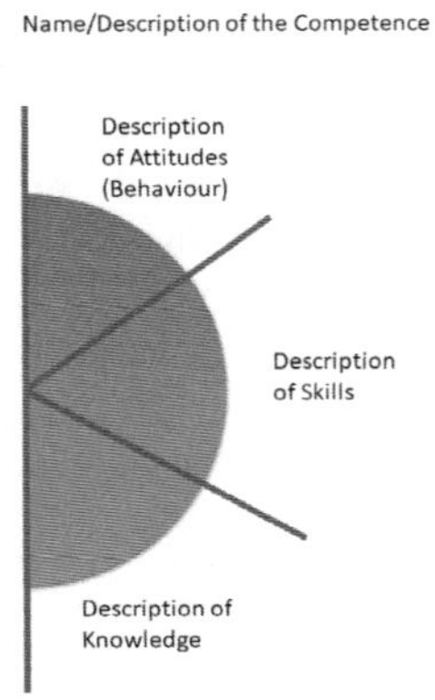

Figure 1. Basic considerations of the depiction (source: Peter Mazohl)

To offer the possibility to express the self-estimation in the three fields each field is split into four areas. These areas represent the various levels (worst level near the middle point of the half circle, best value in the area with the biggest distance of the middle point.

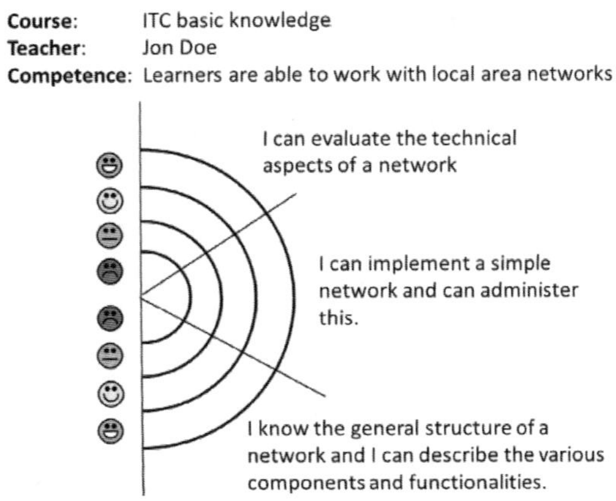

Figure 2. The mandala with four different levels for each part of the competence (source: Peter Mazohl)

In contrast to the classical levels of Likert based scale (which uses five levels) the neutral midlevel was dropped. With four levels, each learner must decide on a valuable level from the beginning. To comply with the educational field emoticons have been selected to express the level of agreement.

Before the course, the learners colour their estimated levels of each item of the competence. This can be done with several different methods:

- Printing the mandala, painting the selected areas with a pencil, taking an image with a smartphone, and finally uploading the image to the learning platform.
- Provision of the mandala in a digital format (for example an image in JPeG or PNG format) and the learners use an image editor to paint the selected areas. This needs digital competences (to download, save, to edit with an image processing or editing program, to save the mandala again, and finally to upload it to the learning platform).

After the course, the empty mandala is taken again and coloured by the learners. The difference between the two mandalas makes the learning success directly visible.

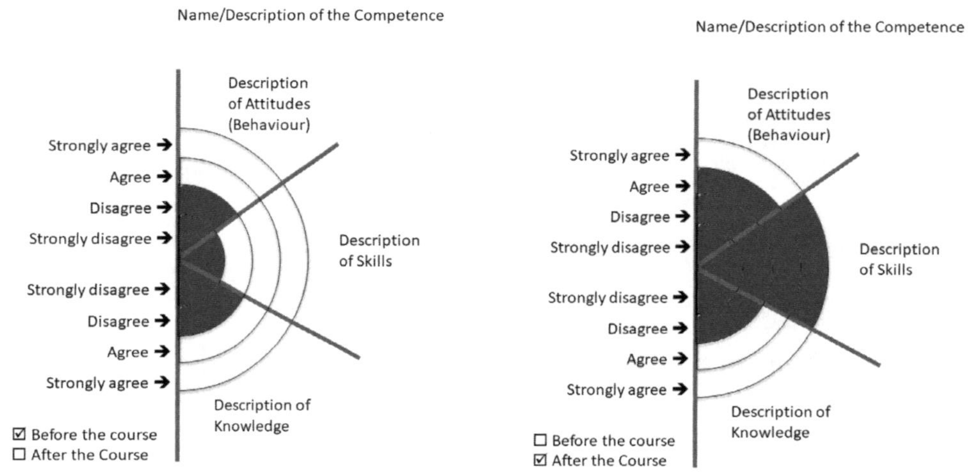

Figure 3. The painted mandala. Left: before the course; right: after the course. (source: Peter Mazohl)

This mandala has been taken from a proposal to implement the mandalas in Adult Education by replacing the emoticons by text.

Course implementation

In the frame of the Virtual Teacher Toolbox project (www.vtt-box.eu) several pilot courses have been developed to test the use of the mandala and to analyse the students' feedback. These courses are distance learning courses performed in school classes with 16 to 18 years old students in different subjects, like language, science, and arts teaching. The courses make intensive use of multimedia and interactive components to develop the required competences. This paper uses the results of the interviews of the course performed in a typical grammar school in Austria in the subject physics.

The course also used the frameworks developed in the frame of the project (pedagogy, quality, and digital competences).

Course analyses

Approximately 120 students were enrolled in the courses. 25 interviews are available (January 2019), the others will be interviewed after passing the courses within the next months. In the mentioned guided interviews students were asked seven basic questions with Likert based on two-level answers. Follow-up questions done individually completed the feedback of the students.

List of questions:

- Mandalas are an appropriate tool for the learning.
- The description of the competences in the mandala is a help for the learner.
- The Mandala itself is more fitting to younger students.
- The evaluation of the learners can be done by the teacher using the mandalas.
- An evaluation of the teacher's success in conveying the foreseen competences is possible.
- The mandala can be handled easily.
- The mandala offers a simple method to make the learning success by comparing the before and after mandala visible.

All students answered correctly to the questions with either "I agree" or "I disagree". Additionally, they could give specific comments, which were discussed between interviewer add students. A summary of the comments was used in the description of the results.

Results

The evaluation and analyses of the interviews was created as a simple yes/no bar chart.

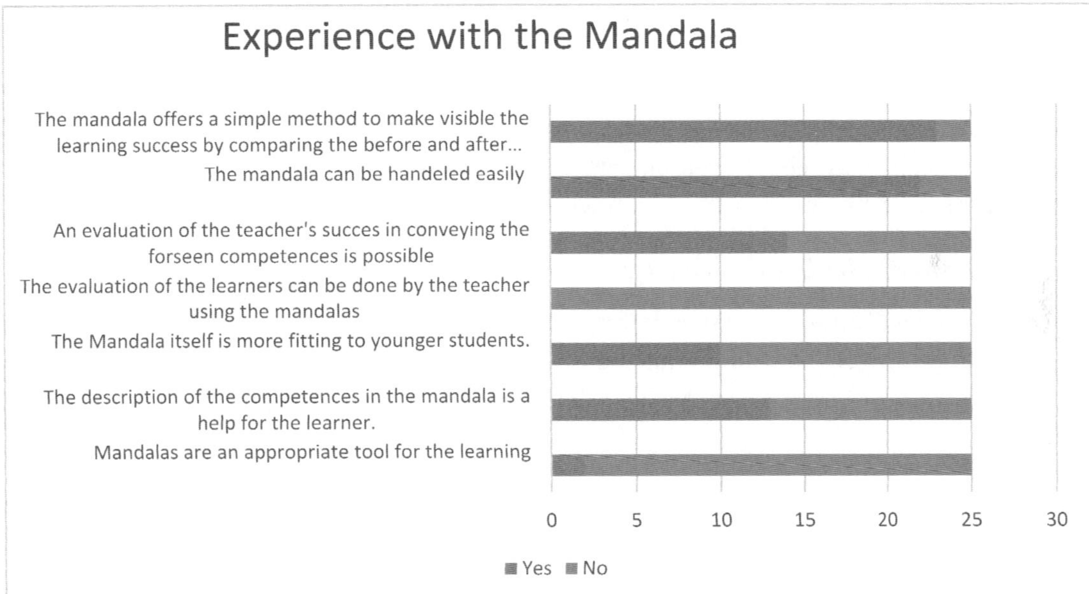

Figure 4. Overview of the answers given in the interview

The students gave individual statements to the various questions which are discussed as follows.

Mandalas are an appropriate tool for the learning

Students do not agree. The majority mentioned that the mandalas are more important to get an overview of the upcoming learning and the depiction provides some information about the expected learning outcomes (described in a competence).

The description of the competences in the mandala is a help for the learner.

Half of the students agree to this statement. The others were asked why they deny. They argued that they are learning in the frame of a curriculum. Therefore, the detailed information was not useful or important to them.

The Mandala itself is more fitting to younger students.

Several students meant that the painting job is "too childish for students". Nevertheless, a minority accepts the mandala as an appropriate tool for them.

The evaluation of the learners can be done by the teacher using the mandalas

Students don't want to be assessed by the mandala method, they prefer an assessment by the teacher. By the way, the students also mention the problem of maturity of learners. Younger students tend to cheat, especially if they know, that their self-estimation in the mandala is used to assess their learning or has an impact on their marks. They think it is not fair that students filling out the mandala honestly have a disadvantage compared with the cheating group.

An evaluation of the teacher's success in conveying the foreseen competences is possible

Students think that the mandala can be used to assess teachers work (under the pre-condition that students don't cheat in compiling the mandala). The comparison of the two mandalas of each student can be an appropriate means to find out what students have learned and how successful the teacher could teach the competences.

The mandala can be handled easily

The asked students think that the handling of the mandala is an easy job. This covers also the digital competences (download the mandala from the learning platform, use an image editor to paint the various areas with a specific colour, save the image and upload it to the learning platform).

The mandala offers a simple method to make the learning success by comparing the before and after mandala visible

Students agree that the learning success and the enhancement of the competences are made visible "by a glimpse". This is also motivating for the learners, because it is easy to realise the progress in enhancing competences. Another issue is the split of the competence into the three characteristic items and in any case, there was an enhancement for each single student minimum in one of the three parts. This obvious progress was mentioned as motivating for the learning.

Conclusion

The feedback of a small group of 25 students gives a first overview of the use of self-evaluation mandalas.

In any case, the self-evaluation mandala forces the teacher (or trainer) to start with a very strict description of the taught competences and the expected learning outcomes in terms of competences. This definition can support students because they also know from the beginning which competence they must develop. The assessment of the students is also an issue – by the well-defined description of knowledge and skills they can prepare perfectly for any assessment.

Self-evaluation mandalas are easily suitable and represent a simple method in the course planning and development. Especially younger learners may appreciate the mandala as an informative tool to document their learning success. Nevertheless, other teacher-controlled objective assessment is necessary to evaluate the learning success (using formative as well as summative methods).

The self-evaluation mandala is an appropriate tool to compare the learning success of the students based on their self-estimation of their knowledge, skills and attitudes of a well-defined competence. The graphical depiction enables to recognize the learning success by a glimpse. In groups with a certain level of maturity the self-evaluation mandala – provided after the course – might be used as an item for the grading of students even if the feedback of the students to this topic was not so positive.

Finally, several remarks are necessary and must be discussed (and further researched in bigger samples and on various national bases is necessary):

- In which way does the maturity of the learner – especially the cheating of students - play a role in using self-evaluation mandalas?
- It is necessary to find out to what extent the age of students plays a role in using the mandala seriously.
- The mandala method must be evaluated in other European countries to exclude typical national behaviour.
- The mandala could be transferred to Adult Education. It is recommended to run pilot courses with adults to find out the acceptance and the usability of the self-evaluation mandala.

References

BusinessDictionary (2018). What is self-evaluation? definition and meaning. Retrieved September 19, 2018, from http://www.businessdictionary.com/definition/self-evaluation.html

Digital Competence Framework: https://ec.europa.eu/jrc/en/digcomp/digital-competence-framework

Lassnigg, L. (2017). Competence-based Education and Educational Effectiveness. In M. Mulder (Ed.), *Competence-based Vocational and Professional Education* (vol., 23, pp. 667–693). Cham: Springer International Publishing (Technical and Vocational Education and Training: Issues, Concerns and Prospects).

Mazohl, P., Ossiannilsson, E., Makl, H., Ampartzaki, M., & Kalogiannakis, M. (2018). An Innovative Tool to Assist the Creation of High Quality Open, and Distance Learning Courses – The Virtual Teachers Toolbox (https://www.vtt-box.eu). In A. Szucs & A. Volungeviciene (Eds.), *Exploring the Micro, Meso and Macro. Navigating between dimensions in the digital learning landscape* (pp. 550–556). EDEN 2018 Annual Conference. Genoa, 17 - 20 June. EDEN. Budapest, European Distance and E-Learning Network.

McLeod, S. A. (2008). Likert Scale | Simply Psychology. Retrieved September 19, 2018, from https://www.simplypsychology.org/likert-scale.html

McMillan, H. J., & Hearn, J. (2008). Student Self-Assessment: The Key to Stronger Student Motivation and Higher Achievement on JSTOR. *Educational Horizons, 87*(1), 40–49. Online resource https://www.jstor.org/stable/42923742?seq=1#metadata_info_tab_contents

Pedagogical Framework: https://www.vtt-box.eu/project/the-products/the-pedagogical-framework

Quality Framework: https://e-xcellencelabel.eadtu.eu

Acknowledges

The authors would like to express acknowledgements and thanks to the European Commission, who is co-funding the VTT-Box project (2017-1-ES01-KA201-038199), under the ERASMUS + KA2-Cooperation for innovation and the exchange of good practice, and KA201 - Strategic Partnership for School Education. The European Commission support for the production of this publication does not constitute an endorsement of the contents which reflects the views only of the authors, and the Commission cannot be held responsible for any use which may be made of the information contained therein.

The authors would like to express acknowledgements and thanks to all partners in the project.

Connecting through Educational Technology
Proceedings of the European Distance and E-Learning Network 2019 Annual Conference
Bruges, 16-19 June, 2019

CONSIDERATIONS FOR QUALITY ASSURANCE OF E-LEARNING PROVISION

Ebba Ossiannilsson, Swedish Association for Distance Education, EDEN, Sweden

Introduction

Today's learning landscape differs greatly from that of a few years ago (Bates, 2015; Daniel, 2016; Mathes, 2019; Ossiannilsson, Williams, Camilleri, & Brown, 2015). The main global challenges highlighted so far and affecting and influencing education are globalization, changing demographics and increasing digitization (Schwab, 2016). The United Nations' UNESCO sustainability goals aim to meet these challenges (2015a; 2015b). In the field of education, the SDG4 focuses on education for all through its core areas of access, equity, equality, equality, inclusion and lifelong learning. Mobile learning is the first choice for most people today. The way learners learn is changing dramatically, due to the fourth industrial revolution, not just the way we learn, but also the way we live, perform, communicate, and interact (Schwab, 2016). Today, learning is possible anywhere, anytime and through any type of device. In the context of globalization and the knowledge-based economy, the quality of higher education is increasingly seen as strategically important for national economic development and competitiveness. High quality and relevant higher education provide students with the knowledge, skills and transferable core competences they need to succeed after graduation, in a high-quality learning environment that recognizes and supports good learning and teaching. The combination of educational technologies is both natural and demanding, so quality aspects must be taken into account (Bates, 2017, Daniels, 2016, Heurtas et al., 2018).

This paper is based on the reflections of the European Association for Quality Assurance in Higher Education (ENQA) Working Group VIII on Quality Assurance and E-Learning on the quality assurance of e-learning services. The report is intended to provide guidance on how European Standards and Guidelines 2015 (ESG) can be applied in the context of e-learning. The recommendations of the ENQA Occasional Paper (Huertas et al., 2018) apply to all forms of e-learning, i.e. learning through the use of information and communication technologies (ICT). The indicators provided are intended to stimulate discussion between stakeholders, both internally and externally. In addition, the applicability and relevance of the standards defined in ESG 2015 are to be investigated. The ENQA report is intended to stimulate discussion and reflection between stakeholders, e.g. universities, quality assurance agencies, etc. In addition to the ESG report, it is based on the European Association of Distance Teaching Universities (EADTU) Quality in E-Learning E-xcellence Benchmarking Framework (Kear et al., 2016). Furthermore, this paper is based on the presentations during the European Distance E-Learning Week (EDLW, 2018) organized by the European Distance and E-Learning Network (EDEN) Special Interest Group on Quality Enhancement (SIG TEL QE on 8 November 2018 on reflections on quality assurance of e-learning based on the ENQA report (Huertas et al., 2018). The challenges of quality improvement in e-learning need to be addressed at all levels, i.e. at the marco, meso and micro levels and not least at the nano level. The nano level refers to people and individuals, the nano level, because ultimately quality is about people, about you and me, that is, not just about indicators or benchmarks, it is about how individuals interpret, follow and apply them.

Aims

The aim of this paper is to raise awareness and stimulate discussion and reflection between the actors involved in quality assurance and quality improvement of e-learning provision, including open online and flexible learning methods such as universities, quality assurance agencies, etc.

Method

This paper is based on the ENQA report on quality assurance considerations for the provision of e-learning by the Working ENQA Group VIII on Quality Assurance and e-learning and the ENQA ESG. It is also based on the framework of the European Association of Distance Teaching Universities (EADTU) Quality in e-learning E-xcellence Benchmarking (Kear et al., 2016). In addition, this paper has its basis in the EADTU SEQUENT project. Furthermore, this paper is based on the presentations during the European Distance E-Learning Week (EDLW, 2018) organised by the European Distance and E-Learning Network (EDEN) Special Interest Group on Quality Enhancement (SIG TEL QE) on 8 November 2018 on reflections on quality assurance of e-learning based on this ENQA report (Huertas et al., 2018).

Results

Even when the ENQA ESG 2015 was introduced, there was no doubt that ESG 2015 would be equally applicable to all forms of teaching and learning, but the need for an appropriate interpretation of its application remains. At that time, it was noted by ENQA that it was still the task of quality assurance agencies and universities to further improve their methodological development. In 2016, the working group decided to set a new focus: the systematic review of both the applicability and the relevance of the standards defined in ESG 2015, taking into account and using existing papers and publications on quality in e-learning offerings. Although it turned out that each standard is fully applicable to e-learning, some standards seemed to require specific guidance on how to apply them. Accordingly, their occasional paper on quality assurance considerations for e-learning services by the Working ENQA Group VIII on Quality Assurance and E-learning aims to provide such guidelines. It is the result of an intensive discussion process both in the working group and with relevant stakeholders of e-learning in Europe (Heurtas et al., 2018).

Its guidelines are to a large extent based on the internationally recognized EADTU Excellence Quality Framework (Kear et al., 2016; Ossiannilsson, Williams, Camilleri, & Brown, 2016), and furthermore it has its basis in the project (Supporting SEQUENT quality in European e-learning networks, 2014-2015) coordinated ENQA by EADTU a partner (Bacsich, 2015; Ossiannilsson, 2015; Williams, 2015). The SEQUENT project aimed to promote excellence in the use of ICT higher education, with the clear objective of preparing European universities in line with the European modernization agenda and better adapting higher education in Europe to cross-border cooperation initiatives in implementing innovative and ICT reinforced partnerships for the purposes of the ENQA report:

> *"...e-learning is understood as any form, including blended learning (except MOOCs and OER), and that which is facilitated by the use of technology" (Heurtas et al., 2018; p.5).*

As a general remark, Heurtega et al., (2018) stressed that e-learning components enable pupils to use personalized and flexible (time and place) pathways while ensuring the achievement of learning outcomes. Content presentation can be more flexible than traditional face-to-face events using online information sources, video and audio channels. However, sometimes personalized and flexible (or innovative) elements of e-learning are not easily understood in a rigid and over-regulated context. It was also stressed that e-learning is a very dynamic and innovative field of learning. The definitions are regularly reviewed and adapted to the new reality.

The guidelines aim to: (i) be generic, non-specific and provide the framework and common basis for national and institutional activities; (ii) apply standards and guidelines for quality assurance, but not for quality as such; (iii) apply e-learning, short courses, to all higher education institutions (EHEA) offered in the European higher education landscape, regardless of the type of study or location (traditional courses); (iv), therefore all types of e-learning and all phases of a learning process (e-assessment) should be considered; and finally, (v) it should apply to all types of quality assurance activities and agencies (quality audits, programme accreditation, institutional assessment). The guidelines consist of three parts, Part 1 Internal quality assurance, Part 2 External quality assurance and Part 3 Quality assurance agencies, as shown in Figure 1. What is new is that the guidelines are aimed both at universities and at quality assurance agencies.

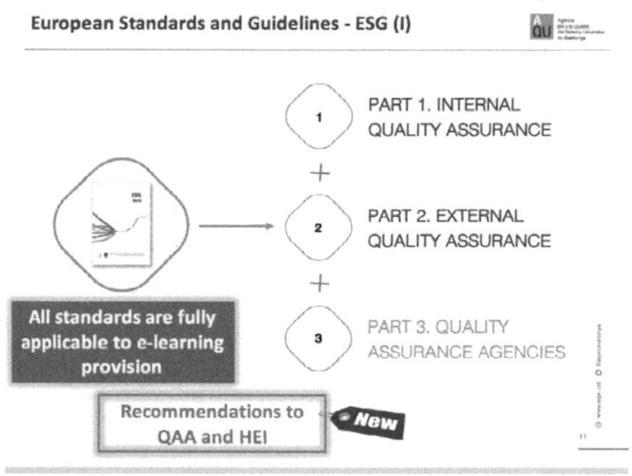

Figure 1. Outline of the Occasional paper on quality assurance considerations for the provision of e-learning (Heurtas, 2018)

In the following the three parts are illustrated, Part I Internal Quality Assurance, Part 2 External Quality Assurance and Part 3 Quality Assurance Agencies.

Considerations for higher education institutions. Part I. Internal quality assurance

- Standard 1.1* – Policy for quality assurance
- Standard 1.2 – Design and approval of programme
- Standard 1.3* – Student-centred learning, teaching and assessment
- Standard 1.4* – Student admission, progression, recognition and certification
- Standard 1.5* – Teaching staff
- Standard 1.6* – Learning resources and student support
- Standard 1.7* – Information management
- Standard 1.8 – Public information
- Standard 1.9 – On-going monitoring and periodic review of programmes
- Standard 1.10 – Cyclical external quality assurance

The ones marked with a star requires particularly special considerations due to e-learning provisions. Below in Figure 2, 3, and 4 Standard 1.1, 1.3, 1.4, 1.5, 1.6, and 1.7 are showed as examples.

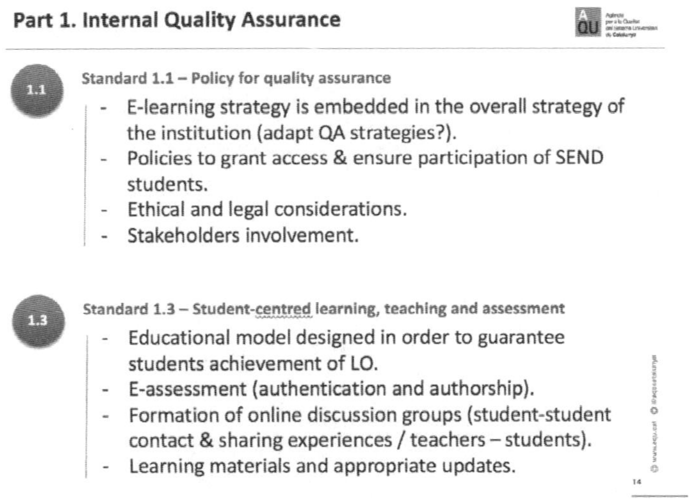

Figure 2. Standard 1.1 and Standard 1.3 (Heuertas, 2018)

In addition, for Standard 1.1 – Quality Assurance Directive, it can be emphasised that the directives are as follows:

The institutional policy for e-learning may also include the constituent quality elements, to which belong:

- institutional support;
- course development;
- teaching and learning;
- course structure;
- student support;
- faculty support with compulsory e-learning training for new members of staff;
- technological infrastructures;
- student assessment (learner authentication, work authorship and examination security) and certification; and
- electronic security measures.

The institution may also define policies to grant proper access and ensure participation for those students affected by disability, illness, and other mitigating circumstances.

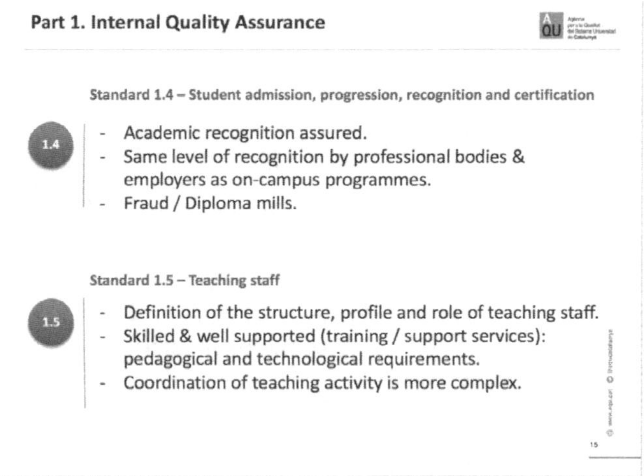

Figure 3. Standard 1.4 and Standard 1.5 (Heuertas, 2018)

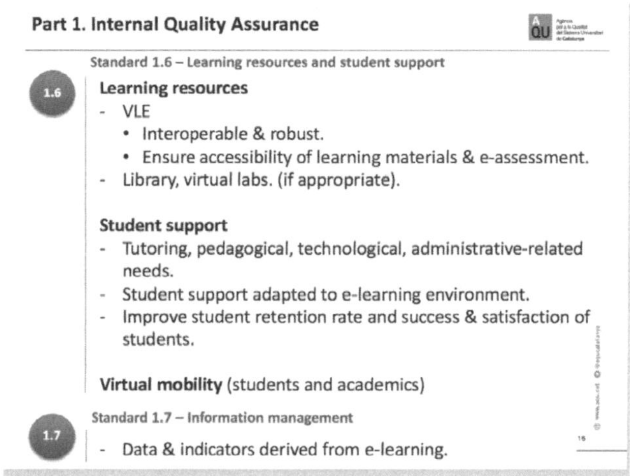

Figure 4. Standard 1.6 and Standard 1.7 (Heuertas, 2018)

Considerations for quality assurance agencies. Part II. External quality assurance

Below considerations for quality assurance agencies are described:

- Standard 2.1 – Consideration of internal quality assurance
- Standard 2.2* – Designing methodologies fit for purpose
- Standard 2.3* – Implementing processes
- Standard 2.4* – Peer-review experts
- Standard 2.5 – Criteria for outcomes
- Standard 2.6 – Reporting
- Standard 2.7 – Complaints and appeals

The ones marked with a star requires particularly special considerations due to e-learning provisions. Some examples are given below. Then Standard 2.2 and Standard 2.3 are shown as examples below in Figure 5. Standard 2.1 is defined, following:

2.1. Consideration of internal quality assurance

Standard: External quality assurance should address the effectiveness of the internal quality assurance processes described in Part 1 of the ESG.

Elements to consider

European, national, and local policies apply also to e-learning, providing institutions with ethical and legal requirements (for example, data privacy or local legal considerations for students with special education needs).

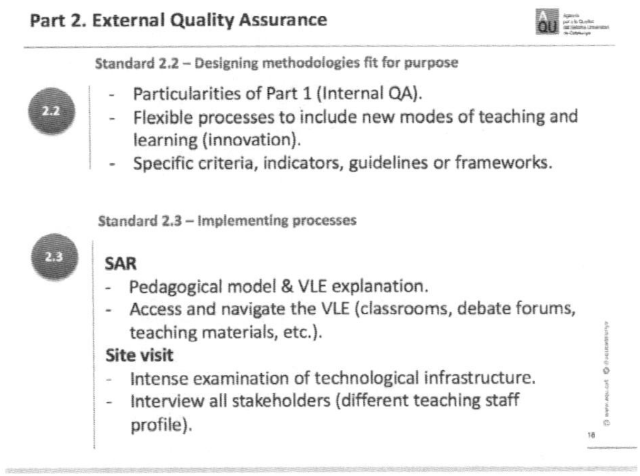

Figure 5. Standard 2.2 and Standard 2.3 (Heurtas, 2018)

The ENQA considerations gives comprehensive guidelines for both internal and external quality assurance and reflect and indicate explicit what has to be taken into considerations by stakeholders involved.

Conclusion

This work by ENQA shows that e-learning is not only ESG applicable, but also illustrates how quality assurance methods can be developed with new indicators.

The current challenge remains with universities and Quality Assurance agencies. On the one hand, Quality Assurance agencies should develop external verification methods that take into account the specificities of e-learning, while on the other hand traditional e-learning or mixed programmes providers should adapt their internal quality assurance systems to ensure the quality of their teaching and learning processes.

This report can be used as a reference for universities and Quality Assurance agencies and could contribute to a common understanding of the concept itself and the relevant terminology. The document can also be useful for training external evaluators and can help to improve the expert profile of the panels.

Two research studies by the International Council for International Council for Open and Distance Education (ICDE) on the quality of open online learning emphasized that important approaches showed that quality assurance models are central and valuable. Areas that do not provide good guidance, guidelines or exchange of good practice face more challenges than others as they have to spend time demonstrating the value of this range of educational modes (Mathes, 2019; Ossiannilsson et al., 2015).

References

Bacsich, P. (2015). *Evaluation SEQUENT University 'showcases' for 'quality in e-learning' procedures.* Retrieved from http://www.sequent-network.eu/images/Guidelines/Sequent_Showcases.pdf

Bates, T. (2015, April 01). Re: Teaching in a digital age: Guidelines for designing teaching and learning for a digital age. [Web log message]. Retrieved from https://opentextbc.ca/teachinginadigitalage/

Bates, T. (2017). Re: What is online learning? Seeking definition [Web log message]. Retrieved from https://www.tonybates.ca/category/teaching-and-learning/blended-learning-teaching-and-learning/

Christensen Institute (2015). Blended learning definitions. Retrieved from https://www.christensenins tute.org/blended-learning-denions-and-models/

Christensen, C., Horn, M., & Staker, H. (2013). Is K-12 blended leaning disrupve? An introduction to the theory of hybrids. Clayton Christensen's Institute for disruptive innovation.

Daniel, J. (2016). *Making sense of blended learning: Treasuring an older tradition or finding a better future?* Contact North Contact Nord Research Associate. Retrieved from https://teachonline.ca/sites/default/files/tools-trends/downloads/makingsenseofblended.pdf

Heurtas, E. (2018). Considerations for quality assurance of e-learning provision. Presentation at the EDEN EDLW 2018, 8 November 2018.

Huertas, E., Biscan, I., Ejsing, Ch., Kerber, L., Kozlowska, L., Marcos Ortega, S., Lauri, L., Risse, M., Schörg, K., & Seppmann, G. (2018). Considerations for quality assurance of e-learning provision. *Occational Paper 26.* Brussels: European Association for Quality Assurance in Higher Education.

Kear, K., Rosewell, J., Williams, K., Ossiannilsson, E., Covadonga Rodrigo, C., (UNED), Sánchez-Elvira Paniagua, A, Santamaría Lancho, M., André Vyt, A., & Harvey Mellar, H. (2016). Final Editing: Karen Kear. K., and Rosewell, J., coordinated by: George Ubachs, G. (EADTU), and Lizzie Konings, L. (EADTU). Quality Assessment for E-learning a Benchmarking Approach (3rd ed.). Heerlen: EADTU.

Mathes, J. (2019). *Global quality in online, open, flexible and technology enhanced education. An analysis of strengths, weaknesses, opportunities and threats.* Oslo: International Council for Open and Distance Education (ICDE).

Ossiannilsson, E. (2015). Evaluation Sequent. Supporting quality in European e-learning networks. Retrieved from https://www.sequent-network.eu/instruments

Ossiannilsson, E. (2017). *Blended learning, the state of nations.* Oslo: International Council for Open, and distance Education (ICDE). Retrieved from https://icde.memberclicks.net/assets/RESOURCES/Blended Learning ICDE Insight Paper 2017 compressed.pdf

Ossiannilsson, E., Williams, K., Camilleri, A., & Brown, M. (2015). *Quality models in online and open education around the globe: State of the art and recommendation.* The ICDE report series. Oslo: The International Council for Open and Distance Education.

Redecker, C., & Punie. Y. (2017). *European framework for the digital competence for educators: The DigCompEdu.* Retrieved from https://ec.europa.eu/jrc/en/publication/eur-scientific-and-technical-research-reports/european-framework-digital-competence-educators-digcompedu

Schwab, K. (2016). *The 4th industrial revolution.* Geneva: World Economic Forum.

UNESCO (2015a). *Education 2030 Framework for Ac on: Towards inclusive and equitable quality education and lifelong learning for all.* Paris: UNESCO.

UNESCO (2015b). *UNESCO and Education 2030: Framework for action and sustainability development goals4, SDG4.* Retrieved from http://en.unesco.org/sdgs

Williams, K. (2015). *Evaluation SEQUENT Supporting Quality in e-learning Europa Networks.* Retrieved from http://www.sequent-network.eu/images/Guidelines/Sequent_Handbook_for_Quality_in_e-learning_procedures.pdf

Acknowledgement

The author would like to express acknowledgements and thanks to the ENQA Working group VIII on Quality Assurance and E-learning. In addition, acknowledgements will be expressed to EADTU and especially the E-xcellence and the SEQUENT team.

CONNECTING EDUCATIONAL TECHNOLOGY TO QUALITY OUTCOMES: THE USE OF QUALITY FRAMEWORKS FOR EFFECTIVE, TECHNOLOGY-ENHANCED DIGITAL LEARNING ENVIRONMENTS

Deborah Adair, Quality Matters, United States of America

The Quality Challenge

Change, propelled by affordances of technology and the rapid development of educational technology tools, is coming to institutions and educators accountable for learning processes and student educational outcomes. For many in higher education, this change is already influencing how the educational experience is structured and how, and with what tools and pedagogies, students are taught. The responsibility of educators remains the – same supporting students and improving learning outcomes – but moving from more traditional approaches to education to more innovative, technology-enabled teaching and learning requires a re-thinking of the standards of practice and methods of evaluation.

Identifying quality, and assuring it, is the next imperative as the pace of change in education technology is much faster than educational research on effective learning environments can address. Instructors and administrators with many years of experience in the face-to-face classroom, supported by well-researched, traditional tools for evaluating effective teaching and learning, may feel they understand and can evaluate quality in that setting. New tools and practices for teaching in new ways will require a fresh look at evaluation. What does quality look like in the integrated use of new technologies to form a robust learning experience? The challenge now is to develop and deploy appropriate quality assurance processes to ensure innovation is advancing student learning.

Overview of the current US-based educational technology landscape

According to the 2018 Higher Education Tech Landscape Report by Encoura Eduventures Research, there are over 300 US-based educational service providers and their products, organized into 38 separate market segments according to 4 major categories aligned to the student lifecycle. Examples for the 38 market segments include solutions and systems for: recruitment management, enrolment analytics, system integration, student information, enterprise content management, student retention, learning analytics, online program management, digital courseware, learning management systems, adaptive learning, competency-based learning, and more. As more tools and related technologies continue to be developed, the rates of adoption of these tools and future plans for such adoption need to be better understood.

Quality Matters and Eduventures have developed some insight through the CHLOE surveys – the Changing Landscape of Online Education (Garrett & Legon, 2019). As a maturing eLearning innovation, online education has grown in reach and application – increasingly embraced, by both students and educators. Chief Online Education Officers, the survey respondents, believe that most of the major changes are now behind them, but those that experienced more significant change in the past were more likely to envision significant future change. Institutions operating online programs at scale were most likely to anticipate major change in the future.

Some of this change will include the use of new pedagogies. Most frequently identified (by 45% of respondents in CHLOE 2) were Badging & Micro-Credentials and Simulations/game-based approaches, followed by Competency-Based Education. The new technologies being considered include adaptive learning and the use of learning analytics and student dashboards, as well as virtual reality. The reason for the adoption of these innovations is made clear in the surveys; overwhelmingly, the goal for new technology adoption is to increase student success. How these institutions are evaluating whether these goals are being achieved is another thing altogether.

Use of quality frameworks in online learning in the United States

There is clear support for the efficacy of identifying and applying quality standards for online learning. According to the CHLOE 3 survey, about 85% of respondents in the U.S. indicate they have quality standards for their courses and programs in the areas of faculty development, course design, program design, student outcomes, and student support services. For all metrics, the majority of institutions represented in the survey were not externally validating the standards.

The sources of these standards are varied, with many institutions using more than one source (see Figure 1 in the CHLOE 3 survey, represented below). Overall, internally generated standards are the most prevalent, particularly for faculty development and support services. Of note is that accreditors' standards pertinent for distance education, particularly the Interregional Guidelines for the Evaluation of Distance Education (2011) and the Twelve Accreditation Standards by the Distance Education Accrediting Commission (2016), are not the primary source of standards for any one metric category although accreditor approval at the institutional level is necessary in the U.S. At the program level, the sources of standards are more evenly distributed, with such external sources as the Hallmarks of Excellence in Online Leadership (UPCEA), the OLC Quality Scorecard for the Administration of Online Programs (OLC), and Online Program Review Criteria (Quality Matters).

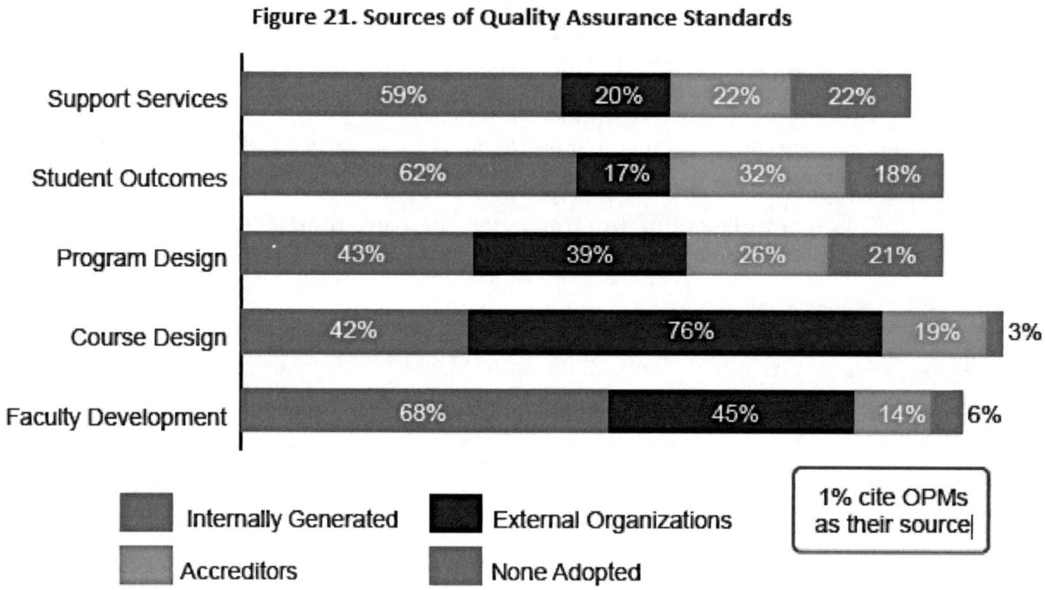

Figure 1. Source of Quality Assurance Standards

At the online course level, external organizations are the most frequently identified source for standards. With over 1400 adopting institutions (1100 in higher education), in all U.S. states and 12 other countries, Quality Matters' Higher Education Standards for Course Design, and its associated review process, is the dominate course evaluation standard in the U.S. Course design, in fact, is the practice most often evaluated whether the standards used are internal, external or a mix of the two. Many options exist for quality standard sets for course design as online learning has matured and instructional design has become a better-known practice. Standards to evaluate student support services have lagged other metrics but have recently grown in popularity.

Institutions in the US are clearly committed to evaluating the quality of their online learning initiatives and do so using a number of standards and benchmarks. Whether these efforts are integrated into a robust quality assurance process, that include external validation of this work, is more difficult to discern. Such processes, however, will be critical for the promise of technology-enhanced education to be achieved. As the pace of innovation continues to accelerate, so must our efforts to assure quality of the teaching and learning experience towards improving student learning outcomes.

Connecting through Educational Technology
Proceedings of the European Distance and E-Learning Network 2019 Annual Conference
Bruges, 16-19 June, 2019

A METACOGNITIVE MOOC FRAMEWORK

Jennifer Roberts, Ignatius Gous, University of South Africa, South Africa

Abstract

MOOC completion rates are well documented as being very low, in most cases, between 5% to 15% (Greene, Oswald, & Pomerantz, 2015; Jordan, 2014). Many reasons have been suggested for the low completion rate. This paper investigates the thesis that one of the predictors of the low completion rates, is that students are not satisfied with the overall experience (structure, content, delivery, etc.) of the MOOC. According to the SERVQUAL measurement scale of satisfaction, service quality can be defined as the difference between expectations and actual experiences. The argument put forward in this paper is that service quality will be enhanced if students' expectation of the MOOC is well understood and that they are properly prepared for what to expect when undertaking the MOOC. This paper follows from an already accepted research paper featuring an auto-ethnographic journey of undertaking a MOOC. The author proposed a metacognitive MOOC framework, from a learner's perspective, based on her MOOC journey. In this paper, this metacognitive MOOC framework is examined in terms of reflective as well as practical components, to assist prospective MOOC students to be prepared for the experience and enhance their satisfaction with their MOOC.

Background and problem statement

MOOCs have been heralded by some as the answer to providing adult education to support lifelong learning (Day, 2014). Others disagree and refer to "nightmare scenarios" if institutions move from traditional student-teacher interaction to the MOOC model (Day, 2014).

One of the major criticisms of MOOCs is the extremely low completion rate (Khalil & Ebner, 2014; Balsh, 2013). Completion rates, particularly in xMOOCs, are acknowledged to be relatively low (Breslow, Pritchard, de Boer, Stump, Ho, & Seaton, 2013). Onah, Sinclair, and Boyatt (2014) suggest many reasons for the low completion rate, with one of them being learner dissatisfaction with the MOOC. They state that many students do not have clear expectations of what the course is about or that their expectations are actually unrealistic.

The satisfaction of college students can be one of the main predictors of their academic success. Quality of service, unlike a product, cannot be easily measured. For example, quality of a product, say an automobile can be easily measured by different parameters like power, torque, fuel consumption, features, time to accelerate, time to brake, crash co-efficient etc. However, in service, the parameters are difficult to measure due to the inherent characteristics of service like intangibility, heterogeneity and inseparability (simultaneous production and consumption). Hence, service quality is more a measure of perception of customer satisfaction, and therefore difficult to have a standard construct. Parasuraman, Berry, and Zeithaml (1991) define service quality as the difference between consumer expectations and perceptions of service performance.

The contention in this paper is that service satisfaction is an intersection between expectation and actual experience. Therefore, the student's expectation of the MOOC will play a role in their overall satisfaction.

Roberts (2019) developed a Metacognitive MOOC Framework for prospective MOOC students (Annex 1). This framework is based on practical as well as metacognitive questions that should assist students to understand and assess their suitability for completing a MOOC. Once their expectations are understood, through the assistance of this framework, then their overall satisfaction level should improve.

This paper therefore takes as its point of departure, the notion that clear and accurate student expectations of undertaking a MOOC will lead to improved satisfaction of the course. The Metacognitive MOOC Framework as proposed by Roberts (2019), is investigated further and substantiated by references to literature on each aspect of the framework.

Methodology

The Metacognitive MOOC Framework article is currently accepted for publication and is based on a qualitative auto-ethnographical research project. It uses a narrative thematic analysis based on Braun and Clarke's (2006) 6 stage analysis. The framework is grounded on the themes that were identified in Roberts's (2019) research. In this paper, the themes (in the form of questions in the framework) are discussed using existing literature on each theme. This is accordance with Ellis (2004; p.198) who states that "the narrative then needs to be surrounded and framed by an analysis of existing literature that should concentrate on how the analysis ties in with or questions existing literature and the accepted theories to which they refer".

Low completion rate of MOOCs

One of the main criticisms of MOOC is their low completion rates. Parr (2013) discusses research that indicates that MOOC completion rates are below 7%. Other authors suggest that completion rates lie somewhere between 5% and 15% (Greene, Oswald, & Pomerantz, 2015; Jordan, 2014). Cognisance should be taken regarding the well-documented low completion rates of distance education students in general (Simpson, 2012). Many people seem eager to disregard MOOCs based on this low completion rate, but accept that it is common in many distance education courses

Conole (2015) discusses a 2-way dilemma in MOOCS. On the one hand MOOCs can be seen as the solution to education challenges in terms of accessibility, affordability and time. On the other hand, low completion rates suggest that MOOCs are not fulfilling this need.

Khalil and Ebner (2013), concur that one of the major concerns regarding MOOCs is the completion rate of the courses. Balsh (2013) supports this. He asserts that the low completion rates are often misleading as MOOC students are more likely to enrol for a course that interest them. Because the MOOCs are very often free of charge, these students are more likely to withdraw before completion.

Onah, Sinclair, and Boyatt (2014) list several reasons that could influence the low completion rate of MOOCs. They state that little research has been carried on the effect size of each of these factors. One of the reasons for high dropout as suggested by Onah et al. (2014) is that many students do not have clear expectations of what the course is about, or that their expectations are unrealistic. They list the following as reasons for the high dropout rate of MOOC students: lack of time; no real intention to complete; course difficulty, starting late; bad previous experience; lack of digital skills and incorrect expectations. Figure 1 shows these reasons, and highlights the possibility that a better understanding of the MOOC process will lead to more realistic expectations and hence a higher level of satisfaction. This is in line with Parasuraman et al.'s (1991) theory that satisfaction is dependent on expected versus actual experience of completing a MOOC. Thesis is therefore that dropout rate will improve if satisfaction of the course is increased.

According to Howarth, D'Alessandro, Johnson, and White (2016), MOOC students are more likely to continue their studies at university if their MOOC experience is satisfying, and that progress in the MOOC is dependent on their goal alignment being maintained. Therefore, it is important to create the correct expectation for prospective students before starting the MOOC. This will reduce the gap between the expected and actual experience of MOOC students. A more realistic expectation should narrow the gap between the expectation and the actual experience and lead to an overall improvement in satisfaction.

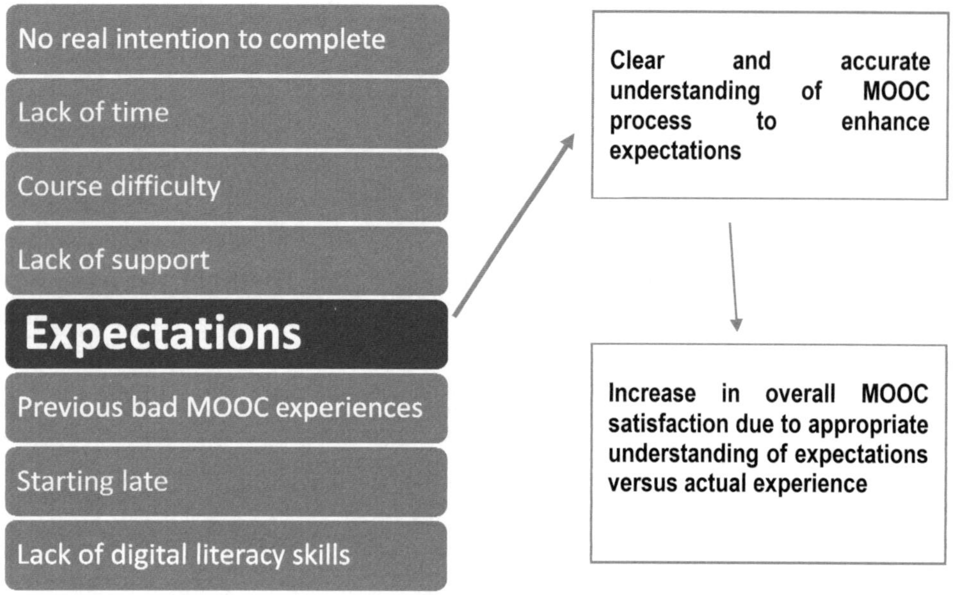

Figure 1. Conceptual framework for increased student satisfaction with MOOCs
Based on Onah et al.'s (2014) reasons for low completion rate of MOOCs

According to Parasuraman et al. (1991), satisfaction is dependent on expected versus actual experience, and therefore, satisfaction levels of MOOCs can be increased by a clear and accurate understanding of the MOOC expectations. One way of doing so is to use the Metacognitive MOOC Framework (Roberts, 2019) that is based on both reflective as well as practical questions.

Flavell's theory of metacognition and reflection

According to Flavell (1976; p.232), "metacognition refers to one's knowledge concerning one's own cognitive processes or anything related to them". Flavell (1979) divides metacognitive knowledge into four categories: knowledge of self, goals, tasks and strategies. In the framework proposed by Roberts (2019) each question is framed around one of these four variables.

Self-reflection has been identified as an important aspect of general learner development in recent years (Park, 2003; Belobrovy, 2018). Self-reflection can play a significant role for learner's taking responsibility for their studies, their own empowerment and motivation. Davis, Herbst, and Busick (2013), state that the process of self-reflection can contribute to the students understanding their own learning process. Metacognition can therefore be a type of reflection – thinking about your own thinking – with the result of enhancing the learning experience.

Roberts (2019) proposed a metacognitive MOOC Framework based on her auto ethnographical research journey on completing a MOOC. The framework is based on the analysis of her reflections and journal entries as a learner participating in her first MOOC. This framework should assist first time MOOCers with understanding their own human factors that could possibly influence their satisfaction with the MOOC journey. The framework can be used by both the MOOC providers, as well as the learners themselves.

The framework is divided into practical and metacognitive questions that any prospective MOOCer should understand.

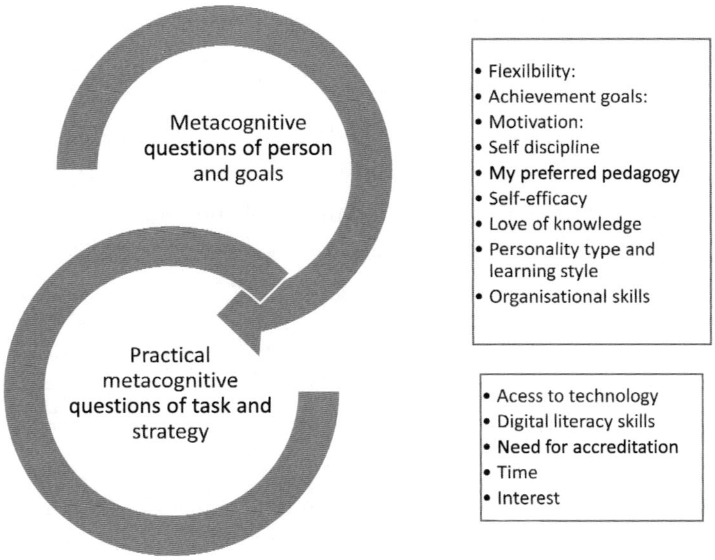

Figure 2. The Metacognitive MOOC Framework (Roberts, 2019)

Unpacking the framework

The research that lead to this framework is currently in print in "Distance Education in China, Vol. 11". The aim of this paper is to unpack the different elements of the framework, relate them to Flavell's (1979) variables of metacognitive knowledge and connect their validity to previously published research on each of the elements of the framework. The reason for this is that the potential MOOCer can create a realistic expectation around the MOOC, to enhance satisfaction. The framework makes a distinction between practical questions that could influence MOOC satisfaction and metacognitive reflective questions, which together will prepare the student for a better MOOC experience.

Flavell (1979) refers to metacognitive knowledge in terms of the four variables, i.e. knowledge of self, goals, task and strategy. Figure 1 is hence unpacked in terms of these four variables, although there is a large degree of overlapping between the four variables. Metacognitive knowledge of person includes all knowledge of yourself, your beliefs, your preferred learning style and your understanding of others. Knowledge of task encompasses the ability to understand that some tasks are more difficult than others are. Knowledge of strategies also plays an important role in understanding which strategies will be most effective in carrying out the task.

Desautel (2009; p.1) sums this up by stating that metacognitions can be described as a complex process of thinking that can result in a person obtaining a "nuanced" understanding of themselves.

Metacognitive knowledge of person

This category includes the following aspects of the framework - personality, learning type (self-pedagogy), flexibility, organisational skills, self-efficacy and self-discipline.

Understanding your personality type

Bocchi, Eastman, and Owens-Swift (2004) suggest that many potential MOOC students do not take into consideration their own personality style, but rather focus on the practical considerations of convenience, availability and flexibility of the course. This is supported by Sheard and Lynch (2003) who highlight that one of the problems of web-based learning is that it that seldom considers the differing personality and learning styles of the students.

It is therefore important to understand your strengths and limitations based of your own personality type. Many different personality assessments are available such as the Myers Briggs (MBTI) and the OCEAN (or Big 5). The MBTI, which was developed in the 1960's by Katherine Cook Briggs and Isobel Myers, is based on the personality theories of Gustav Jung (Briggs & Myers, 1980). Another well researched personality test is the OCEAN that describes five broad personality traits: openness to experience, conscientiousness, extraversion, agreeableness and neuroticism (McAdams, 2008).

The question asked in the framework is the following:

> *"Have I ever undertaken a reliable personality type assessment test that frames my strong points as well as draws attention to areas that are more challenging for me? Do I really know and understand my own unique personality?"*

Learning type (self-pedagogy)

Roberts (2019) found that MOOC pedagogy was able to provide her with basic content knowledge but did not necessarily go deep enough to ensure the development of critical thinking, reasoning and argumentative skills. MOOCs are often criticised for their "behaviourist" approach to learning (Kesim & Altinpulluk, 2016; McGuire, Raaper, & Niklova, 2016). However, in a report of learner's experiences of undertaking a MOOC at the University of Southampton, Wintrup, Wakefield, Morris, and Davis (2015) indicated that many MOOC students preferred the linear structure of the MOOC for providing basic content knowledge. Daniel (2012) states that xMOOCs are based on a behavioural epistemology and Amo (2013) postulates that cMoocs – those that focus on a connectivist learning approach

The following question from the framework regarding the type of learning the student requires should therefore be asked:

> *"Do I prefer to learn in a linear behaviourist manner to obtain information and knowledge or would I rather adopt a more social constructivist approach that involves discussion and interactions with other students/course leaders etc.?"*

Flexibility

There are different levels of flexibility for different MOOCs. Some MOOCs have strict start and end dates and deadlines for assignments, quizzes and exams. They work on an inflexible schedule and if the student misses a deadline, they do not receive credit for that part of the course. Other MOOCs are more flexible. Many of them have no fixed start date and the student can start whenever they want to and submit assignments in their own time.

Loya, Gopal, Shukla, Jermann, and Tormey (2015) studied the impact of conscientious behaviour on the completion rate of MOOCs. They found that the flexible nature of some MOOCs is better suited to students who possess high levels of planning, self-discipline and organisational skills. For this reason, a metacognitive understanding of your own levels of these skills is necessary. This is supported by Fasihuddan, Skinner, and Athauda (2013) who suggest that although some students like to learn at their own pace, deadlines from MOOCs could then prove to be challenging. Roberts (2019) found from her research that although she prefers flexibility and less structure, this led to her not completing (or even starting) the MOOC that had open-ended start and end dates. She needed the discipline of a structured MOOC to ensure that she completed it.

Here, it is important to reflect on your own preferred type:

> *"Do I prefer structured courses or those with a flexible deadline? Am I the kind of person who needs deadlines I order to complete a task or do I prefer an environment that I can adjust to my busy schedule?"*

Organisational skills

There are many different formats to MOOCs. Some have strict start and end dates, as well as weekly deadlines and final exams. If the student fails to meet any of the deadlines, then they run the risk of failing the MOOC. Other MOOCs are open-ended – the student can decide when to start the MOOC and move at their own pace. As Roberts (2019) found, unless the student is well organised and able to plan appropriately, there is a danger that a self-paced MOOC will not be completed.

An understanding of your own organisational skills is therefore necessary. This ties in with the time management knowledge which is discussed later in the "Time management" subsection of "Metacognitive knowledge of strategy" section.

> *"How organised and methodical am I really? Do I have a good track record of sticking to a schedule?"*

Self-discipline

Following through on a MOOC requires a relatively high level of self-discipline, in addition to intrinsic motivation, which is discussed in paragraphs of the "Intrinsic motivation" subsection below.

Gillen (2013) discusses four important lessons that he learned from undertaking a MOOC. His lesson two states that for students taking a MOOC, self-motivation and self-discipline are even more important.

> *"One advantage of in-person courses is the expectation that students will show up at certain times. Indeed, during my MOOC experience I felt none of the nagging guilt about skipping class that I experienced in my college years. My ability to work on the course at any time made it easy to put it off. In fact, I'm still working on the last few weeks of course material even though the course is already over. This procrastination wasn't about a lack of time – for instance, I am completely up to date on the TV show The Walking Dead – but rather a lack of self-discipline." (Gillen, 2013)*

This is in line with the experience of Roberts (2019) who found that lack of self-discipline resulted in her not even starting the open ended and flexible MOOC.

> *"Am I impulsive or rational? Do I let my feelings overwhelm me at times? Do I need instant gratification or am I able to see the bigger picture and make sacrifices now to achieve my long-term goal?"*

Self-efficacy

Self-efficacy can be defined as "belief in one's capabilities to organize and execute the courses of action required to produce given attainments" (Bandura, 1997; p.3). It means believing in yourself and that your own efforts are strong enough to see you through a difficult time. A person's sense of self-efficacy is enhanced when they have a strong sense of responsibility for their own situation as well as being able to make decisions about their own circumstances.

Tsai, Chuang, Liang, and Tsai (2011; p.22) recently concluded from a review of the literature regarding self-efficacy in internet-based learning environments that "student's self-efficacy plays a positive role in their attitude towards and their processes and outcomes derived from Internet-based learning".

> *"How confident am I that I will be able to master this course? Do I feel that I have the ability to pass even if the subject is out of my comfort area? Do I believe in my own abilities even if it means that I will have to put in a lot of time and effort?"*

Metacognitive knowledge of goals

Metacognitive knowledge of goals (Flavell's second variable) includes aspects such as motivation, and interest, MOOC achievement goal and the need for accreditation.

Intrinsic motivation

Pintrich (2003) puts forward five different motivational constructs being: interest, achievement goals, value beliefs, self-efficacy and control beliefs. The Metacognitive MOOC Framework (Roberts, 2019) highlights three of these motivational constructs – interest (including love of knowledge), achievement goals and self-efficacy. Interest is discussed in the "Interest" subsection of the "Metacognitive knowledge of task" section below and self-efficacy has been addressed in "Self-efficacy" above.

Intrinsic as well as extrinsic motivational factors need to be considered when deciding to undertake a MOOC. Within the parameter of knowledge of person, intrinsic motivation, which is derived from intangible factors, plays an important role. An example of intrinsic motivation would be when you do something because you want to and find it interesting e.g. dancing or listening to music. You do it because you enjoy it! When you are intrinsically motivated, your behaviour is motivated by your internal desire to carry out the task. Extrinsic motivation, on the other hand, occurs when there is a contributory reason for that behaviour e.g. going for a run, to increase your heart rate for health purposes. This differs from intrinsic motivation where the love of running is the motivational factor.

The potential MOOC student needs to determine their motivation for undertaking the MOOC under consideration. Is it for a thirst for additional knowledge on the subject or a necessity in order to "prove" knowledge for a work promotion etc.? Yama (2017) states that intrinsic motivation is essential for decreasing dropout rates in online learning contexts. Espinosa, Sepúlveda, and Montoya (2015), who found that a lack of learner intrinsic motivation is one of the main reasons for the high dropout rates in MOOCs, support this. Where a MOOC does not offer accreditation and certification, and the main aim is to provide increased knowledge, intrinsic motivation is a prerequisite.

Here, the questions that need to be asked are as follows:

> *"Am I registering for this MOOC to expand and/or supplement my current knowledge on this subject even through it does not necessarily relate directly to my current career? What is my reason for registering for this course?"*

Achievement goal

There are many different reasons for students registering for a MOOC. It is important for the student to fully understand their motivation and reason for undertaking the MOOC and the outcome that they wish to achieve. Some students might wish to participate, with the intention of completing the course, staying the distance, and gaining the full experience of the MOOC. This will be acknowledged through accreditation for completing and passing the

MOOC – through certification, badging or some other form of recognition. Alternatively, the MOOC might be used to simply "fill in" missing content knowledge and thus completion and accreditation are not that important. Other reasons could include: broadening your horizons, professional development, learning a new skill and getting a taste of university teaching. A study by Liu, Kang, and McKelroy (2015), revealed that the majority of MOOC students were professional people who were looking for opportunities to advance their careers without the constraints of time and place.

> *"The question for the construct of achievement goal is thus: What is the result that I want to achieve by taking this MOOC? Do I want to complete the whole course and receive certification for my knowledge and efforts or is it more important to me to only find additional knowledge in the areas that interest me?"*

Metacognitive knowledge of task

The task at hand is the actual MOOC that the student wishes to register for. The student needs to understand the scope of the MOOC, including the content that will be covered. An interest in the topic is a prerequisite as well as aspects such as having a love of knowledge and a desire to learn – all indication of a lifelong learner.

Interest

Ryan and Deci (2000) state that "if a person is simply not interested in a particular learning activity, he will not be intrinsically motivated for engagement". This ties in too with understanding the real reason why the student wants to register for a MOOC. Anderson (2013) suggests that many students are motivated by an initial curiosity in the MOOC content, but their intention is never to complete the MOOC. They might only be interested in certain parts of the MOOC content.

> *"What about this MOOC has sparked my interest? Is it a subject that I am particularly interested in?"*

Love of learning

This theme ties in with achievement goals stated in "Achievement goal" subsection above. It is important for the potential MOOC student to understand the exact reason for undertaking the MOOC. The questions being asked here relates to the reason for registering for a MOOC. If the learner is fully aware of this reason, whether it be for the love of acquiring new knowledge or a necessary way to obtain information and content for a purpose. The potential MOOCer needs to possess a love of learning and an understanding of their achievement goal and then search for MOOCs that relate to their own interests and passions – this could range from building robots to Shakespearean literature and all things in between.

> *"Am I registering for this MOOC to expand and/or supplement my current knowledge on this subject even though it does not relate directly to my current*

studies/career? Am I a lifelong learner who is motivated by a thirst for new knowledge?"

Metacognitive knowledge of strategy

Strategies refers to the tools that are needed and that the student possesses to complete a fully online MOOC.

Time management

Many students seem to underestimate the time needed to successfully complete a MOOC. They see the time guidelines as only a vague indication of how much time is needed. It is therefore imperative that each student thinks conscientiously about the time that they have available and fully understands the time commitment that is necessary. When a student is caught up in the hype of undertaking a MOOC, in their excitement, it is often tempting to register for multiple courses, not fully understanding the time commitment that is required. Many MOOCs provide a fixed and inflexible format in terms of timing (Onah et al., 2014). Smith, Murphy, and Mahoney (2003) state that online readiness for students focuses on time management as well as self-directedness, motivation, learning styles and experiences. These skills are just as necessary in the MOOC era. Students who lack study skills and good work habits run the risk of dropping out of MOOCs (Gutierrez-Rojas, Alario-Hoyos, Perez-Sanagustin, Leony, & Delgado-Kloos, 2014). Effective time management is seen as a critical study skill.

"How much time do I have available to spend on this course? Does it realistically equate to the time suggested by the course provider? Do I have the time to do more than one MOOC or should I rather spread them over a longer timespan?"

Access to technology

Van Dyk and Hacker (2003) classified four types of access to online learning and their barriers: mental access, material access, skills access and usage access.

Prospective MOOC students need to understand that the MOOC is a fully online course and can only be completed if they have access to technology that supports it. Many MOOCs make use of video podcasts, interactive sessions and other continuously evolving technologies. Their hardware must support the instructional design techniques. Anecdotal evidence from observations at the author's own institution show that many students tick the box to say that they understand that the course they are taking is fully online – but afterwards complain that they do not have a laptop or internet connectivity. This problem is prevalent in many developing countries where there is a lack of reliable broadband connectivity, compounded by high costs. Roberts (2019) found that although she had access to a high-quality device, and Wi-Fi connectivity at both work and home, there were times that she experienced levels of frustration because of interruptions in both her connectivity and hardware problems. These challenges may lead to feelings of annoyance and exasperation, which could result in dropout.

It is therefore important to assess your own technology and internet access to be certain that you have the required specifications.

> *"Do I have access to the required technology for this MOOC? Is my internet access easily available and consistent? Do I have internet at home and/or work or do I have to rely on internet hotspots?"*

Digital literacy skills

Many authors have attempted to define digital literacy (Ilomäki, Pavola, Lakkala, & Kantosalo, 2016; Pokpas, 2014; Stordy, 2015). Julien (2015) defines digital literacy as "The set of skills, knowledge and attitudes required to access digital information effectively, efficiently, and ethically".

Drawing once again on van Dyk and Hacker's (2003) classification, one of the barriers to online learning, and by deduction to MOOCs as well, is the necessary levels of digital literacy skills that are required. This is particularly widespread in developing countries where poor infrastructure at school level sometimes results in low levels of digital literacy.

An honest appraisal and assessment of the individual's digital literacy skills is therefore an important aspect of preparing to undergo a MOOC. The question related to this that needs to be asked is:

> *"How would I rate my computer skills? Can I download files, carry out internet searches, and interact with social media?"*

Conclusion

The aim of this paper was to discuss the Metacognitive MOOC Framework proposed by Roberts (2019). The framework was developed to assist would-be MOOC students to better prepare themselves for the MOOC experience. The contention is that if students are well prepared and have realistic expectations, their level of satisfaction will improve. This could, in turn, lead to a higher completion rate of MOOCs.

The framework is based on Flavell's (1979) metacognitive principles of thinking about various aspects related to undertaking a MOOC i.e. thoughts about self, motivation and goals, the actual task and the strategy needed to complete the task. An understanding firstly of oneself – your own personality, and the related aspects of self-discipline and self-efficacy, organisational as well as self-pedagogical understanding, sets the basis for this metacognitive framework. Once the learner has thought about these aspects, then motivation and achievement goals need to be assessed. The framework places an emphasis on understanding your own motivation and the results that you wish to achieve through undertaking a MOOC – whether it be for lifelong learning aspects, an interest in a hobby, professional development or filling a knowledge gap. The framework then homes in to the actual task – in this case the MOOC, and prepares the student to think about the MOOC that they are intending to register for, to understand the content, the structure and the instructional design. Finally, the learner needs to comprehend the types of strategies that they are going to use to achieve their desired outcomes. These are practical questions related to time management, access to technology and digital literacy skills.

All the above are necessary is to avoid a sense of disappointment when the outcomes are not what you expected.

References

Amo, D. (2013). *MOOCs: Experimental approaches for quality in pedagogical and design fundamentals.* Paper presented at the TEEM '13, November 14 - 15 2013, Salamanca, Spain.

Balsh, T. (2013, July 24). Why the "Low MOOC Completion Rate". Statistic is a Bogus Argument. The augmented trader [Blog post]. Retrieved March 13, 2019, from http://augmentedtrader.wordpress.com/2013/07/24/why-the-low-mooc-completion-rate-statistic-is-a-bogus-argument

Belobrovy, A. (2018). *Theories on Self-Reflection in Education.* Paper presented at Conference: IAFOR ACE.

Bocchi, J., Eastman, J., & Owens-Swift, C. 2004. Retaining the online learner: Profile of students in an online MBA program and implications for teaching them. *Journal of Education for Business, March/April,* 245-253. http://dx.doi.org/10.3200%2FJOEB.79.4.245-253

Braun, V., & Clarke, V. (2006). Using thematic analysis in psychology. *Qualitative Research in Psychology, 3*(2), 77-101.

Breslow, L., Pritchard, D., de Boer, J., Stump, G., Ho, A., & Seaton, D. (2013). Studying learning in the worldwide classroom: Research into edX's first MOOC. *Research & Practice in Assessment, 8,* 13-25.

Briggs, I. & Myers, P. (1980). *Gifts differing.* Palo Alto: CA.

Conole, C. (2015). Designing Effective MOOCs. *Educational Media International, 52,* 239–25.

Daniel, J. (2012). Making sense of MOOCs: Musings in a maze of myth, paradox and possibility. *Journal of Interactive Media in Education, 3.* Retrieved December 4, 2018, from https://jime.open.ac.uk/articles/10.5334/2012-18/

Davies, A., Herbst, S., & Busick, K. (2013). *Quality assessment in high schools: Accounts from teachers.* Courtney, BC: Connections Publishing.

Day, D. (2014, April 10). 'MOOC World': Experts clash over differing visions of education technology. Princeton University News. Retrieved May 12, 2018 from https://www.princeton.edu/news/2014/04/10/mooc-world-experts-clash-over-differing-visions-education-technology?section=topstories

Desautel, D. (2009). Becoming a thinking thinker: metacognition, self-reflection, and classroom practice. *Teachers College Record, 111*(8), 1997-2020.

van Dijk, J., & Hacker, K. (2003). The digital divide as a complex and dynamic phenomenon. *Information society, 19*(4), 315-326.

Ellis, C. (2004). *The ethnographic I: a methodological novel about autoethnography.* Walnut Creek: AltaMira Press.

Espinosa, B., Sepúlveda, G., & Montoya, M. (2015). Self-motivation challenges for students involvement in the Open Educational Movement with MOOC. *Revista de Universidad y Sociedad del Conocimiento, 12*(1), 91-103.

Fasihuddin, H., Skinner, G., & Athauda, R. (2013). Boosting the opportunities of Open Learning (MOOCS) through learning theories. *GSTF Journal on Computing, 3*(3). Retrieved December 2, 2018, from https://www.globalsciencejournals.com/content/pdf/10.7603%2Fs40601-013-0031-z.pdf

Flavell, J. (1976). Metacognitive aspects of problem solving. In L. Resnick (Ed.), *The nature of intelligence* (pp 231-236). Hillsdale, NJ: Erlbaum.

Flavell, J. (1979). Metacognition and cognitive monitoring: a new area of cognitive-developmental inquiry. *American Psychologist, 34*(10), 906-911.

Gillen, A. (2013, April 4). The four lessons I learned by taking a MOOC. American Institutes for Research [Blog post]. Retrieved February 3, 2019, from https://www.air.org/edsector-archives/publications/four-lessons-i-learned-taking-mooc

Greene, J., Oswald, C., & Pomerantz, J. (2015). Predictors of retention and achievement in a massive open online course. *American Educational Research Journal, 52*(5), 925-955. doi: 10.3102/0002831215584621

Gutiérrez-Rojas, I., Alario-Hoyos, C., Pérez-Sanagustín, M., Leony, D., & Delgado-Kloos, C. (2014). *Scaffolding Self-learning in MOOCs.* Paper presented et the European MOOCs Stakeholder Summit, 2014.

Howarth, J., D'Alessandro, S., Johnson, L., & White, L. (2016). Learner motivation for MOOC registration and the role of MOOCs as a university 'taster'. *International Journal of Lifelong Education, 35*(1), 74-85. doi: 10.1080/02601370.2015.1122667

Ilomäki, L., Paavola, S., Lakkala, M., & Kantosalo, A. (2016). Digital Competence – an emergent boundary concept for policy and education research. *Education in Technology, 21*, 655-679.

Jordan, K. (2014). Initial trends in enrolment and completion of massive open online courses. *The International Review of Research in Open and Distributed Learning, 15*(1), 133-160. Retrieved March 21, 2019, from http://www.irrodl.org/index.php/irrodl/article/view/1651/281

Julien, H. (2015). *Digital Literacy.* Retrieved March 22, 2019, from https://www.igi-global.com/chapter/digital-literacy/112623

Kesim, M., & Altinpulluk, H. (2015). A theoretical analysis of MOOC types from a perspective of learning theories. *Procedia – Social and Behavioural Sciences, 186*, 15-19.

Khalil, H., & Ebner, M. (2014). *MOOCs Completion Rates and Possible Methods to Improve Retention – A Literature Review.* Paper presented at the World Conference on Educational Multimedia, Hypermedia and Telecommunications 2014 (ED-Media).

Liu, M., Kang, J. & McKelroy, E. (2015). Examining learners' perspective of taking a MOOC: reasons, excitement, and perception of usefulness. *Educational Media International, 52*(2), 129-146. doi: 10.1080/09523987.2015.1053289

Loya, A. Gopal, A. Shukla, I., Jermann, P., & Tormey, R. (2015). Conscientious Behaviour, Flexibility and Learning in Massive Open On-Line Courses. *Procedia – Social and Behavioural Sciences, 191*. doi: 10.1016/j.sbspro.2015.04.686

McAdams, D. (2008). *The person: an introduction to the science of personality psychology* (5th ed.). New Jersey: Wiley.

McGuire, W., Raaper, R., & Nikolova, V. (2106). Three perspectives on hybridizing x and c MOOCs to create an online course. *International Multidisciplinary Journal, 3*(2), 20-33.

Onah, D., Sinclair, J, & Boyatt, R. (2014). Dropout rates of massive open online courses: behavioural patterns. *EDULEARN14 Proceedings*, 5825-5834.

Parasuraman, A., Berry, L., & Zeithaml, V. (1991). Perceived service quality as a customer-based performance measure: An empirical examination of organizational barriers using an extended service quality model. *Human Resource Management, 30*(3), 335-364. https://doi.org/10.1002/hrm.3930300304

Park, C. (2003). Engaging students in the learning process: The learning journal. *Journal of Geography in Higher Education, 27*(2), 183-199.

Parr, G. (2013). MOOC completion rates below 7%. Retrieved March 22, 2019, from https://www.timeshighereducation.com/news/mooc-completion-rates-below-7/2003710.article

Pintrich, P. (2003). A motivational science perspective on the role of student motivation in learning and teaching contexts. *Journal of educational psychology, 95*(4), 667–686.

Pollack Ichou, R. (2018). Can MOOCs Reduce global inequality in education? *Australasian Marketing Journal, 26*(2) 116-120. https://doi.org/10.1016/j.ausmj.2018.05.007

Pokpas, C. (2014). *Towards a framework for the development of e-skills for digital inclusion in the Western Cape.* Retrieved March 12, 2019, from https://etd.uwc.ac.za/xmlui/bitstream/handle/11394/4216/pokpas_c_msc_ems_2014_1.pdf

Roberts, J. (2019) (in print). My MOOC journey: an auto-ethnographical account into lifelong learning. (Junhong Xiao trans.) *Distance Education in China, 11.*

Rosen, G. (2014). 'MOOC World': Experts clash over differing visions of education technology. Retrieved May 12, 2017, from http://www.princeton.edu/main/news/archive/S39/71/57E81/index.xml?section=topstories

Ryan, R., & Deci, E. (2000). Self-determination theory and the facilitation of intrinsic motivation, social development, and well-being. *American Psychologist, 55*(1), 68-78.

Simpson, O. (2013). Student retention in distance education: are we failing our students? *Open Learning, 28*(2), 105-119. doi: 10.1080/02680513.2013.847363

Smith, P., Murphy, K., & Mahoney, S. (2003). Identifying factors underlying readiness for online learning: An exploratory study. *Distance Education, 24*, 57-68.

Stordy, P. (2015). Taxonomy of literacies. *Journal of Documentation, 71*(3), 456-476.

Tsai, C., Chuang, S., Liang, J., & Tsai, M. 2011. Self-efficacy in Internet-based Learning Environments: A Literature Review. *Educational Technology & Society, 14*(4), 222–240.

Wintrup, J., Wakefield, K., Morris, D., & Davis, H. (2015). Liberating learning: experiences of MOOCs. Higher Education Academy. Retrieved November 6, 2018, from https://heacademy.ac.uk/sites/default/files/resources/liberating learning.pdf

Yama, P. (2017). *Learner intrinsic motivation in online social learning platforms: a case study of massive open online course (MOOC) in Thailand.* Retrieved March 3, 2019, from https://eprints.qut.edu.au/108005/5/Pittaya_Yamo_Thesis.pdf

Annex 1. Metacognitive MOOC Framework (Roberts, 2019)

Construct	Questions
Flexibility	Do I prefer structured courses or those with a flexible deadline? Am I the kind of person who needs deadlines to complete a task or do I prefer an environment that I can adjust to my busy schedule?
Time	How much time do I have available to spend on this course? Does it realistically equate to the time suggested by the course provider? Do I have the time to do more than one MOOC or should I rather spread them over a longer timespan?
Organisational skills	How organised and methodical am I really? Do I have a good track record of sticking to a schedule?
Self-discipline	Am I impulsive or rational? Do I let my feeling overwhelm me at times? Do I need instant gratification or am I able to see the bigger picture and make sacrifices now to achieve my long-term goal?
Access to technology	Do I have access to the required technological devices that are required for this MOOC? Is my internet access easily available and consistent? Do I have internet at home and/or work or do I have to rely on Wi-Fi hotspots?
Digital literacy skills	How would I rate my computer skills? Can I download files, carry out internet searches, and interact with social media?
My type of learning	Do I prefer to learn in a linear behaviourist manner to obtain information and knowledge or would I rather adopt a more social constructivist approach that involves discussion and interactions with other students/course leaders etc.?
Love of knowledge	Am I registering for this MOOC to expand and/or supplement my current knowledge on this subject even though it does not relate directly to my current studies/career?
Motivation	Why am I thinking of registering for this MOOC?
Interest	What about this MOOC has sparked my interest? Is it a subject that I am particularly interest in?

Self-efficacy	How confident am I that I will be able to master this course? Do I feel that I can pass even if the subject is out of my comfort area? Do I believe in my own abilities even if it means that I will have to put in a lot of time and effort?
Achievement goals	What is the result that I want to achieve by taking this MOOC? Do I want to complete the whole course and receive certification for my knowledge and efforts or is it more important to me to only find additional knowledge in the areas that interest me?
Personality and learning style	Have I ever undertaken a reliable personality type assessment test that frames my strong points as well as draws attention to areas that are more challenging for me? Do I really know and understand my own unique personality?
Reflexive thinking	Do I spend time thinking deeply about my motivations, goals and plans for the future? Do I reflect on experiences and try to learn from them to avoid recurring problems?
Need for accreditation	For this MOOC, do I really need accreditation for job advancement, to put on my CV or to gain access to further studies? Alternatively, is it more important to me that I gain new knowledge as part of my lifelong learning journey?

APPROACHES AND METHODOLOGIES TO SUPPORT CRITICAL REFLECTION

Jean Claude Callens, VIVES University of Applied Sciences, Belgium

Introduction

During their studies, pre-service teachers are continually asked to reflect (Calderhead & Gates, 1993; Korthagen & Vasalos, 2005; Rodgers, 2002). In teacher education a goal of reflection is to change beliefs about teaching in order to improve practice, and therefore there is a strong connection between reflection and actions of students on the workplace.

It does not seem obvious that students in teacher education reach a critical level in their reflections (Bean & Stevens, 2002). According to Bean and Stevens (2002) effective scaffolding of a reflection process encompasses a number of key features within cognitive and emotional domains. Cognitive features include for instance using hints and leading questions to develop self-regulation. Emotional features include for instance providing a safety net to allow for mistakes. In this study we focus on cognitive features and search for an approach/methodology that may support a reflection process.

Approaches and methodologies to reflect

There are different approaches and methodologies to support students to write their reflections. According to Rogers (2001) the number of steps in the different approaches to reflect varies from zero to eight. Some view the steps in a reflection process as sequential (Seibert & Daudelin, 1999), while others contend that the steps of a reflective process do not need to follow any particular order (Schön, 1983). In this contribution, an approach that contains guidelines that may be considered sequential and step-by-step-structured is described as a linear approach to reflect. In contrast, an approach that does not include sequential, step-by-step-structured guidelines is described as a non-linear approach (van Eekelen, Boshuizen, & Vermunt, 2005).

Besides variations in approaches to reflect, there are also variations in methodologies to support reflection (Callens & Elen, 2012). In line with Callens (2012) we distinguish in this contribution methodologies that are (a) primarily language based or (b) primarily image based and thus more multimedial.

The writing of a learning journal and digital storytelling may be considered as examples of respectively primarily language and primarily image-based methodologies to support reflection. A learning journal is described as a hand-written note that may contain thoughts, reflections, feelings, personal opinions, hopes and fears regarding an educational experience (Mc Garr & Moody, 2010). Banaszewski defines digital storytelling as "The practice of combining personal narrative with multimedia (images, audio and text) to produce a short autobiographical movie" (Banaszewski, 2005; p.1).

It is possible to vary the degree of structure (linear and non-linear approach to reflect) within each of the mentioned methodologies to support reflection (learning journal and digital journal). With the distinction between (a) the linear and non-linear structured approach and (b) primarily language and primarily image based methodologies to reflect 4 combinations are indicated (=linear and non-linear structured learning journal/digital storytelling).

Research questions

In this study we examine which combination of approach to reflect (cf. degree of structure) and methodology to reflect (cf. primarily language and primarily image based) most effectively supports critical reflection. This leads to the following research questions:

- To what extent do student teachers reflect critically?
- Is there an impact of approach to reflect on the degree of critical reflection?
- Is there an impact of methodology to reflect on the degree of critical reflection?
- Is there an interaction effect between an approach and methodology to reflect on the degree of critical reflection?

Design of the study

In order to determine which combination of approach and methodology to reflect most effectively supports the writing of reflection assignments, two studies were conducted. In both studies an experiment was carried out with respectively a pre-test post-test control group design and a post-test only control group design. In each study: (a) participants were student teachers, (b) the theoretical model of Kelchtermans was used to describe critical reflection, (c) the same procedure was used in order to determine the degree of critical reflection in the written reflection assignments, and (d) in both studies variations of the degree of structure (cf. approach to reflect) with respectively a learning journal and a digital storytelling were used.

Participants

In total 164 student teachers participated in the two studies. In the first study participants were 63 primary school student teachers and 101 secondary student teachers in the second. All participants were freshmen.

Material and procedure

Based on the results of an empirical study, Callens (2012) concludes that leading questions may influence the reflections that students make (see also Lai & Calandra, 2010). Therefore, in both studies the same leading questions were used, but the presentation of these questions depended on the condition. With a more linear structured approach to reflect, the leading questions were presented according to the ALACT model of Korthagen. The ALACT model contains 5 sequential steps (*Action*, *Looking back*, *Awareness of essential aspects*, *Creating alternative methods of action*, and *Trial*) (Korthagen & Vasalos, 2002). In a non-linear approach to reflect there was no step-by-step structuring of the leading questions.

The procedures varied. In the first study, students were notified of the experiment by their lecturers. Then, during an information session the participants were given further explanation. There were three class groups, and the same explanation was given by the same person. Afterwards, participants got guidelines for the first reflection assignment (pre-test) by e-mail. The guidelines in the first reflection assignment were the same for all participants (= non-linear structured digital story). Participants were asked to reflect upon a situation (a situation which they assess as difficult) in which they explained something (=content, a skill, a game…) to someone or to a group. Participants were asked to reflect by making a digital story. Because participants were freshmen, it could not be said with certainty that they had sufficient ICT skills to use multimedia in their digital stories. Therefore, a variant of digital storytelling was used and the students were asked to write a digital comic with a Word template. Participants were asked to explain the comic in a speech balloon. In addition to the reflection assignment, the first mail also contains a worked-out example. The second reflection assignment (post-test) was sent with an email after participants had finished the first assignment. The second reflection assignment varied according to the condition participants were randomly assigned to (cf. linear or non-linear structured digital story).

In the second study, students were notified of the experiment by their lecturers. Then the guidelines to make the reflection assignments were sent by email to the participants.

In all conditions, the same worked-out example was used, but the presentation varied according to the condition (whether or not linear structured). The subject of reflection was the same as in the first study but in the second study participants were asked to reflect with a primarily language based methodology, and were asked to write a learning journal (instead of the primarily image based methodology, cf. digital comic in the first study).

In the first study 154 and in the second 126 students were invited to participate. An individual randomization was used. Drop-out and the fact that uncompleted reflections were not taken in the analysis, lead to the fact that in the first study reflections of 101, and in the second of 63 participants were taken in the analysis. Due to the drop-out the conditions used in the two studies contains a different number of participants.

Data analysis

Similar to other approaches to determine the degree of critical reflection (see Granberg, 2010; Carrington & Selva, 2010), a framework was used as coding scheme. This framework is based on the dimensions and domains described by Kelchtermans (2001; 2009).

In both studies, the approach used is based on the method described by Van Beirendonck (1998) to assess competences in an assessment centre. Marking in this context means that if, in a reflection by a participant, one element refers to a dimension or a domain of the mentioned framework, the participant received score one, with two elements score two, and so on.

In the first study (with a pre-test post-test control group design) the reflections from the post-test were analysed, in the second (with a post-test only control group design) all reflections were analysed. This means that a total of 164 reflections in the secondary data analysis were taken in the analysis.

When participants reflected through the writing of a learning journal, this journal was analysed. Because images are difficult to interpret without an explanation of the student (Briell, Elen, Depaepe, & Clarebout, 2010), the analysis of the digital stories was based on the speech balloon, in which participants explain the comic.

Due to the large amount, all reflections in both studies were scored by only one assessor. However, to calculate the inter-rater reliability, in each study 40 reflections were scored by a second assessor. Each of the assessors marked blindly for condition using the coding scheme.

Because the variables are at a ratio scale, the inter-rater reliability was verified by calculating the correlation (using Pearson's correlation coefficient) (Evers & Sermeus, 1998), between the scores of both assessors for: the technical and emotional dimensions, for the political and moral dimensions and for the personal interpretative framework. The correlation coefficients are between 0.78 and 1.00. Because a relatively high inter-rater reliability score was determined, the score of the first assessor – whom analysed all reflections – was taken as result.

Results

To answer the first research question, the results of the first study (in which students reflect by writing a digital story) reveals that participants score low on critical reflection (mean = 0.34; SD = 0.77). In the second study (with a learning journal) the mean score is higher but still low (mean = 0.68; SD = 0.82). In both studies a high SD was found. Overall (results of both studies taken together in the analysis) the mean score is low and there is a high SD (mean = 0.47; SD = 0.81).

To answer the second research question, a one-way ANOVA (with approach to reflect as independent variable and degree of critical reflection as dependent variable) was conducted. For the first study, no significant results could be retrieved ($F(1,99) = 0.22$, $p = 0.64$, $\eta_p^2 = 0.00$). Analysis of the second study reveals a significant weak-to-moderate (according to the guidelines of Nijdam, 2003) main effect of approach to reflect on critical reflection ($F(1,61) = 7.61$, $p = 0.00$, $\eta_p^2 = 0.11$). When participants reflect with a linear structured learning journal (mean = 0.97, SD = 0.96), they score better on the degree of critical reflection than when they reflect with a non-linear structured learning journal (mean = 0.42, SD = 0.56).

To exam the impact of methodology to reflect and to check for interaction between approach and methodology to reflect on critical reflection (cf. third and fourth research question), the results of both studies were taken together in the analysis. A one-way ANOVA shows a significant, weak-to-moderate main effect of methodology to reflect ($F(1,162) = 7.35$, $p = 0.00$, $\eta_p^2 = 0.04$) on the degree of critical reflection. As mentioned earlier, when participants reflect with a learning journal (mean = 0.68, SD = 0.82) they score better than when they reflect by writing a digital story (mean = 0.34, SD = 0.77). Finally, a two-way ANOVA (with approach and methodology to reflect as independent and degree of critical reflection as dependent variables) reveals no interaction effect between approach and methodology to reflect on the degree of critical reflection.

A descriptive analysis give a more detailed view of participants' mean scores (Table 1). The results reveal that a linear structured learning journal most effectively supports critical reflection; a non-linear structured digital storytelling is least effective.

Table 1: Score critical reflection related to the approaches/methodologies to reflect

Approach and methodology to reflect	Mean score on critical reflection	SD	Frequency of reflections participants made
-Linear structured learning journal	.97	.96	30
-Non-linear structured learning journal	.42	.56	33
-Linear structured digital story	.38	.84	48
-Non-linear structured digital story	.30	.72	53
Total	.47	.81	164

Conclusion

The results in this study reveal that the mean score of all reflections on critical reflection is low. This is in line with results from previous studies (Callens et al., 2012; El-Dib, 2007; Dinkelman, 2000).

Second, a high SD is observed. Because of this high SD, the assumption that learner characteristics may have an impact on the degree of critical reflection is – at least partly – confirmed in this study. When asked what characteristics of the students can determine whether a student is able to reflect critically, we refer to Rogers. Rogers (2001) identifies readiness and willingness to engage in the process of reflection and refers to the work of Boud, Keogh and Walker, Dewey, Langer, Loughran, and Mezirow. The importance of willingness is also mentioned by Rodgers (2002), Walkington, Christensen, and Kock (2001) and Tann (1993). Furthermore, a research study conducted by Huy (2008) reveals that both epistemological beliefs and learning approaches may influence reflection processes. The assumed influence of willingness on the process of reflection is indirectly confirmed in a study conducted by Granberg (2010). The analysis of reflection reports (with blogs) and interviews with 13 preschool student teachers revealed that students that complete their reflection assignments only to obtain a degree, do not take enough time to commit themselves to the reflection process and thus to make deeper reflections (Granberg, 2010).

Third, it seems that a linear-structured approach to reflect more effectively supports critical reflection than a non-linear structured one. Several authors stress the importance of a more structured approach to reflect (Gibbs, 1981; Korthagen, Koster, Melief, & Tigchelaar, 2002). According to Korthagen et al. (2002) student teachers sometimes hate to complete reflection assignments because thinking about oneself can be threatening. They argue that student teachers (especially externally oriented, less "reflective" students) are initially in need of much guidance and structure to compensate for (often unconscious) feelings of uncertainty. Bean and Stevens (2002) write that when reflection takes place without adequate guidance, students may see the process as yet another ritual and treat in a cursory fashion. According to Arrastia et al. (2014) pre-service teachers can reflect without guidance or scaffolding, but ill-structured assignments may not lead to deeper reflection.

Fourth, the lower score on digital storytelling (compared to a learning journal) can be explained by the idea that writing digital stories (or writing a comic strip) expects additional skills. According to Banaszewski (2005) digital storytelling requires students to develop enough visual literacy when they are asked to write a digital story. Visual literacy refers to understanding and using images. From this perspective, it seems that a sober methodology to reflect (like a learning journal) more effectively supports a reflection process than a complex methodology (like digital storytelling).

While the results of these two studies are revealing, a number of methodological issues are to be considered.

First, there are additional factors (than approach and methodology to reflect) of a learning environment that may influence the degree of critical reflection and should thus be considered as elements of a learning environment that support pre-service teachers in critical reflection. For instance, Rogers (2001) refers to the following contextual conditions: feedback, autonomy, interaction and facilitating opportunities so that appropriate challenges may emerge. Based on the results of this study, it is unclear what feedback participants have received from their lecturers, the degree of interaction they have had with their peers, and what specific initiatives lectures have taken to stimulate students to reflect. It is possible that these elements may have influenced the reflection of the participants and thus affected the (low) score of critical reflection obtained in this study. Furthermore, a supportive climate seems to be a vital condition in supporting a reflection process (Ramsey, 2010). In these studies, students from only one institution were asked to participate. It is not clear to what extent this institution aims to create a climate that encourages students to have a critical dialogue on their teaching practice and thus have enough confidence to write a reflection report. The results of this study do not clarify whether the low score for critical reflection is due to the students' abilities/characteristics or is affected by contextual conditions of a learning environment (or both).

Second, in the first study participants were secondary school student teachers, in the second primary school student teachers. It is unclear whether the same result could be achieved in case participants in both studies followed the same program.

Third, the results in this study are obtained by analysis from only two experiments with different participants. Although there are a rather large number of participants, it seems that a longitudinal research with the same participants is needed to corroborate the results.

Last, we want to discuss the analysis of the data. In this study, the reflections used in the analysis are reports made by the participants after the 'action' (cf. reflection after action). This approach does raise at least three questions. First, reflection after action is always blended with the reflection that took place prior to and during the action (Ramsey, 2010). With the methodology used in this study, reflections made prior to and during the action are not taken into account. Second, it is unclear whether the participants were sufficiently motivated to write these reports. Third, it is assumed that students may have had difficulty in articulating their experiences in anything other than colloquial terms (Tann, 1993). For these three reasons, it is unclear whether these documents capture all of the reflections of the students.

Regarding further research, as the results of this study refer to freshmen further research could focus on the impact of approach and methodology to reflect with participants whom are more experienced.

Further, the data analysis in this study is based on a quantitative approach. Referring to earlier mentioned reasons (see discussion of analysis of the data) it would be interesting to repeat this study but use a qualitative approach to analyse the reflections participants write.

In conclusion, we recommend – based on the results of this study- a linear structured approach to support first year pre-service teachers when writing reflection assignments. Secondly, it seems that more complicated methodologies are inhibitory for the degree students reflect critically. Therefore, we endorse a simple (for instance text based methodology) to support student to reflect critically.

References

Akbari, R. (2007). Reflections on reflection: A critical appraisal of reflective practices in L2 teacher education. *System, 35*, 192-207.

Arrastia, M. C., Rawls, E. S., Brinkerhoff, E. H., & Roehrig, A. D. (2014). The nature of elementary preservice teachers' reflection during an early field experience. *Reflective Practice, 15*(4), 427-444.

Banaszewski, T. (2005). *Digital storytelling, supporting digital literacy in grades 4-12* (Unpublished master thesis). Georgia Institute of Technology. Retrieved from http://techszewski.blogs.com/techszewski/files/TB_thesis_2006_edits.doc

Bean, T. W., & Stevens, L. P. (2002). Scaffolding reflection for preservice and inservice teachers. *Reflective Practice, 3*(2), 205-218.

Briell, J., Elen, J., Depaepe, F., & Clarebout G. (2010). The Exploration of Drawings as a Tool to Gain Entry to Students' Epistemological Beliefs. *Electronic Journal of Research in Educational Psychology, 8*(2), 655-688.

Calderhead, J., & Gates, P. (Eds.) (1993). *Conceptualizing reflection in teacher development.* London: Falmer Press.

Callens, J. C., & Elen, J. (2012). The impact of approach to reflection and learner control upon critical reflection. *Reflective Practice, 12*(4), 495-506.

Callens, J. C. (2012). *Impact van reflectie-aanpak en learner control op kritisch reflecteren Doctoraatsproefschrift.* Katholieke Universiteit Leuven, Faculteit Psychologie en Pedagogische Wetenschappen, Centrum voor Instructiepsychologie en –technologie, Leuven.

Carrington, S, & Selva, G. (2010). Critical social theory and transformative learning: evidence in pre-service teachers' service-learning. *Higher Education Research & Development, 29*(1), 45-57.

Dinkelman, T. (2000). An inquiry into the development of critical reflection in secondary teachers. *Teaching and Teaching Education, 16*(2), 195-222.

van Eekelen, I. M., Boshuizen, H., & Vermunt, J. D. (2005). Self-regulation in higher education teacher learning. *Higher Education, 50*(3), 447-471.

El-Dib, M. (2007). Levels of Reflection in Action Research: An Overview and an Assessment Tool. *Teaching & Teacher Education: An International Journal of Research and Studies, 23*(1), 24-35.

Evers, G., & Sermeus, W. (1998). Betrouwbaarheid en validiteit van meetinstrumenten. In Evers, G. (Ed.), *Meten van zelfzorg. Verpleegkundige instrumenten voor onderzoek en klinische praktijk.* Leuven: Universitaire Pers.

Gibbs, G. (1981). *Teaching Students to Learn, a student-centered approach.* Milton Keynes: Open University Press.

Granberg, C. (2010). Social software for reflective dialogue: questions about reflection and dialogue in student teachers blogs. *Technology, Pedagogy and Education, 19*(3), 345-360.

Huy, P. (2008). Predicting change in epistemological beliefs, reflective thinking and learning styles: a longitudinal study. *British Journal of Educational Psychology, 78*(1), 75-93.

Korthagen, F., & Vasalos, A. (2002). Niveaus in reflectie: naar maatwerk in begeleiding. *VELON Tijdschrift voor Lerarenopleiders, 23*(1), 29-38.

Korthagen, F., & Vasalos, A. (2005). Levels in reflection: core reflection as a means to enhance professional growth. *Teachers and Teaching: theory and practice,11*(1), 47–71.

Korthagen, F., Koster, B., Melief, K., & Tigchelaar, A. (2002). *Docenten leren reflecteren. Systematische reflectie in de opleiding en begeleiding van leraren.* Soest: Uitgeverij Nelissen.

Lai, G., & Calandra, B. (2010). Examining the effects of computer-based scaffolds on novice teachers' reflective journal writing. *Educational Technology Research and Development, 58*(4), 421-437.

Mc Garr, O., & Moody, J. (2010). Scaffolding or stifling? The influence of journal requirements on students' engagement in reflective practice. *Reflective Practice, 11*(5), 579-591.

Nijdam, A. (2003). *Statistiek in onderzoek, beschrijvende technieken, deel 1.* Groningen: Wolters Noordhoff.

Ramsey, S. (2010). Reflecting on the future, education in the third millennium. *Curriculum and Teaching Dialogue, 5*(2), 123-130.

Rodgers, C. (2002). Defining Reflection: Another look at John Dewey and reflective thinking. *Teachers College Record, 104*(4), 842-866.

Rogers, R. (2001). Reflection in higher education: a concept analysis. *Innovative Higher Education, 26*(1),37-57.

Schön, D. (1983). *The Reflective Practitioner. How Professionals Think in Action.* New York: Basic Books Inc.

Seibert, K. W., & Daudelin, M. W. (1999). *The role of reflection in managerial learning: Theory, research, and practice.* Westport, CT: Quorum.

Tann, S. (1993). Eliciting Student Teachers Personal Theories. In J. Calderhead & P. Gates (Eds.), *Conceptualizing reflection in teacher development* (pp. 53-69). London: Falmer Press.

Van Beirendonck, L. (1998). *Beoordelen en ontwikkelen van competenties. Assessment centers, development centers en aanverwante technieken.* Leuven/Amersfoort: Acco.

Walkington, J., Christensen, H., & Kock, H. (2001). Developing critical reflection as a part of teaching training and teaching practice. *European Journal of Engineering Education, 26*(4), 343-350.

Connecting through Educational Technology
Proceedings of the European Distance and E-Learning Network 2019 Annual Conference
Bruges, 16-19 June, 2019

EXPLORING THE EMOTIONS OF DISTANCE LEARNING STUDENTS IN AN ASSESSED, ONLINE, COLLABORATIVE PROJECT

Jake Hilliard, Karen Kear, Helen Donelan, Caroline Heaney, The Open University, United Kingdom

Summary

Previous research has highlighted the importance of emotions of learners in online learning settings. However, much of this research has tended to focus on individual learning situations rather than social learning activities. The exploration of the emotional experiences of distance learners has also received little attention when compared to other student groups (e.g. full-time or blended learning students). As many distance learners are in full- or part-time employment or have other commitments, the emotions experienced and the reasons for these emotions might be greatly different to other student populations. This study investigated these issues by exploring the emotional experiences of distance learners when undertaking an assessed, online, collaborative group project. Self-report data about the emotions experienced and their causes were gathered using a structured diary at six times points during the group activity. Findings revealed that learners experienced a ranged of pleasant and unpleasant emotions before, during and after the collaborative activity. Feelings of satisfaction and relief were the most reported pleasant emotions and feelings of anxiety and frustration were the most frequently reported unpleasant emotions. To conclude this paper, implications for educators are briefly discussed and reflections on using an online diary to explore student emotions are provided.

Introduction

The UK Open University (OU) is currently one the largest Higher Education (HE) institutions in Europe, with a student population of around 120,000 (Higher Education Student Statistics, 2019). The OU is based on a unique distance education method called "Supported Open Learning". This method offers a flexible approach to education, with students having much greater freedom to study where and when they like, compared to traditional campus based universities. OU students come from diverse backgrounds; for instance, their age (OU students are typically older than those who attend typical HE institutions); location (located all over the UK and around the world); previous levels of education (the OU require no formal entry qualifications); and employment status (many OU students are in full-time or part-time employment) will vary greatly. Additionally, there are a higher portion of students with disabilities and with additional needs/requirements studying at the OU in comparison to other UK universities (The Open University, 2018). Flexibility is therefore central to underpinning the OU's mission of being open, and is essential for learners studying at the OU.

To deliver Supported Open Learning, the OU makes considerable use of online provision. Students use a virtual learning environment (VLE) which provides access to course content (e.g. weekly study material, interactive quizzes, podcasts) and supports student interaction with peers and tutors using asynchronous (i.e. online forums) and synchronous (i.e. using messenger and video chat via Adobe Connect) communication methods. With changes in education policy (e.g. the recent Teaching and Excellence Framework in the UK) and the need to ensure employability skills, such as teamwork competencies and collaboration skills, are developed, teaching and learning in HE is changing. Traditional methods of instruction, such as one-way transmission of knowledge from teacher to student, are being replaced by active learning through interacting with fellow students. This has led to an increased prevalence of social and collaborative activities being incorporated into online learning programmes (Järvelä et al., 2015). At the OU, for instance, learning and assessment activities which encourage interaction and collaboration are being increasingly advocated (Evans & Galley, 2016; Rienties & Toetenel, 2016). The integration of such collaborative activities (either in assessed or non-assessed formats) into the Supported Open Learning model at the OU does, however, pose challenges. For example, due to the shared discussion, planning and creation often involved in collaborative learning, students may feel that their study flexibility has been reduced. It has also been found that some students may experience increased levels of unpleasant emotions, such as anxiety and frustration, when working collaboratively online (Donelan & Kear, 2018; Hilliard, 2017) and are less satisfied with social learning activities when compared to other approaches to teaching and learning (Rienties & Toetenel, 2016).

Over the last two decades, the importance of emotions in academic learning has been evidenced. Research has shown that emotions play a vital role in student motivation, self-regulation and academic achievement (Rienties & Rivers, 2014). Although much research has focussed on the impact of emotions in face-to-face learning contexts, more evidence is being found for the importance of understanding emotions in online learning settings (e.g. Artino, 2012; Marchand & Gutierrez, 2012). Much of this work has concentrated on individual learning situations, with less attention being paid to the social and collaborative elements of online learning. In a recent study, Reis et al. (2018) reviewed existing literature to explore the emotions reported during online collaborative learning. Results revealed both pleasant (e.g. surprise, joy, excitement) and unpleasant (e.g. frustration, anxiety, anger) emotions amongst the most frequently mentioned. As well as limited exploration of emotions in online collaborative settings, there is currently little research exploring the emotions of distance learners. The emotional experiences of these students may be impacted by the additional commitments many of them have, such as being in full-time or part-time employment. Gaining a greater insight into the emotional experiences of distance learners undertaking assessed, online, collaborative activities will be of great value to educators and institutions who have adopted, or who are planning to adopt this pedagogical approach. Findings may help with the design of future collaborative activities and support strategies for students who may experience unpleasant emotions.

Purpose and Research Questions

The main purpose of the study reported in this paper was to explore undergraduate distance learners' emotional experiences in an assessed, online, collaborative project. The following research questions were addressed:

- What emotions do learners self-report before, during and after an assessed, online, collaborative project?
- What are the perceived reasons for the self-reported emotions before, during and after an assessed, online, collaborative project?

Study Context

The study was undertaken using students from OU who were studying an undergraduate physics and astronomy module. As part of the module, students were required to work in teams to undertake a group project based around the modelling processes of the Earth's atmosphere. Students worked in teams of up to ten, sub-divided into three smaller specialist teams – one team undertook experiments, one mathematical modelling and one a literature survey (see Figure 1). After completing their tasks in the specialist teams, students combined results to produce the core of a scientific report (results and discussion sections). Students were individually required to produce the remaining sections of the report (abstract, introduction, and conclusion). Collaboration within the main team and specialist teams was expected throughout the duration of the 8-week team project. A student's overall grade for the project was made up of both individual (75% of overall grade) and group marks (25% of overall grade) (see Figure 1).

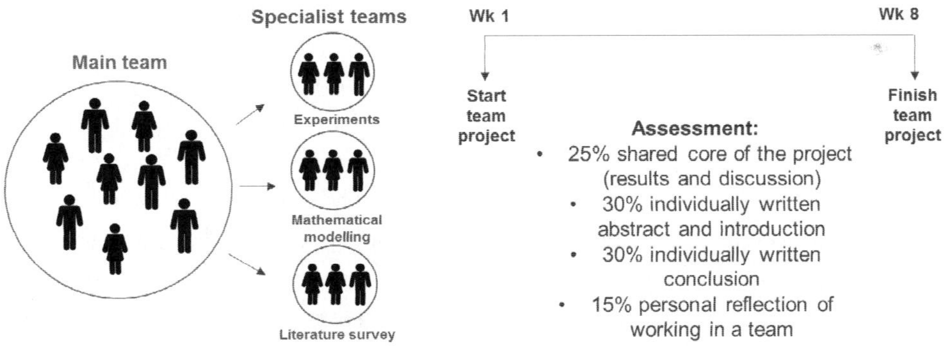

Figure 1. An overview of the assessed collaborative group project

Methods

Sample and Procedures

Seventeen students volunteered to participate (13 males and 4 females). The age of participants varied: 3 were aged under 25 years; 4 were aged between 26 – 35 years; 6 were aged between 36 – 45 years; and 3 aged were aged 56 years and over. One participant withdrew from the study 2 weeks into the collaborative project due to personal reasons (male, aged between 36-45 years).

Before contacting students about taking part in this diary-based study, ethical approval was gained from The Open University's Human Research Ethics Committee (HREC) and Student Research Project Panel (SRPP). Invitation emails stating the purpose of the study, and informing students that taking part would have no effect on any aspect of their module or university study, were sent to 83 of the 158 students that studied the module that year. Some students could not be included because of rules observed by SRPP. Over a 9-week period, students were sent a link to six online diary entries (created using JISC Online Surveys). The first entry was to be completed before the start of the collaborative project, the next four during the project and the final entry after the project had been completed. Students were briefly instructed on how to fill out the diary entries after agreeing to take part in the study. Students had 48 hours to complete each diary entry; after this time, they were unable to access the online form. In total, 93 diary entries were completed out of a possible 102 (91.2% completion rate). Four uncompleted diary entries were due to the one participated withdrawing from the study, whilst the remaining five were due to participants not completing the entry on time. For participating in the study, participants who completed four or more entries received a £20 Amazon voucher.

Measures

Diary methods have been used previously to explore student experiences of emotion in various learning contexts (e.g. Peterson, Brown, & Jun, 2015; Zembylas, 2008). This method has many advantages, such as being able to explore temporal variations in emotions and minimising the retrospective bias that can be caused when using other data collection methods (Becker, Keller, Goetz, Frenzel, & Taxer, 2015). Each of the six diary entries were structured, asking questions about the types of emotions experienced during a specific time period and their causes. Both quantitative and qualitative data were gathered.

Type of emotion

Students were asked to select (by ticking a check box) which emotions they had experienced in relation to the online collaborative project for the specific time period stated in each diary entry (e.g. the time since the previous diary entry). Students could select from six pleasant (enjoyment, excitement, pride, satisfaction, relief, hope) and eight unpleasant (boredom, frustration, disappointment, anxiety, anger, embarrassment, dissatisfaction, confusion) emotions. These emotions were selected based on previous research which has investigated emotions in online collaborative activities, face-to-face collaboration, and individual online learning settings. An "other" option was also provided so that students could identify any other emotions they had experienced. Additionally, a question at the end of each diary entry asked students to select the most dominant emotion they had experienced for the specific time period (from the fourteen previously stated emotions or an "other" option).

Cause of emotion

If students identified that they had experienced one or more pleasant emotions, they were asked to explain (in an open-ended text box) the cause of one of these emotions for a specific occasion. This was repeated for unpleasant emotions.

Analysis

Quantitative data relating to the type of emotions experienced by students in relation the online collaborative project were analysed using descriptive statistics. Frequencies (*n*) and percentages (%) were calculated and transformed into tables in Microsoft Excel 2013. Qualitative data for the causes of emotions were analysed using classical content analysis (Leech & Onwuegbuzie, 2008), using an inductive approach. This approach initially involved reading and re-reading the qualitative data to become familiar with the content. Data were then systematically worked through and interesting features coded. Codes were then grouped into higher level categories and these were quantified by counting the number of instances they were used in the text.

Results

Types of emotions

Frequencies and percentages of emotions reported during each of the six diary entries are reported in Table 1. Overall, slightly more pleasant emotions were reported over the six entries than unpleasant emotions (pleasant: 53.5%; unpleasant: 46.5%). More pleasant emotions than unpleasant emotions were reported in diary entries 1, 2 and 6, whereas more unpleasant emotions were reported in diary entries 3, 4 and 5. The total number of reported emotions was highest in diary entry 3 and lowest in diary entry 2. Of the six pleasant emotions, *satisfaction* and *relief* were reported most overall. Both of these emotions were reported by a large proportion of students in diary entries 5 and 6. Satisfaction was also highly reported during diary entry 3. *Hope* and *excitement* were more frequently reported in entries 1 and 2 than in any of the other four entries. Apart from *pride* in entry 6, both *enjoyment* and *pride* were reported less frequently than other pleasant emotions. In addition to the eight unpleasant emotions listed, three further unpleasant emotions were reported by students (*trepidation, unconfident, sadness*). Of these eleven unpleasant emotions, *anxiety* and *frustration* were reported most overall. *Anxiety* was the most reported emotion during diary entry 1 and was highly reported during diary entry 3. *Frustration* was most reported during diary entry 5 and was also the most highly reported unpleasant emotion in diary entries 3 and 4. Other unpleasant emotions were less frequently reported.

Analysis of the most dominant emotion self-reported by participants in each entry (results table not reported), revealed that *anxiety* was the most reported emotion. This emotion was heavily reported in diary entry 1. The second most self-reported dominant emotion was *satisfaction*. This was reported most frequent in diary entries 3 and 4.

Table 1: Self-reported pleasant and unpleasant emotions before, during and after the online collaborative project

Emotion	Diary 1 (before)		Diary 2 (during)		Diary 3 (during)		Diary 4 (during)		Diary 5 (during)		Diary 6 (after)		Overall	
	n	%	*n*	%	*n*	%	*n*	%	*n*	%	*n*	%	*n*	%
Pleasant	22	61.1	19	61.3	28	48.3	21	45.7	23	42.6	25	75.8	138	53.5
Satisfaction	3	8.3	5	16.1	8	13.8	5	10.9	8	14.8	8	24.2	37	14.4
Relief	5	13.9	2	6.5	6	10.3	5	10.9	8	14.8	11	33.3	37	14.4
Hope	4	11.1	5	16.1	5	8.6	4	8.7	3	5.6	1	3.0	22	8.5
Excitement	6	16.7	4	12.9	4	6.9	3	6.5	2	3.7	1	3.0	20	7.8
Enjoyment	3	8.3	2	6.5	3	5.2	3	6.5	1	1.9	1	3.0	13	5.0
Pride	1	2.8	1	3.2	2	3.4	1	2.2	1	1.9	3	9.1	9	3.5
Unpleasant	14	38.9	12	38.7	30	51.7	25	54.3	31	57.4	8	24.2	120	46.5
Anxiety	9	25.0	4	12.9	7	12.1	5	10.9	5	9.3	2	6.1	32	12.4
Frustration	1	2.8	3	9.7	8	13.8	6	13.0	10	18.5	1	3.0	29	11.2
Dissatisfaction	1	2.8	2	6.5	4	6.9	2	4.3	5	9.3	3	9.1	17	6.6
Disappointment	0	0.0	1	3,2	4	6.9	4	8.7	3	5.6	1	3.0	13	5.0
Confusion	0	0.0	0	0.0	3	5.2	3	6.5	2	3.7	1	3.0	9	3.5
Anger	0	0.0	1	3,2	0	0.0	2	4.3	3	5.6	0	0.0	6	2.3
Embarrassment	1	2.8	0	0.0	2	3.4	1	2.2	2	3.7	0	0.0	6	2.3
Boredom	1	2.8	1	3.2	2	3.4	1	2.2	0	0.0	0	0.0	5	1.9
Trepidation	1	2.8	0	0.0	0	0.0	0	0.0	0	0.0	0	0.0	1	0.4
Unconfident	0	0.0	0	0.0	0	0.0	1	2.2	0	0.0	0	0.0	1	0.4
Sadness	0	0.0	0	0.0	0	0.0	0	0.0	1	1.9	0	0.0	1	0.4
Total	36	100	31	100	58	100	46	100	54	100	33	100	258	100

Reasons for emotions

Approximately 119 answers were provided when students were asked to describe the cause of emotions experienced in the online collaborative project. Seventy of these were for occasions when participants had experienced a specific pleasant emotion and 49 were related to specific unpleasant emotions. As more than one cause may have been stated in each response, a total of 141 descriptions of the causes of emotions were found. After initial analysis, 13 categories for the causes of emotions were identified. These were (frequencies provided in brackets): *completion of project or module* (24); *participation and engagement from others* (18); *task progress* (18); *working and collaborating with others* (17); *performance in the project or module* (15); *self-belief* (15); *the task itself* (11); *guidance and support* (8); *workload and assessment timing* (7); *time availability* (3); *technology and software* (2); *external factors* (2); and *other* (1).

Pleasant emotions

All causes in the *completion of project or module* category were related to pleasant emotions (24 out of 24). Many of these related to the *relief* and *satisfaction* of completing the project, whilst other answers related to the anticipation of finishing the project and ultimately the module. The majority of causes in the *task progress* category were also related to pleasant emotions (15 out of 18). These included both individual and group progress that had been made in the project. A number of pleasant emotions were caused by *working and collaborating with others* (10 out of 17). Reasons varied from the general *enjoyment* of meeting and working with others to the positive social interactions between group members. For instance, one student stated student "I enjoyed collaborating as part of the modelling team". *Participation and engagement from others* also led to a number of pleasant emotions (9 out of 18). This category referred to the participation and engagement of other students in the task. For instance, one student wrote "Relief that the rest of my group also seems motivated to get the project completed". Aspects of the *task itself* also caused a number of pleasant emotions (7 out of 11). For example, one student was satisfied because the project resembled a "real world" investigation and *enjoyed* being able to undertake a "massive group project". From the remaining six categories, only one pleasant emotion was related to the *self-belief* category and there were no pleasant emotions from the remaining five categories.

Unpleasant emotions

Many unpleasant emotions stemmed from the *self-belief* category (14 out of 15). Reasons for these emotions predominantly related to having self-doubts about their own ability, or thoughts of letting themselves or others down in the project. These responses mainly occurred in diary entries 1 and 2 and were often related to feelings of *anxiety*. A number of unpleasant emotions were caused by *participation and engagement from others* (9 out of 18). These often related to other students not communicating or participating in the activity and were often linked to *frustration*, *disappointment* and *anxiety*. *Performance in the project or module* (8 out of 15) was another cause of unpleasant emotion. Many reasons related to the final quality of the report for the project. A lack of *guidance and support* (8 out of 8) predominantly from the course content and tutor were a source of unpleasant emotion for some learners. For example, a student wrote "Lack of instruction about what needs to be done from OU". These responses were often linked to *frustration* and *confusion*. Categories of *working and collaborating with others* (7 out of 17) and *workload and assessment timing* (7 out of 7) were also commonly cited reasons for unpleasant emotions. Fewer unpleasant emotions stemmed from the remaining six categories. From these, unpleasant emotions related to *time availability* category (3 out of 3) stemmed from not having enough time to complete the project. For instance, one student stated that they felt *anxious* "...about being able to find the time required to do the necessary work". The difficulty of the task was found to be a reason for unpleasant emotion for the *task itself* category (4 out of 11). *Technology and software* caused a small number of unpleasant emotions during the project (2 out of 2).

Conclusion

Findings revealed that learners experienced a range of pleasant and unpleasant emotions in relation to the assessed, online, collaborative project. The use of qualitative data also allowed for numerous reasons for emotions to be identified. There are a number of implications for educators and learning designers from these findings. Firstly, before the activity began anxiety was by far the most commonly reported emotion, often resulting from low self-belief and the fear of lettings others down. The use of prior activities aimed at increasing confidence and trust in learners when interacting and collaborating online is one way that may help reduce these unpleasant feelings. Secondly, it was reported that a lack of guidance and support during the project resulted in frustration and confusion. Ensuring activity guidelines are clear and that support can be gained when needed (e.g. from tutors), will hopefully help create a more positive learning environment. Thirdly, the "real world" value and ability to use skills learnt previously in the module were stated as reasons for pleasant emotions by students. This finding highlights the importance of task value and authenticity when designing assessed, online, collaborative activities.

The use of a structured online diary proved to be an effective way of gathering data about student emotion during an assessed, online collaborative project. When compared to other data collection methods more commonly used to explore student emotions (e.g. surveys, interviews), diaries allowed for a reduced recall period helping to overcome issues of memory decay and retrospective bias which are often associated with these other methods. Being able to explore emotions and their causes at multiple time points also allowed for temporal variations and within person changes to be explored. One concern that researchers may have when using an online diary is the potential for large dropout rates or an increased number of incomplete entries. However, in this study we observed a small dropout rate (one student due to personal reasons) and a high diary entry completion rate (91.2%).

References

Artino, A. (2012). Emotions in online learning environments: Introduction to the special issue. *The Internet and Higher Education, 15*(3), 137–140.

Becker, E. S., Keller, M. M., Goetz, T., Frenzel, A. C., & Taxer, J. L. (2015). Antecedents of teachers' emotions in the classroom: an intraindividual approach. *Frontiers in Psychology, 6*(635).

Donelan, H., & Kear, K. (2018). Creating and collaborating: students' and tutors' perceptions of an online group project. *International Review of Research in Open and Distributed Learning, 19*(2).

Evans, G., & Galley, R. (2016). *Collaborative online activities: a guide to good practice.* Milton Keynes: The Open University.

Higher Education Student Statistics (2019). Who's studying in HE?: Personal characteristics. Retrieved January 30, 2019, from https://www.hesa.ac.uk/data-and-analysis/students/whos-in-he/characteristics

Hilliard, J. (2017). *Students' Perceptions and Experiences of Anxiety in an Online Collaborative Project.* The Open University.

Järvelä, S., Kirschner, P. A., Panadero, E., Malmberg, J., Phielix, C., Jaspers, J., Koivuniemi, M., & Järvenoja, H. (2015). Enhancing socially shared regulation in collaborative learning groups: Designing for CSCL regulation tools. *Educational Technology Research and Development, 63*(1), 125–142.

Leech, N. L., & Onwuegbuzie, A. J. (2008). Qualitative data analysis: A compendium of techniques and a framework for selection for school psychology research and beyond. *Psychological Association, 23*(4), 587–604.

Marchand, G. C., & Gutierrez, A. P. (2012). The role of emotion in the learning process: Comparisons between online and face-to-face learning settings. *The Internet and Higher Education, 15*(3), 150–160.

Peterson, E. R., Brown, G. T. L., & Jun, M. C. (2015). Achievement emotions in higher education: A diary study exploring emotions across an assessment event. *Contemporary Educational Psychology, 42*(1), 82–96.

Reis, R. C. D., Isotani, S., Rodriguez, C. L., Lyra, K. T., Jaques, P. A., & Bittencourt, I. I. (2018). Affective states in computer-supported collaborative learning: Studying the past to drive the future. *Computers & Education, 120*, 29–50.

Rienties, B., & Rivers, B. (2014). *Measuring and understanding learner emotions: Evidence and prospects.* Learning Analytics Community Exchange (LACE).

Rienties, B., & Toetenel, L. (2016). The impact of 151 learning designs on student satisfaction and performance: social learning (analytics) matters. *Proceedings of the Sixth International Conference on Learning Analytics & Knowledge – LAK '16*, 339–343.

The Open University (2018). Strategy and policies: Facts and figures. Retrieved January 30, 2019, from http://www.open.ac.uk/about/main/strategy-and-policies/facts-and-figures

Zembylas, M. (2008). Adult learners' emotions in online learning. *Distance Education, 29*(1), 71–87.

DISCLOSING LEARNERS' BEHAVIOUR AND ENGAGEMENT INTO ONLINE AND BLENDED COURSES: CASE STUDY OF VYTAUTAS MAGNUS UNIVERSITY

Giedrė Tamoliūnė, Margarita Teresevičienė, Vytautas Magnus University, Lithuania, Josep M. Duart, Universitat Oberta de Catalunya, Spain, Justina Naujokaitienė, Vytautas Magnus University, Lithuania

Abstract

Interfaces between students' participation, number of submissions to discussion forums, attendance of online lectures and students' performance on their assignments are significant for students' success and achievements. Teachers' activities become more significant when delivering blended or online courses and their role changes from knowledge deliverer to learning designer. Therefore, teachers are challenged to recognize new learning behaviour models and find new ways to engage and motivate learners. Universities offering study programs in blended or online way need to recognize learners' behaviour, know how to analyse the data, make it "understandable" to teachers and learners, and learn how to adapt course curriculum based on this data. Results of the case study conducted at Vytautas Magnus University revealed that after logging in to Moodle learning platform, students tend to spend time checking forums or course assignments rather than browsing another course content. Moreover, a significant drop-out rate was noticed after the 4th click, when 24% of students tend to quit the session. The results of this research confirm the fact that online learners' behaviour is changing rapidly, and teachers should be aware of that, understand preferred learning patterns and develop course content based on this data.

Theoretical background

Online learning platforms like MOOCs and Moodle access and collect large amounts of data allowing to observe and analyse learners' interaction, behaviour and engagement into study process at macro and micro levels. When engaging in online or blended courses, learners have various intentions and experiences, and therefore they demonstrate different learning behaviours. To recognise learning behavioural patterns, teachers aim to master how to access the data, understand it, rethink course content based on this data and improve curriculum. Learning analytics help to understand and optimise learning processes and environments where this learning happens. Moreover, it could also help to measure learners' engagement, suggest study materials and resources based on test results, personalise learning experiences, provide feedback for the submitted work (Radu, 2017) and encourages teachers' metacognition related to their teaching practice. LA serves as a metacognitive tool encouraging and allowing teachers to improve the way they teach and organise their teaching, helping students to learn and monitor their learning process. These decisions and observations could be made by using structured analysis techniques.

LA can provide evidence of students' learning performance and behaviour in educational settings and consequently teaching strategies and instructional measures can be taken based on the presented facts. This also implies that such evidence will allow teacher to employ needed strategies and use personalized interventions as well more attention might be paid to low achievers. Learners' engagement in discussion forums and attendance of online lectures were found to be positively associated with each other, moreover, submissions to the discussion forums and amount of interaction online (Ellis, Han, & Pardo, 2017) were directly related with a positive effect on learners' final exam grades.

These finding confirm that teachers' activities become more significant when both, recognising trends and challenges of learners' behaviour in online or blended course, or organising the learning and teaching curriculum by, for example, establishing a minimum reply requirement, drawing one's attention to others' ideas on a discussion topic, phrasing question in way motivates and engages as many students as possible (Kim et al., 2016). All these transformations of teachers' activities demonstrate their changing role, from being knowledge deliverer to becoming learning designer (Buckingham Shum & Crick, 2016), being able to recognise learners' behaviours and respond to their learning needs.

Learners' behavioural patterns in online courses

When discussing learners' behaviour and engagement into online and blended courses, it is important to note, that open online or blended courses offer the unique possibility to uncover different and diverse student behaviours. And this is one of the significant aspects that differentiates open online courses from traditional courses (Anderson et al., 2014).

There are number of different categorisations and clusters identified based on various criteria related to learners' engagement with one or the other learning resource or task. Douglas et al. (2016) clustered learners into five groups based on their material usage: (a) *fully engaged learners*, with regular participation; (b) *consistent viewers*, who do not regularly access the course assessment materials (c) *two-week engaged learners*, participating first two weeks of the course (d) *one-week engaged learners*, who fully access the first week's materials and (e) *sporadic learners* who randomly access materials. Learners engagement into the course through video lectures and assignments for credits was observed by Anderson et al. (2014). As previous authors, they have identified 5 behavioural patterns which described learners as *viewers* (primarily watching videos; submitting only few assignments); *solvers* (primarily submitting assignments; watching few if any videos); *all-rounders* (equally engaging when watching videos and preparing assignments); *collectors* (primarily downloading video lectures but not necessarily watching them, presenting few assignments if any); and *bystanders* (signing up for the course but demonstrating extremely passive engagement). Other behavioural clusters like *passive participants*, *active participants*, *community contributors* (Koller, Ng, & Chen, 2013), *dropouts*, *excellent students*, *gamblers or learners who played with the system*, and *social learners* (Khalil, Kastl, & Ebner, 2016) demonstrate closely related features of learners' behaviour, although it is important to distinguish that they identify learners' need for socializing and networking. These learners tend to engage in course activities but they demonstrate specific interest in facilitating forum discussions or contributing and helping other learners by, e.g. providing foreign language subtitles (Koller, Ng, & Chen, 2013).

Based on these learning trends, Kim (2016) suggest to pay attention to encouragement of students before the mid-term by shifting from course related material to discussion and allowing learners to progress with more in-depth analysis and understandings in the class or team based discussions. Aiming to increase learners' engagement, Universities, together with administrators of virtual learning platforms and teachers, deployed a system of badges and conducted an experiment where this system was presented to different learners' sub-populations. Research results demonstrated that badge system had a positive impact on learners' participation and engagement (Anderson et al., 2014).

Thus, teachers should be able to understand how different measurement approaches could help them to monitor learning process and improve teaching process. Gašević, Dawson, and Siemens (2015) pointed out the important learning evidence possibilities to collect by observing completion of online quizzes or course grades, which did not accurately measure learning outcomes but rather academic performances at a given point in time.

To sum up, clustering can help to illustrate learners' profiles based on their behaviours, like time spent of doing and completing the assignment, test or other learning activity, group learning, or time of one's engagement into specific activity (Antonenko, Toy, & Niederhauser, 2012; Dutt, Ismail, & Herawan, 2017). Dutt, Ismail, and Herawan (2017) emphasize that regarding variety of methods and algorithms for data clustering, teachers and researchers should keep in mind their research aim and be very careful when choosing the most appropriate method for collecting valid data.

It is important to note, that despite the variety of data visualisation tools and huge amounts of statistical data, researchers (Gašević, Dawson, & Siemens, 2015; Derr, 2017) are emphasizing the importance of qualitative studies in this field, which would give better understanding of learners' behaviour, e.g. through the texts created in discussions or blogs.

Research methodology

This study aims to present trends and challenges of learners' engagement into online and blended courses at Vytautas Magnus University. Desk research and interviews with teachers were conducted to collect data related to our research topic. Desk research was implement to recognise and observe which learning activities teachers tend to organise when delivering online or learning courses and how, what behavioural patterns can be recognised from macro level, etc. These observations and results were further validated and exploited with the empirical research based on semi-structured interviews with teachers, more in-depth analysis of their module curriculum and their metacognitive activities for curriculum redesigning.

Findings

This University offers traditional study courses mainly, although two online study programs are offered and delivered to learners worldwide. Other study programs are free to choose how study courses are delivered, i.e. face-to-face, blended or online courses. Even though teachers are not obliged to deliver blended or online courses, they are required to upload their courses on Moodle platform. Therefore, since 2013 when Rector's order was released, a significant growth of online study modules can be noted (see Figure 1)

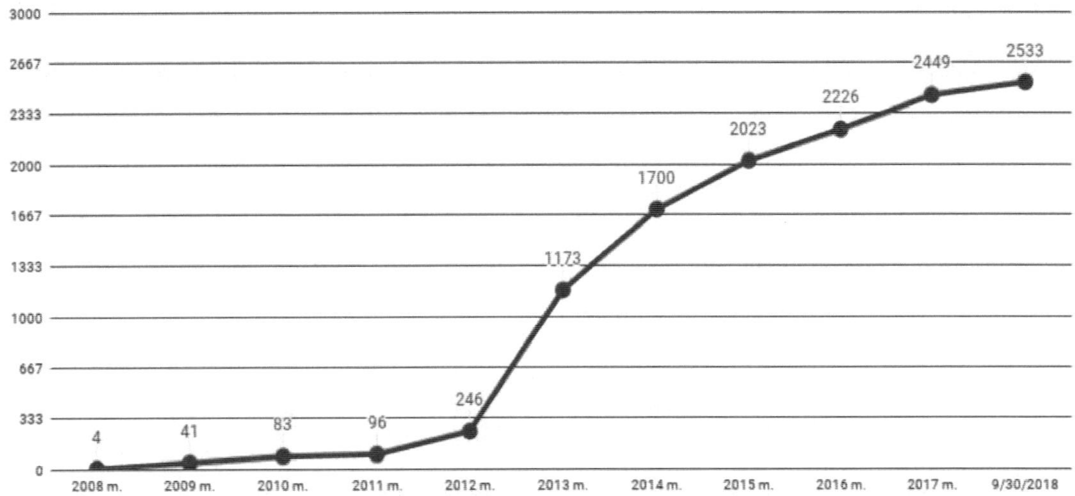

Figure 1. Number of online study modules at VMU

Until now there are 211 modules accredited as high quality blended courses on Moodle platform, and 101 courses are accredited and delivered fully online. Most of the fully online module are the ones delivered in online study programs, although there are some teachers from traditional study courses aim to modernize their modules and deliver it online.

When considering the variety of tools that are used by teachers in Moodle, the data reveal that forums and assignments have increased significantly since 2012 (see Table 1) and are much more elaborated than tools for, e.g. providing feedback or constructing mind-maps. The number of quizzes have increased significantly and it may reflect teacher's aim to engage students into the learning process.

Table 1: The use of Moodle learning activities

Tool	2012	2013	2014	2015	2016	2017	2018
Assignment	*1045*	*1465*	*2185*	*3069*	*4426*	*5824*	*6569*
Chat	215	247	226	225	258	285	290
Choice	73	83	118	148	259	351	401
Feedback	20	33	90	100	152	191	257
Forum	*1928*	*2884*	*4170*	*4772*	*5802*	*6526*	*6515*

Glossary	190	229	232	249	257	286	319
Group choice	8	38	47	78	140	199	210
HotPotatoes	748	908	933	1085	1141	1286	1268
Mindmap	12	37	53	79	155	165	134
Quiz	*922*	*1023*	*1092*	*1187*	*1568*	*1940*	*1939*
Wiki	56	73	156	187	234	252	270
Workshop	38	55	71	89	66	71	62
Database					45	66	76

To increase learners' engagement and participation in learning activities, badge system has been introduced to teachers. Even though this, conditionally innovative motivation system has not been used over modules widely, there are some teachers who have integrated badges into their courses already.

All the above discussed tools and learning activities are organised by teachers who are willing to encourage learners to become active learners, participating in interactive activities, discussing in forums, monitoring their learning process and reflecting on it. Recent data of learners' behavioural flow reveal that students tend to check the course material in "4 clicks" (see Figure 2). The significant drop-out rate was noticed after the 4th click, when 24% of students tend to quit the session.

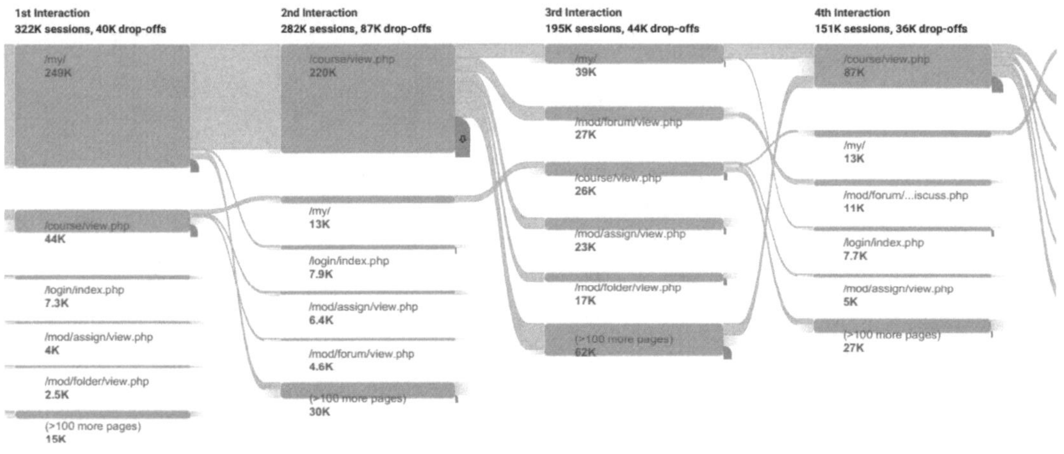

Figure 2. VMU learners' behavioural flow

The results of this research confirm the fact that online learners' behaviour has changed significantly as now part of the learners aim to receive information very quickly and in small pieces, without spending much time searching or reading additional learning resources. Teachers should be aware of that, understand these learning patterns and redesign their module curriculum based on this data. Despite the ongoing discussions about improvement of online or blended courses, in many occasions, there is a gap between knowing that a certain data about learners' behavioural patterns are significant and knowing how to make changes upon it encouraging their engagement into study process.

Conclusions

When learning in a blended or online study courses, students demonstrate their need for an easily-absorbed information in small pieces. As data has shown, learners do no spend much time analysing course content, mainly focusing on the latest topic and news forum. For us, as researchers, this data analysis allowed to distinguish some aspects that our future research should focus on, e.g. how teachers apply LA data for their course improvement, do they recognise how this data should be monitored, what data do they monitor, and how they facilitate learners' discussions? To answer these questions, qualitative research will be conducted, providing a more in-depth and experience-based data on learners' behavioural patterns and teachers course organising reflecting these patterns.

References

Anderson, A., Huttenlocher, D., Kleinberg, J., & Leskovec, J. (2014). Engaging with massive online courses. *Proceedings of the 23rd international conference on world wide web (WWW'14)*, 687-698. Retrieved from https://www.cs.cornell.edu/home/kleinber/www14-courses.pdf

Antonenko, P. D., Toy, S., & Niederhauser, D S. (2012). Using cluster analysis for data mining in educational technology research. *Educational Technology Research and Development, 60*(3),383-398. Retrieved from http://www.jstor.org/stable/41488590

Buckingham Shum, S., & Crick, R. D. (2016). Learning Analytics for 21st Century Competencies. *Journal of Learning Analytics, 3*(2), 6-21. https://doi.org/10.18608/jla.2016.32.2

Derr, K. K. (2017). Identifying Consistent Variables in a Heterogeneous Data Set: Evaluation of a Web-Based Pre-Course in Mathematics. *Electronic Journal of E-Learning, 15*(1), 82-93. Retrieved from https://eric.ed.gov/?id=EJ1140127

Douglas, K. A., Bermel, P., Alam, M. M., & Madhavan, K. (2016). Big Data Characterization of Learner Behaviour in a Highly Technical MOOC Engineering Course. *Journal of Learning Analytics, 3*(3), 170-192. https://doi.org/10.18608/jla.2016.33.9

Dutt, A., Ismail, M. A., & Herawan, T. (2017). A Systematic review on educational data mining. *IEEE Access, 5*, 15991-16005. doi: 10.1109/ACCESS.2017.2654247

Ellis, R. A., Han, F., & Pardo, A. (2017). Improving Learning Analytics – Combining Observational and Self-Report Data on Student Learning. *Journal of Educational Technology & Society, 20*(3), 158-169. Retrieved from http://www.jstor.org/stable/26196127

Gašević, D., Dawson, S., & Siemens, G. (2015). Let's not forget: Learning analytics are about learning. *Techtrends: Linking Research & Practice to Improve Learning, 59*(1), 64-71. doi:10.1007/s11528-014-0822-x

Khalil, M., Kastl, Ch., & Ebner, M. (2016). Portraying MOOCs learners: A clustering experience using learning analytics. *Proceeding of the European MOOC Stakeholder Summit 2016*, 265-278. Retrieved from https://pure.tugraz.at/portal/files/3217512/komplette.265_278_1_.pdf

Kim, D., Park, Y., Yoon, M., & Jo, I. (2016). Toward evidence-based learning analytics: Using proxy variables to improve asynchronous online discussion environments. *Internet & Higher Education, 30*, 30-43. doi: 10.1016/j.iheduc.2016.03.002

Koller, D., Ng, A., & Chen, Zh. (2013, June 3). Retention and intention in massive open online courses: In depth. Educause review [Blog post]. Retrieved from https://er.educause.edu/articles/2013/6/retention-and-intention-in-massive-open-online-courses-in-depth

Radu, I. R. (2017). Emergent technologies for learning analytics. *Elearning & Software for Education*, 509-514. doi:10.12753/2066-026X-17-157

Acknowledgments

Preliminary findings presented in this study will serve as a basis for further empirical research conducted in the four year-long scientific research project "Open Online Learning for Digital and Networked Society" (3.3-LMT-K-712-01-0189). The financial support provided by the ESF and Lithuanian Research Council under High Level R&D grant is gratefully acknowledged.

Connecting through Educational Technology
Proceedings of the European Distance and E-Learning Network 2019 Annual Conference
Bruges, 16-19 June, 2019

STUDENT PREFERENCES WITHIN A HOLISTIC BLENDED LEARNING ENVIRONMENT

Bernice Beukes, Karin Barac, Lynette Nagel, University of Pretoria, South Africa

Abstract

Extant research shows that blended learning environments are widely accepted by students mainly because of the flexibility it offers. However, there is very little research that focuses on students' preferences within a holistic blended learning environment and the contribution that a component makes to the learning of the subject matter, especially in large class settings.

The purpose of this study is to investigate students' perceptions of blended learning components in a holistic blended learning environment and whether these perceptions vary for students with different academic performance levels. A mixed method approach was used in this study performed at a residential university in South Africa and the results indicate that auditing students do have a clear preference for specific components within the environment and significant differences exist between the preferences of different academic performance levels. Such insights allow lecturers to adjust the resources and focus of the different components implemented in a blended learning environment.

Introduction

Technology enables educators to reach every student in every class every day (Bergmann & Sams, 2012). How the technology is applied within the educational context impacts on the level of reach into the student's personal learning sphere and in turn, impacts the learning of that student. The literature on blended learning initiatives is widespread. However, research on a holistic blended environment and its components is in short supply. This gap informs the twofold reach questions in this study. How do students perceive the combination of components in a holistic blended learning environment on their learning and whether differences exist between students with varying academic performance levels?

The use of blended learning has proliferated over the years as more and more educators adapt the methodology to enhance student learning. The growing body of research confirms that blended learning environments have been readily accepted by residential students (Bonk & Graham, 2012; Du, 2011; Garrison & Kanuka, 2004; Means, Toyama, Murphy, & Baki, 2013), and that students understand the benefit of having information readily available. However current literature on blended learning tends to focus on either instructional design considerations, comparisons of either purely online, blended or purely face-to-face teaching environments or investigating the effect of one blended learning component implemented in the learning environment (Dellaportas & Hassall, 2013; Dombrowski, Smith, & Wood, 2013; Massey, Poli, & Proctor, 2002; Tonge & Willett, 2012). These studies are also conducted in small to medium settings (less than 150 students) and mostly ignore large class settings (class more than 150 students).

By providing a deeper understanding of blended learning environments, this study aims to expand the literature in two ways. First the study adds a large class setting perspective; second, it presents a multifaceted view on blended learning by examining different components in a holistic blended learning environment. Educators, students and university policymakers can benefit from this research by improving the pedagogy and reaching an effective balance between components for optimum learning

A mixed method approach was used for this study. A survey was administered to third-year undergraduate auditing students at a South African residential university, where a holistic blended learning environment (five components) was implemented in a large class setting. Students had to indicate the perceived level of contribution that each component in the blended learning environment had on their learning of the subject matter on a Likert-type scale and also offer reasons as to how the component contributed to their learning in open-ended questions. The student data was then analysed overall and also by performance level groups (high, medium and low), based on an average for the formative assessments obtained to determine whether differences in preferences between these groups exist.

The results indicate clear preferences as to which components were perceived to contribute more to student learning. Two distinct groupings within the components in the holistic blended learning environment were identified. In general, students perceive activities driven by the lecturer (online videos, lecture and tutorial) to contribute more to their learning, compared to the student-driven activities (simulation and peer-review/mentoring). There were significant differences in these preferences between the performance levels and the reasons as to how the components contributed to the learning were more distinct between the groupings.

The next section of this paper presents the literature review. This is followed by the description of the research setting and methods used. Thereafter the results are presented and discussed. The paper concludes by identifying areas for future research.

Literature review

The body of knowledge on blended learning has grown incrementally over the past 15 years covering an array of topics. These include describing the transformative power of blended learning (Garrison & Kanuka, 2004), identifying best practices to implement blended learning (Alonso, López, Manrique, & Viñes, 2005; Singh, 2003) and developing a framework for the design of blended learning environments. A thematic review which identified the main themes of blended learning addressed by scholars in higher education, which was originally performed by Halverson, Graham, Spring, Drysdale, and Henrie (2014) and later expanded on by Pima, Odetayo, Iqbal, and Sedoyeka (2018). It highlights four broad themes which represent approximately 70% of literature published between 2000 and 2016 on blended learning (Pima et al., 2018). The most prominent theme identified relates to instructional design considerations (approximately 30% of literature). This stream of research, which include different perspectives on teaching models and strategies, best practices, implementation and environment matters, guidance, frameworks and the adoption of blended learning (Pima et al., 2018) indicates that blended learning is becoming a common instructional model in higher education, while educators seek to integrate the strengths of both online and face-to-face learning and blend these two modes of teaching so that they become blurred and seamless transitions between them can be achieved (Garrison & Kanuka, 2004; Pima et al., 2018).

Although research on the instructional design of blended learning appears comprehensive, little is known about students' preferences within a holistic blended learning environment. Most previous studies have either focused on broad design considerations, or have considered the effect of only one or two components in the blended learning environment (Bonk & Graham, 2012; Ellis, Goodyear, O'hara, & Prosser, 2007).

It is important to understand what is meant by learning in this context. The definition by Ambrose, Bridges, DiPietro, Lovett, and Norman (2010; p.3) that learning is "a process that leads to change, which occurs as a result of experience and increases the potential for improved and future learning" encapsulates all three core elements (behaviourism, cognitivism and constructivism) of learning theory and is applied as a benchmark for learning in this study. Within this complex construct, blended learning leans more to the constructivism paradigm in that students should construct their own knowledge through experience (Bates, 2016). Therefore, active learning activities are commonly incorporated into a blended learning environment, which includes experiential learning, problem-based learning and cooperative learning activities (Watkins & Beckem II, 2012; Donnelly, 2010). Deciding which components to incorporate into a blended learning environment vary and is largely influenced by the objective of the blended learning approach and the environment in which the learning takes place. However, it is reasonable to expect that students may have preferences for particular components within a blend and that these preferences will differ within the cohort of students in a class.

Academic performance has been widely used by scholars as a benchmark to determine the effectiveness of educational interventions (Asarta & Schmidt, 2017; Hun, Loy, & Hansaram, 2013; McKenzie & Schweitzer, 2001; Schmulian & Coetzee, 2011), and as a differentiation mechanism to determine if students with different academic performance capabilities experience a teaching intervention differently (Owston, York, & Murtha, 2013). The premise for this differentiation is that students with different capability levels approach their studies differently and also learn differently (Honicke & Broadbent, 2016). Asarta and Schmidt (2017) explained that when students were divided into high, medium or low performing groups, based on their grade point average (GPA), the low performance group achieved higher performance in the traditional approach, compared to the blended learning approach, while the medium group did not indicate any significant difference in their final grades. Sanford

(2017) found similar results with low achieving students but contradicts the result on medium and high achieving students, stating that all students benefit more from face-to-face formats. Owston et al. (2013) considered satisfaction, convenience, engagement and learning in a blended format based on achievement, and their results are in line with that of Asarta and Schmidt (2017). They found that high achieving students were more satisfied with the blended format. These students also experienced it as more convenient, felt more engaged and believed that they understood key concepts better with the blended format (Asarta & Schmidt, 2017). The aforementioned studies offer insights into students' preferences, but since these studies are comparisons between face-to-face and online learning, it does not take cognisance of student preferences within a holistic blended learning environment, a notion pointing towards the relevance of our study.

Research setting and methods

The study was conducted at a South African university with scheduled weekly contact sessions between students and lecturers. The student cohort is culturally diverse, with approximately a third English first language speakers, a third Afrikaans first language speakers and a third indigenous African languages speakers.

The study focuses on an auditing module presented to students in their third year (final year) of specialised accounting undergraduate degree programming. Since 2015, this module was presented in a blended learning environment which was adjusted in 2016 to a holistic blend with a more coherent integration of the different components. The components implemented in the blended learning environment were (a) a flipped classroom (online videos and lectures), (b) a weekly tutorial, (c) an online simulation and (d) finally peer-mentoring and peer feedback.

For the *flipped classroom*, theoretical videos (referred to as online videos) explaining the basic concepts were recorded and made available on Bb. Students had to watch the videos as preparation for the lecture. During the lecture, the information in the video was placed in context and elaborated upon if necessary, whilst also adding more active learning activities during the session.

The *tutorials* required students to prepare case study questions at home and then bring the attempted solution to the tutorial for discussion. For tutorials, students were divided into six smaller groups and the focus of the discussion was on how students could improve the quality of their work by demonstrating appropriate examination techniques.

The *simulation* (called AuditSIM) provided students with an opportunity to practice theoretical auditing concepts in a practical situation, thus mirroring a real audit client. Students had to access client information through Bb and perform specific tasks in a group in a wiki throughout the year.

For the *peer feedback* (called TUTBuddy), students had to complete a case study question and then exchange their attempted solution with another group member (the same groups used in the simulation were used for the peer feedback). The group member then had to review the attempted solution and provide comments with regard to examination technique displayed and presentation. After completion, students had to complete an online logbook reflecting on the experience. With the *peer-mentoring* (called BuddyM), students in their third year of undergraduate study had to mentor a second-year student by sharing experiences and giving advice. A minimum of 14 hours had to be spent with the mentee and again students had to record their engagement by completing an online logbook.

Method and data collection

This study followed a mixed method research approach. A custom-developed survey instrument was used to collect both quantitative and qualitative data. The instrument had to be custom-developed, as a suitable instrument to address the research question of the study could not be identified. In order to expedite completion of the survey, the first part (part A) of the survey (quantitative data) was administered online, using Qualtrics (online survey software). The second part (part B) of the survey was open-ended questions and was distributed manually during the last contact session for the year. The quantitative data were subsequently prepared for statistical analysis and analysed using the Statistical Package for Social Sciences (SPSS), while the qualitative data were captured and analysed using AtlasTi.

Part A of the survey instrument consisted of eight demographical and two questions with sub-questions on the blended learning components. A 5-point Likert scale ranging from 1 – *not at all contributing* to 5 – *contributing a great deal* was used to determine how students perceived each of the components contributed to their learning of the subject matter. In part B of the survey, students were requested to comment on how each component in the blended learning environment contributed to their mastering of the subject matter.

The population of this study was the students registered for the B Com Accounting Sciences degree and who enrolled for the third-year module at the university where the study was performed in 2016. All these students were exposed to the holistic blended learning environment in the module and in 2016 there were 651 students enrolled for the module.

The final sample size for the research was 461 responses. Table 1 presents a profile of the sample. An overall response rate of 71% was obtained. The response rate is high for an online questionnaire, as online surveys typically have lower response rates (Cook, Heath, & Thompson, 2000). The gender distribution mirrors the gender distribution of the population. For both male and female respondents, a 2.5% - 3% difference was found. Male respondents in the sample were slightly underrepresented (38.2% to the population of 41%), while female respondents were slightly over-represented (61.6% to the population of 59%). Taking into account the high response rate of 71%, as well as the gender distribution of the respondents, the sample appears to be representative of the population.

Table 1: Overall response rate

	Total			
	Population		Sample	
	Total	%	Total	%
Response rate	651	100%	461	71%
Males	267	41.0%	176	38.2%
Females	384	59.0%	284	61.6%
Missing data (gender not indicated)			1	0.2%

Results

In answering the twofold research question (How students perceived the contribution of the components in a holistic blended learning environment on their learning and differences between academic performance levels), descriptive and inferential statistics analysis was performed on part A of the survey. External validity was achieved since the study was performed in a real-life setting and a representative sample was obtained.

The mean scores for the six component questions were calculated and ranked and presented in Table 2.

Table 2: Perception of the level of contribution of blended learning components on respondents' learning

Reference	Question	Mean (out of a possible 5)
Tutorials	Attending the weekly tutorials	4.08
Online videos	The theory videos explaining the basic concepts	3.97
Lectures	Attending the weekly formal lectures	3.48
TUTBuddy	Engaging with my TUT Buddy group on the Buddy questions	2.85
AuditSIM	Completing the tasks on the AuditSim	2.79
BuddyM	Engaging with my BuddyM mentee	2.33

Table 2 shows that the first three components displayed higher mean scores (above 3.0) compared to the latter three (means below 3.0). The mean scores suggested that the tutorial appears to be the blended learning component that contributed highly to the learning of the subject matter, obtaining the highest value (4.08). It is followed by the online videos (3.97) and formal lectures (3.48) which are regarded as contributing moderately to the learning (between 3.0 and 3.9) of the subject matter. The other three blended learning components have a mean score of below 3, indicating that respondents perceive these components to contribute in a limited way to the learning of the subject matter.

The responses were divided into three performance level groups. Academic performance for this study was based on the year mark obtained in the module which was presented as a year module. This year mark was calculated by taking both the formative assessments (85% contribution to mark) completed during the year and other activities such as the simulation, tutorial attendance, Buddy and class activities (15% contribution to mark) into consideration.

Students indicated their own year mark on the anonymous survey. The questionnaire provided five intervals for the year mark, 1 – *below 50%*, 2 – *50% – 57%*, 3 – *58% – 63%*, 4 – *64% – 69%* and 5 – *70% and above*. These intervals divided the population into approximately five equal sized groups. In order to reduce the number of groups, responses were redistributed as *low* (<57%), *medium* (58% – 69%) and *high* (>70%) performing students for the analysis. This was based on an analysis showing the year marks were inflated with marks attributed to participation in class activities, tutorial attendance and Buddy activities. When solely based on formative assessments, the marks would be 7% –10% lower. Table 3 sets out the details of the adjusted groups and the gender distribution within these performance level groups.

Table 3: Distribution of respondents' year mark for the module in 2016, after redistribution

Performance group	Interval	Population		Respondents		Male* respondents		Female* respondents	
		Total	%	Total	%	Total	%	Total	%
High	>70%	118	18%	108	24%	38	35%	70	65%
Medium	58% – 69%	296	46%	212	46%	73	35%	138	65%
Low	<57%	237	36%	139	30%	64	46%	75	54%
Missing data				2		1		2	
Total		651	100%	461	100%	176		285	

* Percentage of the respondents per category: high, medium and low

The blended learning components were analysed to determine whether students with different academic performance levels perceived the contribution of the components to their learning differently. The results are presented in Table 4 and Figure 1.

Table 4: Mean scores for learning per performance group and blended learning component

	Tutorial		Video		Lecture		TUT Buddy		AuditSIM		BuddyM	
	Mean	SD#	Mean	SD	Mean	SD	Mean	SD	Mean	SD	Mean	SD
High$	4.19	1.05	4.10	0.99	3.34	1.11	2.59	1.16	2.46	1.14	2.17	1.11
Medium$	4.16	1.06	3.99	1.07	3.51	1.21	2.88	1.08	2.66	1.15	2.33	1.12
Low$	3.89	1.15	3.83	1.14	3.52	1.20	3.01	1.09	3.24	1.15	2.46	1.13

\# Standard deviation
$ Performance group

In Figure 1, the difference in perceptions between respondents in different performance groups is portrayed graphically making the differences more visible.

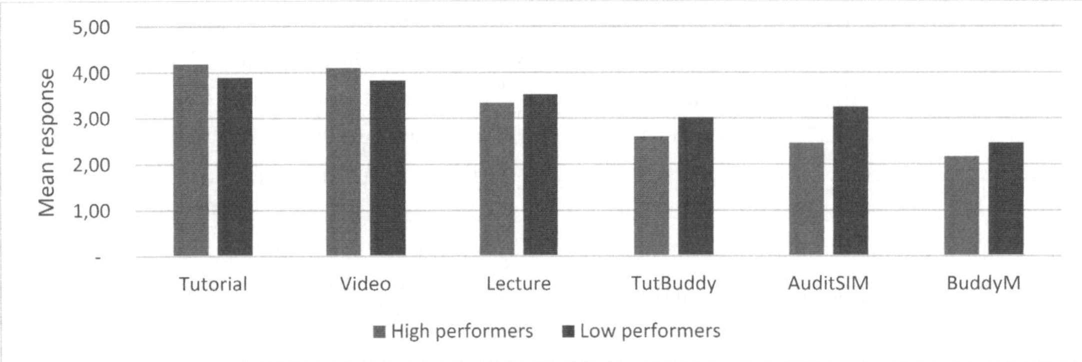

Figure 1. Mean scores for the perception of learning per high and low performance group for each blended learning component

The mean scores of the medium performing respondents followed a consistent pattern between the high and low performing respondents and will therefore not be addressed specifically. The high performing respondents scored their perception of the learning value of tutorials and videos higher compared to the low performing group. This pattern was reversed in the perception of learning in lectures, TUT Buddy, AuditSIM and BuddyM, with the high performers rating those components lower than the low performers. According to the high performers, the tutorial (mean score of 4.19) and videos (mean score of 4.10) contributed highly to their learning, while the formal lectures (mean score of 3.34) contributed moderately. The TUT Buddy, AuditSIM and BuddyM components only had a limited contribution (mean scores of 2.59, 2.46 and 2.17 respectively) to their learning of the subject matter.

Low performing respondents perceived most of the blended learning components to contribute moderately (mean scores between 3.0 and 4.0) to their learning of the subject matter, except for the BuddyM (mean score of 2.46) of which they perceived limited contribution to their learning.

Observing the trends within the groups indicate that the higher the grades, the more the respondents valued the tutorials and videos, and the lower the grades, the more they valued the lectures, TUT Buddy, AuditSIM and BuddyM.

The Kruskal-Wallis test was conducted to determine if statistically significant differences exist between the three performance groups with regard to the blended learning components. The test was used due to the ordinal nature of the data and the results are presented in Table 5.

Table 5: Kruskal-Wallis test results

	Test Statistics [a,b]					
	Videos	Lectures	Tutorials	AuditSIM	BuddyM	TUT Buddy
Chi-Square	3.371	1.876	6.896	28.985	4.919	7.249
df	2	2	2	2	2	2
Asymp. Sig.	Not significant (p = 0.185)	Not significant (p = 0.391)	5% (p = 0.032)	1% (p = 0.000)	10% (p = 0.085)	5% (p = 0.027)

a Kruskal-Wallis Test
b Grouping Variable: year mark – high, medium and low performance groups

The results of Table 5 indicate that statistically significant differences were identified between performance levels. There is a strong statistically significant difference, with regard to the AuditSIM between performance groups ($p = 0.000$) and a statistically significant difference exists at the 5% level of significance for attending the weekly tutorials ($p = 0.032$) and engaging with the TUT Buddy ($p = 0.027$).

Discussion

In this section, students' comments are included to deepen the understanding of how the components in the holistic blended learning environment influenced their learning. The study shows students perceived the video, lecture, and tutorial components of blended learning to contribute more to their learning than the other components. They preferred lecturer driven components where the lecturer controls the format and pace of these activities. The AuditSIM and two Buddy components, the more student-driven components that require more active student participation and cooperation with peers, were perceived as less favourable. These components also aimed at developing additional skills (communication, computer and co-operation) that employers require graduates to possess at entry level into the workplace. This finding suggests that students' perceptions of learning are short term orientated (to pass the module), which does not consider their development in generic skills. Based on the mean scores, this tendency was found for high performing respondents who perceived the lecturer driven activities (flipped classroom and tutorial) to contribute more to their learning, whilst the low performing respondents, with the exception of BuddyM, found relatively more value from both the lecturer and student-driven activities than the higher performing students.

The component that all respondents perceived as highly contributing to their learning was the tutorials. Respondents confirmed this preference in the open-ended question, as illustrated by comments "learned a lot" or "I gained the most here" were made by them. Even though research cautions that tutorials should not be the only mode of teaching (Sweeney, O'donoghue, & Whitehead, 2004), Zhou and Chua (2016) have found in a similar context, that students preferred tutorials above other blended learning interventions. In our study, the number of students per tutorial group (between 60 and 100) was much higher than the norm of one-to-one or one-to-few suggested in the literature (Frey & Reigeluth, 1986; Sweeney et al., 2004), and therefore not optimal and respondents still perceived tutorials as contributing highly to their learning. They still felt comfortable in a smaller and more informal setting, which allows for frequent questioning (Gordon, 2009). Between the three lecturer-driven components, the tutorial is the element that requires most active participation from students. As this is the preferred element in the holistic blend, this finding is in line with that of Yoder and Hochevar (2005), that active learning activities could improve understanding and performance.

Based on the results, the second and third highest scoring components in the model were also part of the flipped classroom (videos and lecturing) which were perceived as moderately contributing to respondents' learning. The positive view of the flipped classroom agrees with Butt (2014), who viewed the concept from an Australian perspective, with actuarial students.

Based on mean scores, theoretical videos are in the second position of the different blended learning components. Comments of respondents indicated that they value the fact that videos could be viewed repeatedly, in their own time and that this saved time to gauge an overview of the topics. If therefore appears respondents made use of theoretical videos as and when the need arises, and they developed in more self-regulated learners with the guidance provided in the videos. Respondents perception that the videos contributed more to their learning, is in line with previous research (Gilboy, Heinerichs, & Pazzaglia, 2015; Little, 2015).

According to Crook and Schofield (2017), it is easy to capture a lecture in digital format and the resultant videos allow for the additional benefits of going back, recapping, note taking and revision. Respondents' perception of a moderate contribution of these components towards their learning could be because videos were seen as an integral part of the lecture. This possibility supports the notion by Gorissen, van Bruggen, and Jochems (2012) that students prefer accompanying online content with their lectures. A factor that could have influenced respondents' perception regarding videos explaining theoretical concepts is their previous exposure to it during their second year in the accounting module.

When comparing the perceptions of the components in the blended learning environment per performance group, more specific differences emerge. With regard to the contribution made for learning, high performing respondents scored the tutorial sessions and videos higher than the low performing respondents, but for the other components, the low performing respondents scored these components higher than the high performers (refer to Table 4 and Figure 1). This difference for the tutorials proved to be statistically significant. A possible explanation is a difference in approach to their studies between the groups. The tutorial requires prior preparation and participation during the session to be effective, and the literature confirms that high performing students are more self-directed learners and willing to work on their own (Owston et al., 2013). This finding is also in line with the tutorial attendance for the population (the class at large), based on weekly attendance registers. The low performing group averaged at 63% attendance, the medium performing group at 78% and the high performing group at 87% attendance. This confirms the high performing respondents' perception that the tutorial sessions contribute to a larger extent to their learning of the subject matter, as compared to their low performing counterparts. This finding, where higher performing students perceived tutorials to highly contribute to their learning, is in line with conclusions reached by Gordon (2009).

In relation to learning, the high performing respondents scored the videos higher, but the lectures lower, compared to the low performing respondents. This indicates that high performing respondents perceived videos explaining the concepts as contributing more to their learning, while this is not the case with formal lectures. The deduction could be made that, as mentioned previously, high performing respondents are self-directed learners who can work on their own (Owston et al., 2013), and have become less dependent on lectures. The fact that the technology element (videos) was scored higher compared to the lectures, confirms the tendency that preference for a specific singular mode of instruction (face-to-face only) is declining, and that respondents are becoming more comfortable with alternative modes of instruction, but with available support, a notion supported by the literature (Dziuban & Moskal, 2011; Kelly, Ponton, & Rovai, 2007).

The three student-driven components were perceived to contribute moderately to the learning of the low performing respondents but were perceived as limited in contribution for the high performing respondents. Statistically significant differences were identified between the three performance groups with regard to the AuditSIM and the TUT Buddy component. Even though respondents did not perceive these components to contribute highly to their learning of the subject matter, they did realise the benefits that these components could offer in "giving a practical view of how it [an audit] is done" and working in groups and learning from peers. This agrees with the literature on cooperative learning that even though cooperative learning does not impact on students' performance, students are generally positive about the mode of learning (Ballantine & McCourt Larres, 2009; Johnson, Johnson, & Smith, 2014; Ravenscroft, Buckless, & Hassall, 1999). The deduction could thus be made that, regardless of their performance, low performing respondents still perceived the student-driven components to contribute moderately to their learning. It is also important to recognise that because the low performing respondents also rated the tutorials and videos to contribute more to their learning, they also prefer the blended learning environment, which is in contrast with conclusions reached by Asarta and Schmidt (2017) and Sanford (2017).

Conclusion

This study sets out to determine how students perceived the contribution of certain components in a blended learning environment on their learning and whether these differed based on academic performance levels. The results indicate that respondents displayed a clear preference for specific components within a blended learning environment and they perceived tutorials to contribute most to their learning of the subject matter.

Significant differences were noted between the different performance groups, and these could be explained because high performing students are more self-directed learners, whilst low performing students scored the student-driven activities higher preferred the social activities more than the high performing counterparts.

The implications of the study are that lecturers can now tailor the environment to suit both high and low performing students and that more autonomy can be given to high performing students, allowing more time to focus on support for low performing students during the contact sessions. Knowing differences exist, lecturers could plan time and resources to allocate to the different blended learning components better, when developing a holistic blended learning environment.

As with any study, there are limitations. This study was performed in a holistic blended learning environment, which might not always be possible to replicate, but the highlights on the individual components and the order of the preferences should make it possible to consider in any blended learning environment.

This study suggests that a holistic blended learning environment with a balance between lecture driven and student-driven activities covers the needs of high and low performing students. Further research could determine the ideal balance which could guide university policymakers and educators. Future research can repeat the investigation of a holistic blended learning environment but use different variables. For example, the level of technology adoption or comparing preferences between undergraduate and postgraduate modules, in order to determine whether students' maturity could influence the preferences.

References

Alonso, F., López, G., Manrique, D., & Viñes, J. M. (2005). An instructional model for web-based e-learning education with a blended learning process approach. *British Journal of Educational Technology, 36*(2), 217–235.

Ambrose, S. A., Bridges, M. W., DiPietro, M., Lovett, M. C., & Norman, M. K. (2010). *How learning works: Seven research-based principles for smart teaching.* John Wiley & Sons.

Asarta, C. J., & Schmidt, J. R. (2017). Comparing student performance in blended and traditional courses: Does prior academic achievement matter? *The Internet and Higher Education, 32*, 29–38. https://doi.org/10.1016/j.iheduc.2016.08.002

Ballantine, J., & McCourt Larres, P. (2009). Accounting undergraduates' perceptions of cooperative learning as a model for enhancing their interpersonal and communication skills to interface successfully with professional accountancy education and training. *Accounting Education: An International Journal, 18*(4–5), 387–402.

Bates, T. (2016). *Teaching in a digital age.* Creative commons – BY-NC. Retrieved from https://www.tonybates.ca/teaching-in-a-digital-age/

Bergmann, J., & Sams, A. (2012). *Flip your classroom: Reach every student in every class every day.* International Society for Technology in Education.

Bonk, C. J., & Graham, C. R. (2012). *The handbook of blended learning: Global perspectives, local designs.* John Wiley & Sons.

Butt, A. (2014). Student views on the use of a flipped classroom approach: Evidence from Australia. *Business Education & Accreditation, 6*(1), 33–43.

Cook, C., Heath, F., & Thompson, R. L. (2000). A meta-analysis of response rates in web-or internet-based surveys. *Educational and Psychological Measurement, 60*(6), 821–836.

Crook, C., & Schofield, L. (2017). The video lecture. *The Internet and Higher Education, 34*, 56–64.

Dellaportas, S., & Hassall, T. (2013). Experiential learning in accounting education: A prison visit. *The British Accounting Review, 45*(1), 24–36. https://doi.org/10.1016/j.bar.2012.12.005

Dombrowski, R. F., Smith, K. J., & Wood, B. G. (2013). Bridging the education-practice divide: The Salisbury University auditing internship program. *Journal of Accounting Education, 31*(1), 84–106. https://doi.org/10.1016/j.jaccedu.2012.12.003

Donnelly, R. (2010). Harmonizing technology with interaction in blended problem-based learning. *Computers and Education, 54*(2), 350–359.

Du, C. (2011). A comparison of traditional and blended learning in introductory principles of accounting course. *American Journal of Business Education (AJBE), 4*(9), 1–10.

Dziuban, C., & Moskal, P. (2011). A course is a course is a course: Factor invariance in student evaluation of online, blended and face-to-face learning environments. *The Internet and Higher Education, 14*(4), 236–241. https://doi.org/10.1016/j.iheduc.2011.05.003

Ellis, R. A., Goodyear, P., O'hara, A., & Prosser, M. (2007). The University Student Experience of Face-to-Face and Online Discussions: Coherence, Reflection and Meaning. *ALT-J: Research in Learning Technology, 15*(1), 83–97.

Frey, L. A., & Reigeluth, C. M. (1986). Instructional Models for Tutoring: A Review. *Journal of Instructional Development, 9*(1), 2–8.

Garrison, D. R., & Kanuka, H. (2004). Blended learning: Uncovering its transformative potential in higher education. *The Internet and Higher Education, 7*(2), 95–105.

Gilboy, M. B., Heinerichs, S., & Pazzaglia, G. (2015). Enhancing Student Engagement Using the Flipped Classroom. *Journal of Nutrition Education and Behavior, 47*(1), 109–114. https://doi.org/10.1016/j.jneb.2014.08.008

Gordon, E. E. (2009). 5 Ways to Improve Tutoring Programs. *The Phi Delta Kappan, 90*(6), 440–445.

Gorissen, P., van Bruggen, J., & Jochems, W. (2012). Students and recorded lectures: survey on current use and demands for higher education. *Research in Learning Technology, 20*(3), 17299. https://doi.org/10.3402/rlt.v20i0.17299

Halverson, L. R., Graham, C. R., Spring, K. J., Drysdale, J. S., & Henrie, C. R. (2014). A thematic analysis of the most highly cited scholarship in the first decade of blended learning research. *The Internet and Higher Education, 20*(2), 20–34.

Honicke, T., & Broadbent, J. (2016). The influence of academic self-efficacy on academic performance: A systematic review. *Educational Research Review, 17*(Supplement C), 63–84. https://doi.org/10.1016/j.edurev.2015.11.002

Hun, T. L., Loy, C. K., & Hansaram, R. M. S. K. (2013). A Study on Predicting Undergraduate's Improvement of Academic Performances based on their Characteristics of Learning and Approaches at a Private Higher Educational Institution. *Procedia – Social and Behavioral Sciences, 93*(Supplement C), 1957–1965. https://doi.org/10.1016/j.sbspro.2013.10.148

Johnson, D. W., Johnson, R. T., & Smith, K. A. (2014). Cooperative learning: Improving university instruction by basing practice on validated theory. *Journal on Excellence in University Teaching, 25*(4), 1–26.

Kelly, H. F., Ponton, M. K., & Rovai, A. P. (2007). A comparison of student evaluations of teaching between online and face-to-face courses. *The Internet and Higher Education, 10*(2), 89–101. https://doi.org/10.1016/j.iheduc.2007.02.001

Little, C. (2015). The flipped classroom in further education: literature review and case study. *Research in Post-Compulsory Education, 20*(3), 265–279.

Massey, D. W., Poli, P., & Proctor, R. (2002). *The development and evaluation of a team-based audit simulation in the introductory auditing course.* Digitalcommons Fairfield University.

McKenzie, K., & Schweitzer, R. (2001). Who Succeeds at University? Factors predicting academic performance in first year Australian university students. *Higher Education Research & Development, 20*(1), 21–33. https://doi.org/10.1080/07924360120043621

Means, B., Toyama, Y., Murphy, R., & Baki, M. (2013). The effectiveness of online and blended learning: A meta-analysis of the empirical literature. *Teachers College Record, 115*(3), 1–47.

Owston, R., York, D., & Murtha, S. (2013). Student perceptions and achievement in a university blended learning strategic initiative. *The Internet and Higher Education, 18*(3), 38–46.

Pima, J. M., Odetayo, M., Iqbal, R., & Sedoyeka, E. (2018). A Thematic Review of Blended Learning in Higher Education. *International Journal of Mobile and Blended Learning (IJMBL), 10*(1), 1–11.

Ravenscroft, S. P., Buckless, F. A., & Hassall, T. (1999). Cooperative learning-a literature guide. *Accounting Education, 8*(2), 163–176.

Sanford, D. (2017). Course format and learning: The moderating role of overall academic performance. *The International Journal of Management Education, 15*(3), 490–500. https://doi.org/10.1016/j.ijme.2017.08.003

Schmulian, A., & Coetzee, S. A. (2011). Class absenteeism: Reasons for non-attendance and the effect on academic performance. *Accounting Research Journal, 24*(2), 178–194.

Singh, H. (2003). Building effective blended learning programs. *Educational Technology-Saddle Brook Then Englewood Cliffs NJ-, 43*(6), 51–54.

Sweeney, J., O'donoghue, T., & Whitehead, C. (2004). Traditional face-to-face and web-based tutorials: a study of university students' perspectives on the roles of tutorial participants. *Teaching in Higher Education, 9*(3), 311–323.

Tonge, R., & Willett, C. (2012). An audit learning experience: A pilot project through cooperation with a third sector organization. *Accounting Education, 21*(2), 171–185.

Watkins, M., & Beckem II, J. M. (2012). Bringing life to learning: immersive experiential learning simulations for online and blended courses. *Journal of Asynchronous Learning Networks, 16*(5), 61–71. Retrieved from https://olj.onlinelearningconsortium.org/index.php/olj/article/view/287

Yoder, J. D., & Hochevar, C. M. (2005). Encouraging active learning can improve students' performance on examinations. *Teaching of Psychology, 32*(2), 91–95.

Zhou, M., & Chua, B. L. (2016). Using Blended Learning Design to Enhance Learning Experience in Teacher Education. *International Journal on E-Learning, 15*(1), 121–140.

Connecting through Educational Technology
Proceedings of the European Distance and E-Learning Network 2019 Annual Conference
Bruges, 16-19 June, 2019

EFFECTS OF ONLINE COURSE LOAD ON DEGREE COMPLETION, TRANSFER, AND DROPOUT AMONG COMMUNITY COLLEGE STUDENTS OF THE STATE UNIVERSITY OF NEW YORK

Peter Shea, University at Albany, State University of New York, Temi Bidjerano, Furman University, United States of America

Abstract

Past research suggests that some students are at risk of lower levels of academic performance when studying online compared to students who take coursework only in the classroom. Community college students appear to be among those that struggle in online settings. In this paper, we hypothesize that online course load may influence outcomes for such students, especially those at risk for lower levels of degree attainment. To examine this, we conducted a state-wide study using data from the 30 community colleges (n = 45,557) of the State University of New York, to understand online course-load effects on degree completion, transfer, and dropout. We conclude that when controlling for covariates known to impact degree completion, community college students who successfully complete online courses nearly double their chances (odds ratio = 1.72) of earning a degree or transferring to a 4-year college. However, racial minorities had reduced outcomes and additional research is warranted.

Post-secondary completion is a significant predictor of a host of individual and societal benefits. Online education has increased access to post-secondary credentials for millions of people. (Allen & Siemen, 2016). Community colleges enrol a higher proportion of online students than other institution types (NCES, 2017). However, concerns exist about outcomes for community college students who take online coursework, especially the effect of higher online course loads. The next section briefly summarizes relevant literature reflecting those concerns.

Review of Related Research

While results are not unanimous (e.g. Wladis, Conway, & Hachey, 2016), several large-scale studies clearly identify community college students to be at risk of significantly worse outcomes online than in face-to-face settings. One consistent finding is that online course load has a negative influence on academic performance. For example, in large, state-wide studies in both Virginia and Washington students who took a higher proportion of credits online were less likely to obtain a degree or transfer to a four-year institution than students who took lower proportions of online credits (Jaggars, Edgecombe, & Stacey, 2013). Further, among the institutions studied in the PAR framework (James, Swan, & Daston, 2016) odds ratio analysis indicated that students mixing online and face-to-face courses or taking only face-to-face courses had up to 1.6 times greater odds of being retained than fully online students. Shea and Bidjerano (2017) found similar results for students in New York State. The odds of degree completion were about 1.5 times greater for SUNY students with a combination of online and traditional courses compared to students with classroom courses only. However, the odds of degree attainment were about 2 to 3 times lower for fully online students relative to students with a mix of online and classroom courses. Taking online courses results appears to result in diminishing returns regarding the attainment of a college degree indicating a curvilinear relationship (Shea & Bidjerano, 2018). We know that taking some courses online assists students toward the beneficial goal of degree attainment, however, prior research has indicated that taking online courses exclusively results in lower levels of retention across major studies in which this outcome is assessed. However, prior research has not included methodology that might account for the curvilinear relationship indicative of diminishing returns for increased online course loads. Specifically, previous research has not looked at the effects of course completion rates in online and classroom settings.

Purpose and Research Questions

This current study seeks to re-investigate the "tipping point" at which the proportion of online course enrolment leads to impaired degree completion using different analytic approaches. Specifically, this paper investigates the research questions below.

- RQ1: Using survival analysis methods, is there a threshold for online course enrolment intensity that jeopardizes one's prospects for successful completion of a college degree and increase risk of dropout when controlling for course completion rates?
- RQ2: Does the intensity of online coursework modify the effect of traditional predictors of degree completion such as remedial education, GPA, minority status etc. when controlling for course completion rates?

The purpose of the study was to examine the effect of intensity of online coursework at a community college level on the probability of experiencing one of three outcomes: degree completion, transfer to a 4-year institution, and dropout. We have reasons to believe that the relation between online education and indicators of college success is far more complex to be adequately captured by conventional linear statistical models (Shea & Bidjerano, 2018; Jaggars & Xu, 2010; Xu & Jaggars, 2011; 2013). Previously we concluded that participation in online coursework has a non-linear effect on the odds of degree, transfer, and dropout at any time of a student career. We asked also what specific factors explain the intricate relationships between online coursework and prospects for attaining any of the three outcomes. To extend our prior investigation, in this study we use competing-risk discrete time-event history analysis, also known as survival analysis. This method offers several advantages over traditional regression analysis. A unique feature of survival analysis is in its capacity to model both the likelihood of an outcome and the timing of the outcome (Singer & Willett, 2003) by accounting for cases for which the outcome is missing or unknown (also called censoring) thus allowing precise estimates of not only when an outcome comes about but also of how it comes about. It is a flexible longitudinal method showing how processes may unfold contingent upon characteristics that remain constant and /or may change with time; that is, the method allows the incorporation of predictors of outcomes with fixed values as well as of variables that change values over time. In the context of a competing-risk discrete model, time is conceived as discrete (as opposed to continuous) and the propensity for multiple mutually exclusive outcomes is studied simultaneously. In essence, modelling revolves around estimating (a) the probability of each outcome occurring at a given point in time (known as risk or hazard) provided that the alternative outcomes have not occurred at a previous time and (b) the change in the risk for the outcome as a function of one or more predictors.

Method

Sample

The study uses institutional data on first-time community college students enrolled in a degree program in one of the 30 community colleges part of the SUNY system. The dataset contained archival program and course enrolment records of all students (n = 45,744) who were enrolled in a 2-year degree granting institution from Fall 2012 to Fall 2017. The vast majority of the students in the sample (91.52%) were between 16 and 25 years old with less than 3% being older than 45.

Measures

Time and Outcome Variables. We considered three competing risks: departure from a 2-year institution for academic or other reasons (dropout); attainment of an educational credential; and transfer to a four-year institution. Transfer and degree attainment were combined in one outcome variable due to some methodological considerations. In the context of competing risk survival analysis, an individual is at risk for multiple events at any given time but can experience only one of the series of events. One event cancels the risk for another event. A sizable portion of sample members had completed a degree and immediately transferred to a 4-year institution or earned their 2-year degree during their transfer semester. Had we coded these students as "degree completers" as opposed of "transfers", we would have had underestimated the hazard (probability) of transfer.

The available data encompassed the enrolment histories of the sample members over the course of 21 consecutive semesters including major (spring and fall) and interim (winter and summer) terms. The last four semesters of data were used in a limited way – only as a means of identifying the subset of students who dropped out or departed (described below). The remaining 17 semesters were collapsed. This resulted in nine discrete time intervals each comprised of two consecutive semesters.

In each observation period, a student faces two distinct outcomes: the desirable outcome of graduation from their two-year institution or transfer to a 4-year one or the negative outcome of departure or dropout from a two-year institution. Dropout/departure functions as a competing risk to graduation or transfer and vice versa. The combined outcome degree or transfer was defined as completion of a degree without evidence of subsequent return or transfer to a four-year baccalaureate program, whichever occurred first.

Independent Variable and Covariates. The majority of students in these community colleges mixed online and classroom study. The focal variable of interest was exposure to online coursework, operationalized as online course load or the proportion of online credits attempted relative to all credits attempted in a given time interval. We controlled for both time-dependent and time-independent covariates. These included a set of conventional predictors of college success such as age, gender, race/ethnicity indicators (Caucasian, Asian, African-American, Hispanic, and other race), international student status, level of academic preparation (whether the student qualified for remedial coursework at time of entry), student determination (whether the student had a goal to complete a degree or transfer to a four-year institution) and type of program (Humanities, STEM or other) at exit. Age was defined as the age in 2012. Except for age, all time-independent variables were categorical.

In the case of time-dependent covariates, the value of the variable changes from one-time period to the next and the hazard of an event at a given time depends on the value of the covariate at that time. Time-varying covariates were selected based on both theoretical and empirical grounds; the set included: number of credits earned as recorded at the end of each time interval, student status (whether the student was full-time in both terms in a time interval), end-of time-interval grade point average (GPA) and financial aid status indicators (whether a student was a federal Pell grant recipient or a New York State grant (TAP) recipient at a time).

Results

The unique risk (probability) associated with an outcome is also the proportion of students who experienced that particular outcome at a given time. As seen, the probability for a degree and/or transfer is low at first then it peaks initially during the fourth time interval. The hazard for dropout remains relatively constant across time. The plots suggest also that events of occur mostly in the spring and summer terms. The corresponding cumulative functions are profiled in Figure 1.

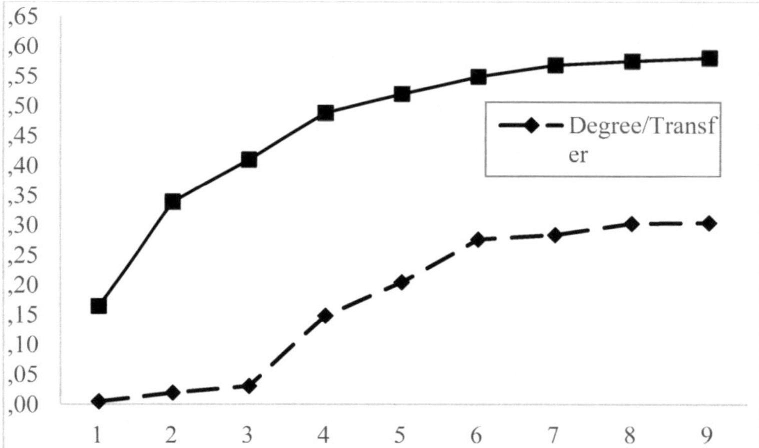

Figure 1. Cumulative hazard probability by time interval

The cumulative hazard represents event rates or the cumulative proportions of students with an event up to a particular time interval. The cumulative hazard probability of degree/ transfer increases slowly in the first terms when the hazard is low, then it increases steadily. With respect to departure/ dropout, the probability increases more rapidly in the first 2 years of college. In both cases, there is little change in the cumulative hazard probabilities after the third year in college. The median time-to-transfer or degree is 3 years, whereas the median time-to-dropout or departure was found to be 2 years. Overall, by the end of the second year of college, 50% of the sample members had experienced one outcome or another.

The Effect of Semester Online Course Load

The addition of course load with its square term as a predictor resulted in substantial improvement in model fit. Students who opt for more online courses in any given time have a higher conditional probability of degree or transfer but, in this model, benefits wear off at higher levels of online course intensity (see Figure 2).

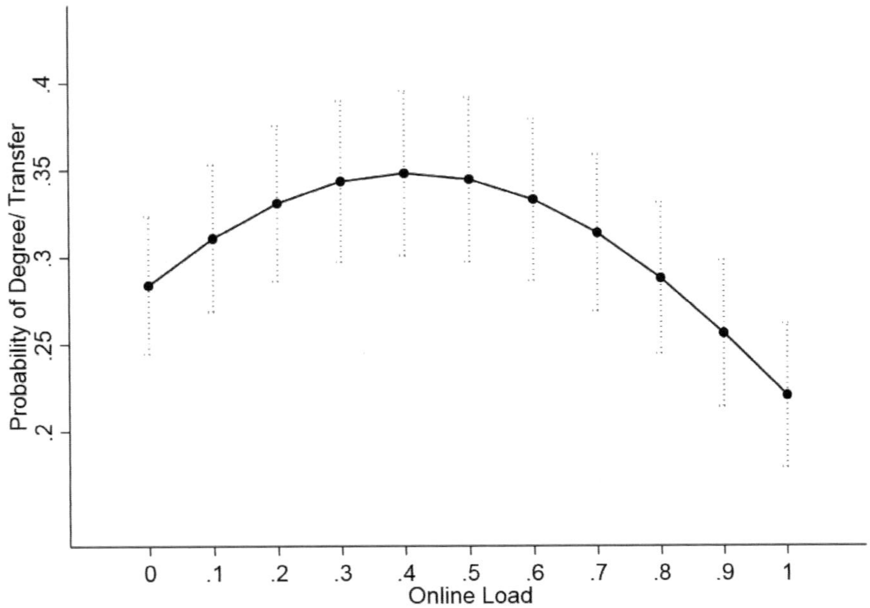

Figure 2. Probability of degree/ transfer at Time 4 by online load

Conversely, increasing levels of online load decreases the hazard of dropping out in any given term to a point at which each additional credit is likely to result in increased risk for dropping out (see Figure 3).

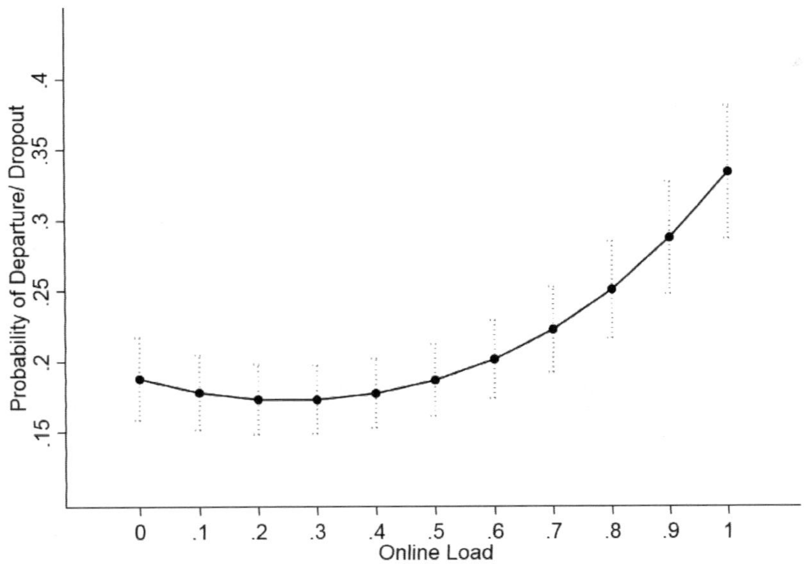

Figure 3. Probability of departure/ dropout at Time 4 by online load

The hazard associated with online course load was found to be invariant across time intervals. Contrary to previous research, our initial results suggest that effect of the intensity of online coursework is not linear in nature. This curvilinear relationship is lost however when course completion rates are included in the analysis.

Covariate Effects and the Relationship between Online Load and Outcomes

With the last set of models shown in Table 1, we addressed the question of whether the effect of online load changes in the presence of other well-known predictors of college success. Our analysis indicates that effect of online load remained notable after controlling for a host of traditional indicators of degree completion, transfer and dropout. Conventional demographic predictors of college success behaved in predicable fashion when the time-varying predictors of semester GPA and online coursework were not considered (Model 3). Model 4 indicates that an upward shift in semester GPA increases the hazard (likelihood) of positive outcomes as well as decreases the hazard of negative outcome.

Table 1: Results from Multilevel Multinomial Logistic Regression: Time to Degree/ Transfer and Time to Departure/ Dropout

Predictors	Model 2				**Model 3**				Model 4				Model 5			
	Deg/Tr		Depart		Deg/Tr		Depart		Deg/Tr		Depart		Deg/Tr		Depart	
	Est	OR	Est	OR	Est	OR	Est	OR	Est	OR	Est	OR	Est	OR	Est	OR
On	1.44^{***}	4.20	$-.86^{***}$	.42	1.08^{***}	2.95	$-.53^{***}$	.59	1.35^{***}	3.85	$-.47^{***}$	.63	$.54^{**}$	1.72	.00	1.00
On2	-1.65^{***}	.19	1.65^{***}	5.2	-1.25^{***}	.29	1.27^{***}	3.56	-1.35^{***}	.26	$.71^{***}$	2.04	-.23	.79	.06	1.06
Age					$-.10^{***}$	.91	$.09^{***}$	1.09	$-.15^{***}$	.86	$.15^{***}$	1.16	$-.15^{***}$	.86	$.11^{***}$	1.12
Age2					$.00^{***}$	1.00	$-.00^{***}$	1.00	$.00^{***}$	1.00	$.00^{***}$	1.00	$.00^{***}$	1.00	$.00^{***}$	1.00
Female					$.07^{***}$	1.07	$-.27^{***}$	.76	$-.05^{*}$	.95	$-.08^{***}$	.92	-.05	.95	$-.10^{***}$	.90
Asian					$-.14^{**}$	.87	$-.28^{***}$	.75	-.15	.86	$-.30^{***}$	.74	-.18	.84	$-.31^{***}$	.74
Black					$-.27^{***}$	.77	$.34^{***}$	1.40	-.08	.92	.01	1.01	$-.10^{*}$	.91	.01	1.01
Hisp					$-.28^{***}$	.76	$.17^{***}$	1.19	$-.25^{***}$	.78	.02	1.02	$-.22^{***}$	.80	-.01	.99
Rc_oth					$-.24^{**}$	.79	$.53^{***}$	1.70	$-.24^{*}$	.79	$.28^{***}$	1.33	$-.23^{*}$	.79	$.26^{***}$	1.29
Rc_mi					$-.56^{***}$	.57	$.45^{***}$	1.57	$-.60^{***}$	.55	$.35^{***}$	1.42	$-.55^{***}$	.58	$.34^{***}$	1.40
Rem					$-.97^{***}$	.38	$.17^{***}$	1.19	$-.81^{***}$	.45	$-.12^{***}$	.89	$-.84^{***}$	.43	$-.24^{***}$	.79
Goal					.04	1.04	-.04	.96	.08	1.08	-.03	.97	.05	1.05	-.01	.99
Intern					$.76^{***}$	2.13	$-.39^{***}$	.68	$.64^{***}$	1.90	.15	1.17	$.41^{**}$	1.50	$.37^{*}$	1.44
Sta					$.41^{***}$	1.51	$-.13^{***}$	.87	$.48^{***}$	1.62	$-.14^{***}$	.87	$.29^{***}$	1.34	$.11^{***}$	1.12
Pell					$-.13^{***}$	.87	$.32^{***}$	1.38	-.09	.91	$.19^{***}$	1.21	-.05	.95	$.17^{***}$	1.18
TAP					$.14^{***}$	1.15	$-.59^{***}$	.56	$.10^{***}$	1.11	$-.41^{***}$	.66	-.04	.96	$-.30^{***}$	.74
Hum					$.23^{***}$	1.25	$.24^{***}$	1.27	$.25^{***}$	1.28	$.21^{***}$	1.23	$.33^{***}$	1.38	$.17^{***}$	1.18
STEM					-.08	.93	.02	1.02	-.09	.91	-.03	.97	-.10	.90	-.02	.98
GPA									$.81^{***}$	2.24	$-.89^{***}$	.41	$.70^{***}$	2.02	$-.48^{***}$	.62
Cred													$.11^{***}$	1.11	$-.14^{***}$	.87
Var Camp	11^{***}				$.12^{***}$				$.08^{***}$				$.11^{***}$			
Var Prog	12^{***}				$.11^{***}$				$.08^{***}$				$.10^{***}$			
LL	-102,004.2				-98,417.27				-85,676.00				-82,269.46			
AIC	204,056.40				196.910.50				171,427.90				164,612.90			
BIC	204,296.20				197,290.20				171797.60				164,982.60			

Note. $^{***}p <001$, $^{**}p <05$, $^{*}p<.01$. Coefficients (Est) represent the change in the baseline logit hazard (log odds) for a unit increase in the predictor's value. The odds ratio are also given for ease of interpretation. Time intercepts are omitted. The baseline outcome category is 'no-event'.

In terms of the study's central question, it appears that the curvilinear effect of online course load on dropout/departure can be fully attributed to course completion rates. In terms of degree/transfer, when course completion rates are accounted for, an increasing online load is linearly associated with increased likelihood of degree completion/ transfer (see Model 5). For a one-unit increase in online load, we expect to see about 72% increase in the odds of degree or transfer holding the remaining predictors constant ($bOn = .54$, $OR = 1.72$, $p = .008$).

Holding other predictors at a fixed value, a unit increase in GPA translate into two-fold increase (Bgpa = .70, OR = 2.02, $p < .001$) and a unit increase in credits earned about an 11% increase (bCred = .11, OR = 1.11, $p < .001$) in the odds of degree/ transfer. The odds for minority students are up to 29% lower than the odds for Caucasian students.

When it comes to departure or dropout, with credits earned entered as a predictor, the constant effect of online load on prospects of departure/ dropout is virtually zero (bOn = 0.00, $p = .567$, bOn2 = .06, $p = .091$). Compared to male students and Caucasian students, female students and Asian students are 10% and 26% less likely to dropout, respectively. As expected, the effect of GPA and credits earned on the odds of departure is negative with a unit increase in both predictors lowering the odds of a negative outcome by 38% (Bgpa = -.48, OR = .62, $p < .001$) and 23% (bCred = -.14, OR = .87, $p < .001$), respectively. The coefficient for remedial status at Time 1 is negative (b = -.24, OR = .79, $p < .001$) suggesting a 21% lower risk for departure/ dropout for remedial students. Albeit counterintuitive, this result is not surprising; if the mission of a community college is to provide a venue for students to compensate for prior academic deficiencies, students in need of remediation should be expected to remain longer in the pipeline.

To qualify findings further, we sought to examine if the effect of online load may potentially depend on demographic and academic factors. Therefore, as a follow-up, we probed all two-way and three-way interactions between online load and time-invariant and time-varying covariates in the context of multilevel logistic regressions. With respect to the outcome departure/ dropout, the effect of online load is contingent upon GPA in any given time period and race (Caucasian vs. other). As indicated in Figure 4, it appears that online course intensity adversely affects the subpopulation of minority students who are academically stronger; these students are significantly more likely to depart/ dropout when the majority of their courses are fully online.

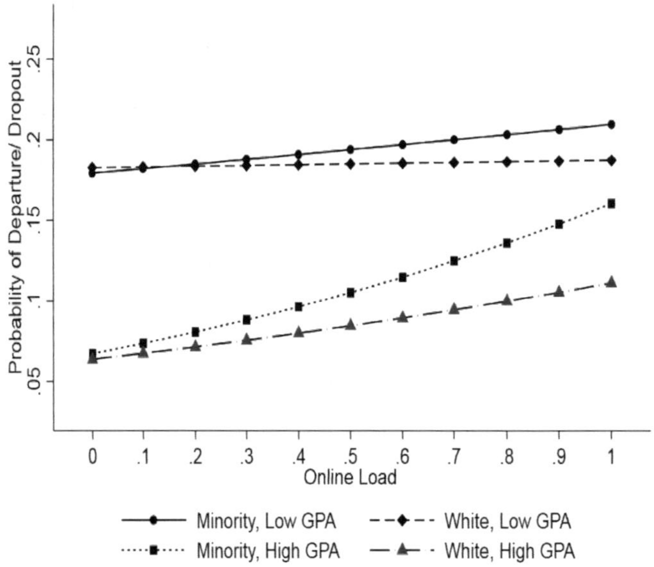

Figure 4. Probability of departure/ dropout as a function of online load, GPA and Race

Discussion

The current study provides new insight through an analysis of prior variables while simultaneously considering course completion rates. It appears that online course completion significantly improves the odds of earning a degree. Unlike previous research (e.g. Shea & Bidjerano, 2018), in the present study, where course completion rates are accounted for, an increasing online load is linearly associated with increased likelihood of degree completion/ transfer. For each additional unit of successful online study, the odds of degree completion/transfer increase by 1.72. Additionally, the constant effect of online load on prospects of departure/ dropout is virtually zero. While this is good news for the average online student, certain subpopulations are at risk relative to the average. Of particular concern are academically stronger minority students; these students are significantly more likely to depart or dropout as their online load increases relative to other subgroups. Further study is warranted to understand the cause and possible interventions to address these issues.

References

Bettinger, E., Fox, L., Loeb, S., & Taylor, E. (2017). Changing distributions: How online college classes alter student and professor performance. *American Economic Review, 107*(9), 2855-2875.

Jaggars, S. S., Edgecombe, N., & Stacey, G. W. (2013). *What we know about online course outcomes: Research overview.* New York: Columbia University, Community College Research Center. Retrieved from https://ccrc.tc.columbia.edu/media/k2/attachments/what-we-know-about-online-course-outcomes.pdf

Jaggars, S. S., & Xu, D. (2010). *Online learning in the Virginia Community College system.* New York, NY: Columbia University, Teachers College, Community College Research Center.

James, S., Swan, K., & Daston, C. (2015). Retention, progression and the taking of online courses. *Online Learning, 20*(2). http://dx.doi.org/10.24059/olj.v20i2.780

Johnson, H., Cuellar Mejia, M., & Cook, K. (2015). *Successful online courses in California's community colleges.* San Francisco, CA: Public Policy Institute of California.

National Center for Educational Statistics (2017). *Number and percentage of students enrolled in degree-granting postsecondary institutions, by distance education participation, location of student, level of enrollment, and control and level of institution: Fall 2014 and fall 2015.* Retrieved from https://nces.ed.gov/programs/digest/d16/tables/dt16_311.15.asp

Scott, M. & Kennedy, B. (2005). Pitfalls in pathways: Some perspectives on competing risks event history analysis in educational research. *Journal of Educational and Behavioral statistics, 30*(4), 413-442.

Shea, P., & Bidjerano, T. (2016). A national study of differences between distance and non-distance community college students in time to first associate degree attainment, transfer, and dropout. *Online Learning, 20*(3), 7-19.

Shea, P., & Bidjerano, T. (2017). Online learning in the 30 community colleges of the State University of New York: Differences in outcomes between classroom and online coursework. In J. Johnston (Ed.), *Proceedings of EdMedia: World conference on educational media and technology 2017* (pp. 1192-1198). Waynesville, NC: Association for the Advancement of Computing in Education (AACE).

Shea, P., & Bidjerano, T. (2018). Online Course Enrollment in Community College and Degree Completion: The Tipping Point. *The International Review of Research in Open and Distributed Learning, 19*(2). http://dx.doi.org/10.19173/irrodl.v19i2.3460

Singer, J. D. & Willett, J.B. (2003). *Applied longitudinal data analysis: Modeling change and event occurrence.* New York, NY, US: Oxford University Press.

Wladis, C., Conway, K., & Hachey, A. (2016). Assessing readiness for online education — Research models for identifying students at risk. *Online Learning, 20*(3). http://dx.doi.org/10.24059/olj.v20i3.980

Xu, D., & Jaggars, S. S. (2011). *Online and hybrid course enrollment and performance in Washington State community and technical colleges* (CCRC Working Paper No. 31). New York, NY: Columbia University, Teachers College, Community College Research Center.

Xu, D., & Jaggars, S. S. (2013). *Adaptability to online learning: Differences across types of students and academic subject areas* (CCRC Working Paper No. 54). New York, NY: Columbia University, Teachers College, Community College Research Center.

A NEW APPROACH TO TEACHING INTRODUCTORY COMPUTING AND INFORMATION TECHNOLOGY BY DISTANCE LEARNING – ADDRESSING KEY ISSUES

Elaine Thomas, The Open University, United Kingdom

Abstract

New introductory level 1 curriculum has been developed for the open-entry Computing and information technology (IT) degree programme in the School of Computing and Communications in the Open University (OU UK). Three key issues in Computing and IT teaching had been identified, namely: student retention, declining participation by women in Computing and IT modules, and the teaching of introductory programming at level 1. Dealing with these issues formed part of the rationale for developing the new curriculum. Computing and IT students at the OU are part-time distance learners and there is a diverse student population with a range of learning needs. Two-thirds of students are in employment, so it is important their work-life balance is considered in the design of new curriculum.

Retention of students is an important issue in distance education (Simpson, 2012) as drop-out rates are high. Students study the new level 1 course "TM111 Introduction to Computing and Information Technology 1" first followed by "TM112 Introduction to Computing and Information Technology 2". Both module production teams engaged in a learning design process to assist with the management of student workload and to ensure coherence and consistency across both modules. The declining rate of participation by women in Computing and IT is a source of concern across both the employment and the higher education sectors (BCS, 2016). In developing TM111 care was taken in the selection of examples and images to ensure that female Computer Scientists were adequately represented so as to provide suitable role models for female students (Frieze & Quesenberry, 2019). Students often struggle with computer programming but easing "cognitive load" (Sweller, 1988) may be helpful, especially in a distance learning context. TM111 uses its own customised version of Scratch, called OUBuild, to assist students in acquiring foundational programming skills. TM111 is presented using a blend of traditional print materials plus online learning and also specialised software. The module is designed to appeal to a wide range of students with a variety of study intentions and learning needs, many of whom have few formal qualifications (or none at all).

TM111 has proven to be very attractive to students and participation by female students has increased to 24%, at least four percentage points over the previous module. Student responses to the module as a whole and the teaching on programming has been positive overall. More work is needed to evaluate the impact of the new modules in equipping students with the necessary programming skills to succeed with programming at level 2.

Introduction

This paper discusses the design and development of a new level 1 course, "TM111 Introduction to Computing and Information Technology 1" which was first presented by the School of Computing and Communications of the Open University (OU UK) in autumn 2017. The rationale for developing the new curriculum is explained and also the measures that the module production team used to address key issues in our level 1 undergraduate Computing and IT programme which are: retention of students in level 1; recruitment and retention of female students to Computing and IT modules, and equipping students with the necessary programming skills to succeed with programming at level 2. Engaging in a learning design process assisted with the management of student workload – an important factor in student retention. The structure and content of the module including the assessment methods are described. Finally, the students' reception of the first presentation in October 2017 will be briefly reported.

Rationale

Major aims of developing the new curriculum were (a) to improve general completion and progression rates in our Computing and IT level 1 modules (b) to address and increasing imbalance between male and female students in our Computing and IT modules (c) to improve skills development, particularly in the area of coding and software development, but also to develop general study competences (Havergal, 2015).

Retention and progression

Our "open" mission means that the OU(UK) does not require entrance qualifications so the University provides for a diverse range of students with a range of learning needs. Around 40% of students studying introductory Computing and IT modules with the OU(UK) have lower than A level qualifications or none at all. Most of our students are mature students and only around 11% of those studying level 1 Computing and IT modules are under 21 years of age. Two-thirds of our students are in employment, but a key motivation for studying is to advance or change their career. Student drop-out is a major problem in distance education which Simpson (2012) has labelled the "distance education deficit" and argues that it is important to strengthen students' learning motivation and their resilience. The "growth mindset" theory (Dweck, 2015) suggests that being able to try new strategies and cope with setbacks are very important. The OU(UK) surveys students who drop out of its modules and a common response is that an unexpected work or family issue has resulted in the student falling behind with their studies. Student workload is recognised as an important issue in student retention (Whitelock et al., 2015). It is important to recognise the student's work-life balance whilst ensuring the modules meet the required learning outcomes.

Attracting women students

At a time when the Computing and IT jobs market is growly strongly, the declining participation rates of women is a source of concern across the sector. Women account for 56% of all higher education graduates, but only 17% of graduates in IT related subjects are women. Only 15% of applicants to Computer Science courses in higher education were female, according to the "Women in IT Scorecard" (BCS, 2016). Participation by female students in the OU(UK)'s level 1 Computing and IT introductory modules had declined from around 33% fifteen years ago to under 20% in more recent times. Cross-cultural studies indicate differences between cultures and countries, for example, India has equal representation between men and women entering careers in Computing and IT (Sondhi, Raghuram, & Herman, 2018). Also, Frieze and Quesenberry (2019) report studies in the US showing that the curriculum was not the cause of the problem, and that cultural differences rather than gender differences were important in attracting and retaining female students. For example, providing female role models greatly improved participation by women students.

introductory programming

Students often find programming difficult and they can easily lose motivation. There is an ongoing debate about the most effective way to teach programming, especially as skills and understanding of one programming language does not necessarily transfer easily into other programming situations. Cognitive Load Theory (CLT) (Sweller, 1988) which focuses on the structure and limitations of the working memory provides a useful explanation of why some subjects are difficult to learn. Struggling with syntax in a text-based programming language is particularly difficult and frustrating for novice programmers in a distance learning context. The *intrinsic* factors (Sweller et al., 1998) in computer programming involve interaction between the syntax of a particular programming language and programming concepts, such as loops, variables etc. Jenkins (2002) argues that it is the blend of learning types required: surface learning for remembering features such as syntax and order of precedence, and deep learning in the understanding of concepts and development of true competence, makes programming difficult. Using a visual programming environment, such as Scratch avoids this problem.

The predecessor module, "TU100 My digital life", used "Sense", which is a visual programming environment specially adapted from Scratch (n.d), to provide a "gentle" introduction to programming skills for our extremely diverse student cohorts. The programming teaching was introduced early in the module, but programming activities were woven through the study material across the whole module, although they formed only one aspect of the overall study. Our research suggested that Sense had been far more successful in engaging students in programming than the textual language used in a previous level 1 module (Thomas et al., 2018). However, feedback from some students in the University's SEaM (Student Experience on a Module) survey suggested that (a) learning programming alongside other topics was confusing for novice students and (b) studying an introductory programming language across a 30-week module was too long for students with prior experience of programming. In addition, there were concerns that students were not being sufficiently well-prepared for study at level 2 in terms of understanding problem-solving and heuristics.

Designing the module

The existing 60 credit module was redesigned as two 30 credit modules "TM111 Introduction to Computing and Information Technology 1" and "TM112 Introduction to Computing and Information Technology 2". Both modules consist of 21 weeks (approximately 14 hours of student workload per week) and are presented in October and April. Students start with TM111 and progress to TM112 on successful completion and pass of TM111.

Early in the production process the teams of academics developing the two modules engaged in a learning design process together. The term *learning design* refers to the educational processes involved in teaching and learning to ensure that the time that students spend studying is as productive and effective as possible (Whitelock et al., 2015). We discussed our ideas for the content and design of each module to ensure consistency across the modules and to avoid duplication of topics in a learning design workshop. A central part of the learning design process is the use of an activity planner which is a graphical online tool that captures descriptions of student activity and also the amount of time that we expect students to spend on each activity. The planner aids the module teams in separating out the teaching and learning involved and in mapping this onto a learning activities taxonomy (Conole et al., 2004), i.e. categorising the activities as: Assimilative; Finding and handling information; Communication; Productive; Experiential, and Adaptive/Interactive.

Figure 1 shows the first draft of the activity planner for TM111 with the first three study weeks of study completed. At an advanced stage in the production process, a member of staff who was not involved in production, worked though the materials and completed the workload planning section of the activity planner to ensure that the workload was balanced across the module.

formation Technology 1 *Add module title here...*

Week / Topic / block or theme / key concepts	Learning outcomes and skills	**Assimilative** e.g. Read, Watch, Listen, Think about, Observe, Review	**Finding and handling Information** e.g. Analyse, Collate, Plot, Discover, Use, Order, Classify, Select	**Communicate** e.g. Debate, Discuss, Argue, Share, Report, Collaborate, Present, Describe, Question	**Productive** e.g. Create, Build, Write, Make, Design, Construct, Produce, Draw, Compose, Remix	**Experiential** e.g. Practice, Apply, Experience, Perform	**Interactive/ adaptive** e.g. Explore, Experiment, Trial, Mimic, Improve, Model, Simulate	**Assessment** Include low/no, medium (e.g. TMAs) and high stakes assessment (e.g. Exam) e.g. Write, Present, Report, Demonstrate, Critique
Block 1 Part 1 Orientation; Why study Computing & IT?	Relates to KU1: major trends; KS2 PPS1 C&IT skills	Read printed study material	Explore and become familiar with online resources e.g. module website; visit library	Introduce yourself; Present an image to other students using OpenStudio e.g. of a favourite piece of C&IT technology				Questions in iCMA01 (low weighted)
Block 1 Part 2 Development of computing & communications systems	Relates to KU1 major trends; Moore's law KS3 numerical skills e.g. binary logic, prefixes for large units; bits and bytes	Read printed study material; watch online video				Practice numeracy skills		Questions in iCMA01 (low weighted)
Block 1 Part 3 Capturing sound and vision; Web 2.0 services	Relates to KU1: Analogue to digital conversion; Processing audio and image files; Compression; Also KU3: Web 2.0 user-generated content; Web 2.0 communities & KS2, KS4, PPS1	Read printed study material;	Explore Web 2.0 resources	Share presentation in OpenStudio; comment on other students' work (optional)	Develop audio-visual presentation		Experiment with different forms of compression	Question in TMA01 related to this part, also a short question in iCMA02

Figure 1. The first draft of the TM111 activity planner for weeks 1-3

Module design and content

There are three blocks of study in TM111, each block consists of six Parts and covers six weeks of study, followed by a week for completing an assessment. Most of the materials are in print but guided by an online study calendar and supported by online materials, online audio-visual resources, and module forums. Full consideration was given to the cognitive load imposed by the instructional design itself (Sweller et al., 1998) in the development of the TM111 study materials. Tight control was kept over the wordcount and workload of each Part during production. The programming in TM111 is designed to be covered in one block of study (100 hours) over a period of six weeks with a seventh week allocated for completing the programming assessment. The intention is to reduce cognitive load by allowing students to focus on learning to program and closely-related concepts and skills i.e. developing simple algorithms, problem-solving and testing and debugging of programs.

Block 1: The digital world

The workload for Block 1 takes account of the "distance learning deficit" (Simpson, 2012) in that time is allocated in the first two weeks to allow students to find their way around University systems. This is especially important as many students are new to the University. Block 1 commences with the student's own experience of using computing and IT systems, covering a range of topics. Students explore how computers and networks developed; how analogue images and sounds are converted into digital formats; and how data is stored and managed in databases (including *big data*). They also gain practical experience of constructing webpages, and, in the final week, they consider how interfaces help us to interact with computers successfully. Positive role models of women in computer science (Raghuram et al., 2018; Frieze & Quesenberry, 2019) are well represented in the materials e.g. a photograph of Grace Hopper (the inventor of the COBOL programming language) standing beside a 1950s computer was chosen to illustrate the development of computers in Part 2 to show that women used to be well represented in computer science in the past.

Block 2: Creating solutions

We chose the title of Block 2 "Creating solutions" to encourage the idea that programming is about being creative in solving problems. The idea was that we should attempt to appeal to a diverse range of students which would have the effect of improving participation by women. After careful consideration, we opted to use the visual programming approach on TM111 developing OUBuild (2017) from the open source version of Scratch 2.0 (n.d.). In addition to providing an appropriate introduction to programming skills, this promotes engagement with programming at level 1 (Thomas et al., 2018) and also helps to raise students' awareness of the strengths and weaknesses of different types of programming. Students explore a variety of programming techniques, such as sequencing, iteration and selection and are encouraged to be creative in developing simple animations and simulations. They create programs involving animation, sounds, numbers and text. Students are also taught how to test and debug their programs. The activities highlight enjoyment in programming, whilst developing the foundational skills and knowledge necessary for university study. The block ends by exploring algorithms, what they actually are, and considers some of their strengths and weaknesses.

Block 3: Connecting people, places and things

In the final block students are introduced to communication networks, including the structure and operation of the internet, and wired and wireless systems. The first three parts of the block explore transmission media, the electromagnetic spectrum, the structure and operation of the internet, and introduces wireless communication. Students gain an understanding of different types of wireless communication including mobile telephony, WiFi, Bluetooth, ZigBee and RFID. The final three parts discuss the Internet of Things (IoT), on-line communication, and issues of security, gender, health care, democracy, and the "digital divide" in ICT. The material on IoT covers topics such as home automation (including coping with signal obstructions), energy harvesting, low-power WANs, and the future of the IoT. The Online Communication's part explores a wide range of asynchronous and synchronous activities, such as forums, group communications, online communities. The important issues relating to social networking are discussed, such as privacy and safety, along with concepts of social presence and awareness. The final part, "The networked society", addresses the use of networked computer systems by government and the health service including biometrics and DNA information. Audio interviews are included with three researchers who have investigated the impact of mobile phone use on the lives of socially excluded young women.

Throughout all three blocks of the module, students develop skills in communication, numeracy, digital and information literacy (DIL) and employability as well as their study skills which are so important for their undergraduate work (Havergal, 2015).

Students study in tutor groups of around 20 students run by associate lecturers. Although distance learning tends to be a rather solitary pursuit, the module team aims to create a strong sense of a learning community through the use of online asynchronous communication tools, such as forums, blogs and wikis are used for communication between students and their peers, their tutors and the module team. Creating a sense of community is particularly important in Block 2 where there are specific online activities to support the teaching of programming and problem-solving.

Assessment

The module uses continuous assessment which consists of three interactive computer-marked assignments, iCMAs and three tutor-marked assignments (TMAs) marked by associate lecturers. The iCMAs consist mainly of short-answer and multiple-choice questions to check knowledge and understanding. The cut-off date for the first iCMA (iCMA41) occurs early in the module, to ensure that students are engaging with the module in the early stages. Advice can be provided if students do not submit or perform poorly in the first iCMA. The second and third iCMAs are scheduled midway through blocks 2 and 3 respectively. Assignment iCMA42 tests numeracy, problem-solving and programming, and iCMA03 further tests knowledge of networks and numeracy associated with networks. The TMAs occur at the end of each block of study and assess the content covered in the block. The TMAs provide an opportunity for personalised tutor feedback and assist a student's progression to the following module, TM112. Tutors are encouraged to promote a "growth mindset" (Dweck, 2015) in their feedback on assessments to encourage students to experiment and learn from their mistakes, particularly in programming. For most students, this module will be followed by "TM112 Introduction to Computing and Information Technology 2". This module uses Python (Keopke, 2010), to broaden and deepen students' understanding of coding, algorithmic thinking and problem-solving. (For further details on the teaching of programming in TM112 see Piwek et al., 2019).

Reception by students and pass rates

TM111 recruited over 2,500 students, more than expected, of these 67% were new students. Female students accounted for 24% of the total number, which is 4-5 percentage points more than the previous module. Retention and pass rates were also higher than other 30 credit level 1 modules in Computing and IT.

The results of the student satisfaction survey (SEaM) at the end of the module were very positive with 91.9% of respondents agreeing that they would be happy to recommend OU study to other students, suggesting that they were satisfied with the module. The module team were particularly concerned about how students would receive the programming in OUBuild. A sample of the open text comments from the SEaM survey is shown in Table 1. The comments from students A and B are more representative of student feedback which suggests that using OUBuild has been successful. Student C's comment suggests that they were not convinced about OUBuild, but this was not typical of the cohort, and the student will progress to using Python on the next module.

Table 1: A sample of responses in the SEaM survey

Student	Response
A	I have really enjoyed the challenge of my first OU module. It has been hard work but it is great to be learning and the online student forums mean you are never alone and if you get stuck there is always someone ready and able to help.
B	I enjoyed study this module very much. The best part for me was Block 2 as I am interested in programming. It was great to start Programming with OU Build because it helped me to learn basic programming skills.
C	I didn't really enjoy OU Build but that could just be me, it didn't feel like I was learning anything meaningful and would have preferred to have gone straight into simple source programming. The math exercises I found very interesting and informative.

Conclusion and further work

The new OU(UK) module "TM111 Introduction to Computing and Information Technology 1" adopts a very broad approach to the introduction of foundational Computing and IT knowledge and skills to take account of the learning needs of a diverse cohort of students. The module addresses key issues in education namely: student retention; recruitment of female students and the teaching of programming to novice students. The teaching and learning materials include a coverage of theory, technology, practical skills development, and the wider socio-technological issues in the Computing and IT field. Traditionally, students have found many of these concepts, particularly programming and mathematical topics, problematic, so great care has been taken with student workload, the mix of study materials (print, online resources, and a file-sharing environment), the choice of programming environment and to the staged development of skills throughout the course. Although TM111 has been well-received by students (and TM112 also) to date, more work is planned to evaluate the impact of the design of the new curriculum on students' performance in programming at level 2. Further research will involve tracking new students from TM111 and TM112 through onto second level programming modules.

References

BCS (2018). *Women in IT Scorecard: A definitive up-to-date evidence base of data and commentary on women in IT employment and education.* BCS, The Chartered Institute for IT and the Tech Partnership. Retrieved from https://www.bcs.org/upload/pdf/women-scorecard-2016.pdf

Bissell, C. (2017). A new approach to the introductory teaching of Computing and IT at the Open University UK. In J. Domenech i Soria, V. Vela, M. de la Poza, & B. Desamparados (Eds.), *Proceedings of the HEAd'17. 3rd International Conference on Higher Education Advances, Universitat Politècnica de València, València*, 101–108.

Conole, G., Dyke, M., Oliver, M., & Seale, J. (2004). Mapping pedagogy and tools for effective learning design. *Computers and Education, 43*, 17–33.

Dweck, C.S. (2015). Growth. *British Journal of Educational Psychology, 85*(2), 242-245.

Frieze, C., & Quesenberry, J. L. (2019). How Computer Science at CMU Is Attracting and Retaining Women. *Communications of the ACM, 62*(2), 23-26. Retrieved from https://cacm.acm.org/magazines/2019/2/234346-how-computer-science-at-cmu-is-attracting-and-retaining-women/fulltext?otl

Havergal, C. (2015, December 10). UK Engagement Survey: universities have limited impact on students' 'soft' skill development. Times Higher Education [Blog post]. Retrieved from https://www.timeshighereducation.com/news/uk-engagement-survey-universities-have-limited-impact-students-soft-skill-development

Jenkins, T. (2002). On the Difficulty of Learning to Program. *Proceedings of the 3rd Annual HEA Conference for the ICS Learning and Teaching Support Network*, 1-8.

Koepke, H. (2010). Ten reasons Python rocks for research (and a few reasons it doesn't). Retrieved from https://www.stat.washington.edu/~hoytak/blog/whypython.html

OUBuild (Software) (2017). The Open University. Retrieved from https://bitbucket.org/lts-imd/public-tm111

Piwek, P., Wermelinger, M., Laney, R., & Walker, R. (2019). *Learning to program: from problems to code.* Paper presented at the Third Conference in Computing Education Practice (CEP), Association for Computing Machinery (ACM), Durham, United Kingdom. Retrieved from http://oro.open.ac.uk/58202/

Raghuram, P., Herman, C., Ruiz B. E., & Sondhi, G. (2018). *Women and IT Scorecard – India 2018.* The Open University. Retrieved from http://gsm-it.com/userassets/Publications/GSM-IT_SCORECARD-INDIA_2018_Final.pdf

Scratch 2.0 (Software) (n.d). MIT Media Lab. Retrieved from http://scratch.mit.edu

Simpson, O. (2012). *Supporting Students for Success in Online and Distance Learning* (3rd ed.). London: Routledge.

Sweller, J. (1988). Cognitive load during problem-solving: Effects on learning. *Cognitive Science, 12*(2), 257-28.

Sweller, J., van Merriënboer, J., & Paas, F. (1998). Cognitive architecture and instructional design. *Educational Psychology Review, 10*(3), 251–296. doi:10.1023/A:1022193728205

Thomas, E., Kouadri Mostéfaoui, S., & Jefferis, H. (2018). Visualising the code: a study of student engagement with programming in a distance learning context. In M. Bajić, D. N. Dohn, M. de Laat, P. Jandrić, & T. Ryberg, (Eds.), *Proceedings of the 11th International Conference on Networked Learning 2018* (pp. 140-148). Springer. Retrieved from https://www.networkedlearningconference.org.uk/abstracts/thomas.html

Whitelock, D., Thorpe, M., & Galley, R. (2015). Student workload: a case study of its significance, evaluation and management at the Open University. *Distance Education, 36*(2), 161-176, doi: 10.1080/01587919.2015.1055059.

UNRAVELLING LEARNING ENGAGEMENT IN THE HYBRID VIRTUAL CLASSROOM

Annelies Raes, Pieter Vanneste, Marieke Pieters, Ine Windey, Wim Van Den Noortgate, Fien Depaepe, KU Leuven Kulak, Belgium

Connecting learners and crossing borders through the hybrid virtual classroom

Based on current societal transitions and in the context of lifelong learning, both upper secondary education, higher education and vocational training are invited to think about how to enable people, at any stage of their life, to take part in stimulating learning experiences. The expectancy to be present at one core location is getting more and more difficult in this (inter)national society. In addition, the student population is changing and balancing work and family life becomes an important point of priority. Therefore, it is important to make education less dependent on location and time and improve flexibility within the learning trajectory (Lakhal, De Sherbrooke, & Bateman, 2017). Next to this, there are growing insights about the need to collaborate over the borders of the institution to implement expertise from partner organisations.

To deal with these shifts in education, a university project invested in the design, research and development of a *hybrid virtual classroom*, as displayed in Figure 1, in collaboration with two industry partners. This *hybrid virtual classroom* creates not only opportunities for on-campus face-to-face (F2F) learning, but also for connecting remote individuals synchronously, overcoming distance limitations to enable remote interactions between students and teachers and among students. All students have access to an interactive platform, allowing them to participate in the course, either on-site or from a remote location. The platform gives access to the sources the teacher is using during his lecture (e.g. power point slides or annotations made on the Wacom), the platform facilitates launching interactive quizzes and polls and a chat room is integrated which gives students to chat with each other during the lecture.

Figure 1. Left picture displays the hybrid virtual classroom including both F2F and remote individual students.
Right picture displays the platform visible for the students

Engagement of remote students from a self-determination perspective

Based on previous research literature, it is known that in case of synchronous hybrid learning, it gets more difficult to activate and engage the *remote students* to the same degree as the students attending *F2F*. In the study of Weitze (2015) for example, *Global Classroom* was investigated as an innovative synchronous hybrid videoconference concept, where adult students could choose between participating in class on campus or from home via videoconference. In this study both students and teachers stated in the questionnaires and in the interviews that – compared to students attending the lesson F2F – *remote students* learned less, were generally more passive and often behaved like they were watching TV and not attending a lesson. One of the reasons for this finding was that teachers gave classes according to more monologue-based teaching strategies, which are not well-suited for this kind of learning settings. *Remote students* also indicated that it was difficult to make the teacher aware that they wanted to answer a question, which made them feel frustrated and uninvolved, leading to a significant sense of distance from their institution, their teacher and their peers.

These low levels of engagement for remote students need to be taken seriously as student engagement is associated with positive learning outcomes (Fredricks, Blumenfeld, & Paris, 2004). Based on previous research, we can state that engagement particularly involves three dimensions or components, (a) *behavioural* (e.g., focus, attention, participation, effort or involvement), (b) *affective* (parameters like interest, boredom, frustration or enjoyment), and (c) *cognitive* engagement (including learning outcomes, metacognition and self-regulated learning). This three-component model is displayed by the three circles in Figure 2 and has been used by several researchers in the past (e.g. Dobbins & Denton, 2017; Gobert, Baker, & Wixon, 2015).

In this study, we are particularly interested in unravelling the affective engagement which is the highlighted circle. We further operationalized affective engagement based on the *self-determination theory* (SDT; Deci & Ryan, 1985). SDT has been established as a well-validated and coherent framework for the conceptualization and investigation of motivation in education (e.g. Raes & Schellens, 2015; Vansteenkiste, Sierens, Soenens, Luyckx, & Lens, 2009), and provides theoretical grounds for examining how the social context of a learning environment can influence the motivation for one's learning experience. According to Deci and Ryan's SDT, motivation can be distributed along a continuum from low to high levels of self-determination. The most self-determined style of motivation is intrinsic motivation (IM) and as displayed in Figure 2, it is maintained that IM can be fostered when the context facilitates the satisfaction of three basic needs: students' need for autonomy, competence, and relatedness (Vansteenkiste et al., 2009).

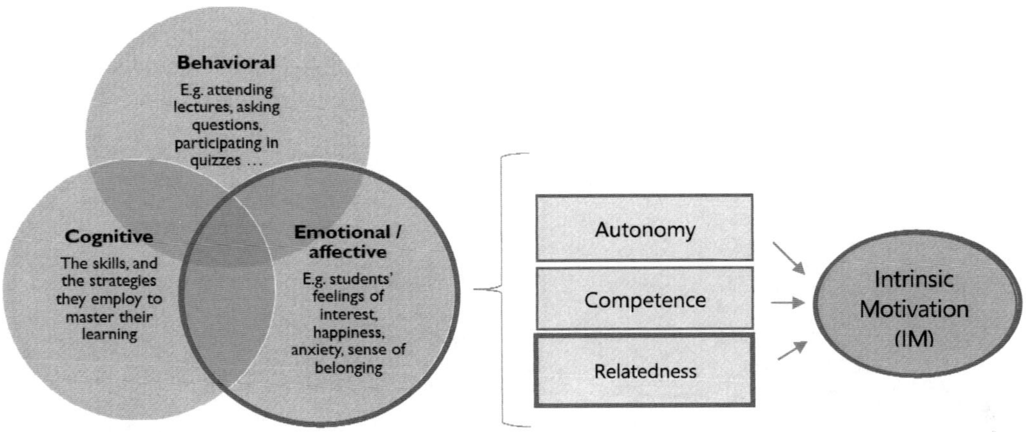

Figure 2. Aspects of student engagement within taught contexts (Dobbins & Denton, 2017) and affective engagement perceived from the self-determination theory (Deci & Ryan, 1985). The affective component and the basic need of relatedness are highlighted as these constructs represent the main focus of this study.

Research scope & methodology

As stated before, the satisfaction of the need for relatedness can be problematic in the context of a hybrid virtual classroom, particularly for the remote students. Previous research has shown that remote learners feel a significant sense of distance from their institution which illuminates the need to address the perceived distance between remote students and their teachers and F2F classmates by establishing some sort of connectedness (Ramsey, Evans, & Levy, 2016). Therefore, in this study we focus on how the basic need of relatedness is experienced by students in the hybrid virtual classroom and how this affects IM as proxy of students' affective engagement. Based on previous research it is hypothesized that the more related students feel with their peers and their teacher the better IM in learning is supported (Hutchinson, Lauckner, Meisner, Gallant, & Silversides, 2017). Given the educational setting, it is hypothesized that students will be most motivated in the F2F setting and least motivated in the remote setting. Previous studies who investigate motivation in a hybrid virtual learning context comparing the experiences of F2F and remote students are limited and mostly based on qualitative methods (e.g. Weitze, 2015). This study aims to fill this research gap by systematically investigating both relatedness and IM in the hybrid virtual classroom through a quasi-experimental within subjects' design (see Figure 3) comparing three learning settings. We collaborated with one teacher of secondary education and his 14 students of Grade 12 (average age of 17) following the course "Economics". Four students were girls and ten were boys. During six consecutive courses (100 minutes per week), the teacher came to the University and taught his lecture in the *hybrid virtual classroom*. As displayed in Figure 3, during Lecture 1 and Lecture 2, all students followed the course F2F. In Lecture 3 and Lecture 4, the students participated in the hybrid setting, the student group was split up and half of the students were following the course virtually and half of the students were following F2F. The groups were swapped after Lecture 3, so all students could experience both perspectives in the hybrid classroom. In Lecture 5 and 6 all students followed the course virtually, whereas the teacher was present in the *hybrid virtual classroom.* As a result, four conditions can be distinguished: a pure face-to-face condition (F2F), a hybrid session followed face-to-face (hybrid-F2F), a hybrid session followed remotely (hybrid-remote) and a pure virtual condition (Virtual).

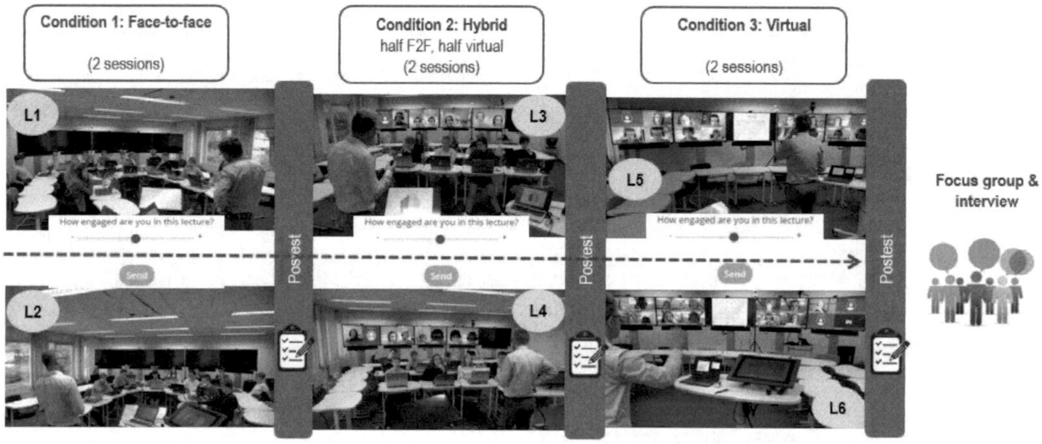

Figure 3. Quasi-experimental within-subjects design in which one teacher and 14 students were followed during six lectures

Data has been collected from a *mixed methods approach* (i.e., the combination of quantitative and qualitative research methods) as this strengthens the inferences in both processes and outcomes of data analysis (Cohen, Manion, & Morrison, 2011).

Quantitative data consisted of a post-test survey administered four times: (a) after the two F2F sessions, (b) after the first hybrid session in which half of the students followed virtually, the other half F2F, (c) after the second hybrid session, (d) after the two virtual sessions. The post-test included existing scales of the Intrinsic Motivation Inventory (IMI) (Deci &, Ryan, 1985) consisting of Likert-scale questions using six-point agreement levels from 1 – *strongly disagree* to 6 – *strongly agree.* The instrument assesses participants' interest/enjoyment, perceived competence, effort, value/usefulness, felt pressure and tension, perceived choice, and experience of relatedness during a certain activity, thus yielding seven subscale scores. In this study, we will only report on the relatedness scores and the scores for the interest/enjoyment subscale which is considered the self-report measure of IM. The perceived relatedness in this study is operationalized as relatedness towards peers (Rel_Peers) and relatedness towards teacher (Rel_Teacher) and these constructs are theorized to be positive predictors of self-report measures of intrinsic motivation (Niemiec & Ryan, 2009).

The self-reports conducted at the end of each session have some shortcomings and biases as they are a snapshot articulation of engagement rather than an examination of how emotion unfolds in an interactive context (Scherer, 2005). Conducting self-reports only at the end of the course will result in a rather poor statistical power and does not allow to capture evolutions in engagement during the course. To counter this, a second measure of IM was added. During the six sessions, all students were registered on the platform and for the purpose of this study, we also build an engagement pop-up containing one question "How engaged are you now?" (displayed on Figure 3) which students could answer on a slider allowing for continuous variables. Students got this pop-up during all lectures at random intervals between 5 and 12 minutes.

Also *qualitative data* have been obtained through open-ended questions in the post-test, a semi-structured interview with the teacher and a semi-structured focus group with all students, one month after the last session. Both the interview and the focus group were audio recorded and fully transcribed afterwards. Based on the transcriptions, content analysis (Cohen, Manion, & Morrison, 2011) was used to generate common experiences and valuable feedback regarding learning and teaching in the hybrid virtual classroom.

The results section includes the descriptive statistics and the main results of the qualitative analyses. In addition, the post-test data are analysed by using for each outcome variable separately a multilevel model containing fixed effects for the categorical independent variable (i.e., the educational setting). In our analysis four levels of the categorical classroom were distinguished as the hybrid condition included F2F and remote students: F2F, hybrid-F2F, hybrid-remote and Virtual. Students' effects are included as random effects to deal with the non-independence of a subject's residuals.

Results

Figure 4 presents the post-test results for the subscales IM (orange bars), Rel_Peers (green bars) and Rel_Teacher (blue bars) and illustrates the conclusions from the multilevel analyses that are discussed below.

- *Relatedness to teacher:* As hypothesized given the educational setting in the different conditions, Rel_Teacher is high in both the F2F and the hybrid-F2F setting, whereas Rel_Teacher is low in the virtual and hybrid-remote setting. The reported Rel_Teacher was the highest in the hybrid-F2F setting.
- *Relatedness to peers*: It was found that students' Rel_Peers was the highest in the F2F setting. A significant difference was found comparing with the hybrid-F2F setting and with the virtual. Rel_peers in these two settings did not significantly differ from each other, but was significantly higher than the hybrid-remote setting, which turned out to be the worst condition in terms of Rel_Peers.
- *Intrinsic motivation*: IM was the lowest in the hybrid-remote setting, compared to the three other settings.

These quantitative results are in line with the qualitative results as both the teacher and the students mentioned that the hybrid sessions were the most puzzling to follow on the one hand and to teach on the other hand.

The teacher in that sense expressed the following:

> *"It is not always easy to divide the attention between the F2F students and the remote students."*

On the students' side, one of the obstacles which were mentioned is that the F2F students had to use the microphone when reacting orally to make sure that the remote students could hear them. They expressed that this did not feel naturally. A student also indicated that he often turned his head during the lesson to see the faces of his peers on the screens in the back. Another student also explicitly mentioned to feel a distance from their peers and the teacher and expressed that it was like watching a movie without feeling real contact. This student mentioned that is was boring and weird to be separated from the others in the hybrid-remote setting. Students also indicated that following the lecture virtually was more tiring and that this kind of learning is only suitable for certain courses with a maximum of 2 hours a day. Yet, students mentioned that the available chat box might have helped in establishing some sort of connectedness with their peers. Overall, most students did also mention that they experienced the remote learning positively and stressed that they were surprised about the possibilities of the new technology and students found it easy to use.

This positive evaluation was also shared by the teacher. During the final interview, conducted at the end of the experiment, the teacher expressed his enthusiasm about this educational experiment and mentioned that the experience exceeded his expectations. He stated this as following:

> *"I thought that teaching to virtual students would have been very artificial and weird, but this was not the case at all. I had the feeling that my students were very close to me and could see their faces and expression quite good;… I could easily interact with them as I do in a normal class setting and I had the feeling my students were very attentive."*

The teacher also stated that the educational setting had not influenced his style of teaching. He mentioned that he could easily start a dialogue and stated that the students who were most interacting are the same as in normal F2F classes. Yet, he expressed that he missed his traditional white board. Although there is a white board function in the platform, the teacher did not use it because he was not used to it and was afraid that it would not work.

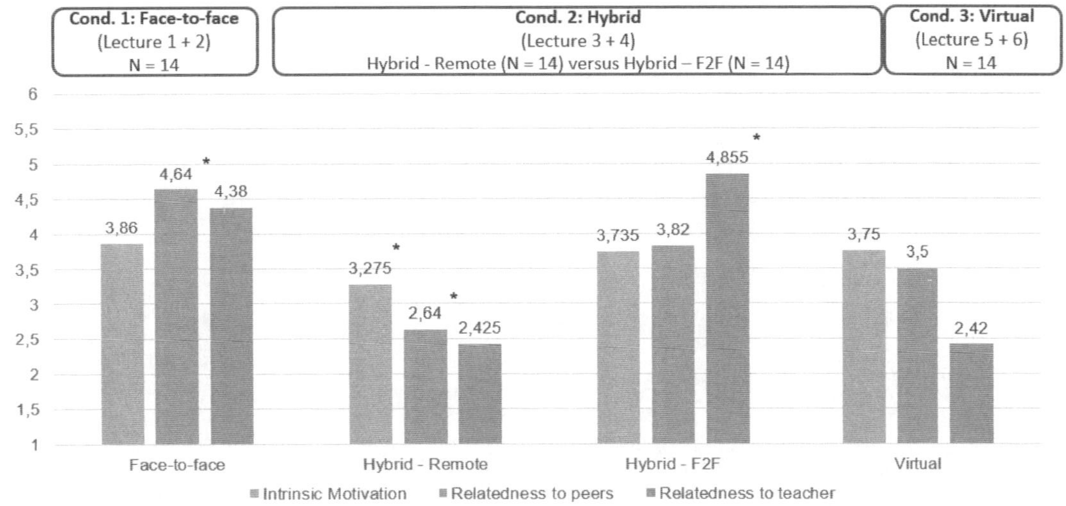

Figure 4. Post-test results of the subscales IM and relatedness in the three learning conditions.

Figure 5 presents the results of the engagement pop-up visualizing how affective engagement of the 14 students evolved during the six lectures. The Y-axis presents students' answers on the question "How engaged are you now?" which students could answer on a slider with a maximum value of 2 – *very engaged* and a minimum of 0 – *very disengaged*. A score of 1 represents a neutral engagement state. The slider always started at the neutral score. The X-axis presents the time point on which the pop-up was received. Further analysis of these digital self-reports confirmed the findings from the self-reports at the end of the course. The results indicated that engagement scores were the highest when all students were physically present in the classroom and were the lowest for remote students in the hybrid setting.

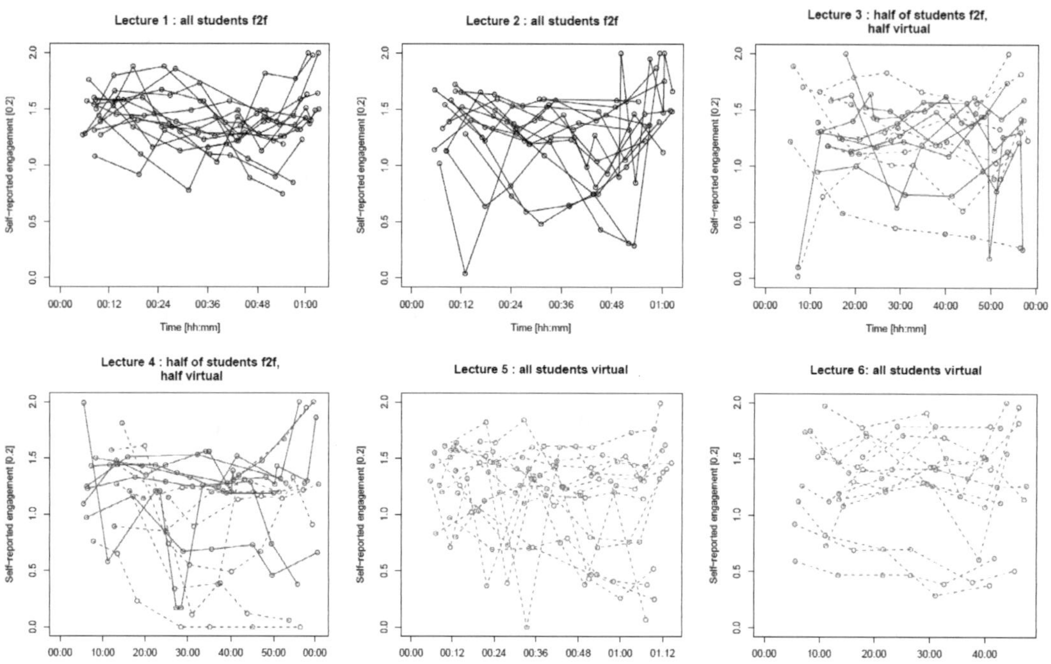

Figure 5. Results of the engagement pop-up. Solid lines apply to students who were following the lecture F2F;
dashed lines apply to students who were following the lecture remotely.

Conclusion

Based on previous literature and more specifically based on the self-determination theory, this study hypothesized that the more related students feel with their peers and their teacher, the better IM in learning is supported (Hutchinson et al., 2017). It was hypothesized that students would be most motivated in the F2F setting and least motivated in the remote setting. This hypothesis is partly confirmed, as the lowest IM was found in the hybrid-remote setting. However, no significant difference was found between the pure F2F and virtual setting. If students were asked which educational setting they prefer, most students still prefer the F2F sessions, but we can conclude that both the teacher and the students were positive about the hybrid virtual classroom and approved the benefit that students are able to attend courses in a flexible way (Lakhal et al., 2017). Yet, our study shows that particularly the hybrid setting is challenging for the remote students as it combines the F2F and remote perspective. These findings confirm previous findings of Ramsey, Evans, and Levy (2016) that remote learners indeed feel a significant sense of distance between remote students and their teachers and face-to-face classmates. Future research should investigate how this connectivity can be approved by means of instructional interventions like collaborative breakout-sessions between F2F and remote students and interactive quizzes and polls.

References

Cohen, L., Manion, L., & Morrison, K. (2011). *Research Methods in Education* (7th ed.). London: Routledge.

Deci, E. L., & Ryan, R. M. (1985). The General Causality Orientations Scale - Self-Determination in Personality. *Journal of Research in Personality, 19*(2), 109–134.

Dobbins, C., & Denton, P. (2017). MyWallMate: An Investigation into the use of Mobile Technology in Enhancing Student Engagement. *TechTrends, 61*(6), 541–549. https://doi.org/10.1007/s11528-017-0188-y

Fredricks, J. A., Blumenfeld, P. C., & Paris, A. H. (2004). School Engagement: Potential of the Concept, State of the Evidence. *Review of Educational Research, 74*(1), 59–109. https://doi.org/10.3102/00346543074001059

Gobert, J. D., Baker, R. S., & Wixon, M. B. (2015). Operationalizing and Detecting Disengagement Within Online Science Microworlds. *Educational Psychologist, 50*(1), 43–57. https://doi.org/10.1017/CBO9781107415324.004

Hutchinson, S. L., Lauckner, H., Meisner, B. A., Gallant, K., & Silversides, K. (2017). Fostering self-determination and sense of belonging through leisure education: reflections on the Steps to Connect program. *Loisir et Société / Society and Leisure, 40*(3), 360-376. doi: 10.1080/07053436.2017.1378503

Lakhal, S., De Sherbrooke, U., & Bateman, D. (2017). Blended Synchronous Delivery Mode in Graduate Programs: A Literature Review and its Implementation in the Master Teacher Program. *Collected Essays on Learning and Teaching*, 47–60. https://doi.org/10.22329/celt.v10i0.4747

Niemiec, C. P., & Ryan, R. M. (2009). Autonomy, competence, and relatedness in the classroom: Applying self-determination theory to educational practice. *Theory and Research in Education, 7*(2), 133–144. https://doi.org/10.1177/1477878509104318

Raes, A., & Schellens, T. (2015). Unraveling the motivational effects and challenges of web-based collaborative inquiry learning across different groups of learners. *Educational Technology Research and Development, 63*(3), 405–430. https://doi.org/10.1007/s11423-015-9381-x

Ramsey, D., Evans, J., & Levy, M. (2016). Preserving the Seminar Experience. *Journal of Political Science Education, 12*(3), 256–267. https://doi.org/10.1080/15512169.2015.1077713

Scherer, K. R. (2005). What are emotions? And how can they be measured? *Social Science Information, 44*, 693–727.

Vansteenkiste, M., Sierens, E., Soenens, B., Luyckx, K., & Lens, W. (2009). Motivational Profiles from a Self-Determination Perspective: The Quality of Motivation Matters. *Journal of Educational Psychology, 101*(3), 671–688. doi: 10.1037/A0015083

Weitze, C. L. (2015). Pedagogical innovation in teacher teams: An organisational learning design model for continuous competence development. In A. Jefferies, & M. Cubric (Eds.), *Proceedings of 14th European Conference on e-Learning ECEL-2015* (pp. 629-638). Reading, UK: Academic Conferences and Publishing International.

Acknowledgements

This research is partially funded by imec through ICON LECTURE+. LECTURE+ is a project realized in collaboration with imec, with Barco, Televic Education and Limecraft as project partners and with project support from VLAIO.

IMPROVING THE FINANCIAL KNOWLEDGE OF THE OLDER GENERATION – THE PLEKHANOV UNIVERSITY EXPERIENCE

Olga A. Grishina, Dinara R. Tutaeva, Alexey I. Grishin, Plekhanov Russian University of Economics, Russia

Older people in the modern labour market

It is not a secret that the level of social development of some certain society is not least of all characterized by the attitude towards the senior and older people. The problems and challenges faced by these groups of citizens have never been easy to solve, and in the modern world, they became even more complicated. Among the challenges that have become particularly relevant in recent years, the first that is worth mentioning is the accelerated development of technologies, above all – informational ones. Often, senior and older people are not able to adapt quickly to these changes, and at best, they experience problems in their daily life. In the worst case, this situation leads to the fact that these categories of citizens become "lagging behind", which is especially painful for people who are specialists in their fields. Despite their knowledge and often invaluable experience, their working competencies are rapidly becoming obsolete. This not only significantly hinders the effective work of such people, but also puts them in a vulnerable position in the labour market, and often becomes the cause of personal psychological problems.

This problem is very serious for countries with the *constructive* (*regressive* by Sundberg's classification) model of the population pyramid, which is characterized by the so-called "mound of the elders". One of the characteristic features of this demographic situation is the massive presence in the labour market of people of pre-retirement age, as well as a significant percentage of pensioners who continue to work. Russia is among the countries experiencing this situation to the full extent. The dynamics of the number of working citizens of Russia of pre-retirement age and retirement age in recent years According to data of the Russian Federal State Statistics Service (FSSS) is shown in the table 1:

Table 2: The number of working citizens of Russia of pre-retirement age and retirement age

Year	Citizens of pre-retirement age (men of 55-59 y.o.; women of 50-54 y.o.), thous.	Citizens of retirement age (men of 60-72 y.o. / women of 55-65 y.o.), thous.
2009	8,316	5,802
2011	8,571	6,288
2013	8,666	6,563
2015	8,907	7,106
2017	8,690	7,315

Thus, with relative stability (in absolute digits) in the number of working citizens of pre-retirement age, there is a steady increase in the number of working retirees. Thus, in accordance with FSSS data for 2017, out of a total number of Russian retirees of 42.7 million people, about 13.1 million continued to work, forming the proportion of about 30.7%. It is also worth mentioning that out of this total number of retirees, about 35.3 million people (82.7%) receive an old-age insurance pension; 7.4 million people (17.3%) receive a social retirement pension.

Of course, older workers have a number of guarantees, including legislation ones. Thus, in accordance with the Labour Code of the Russian Federation, age is not a reason for dismissing an employee, and unreasonable dismissal of an employee of pre-retirement age at the initiative of the employer entails criminal liability in accordance with article 144.1 of the Criminal Code of the Russian Federation (which is in force since 2019). According to the same article, the employer is also responsible for the unreasonable refusal to hire persons who will have a retirement age in the next five years or less (under labour law, responsibility arises on the basis of article 64 of the Labour Code of the Russian Federation). None of the above, however, is able to protect older workers from the problems identified at the beginning of the article.

What makes older people work

So, what makes older people work? Various surveys conducted in Russia over the past four years allow us to highlight the following key drivers:

- low pension (the desire to receive additional income);
- need for communication;
- habit of work;
- striving for financial independence.

Somewhat different results were obtained from the study conducted in 2018 by the Silver Generation University of the Plekhanov Russian University of Economics. Founded in 2014 by Plekhanov RUE Faculty of Distance Learning, the Silver Generation University studies the needs of the older generation, organizes and conducts educational activities aimed at improving the performance of active retirees, as well as enhancing the interaction of the younger and older generations. The events of the Silver Generation are aimed at supporting the personal and social status of the elderly person, prolonging maximally the active lifestyle of the older generation, as well as organizing leisure activities taking into account the interests of the elderly and thus contributing to the formation of a stable emotional state for them. The results of the aforementioned study revealed the following reasons that drive pensioners to continue working:

- fear of poverty;
- love to work;
- the desire to help children / grandchildren.

It can be said for certain that the main reason why older people continue to work is of a financial nature. In this light, the key task facing the society as a whole and the employer in particular is to help older workers overcome the fear of a subsequent life for an insufficient pension, that is, the fear of poverty. The results of the Silver Generation University activity allowed to formulate three main directions for solving this problem:

- ensure the employer's interest in preserving jobs for older workers;
- providing psychological support;
- enhance personal applied financial literacy.

In the case of the first direction, the main objects of work of the University were enterprises-employers. Their interest in keeping older employees in the workplace was decided to increase, relying on the role of employees' confidence in the future in increasing loyalty to the employer. The latter, in turn, ensures steady growth in the productivity and efficiency of workers. The provision of psychological support has been delegated to invited experts in this field. The direction connected with the increase of personal applied financial literacy, as carrying educational nature, was considered a priority for the Silver Generation University and required the development of special educational programs.

How to teach older people on a working place?

In developing the content of the relevant educational programs, it was decided to rely on the following topics:

- personal finance planning, cost optimization, and passive income management;
- acquaintance with various kinds of frauds in the financial environment (including using modern information technologies) in order to reduce the risk of becoming a victim.

The most significant problem was the choice of educational practices, which would meet best the needs of the audience (working men aged 55–70 years and working women aged 50–65 years). According to target audience surveys, a number of educational practices have been selected and implemented within the bounds of the pilot project. The latter was conducted by the Silver Generation University from September to December 2018 at the Sberbank of Russia Centre of Client Operations Support (CCOS), which employs about 3,500 people at the same time, of which about 1,000 are pre-pension and retirement age. In total, 482 employees took part in the project.

Within the pilot project, the following educational practices were used:

- On-line trainings. Within the framework of this format, educational and training materials were sent to audiences via e-mail. Special attention was paid to the structure of the information in the distributed materials, which was supposed to be quite intelligible, but at the same time maintaining academic integrity. In particular, a number of case-studies and step-by-step algorithmic instructions were included.

- Webinars organized before or after the workday. At the same time, given that the webinars have practically 'lengthened' the working day, the organizers limited the length of these webinars to 30 minutes.
- "Live" (face-to-face) short-term sessions. These were also organized before or after the work day, as well as during the lunch break, and included mostly practical exercises and Q&A sessions.
- Demonstration of short fascinating videos on financial literacy on TV screens installed in the CCOS canteens. This format turned out to be unexpectedly popular – afterwards, many listeners noted that they had discussed with interest what they had just seen with their colleagues right here, when having a meal.

In the course of the project, a very specific problem was noted – a significant proportion of listeners faced a notable "last mile" effect. After obtaining the necessary knowledge, the direct implementation of certain actions (for example, registration in the on-line banking system) still caused difficulties. Also, the high value of teamwork for older listeners was noted – the implementation of certain tasks was greatly facilitated if they were performed together with colleagues. Therefore, it was decided to include the implementation of such tasks in the "live" sessions mentioned above, and invite specialists – managers of banks, insurance companies, tax consultants, etc. – who would act as instructors during these sessions.

After the completion of the pilot project, a survey was conducted with the purpose of feedback receiving. The survey consisted of a set of questions of a digital evaluative type, as well as a series of open questions. In the set of 20 questions of a digital evaluative type, a modified Likert scale was used (from 1 to 5); the average score was 4.61. According to the analysis of answers to open questions, it was found that the audience as a whole was satisfied with the organization of the learning process. Wishes were expressed to increase the number of short-term 'live' sessions, as well as to include in the program some basic information about the organization of small business and various forms of earnings on the Internet. The Sberbank of Russia CCOS management was satisfied with the program, which was recommended by them to be implemented by other Russian banks – members of the Association of Russian Banks (ARB).

Thus, the experience of the Plekhanov RUE Silver Generation University shows that the highest effectiveness in solving the problem of increasing the financial literacy of older people may be achieved only by combining of educational techniques selected specially in regards to this particular audience's features. The development of educational programs in this field continues and will undoubtedly lead to a further increase in the effectiveness of measures to improve the quality of life of older citizens.

References

Dirksen, J. (2015). *Design for How People Learn (Voices that Matter)* (2nd ed.). Berkeley, CA: New Riders. 1249 Eighth Street.

NewtoNew (2018). How do those who are over 50 study in Russia? (Как учатся в России те, кому за 50 in Russian). Retrieved 11 March, 2019, from https://newtonew.com/culture/kak-uchatsya-v-rossii-te-komu-za-50/

Russian Federal State Statistics Service official web-site. Population data (2009-2017). Retrieved 11 March, 2019, from http://www.gks.ru/wps/wcm/connect/rosstat_main/rosstat/en/figures/population/

PRECARIOUS VOICES: THE SHARED HOPES AND DREAMS OF THOSE TEACHING AND SUPPORTING LEARNING IN DIGITAL CONTEXTS

Peter Bryant, University of Sydney, Australia, Donna Lanclos, Anodyne Anthropology, LLC, United States of America, David White, University of the Arts London, United Kingdom

Abstract

University staff in learning technology related roles are critical to the capability of the institution to effectively enhance the student experience, deliver an engaged curriculum and achieve significant pedagogical change. However, their perceptions of identity, *precarity*, status and capability and the locations and roles they are located in within many institutions can challenge that capability. Drawing on data gathered about the hopes and dreams of over two hundred learning technology related staff at three workshops held in the United Kingdom, Australia and Germany, this paper will explore the contradictions and paradoxes that impact on the capability of staff in learning technology related roles to influence and shape pedagogical and technological change.

Introduction

Designing and implementing strategic pedagogical change is a critical and sometimes intractable challenge for higher education institutions. The imperative to deliver the ambitions of these strategic plans is in part driven by policy agendas that enshrine an internationalised and globalised agenda to compete and be measured against collegiate institutions to ensure survival in a higher education marketplace (Hemsley-Brown & Oplatka, 2006). Many institutions have found or seek to find competitive advantage through designing or replicating pedagogy and curriculum practices and the application and leveraging of educational technologies (and the data they generate) (Marshall, 2011). This has led to weaponization of practices such as learning analytics, online learning, social media learning and co-design in the fight to ensure survival and success of institutions in an increasingly competitive higher education market (Daniel & Butson, 2014; Nord, Paliszkiewicz, & Koohang, 2014; Watters, 2017; Yuan & Powell, 2013).

How institutions are designing and implementing these strategies for change is fuelling debate that centres on the disruption of the economic and social model of traditional universities and heralding the arrival of new, transformative players (e.g., Christensen, 2013; Weller, 2018). Some writers (e.g., Tapscott & Williams, 2010) argue that technology is the pivotal force in shaping learning for the emerging "customers" of the modern university. Selwyn (2016a) observes (perhaps slightly wryly) that "…all told, the overriding sense is of the fundamental re-alignment and reform of university teaching and learning along digital lines" (Selwyn, 2016a; p.1006). There is little universality in that opinion with other writers (e.g., Blin & Munro, 2008) running from the benign to the sometimes hostile in describing the impacts of technology on learning and teaching despite how integrated technology is into the delivery of education (Selwyn, 2016b)

One consequence of this strategic activity and competitive frisson has been a growing sense of job insecurity and uncertainty experienced by many higher education staff (both academic and professional) (Pucciarelli & Kaplan, 2016; Ylijoki & Ursin, 2013). McNaughton and Billot (2016) argue that teaching and related staff are amongst the first people in institutions to experience challenges to their perceptions of academic identity within the constantly shifting and uncertain institutional discourses on pedagogy and technology. The staff in learning technology related roles (which includes learning technologists, data or technology specialists, designers, academics and educational developers) have a diverse range of influence, agency and authority in the institutional strategic discourse and subsequent actions arising from it (Austen, Parkin, Jones-Devitt, Mcdonald, & Irwin, 2016; Bryant, 2015; Mitchell, Simpson, & Adachi, 2017). There is also significant variation in how visible or present they are in the integration of technology into wider strategic initiatives and how they understand or share their own sense of identity, either collectively or institutionally in that context (Browne & Beetham, 2010; Fox & Sumner, 2014; Walker & MacNeil, 2015). This places staff in these roles in institutional positions that are rent with contradictions, centred on where they act in supporting and leading technological change in institutions. The can make their job role feel "...often marginalised and sometimes precarious" (Fox & Sumner, 2014; p.94)

Addressing precarity, marginalisation and being: Future Happens changehacks

In response to our own experiences in a variety of University roles that were a part of or led pedagogical and technological change, we came together in 2016 to design a series of workshops that afforded participants the opportunity to share their experiences and fears about the role of technology related staff in the development and delivery of institutional pedagogical change. We called the workshop "Future Happens" as a counter to the narrative that the significant impacts and benefits of learning technology were unrealised and simply "potential" in many institutions (e.g. Christensen & Eyring, 2011; Kirkwood & Price, 2014; Selwyn, 2016b). This narrative had been used in all our institutions to simultaneously advocate for more learning technology and to resist and rebel against its use. Future Happens set the marker in the sand that at least for the duration of the workshop, there was no need to debate the arrival and influence of technology in education, it had already happened. We felt it critical to address the impacts of the variability of agency, experience and identity by affording participants the opportunity to collectively define and describe the narrative behind their beliefs and ambitions for technology and pedagogy, rehearsing the words in the safe space of engaged peers and stakeholders.

The Future Happens workshops involved a mix of invited and self-selected learning technologists, University management, stakeholders such as industry bodies and students and academics brought together to determine how they could be empowered and enabled to be the nexus between practice and strategy. The intention of these workshops was to encourage participants to be part of the discourse at their institution by generating, sharing and challenging the key messages, tools and strategies necessary to put the digital in the heart of the conversation with senior University management (such as the Vice-Chancellor).

Future Happens workshops was run across three countries (the United Kingdom, Germany and Australia) over two years and brought together over two hundred participants from approximately 100 institutions and groups to address the wicked problem of how to be a part of the dialogue around pedagogical change (using several different filters such as social media and scalability and sustainability). Each workshop generated individual and collective outputs centred on the participants themselves (the *Burnt* activity) and their crowdsourced response to the challenge of integrating technology at a strategic level (the *Hacks*). The analysis of this paper is focusing specifically on the three workshops we called Future Happens 3 ran in 2017. We have chosen to focus in particular on the critical reflections of participants in learning technology related roles that emerged in the Burnt activity. In Burnt, we sought to sharpen the focus on being a part of the pedagogical change process without the *baggage* of rehearsed excuses, fears, past experiences or overly ambitious aspirations, before moving on to engaging in collectively participating in participating in defining change through the *changehack*.

Changehack design

Building on the practices of a hack which seek to spin scenarios and collectively solve and technology problems, a changehack uses similar principles of time limited engagements, specific rules of participation and a casual but slightly pressured environment of crowdsourcing, to bring together people into a learning community to collectively solve educational and organisational problems (Bryant, Lanclos, & White, 2016). Before we engaged participants in the hacking process, we wanted to expose and explore their frameworks and experiences of how technology and pedagogical change have impacted them in their own personal experiential frame. Each changehack brought together a disparate, unconnected and unfamiliar group of people, with their own institutional tensions, victories and lenses. The conceit of the workshop was predicated on how these people could imagine an institutional world separate but the same as theirs, free from the things that hold back engagement with pedagogical and technological change.

We opened each changehack with "Burnt" – a simple, but powerful activity. We told participants at each Future Happens 3 workshop (the first in Liverpool, United Kingdom at ALT-C, the second at ASCIILITE in Queensland, Australia, and the third at Online Educa in Berlin, Germany) that we wanted to give them a chance to reflect on their own practices and contexts before we began the changehack itself. Whilst individual and organisational experience and memories are critical to designing and implementing effective change, enabling authenticity and practice to inform the discourse (Walsh & Ungson, 1991), they can also be a rationale to resist or repel change (Bryant, Coombs, & Pazio, 2014). We told participants that before we could plan for scenarios and imagine new ways of working and thinking, we needed to clear the air and vent their assumptions that might get in the way.

We ask participants to write down their "Hopes and Dreams" for the kind of work they did in education and technology. We then asked for "Victories", moments where they really thought they were successful in their work at their institution (or a previous institution). The final category was "Disasters", a moment where everything went terribly wrong. All of these post-its went on the wall of the workshop room to be shared with the entire group. We did a brief reflection on these post-it notes before moving on with the workshop. We chose to use value laden words to prompt engagement with these categories (hopes and dreams, victories, fears, dumb things/nightmares). We wanted the words to be sharply evocative, to provide shortcuts to people being able to unpack swiftly their personal experiences, internal reflections and examples of successful and unsuccessful change. The openness of these terms was a deliberate attempt to create broad areas in which whatever was foremost in a participant's mind could be expressed. We also added a time pressure to the activity to tease out immediate and hopefully more viscerally felt responses.

Hopes and Dreams: exposing the paradoxes of learning technology related roles

As the rest of the workshop progressed, Donna Lanclos (the anthropologist on the team) spent time sorting through each of the larger Burnt categories to find emergent themes, which we then discussed and preliminarily verified with the workshop participants in the final stages of workshop. We transcribed each of the post-it notes into a spreadsheet, with initial analytical codes generated in the room in the UK and remotely in Australia and Germany. Fundamentally, this was an analytical coding exercise, where we were treating each post-it note as a piece of data (for a total of 300 data points). We applied an inductive analysis methodological approach to the data, which allowed the themes to emerge from what was submitted, rather than imposing the categories we thought would be important from the outset. The themes initially identified by Lanclos, were further verified and refined by all of us in an iterative asynchronous process, primarily within the spreadsheets.

For this paper, we have chosen to focus on the Hopes and Dreams responses only. These responses represented an aspirational, personal perspective on the role of the learning technology related staff, one which was essentially positive and forward thinking. They provided an insight into a vision for the future that contributed towards how the participants understood and participated in the strategic direction of the institution. In describing Hopes and Dreams, participants were describing perceptions, ambitions and states that were not currently present in their working lives. These were transitory states, however much driven by uncertainty, experience or faith and the actions required to move between states of change, are critical components of successful organisational change. Hopes and Dreams were descriptors of both the context and the end point of transition, which was critical to success the workshops and for this analysis.

The shared themes that emerged from within Hopes and Dreams were:

- Theme 1: Structural Institutional Support,
- Theme 2: Respect and Social Capital for Tech and Instructional Design,
- Theme 3: Integration of Teaching and learning into Technology,
- Theme 4: Confident Staff and Students,
- Theme 5: Digital Thoroughly Embedded across the whole institution and Theme 6: Digital Facilitating Transformation.

These themes emerged as common in all three workshops, and were not impacted by the geographic location or cultural or institutional role of the participants. The unanimity of the responses was not expected in the design of Burnt. We hypothesized that the diversity of voices in the room and the complex and unique policy frameworks impacting on each University sector would generate very different experiences for people in learning technology related roles. Whilst the change occurring at their institution might have been radically different (or strikingly familiar), how those changes made them feel, how they learnt from it, how they located where the pressure or pain points were and how they understood their own reactions and emotions were experientially common. The Hopes and Dreams responses also explored the enablers and barriers within an institutional system, offering insights into how the participants were not entirely in control (and sometime not at all) of their own actions. The institutional environment, the limitations of technology (and potentially technological determinism) and interactions with other players in the process (and their own reactions and responses) emerged. Hopes and Dreams exposed a complex human ecosystem that may not be visible to those determining the types of pedagogical change occurring in institutions.

Theme 1: Structural Institutional Support

The desire for greater institutional support for the work of technology in education cannot always be reduced to the claim for "adequate (or more) funding" but that was certainly one of the things highly visible within this theme. However, Hopes and Dreams that referenced "Support" went past the requirement for more money. There was a real and recognised need for the integration of learning technology related professionals and their expertise into the structures and standardised workflows of their respective institutions. People wanted to be a part of "how we do things" not just an optional add-on, or an after-the fact gloss to decisions that had already been made around process and pedagogy. This desire to be part of the structures determining the direction of education and the student experience was a key insight. How staff in learning technology related roles valued what they could bring to the discourse and how their skills and knowledge could make the strategy better was strongly present in the responses, best demonstrated by this response from a UK participant, "Being able to have projects from any part of the university bid for time for it (to) be an active community of support".

Theme 2: Respect and Social Capital for Technology and Instructional Design

The desire to be treated as a professional in their own right, with expertise and a clear, defined voice in change that impacts directly on their identity and self-belief was a necessary accompaniment to the need for structural support. Allusions to an academic-professional staff divide emerged within this theme and it feels important to note that if people experienced such professional respect in their everyday lives, it may not be in the "Hopes and Dreams" responses, but in the "Victories" one. One post-it summed this up noting, "Professional staff are recognised as professionals". This theme was closely related to the first theme, but that critical importance of the social capital participants could add to the organisations through their engagement with change was the distinguishing factor, with one participant in the UK hoping for "Learning technology to be taken seriously as a profession within institution". It was also representative of the critical factors that underpin the professional identity of people in learning technology related roles; respect for expertise, the capacity to make things better and the ability to contribute were all key to defining identity.

Theme 3: Integration of Teaching and learning into Technology

This theme represented the idea that the work of technology and teaching (and learning) could not be separated, but was entwined via the skills and expertise of many professionals working together on curriculum development and delivery in both physical and digital places. It was clear that participants felt separated from the teaching and learning processes and conversations in their institutions, and that their expertise was not being used by their fellow teaching academics (as opposed to senior management or the institution more broadly). One respondent described this as a hope that "Technology (is) used to support quality pedagogy". Another aspect of this theme was the hope that the pejorative positioning of the digital as a second-class or inferior form of teaching and learning would end, as one UK participant noted "Stitch the digital and the physical into the fabric of learning – no more digital divide".

Theme 4: Confident Staff and Students

The words *engaged* and *comfortable* and *collaborative* were visible in this theme, speaking to a desire for academics and students alike to be willing to try what might be possible with technology in education, and to be provided opportunities to see what happens when they do try (even if it doesn't all go according to plan). Students and academic staff were seen as unwilling (and sometimes unable) to wrangle tech for themselves such that they could get to a point where new modes of teaching and learning might be possible. Confidence in success or achievement was also a factor of institutional support, not just individual initiative, as one European participant noted "More positive attitude to change – only positive attitude is way to survive and tackle challenges".

Theme 5: Digital Thoroughly Embedded across the whole institution

Closely aligned to theme 3, Digital Thoroughly Embedded took a more holistic and University-wide perspective on the importance of digital to institutional change, as one UK participant noted, "Not needing to put the word 'digital' in front of things anymore". The responses in this theme provided evidence that respondents hoped that technology will become an integral part of the way their institution imagines, creates, and delivers educational experiences. There was a realisation in some responses that this would provide a new set of challenges for people whose work is defined by technology, but that it also might provide opportunities for everyone in educational environments to embed their practice at the DNA level of change. This ambition was described by this European participant hoping, "To get every professional category at university actively engaged in digital education, i.e. teachers, researchers, librarians, ICT-pedagogues, staff support, student support. We're all in it together to put student learning in focus."

Theme 6: Digital Facilitating Transformation

The stated desire in this theme was for technology to do far more than make things efficient, or to replicate or replace old ways of doing things. Participants wanted to see more of what might be possible that hasn't already been imagined, for digital technology to open space for new and previously untried ways, places, and possibilities within education. This desire for transformation was in tension with the current state of their work, which included tasks around maintaining systems that support traditional modes of teaching and learning (lecture capture, assessment, etc.). This desire for the true transformative potential of technology to be realised was described by this European participant, "Showing that technology can make the learning/education better and that it's not the goal to replace everything with technology, because there still is a lot of reluctance among teachers and students".

Conclusions

Burnt was designed as an icebreaking activity to start the overall changehack process. However, the "open" character brought to the surface themes which we discovered were shared across numerous institutions and may not have been exposed in the participants' day-to-day work. What the Hopes and Dreams responses clearly demonstrated were the institutional and human reactions to pedagogical change. At an institutional level, the responses highlighted that staff in learning technology related roles often frame the institution as a blocker, and themselves as an "outsider" (this can take many forms) rather than understanding the process of practice and culture change as the central task in hand. One of the ways this manifests itself is the feeling of "not being in the room" where critical strategic decisions are made. This can lead to a sense of "them and us" which often emerges as a lack of agency to shape institutional agendas and the sense that one's own work is at the mercy of senior management who do not share the same educational or institutional philosophy as your own. The themes that emerged from the Hopes and Dreams responses suggest that there is in fact more than one "room" and that people who are classed as learning technology related staff are often in it. And still, status, structures, and siloes get in the way of the work to be done. It also exposed a perception of institutional failures to centre people and process rather than systems and products. This paradox was informed by critical issues of professional identity and respect that shaped the motivation of staff in learning technology related roles to become involved in change, sometimes revelling in their perceived role as outsider.

At a human level, how that change made them feel, how they learnt from it, how they located where the pressure or pain points were and how they understood their own reactions and emotions were critical underpinnings to the responses. Despite the intention of the Hopes and Dreams activity to draw the participants into the future through aspiration and grounded fantasy, the frame of current experiences, frustrations and disappointments was front of mind for many participants. Experience and memory are powerful human traits. They are also critical in the process of designing and implementing pedagogical change, bringing to the discourse a sense of authenticity and practice. However, they are also often a rationale or an excuse to resist or repel change. They become rehearsed lines, inculcated in the culture of protecting the ways we do things. In essence, staff become jaded, inured to what appear to be intractable structural and institutional-cultural situations. Within the themes, that sense of defence came through in calls for funding, the declarations of much needed respect and the implicit referencing of those unnamed and unspoken of people who did not want the digital embedded in their institution. There was a further implicit inference in the framing of the responses that suggested a techno-solutionist approach was being taken by "senior management" which squeezed out their teaching and learning expertise in favour of the more utilitarian "keep the technology running" mantra. This may have been driven by pressures on senior management to be expansionist and metrics-driven, while learning technologists and more practice-based staff focus on pedagogy and the quality or character of teaching and learning. The further analysis of the other two Burnt activities could provide some verification of these assertions as in the main they were the unspoken antithesis to the stated hopes and dreams.

Returning to the paradoxical and precarious role of learning technology related staff, it was demonstrable in the responses that our participants identified significant changes that needed to occur within their institutions. In the main these were not related to the purchase of a new piece of technology and neither were they declarations of techno-superiority that simply wished for people to use the technology better. They were pointers to some of the existential threats challenging their ongoing viability of their roles and more widely the notions of teaching and learning itself. Perhaps, the unseen elephant in the room of those who did not share their hopes and dreams may highlight that we as a sector have not fully come to terms with the massification and marketisation of higher education, leading to institutions where the tension between the pressure to expand and survive and holding onto laudable pedagogical approaches has found its nexus in digital technology and the staff employed to inspire others to integrate it into teaching and learning, with the end result being the marginalisation of those critical voices.

References

Austen, L., Parkin, H., Jones-Devitt, S., Mcdonald, K., & Irwin, B. (2016). *Digital capability and teaching excellence: an integrative review exploring what infrastructure and strategies are necessary to support effective use of technology enabled learning (TEL).*

Blin, F., & Munro, M. (2008). Why hasn't technology disrupted academics' teaching practices Understanding resistance to change through the lens of activity theory. *Computers & Education, 50*(2), 475-490.

Browne, T., & Beetham, H. (2010). *The positioning of educational technologists in enhancing the student experience. Report funded by The Higher Education Academy under its Call4: Enhancing Learning and Teaching through the use of Technology.* An ALT Occasional Publication. Retrieved from http://repository.alt.ac.uk/831/1/Tom_Browne_Helen_Beetham_HEA_finalweb.pdf

Bryant, P. (2015). *From the middle out: Flipping the role of learning technology from supporting practice to leading change.* Paper presented at the apt2015.

Bryant, P., Coombs, A., & Pazio, M. (2014). Are we having fun yet? Institutional resistance and the introduction of play and experimentation into learning innovation through social media. *Journal of Interactive Media in Education, 2014*(2), a4.

Bryant, P., Lanclos, D., & White, D. (2016). *What is Future Happens?*

Christensen, C. (2013). *The innovator's dilemma: when new technologies cause great firms to fail.* Harvard Business Review Press.

Christensen, C., & Eyring, H. J. (2011). *The innovative university: Changing the DNA of higher education from the inside out.* John Wiley & Sons.

Daniel, B., & Butson, R. (2014). *Foundations of big data and analytics in higher education.* Paper presented at the International conference on analytics driven solutions: ICAS2014.

Fox, O., & Sumner, N. (2014). Analyzing the roles, activities, and skills of learning technologists: A case study from City University London. *American Journal of Distance Education, 28*(2), 92-102.

Hemsley-Brown, J., & Oplatka, I. (2006). Universities in a competitive global marketplace: A systematic review of the literature on higher education marketing. *International Journal of public sector management, 19*(4), 316-338.

Kirkwood, A., & Price, L. (2014). Technology-enhanced learning and teaching in higher education: what is 'enhanced' and how do we know? A critical literature review. *Learning, Media and Technology, 39*(1), 6-36.

Marshall, S. (2011). Change, Technology and Higher Education: Are Universities Capable of Organisational Change? *Journal of Asynchronous Learning Networks, 15*(4), 22-34.

McNaughton, S. M., & Billot, J. (2016). Negotiating academic teacher identity shifts during higher education contextual change. *Teaching in Higher Education, 21*(6), 644-658.

Mitchell, K., Simpson, C., & Adachi, C. (2017). What's in a name: The ambiguity and complexity of technology enhanced learning roles. ASCILITE 2017. Retrieved from http://2017conference.ascilite.org/program/whats-in-a-name-the-ambiguity-and-complexity-of-technology-enhanced-learning-roles/

Nord, J. H., Paliszkiewicz, J., & Koohang, A. (2014). Using social technologies for competitive advantage: impact on organizations and higher education. *Journal of computer information systems, 55*(1), 92-104.

Pucciarelli, F., & Kaplan, A. (2016). Competition and strategy in higher education: Managing complexity and uncertainty. *Business Horizons, 59*(3), 311-320.

Selwyn, N. (2016a). Digital downsides: exploring university students' negative engagements with digital technology. *Teaching in Higher Education, 21*(8), 1006-1021.

Selwyn, N. (2016b). *Is technology good for education?* John Wiley & Sons.

Tapscott, D., & Williams, A. D. (2010). Innovating the 21st-Century University: It's time! *Educause review, 11.*

Walker, D., & MacNeil, S. (2015). Learning Technologist as Digital Peadgogue. In D. Hopkins (Ed.), *The Really Useful #edtech Book* (pp. 91-106). David Hopkins.

Walsh, J. P., & Ungson, G. R. (1991). Organizational memory. *Academy of management review, 16*(1), 57-91.

Watters, A. (2017). *The Weaponization of Education Data.* Hackeducation.com.

Weller, M. (2018). The Digital Scholar Revisited. *The Digital Scholar: Philosopher's Lab, 1*(2), 52-71.

Ylijoki, O.-H., & Ursin, J. (2013). The construction of academic identity in the changes of Finnish higher education. *Studies in Higher Education, 38*(8), 1135-1149.

Yuan, L., & Powell, S. (2013). *MOOCs and open education: Implications for higher education – White Paper.*

DIGITAL (4) EDUCATION – A NATIONAL DIGITAL STRATEGY IN THE CONTEXT OF THE TRANSFORMATION OF A COUNTRY INTO A DIGITAL NATION

Serge Linckels, Ministry of Education, Luxembourg

Introduction

This paper describes Luxembourg's strategy "Digital (4) Education" by the Ministry of Education, Children and Youth to leverage learning to the 21st century. It is divided into three areas: media literacy, educational technologies, and promotion of STEM. The strategy is embedded into the overarching national strategy "Digital Luxembourg" which is the governmental programme to transform the country into an IT nation.

Disclaimer

The following text is for general information purposes only. Although the author was professionally implied in the creation of the Digital (4) Education strategy, this paper presents the author's personal and subjective view and interpretation and does not reflect the ministries position or intentions.

General governmental context

Governmental programme

On 10 December 2013, Luxembourg's Prime Minister Xavier Bettel presented the governmental programme to the national parliament. This programme recommends, at a policy level and among other things, using more modern teaching material and in particular influencing the quality of daily work.

> *"To ensure more individual care of the student in teaching, emphasis should be placed on factors that directly influence the quality of classroom work. The aim will be to ensure better teacher training, more modern teaching material and a contribution to new didactic ideas in the daily work of teachers."*

In November 2018, a new Ministry of Digitalisation was created, whose mission

> *"is to sustain the general technological development in the areas important to Luxembourg's economy and to develop new strategies for Luxembourg to move forward, but also to improve the daily lives and the various administrative processes. Much of the work of the ministry is focused on making people's lives easier."*

In January 2019, the Prime Minister announced a national strategy on artificial intelligence and stated that if Luxembourg wants to continue positioning itself in the digital world, artificial intelligence appears as a new pillar to build.

> *"We will federate the ecosystem of skills, for example by supporting courses in the field, from an up skilling perspective, but also research. And we will showcase those who are already champions in artificial intelligence, to attract those who need these skills."*

Digital Luxembourg

On 20 October 2014, Prime Minister and minister of Communications and Media, Xavier Bettel, presented "Digital Luxembourg" as an initiative, which aims to strengthen and consolidate Luxembourg's position in the field of information and communication technologies (ICT) and to make the Grand Duchy a real centre of high-tech excellence. It focuses on the six topics: infrastructure, eSkills, innovation, FinTech, e-Administration, and promotion (see Figure 1).

As part of the strategy, Luxembourg's schools must train young people who will be able to adapt to the acceleration of change, i.e. who will be characterised by their openness to innovation and their ability to take advantage of the uncertainty generated by an unknown future. Digital technologies can also be an important factor in reducing inequalities. On the one hand, it provides all students, regardless of their social background, with access to quality cultural and educational information and resources. On the other hand, digital technologies make it possible to diversify learning methods and to better adapt teaching to the needs and pace of each individual.

Within the eSkills theme, education has developed its Digital (4) Education strategy.

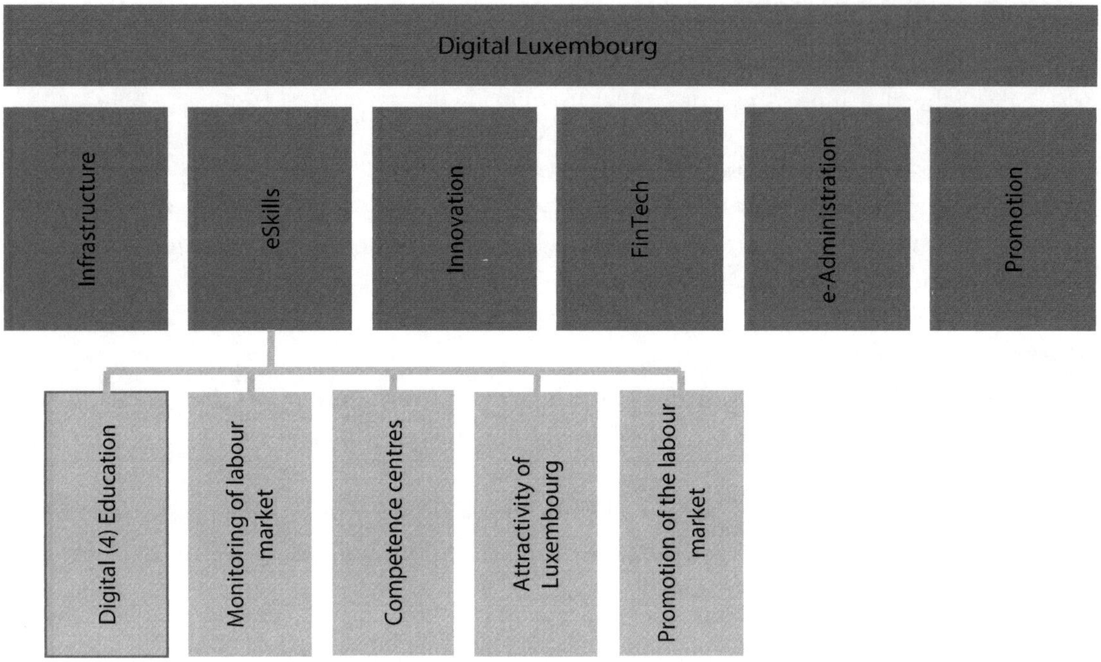

Figure 1. Themes of the national strategy "Digital Luxembourg"

Digital (4) Education

On May 20 2015, Claude Meisch, Minister of Education, Children and Youth, presented the strategy "Digital (4) Education". The name of the strategy allows for a double reading that perfectly illustrates the two priority objectives:

- *Digital education*: the preparation of young people for a complex and constantly changing working environment and their role as citizens in the private and public sector.
- *Digital for education*: the promotion of new learning strategies and innovative pedagogical projects, using digital technology in schools and in the extracurricular world.

The Digital (4) Education strategy is structured around the following five dimensions:

- *Digital citizen*: The school will introduce students to key computer applications that are essential in their future lives as citizens, such as: administrative procedures, communication with the authorities, and e-banking.
- *Digital peer*: Young people will learn to use ICT in a more secure and responsible way. In particular, Internet safety, moral harassment in social media, and image rights will be discussed.
- *Digital learner*: To create learning situations that foster the development of 21st century skills, a learning and teaching environment with appropriate resources will be made available to teachers and students.

- *Digital worker*: Students will be encouraged to develop the skills necessary to handle basic technological tools in their future professional life.
- *Digital entrepreneur*: Activities are being implemented to stimulate talent, encourage young people to take an interest in technological tools and thus contribute to the training of future specialists in the digital economy.

Digital (4) Education's three focus areas

The Digital (4) Education strategy is based on five dimensions presented in the previous section that are broken down into specific projects. These precise actions are grouped in three areas: media literacy, educational technology, and promotion of STEM (see Figure 2). Each project provides school or extracurricular actors with the necessary tools (software, hardware, pedagogical resources, pedagogical scenarios, learning places...) to create learning situations that promote the development of skills for the 21st century.

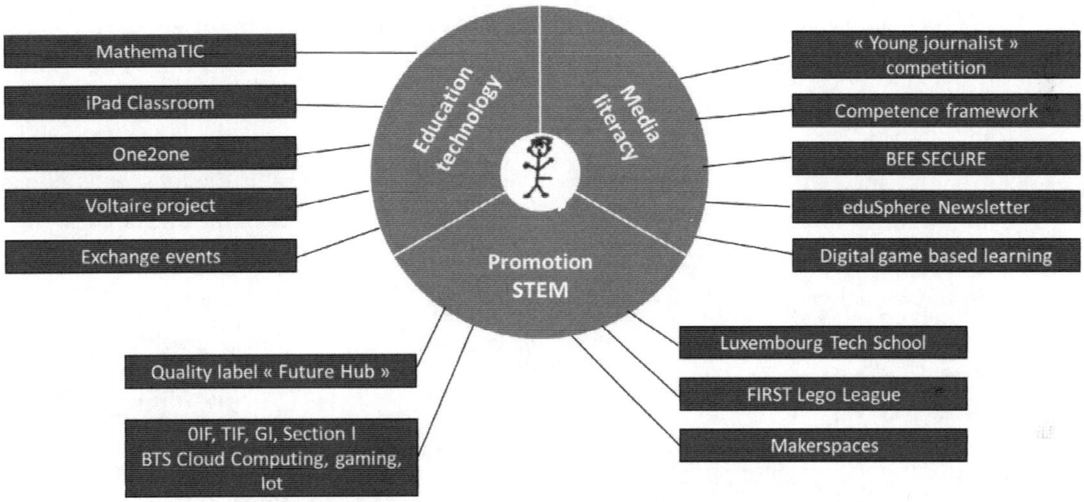

Figure 2. Areas of activities of the strategy "Digital (4) Education"

Area 1: Media Literacy

The objective is to prepare young citizens to become members of a modern and highly technical society with all its opportunities, challenges and dangers. Today's children are natives of the digital age. However, the challenges of education and the extracurricular world related to technological tools remain enormous. How can we prevent young people from becoming passive consumers switching from one medium to another, without being able to appropriate the information? How to develop the knowledge, skills, and attitudes they will need to find jobs in emerging or evolving sectors?

Education has the obligation to equip young people with the skills and knowledge they will need to adapt in our changing world. These skills are two-folded:

1. To prepare young people to live in a complex and constantly changing work environment. Therefore, education must develop skills in four key areas: communication, collaboration, creativity, and critical thinking.
2. To prepare young people to assume their role in the private and public domain. Therefore, education must offer learning situations that foster understanding of the world and society, personal development, and well-being.

Precise actions have been put in place. Here is a non-exhaustive list:

- In collaboration with the national press council, the *young journalist contest* aims at explaining the process of news-creation, the importance of the quality of the source of information, the danger of fake news, etc. to the students. Journalists visit primary and secondary schools and help the students produce a journalistic work. The best submissions are presented in a traveling exhibition.
- "BEE SECURE" is a programme to inform students, parents, and teachers in a simple language about the dangers on the Internet. Workshops are organised, pedagogical material is made available in different languages, and experts visit schools. Every year, a campaign is launched with a specific topic, e.g. Love stories (2018-2019) and Big data (2017-2018).
- In compliance with the European model "DigComp", a national *digital competencies framework* is under development that apply for all grades (primary and secondary). Among the 16 competencies grouped into five areas (see Figure 3), lesson plans, best practices, teacher trainings, events, etc. will be part of the whole package.

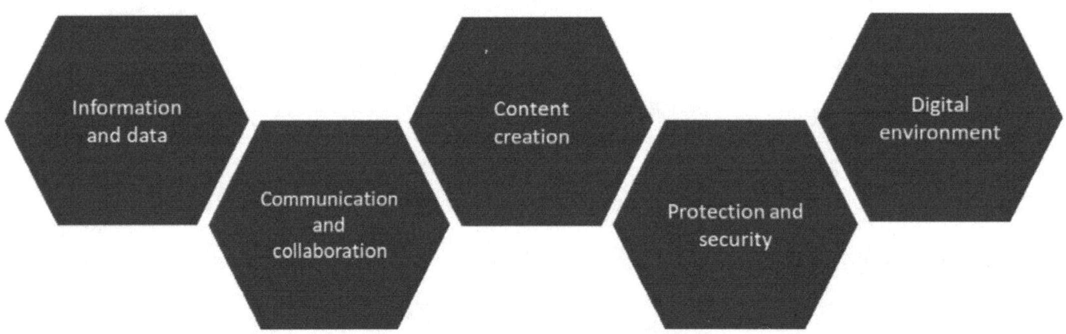

Figure 3. Five areas of the European digital competencies framework (DigComp)

- In its efforts to inform all teachers about new trends, events, challenges, trainings, etc. the Ministry of Education publishes every month the "eduSphere newsletter" and organises as a key event called "eduSphere day", which is a whole day of practical training for teachers. The workshops present inspiring practices and allow teachers to exchange their experiences. The topics range from 3D printing, laser cutting, robotics, green screen towards the use of specific apps and tablets in class.
- To learn about the potential of *digital game based learning* in education, experiments were made in different schools (primary and secondary) in cooperation with the University of Luxembourg and the Donau University in Krems (Austria). First

promising results were presented in January 2019 at a meeting of the European Commission's DG EAC working group on digital education. Additionally, the creation of national and international networks as well as the elaboration of appropriate learning resources, i.e. games, are all initiatives that allow the strategic development and implementation of this pedagogical approach.

Area 2: Educational technology

The objective of the activities in this area are to support learning with digital tools (hardware and software) which shall foster a more student centred and practical learning. The following incomplete list illustrates some of the actions put in place.

- "MathemaTIC" is a personalised learning environment for mathematics. It allows students to learn in an individual way at their pace by using interactive learning activities. All exercises are consistent with the curriculum and its objectives. Due to Luxembourg's multi-linguistic population, the content is available in four languages: German, French, Portuguese and English. The particularity of MathemaTIC is that students are provided with learning activities that best fit their current level of knowledge. The system provides teachers with a constant overview of their students' performance.
- The programme "one2one" was initiated to reduce inequalities and to allow every student, independently of their social background, access to digital learning resources. Tablets are deployed under a leasing contract to ensure that all students will be able to own such a device. In pair with the one2one program, new learning scenarios and digital resources are made available to profit as much as possible of the added values of the tablets.
- As teachers are the key component of the success of any educational approach, their *continuous professional development* is essential. The national training institute for teachers (IFEN) offers a large variety of courses in the domain of media literacy and educational technology, as well as on other connected topics like GDPR, author rights and deontology on social networks. Such courses were also integrated into the initial teacher training (primary and secondary).
- The Ministry of Education is in the process of *updating existing curricula* in order to adapt them to the digitalisation of daily life. For the sake of illustration, the classical "Technician in electrical engineering" is transformed into "Technician in smart technologies" to prepare the students to technologies on industry 4.0, smart home, renewable energy and electric mobility. *New curricula* are created, e.g., in eCommerce and computer sciences.

Area 3: Promotion of STEM

According to Cedefop (European skills and jobs survey, 2018), 43% of adult employees in the European Union have recently been affected by digitisation in their jobs, e.g. by the introduction of a new ICT tool or processes to automate tasks. More specifically, the study suggests that 14% to 18% of jobs are at risk and that future employees will need to have the know-how required by this new way of working in a digital world. This risk is greater for routine jobs and is likely to affect mainly lower-skilled workers. However, other positions in the tertiary sector are also concerned and traditional tasks such as document management are impacted by digitisation.

A Eurofund study (Overview of new forms of employment, 2018) found that it is not only a question of job substitution, but that digitisation also implies that new tasks must be considered in old jobs. As a result, continuous professional development is more necessary than ever to acquire digital skills such as coding.

According to the European Commission (Digital Skills & Jobs, 2019), up to 500.000 ICT jobs will remain vacant in Europe by 2020. However, the number of graduates leaving education does not meet that demand.

Luxembourg is lacking not only of (highly) qualified experts, but also youngsters that are interested in ICT studies or trainings. Therefore, the aim of this third area of Digital (4) Education is to modernise the offer of curricula and to attract more students to this sector of the labour market. The 2018-2023 coalition agreement of the Luxembourg government sets the political priority to equipping students with the skills that are required by the digitalisation of the labour market. Some specific initiatives are listed here as illustration.

- The Ministry of Education created the label "Future Hub" to promote secondary schools that are open to technology and innovative learning from science, technology, engineering, and mathematics (STEM). The Future Hub schools integrate a variety of training and specialisation courses with technological characteristics in their school offer. The integration of technologies in learning methods while promoting students' creativity and sense of initiative is fostered.
- New *ICT curricula* were created at different levels of the school system, from lower secondary, over VET, towards higher secondary. These offers have a strong focus on computer sciences and communication, and allow graduates access to university studies in the related field.
- Following a strong demand from industry on highly qualified and immediately operational work force, a two year curricula of higher education was extended to computer science topics. This "Brevet de Technicien Supérieur" (BTS) is offered in different secondary schools according to their local speciality and orientation, e.g. Internet of Things (IoT), Game Art & Game Design, Game Programming & Game Design, and Cloud Computing. Collaboration with external actors in these fields allows developing and adapting a leading-edge school offer.
- The "Luxembourg Tech School" is a new extracurricular programme that supports the development of future digital leaders. It is aimed at 15-19 year-old learners who are passionate about the digital environment and eager to learn about the use and application of technology in a real business context. The activities cover different topics, e.g. game development, big data, FinTech, and space.

- "BEE CREATIVE" is a project which aims to motivate students to create using technical tools and to promote entrepreneurship. The project culminated in 2015 in the launch of several educational *makerspaces*. A makerspace is a place where young people can discover and create. It is also an opportunity to meet other young people and embark on maker-projects together. Such sessions are always free of charge and are accompanied by experts in the field. Learners can accomplish projects such as: build their own drone or robot, develop their own video game, or create their own music.

Conclusion

Digital (4) Education is an ongoing strategy by Luxembourg's Ministry of Education, Children and Youth and is constantly extending its broad variety of activities in formal, non-formal and in-formal education according to its key objectives.

References

Cedefop (2018). European skills and jobs (ESJ) survey. Retrieved March 10, 2019, from http://www.cedefop.europa.eu/en/events-and-projects/projects/european-skills-and-jobs-esj-survey

Eurfound (2018). Overview of new forms of employment. Retrieved March 10, 2019, from https://www.eurofound.europa.eu/sites/default/files/ef_publication/field_ef_document/ef18050en.pdf

European Commission (2019). Digital Skills & Jobs. Retrieved March 10, 2019, from https://ec.europa.eu/digital-single-market/en/policies/digital-skills

EDUCATING FOR INTERDISCIPLINARY COMPETENCES: A VIVES-FRAMEWORK

Elien Sabbe, David Wemel, VIVES University of Applied Sciences, Belgium

Situating interdisciplinarity in VIVES

Nowadays professionals function in a society that is changing faster and faster. They face complex questions and challenges for which a mere (mono)disciplinary approach is no longer sufficient (Holley, 2017; Spelt, Biemans, Tobi, Luning, & Mulder, 2009). For VIVES, it is therefore both a necessity and an asset that students are equipped with solid domain specific knowledge and skills as well as with broader competences, the so-called competences for the 21st century. One of those broader competences is the competence for interdisciplinary cooperation.

VIVES is investing a lot in interdisciplinarity. In our VIVES-research (VIVES, 2016), we explicitly choose for interdisciplinary centres of expertise. Also in the lab-approach of education, our make-lab, a care-lab and a simulation-lab are seen as real hubs for interdisciplinarity. In our VIVES-vision on education, we aim to prepare student for the jobs and the society of tomorrow (VIVES, 2014). That is why we so strongly stress the importance of interdisciplinary competences in our policy documents: the VIVES vision on education, the VIVES-competences for the 21st century and the VIVES-framework for quality assurance of our study programmes (VIVES, 2018). Our educational policy plan for the period 2017-2022 points out the necessity to create enough space for interdisciplinary cooperation in the curricula and demands that every study programme is cooperating interdisciplinary with at least one other study programme in at least one course (VIVES, 2017).

Students don't learn to cooperate interdisciplinary on their own (Holley, 2017; Spelt, Biemans, Tobi, Luning, & Mulder, 2009). It is therefore crucial for study programmes to choose explicitly for well targeted learning activities and assessments that really contribute to the acquisition of interdisciplinary competences. Moreover, those activities are stronger if they are embedded in what we call "connected curricula" (VIVES, 2017). We shouldn't treat interdisciplinarity as something separate or besides the curriculum, but as fully integrated in the existing curricula. To support this vision and in order to get a clear view on the level of integration of interdisciplinarity in our curricula, VIVES has developed the framework we will describe below.

The framework

The 7 axes

Designing curricula that stimulate interdisciplinary cooperation is a complex interaction between content, methods and organisation. In order to make this complex reality comprehensible, we have selected seven core-elements to build the framework. These 7 elements are based upon research results and practical experience in literature (Holley, 2017; Hogeschool UC Leuven-Limburg, 2017; Spelt, Biemans, Tobi, Luning, & Mulder, 2009). and in practice. For each of the elements we have developed an axe on which the single course or the entire curriculum can be positioned.

1. *Students*: Which students encounter interdisciplinarity in their programme? (Individual students → All students)
2. *Society and professional field*: How do students experience interdisciplinarity in their contacts with the professional field or broader society? (Exploration → Interdisciplinary cases by and for professional partners)
3. *Level of interdisciplinarity*: Multidisciplinarity → transdisciplinarity
4. *Scope*: Different study programmes in the same faculty (narrow scope) → Interdisciplinary cooperation between faculties (large scope)
5. *Embeddedness*: Impact of interdisciplinary cooperation on the educational activities. (interdisciplinary cooperation between teachers (to enrich their content) → interdisciplinarity as a learning outcome)
6. *Alignment*: Level of alignment between learning outcomes, learning activities and assessment (Biggs, 1996)
7. *Coherence*: The way in which activities aimed at interdisciplinarity are connected. (individual or isolated activities or courses → strong integration in the whole curriculum)

For each of the axes, a 3-level scale with a description for each level has been developed.

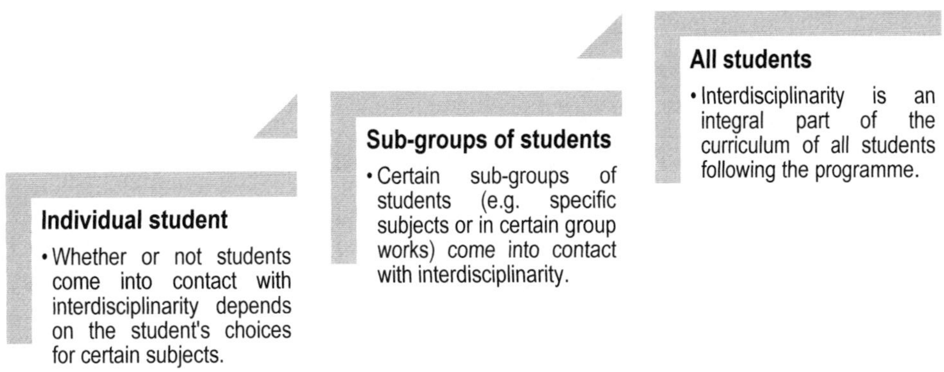

Axe 1: Students

Exploration of interdisciplinarity in the professional field/society

- Students get to know the interdisciplinary character of the professional field/society through company visits, practical examples, cases,...
- Students do not actively work interdisciplinarily in and with the professional field/society.

Interdisciplinary cases from the professional field/society

- Students actively work with interdisciplinary cases/assessments/problem propositions from the field or society.
- Students must be able to connect core concepts from their own discipline with other relevant disciplines in a (simulated) educational situation.
- The guidance and evaluation in the elaboration of the cases by the students takes place within (simulation-education in) VIVES.

Interdisciplinary cases with and for the professional field

- Students actively work with interdisciplinary cases/assessments/problem propositions with and for the field of work or society.
- Students connect core concepts from their own discipline with other relevant disciplines in order to contribute to a solution/execution of the case with and for the field of work or society.
- The guidance and evaluation in the elaboration of the cases takes place in collaboration with the interdisciplinary field of work or society.

Axe 2: Society and professional field

Multidisciplinary

- Different disciplines each contribute with their own expertise.
- Expertise remains side by side.
- There is no knowledge transfer or integration between disciplines.

Interdisciplinary

- Interaction between experts and integration of expertise from different disciplines.
- Boundaries between the different disciplines remain.
- Common goals and products (which could not arise from the individual discisplines).

Transdisciplinary

- Co-creation by experts from different disciplines and non-experts (experts by experience).
- Boundaries between disciplines disappear, people (partially) move into each other's field of work or environment.
- A new set of shared knowledge or solutions is created for a discipline-transcending authentic problem.

Axe3: Level of interdisciplinarity

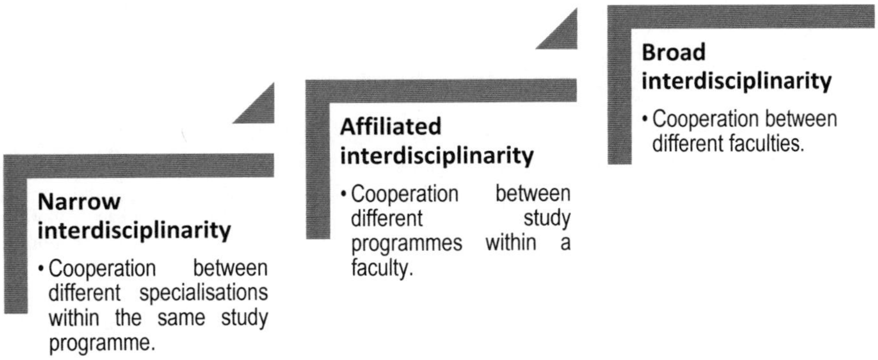

Axe 4: Scope

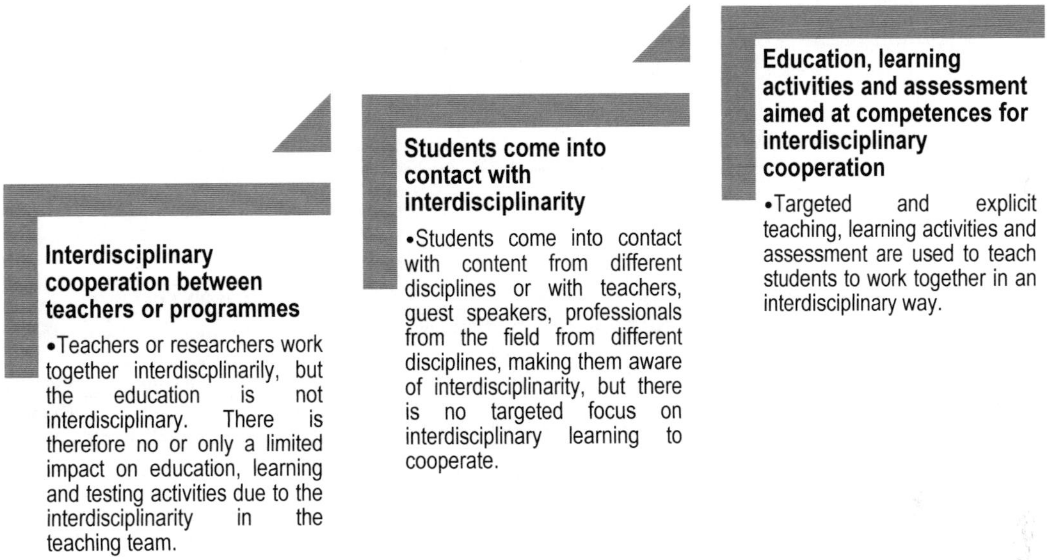

Axe 5: Embeddedness

Is implicitly addressed

- The curriculum includes interdisciplinary initiatives, but these are not named as such or the intended competences for interdisciplinary cooperation are not explicitly formulated or communicated to the students.

Explicit purpose of teaching and learning activities

- The curriculum explicitly aims at competences for interdisciplinary cooperation and contains deliberately chosen teaching and learning activities.
- Students are explained why they have opted for certain teaching and learning activities based on competences for interdisciplinary cooperation and what the expectations are.

Systematically assessed

- Throughout the programme, the competencies for interdisciplinary cooperation are assessed formatively or summatively (preferably at different moments in the programme).
- Students reflect and/or receive (preferably interim) feedback on the extent to which they have acquired competencies for interdisciplinary cooperation.

Axe 6: Alignment

Separate initiatives of individual teachers

- Individual teachers use interdisciplinary teaching, learning activities or assessment on their own initiative.
- Interdisciplinarity occurs in one or more subjects and is separate from other educational, learning activities, assessment or learning objectives in the programme.

Several related initiatives

- In the curriculum there are some interdisciplinary initiatives which are to a limited extent interlinked or coordinated with other educational, learning activities and assessment.

Integrated perspective

- Interdisciplinary teaching, learning and assessment activities are integrated by the training team into the curriculum in a balanced, coherent and targeted way.
- Moreover, there is an accumulation in complexity, difficulty and degree of integration in the interdisciplinary teaching, learning activities and assessments throughout the different phases of the programme.
- The acquisition of competences for interdisciplinary cooperation or underlying competences is preferably linked to the acquisition of other related competences (e.g. cooperation and communication, research competences, critical-reflexive competences, etc.).

Axe 7: Coherence

Interdisciplinary profile

(Teams of) teachers can now build an interdisciplinary profile of their course or their study programme. We bring together the seven axes in a spider diagram in order to visualise the level of interdisciplinarity for a course or a study programme. The diagram can be used in a static way, by using it to take a picture from the current level of interdisciplinarity (as is), or it can be used in a more dynamic way, by also visualising the desired level of interdisciplinarity (as should be) in the same diagram.

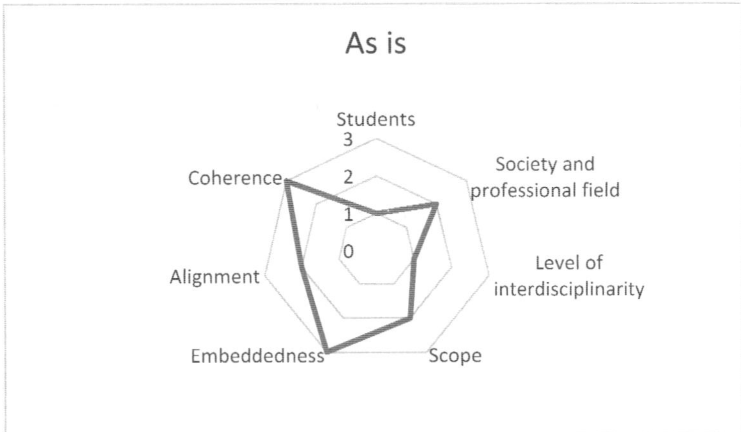

Figure 1. Static use of the spider diagram

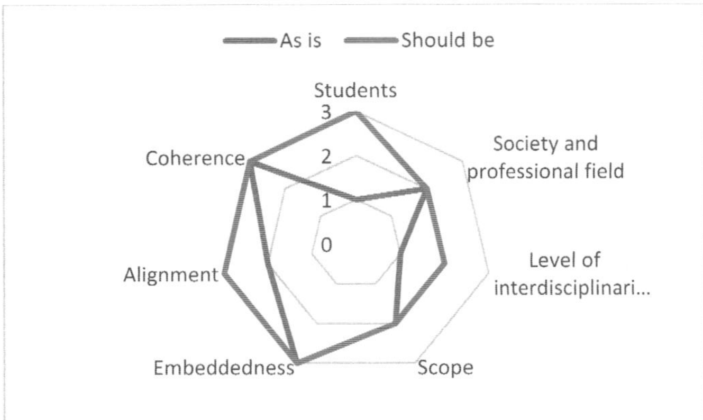

Figure 2. Dynamic use of the spider diagram

Action plans

A next step for teacher teams can then be to make up an action plan to make the shift from the situation "as is" towards the situation "as it should be".

Discussion

In VIVES, our educational policy plan for the period 2017-2022 points out the necessity to create enough space for interdisciplinary cooperation in the curricula and demands that every study programme is cooperating interdisciplinary with at least one other study programme in at least one course (VIVES, 2017). This framework offers a tool for teacher teams to "score" the level of interdisciplinarity in their study programme. For some of the axes we pointed out a minimum score to make clear what is the absolute minimum level of interdisciplinarity we expect from our different study programmes. In other words, this is where the "as is" line needs to be for every single study programme by the end of 2022. Off course, we stimulate our teachers to be more ambitious in their positioning of the "should be" line, but we also recognise that the desired level of interdisciplinarity can be different for every study programme due to, among other things, context reasons.

In our quest for more education for interdisciplinary competences, we often encounter practical obstacles. When two or more study programmes need to collaborate, time and space issues appear. In the case of VIVES for example, our campuses are located in five different cities across the province. Therefore, interdisciplinary courses often require mobility between two or more campuses. This is considered time consuming, inefficient and less sustainable. Moreover, the issues of time and space are even more present in a context of distance education.

An emerging question is how to develop distance education curricula with components of interdisciplinarity and how educational technology can help us to overcome issues of time and space in a context of interdisciplinary education both for distance education as for regular study programmes.

References

Biggs, J. (1996). Enhancing teaching through constructive alignment. *Higher Education., 32*(3), 347.

Holley, K. (2017). *Interdisciplinary Curriculum and Learning in Higher Education.* Oxford Research Encyclopedia, Education.

Hogeschool UC Leuven-Limburg (2017). Transdisciplinair onderwijs. Inspiratiegids. Onderwijsontwikkelingsfonds (OOF) Horizon.

Lattuca, L. (2001). *Creating interdisciplinarity: interdisciplinary research and teaching among college and university faculty.* Nashville: Vanderbilt University Press.

Spelt, E. J. H., Biemans, H. J. A., Tobi, H., Luning, P. A., & Mulder, M. (2009). Teaching and Learning in Interdisciplinary Higher Education: a systematic review. *Journal of Educational Psychology Review, 21*(4), 365-378.

VIVES dienst onderwijsbeleid (2014). De missie, strategische krachtlijnen en onderwijsvisie van VIVES. DO@Vives nr. 1.

VIVES dienst onderwijsbeleid (2016). Competent voor de 21e eeuw. DO@Vives nr. 8.

VIVES dienst onderwijsbeleid (2017). Onderwijsbeleidsplan 2017-2022. DO@Vives, nr. 12.

VIVES dienst onderwijsbeleid (2018). Kwaliteitszorg van een opleiding. VIVES-referentiekader 2017-2022. DO@VIVES nr. 15.

VIVES dienst onderzoek en dienstverlening (2016). Onderzoeksbeleidsplan 2016-2020. Kortrijk: hogeschool VIVES.

10 YEARS OF LEARNING DESIGN AT THE OPEN UNIVERSITY: EVOLUTION, FINDINGS AND FUTURE DIRECTION

Gerald Evans, The Open University, United Kingdom

Overview

Over the past 10 years The Open University has embedded an institutional approach to Learning Design, with use of the approach mandated as part of the curriculum design process.

This paper will explore how that approach has developed over time, as practitioners have learnt from and developed the offering, and as requirements on the institution and on curriculum production have changed. This evolution has seen the approach develop into an end-to-end process of design and evaluation and brought to bear the power of learning analytics into curriculum design.

The paper will also explore the various internal and external research outputs, synthesising these into some key lessons that have been learnt over the past ten years.

Finally, the paper will look ahead, to see how the next ten years might look and how the role of Learning Design may adapt over this time.

Evolution of process

There are a number of reasons for The Open University, and distance learning providers more generally, to take an institutional level approach to Learning Design, but two stand out:

- Our students learn at a distance, so it is important that a broad picture of the structure and pedagogy of a piece of curriculum can quickly and effectively be communicated to tutors and students.
- It is much more difficult for us to identify and fix problems when a module is in presentation than in a conventional university, and problems are often easier to spot when information is presented in a visualised form rather than a descriptive narrative.

Back in 2009, when starting out on the implementation of Learning Design at The Open University, the approach was based around three key principles (Galley, 2015):

- mechanisms to encourage design conversations across disciplines and expert roles;
- the use of tools and instruments as a means of describing and sharing designs;
- the use of information and data to inform the conceptual tools and frameworks that guide the decision making process.

These manifested themselves through the core suite of tools that the Learning Design approach embedded as part of business as usual for The Open University, and included the following set of resources.

Learning Design workshops

These were established as key interventions bringing together the module team and holding a facilitated conversation with the team to help them to articulate and capture the learning journey for the module. The Learning Designer facilitates the workshop and the module team bring their subject expertise to the table to work with the designer to flesh out the plans for the module.

Learning Design views

A number of core Learning Design views were established early on which acted as core mechanisms for developing shared understanding of Learning Designs. This included common templates to be used to capture the designs and common terminology enabling the University to establish a shared language for describing completed learning designs.

Online tools and learning analytics

As the views and approach to workshops developed, online versions of the views were created enabling the University to start to develop learning analytics from completed learning designs. This included a tool for logging the student workload down to activity level.

Other initiatives

Alongside the development of Learning Design, there have been two new initiatives developed internally that have now been integrated into the full end-to-end Learning Design and evaluation model:

- Firstly, development of approaches within the University's production teams to support teams with detailed-level technology support and design. This was initially called TEL design and sought to bridge the gap between creation and implementation of a given learning design.
- Secondly, the development of learning analytics views, culminating in a programme of work around this area from 2013 which sought to create a step change in the University's adoption of learning analytics. A key part of this initiative was the idea of using learning analytics to inform evidence-based change in presentation. This approach was labelled Analytics4Action.

Over the past three years the Learning Design team at The Open University have carefully integrated both of these initiatives together with the original Learning Design tools to create the end-to-end support for Learning Design and evaluation at the OU. This revised process, as outlined in Figure 1, is bringing to bear the full benefits of learning analytics as a tool to support evaluation of learning design work.

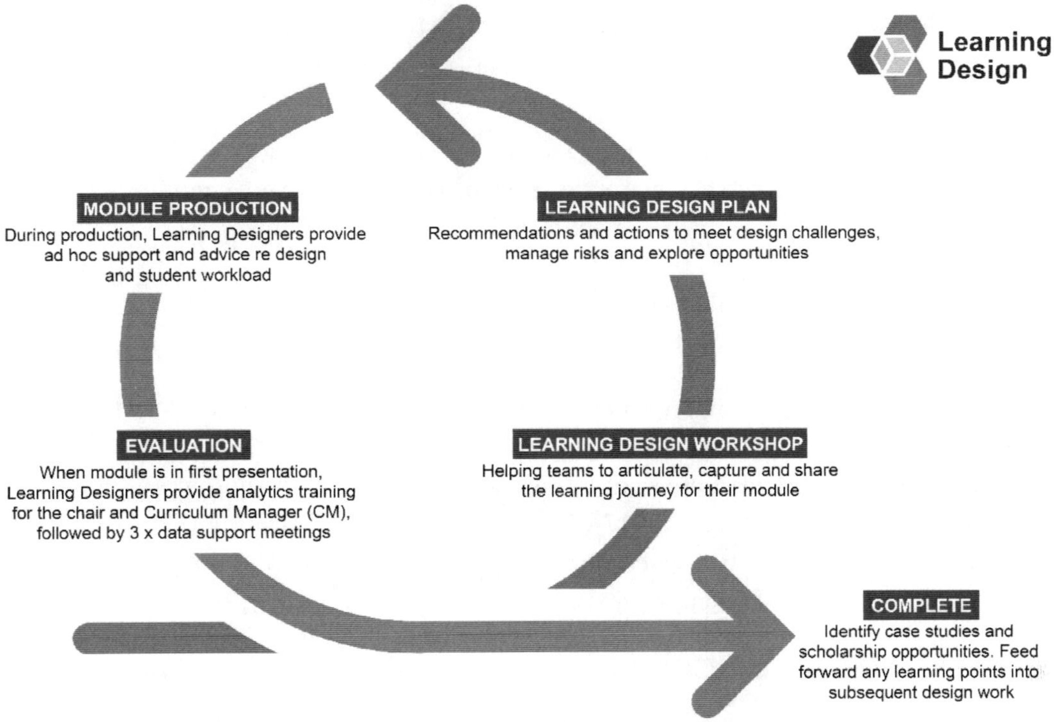

Figure 1. The Open University Learning Design process

Key to the success of the approach is the people-based nature from start to finish. The workshop, Learning Design Plan and analytics training all aim to handhold and bring people along with the Learning Designer in a collaborative manner. In particular, the approach to training and supporting teams with Evaluation has led to very positive feedback from participants and has encouraged even analytics sceptics to work with us and engage with the learning analytics.

Research outputs and findings

Over the past ten years, a large volume of research has been undertaken by staff at The Open University looking at the outputs and findings from our Learning Design approach. This has also helpfully been collated into a paper reviewing the alignment of learning design with learning analytics which summarises eight empirical studies linking learning analytics with Learning Design (Rienties et al., 2017).

These studies have found a number of key conclusions, including:

- That educators working with Learning Design views have adjusted their designs toward more student-active activities such as communication and finding and handling information (Toetenel & Rienties, 2016).
- That communication activities are a key predictor of academic retention in learning designs (Rienties & Toetenel, 2016).
- That learner satisfaction is strongly influenced by learning design (Rienties & Toetenel, 2016).

- That learning designs vary considerably across disciplines (Nguyen et al., 2017).
- The OU Learning Design taxonomy needed to be adjusted for the languages context (Rienties et al., 2018).

Further studies have led to the creation of a series of principles for design for retention (van Ameijde et al., 2018). These are based around seven principles, and more commonly known as the ICEBERG model as an acronym of the combined principles (Integrated, Collaborative, Engaging, Balanced, Economical, Reflective and Gradual). These principles have been integrated into the approach taken to Learning Design and new resources have been created to support teams in implementing the principles.

Additionally, the Learning Design team have generated improved institutional understanding into the challenges of collaborative learning activities and provided tips on designing these (Evans & Chang, 2017), and prototyped a number of innovative design approach, such as adaptive learning (Evans & Gallen, 2017). Designing these and delivering them at scale is a significant challenge and an area where Learning Design can help educators to both design effective solutions and avoid potential pitfalls.

Future direction and conclusion

So the first ten years of embedding Learning Design at The Open University has led to a substantial amount of change in terms of completeness of the process and with that a far more nuanced understanding of what works for our students. This has been a process of evolution and looking for opportunities to link up the existing process with new initiatives aimed at improving student retention and with a strong link to Learning Design.

The coming years are likely to see similar adaptations as improved understanding of the approaches used enables us to further develop the model.

In the short-term, developments in the learning analytics model will enable improved insight into student engagement with learning activities. These will help us to pinpoint where students are hitting challenges in their learning and most importantly to understand where they disengage from the learning process.

In the medium-term there are developments in the field of Artificial Intelligence (AI) which could significantly improve the support we are able to offer to content creators by offering real-time Learning Design advice based on machine learning. This work is underpinned by work to review the usage of the existing Learning Design taxonomy and to ensure that machine learning is able to pick up the distinctions between various types of activity.

Any further developments will be built upon what is a very strong base, but will also need to take into account any changing dynamics for curriculum production at the University. For instance, the University is seeing an increase in students wishing to study at full-time intensity. With curriculum designed for part-time study intensity this creates a series of new challenges and the Learning Design approaches will need to support teams with meeting these challenges.

Conclusion

As a fully established and matured process, Learning Design at The Open University has become a part of the norm for curriculum design and is growing from strength to strength as it learns from new initiatives and is able to build these into the work of the team and University. The original creators of the OU Learning Design process would never have wished for their creation to stand still and the hard work of the practitioners and researchers at the University is ensuring that there is an ongoing evolution of approach.

By continuing to learn from these new initiatives and being able to both develop staff and adapt the process, Learning Design has been able to move with the times and adapt to change both internally and externally. This requirement seems likely to remain as a key factor for the University as the sector and picture for distance learning continues to change at pace. It's a big strength of the process that it is able to adapt and that will be key to the ongoing success of Learning Design at The Open University in the coming years.

References

van Ameijde, J., Weller, M., & Cross, S. (2018). Learning Design for student retention. *Journal of Applied Perspectives in Applied Academic Practice, 6*(2), 41-50.

Evans, G., & Chang, D. (2017). Collaborative online learning at a distance – a case study and developing the knowledge base. *Book of abstracts and synergy projects, Eden Conference 2017.*

Evans, G., & Gallen, A. (2017). Adaptive learning as a tool for supporting diverse students with threshold concepts at a distance. *Book of abstracts and synergy projects, Eden Conference 2017.*

Galley, R. (2015). *Learning Design at The Open University.* The Open University: Milton Keynes.

Nguyen, Q., Rienties, B. & Toetenel, L. (2017). Unravelling the dynamics of instructional practice: a longitudinal study on learning design and VLE activities. *Proceedings of the Seventh International Learning Analytics & Knowledge Conference, Vancouver, British Columbia, Canada 2017*, 168-177. ACM, New York, NY, USA.

Rienties, B., Lewis, T., McFarlane, R., Nguyen, Q., & Toetenel, L. (2018). Analytics in online and offline language learning environments: the role of learning design to understand student online engagement. *Journal of Computer-Assisted Language Learning, 31*(3), 273-293.

Rienties B., Nguyen Q., Holmes W., & Reedy K. (2017). A review of ten years of implementation and research in aligning learning design with learning analytics at the Open University UK. *Interaction Design and Architecture(s) Journal, 33*, 134-54.

Rienties, B., & Toetenel, L. (2016). The impact of learning design on student behaviour, satisfaction and performance: a cross-institutional comparison across 151 modules. *Computers in Human Behavior, 60*, 333-341.

Toetenel, L., & Rienties, B. (2016). Learning Design – creative design to visualise learning activities. *Open Learning, 31*(3), 233-244.

MASSIVE, PARTIALLY ONLINE CS1 COURSE

Tamar Vilner, Ela Zur, The Open University of Israel, Israel

Abstract

The Open University of Israel (OUI) has an open admissions policy and is based primarily on distance learning. As in other universities, our CS1 course includes the topics recommended in the Computer Science Curricula (2013). The large number of students who register for the course (from 700-900 students per semester) presents us with unique challenges in management. In this paper, we describe the efforts we have devoted to making the learning and teaching process as uniform as possible for all students taking the course. We describe the research we conducted in order to ascertain whether there is a correlation between regular or intensive tutoring groups and student success in CS1 and whether the specific tutors affect student success. We were satisfied that the teaching of our course is quite uniform.

Background

The Open University of Israel

The OUI features an open admissions policy and study programs based primarily on distance learning. The university offers a variety of undergraduate and graduate degree programs (see the OUI website), which rely almost entirely on independent study. Courses are taught through course books developed at the OUI which also benefit students at other universities, and videotaped lectures designed specifically for OUI students. OUI courses feature optional face-to-face small group tutorials and a predefined assignment submission schedule. In order to receive credit, students must successfully pass a final exam. The OUI also makes use of advanced web-based technologies (Gal-Ezer, Vilner, & Zur, 2009) in order to facilitate its distance-learning methodology.

The CS1 Course

Course Material and Assignments

The CS1 course, Introduction to Computer Science Using Java, is based on the textbook "Java Software Solutions", by Lewis and Loftus (2012). Dr. Amir Goren and Tamar Vilner, of the OUI mathematics and computer science department, present a series of lectures which are available on the course website, and which contain all material covered in the course. As in introductory courses at other universities, our course includes the topics recommended in the Computer Science Curricula (2013). We teach Java using the BlueJ environment (BlueJ Website).

Along with the course material, we include eight assignments, of which students are required to submit at least five, according to the deadlines. The assignments are graded, and calculated into the final grade of the course. Each assignment includes questions that relate to various theoretical subjects, and that require writing Java programs.

Face-to-Face Meetings

CS1, like all OUI courses, incorporates face-to-face meetings held at OUI study centres throughout the country. The tutorials are offered in *regular mode* – two-hour meetings held every other week, and *intensive mode* – three-hour weekly meetings. Registration for the course is based on signing up for one of the two tutorials. Although attendance is not mandatory, it is highly recommended. The intensive mode costs more than the regular one. To assist students who live far from a study centre, or those who cannot attend face-to-face meetings, a "Zoom" group allows an instructor to teach a live class remotely from a studio on the OUI campus.

Course Website

The course website, which serves as an interactive learning environment, provides two types of communication channels – an administrative channel and an academic channel that includes a message board, discussion forums and enrichment materials. These include supplementary study materials, exercises, and exams for self-assessment, demonstrations, feedback on assignments, links to the recorded lectures and videotaped tutorial sessions, and links to relevant websites. The website also contains sample exams from previous semesters.

Managing a Massive Open Online Course

In recent years, many universities have begun to offer Massive Open Online Courses (MOOCs), which have become a popular topic in academic discussions. Although our CS1 course in not considered a MOOC, the issues we deal with are similar, and thus, we have checked the literature regarding managing a course with numerous students, especially with regard to grading assignments and exams.

MOOCs offer internet-based university-style courses for large numbers of learners. Staubitz et al. (2016) takes a closer look at peer assessments as a tool for delivering individualized feedback and assignments to MOOC participants. The paper describes a peer assessment workflow and its implementation on the openHP1 and open SAP MOOC platform.

Vihavainen, Paksula, and Luukkainen define an Extreme Apprenticeship model that is based on a set of values and practices that emphasize learning by doing together, with continuous feedback, as the most efficient means for learning (2011). They demonstrate how the method has been applied to a CS1 programming course. Vihavainen, Luukkainen, and Kurhila (2013) used this method in their MOOC introductory programming course, thus ensuring that students proceeded step-by-step in the desired direction. The feedback was provided by human advisors (teachers), however, they don't describe how they maintain uniformity when checking assignments.

Stephenson (2018) reports on a recent experience using exams that include two portions: one, a closed book multiple choice test answered on paper, and the other, a computerized programming portion where students were asked to create small programs using their usual development tools and reference materials. They tried this version instead of exams that asked students to write small programs on paper, after the students expressed the opinion that exams on paper were not reflective of the "real world", and thus their grades on such exams would not accurately reflect their programming ability. They found that both the students and the course instructors preferred the exams that included computerized programming questions.

The use of automatic assessment has been less extensive, mainly because almost all existing systems are based on output comparison. If the output is the expected, the code is correct. Otherwise, it is reported as wrong, even if there is only one typo in the code. Insa and Silva (2015) introduce a new code assessment method that also verifies properties of the code, thus marking the code even if it is only partially correct.

Ju et al. (2018) describe a system that "enables realistic in-class coding-based exams with broad Internet access". They report on "lessons and experience creating and administering such exam, including autograding-related pitfalls for high-stakes exams"".

Managing our CS1 Massive Course

Each semester, about 700-900 OUI students enrol in the CS1 course, which is mandatory for all undergraduate computer science programs. The students are located all over the country, and attend face-to-face study groups led by about twenty tutors. Great effort is made by the course coordinator to ensure that the teaching is as consistent as possible for all the students in all the groups.

First, a tutors meeting is held immediately preceding each semester. Tutors discuss issues regarding teaching. Each course has its own timetable (scheduling, dates for submitting assignments, etc.), so tutors attempt to teach more or less the same materials. The course coordinator provides the slideshows for each face-to-face meeting and tutors try to present similar examples and to give the students the same problems to solve.

As mentioned above, before the start of each semester, students receive the assignments which they will need to submit, along with a list of deadlines. Naturally, all students receive the identical exercise booklet, and the course coordinator tries to make assignment grading as consistent as possible. For that purpose, tutors are divided into eight teams of two or three for the purpose of preparing one assignment each. This includes preparing a solution for that exercise, a tester for checking the code of the exercise, and a guide of typical errors and number of points to subtract from the grade when such errors occur. This creates an optimal environment for grading the exercises consistently in all groups by all the tutors. Since each assignment in the course web has a discussion group, in which students may ask questions, the team responsible for a particular assignment is expected to answer the students' questions in this forum. This helps the students receive uniform answers to their questions, and other tutors need not enter the forums to answer the many questions. Each tutor is responsible for one assignment only, and shares information for the other assignments with his or her colleagues.

Student Support

Tutors are also expected to provide student support during the learning process. Each tutor has a specific hour during the week which is dedicated to answering student questions by phone. As there are about twenty tutors, and a student is not required to call his or her own tutor, assistance is available to students for about 15 hours per week (there is some overlap of tutor hours, of course.) Email and discussion groups on the course website are the most popular channels used by students to contact tutors and other students. We know, of course, that the students also have closed groups on Facebook and WhatsApp, but we do not interfere, although we know that many of the exercise solutions are published there.

Final Exams

As already mentioned, in order to complete a course, students must submit assignments throughout the semester and pass the final exam. Exams are held at OUI study centres throughout the country, and in embassies worldwide for those studying abroad. At the end of the exam, they are collected and sent back to OUI headquarters, where they are distributed to the course coordinators for grading. In order to ensure that the exams are graded fairly, all exams are graded by the course coordinator, usually with help of one or two tutors. Each grader checks the same questions across the board. In this way, different grading styles balance each other out, ensuring uniformity.

As one can see, we expend much effort in order to create a consistent and uniform learning and teaching process. We decided to evaluate whether these efforts are beneficial. In the following sections we will describe our research.

Research Methodology

Research Questions

- Is there a correlation between student success in CS1 and participation in regular or intensive tutoring?
- To what extent is there a connection between specific group tutors and student success in CS1?

Research Population and Research Tools

The study included 12,242 students enrolled in our CS1 course during the years 2010-2018. The data is taken from the university's enrolment and grade database.

Results

Background Details of Students

Figure 1 shows the number of students enrolled in the CS1 course over the years. As is evident, the numbers have been increasing since 2011.

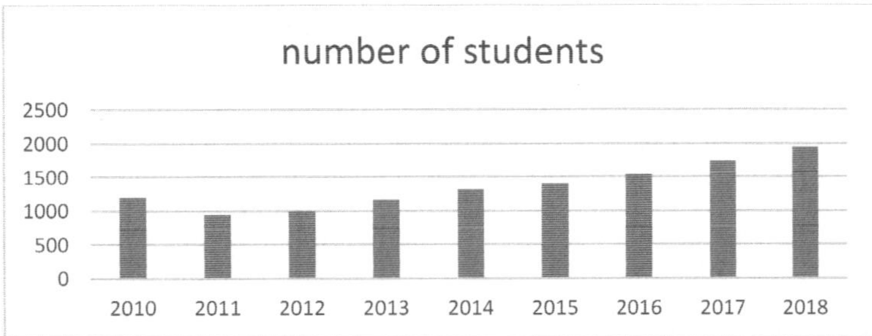

Figure 1. Number of students enrolled in CS1 since 2010

We collected some background details about the students:

- As can be seen worldwide, most of the student population is male, while females are in the minority. We found that the percentage of female computer science students has been hovering at around 20%, having dropped to 19% in 2013-2014 and having increased to 21% in 2018 (Vilner & Zur, 2006; Barr, 2018).
- There has been an increase in students completing their high school matriculation exams. So, although the OUI has an open admission policy, even for applicants who haven't complete high school, we found that the majority of the students attended high school. And while only 62% declared that they had a matriculation certificate in 2010, by 2018, 77% of OUI students were high school graduates.
- The average age of students enrolled in the CS1 course over the years has remained between 26 and 27.
- Since CS1 is the first course in the undergraduate computer science program, and must be passed in order to continue with the program, we found that about 10-11% of the students repeated this course.
- The majority of students chose to register for intensive tutoring. However, this percentage is dropping. While 81% of students studied in intensive groups in 2010, only 67% chose to do so in 2018. An explanation for this might lie in the development of technologies that we use in our tutoring sessions, such as the Zoom group.

Student Advancement over the Course of a Semester

The course does not require any previous programming knowledge, and even students with no background at all can achieve a high level of success. Since we have an open admission policy, and this is usually the first course students take towards an undergraduate degree program in CS, the students are very heterogeneous in their level of knowledge and skills when beginning the course. Some students have studied CS in high school, some are already programmers in the high tech industry, and some have no knowledge at all. As a result, the dropout rate is quite high. Figure 2 shows student advancement over the semester. One can see that while 93% of the students enrolled in the course submit at least one assignment during the semester, only 71% complete all the exercise requirements. Only 64% of the students attended the final exam, and just 42% succeeded in the course.

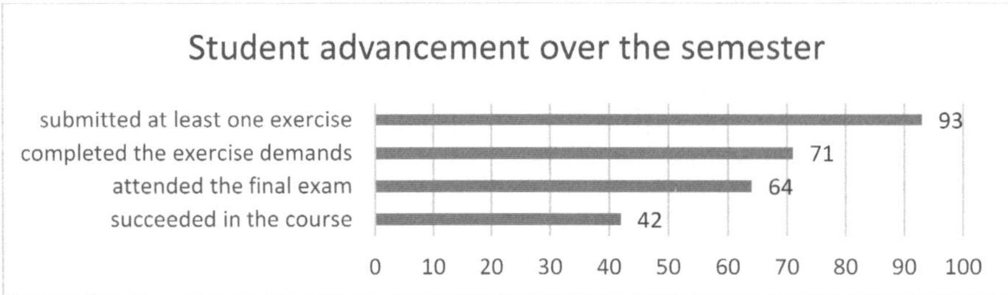

Figure 2. Student advancement over the semester

Intensive Tutoring Versus Regular Tutoring

For our research, we conducted an evaluation of all students in every study centre, but for this paper, we focused on students at our Tel-Aviv site. Table 1 shows how many students enrolled in this large central-Israel study centre, which hosts more than ten CS1 study groups per semester; 5-6 in regular-tutoring mode, and the rest in intensive mode. We chose this particular site as the focus of our research, since the large number of groups means that there is at least one group per day, which allows students to choose a group according to their preference for particular days of the week and convenience. The groups are therefore heterogeneous as far as student level, with no one group containing only stronger or weaker students. The exception is the separation between regular and intensive groups. Usually, most of the students who choose the regular groups have a background in programming and prior knowledge, particularly in Java.

Table 1: No. of students who studied in Tel-Aviv centre

Year	2010	2011	2012	2013	2014	2015	2016	2017	2018
Regular	177	164	182	283	317	343	471	514	634
Intensive	277	231	278	274	336	347	374	470	437
Total	454	395	460	557	653	690	845	984	1071

We found differences in the rate of success between students who participated in the regular and intensive modes, with significant differences between the modes noted in the percentage of students who passed the course, in exam scores, and in the final grades (which take into account assignment scores, and are much higher than the exam scores). We found that the students who chose the regular groups had higher success rates. This can be explained by the fact that most of these students already had programming experience and registered for the regular groups since they did not intend to attend the meetings anyway.

Here are some examples:

- During the first semester of 2010, 54.4% of the students in the regular group passed the course, as compared to 38.3% of the students in the intensive group. The average exam score was 68.36 versus 55.18, and the average final grade was 83.12 vs 77.82 for the students who chose regular tutoring. All of these results are significant ($p < 0.05$).

- In the first semester of 2013, the success rate was 58.4% as compared to 41.5%; 75.92 vs 64.02 on the exam scores, with no significant differences in the final grades.
- During semester B of 2014, significant differences were noted in the exam scores between the two tutoring modes. While the regular students achieved 70.04, students enrolled in intensive groups only scored 62.43 ($p = 0.034$). there were no significant differences in success rates and in the final course grades.
- Please note that we did not find that all regular groups consistently scored better than the intensive ones, although this was the case in the earlier years. But in later years, more students in general (not only stronger students) tended to register for the regular mode. This may be explained by the fact that registering for either mode entitles students to watch the recorded Zoom group, (an intensive mode), without paying extra

Tutors

When we evaluated the groups according to specific tutors, we found no significant differences. Sometimes we found one group to be better or worse. But we found that identity of the tutor, day of the week, time, etc. made no difference. We occasionally noted that a group contained several students who were taking the course for the second time; or that had a background in math (studied at the OUI), but no consistent patterns were found.

Discussion and Conclusions

In this paper we evaluated student success in CS1 courses which included tutoring in the Tel-Aviv study centre groups. We chose to focus on this particular site because of the variety of groups offered. Different groups meet each day of the week, allowing students to choose the group that is most convenient to them. This leads to heterogenic groups that are usually at the same level. We occasionally found one group that was better or worse than the others in a particular semester, but we found no correlation between the success of a particular group with a specific tutor, day of the week, or any other factor. We were glad to find no significant differences between the groups, which shows that the teaching and the learning process of our CS1 course is consistent all over the country.

In the following paragraphs we will explain the factors leading to this result, and how we manage the course in order to achieve this uniform teaching process.

- All OUI students enrolled in a particular course receive identical mandatory course materials at the beginning of each semester, as well as supplementary study materials found on the course website. The face-to-face meetings with tutors are designed to summarize and reinforce the information taught during the course. Although it is very helpful to attend these sessions, no extra topics or skills are taught.
- At the beginning of each semester, students receive a timetable which details the syllabus, including which unit will be taught each week, and which assignments must

be submitted. As a result, the course progression is unified at all study groups all over the country.

- Before the start of each semester, a tutors meeting is held, in which we gather to discuss pedagogic issues. We share insights about the teaching process for this particular course, and discuss student misconceptions relating to the course which are encountered during tutoring sessions or in assignments, as well as solutions to the issues raised. The tutors share their thoughts about how to teach difficult topics and provide examples they use to demonstrate these issues. They collaborate to design good presentations which can be helpful to all the tutors.
- During the semester, the tutors and the course coordinator keep in touch by email or in a special forum, to help each other solve problems which may arise that are connected to the teaching process.
- Study centre teams are made up of mainly veteran tutors. Turnover is quite low, and most tutors are experts who remain in their positions for several years. Occasionally tutors leave and/or others join.
- In order to make the assignment checking process as consistent as possible, we use this system: Each pair of tutors is given one exercise out of the eight assigned and are expected to prepare a guide detailing how to score the solution, how many points to reduce for each common error etc. The checking process includes two parts: (a) *machine checking*, which checks the correctness of the solution, and (b) *human checking* where the tutor reads the code and examines the programming style, the efficiency of the solutions etc. The guide prepared by the two tutors deals with these subjects as well.
- Different forums are provided for students to ask questions about each exercise, and the two tutors are responsible for answering the questions in the forum, so the feedback is uniform for all students.
- For final exams, the course coordinator, assisted by one or two tutors, checks all the exams of all the students. Prior to commencing the grading process, they meet to discuss the errors commonly expected, and how to grade the solutions. Each tutor grades the same question in all the exams. In this way, we guarantee that the checking process will be uniform.

As mentioned above, this course is not considered a MOOC. Although we have an open admissions policy, the teaching of this course is not exclusively online, and, it is part of studies leading to a BSc in computer science. We hope, however, that our many years of experience managing a course with numerous students and the uniform results we achieve can, through this paper, help others who manage MOOCs courses.

References

Barr, V. (2018). Different Denominators, Different Results: Reanalyzing CS Degrees by Gender, Race, and Ethnicity. *ACM Inroads, 9*(3), 40-47.

BlueJ – http://www.bluej.org

Computer Science Curricula (2013). *The Joint Task Force on Computing Curricula. Association for Computing Machinery (ACM) & IEEE Computer Society.* Final Report. Retrieved from https://china.acm.org/SIGCSE/static/images/CS2013-final-report.pdf

Gal-Ezer, J., Vilner, T., & Zur, E. (2009). The Professor on Your PC: A Virtual CS1 Course. *Proceedings of the 13th annual conference on innovation and technology in computer science education*, 191-195.

Insa, D., & Silva, J. (2015). Semi-Automatic Assessment of Unrestrained Java Code. *ITiCSE'15 – Proceedings of the 2015 ACM Conference on Innovation and Technology in Computer Science Education*, 39-44.

Ju, A., Mehne, B., Halle, A., & Fox, A. (2018). In-Class Coding-Based Summative Assessments: Tools, Challenges, and Experience. *ITiCSE'18 – Proceedings of the 2018 ACM Conference on Innovation and Technology in Computer Science Education*, 75-80.

Lewis, J., & Loftus, W. (2012). *Java Software Solutions* (7th ed.). Pearson Education.

The Open University of Israel (2018). https://www.openu.ac.il/en/pages/default.aspx

Staubitz, T. et al. (2016). Improving the Peer Experience on MOOC Platforms. *L@S '16 – Proceedings of the 3rd ACM Conference on Learning @ Scale*, 389-398.

Stephenson, B. (2018). An Experience Using On-Computer Programming Questions During Exams. WCCCE – *Proceedings of the 23rd Western Canadian Conference on Computing Education*, 1-6.

Vihvainen, A., Paksula, M., & Luukkainen, M. (2011). Extreme Apprenticeship Method in Teaching Programming for Beginners. *SIGCSE'11 – Proceedings of the 42nd ACM Technical Symposium on Computer Science Education*, 93-98.

Vihavainen, A., Luukkainen, M., & Kurhila, J. (2013). MOOC as Semester-Long Entrance Exam. *SIGITE'13 – Proceedings of the 2013 ACM SIGITE Annual Conference on Information Technology Education*, 177-182.

Vilner, T., & Zur, E. (2006). Once She Makes it, She is There: Gender Differences in Computer Science Study. *ACM SIGCSE Bulletin, 38*(3), 227-231.

Connecting through Educational Technology
Proceedings of the European Distance and E-Learning Network 2019 Annual Conference
Bruges, 16-19 June, 2019

REASONS FOR ATTENDING A MOOC: A SURVEY ON EDUOPEN LEARNERS

Annamaria De Santis, Katia Sannicandro, Claudia Bellini, Tommaso Minerva, University of Modena and Reggio Emilia, Italy

Introduction

In the Italian university context, starting from 2016, EduOpen portal (https://learn.eduopen.org) was launched. It was realized within a project funded by the Italian Ministry of Education, University and Research (MIUR) for an extraordinary intervention based on art. 11 of the Ministerial Decree of November 4 n. 815 (distribution of the Ordinary Financing Fund). The MOOC platform is made up of 17 Italian universities and a set of selected partners; the network is open to the access of other universities and institutions, associations of scientific and cultural relevance.

The registered users are about 50,000 (February 2019). Till now, 208 courses and 26 *pathways* (training courses dedicated to the construction of complex knowledge and composed by multiple MOOCs and intermediate and final assessments) were produced. At the completion of each course the user acquires an attendance certificate and an open badge (currently distributed by Bestr, www.bestr.it). Moreover, users can acquire ECTS by attending EduOpen MOOCs: there are two Professional Masters and some curricular courses that provide academic credits for students that formalize the enrolment at the reference universities of the network.

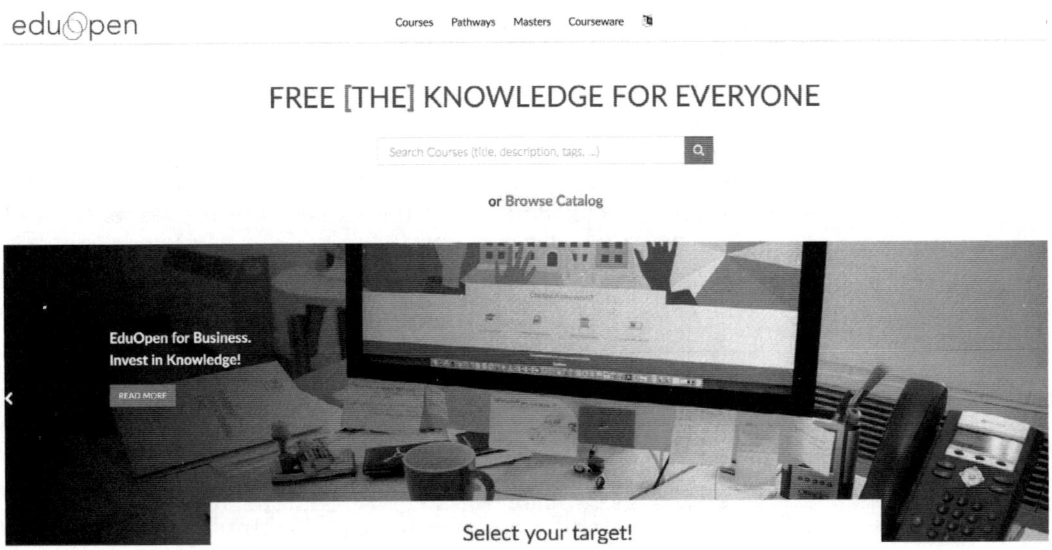

Figure 1. EduOpen Homepage – https://learn.eduopen.org

The continuous development of the project concerns not only the access of new universities and the consequent initiatives – such as the activation of Professional Masters as MOOCs, first in Italy – but also the constant increasing of the number of registered students in EduOpen. It requires updating of the user interface and technical functions, together with a reflection on the instructional design based on users' training needs.

The paper shows an early analysis of the training needs of users enrolled in the courses on EduOpen through the study of motivations that lead them to register in the portal and, so, to enrol in training paths offered in *open* mode in the Italian context (especially in the EduOpen environment). We start a reflection on users' expectations and on the reasons for drop out. In a wide research perspective, the analysis conducted will help us to understand how students use the portal and reply to the following research questions: how to promote the continuous development of skills related to the professional expectations of EduOpen users? Which can be effective tools and strategies for rethinking the instructional design of the courses, starting from the training needs of the users?

Methods

The tool used for the research consists of a questionnaire of 35 queries of which two open-ended and 33 with closed answers. The survey, designed to define the characteristics, the motivations and the kind of portal use by registered users, is divided into two areas. The first part (18 closed questions) focuses on defining the users' personal data; the second part (13 closed questions and 2 open questions) focuses on: the level of digital competence (declared and perceived); reasons to enrol and abandon the courses; devices and softwares used to navigate the pages in the platform; registration on other national and international MOOC platforms; most appreciated course topics; number of completed courses and badges acquired; satisfaction in using EduOpen.

The following section describes the answers to 3 questions belonging to the second part of the questionnaire that allow to define motivations, expectations and needs of the users. We investigate the reasons that push to register in an *open* portal along with those that lead to abandoning courses that are attended free and voluntary. At the same time, we aim to verify the interest shown for the topics of study (categories) in which the courses on EduOpen are grouped, describing the themes that, being the focus of the attention of the students, can be considered indicative of their training needs. The results obtained from the analysis of the three questions are presented in relation to the survey data obtained from the first part of the questionnaire and already presented in other works (De Santis et al., 2018).

Results

The questionnaire was answered by 1982 users, that is 6.6% of those enrolled when the survey was launched. To date, no sample significance testing has been conducted, but the high number of answers qualitatively supports the hypothesis that the sample is significant and representative of the whole population.

The analysis carried out on the users' personal data, that we can read in the first part of the questionnaire, shows some features of EduOpen users, partly in common with the international descriptions related to learning environments that offer MOOCs (OECD, 2017). The users are mainly adults: 49.5% of respondents are of age 45 to 64 and 59.7% of the sample completed at least a bachelor's degree.

Referred to occupational and marital status, survey reveals that 62.7% of users attending courses on EduOpen are employed, 15.0% occasional workers, a further 14.5% unemployed:

- the first ones (employed) are adults over the age of 40, mainly married/cohabiting, with an educational attainment equal or higher than the master's degree (58.5%);
- the second ones (occasional workers) are under the age of 40 years, attending university (both undergraduate and graduate) courses and 56.5% have an educational qualification equal or lower than bachelor's degree, 40.2% are married/cohabitant;
- the third ones (unemployed) are single, in education, under the age of 30, with a secondary (51.1%) and tertiary (44.7%) educational qualification.

These elements are used in this paper to analyse the answers to the three questions selected for the discussion; they allow us to read more deeply into the results obtained.

Table 1 shows the reasons that led the users to register in EduOpen. The main options selected are training needs (65.7%) and interest in course topics (44.9%). Continuing, we found the need for professional updating (37.3%), the possibility of using open and free materials (30.4%) and obtaining certification for the courses attended (28.7%). We analyse these data through some categories used to describe the demographic features: age, employment status, marital status. The main evidences emerged are below: the mode for all the categories analysed is the answer: "for my training needs, I would like to acquire/improve my knowledge and skills".

Age

Less than 40 years old (N = 676); more than 40 years old (N = 1173).

Dividing the sample by age into two groups (the central value – 40 years – was chosen starting from the demographic and occupational elements previously described), the main differences are noted in correspondence of the following response options:

- "for professional updating" – 28.1% for under 40, 42.6% for over 40;
- "to obtain certifications" – 32.1% for under 40, 26.8% for over 40;
- "to complete my university training" – 19.4% for under 40, 5.2% for over 40;
- "at the suggestion of the teachers of my degree course/of my school" – 13.3% for under 40, 1.4% for over 40.

In line with these results, the users aged under 40 years old, mostly unemployed or occasional workers, are university students and need certification of acquired skills; instead, the over 40s – that are employed –, are more interested in professional training courses.

Employment Status

Unemployed (N = 263); occasional workers (N = 271); employed (N = 1146).

In the same way, also in this categorization, the answer options with more relevant variations are: "for professional updating" with values respectively for the three groups equal to 19.4%, 33.6% e 44.9%; "at the suggestion of the teachers of my degree course/of my school" with 16.0%, 11.4%, 2.2%; "to complete my university training" with 22.4%, 15.5%, 5.8%. A slight variation, not appreciable in the other two demographic categories, is related to the response: "to attend courses offered by universities that in my opinion work seriously and effectively". This option is more frequently observed among workers (occasional 22.1%, employed 23.1%) than unemployed (17.5%).

Marital Status

Married/cohabiting with children (N = 695); married/cohabiting without children (N = 401); no married/cohabiting (N = 726).

A new confirmation in the correspondence between reasons of registrations and personal data comes from this categorization where the variations regard the options: "for professional updating", "at the suggestion of the teachers of my degree course/of my school", "to complete my university training". The percentages of married/cohabitants with children interested in the professional updating amount to 42.7%, the percentages for married/cohabitant without children is 42.9%, for singles the value drops to 29.2%. The university training is a reason for registration in the portal for 16.4% of no married/cohabitants and for 6.2% of married users with children, 6.7% for married without children. The teachers' suggestion is essential for 11.8% of singles, only 1.4% of married with children, 2.5% of married without children. Comparing the trends of the two distributions for the conjugates (with and without children) there were no relevant changes in the resulting percentages (among the no married/cohabitants it was preferred not to distinguish the data relating to users with and without children because the number of singles registered at the portal that have children is very low).

Table 1: You decided to register in EduOpen... (max 3 answers) – N = 1850

Reasons to register to EduOpen	% users
for my training needs, I would like to acquire/improve my knowledge and skills	65.7%
for curiosity/interest in the topics of the courses	44.9%
for professional updating	37.3%
to learn free, open and online materials	30.4%
to obtain certifications	28.7%
to attend courses offered by universities that in my opinion work seriously and effectively	21.8%
to learn by overcoming geographical limits	12.9%
to complete my university training	10.4%
to join a learning community on the topics of my interest	9.8%
for a professional reorientation	8.1%
at the suggestion of the teachers of my degree course/of my school	5.8%
to attend courses by one or more teachers I like	4.0%
at the suggestion of my director/manager	1.0%
other	2.0%

The main interests of EduOpen users regard "Social sciences, Computer and data sciences, Arts and humanities" (see Table 2). We present the training needs of users starting from the categorization of courses topics based on users' personal data. If we categorize the data with reference to age and marital status, the trends are not very discordant. Instead, the histograms in Figure 2, 3 and 4, show the most significant variations obtained by grouping data by gender, employment situation and educational attainment. Women prefer courses about Social sciences and "Arts and humanities" more than men that, on the other hand, are more interested in "Computer and Data Sciences, Technologies, design and engineering" and "Science". "Computer and data sciences", as well as "Social Sciences", are the areas in which the most relevant differences occur based on the employment situation. Frequency trends, if the educational attainment is considered the variable, are quite changing: users with a secondary education qualification are interesting in courses regarding "Computer and data sciences" and "Social sciences"; users with a degree or over are interested in "Social sciences" and "Arts and humanities".

Table 2: EduOpen courses are divided into 6 topics (categories). Which of these are you most interested in? (more answers possible) – N = 1788

Course categories	% users
Arts and humanities	41.2%
Computer and data sciences	42.8%
Health and pharmacology	15.0%
Science	29.0%
Social sciences	53.9%
Technologies, design and engineering	23.8%

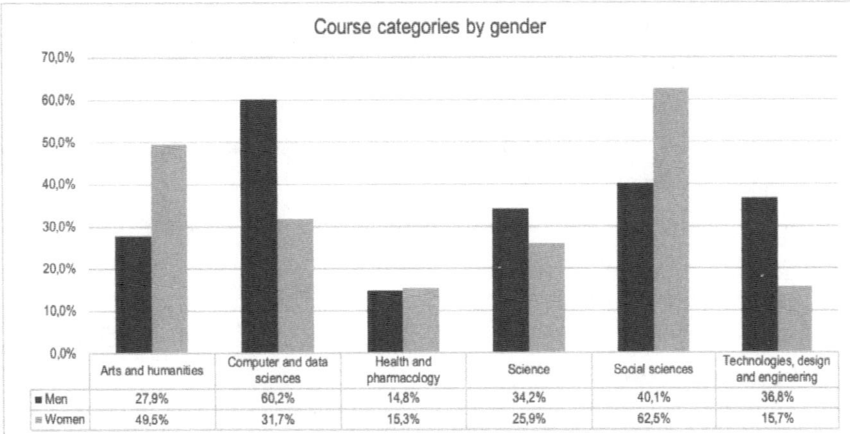

Figure 2. Course categories by gender

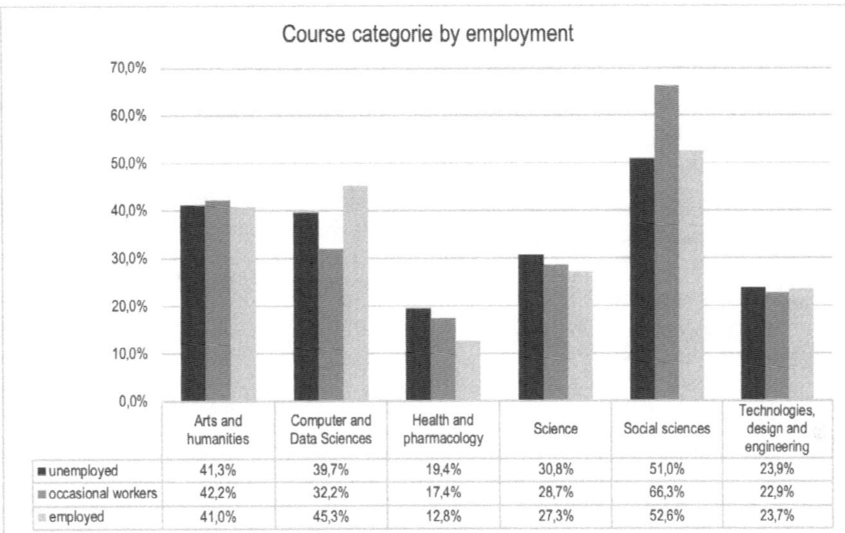

Figure 3. Course categories by employment

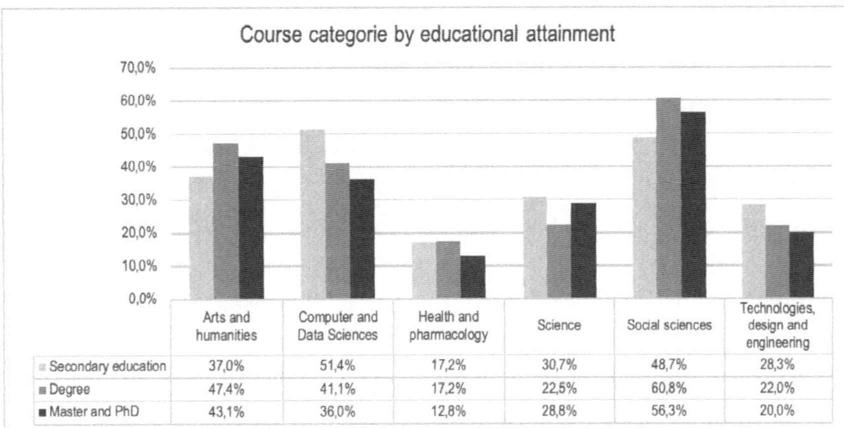

Figure 4. Course categories by educational attainment

Last issue in our discussion regards the reasons for users drop out of courses. Table 3 shows that for almost all items, adding the percentages calculated for the two positive options (*agree* and *completely agree*) and for the two negative ones (*completely disagree* and *disagree*), the population tends not to consider as relevant for dropping out a course the unsatisfactory interaction with classmates (83.7%) and with instructors (64.6%), the use of a transmissive teaching method (63.2%), the presence of demanding tasks (58.2%), difficult in navigation of the platform (54.5%). The sample is divided into two groups of almost similar size on the items referred to audio-visual quality of the teaching materials (52.3%) and the definition of deadlines for assessments (50.8%). The only two items for which the percentages of disagreement are below 50% are related to instructional design of the course (45.6%) and personal commitments (22.6%).

Table 3: Which of the following reasons could push you or (pushed you in the past) to drop out a MOOC? – N = 1602
The answers to each item were structured on a 4-level Likert scale: 1 – *completely disagree*, 2 – *disagree*, 4 – *agree*, 5 – *completely agree*

Reasons to drop out a MOOC	1	2	4	5
unsatisfactory interaction with classmates	52.1%	31.6%	12.7%	3.6%
unsatisfactory interaction with instructors (communication, support, feedback)	35.7%	28.9%	28.0%	7.4%
inadequacy of the instructional design of the course (structure, materials, activities)	25.4%	20.2%	33.3%	21.1%
demanding tasks	23.7%	34.5%	33.4%	8.4%
definition of deadlines for assessments	18.9%	31.9%	37.5%	11.6%
use of a transmissive teaching method	25.3%	37.8%	29.0%	7.9%
difficult navigation of the platform	30.0%	24.5%	29.7%	15.8%
inadequate audio-visual quality of the teaching materials published in the course	27.2%	25.1%	30.8%	16.9%
unforeseeable personal commitments	9.9%	12.8%	42.2%	35.0%

Some reflections:

- It's relevant that an unsatisfactory interaction with colleagues doesn't represent a valid reason to stop attending a course. The result is in contrast with some recent researches that explored the online textual interactions between users, concluding that, even today, connections among tutors, staff and peers represent the most important support for learning (Reich & Rupierez-Valiente, 2018; Xu et al., 2018). On the contrary, it supports the hypothesis that the motivations of EduOpen users have a predominantly intrinsic connotation. The factor is confirmed by the answers to question Q21 in which the highest percentages of reasons for registering to the portal are referred to training needs, interest and curiosity in the topics and not, among those proposed, to joining in learning communities.
- The instructional design is an issue of interest for users enrolled in the courses. The term *instructional design* is not used as a synonym of active or collaborative teaching methods by users. In fact, the use of a transmissive teaching method, distinguishing of

the so-called xMOOCs, is not considered by over 60% of users as a valid reason to drop out the courses.

- The opinions of users about the navigation of the platform and the production of multimedia materials are mostly equally divided into critical and uncritical. The data will have to be analysed in relation to the questions that define the digital skills and the number of completed courses by the students.

Conclusions

The analysis conducted shows the below main elements:

- the main reasons for registration of EduOpen learners are to be found in a personal training needs and curiosity/interest in the topics of the courses;
- the learners don't see in the interaction with classmates a motivation that lead them to leave participation in a course;
- users place greater emphasis on interaction with teachers than one with classmates and on a friendly interface.

Despite these results – we believe in the relevance of peer-interaction in online learning context – we recently stimulated a learning users' community where we invite learners to be involved as *mentor*, a facilitator profile who will try to support and increase communication among the students.

The trends emerged from the answers about the instructional design of the courses opened a discussion on the profile of the EduOpen's Instructional Designers, technological tools and teaching strategies that allow to realize courses starting from the training needs of the users. We pursue this goal in agreement with recent research highlighting that demonstrate close link between design, development of teaching strategies and learning processes in MOOCs (Jung & Lee, 2018).

References

De Santis, A., Sannicandro, K., Fazlagic, B., Bellini, C., Tedeschi, C., & Minerva, T. (2018). Gli Open Learners di EduOpen: numeri e prospettive. In A. Volungeviciene, & A. Szűcs (Eds.), *Exploring the Micro, Meso and Macro. Navigating between dimensions in the digital learning landscape. EDEN 2018 Annual Conference, Genoa, Italy 17-20 June 2018* (pp. 887-94). Budapest: European Distance and E-Learning Network.

Jung, Y., & Lee, J. (2018). Learning engagement and persistence in massive open online courses (MOOCS). *Computers & Education, 122*, 9-22.

OECD (2017). *Education at a Glance 2017: OECD indicators.* Paris: OECD Publishing. Retrieved http://dx.doi.org/10.1787/eag-2017-en

Reich, J., & Rupérez-Valiente, J. A. (2018). The MOOC Pivot. What happened to disruptive transformation of education? *Science, 363*(6423), 130-131.

Xu, D., Solanki, S., & McPartlan, P. (2018). EASing students into college: the impact of multidimensional support for underprepared students. *Sage journals, 7*(47), 435-450.

Connecting through Educational Technology
Proceedings of the European Distance and E-Learning Network 2019 Annual Conference
Bruges, 16-19 June, 2019

BACK TO THE FUTURE, THE LEARNER STRIKES BACK: FEEDBACK AND REFLECTION AS KEY ELEMENTS IN MOOC RE-DESIGN

Conchúr Mac Lochlainn, Mairéad Nic Giolla Mhichíl, Elaine Beirne, Mark Brown, Dublin City University, Ireland

Abstract

A general trend within research into Massive Open Online Courses (MOOCs) has been the study of learner behaviour and motivations using large-scale, quantitative studies to measure, correlate and predict forms of interaction and participation. Far few studies have focused on contextual, local and qualitative forms of inquiry, despite the great potential of such methods. In this paper, we discuss a preliminary study making use of qualitative data generated on an Irish language MOOC, namely learner comments on reflective steps each week. This data was analysed using an interpretive framework for elucidating both positive and negative forms of learner feedback. Three major themes are defined, relating to opinions regarding course materials, positive attitudes towards interaction and a broad metacognitive awareness of the process of learning. Implications for the design process and the importance of using such methods are briefly discussed.

Introduction

What motivates learners to study in MOOCs is a question that has been contemplated by researchers ever since MOOCs became part of the global learning ecology (e.g. Kizilcec & Schneider, 2015). Primarily, this interest stems from the perceived close relationship between completion and participation, with a positive correlation usually theorised between these concepts. We view participation, as a complex and nuanced concept with many competing contextual and influencing factors. Researching such factors requires careful methodological consideration. The majority of MOOC-based research in this area adopts a distinctive quantitative approach when considering participation (e.g. Wang & Baker, 2015; Jordan, 2015). While studies in related fields such as computer assisted language learning and distance learning have considered qualitative perspectives (see Murphy, 2011; Hurd, 2008), they are not as common among MOOC-centred studies. To address this gap in the empirical literature, this brief paper employs a qualitative, interpretive approach to analysing the motivations of MOOC learners over the length of a course at weekly intervals. The paper draws on Anderson's (2003) framework of learner interaction in online learning as a conceptual tool to consider participation. Data is primarily derived from a corpus of learner comments collected from the three week, Irish-language and culture MOOC, Irish 101, which is delivered through the FutureLearn platform. This is coupled with data derived from self-reported course survey instruments. The paper critically-reflects on the importance of such methodological and conceptual innovation and the importance of listening to "the learner voice" (Conole, 2008; p.126). The process by which that voice influenced learner design and redesign is also explored. The findings illustrate that participants' reasons for engagement suggest a form of integrated, self-regulated learning (Zimmerman & Schunk, 1989), at least amongst those who comment. The study also highlights the impact of language learning nuances on learner participation as well as the impact of broader contextual dimensions beyond subject area.

Background and Literature on MOOC learner motivations and continuation

Understanding the motivations of those who participate in a MOOC is akin to opening a proverbial black-box. While several large meta-analyses exist on learner participation, they have primarily been concerned with uncovering trends and focuses. Studies such as Kizilcec, Piech, and Schneider (2013) and Ferguson and Clow (2015) take a macro-level approach to parsing behavioural patterns and suggest that taxonomies or clusters of learner engagement patterns exist. Research in the vein of Clow (2013) uses metaphors such as the funnel of participation to explain learner participation and completion while Wang and Baker (2018) employ psychological variables such as learner grit or persistence. Others have focused on the traits and characteristics of learners who have completed their studies (Breslow et al., 2013). The underlying premise of this research is that of a variance-based understanding of participation (Mohr, 1982). Learner responses are typically aggregated and averaged. Such studies are increasingly-prevalent across all domains of educational research (Ferguson et al., 2016) and they have provided insights into typical patterns of learner behaviour whilst also providing a basis by which to compare modalities of learning. Their contribution to learner participation in MOOCs is relatively limited, however, when attempting to uncover contextual factors. The limitations and scope of such MOOC-based studies are identified by Veletsianos, Collier, and Schneider (2015; p.574), as they critique a general discourse which suggest that "teaching and learning can be fully analyzed, understood and designed for by examining clickstream data". Many of these studies focus on what can be readily measured i.e. behaviour or activity within a MOOC-platform, or Twitter-related feed, and such measurements only provide a partial view of the habits and indeed "lifeworld" of such learning, as embedded in personal, social and contextual relations (Veletsianos, Reich, & Pasquini, 2016; p.6). A promising development marrying the best of both worlds in this regard may be to use an analytical framework such as Henderikx, Kreijns, and Kalz's (2018: 358-60). This focuses specifically on measuring learner goals in a localised, contextual sense by asking whether they achieved their particular expectations from a MOOC. Anderson's updated (2003) model of online interaction provides a nuanced understanding when considering the broader concept of learner participation. Though, pre-dating MOOCs, it delineates between interactions between (a) learner and content, (b) the learner and instructor, and (c) the learner and other learners. Regarding the first and third aspects, Ferguson and Clow's (2015: 8) study found a general link between posting comments and course completion, whilst Swinnerton, Hotchkiss, and Morris' (2017; p.61) study distinguishes between MOOC-commenters and non-commenters in discussion forums. Furthermore, commenting in MOOCs can be considered not only from the perspective of those learners who comment or those who do not. It can also be viewed from the perspective that the presence of comments represents an active and engaged learning space for all learners (Hart, 2012) which may help to reduce perceived or actual social isolation (Gasevic et al., 2014).

Methodology

1,081 comments, providing a corpus of 52,000 words, were posted by learners in three weekly "review of the week" discussions on the Irish 101 MOOC. The total comments posted in the Irish 101 MOOC were 25,000, across approximately 90 learning steps. 5 standard questions were asked each week in this review step e.g. "what did you find difficult about week X? What was easy?". A broadly interpretive (Merriam, 2002; pp.6-7) approach to data analysis was adopted, with a focus on contextualising the interaction within wider MOOC participation. Leximancer, a qualitative data analysis tool, was used to analyse and thematically group comments. This was then crosschecked by the researchers to ensure an accurate fit to the semantic meaning of the data. This approach was adopted to increase validity and consistency (Creswell & Miller, 2000). Three key non-language specific themes emerged consistently: (a) Attitudes towards course design and content (b) Enjoyment of social interaction (c) Metacognitive awareness of learning. The following section briefly sets out the findings in these three areas.

Findings

Theme 1 – Attitudes to course design

Many of the comments grouped under the attitudes towards course design theme illustrated that the learners were both agentful and reflexive regarding their learning, in addition to being quite willing to comment on aspects of course structure and design. Frequently, within comments they benchmarked MOOC learning content with their own particular learning goals and expectations (which may vary greatly (Ho et al., 2014; p.6)) regarding learning resources and activities within the MOOC:

> *"I enjoyed the materials and that new words are connected with my favourite activities: listen and repeat. I also liked to learn words. Well-done materials!" (Learner A)*

For some, materials were extremely beneficial and aligned with expectations whilst others formulated suggestions within comments, these changes were integrated where possible in the iterative refinement of the MOOCs learning design:

> *"I think my main feedback to the educators is the need for more downloadable material of the sound bites in the presentations so those of us who are absolute beginners can hear them and then practise." (Learner B)*

These attitudes provide a central insight regarding MOOC learners: as typically-educated, aware and active learners, any design or instructional experience is at least on some level a process of co-construction, and this aspect of the learner voice is deeply valuable in providing solid feedback relating to provision, design and dissemination.

Theme 2 – Enjoyment of interaction

The second theme, enjoyment of interaction, centred on the importance and role of the interaction of learners with their peers, instructors and with other learners within the MOOC, in keeping with Anderson's framework:

> *"I also want to thank everyone both teachers and learners in this course that made me feel like I was a member of a community of like-minded people." (Learner C)*

This comment illustrates that building "a bounded group motivated by learning and creating the terms for such learning through socially shared interactions" (Oleksandra & Dawson, 2016; p.208) is an important outcome of good learning design but may also impact sustained motivation. Learners engaged in interactions with each other by providing advice and feedback could also be viewed as a factor in the construction of this community.

A sub-theme related to the interactional challenges was associated with the disciplinary area of learning a language. In keeping with several motivational theories common to both language learning and wider educational psychology, such as the concept of mastery orientation (Ames & Archer, 1988) or intrinsic motivation – accomplishment (Noels et al., 2000; p.61), the difficulty of the language was both potentially demotivating (if the learner believed it was too difficult for them to achieve gains in) and a potential intensifier of motivation, as the challenge appealed to many learners:

> *"Lenition is giving me brain freeze and I think my pronunciation would make most people cry – it does me – but I'm enjoying the challenges and also the community!" (Learner D)*

> *"The language is a tricksy one – difficult to catch hold of but I don't mind because my main reason for being here is to find out. About the complexity, the history, the tangles and tales of a fascinating country and people. Loving it." (Learner E)*

This desire for greater interaction and the great enthusiasm for the subject matter shows language learning as deeply social and interactive, and as acknowledged in the distance language-learning literature (Carrió-Pastor, 2018; p.205), speaks to a particular pedagogical challenge faced by disciplines where the acquisition of knowledge and skills both play central roles.

Theme 3 – Metacognitive awareness

The final theme, metacognitive awareness, is perhaps the most relevant to learning motivation and learning in MOOCs, beyond the context of learning languages. Comments demonstrated awareness that learning takes time, while also sharing strategies for learning. A common trend was that many felt that more time was needed to complete the MOOC. Comments also alluded to the adoption of learning activities outside of the MOOC to aid progress:

> *"I have enjoyed it but need more time to study the pronunciation. I don't imagine I will learn to speak the language in this short time but it gives me an insight and widens my knowledge of all things Irish. The course is detailed and more challenging than others I have undertaken." (Learner H)*

> *"I'm thoroughly enjoying this course! And I'm finding myself taking it quite seriously as I spread flash cards and other helpful ways to learn around my house!" (Learner I)*

This awareness may be a core feature in positive MOOC learning, and a source of sustained motivation. Indeed, this ability, to reflect, and to create strategies that may contribute to goal achievement, might be critical, in the ability to be "motivationally, meta-cognitively and behaviourally active participants in their own learning process" (Zimmerman & Schunk, 1989; p.329). Empirical evidence supports the distinction between high and low self-regulated learners in terms of MOOC outcomes, with high self-regulation associated with continuation (Littlejohn et al., 2016; pp.42-44). Fostering this sense of self-regulation is not easy, but it may be critical to ensure the largest number of persons possible can benefit from their participation in a MOOC.

Discussion and conclusion

Two conclusions can be drawn from the reporting of this preliminary research. The first is that discussion comments, particularly at points geared at generating reflective feedback, provide researchers with a wealth and depth of contextual information, which is not easily accessed through survey instruments. A wide array of social, affective and metacognitive forms of feedback and self-regulation were present within the data, with variation both from week to week and from learner to learner. In keeping with Zheng et al. (2015; p.1891), we hold that this research may afford researchers the ability to provide a "vivid picture of learning patterns", and to see how learners construe their own progress as it unfolds organically. By adopting a reflexive, interpretative approach and methods, it may be possible to "make the massive humane" (Sokolik, 2014; p.20) and indeed to listen to the learner voice (Conole, 2008).

Our second conclusion relates to the provision of these steps themselves, namely that they are a highly useful aspect of MOOC course design. Evidenced in this paper but also our experiences as learning designers and instructors, is that these spaces are highly useful in enabling learners to provide feedback that can be very valuable in MOOC redesign. Several trends from this initial analysis, such as providing more audio support, video provision and opportunities for social practice, have directly affected the re-design of subsequent runs of the course. Others, such as the general consensus on the difficulty of the language, have led to a focus on providing additional time estimates for task completion, and to restructure material substantially. Given that behind every course is a collection of research, experience and agency, there is particular value in harnessing these design affordances and the learner generated reflective evidence-base to inform the design and redesign process.

References

Ames, C., & Archer, J. (1988). Achievement goals in the classroom: students learning strategies and motivation processes. *Journal of Educational Psychology, 80*(3), 260-267.

Anderson, T. (2003). Getting the mix right: An updated and theoretical rationale for interaction. *The International Review of Research in Open and Distributed Learning, 4*(2).

Breslow, L., Pritchard, D., DeBoer, J., Stump, G., Ho, A., & Seaton, D. (2013). Studying Learning in the Worldwide Classroom: Research into edX's first MOOC. *Research and Practice in Assessment, 8.*

Carrió-Pastor, M. (2018). *Teaching language and teaching literature in virtual environments.* Springer Press.

Clow, D. (2013). MOOCs and the funnel of participation. *Proceedings of the Third Conference on Learning Analytics and Knowledge (LAK), 2013,* 185-189.

Conole, G. (2008). Listening to the learner voice: The ever changing landscape of technology for language use. *ReCALL, 20*(22). 124-140.

Creswell, J., & Miller, D. (2000). Determining Validity in Qualitative Inquiry. *Theory into Practice, 39*(3). 124-130.

Ferguson, R., & Clow, D. (2015, March). *Examining engagement: Analysing learner subpopulations in Massive Open Online Courses (MOOCS).* Paper presented at the 5th International Learning Analytics and Knowledge Conference, 16-20 March.

Ferguson, R., Brasher, A., Clow, D., Cooper, A., Hillaire, G., Mittelmeier, J., Rienties, B., Ullman, T., Vuorikari, R., & Castano, J. (2016). *Research evidence on the use of Learning Analytics: Implications for Education Policy.* EUROPA Scientific and Technical Reports.

Gasevic, D., Kovanovic, V., Joksimovic, S., & Siemens, S. (2014). Where is Research on Massive Open Online Courses Headed? A Data Analysis of the MOOC Research Initiative. *The International Review of Research in Open and Distributed Learning, 15*(5). 134-176.

Hart, C. (2012). Factors Associated with Student Persistence in an Online Program of Study: A Review of the Literature. *Journal of Interactive Online Learning, 11*(1). 19-42.

Henderickx, M., Kreijn, K., & Kalz, K. (2018). Refining success and dropout in Massive Open Online Courses. *Distance Education, 38*(3). 353-368.

Ho, A., Chung, I., Reich, J., Coleman, C., Whitehall, J., Northcutt, C., Williams, J., Hansen, J., Lopez, G., & Petersen, R. (2015). *HarvardX and MITx: Two years of open courses.* HarvardX working paper.

Hurd, S. (2008). Affect and strategy use in independent language learning. In S. Hurd, & T. Lewis (Eds.), *Language Learning Strategies in Independent Settings. Second Language Acquisition* (pp. 218–236.). Bristol, UK: Multilingual Matters.

Jordan, K. (2015). Massive Open Online Courses completion rates revisited: Assessment, length and attrition. *The International Review of Research in Open and Distributed Learning, 16*(3).

Kizilcec, R., Piech, C., & Schneider, E. (2013). *Deconstructing disengagement: analysing learner subpopulations in Massive Open Online Courses.*

Kizilcec, R., & Scheider, E. (2015). Motivation as a lens to understand online learners: towards data-driven design with the OLEI scale. *Computer-Human Interaction, 22*(2), Article 6. ACM Trans.

Littlejohn, A., Hood, N., Milligan, C., & Mustain, P. (2016). Learning in MOOCs: Motivations and self-regulated learning and MOOCs. *The Internet and Higher Education, 29*, 40-48.

Merriam, S. (2002). *Qualitative Research in Practice: Examples for Discussion and Practice.* San Francisco, CA: Wiley and Sons.

Mohr, L. B. (1982). *Explaining Organizational Behavior.* San Francisco, CA: Jossey-Bass.

Murphy, L. (2011). Why am I doing this? Maintaining motivation in distance language learning. In G. Murray, G. Xuesong, & T. Lamb (Eds.), *Identity, Motivation and Autonomy in Language Learning* (pp. 107-124).

Noels, K., Pelletier, L., Clément, R., & Vallerand, R. (2000). Why are you learning a second language? Motivational orientations and self-determination theory. *Language Learning, 50*(1), 57-85.

Oleksandra, P., & Dawson, S. (2016). Untangling MOOC Learner Networks. *Proceedings of the Sixth International Conference on Learning Analytics and Knowledge, LAK '16*, 208-212.

Sokolik, M. (2014). What constitutes an effective language MOOC? In E. Martín-Monje, & E. Bárcena (Eds.), *Language MOOCs: Providing learning, transcending boundaries* (pp. 16-32). Berlin: DeGruyter

Swinnerton, B., Hotchkiss, S., & Morris, N. (2017). Comments in MOOCs: Who is doing the talking and does it help? *Journal of Computer Assisted Language Learning, 33*(1). 55-64.

Veletsianos, G., Collier, A., & Schneider, E. (2015). Digging deeper into learners' experiences in MOOCs: Participation in social networks outside of MOOCs, notetaking and contexts surrounding content consumption. *British Journal of Educational Technology, May 2015*, 570-587.

Veletsianos, G., Reich, J., & Pasquini, L. (2016). The life between big data log events: Learners' strategies to overcome challenges in MOOCs. *AERA Open, 2*(3). 1-10.

Wang, Y., & Baker, R. (2015). Content or platform: Why do learners complete MOOCs? *MERLOT Journal of Online Learning and Teaching, 11*(1), 17-30.

Wang, Y., & Baker, R. (2018). Grit and intention: why do learners complete MOOCs? *International Review of Research in Open and Distributed Learning, 19*(3). 20-42.

Zheng, S., Rosson, M., Shih, P., & Carroll, J. (2015). *Understanding Student Motivation, Behaviors, and Perceptions in MOOCs.* Paper presented at the Motivation and Dynamics in the Open Classroom, CSCW 2015.

Zimmerman, B. J. & Schunk, D. H. (Eds.). (1989). *Self-Regulated Learning and Academic Achievement: Theory, Research and Practice.* New York: Springer-Verlag.

Acknowledgement

This study was conducted as part of the "Fáilte ar Líne" project which is co-funded by the Irish Government, Department of Culture, Heritage, and the Gaeltacht, under the Twenty-Year strategy for the Irish Language, with support from the National Lottery.

MOOCS INTEGRATION INTO CAMPUS-BASED CURRICULA: THE CASE FOR RUSSIA

Tatiana Semenova, Ksenia Vilkova, National Research University Higher School of Economics, Russian Federation

Abstract

Massive open online course (MOOC) is a relatively new format of online learning; despite this, it is actively integrated into the educational process of universities. Using data from publications, regulatory documents of universities, official websites of educational institutions, as well as data from expert interviews, this paper summarizes the experience of Russian universities on MOOC integration into campus-based curricula. The main models of MOOC integration into the educational process were highlighted: (a) embedding the MOOC into the blended learning format, (b) replacing part of the offline courses of the academic program with MOOCs, (c) creating an online master's program with MOOCs.

Introduction

Initially, the format of massive open online courses (MOOCs) appeared as part of blended learning technology to replace face-to-face lectures with watching videos outside the classroom with tests and quizzes (Hollands & Tirthali, 2014b). Leading American universities began to create MOOCs by transforming and transferring their offline courses to an online environment. The practice of integration own MOOCs into the academic program has come along with the practice of buying a license to use the content of MOOCs developed by another university (Sandeen, 2013). Over time, the format of using MOOC in the educational process was transformed: MOOC was used not only as part of blended learning but also as an alternative to traditional courses. Since 2012, the practice of recognizing MOOC certificates has been taking shape, i.e. it becomes possible to get credits for MOOCs. At the same time, there are not only isolated cases of replacing traditional courses with MOOCs (Israel, 2015) but also the embedding MOOCs in the curricula as mandatory ones. Also, universities together with online platforms have started to create academic programs based on MOOCs.

At the moment, the question of the effectiveness of replacing traditional courses with the MOOC, as well as the creation of academic programs based on the MOOC, remains open. Despite this, MOOCs continue to be actively integrated into the educational process in foreign and Russian universities. It is believed that the MOOC integration into campus-based curricula allows applying and refining innovative methods in teaching in practice, improving the students' academic outcomes, bringing the effect of internationalization and co-studying from participating in the MOOC with different learners (Sandeen, 2013; Hollands & Tirthali, 2014a; Belanger et al., 2013; Kizilcec & Brooks, 2016).

In several studies, the following models of the MOOC integration are highlighted: (a) recognition of credits received for passing the MOOC, (b) purchasing licenses for the content of MOOC created by another university, (c) establishing mutual agreement regarding the credits for the MOOC created by another university for solving a problem with organizing an expertise of courses (Sandeen, 2013), (d) embedding the MOOC into the blended learning format, (e) the use of MOOC as an additional source of knowledge and skills, (f) the use of MOOC for teachers skills development (Chamchiyan, 2014; Makoveychuk, 2015). Due to the fact that the models in these papers were formulated and described four-five years ago, they no longer cover new forms of MOOC integration into campus-based curricula.

In this paper, we identify and describe the existing models of MOOC integration into campus-based curricula based on the research of practices accepted in Russian universities. For the description of the practices, data from publications, regulatory documents of universities, official websites of institutions, as well as data from expert interviews conducted with managers and employees of centres for online education at leading universities in Russia were used.

Models of MOOC integration into campus-based curricula in Russian universities

The practice of MOOC integration in curricula has not become widespread in Russian universities. However, no legal restrictions were found for the integration of the MOOC into the educational process. Thus, according to the Law on Education, each student has the right to form his educational path. At the moment, three models of MOOC integration into campus-based curricula in Russian universities can be marked:

1. Embedding the MOOC into blended learning format;
2. Replacing part of the traditional courses of the academic programs with MOOCs;
3. Master's programs with MOOCs.

The first model of integration is associated with the use of MOOC content in a blended learning format. Teachers can use materials of MOOCs created by their university, and/or by other universities, including courses in a foreign language, in their traditional courses. There are several options for implementing a blended learning format with MOOCs, each of which will differ in the proportion of offline interaction between the student, teacher and tutor of online learning, as well as the proportion of interaction with MOOC content. For example, students may take a MOOC along with the attending seminars, or students may be exempted from seminars, subject to obtaining a MOOC certificate and passing an offline exam to a university teacher.

The second model of integration – the replacement of part of the traditional courses of the academic program with MOOCs, which can be implemented both at the individual and institutional levels. At the individual level, the replacement of the traditional course with a MOOC is an initiative of the student himself. In this case, a student can use not only the MOOC of his university but also online courses from other universities. Instead of a traditional course, students take a MOOC, which they choose from a list of recommended online courses, or independently. The list of recommended MOOCs can be compiled by a separate centre of online education, or academic leader of an educational program, or program manager together with teachers, or methodical committee of departments, or by vice-rector for academic work. When the selected MOOC is not included in the list of recommended, the commission of experts evaluates the characteristics of the course and decides whether to add the course to the list.

The main requirement for getting credits for MOOC is to receive a certificate of MOOC completion with a description of the main characteristics of the course required for the transfer procedure. Also, in most universities, a student has to undergo a proctoring procedure with personal identification in order to eliminate unfair passing of the course. In some cases, a certificate of MOOC completion is a necessary but not sufficient condition: the student also has to pass an oral consultation/exam with the teacher.

At the institutional level, the MOOC is included in the curriculum of the academic program, which students must pass it. The curriculum of the academic program may include MOOCs, developed by the teachers of both their university and another university.

The third model of MOOC integration, which currently exists in Russian universities, is the online master's program. The first online master's program, devoted to the issues of modern combinatorics, was launched in the fall of 2016 in one of the highly selective universities of Russia. The structure of this program has significant differences from the foreign online master's programs. For example, even though the program is implemented online, applicants are required to pass offline written exams in mathematics and computer science. State examinations and the defence of diplomas are held in traditional format too. Also, the number of places per program, and the cost of the program are equivalent to the cost of a traditional (offline) program in combinatorics.

Conditions for successful integration of MOOCs into the educational process of Russian universities

In our research, we highlight some conditions necessary to ensure the successful integration of MOOCs into the educational process of Russian universities based on data obtained from expert interviews. These conditions can be divided into three groups: (a) staff, (b) administration of the integration process, and (c) functionality of the online platform.

The first group includes university staff, tutors and assistants, who provide support for online learning and track the results of the educational process, as well as those engaged in designing online master's programs consisting of MOOCs from different universities. Participation in the MOOC requires a high degree of independence, time management skills, as well as motivation to complete the course (Onah, Sinclair, & Boyatt, 2014). If students cannot properly allocate their time, if they have any questions during the course (for example, they do not know how to go through the proctoring procedure), then they can contact the online tutor/assistant, who will help to solve emerging problems.

The second group includes conditions related to creating a transparent and flexible system at university, which allows using MOOC as part of the educational process and getting credits for it. Thus, the university should establish a centre that is responsible for administering the process of integrating the MOOC into the curriculum, developing the necessary documents on online learning and concluding agreements on the use of the MOOC of another university.

The third group includes conditions related to the operation of the platform, whose courses are used in the educational process. The online platform should provide a good visualization of studying both for students, who could track their process of learning, and for the teachers, who may receive a quick summary of the course progress among their students.

Conclusion

The analysis of experience in MOOC integration into campus-based curricula allowed to identify three main models of MOOC integration: (a) embedding the MOOC into blended learning format, (b) replacing part of the traditional courses of the academic program with MOOCs, (c) creating an online master's program with MOOCs. In foreign universities, MOOCs are becoming an integral part of education, creating new conditions for getting an education. At the same time, a regulatory framework already exists in Russian higher education system that allows MOOC integration into the educational process. However, this practice has not gained widespread acceptance. This may be due to the low awareness of both universities and students about the possibility of using the MOOC in the educational process. For example, as was shown in (Balyasin & Semenova, 2016), every fifth student of leading universities in Russia did not hear anything about MOOC. Also, there is no established practice of integrating the MOOC into the educational process due to lack of necessary information on how to recount the results of the online course, how to organize the process of integrating the MOOC into the curriculum, and how legally and financially solve the issue of its using. However, there are some advantages of MOOC integration into campus-based curricula. First, universities can use the MOOC as training for a specific university life for new students, freshmen. Such MOOCs will allow to incorporate new student rapidly into the university environment, as well as to generate certain knowledge necessary for mastering the disciplines (Firmin et al., 2014; Docq & Ella, 2015). Secondly, universities can integrate the MOOC in curricula in order to optimize the costs of their educational activities. For example, a university may purchase a MOOC of a famous professor instead of searching for and hiring a qualified teacher. Thirdly, the MOOC integration into educational process allows increasing the variability of the curriculum and expanding the possibilities for creating an individual educational trajectory. And, finally, embedding the MOOC into the educational program may allow improving the educational process, freeing up time for more active practices used at seminars.

At the same time, despite all the advantages of MOOC integration into campus-based curricula, this practice has its risks. First, the studies have not yet revealed a single standard for organizing a blended format course. Each teacher is faced with the question of constructing a course that combines face-to-face classes and MOOCs (for example, they have to decide, how to correctly combine MOOC content with the content of the traditional course, how to properly allocate time, how to choose a MOOC). Secondly, there is no uniform standard for assessing the quality of the MOOC. The centre for online education and the teacher who plans to use the MOOC should develop mechanisms to assess the quality of the online course. Third, the economic and educational effects of the MOOC integration in university curricula, as well as the business model of online education, are still unclear. Fourth, not all courses can be converted to MOOC format. Also, this format is not suitable for all students, because studies show that the probability of successful completion of a MOOC is higher for those who already have a higher education, online learning experience, and experience on the course subject (Kizilcec et al., 2017; Semenova & Rudakova, 2016; Goldberg et al., 2015; Hansen & Reich, 2015; Engle, Mankoff, & Carbrey, 2015). Fifthly, there is resistance from teachers on the MOOC integration and their low interest in using online courses as part of the curriculum.

However, most of these limitations are removed based on the results of research, which will show (a) how effective the MOOC format is when it is used in educational process of universities, (b) which model is most beneficial both from the economic side and from the maximization of students' academic outcomes, and (c) how evaluate the quality of the course and embed it in the curricula.

References

Balyasin, M., & Semenova, T. (2016). Engaging students in online learning. Federal Guide. *Education in Russia Moscow, 1*, 290-298.

Belanger, Y., Thornton, J., & Barr, R. C. (2013). Bioelectricity: A quantitative approach – Duke University's first MOOC. *EducationXPress, 2013*(2)

Chamchiyan, A. (2014). To the question of the possibility of using MOOC and the traditional form of education. *E-learning in continuing education, 1*(1), 339-347.

Docq, F., & Ella, H. (2015). Why make MOOCs? Effects on on-campus teaching and learning. *Proceedings of the European MOOC stakeholders summit*, 18-20.

Engle, D., Mankoff, C., & Carbrey, J. (2015). Coursera's introductory human physiology course: Factors that characterize successful completion of a MOOC. *The International Review of Research in Open and Distributed Learning, 16*(2).

Firmin, R., Schiorring, E., Whitmer, J., Willett, T., Collins, E. D., & Sujitparapitaya, S. (2014). Case study: Using MOOCs for conventional college coursework. *Distance Education, 35*(2), 178-201.

Goldberg, L. R., Bell, E., King, C., O'Mara, C., McInerney, F., Robinson, A., & Vickers, J. (2015). Relationship between participants' level of education and engagement in their completion of the Understanding Dementia Massive Open Online Course. *BMC medical education, 15*(1), 60.

Hansen, J. D., & Reich, J. (2015). Democratizing education? Examining access and usage patterns in massive open online courses. *Science, 350*(6265), 1245-1248.

Hollands, F. M., & Tirthali, D. (2014a). Why Do Institutions Offer MOOCs? *Online Learning, 18*(3), n3.

Hollands, F. M., & Tirthali, D. (2014b). *MOOCs: Expectations and reality. Full report.* NY: Center for Benefit Cost Studies of Education, Teachers College, Columbia University.

Israel, M. J. (2015). Effectiveness of integrating MOOCs in traditional classrooms for undergraduate students. *The International Review of Research in Open and Distributed Learning, 16*(5).

Kizilcec, R. F., & Brooks, C. (2017). Diverse big data and randomized field experiments in MOOCs. *Handbook of Learning Analytics*, 211-222.

Kizilcec, R. F., Saltarelli, A. J., Reich, J., & Cohen, G. L. (2017). Closing global achievement gaps in MOOCs. *Science, 355*(6322), 251-252.

Makoveychuk, K. (2015). Prospects of using MOOCs in basic educational programs of higher education in Russia. *International Research Journal, 6*(37), 66-67.

Onah, D. F., Sinclair, J., & Boyatt, R. (2014). Dropout rates of massive open online courses: behavioural patterns. *EDULEARN14 proceedings, 1*, 5825-5834.

Sandeen, C. (2013). Integrating MOOCs into traditional higher education: The emerging "MOOC 3.0" era. *Change: The magazine of higher learning, 45*(6), 34-39.

Semenova, T. V., & Rudakova, L. M. (2016). Barriers to taking massive open online courses (MOOCs). *Russian Education & Society, 58*(3), 228-245.

Connecting through Educational Technology
Proceedings of the European Distance and E-Learning Network 2019 Annual Conference
Bruges, 16-19 June, 2019

AUTOMATIC TRANSCRIPTION SOFTWARE: GOOD ENOUGH FOR ACCESSIBILITY? A CASE STUDY FROM BUILT ENVIRONMENT EDUCATION

Tharindu R. Liyanagunawardena, University College of Estate Management, United Kingdom

Abstract

The increasing use of multimedia in learning resources in higher education poses a challenge for learners with hearing disabilities, unless these are accompanied by transcripts or captions. This paper reports on a small study where six Automatic Transcription Software (ATS) were analysed for their accuracy. Although economical and timesaving, at present, it seems an automatically generated transcript is not yet accurate enough to be an accessibility aid for the subjects relating to built environment sector.

Accessibility

The use of multimedia has allowed the creation of rich learning experiences for students, especially for distance learners. This poses a huge challenge in making these resources accessible. Oxford Living Dictionary (n.d.) defines accessibility as "the quality of being able to be reached or entered". More specifically, the term "Web accessibility" is used to denote that "websites, tools, and technologies are designed and developed so that people with disabilities can use them". That is, people with disabilities can "perceive, understand, navigate, and interact with the Web and contribute to the Web" (W3C, 2018a).

Web Content Accessibility Guidelines (WCAG) is a set of guidelines produced with the goal of creating one international shared standard for web content accessibility (W3C, 2018b). With the recent European Parliament directive on accessibility (Europa, 2016) there will be an increasing need for transcripts/captions to meet the legal requirement of time-based media accessibility.

Accuracy, Cost and Automatic Speech Recognition (ASR)

Transcription services that employ human transcribers can be expensive. In December 2017, the author's institution paid an average rate of £1.30 per minute for instructional videos to be professionally transcribed, amounting to £78 per hour (subjected to a minimum fee and additional cost for more than one speaker). Manchester University guidelines for research students indicate that an hour of recording is likely to take four to seven hours to transcribe (Burke, Jenkins, & Higham, 2010). University of California Berkeley removed over 20,000 videos and podcasts from public access in March 2017, in response to an order by the

Department of Justice to make these contents accessible to people with disabilities because it was deemed "extremely expensive" (Straumsheim, 2017). Prohibitive cost and extensive time requirement are major disadvantages of manual transcription.

Automatic Speech Recognition (ASR) technologies have improved rapidly with both IBM and Microsoft reaching 5.5% (Fogel, 2017) and 5.1% (Lant, 2017) Word Error Rate (WER) respectively, almost on a par with a professional human transcriber. Today, off-the-shelf Automatic Transcription Software (ATS), for example Nuance Dragon Professional Individual v15, promises 99% accuracy once the software is trained for the speaker's voice (Dragon Speech Recognition, 2016). However, automatically generated captions/transcripts, can sometimes fail to convey the meaning accurately; it can be humorous or intelligible, but for people with hearing-impairments this can result in inaccessible content. Bokhove and Downey (2018) argue that given the quality of ATS is sufficient, these tools could provide a useful first draft for transcription creation.

In this context, this paper reports an experiment conducted at University College of Estate Management (UCEM) to assess the suitability of using ATS in the built environment sector subject disciplines.

University College of Estate Management

UCEM, previously known as the College of Estate Management, is a leading supported online learning provider for the built environment. Celebrating its centenary in 2019, UCEM was originally a postal distance education provider until 2014 when it offered fully online modules to students. Since then UCEM has been offering almost all courses fully online. The core purpose of UCEM, as described in its vision statement, is to "provide truly accessible, relevant and cost-effective education". UCEM caters for students in various circumstances; due to their circumstances some of them would not have had an opportunity to gain professional recognition in built environment in a more traditional university setting. The institution also has a large international student population.

When UCEM achieved the University College status in 2015, the rebranding exercise was taken as an opportunity to improve accessibility of UCEM learning material templates (Liyanagunawardena & Hussain, 2017). UCEM provides transcripts/captions for all pre-recorded audio and video learning materials. Captions for webinars were only provided where this was required for accessibility (Liyanagunawardena, Forster, & Nadan, 2017). However, it is shown that all students benefit from closed captions (Linder, 2016). Therefore, UCEM is keen to explore capability of ATS to improve webinar recording accessibility to all students. UCEM webinars are generally an hour long and conducted using Blackboard Collaborate. For UCEM students, studying at a distance, webinars are important for real-time interaction with tutors and peers. Due to the volume of webinars conducted it is not feasible to source manual transcription – both due to time and cost implications.

The Study

With this backdrop, this study investigated whether off-the-shelf automatic transcription software (ATS) is good enough to be used as an accessibility tool in the built environment sector?

Many commercial ATS are available that accept a variety of file formats and offer additional features such as human involvement as add-on services. In identifying a small set of software to be trialled, first the Association for Learning Technology community mailing list was consulted for recommendations. The cost and the availability of a free trial were also considered and the following software were selected: Descript (www.descript.com), IBM Watson Speech to Text (Watson) (www.ibm.com/watson/services/speech-to-text/), Sonix (sonix.ai), Synote (www.synote.com), Trint (trint.com) and Zoom (zoom.us). Synote, Zoom and IBM Watson were selected for the trial as UCEM was already using one or more of their services.

The research obtained ethical approval from the UCEM Research Ethics Committee prior to the data collection. A built environment specific text, containing 1000 words, was created for the experiment. In sourcing this text, expert tutors in were consulted and a section of text (200-500 words) containing subject specific terminology was requested. Four submissions were selected, covering the subject areas of property management, construction management, property and contract law, and building pathology were selected. These submissions were compiled to create the experiment text.

A purposely selected sample of 14 participants, all UCEM employees, with a range of native and non-native English accents, were invited to participate. This small sample was selected to maximise the project's benefits, within the available time, by representing the diversity of UCEM staff and students in webinars. A course, "Transcription testing" was set up on the institutional VLE, Moodle 3.4. This course contained an information sheet, consent form, instructions, the experiment text to be read and a Blackboard Collaborate webinar to create the voice recording. Out of the 14 invited participants, ten who expressed an interest in the study were enrolled on the course. After receiving consent, they were directed to the webinar setup in the course to create a recording of their voice. Seven participants created recordings; four had to be re-recorded due to recording errors. All recordings were created between 17th July and 30th August 2018. Participant demographics is provided in Table 1.

The recordings were downloaded in MP4 format. Whenever MP4 files were supported these were used, otherwise the recordings were converted into a compatible format using Camtasia Studio 8 software.

All transcriptions, except Zoom and Synote were created using each provider's free web service. With Zoom, a trial Zoom Webinar license provided to UCEM was used. The existing Synote workflow at UCEM was followed with Synote. All automatic transcriptions were generated during the period July to October 2018. The transcripts were then extracted into

Microsoft Word 2016 documents and any additional information such as timings for captions were removed manually. Altogether there were 42 transcripts containing 42,000 words to be analysed

Table 3: Participant demographics

Participant	Gender	Native English Speaker	English Accent (as identified by participant)	Length of Recording (min)
1	Male	Yes	Generic British	6:02
2	Female	No	South American	7:49
3	Male	Yes	Generic Scottish	6:32
4	Male	Yes	Generic British	6:36
5	Female	No	South Asian	6:59
6	Male	No	Greek	5:57
7	Male	No	African	8:21

Analysis

The voice recordings were first compared with the experiment text and variations were noted. For example, instead of "bond yields by contrast" a participant read "both yields by contrast". Each automatic transcription was then compared against the transcript of the voice recording (what the participant read) using Microsoft Word 2016 "Compare" function and a new document was generated where comparison was shown as track changes. These documents were then manually checked. Contractions, punctuations and capitalisation differences were ignored. Transcription of numbers and dates either using word or digits were accepted. Spelling mistakes, tense or singular/plural mismatches were considered as errors. However, where a word such as "webcam" was being transcribed as "web cam" this was ignored (not considered an error).

Once this pre-processing was completed, a manual colour coding was applied to identify substitutions, deletions and insertions. To verify consistency, another member of the Learning Technology Research team was asked to perform the coding on a sample of transcripts and these were compared. Manual comparison was time consuming; however, this was chosen over calculating similarity with a software as used in Bokhove and Downey (2018) due to the high level of differences shown by the Microsoft Word "Compare" function when in fact they were presentation differences. In this study only the meaning of the text was important and presentation differences were not relevant.

Transcript accuracy was checked using the measure Word Error Rate (WER), which was calculated using the formula: WER = (Substitution + Deletion + Insertions) / N; where N is the total number of words in the reference transcript (Apone, Botkin, Brooks, & Goldberg, 2011).

WER calculation for the first few ATS showed that Participant 1's recording was an outlier. In fact, Participant 1 had recorded the voice using laptop microphone while all other participants had used headset microphones mimicking the UCEM setup for webinars. This difference was evident in the quality of the recording and thus Participant 1's recording was eliminated from the experiment to manage the like for like comparison.

Subject matter experts were contacted to get their opinion of the automated transcript's quality. Only the transcripts created by the best performing ATS on WER measure was presented to them. Separate documents were created for each subject area consisting only of the text and transcriptions relevant to the subject area. At the top of the document was the original text followed by each of the six (Participants 2-7) numbered transcriptions. Experts' opinion whether each was "good enough" for a student to understand the meaning of the original text was recorded.

Results

Table 2 shows the calculated WER for each software. Some recordings created by non-native speakers performed better than native English speakers' recordings on the WER. For example, Participant 5 (South Asian accent) recorded lower WER than Participant 3 and Participant 4 in all except one. Furthermore, Participant 7 (African accent) recorded lower WER than Participant 3 in three software: Sonix, Descript and Zoom.

Some ATS seemed to have worked better than others in the experiment. For example, Synote has a low WER for Participant 4 (Generic British English accent) but relatively higher WER for all other participants while IBM Watson recorded the highest WER in the experiment for all except one participant. Descript have performed consistently for all participants in the experiment. Table 3 provides details of the total errors and average errors per each software considered and calculated average accuracy. Descripts has the highest average accuracy in this experiment followed by Trint, Sonix, Zoom, Synote and Watson.

Table 2: Word Error Rate for automatic transcription services

Participant	Trint	Sonix	Descript	Watson	Zoom	Synote
2	0.277	0.275	0.181	0.490	0.292	0.471
3	0.168	0.301	0.176	0.412	0.274	0.277
4	0.120	0.140	0.110	0.434	0.245	0.139
5	0.115	0.108	0.101	0.428	0.211	0.359
6	0.392	0.383	0.254	0.555	0.293	0.689
7	0.226	0.147	0.159	0.560	0.263	0.473

Table 3: Average errors per each software

Software	Trint	Sonix	Descript	Watson	Zoom	Synote
Total errors	1098	1354	981	2879	1578	2408
Average errors per transcript (1000 words)	216.33	225.67	163.50	479.83	263.00	401.33
Average accuracy (%)	78.37	77.43	83.65	52.02	73.70	59.87

Expert opinion of the automatic transcripts is provided in Table 4.

Table 4: Expert opinion of Descript transcripts

Subject area/ Participant	Property Manageme nt	Construction Management		Building Pathology		Property and Contract Law	
	Expert 1	Expert 2	Expert 3	Expert 4	Expert 5	Expert 6	Expert 7
2	x	x	x	x	x	x	x
3	x	x	x	x	x	x	x
4	x	Good enough	Good enough	x	Good enough	Good enough	x
5	x	Good enough	x	Almost good enough	x	x	x
6	x	x	x	x	x	x	x
7	x	x	x	x	x	x	x

Despite receiving the lowest WER for Descript software, Participant 5's transcript was "not good enough" as an accessibility aid in its original form except for the Construction Management section and the Building Pathology section where it received an "almost good enough" rating. On the other hand, Participant 4's transcripts received "good enough" rating from four experts. It was also interesting to see that in some instances two experts in the same discipline having conflicting views on acceptability of a transcript. None of the transcripts received a "good enough" rating in the subject discipline Property Management. The selected section was on property and bonds. However, the word "bonds" was transcribed as "bumps", "bones", "blondes", "buttons" deeming them not good enough from the outset. ATS also struggled with a range of other technical terms in the valuation section such as inflation, liquidity, yield, hedge and redemption.

Discussion

Accuracy of transcriptions is an important factor to be considered especially when they are used as accessibility aids. Though WER is used as a common measure of transcription accuracy, there are issues with measuring transcription accuracy this way (Apone et al.,2011). Even though WER considers all words to be equally important, in a technical discipline to make sense of a paragraph an error in an article such as "the" or "a" may be insignificant compared to an error in a key technical term. To address this issue, instead of relying only on the WER, the study was designed to seek the opinion from subject matter experts so that the findings would be more robust. This in fact was reflected in the results of the study, where Participant 4's transcription with slightly higher WER than Participant 5's was judged to be better by the experts.

Providing accessible material is a legal requirement and even when automatic captioning is provided, if they are not "good enough" an institution could be found to be in breach of law. For example, the lawsuit by National Association for the Deaf against Massachusetts Institute of Technology (MIT) and Harvard University stated that "Much of Harvard's online content is either not captioned or is inaccurately or unintelligibly captioned, making it inaccessible for individuals who are deaf or hard of hearing" (Lewin, 2015). As this study has shown, some automatic transcripts may not be "good enough" for the students who are hearing-impaired as technical terms have been transcribed incorrectly. Therefore, it is important that the generated automatic transcripts are checked for meaning before being made available to students.

The quality of the recording also plays a role in how well they can be transcribed automatically. In this study, despite Participant 1 being a native English speaker, all ATS struggled to transcribe the recording. The only difference between this recording and other recordings was the use of laptop's built-in microphone as opposed to a headset microphone. This shows the need to use suitable devices/tools to create good quality recordings when ATS is to be employed.

Recording of Participant 5 with a South Asian accent was more accurately transcribed (in terms of WER) than native English speakers. Furthermore, two of the experts rated passages from Participant 5's transcript as "good enough" while none of the passages from the native English speaker Participant 3's transcript was rated "good enough". This may be an indication that the ATS has improved over the years to consider accents other than standard British and standard American accents.

Experiments have shown that even when letters are transposed ("jumbled word effect") due to the way the human brain works, they are still able to recognise the word but at a slower pace (Davis, n.d.) and that the context plays an important role in understanding words. Many transcripts with lower WER were rated "not good enough" by the subject experts. But if these transcripts were presented to hearing-impaired students who have developed various skills in negotiating similar situations – for example, considering the transcript with lip reading or simply contextualising to correct errors – whether these transcripts would have been considered "good enough" is a question worth exploring. Due to the limitation of not having access to hearing-impaired learners as quality assessors this project was unable to explore this interesting avenue.

Limitations

The small sample of transcription software used for this research was selected based on the requirements of the institution. The research was conducted using freely available versions of selected transcription software and if the paid-for version was better than that of the trial version on the web, this would not be reflected in the results. Due to the small sample size, results of this experiment cannot be generalised. Participants were aware of the research and could have consciously read the text for the experiment, rather than the way they would normally communicate. Nevertheless, this study it is a useful reminder that WER on its own cannot be considered as a quality measure for transcription in technical subjects. Using subject experts to assess the quality of the transcripts rather than having a pool of hearing-impaired students was another limitation; as the later would have better reflected the quality of the transcript as an accessibility aid.

Conclusion

This study analysed six types of off-the-shelf automatic transcription software with a variety of native and non-native speakers' voice recordings to explore whether the transcripts created were "good enough" as accessibility aids in the built environment discipline. The quality of the recording affects the automatic transcription and it is important to take great care in selecting suitable recording devices. In a technical discipline, where key technical terms are of great importance to convey the meaning of a text, Word Error Rate (WER) on its own may not be a sufficient predictor of the quality of a transcript. Automatic transcriptions created using a software with a lower WER could be a great time saving first draft, that could then be checked for meaning and made available to students as an accessibility aid. At present, it seems off-the-shelf automatic transcription software does not produce a high enough level of accuracy for the creation of accessibility aids for the built environment sector even though they are economical and time saving.

References

Apone, T., Botkin, B., Brooks, M., & Goldberg, L. (2011). *Caption Accuracy Metrics Project: Research into Automated Error Ranking of Real-time Captions in Live Television News Programs.*

Bokhove, C., & Downey, C. (2018). Automated generation of 'good enough' transcripts as a first step to transcription of audio-recorded data. *Methodological innovations, 11*(2), 1-14. doi: 10.1177/2059799118790743

Burke, H., Jenkins, L., & Higham, V. (2010). *Realities Toolkit #8: Transcribing your own qualitative data.* Retrieved from http://eprints.ncrm.ac.uk/973/2/08-toolkit-transcribing-your-qual-data.pdf

Davis, M. (n.d.). Psycholinguistic evidence on scrambled letters in reading. Retrieved from http://www.mrc-cbu.cam.ac.uk/people/matt-davis/cmabridge/

Dragon Speech Recognition (2016). Nuance Dragon Professional Individual: Data Sheet. Retrieved from https://www.nuance.com/content/dam/nuance/en_uk/collateral/dragon/data-sheet/ds-dragon-professional-individual-v15-en-uk.pdf

Europa (26 October 2016). Directive (EU) 2016/2102 of the European Parliament and of the Council of 26 October 2016 on the accessibility of the websites and mobile applications of public sector bodies. Retrieved from https://eur-lex.europa.eu/legal-content/EN/TXT/HTML/?uri=CELEX:32016L2102&from=EN

Fogel, S. (2017, October 3). IBM inches toward human-like accuracy for speech recognition. Engadget [Blog post]. Retrieved from https://www.engadget.com/2017/03/10/ibm-speech-recognition-accuracy-record/

Lant, K. (2017, August 23). Microsoft's Speech Recognition is Now as Good as a Human Transcriber. Futurism the Byte [Blog post]. Retrieved from https://futurism.com/microsofts-speech-recognition-is-now-as-good-as-a-human-transcriber

Lewin, T. (2015, February 12). Harvard and M.I.T. Are Sued Over Lack of Closed Captions. The New York Times [Blog post]. Retrieved from https://www.nytimes.com/2015/02/13/education/harvard-and-mit-sued-over-failing-to-caption-online-courses.html

Linder, K. (2016). *Student uses and perceptions of closed captions and transcripts: Results from a national study.* Corvallis, OR: Oregon State University. Retrieved from http://info.3playmedia.com/rs/744-UDO-697/images/Student-Survey-Report-10-25-16-Final.pdf

Liyanagunawrdena, T.R., Forster, S. & Nadan, T. (2017, September). *Captioning videos for accessibility: A case study of University College of Estate Management.* Paper presented at the 24th Annual Conference of the Association for Learning Technology, 5 – 7 September 2017, Liverpool. Retrieved from https://altc.alt.ac.uk/2017/sessions/captioning-videos-for-accessibility-a-case-study-1676/

Liyanagunawardena, T. R., & Hussain, A. (2017). Online Distance Education Materials and Accessibility: Case Study of University College of Estate Management. *Proceedings of the E-Learning, E-Education, and Online Training. Third International Conference, eLEOT 2016, Dublin, Ireland, August 31 – September 2, 2016*, 79-86. doi: 10.1007/978-3-319-49625-2_10

Oxford Living Dictionary. (n.d.). Accessibility. Retrieved from https://en.oxforddictionaries.com/definition/accessibility

Straumsheim, C. (2017, March 6). Berkeley Will Delete Online Content. Inside Higher ED [Blog post]. Retrieved from https://www.insidehighered.com/news/2017/03/06/u-california-berkeley-delete-publicly-available-educational-content#.W-QIwc1SSlI.link

W3C (24 March 2018a). What is Web accessibility. Retrieved from https://www.w3.org/WAI/fundamentals/accessibility-intro/#what

W3C (22 June 2018b). Web Content Accessibility Guidelines (WCAG) Overview. Retrieved from https://www.w3.org/WAI/standards-guidelines/wcag/#intro

Acknowledgement

I would like to thank Graham North, Dr Peter and Dr Adrian Shell for their support.

INNOVATING A FLEXIBLE CONCEPT BASED CURRICULUM IN A COURSE: AN EXPERIENCE USING FRACTAL MODEL

Larisa Enríquez Vázquez, Universidad Nacional Autónoma de México, Mexico

Summary

Fractal is an educational model that tries to respond to the new learning contexts in which we find ourselves, which are characterized by the need to learn and update knowledge continuously and constantly and with the opportunity to access a large number of options for learning and training through the use of technologies, computer networks and digital environments, among others. The fractal model considers four interrelated elements but one element particularly stands out; it is the curriculum based on concepts that allows to expand and integrate different areas of knowledge to a specific, initial perspective. In addition, Fractal presents aspects that can be linked to connectivism and rhizomatic learning, through a concrete proposal of flexible learning design, which can be useful for formal and non-formal courses. The following Master's program at the University of La Sabana, in Colombia, presents an experience applying the model in a close context (https://www.unisabana.edu.co/programas/posgrados/centro-de-tecnologias-para-la-academia/maestria-en-innovacion-educativa-mediada-por-tic-virtual/nuestro-programa/).

Introduction

Fractal is an educational proposal to face some of the challenges and demands that today's society expects universities to address. To do this, it considers flexible and open teaching models in which formal and non-formal education converge. In 2017, Enriquez referring to several authors, such as Bates (2011), Tünnerman (2003), González Casanova (2001), points out the need to adapt university models to those that are more in line with the current context we live in, considering pedagogical methods centred on collective and self-directed work which allow, through curricular flexibility, personal learning paths with interdisciplinary approaches (Enríquez, 2017; p.375). The model has four elements that contribute to the following four dimensions: curricular flexibility, adaptability to environment, academic relevance and accessibility, in several ways. The elements proposed to achieve this goal are based on concepts curriculum, student-centred teaching, academic openness and promotion of heutagogy. The continuous execution of each one of them shows a Fractal figure (Figure 1).

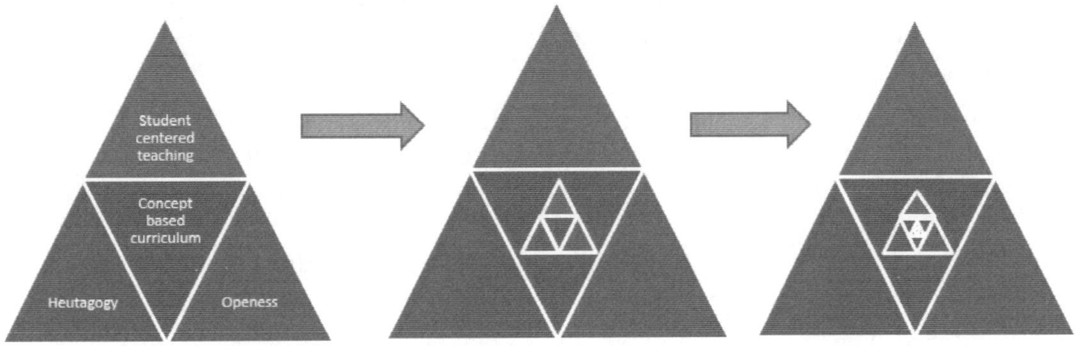

Figure 1. Fractal's elements and its iterations

Concept based curriculum

It is common to find in traditional models of education that the content of the academic programs is designed by topics or units which has generated, among other things, extensive detailed programs that, in the vast majority of cases, isolate a topic from others. However, if we consider the essential concepts of a syllabus, we can optimize teaching and learning by concentrating on deep understanding of each term which, depending on the context to which it is translated, takes on new meanings.

According to Erickson (2008), concept-based curriculum design not only reduces curricular load in a course, but also helps to focus teaching on broad and relevant situations at the same time that it enhances more flexible learning methods and strategies.

Erickson herself points out that concept-based design, when it is connected to prior knowledge, brings relevance and meaning to students' learning while causing students to process facts and skills on deeper intellectual levels, as they relate to facts, strategies and skills linked to key concepts, their generalizations and principles. It also increases the motivation for learning by involving personal knowledge and increases the fluency of language when students explain and defend their own understanding with reliable information. (Erickson, 2008; p.83).

On the other hand, Siemens (2005) and Cormier (2008) point out that learning that is sought from a pre-established curriculum transmits the idea that knowledge is static and closed, in which information is hardly updated or responds to new contexts. Enriquez points out that concepts are cognitive units of meaning, that arise from the interaction with the environment and the previous knowledge we have, and it is through continuous interaction with ourselves and others that we can create new knowledge and new concepts (Enríquez, 2017; p.377). In this sense, Fractal presents a curriculum based on concepts that, for the students, can be represented by conceptual maps.

Under this perspective, curriculum changes constantly when new concepts are introduced that arise from the interaction with different people, groups and resources. All of these new concepts are selected freely and independently by each of the students with the guidance of the teacher. While there is a starting point for the development of the fractal, represented by a concept map that presents a general idea of the teacher to address the course, new concept maps emerge from the specific context in which learning takes place, the prior knowledge and the specific interests of each student. The initial concept map is called Concept domain, while the new concept maps are called Personalized concept domains (see Figure 2).

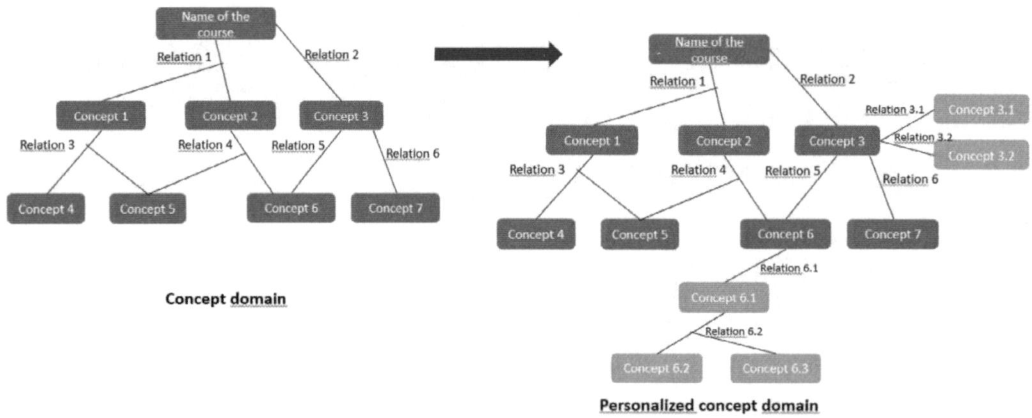

Figure 2. Concept domain and 1st iteration

Although Fractal tries to open up new ways to explore more significative, open and flexible experiences in which formal and non-formal education are intertwined, it is difficult for traditional schools and programs to make dramatic changes to their teaching models. In this sense, Fractal can also be used to design flexible courses within a specific academic degree program to enhance curricular flexibility through self-determination of students.

An online experience using Fractal

The Master's degree in Educational Innovation mediated by ICT (Information and Communication Technologies), from the University of La Sabana, in Colombia, is a recently created online master's degree, which began activities in 2018. Within the Master's program, there is a course called "Innovation Project II", for which this author was invited to design and teach the content. Although the general structure of the program maintains a slightly more traditional structure, it was possible to propose a way to approach the course in a more flexible and connectivism way using the Fractal model. In this sense, the following was taken into considerations for the course:

- To have a conceptual domain that would guide the analysis of at least five concepts.
- To invite students to develop a personal work log for self-tracking, self-reflection and self-evaluation.
- To provide materials and experiences close to students' personal project and interests.
- To search for communities of experts on topics of interest to students.

The course spanned over twelve weeks with three registered students. The Concept domain that was presented at the beginning of the course and considered five main concepts (educative innovation, educative research, models, processes and indicators). The initial relations suggested among these concepts can be seen in Figure 3.

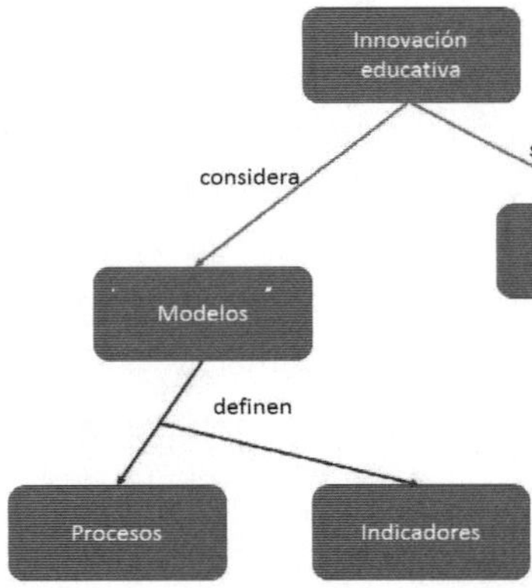

Figure 3. Course's Concept domain map

A brief introduction together with some suggested readings was given to review each of the concepts, to start analysis and reflection. Likewise, guiding questions were included to help students to work in a general way on the understanding of the concept, as well as to anchor it in their personal projects so that they could refine and improve it. For the specific review of students' understanding of the concepts, they were invited to work continuously on their personalized concept domain maps. Figure 4 and Figure 5 show a student's first and second iteration for the Concept domain. The yellow square emphasizes the concepts that were modified and widened, after completing some readings and having interactions through the virtual classroom. Figure 6 shows the fourth iteration where the student's progress can be seen as she is advancing in the review of the different concepts proposed in the Concept domain.

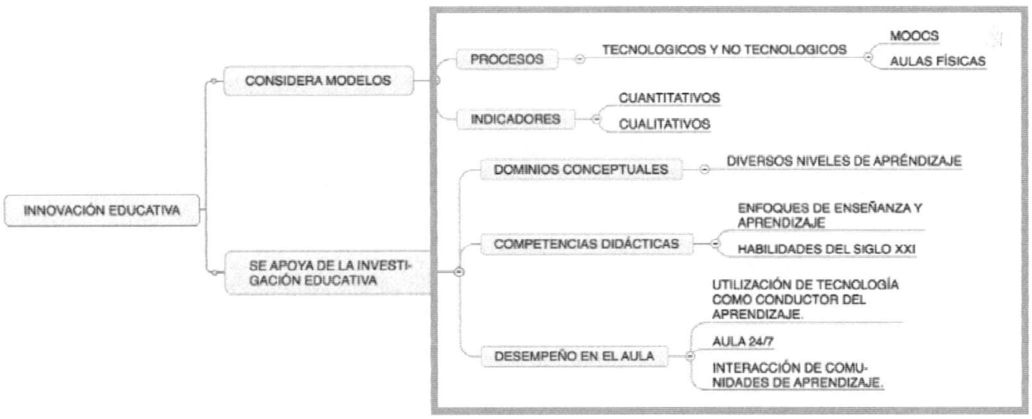

Figure 4. Student A, personalized concept domain, 1st iteration

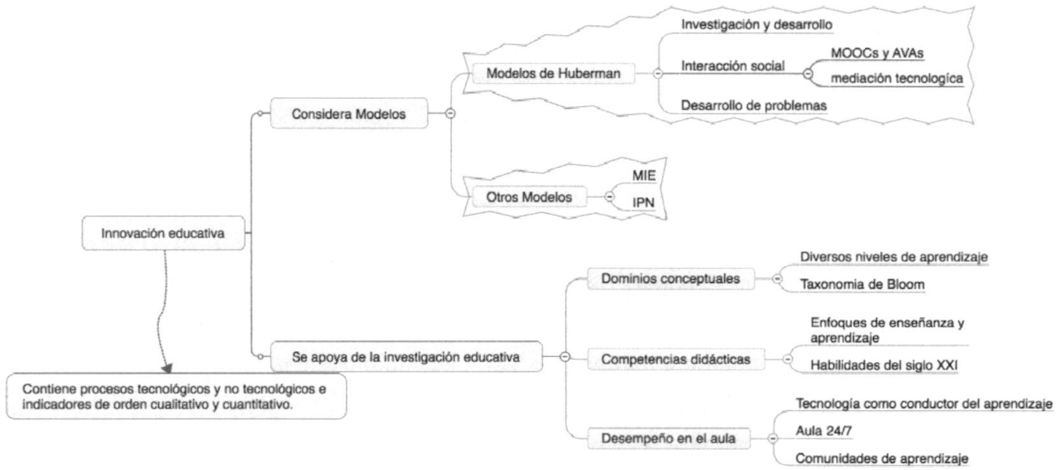

Figure 5. Student A, personalized concept domain, 2nd iteration

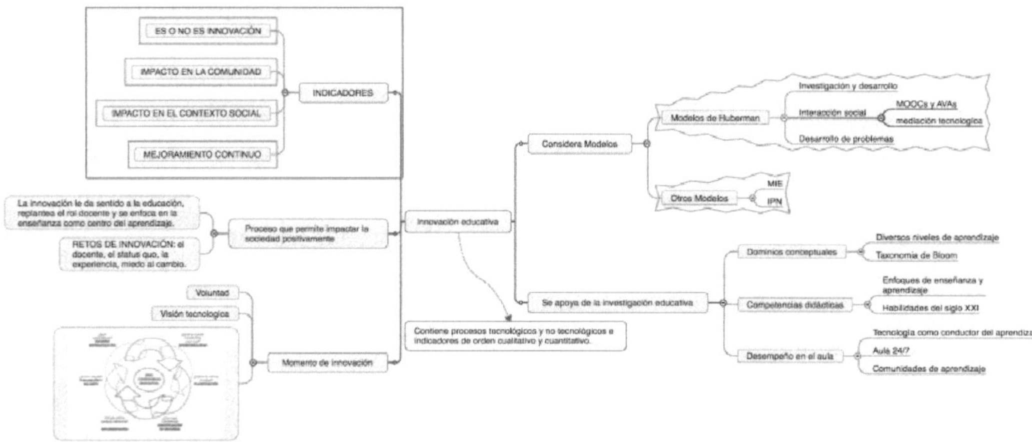

Figure 6. Student A, personalized concept domain, 4th iteration

On the other side, we may expect that working individually with the Concept domain should bring different Personalized concept domains. In Figure 7 we can see another student's 2nd iteration personalized concept domain, after she studied the concept called Educative research. In the concept map presented, it can be seen that the student classified the different kinds of educational research. Some of them were classified from the perspective of the methodologies used, some of them were classified according to the kind of variables they manage, or according to the moment in which they take place. The student even integrated specific documents for different concepts to support her point of view. Nevertheless, the personalized concept domain not only proves the approach and specific interests that student B had, but it is also evidence of the personal trajectories that each student has. It further shows the different understandings that take place in this learning experience. While the 2nd iteration of student A personalized concept domain mentions different educational areas in which research is taking place (she even points out some examples), student's B personalized concept domain brings a variety of classifications that have been used in educational research. It is interesting to see that both student C and student A included in some way the topic they are working with as part of their personal research project (in the case of student C, digital resources and in the case of student A, MOOC's).

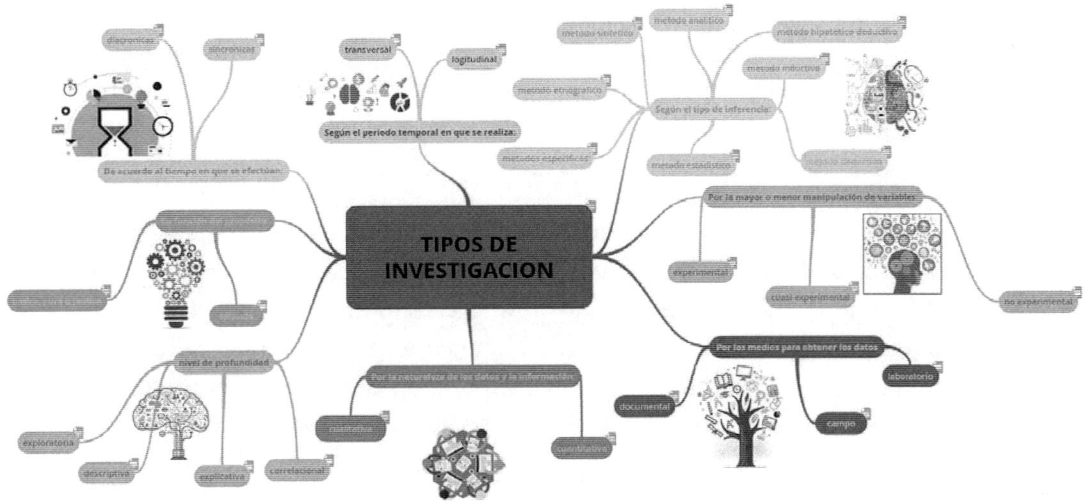

Figure 7. Student B, personalized concept domain, 2nd iteration

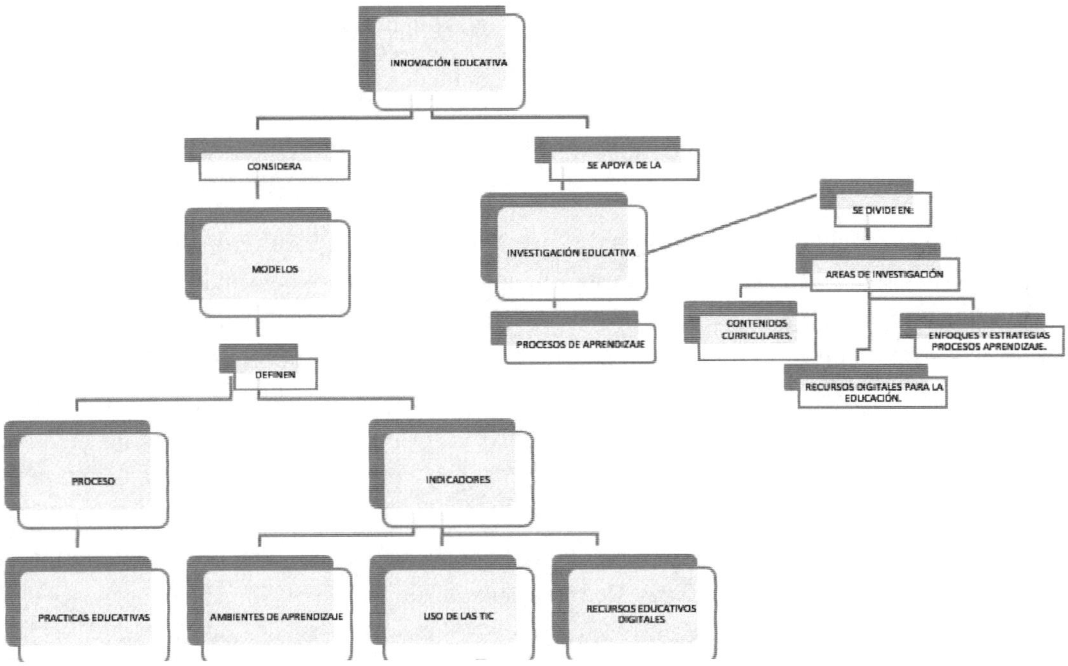

Figure 8. Student C, personalized concept domain, 2nd iteration

Results

As has been said, the Fractal educational model is composed of four elements that aim to promote student-centred teaching, curricular flexibility, students' self-determination and the possibility of connecting with other communities. The first two elements which are curriculum based on concepts and students' self-determination were those that were exercised to a greater degree while the last two elements were driven to a lesser degree. The students presented, through the personalized concept domains, both knowledge and misinterpretation of the relationships between different concepts. Likewise, it was found that the specific interests of the students (in this case, the topic of the research project they are developing) were also reflected in these personalized conceptual domains.

On the other hand, the research activities that were focused on landing the new knowledge into the degree project, helped to identify problems and doubts about the research topic. This then led to the possibility of connecting with a group of subject matter experts.

Although the Fractal model might present some of the chaotic and rhizomatic principles to which connectivism and rhizomatic learning point, in this case, however, the networks of connections do not reflect the interactions with different communities or with resources but the level of understanding and deepening that is obtained from a concept. At the same time, if we analyse the transformations that happen in each of the personalized conceptual domains, we obtain evidence of the introspective exercise that each student does.

Conclusions

The Fractal model tries to open up new opportunities for universities to explore alternatives for more significant academic experiences. Through this model, particularly considering the concept-based and flexible curriculum design, it is possible to offer a divergent view of the relationships that exist between a group of concepts. Furthermore, it presents the personal learning trajectories through which each student has travelled and how the student considers moving forward.

Also, Fractal through the concept domain, presents a solution to one of the problems that some course designers have found in designing a connectivist or rhizomatic courses. Despite the interesting and rich proposals that connectivism and rhizomatic learning represent, at the end, it is very difficult to design a course under one of these two pedagogical approaches. In this sense, Fractal sets a starting point for a course that it is just this, a starting point for a living, exploratory and personal learning experience.

References

Bates, T. (2011, November 11). European report on the future of learning. Online learning and teaching resources [Blog post]. Retrieved from http://www.tonybates.ca/2011/11/11/european-report-on-the-future-of-learning/

Cormier, D. (2008, June 3). Rhizomatic education: Community as curriculum. Dave's educational blog [Blog post]. Retrieved from http://davecormier.com/edblog/2008/06/03/rhizomatic-education-community-as-curriculum/

Enríquez, L. (2017). Fractal: An educational model for the convergence of formal and non-formal education. *Open Praxis, 9*(4), 375-386. http://dx.doi.org/10.5944/openpraxis.9.4.699

Erickson, H. L. (2008). *Stirring the head, heart, and soul: Redefining curriculum, instruction, and concept-based learning* (3rd ed.). Thousand Oaks, CA: Corwin Press.

González Casanova, P. (2001). *La universidad necesaria en el siglo XXI.* Ed. Era.

Siemens, G. (2005). Connectivism: A learning theory for the digital age. *International Journal of Instructional technology and distance learning, 2*(1). Retrieved from http://www.itdl.org/journal/jan_05/article01.htm

Tünnermann B. C. (2003). *La Universidad Latinoamericana ante los retos del siglo XXI.* México: Unión de Universidades de América Latina.

ELENE4LIFE: ACTIVE LEARNING FOR SOFT SKILLS – UNIVERSITY-CORPORATE CONNECTIONS AND CROSS-FERTILISATION

Deborah Arnold, AUNEGe, France, Mirela Mazalu, European University Colleges Association, Belgium, Matteo Uggeri, Fondazione Politecnico di Milano, Italy

Abstract

According to the 2018 World Economic Forum Report "Towards a Reskilling Revolution: A Future of Jobs for All", the rise of artificial intelligence, robotics and other digital developments is upending the primacy of human expertise in the economy. The individuals who will succeed in the economy of the future will be those who can complement the work done by mechanical or algorithmic technologies, and "work with the machines". The 2018 European Commission Proposal on Key Competences also draws attention to these disruptions affecting European societies and economies, stating that "Skills such as creativity, critical thinking, taking initiative and problem solving play an important role in coping with complexity and change in today's society."

In a previous Erasmus+ project, eLene4work, the development of HE students' (digital) soft skills was experimented through the use of MOOCs and OERs. The results showed that, while autonomous learning indeed played a significant role, real impact would only come from fully integrating these into the curriculum. The project also found a mismatch between employers' expectations and students' perceptions of the labour market with respect to these soft skills.

This paper reports specifically on the initial results of the follow-up Erasmus+ project, eLene4Life: Learning and Interacting to Foster Employability, in the form of a combined foresight analysis exploring how soft skills are and can be developed through active learning in both Higher Education and corporate training. It also highlights the potential for cross-fertilisation of these approaches in both directions and lays the ground for future actions, connections and collaborations.

Background

Many studies (Deloitte, 2017; Manpower Group, 2018; World Economic Forum, 2018) point out that soft skills are becoming as important as hard skills when looking for a job. Yet transversal or soft skills are the hardest skills to document and, at present, there is a mismatch between academic education and the skills required in the labour market.

A number of documents issued by the European Commission confirm that soft skills are "closely connected with employability" (European Commission, 2010; 2012a; 2012b) but they are not thought of as such within many universities. Companies need a more skilled workforce and opportunities should be given to young people to develop those soft skills, such as entrepreneurial skills, coping skills (i.e., the capacity to deal with a problem in a creative way), learning to learn, and other skills (such as the ability to work in teams, to communicate clearly and effectively, to adapt to different cultural contexts, to solve problems, to manage conflicts, and to show endurance in complicated or stressful situations) that will help university students make a successful transition from full-time education to entering the labour market. The importance of these soft skills is also highlighted in the Council Recommendation of 22 May 2018 on key competences for lifelong learning (The Council of the European Union, 2018).

However, at present, different countries have different methodologies and approaches to the teaching and recognition of skills for employability. This has led to a mismatch between academic education and skills required in the labour market. According to Mourshed et al. (2014), providers, employers, and young people seem to live in "parallel universes". For example, in Europe, 74 percent of education providers were confident that their graduates were prepared for work, yet only 38 percent of youth and 35 percent of employers agreed. The existence of such discrepancies implies that cooperation should be strengthened among the different stakeholders to identify and further develop solutions in the form of educational models which mobilise appropriate learning and teaching approaches for the development and recognition of soft skills, embedded within the curriculum.

The eLene4Life project

eLene4Life is an Erasmus+ Key Activity 2 Strategic Partnership project which was launched in September 2018 and runs for three years. It involves 8 partners from 6 countries (France, Italy, Germany, Belgium, Poland, the United Kingdom) and is coordinated by AUNEGe, the French digital university for management and economics.

The project approach is focused on the self-empowerment of students, through a learning process where their independence is fostered (active learning). Soft skills development is embedded in *traditional* courses through appropriate teaching methodologies (case studies, problem-based learning, project-based learning). Some of these methodologies are drawn from the experiences of company training and are based on *experiential learning* through internal (or, in some cases, external) practical activities. In both cases, reflection on the outcomes and student self-assessment will be fostered and enriched by the use of digital technologies.

The project is creating the methodological basis for the interaction with companies to foster a permanent Corporate/Higher Education Community of Practice for innovation in learning and teaching, in which the different stakeholders (teachers/instructors, students, representatives of private companies) will be involved in order to exchange experiences, discuss, update the common knowledge and evaluate the results of the experimentations.

A key point of the project is the analysis of the real practices of companies and their internal dynamics in terms of teamworking, e-collaboration, communication, change management and situations that involve soft skills in general. Both methodologies and tools used by companies to support newly graduated employees offer an interesting point of view from which to start the research activity.

The project supports the co-design between European companies and universities of new teaching/learning practices integrated in to academic curricula, aimed at fostering students' development of transversal skills, while addressing the critical issues faced by many higher education institutions in terms of class size and physical spaces. Indeed, at macro level, the project addresses the need for new, realistic means of interaction and communication between higher education and the corporate sector. Teaching and training methodologies have the potential to become a point of union through which to create a continuum, as behind the choices of companies in training investment, and in applying innovative approaches, there is the awareness of the expected result and of the perceived need. Bringing together these different experiences will open a window in the sometimes-difficult communication between the two sectors.

The variations across member states with respect to University-Corporate collaboration in curriculum innovation mean that a transnational approach is vital for addressing this issue, enabling the partnership to draw on a wide base of experience and to address the inherent cultural differences, for example in terms of attitudes towards and maturity of cross-sectoral collaboration. By bringing together and analysing examples from the different participant member states, the project enables each partner to learn from experiences outside their national context and thus to be in a stronger position to bring about change through the pilot projects they implement, and to feed the results back in to the project in order to develop a truly transnational perspective on cross-sectoral collaboration for the integration of soft skills in the curriculum.

Active learning: what do we mean?

This working definition of active learning is adapted from Bonwell and Eison (1991), Prince (2004), Raynal and Rieunier (2010), University of Minnesota – Center for Educational Innovation.

According to Prince (2004),

> *"It is not possible to provide universally accepted definitions for all of the vocabulary of active learning since different authors in the field have interpreted some terms differently. However, it is possible to provide some generally accepted definitions and to highlight distinctions in how common terms are used. Active learning is generally defined as any instructional method that engages students in the learning process. In short, active learning requires students to do meaningful learning activities and think about what they are doing…[in] the classroom." (Prince, 2004; p.223).*

Active learning refers to a broad range of teaching strategies which engage students or trainees as active participants in their learning. Typically, these strategies involve learners working together during class, but may also involve individual work and/or reflection, as well as group work outside the classroom. The focus is on how to learn rather than what to learn, placing the learner at the heart of the process. Active learning can be on a spectrum of learner and teacher control of the learning process and learning environment.

The main characteristic of active learning is that students are engaged in activities which involve more than just listening and note-taking (e.g. reading, discussing, writing).

One or more of the following should be present to fully exploit the potential of active learning:

- Less emphasis is placed on transmitting information and more on developing students' skills.
- Students are engaged in the (co)creation of new knowledge based on their previous knowledge and socio-cultural context.
- Students are involved in higher-order thinking (analysis, synthesis, evaluation, critical thinking, problem-solving, metacognition and reflexivity).
- Greater emphasis is placed on students' exploration of their own attitudes and values.

Teaching approaches to support active learning range from short, simple activities like journal writing, problem solving and paired discussions, to more complex activities such as case studies, debating, role playing, team-based problem solving, collaborative game-based learning and project-based learning.

Initial results: foresight analysis on active learning for soft skills development

Foresight analysis on innovative higher education learning models for soft skills

Transnational research has been conducted to analyse the state-of-the-art of innovative methodologies and activities which foster the acquisition of soft skills in Higher Education. The main purpose of this research is to provide universities, HE institutions and companies with examples, scenarios and good practices for the improvement of soft skills that are used in HE. Desk research and semi-structured interviews with HE teachers in 5 European countries are combined with the same approach at cross-national level to provide valuable insights in the ways that soft skills are embedded into the curriculum or developed as specific transversal modules.

The data is collected in such a way as to facilitate the creation of a Dynamic Toolkit in the form of practical advice to support the transferability of innovative practices. Questions such as the number of students, the physical environment required for successful active learning and the various assessment methods are covered, as well as issues of institutional support, cost and recognition.

Initial insights from these interviews show a keen understanding of the principles of active learning in accordance with the proposed working definition. In terms of the benefits observed for students, these included:

> *"increased faith in one's own strengths, abilities and skills, identification of own personal and social competences, broadly understood knowledge of interpersonal communication, learning assertive behaviour and effective communication with people, knowledge of the principles of good behaviour, practical interpersonal training" (training provider in HE context, Poland).*

Unexpected benefits were also reported in the form of high participation during discussions and comparisons at class level, as well as students doing things even if they are not mandatory.

There was also a high level of awareness among teachers and trainers of the constraints relating to the physical environment and class size:

> *"A transversal module doesn't depend on any particular teaching department so there is no admin support, you're on your own! Fortunately, organising the course during the holidays means that the gymnasium is available, as well as a classroom in the sports department equipped with chairs on castors and a whole-wall whiteboard." (HE teacher, France).*

> *"The optimal class size is 25, if more then you need to run additional parallel courses. Work in small subgroups requires fluid physical environment where furniture can be moved around easily. It could be possible with up to 80 participants in a large empty room. But a problem with large groups is the loss of spontaneity with respect to oral participation." (training provider in HE context, France).*

> *"High workload for students and difficulties in completing the official programme as lot of time was dedicated to active learning." (training provider in HE context, Italy).*

The question of how, or even whether, to assess soft skills was also raised. Techniques used are often a combination of observation, self-assessment and peer-assessment. In one case, the assessment involved evaluation of project work (group assessment), combined with a written exam (individual grade) and successful participation in a MOOC. In another example, teachers shared the evaluation rubric with students at the beginning of the course and discussed subsequent revisions. A third example consisted of a self-assessment questionnaire (at least once in each phase) to evaluate teamwork and collaborative processes as well as the learners' own contribution. This activity was seen as very useful for students and teachers to reflect on the ongoing collaborative activity and intervene if needed. Finally, several participants questioned whether it is actually possible or desirable to assess soft skills and called for more insights from research that can be applied in practice.

Foresight analysis on innovative corporate training models for soft skills

This analysis captures the state-of-the-art of innovative methodologies and activities, fostering the acquisition of soft skills in the corporate field. Run in parallel to the foresight analysis for higher education, the main purpose is to provide universities with examples, scenarios and good practices for the improvement of soft skills that are used in corporate training. The innovative aspect of this approach resides in breaking down the barrier between "traditional" university teaching methodologies and some of the most active corporate training approaches linked to the concepts of coaching, empowerment and personal development.

In the corporate sector, the question of large groups is less prevalent than in HE, and indeed participants expressed a preference for small groups:

> *"We tend to work with smaller groups, as this makes the reluctant ones more comfortable, so – this way – we can force them to express themselves a bit. In these cases, is also useful to use digital tools (like Sli.do for instance) to allow everyone to answer questions in a short span of time. Otherwise it'll be impossible." (HR manager, Italy).*

In terms of expectations within the corporate sector, some differences of focus were noted, for example one participant had high expectations regarding the soft skills that a new employee could bring to the job, whereas the experience of a training provider put the emphasis on applying these soft skills to a concrete business problem.

> *"When someone new arrives in the company, you do not expect him to bring a new technical know-how, neither on the way to work. Or at least I expect it after a few months. Only after 6 months he can start to bring ideas and solutions opportunities. On soft skills, on the other hand, it could bring innovation to zero time!" (HR manager, Italy).*

> *"Soft skills training for the corporate sector needs to address a specific need, such as customer relations, not soft skills for the sake of soft skills, though there is growing awareness of soft skills nowadays." (Training provider, France).*

Aligned with this is the insight from the same training provider with respect to soft skills training in HE, where "the students' goal is to get a diploma, so they are not interested in soft skills per se, as they are more interested in the discipline itself." Referring to the approach taken by the University of Sherbooke in Canada, the advice is to get students to mobilise and develop soft skills through active learning related to the discipline, for example an engineering project which requires collaboration, negotiation and creativity.

Discussion: cross-fertilisation between the HE and corporate sectors

Examples of successful cross-fertilisation are rare and it is not uncommon to meet with resistance within HE regarding the "interference" of the corporate sector in defining the curriculum, for fear of HE becoming instrumentalised as a "provider of work-ready graduates". However, the focus here is more on the methodologies used in corporate training than the actual content of the curriculum, and few would argue that soft skills do not contribute to the development of socially competent citizens, open to the world, to others and to the challenges of the 21st century. As one participant said:

> *"the main objective is to discover one's own talents within a 'caring' group. Employability is secondary to this. But the mix of ages in the group is an important factor… as it reflects the intergenerational reality of the workplace". (HE teacher, France)*

A concrete example of such cross fertilisation identified during the foresight analysis stage is presented here as an example. One teacher took an interest in a soft skills training initiative, which started out as a project quite separate from the institution. The teacher took a *research inquiry* approach to explore the initiative and to gather enough data to be able to defend the idea to colleagues, who were very reticent at first. He participated in a *soft skills* course as a learner himself, observed other sessions and then made a formal proposal for the creation of a transversal module. He got three of four colleagues from different disciplines on board, who all followed the soft skills course as learners themselves. However, he still met with resistance when seeking to embed a soft skills module within a disciplinary course, suggesting that there is still some way to go before full recognition of the importance of soft skills in the curriculum. Again, the University of Sherbrooke recommendation to embed soft skills within disciplinary courses, rather than develop specific courses, might go some way to getting more HE teachers (and students) on board.

On the issue of barriers to education-business cooperation:

> *"Companies are eager to be in touch with young talent, but we see they are more interested in short term gains because they want to be involved in activities mostly with last year students. But we have soft skills training also for younger students, 1st or 2nd year. This is why we highlight the concept of brand, to present themselves as an attractive company to younger students and build their brand, and have thus a medium-term talent investment approach." (Training provider in HE context, Italy)*

Finally, the following advice was formulated for universities wanting to promote soft skills learning:

- offer teacher training to professors to promote a new approach to didactics through active learning;
- talk with students during and after activities in order to draw out difficulties and needs;
- identify the challenges to changing one's way of teaching: avoid frontal lessons, recognise that it is not possible to cover all contents, think differently about the course structure, add priorities, recognise that probably not everything is necessary;

- develop active learning approaches related to the curriculum, which mobilise soft skills but where soft skills are not the primary focus.

Conclusion

This paper provides some initial insights into the way in which universities are using active learning for the development of soft skills, as well as the point of view of companies and training providers. The consolidated results will enable the creation of a concrete toolkit and a MOOC for all those wishing to develop soft skills training. A transnational University-Corporate Community of Practice will bring together stakeholders from both sectors to further the exchange of innovative practice for cross-fertilisation. In particular, further research on the assessment of soft skills would be welcomed.

The expected outcome for HE teachers will be a heightened awareness of needs and practices in the corporate sector as well as access to human and digital resources in order to bring about curriculum innovation. Similarly, corporate representatives will gain a better understanding of HE practices, with the opportunity to engage in dialogue. Ultimately, the impact for students will be a more relevant learning experience, offering them the chance to develop contextualised transversal skills during the course of their studies and thus be better prepared for the workforce and society in general, as competent and confident 21st century citizens.

References

Bonwell, C. C., & Eison, J.A. (1991). *Active Learning: Creating Excitement in the Classroom. ASHE-ERIC Higher Education Report No. 1.* Washington, D.C.: The George Washington University, School of Education and Human Development.

Deloitte (2017). *Soft Skills for business success.* Retrieved from https://www2.deloitte.com/content/dam/Deloitte/au/Documents/Economics/deloitte-au-economics-deakin-soft-skills-business-success-170517.pdf

European Commission (2010). *An agenda for new skills and new jobs.* Retrieved from https://publications.europa.eu/en/publication-detail/-/publication/7f39a8c6-068e-434d-a7ce-a9665bf227f9

European Commission (2012a). *New skills and jobs in Europe: Pathways towards full employment.* Retrieved from https://ec.europa.eu/epale/en/resource-centre/content/new-skills-and-jobs-europe-pathways-towards-full-employment

European Commission (2012b). *Rethinking education: Investing in skills for better socio-economic outcomes – COM(2012) 669.* Retrieved from https://ec.europa.eu/europeaid/rethinking-education-investing-skills-better-socio-economic-outcomes-com2012-669_en

Manpower Group (2018). *Solving the Talent Shortage: Build, Buy, Borrow and Bridge. 2018 Talent Shortage Survey.* Retrieved from https://www.manpowergroup.co.uk/wp-content/uploads/2018/07/MG_TalentShortage2018.pdf

Mourshed, M., Patel, J., & Suder, K. (2014, January). Education to Employment: Getting Europe's Youth into Work. McKinsey Center for Government [Blog post]. Retrieved from https://www.mckinsey.com/industries/social-sector/our-insights/converting-education-to-employment-in-europe

Prince, M. (2004). Does Active Learning Work? A Review of the Research. *Journal of Engineering Education, 93*, 223-231.

Raynal, F., & Rieunier, A. (2010). *Pédagogie: Dictionnaire des concepts clés.* Paris: ESF.

The Council of the European Union (2018). *Council Recommendation of 22 May 2018 on key competences for lifelong learning.* Retrieved from https://eur-lex.europa.eu/legal-content/EN/TXT/PDF/?uri=CELEX:32018H0604(01)&rid=7

University of Minnesota – Center for Educational Innovation. Retrieved from https://cei.umn.edu/active-learning

World Economic Forum (2018). *Towards a Reskilling Revolution: A Future of Jobs for All.* Retrieved from http://www3.weforum.org/docs/WEF_FOW_Reskilling_Revolution.pdf

SWITCHING CHANNELS: THE CHANGING ROLE OF VIDEO IN EUROPEAN UNIVERSITIES

Sally Reynolds, ATiT, Belgium/Media & Learning Association, Belgium

Most European universities have been using video as a teaching tool for many years. This includes not only the open universities for whom video production has been a stable component right from the start, but also more traditional universities, many of whom supported professional audio-visual production facilities designed to create high-quality educational teaching resources.

At the start, video in education was all about creating resources that could show processes and systems that were otherwise difficult to visualize. It was also about showing situations and contexts that were challenging to reproduce in normal university settings. University audio visual centres, were also charged with putting in place the services and systems to support the types of audio-visual support that academics required ranging from good audio in the lecture theatre to high-quality projection of images. These centres were usually the first to get involved in introducing the first video conferencing services and while the IT services also played a key role here, it was generally the AV staff who were charged with not only the equipment, but also with training academic staff in the use of video conferencing for teaching when this type of teaching became a popular way to reach remote campus locations and students in the 1990's.

Since then, the use of video for teaching and learning has virtually exploded and video technology for higher education has now become indispensable. Whether this is for the capturing and relaying of lectures or for application in high-end virtual reality scenarios, it is almost impossible to imagine a university setting where video does not play some kind of role. The introduction of student video assignments in assessment, the independent creation of knowledge clips by academic teaching staff, the use of subtitling and speech recognition to support access are all practices that place considerable pressure not only on university services but also on common practices and accepted standards within the university. At the same time AI (Artificial Intelligence) and Immersion look set to become common practice in higher education which raises questions that are not only practical in terms of cost but also ethical in terms of how far individual privacy is challenged by video based observation and assessment techniques.

Some of the issues that arise due to the increased dominance of video in university teaching are: How does a university manage the relationship for example between pedagogy and technology? Who decides on how and when new video based services are introduced?

Managing quality and reputation is increasingly a challenge, how can a university best distinguish between materials that are created by and for the academic for use in his or her teaching as opposed to those that are created by a skilled and experienced audio-visual production team with a different set of objectives.

There is the whole discussion about whether video is being used to simply re-enforce what many consider to be the outdated one way transfer of knowledge model commonly seen in many MOOC and lecture capture settings, and if so, how can such uses of video be made more interactive and relevant to today's students. Synchronous virtual classes, with students fully engaged across all modalities are becoming common practice and systems to support learning and assessment in such environments are now possible. But what does this mean for academic teaching staff, how does this affect the process of learning?

For many of us the journey is only beginning.

ATTEMPTING TO REGULATE DISTANCE HIGHER EDUCATION: REFLECTIONS ON THE PORTUGUESE EXPERIENCE

António Moreira Teixeira, Pedro Barbosa Cabral, Maria do Carmo Teixeira Pinto,
Universidade Aberta, Portugal

The continuous expansion in the use of digital technology to enhance teaching and learning experiences has led to a major shift in the Higher Education sector across the world. The large impact of new educational practices and forms of education delivery, as exemplified by the Massive Open Online Courses (MOOC) phenomena, has contributed to accelerate dramatically the digital transformation of Higher Education Institutions (HEI). As a result, an increasingly amount of distance and eLearning provision is now part of HEIs mainstream operations. In this new hybrid environment, the border between formal and non-formal education, as well as virtual and face-to-face becomes blurred. Moreover, the development of online learning has set new challenges to European and national regulation bodies as well as quality assurance systems.

Following the publication of the revised Standards and Guidelines for Quality Assurance in the European Higher Education Area – ESG (ENQA, 2015) specific quality standards and criteria have been developed in order to allow for European quality assurance agencies to appropriately evaluate eLearning delivered programmes (Huertas et al., 2018). However, in what regards regulation only a few countries have issued specific legislation on distance higher education and eLearning so far. The most notable cases being Italy and Brazil. These scarce experiences have generated mixed feelings on the part of the academic community. On one hand, the known examples prove regulation allows to assure transversal quality standards by imposing a number of minimum requirements which are mandatory for all providers. On the other hand, they impose strict rules and models which easily become obsolete in such a rapidly changing technological environment thus hindering continuous pedagogical innovation.

In Portugal, the discussion on the need for development of a specific legislation on distance higher education dates back from 2007. It was initiated by Universidade Aberta (UAb), the Portuguese open university, which is the major provider of online learning in the country. Being the dominant force, the institution feared that the entry of new players in an unregulated sector could lower the quality standards. At that time, a provision in the general legislation regulating HEIs has been made stating that a dedicated distance education act should follow up. However, this didn't happen. As all public HEIs started to provide distance and eLearning programmes, though, it became ever more apparent for most members of the academic community that some sort of regulation was in need. This understanding was shared by the national quality assurance body, the A3ES. The agency felt such regulation was paramount to provide them with a clear framework for evaluating distance and eLearning degrees.

In response to this demand from the stakeholders, the Portuguese Government has drafted a proposal for the Legal Framework for Higher Distance Education (Regime Jurídico do Ensino Superior a Distância – RJED). This is part of the Decree-Law nr. 83/2019. The RJED draft proposal presents a holistic view of how the sector should be regulated, combining a number of requirements for providers, programmes and courses and also a set of criteria to organize its quality assurance. Yet, it also imposes a new strategic ambition for the distance higher education system, by setting a target of 50.000 students enrolled by 2030. In addition, the RJED establishes a new specific role for the UAb within the HEI national public system. According to the draft proposal, the UAb should become the national research and resource centre for distance and eLearning. All other HEIs wanting to provide distance and eLearning are expected to partner with UAb for developing their programmes and courses. The UAb is bound to have all its provision delivered in partnership in order to receive public funding.

This new legislation has been submitted to public discussion in the Spring of 2019 generating significant controversy and wide criticism amongst the higher education system and the academic community. The focal point has been the combination of the regulation of the sector with a restructuring of the UAb mission awarding it a specialized role as a central hub in the distance and eLearning public higher education system.

In this paper, the authors analyse the RJED draft proposal, highlighting its most controversial aspects, as the limitations it imposes to pedagogical innovation and the specialized role it awards to UAb, and discussing the potential impact such regulations can have in the development of the higher education sector in Europe.

THE INTERNATIONALIZATION OF THE XXI CENTURY UNIVERSITIES: UNINETTUNO MODEL

Maria Amata Garito, Università Telematica Internazionale UNINETTUNO, Italy

The Internationalization of the Universities: A Historical Overview

Universities were born as supranational institutions. Earlier, the first cultural centres, named universities by the scholars of the Arab World, such as the al-Qarawiyyin University, or the al-Karaouine University, based in Fes, Morocco, founded in 859 by a woman, Fatima Al-Fihriya, and followed, in a chronological order, by the al-Azhar University, Cairo, Egypt, founded in 975, played an important role in the cultural relationships between the Islamic World and Europe. The texts of the ancient Greeks, from Aristotle to Hippocrates, from Galenus to Euclydes up to Ptolemy, were translated in Arabic, and studied and commented by the Arabic intellectuals. At the beginning of the Middle Ages, Europe received from Arab culture more than it would be able to give. From the 12th century on, the path was traversed backwards. Latin intellectuals moved to Barcelona, Toledo, Sevilla, and in Sicily, where they found the aforementioned texts and translated them into Latin, allowing Arab culture ideas and knowledge, elaborated on the basis of Greco-Roman civilization ideas, to penetrate the European intellectual circuit. Along with those texts, there came also the works by the Arab commentators to Aristotle, like Avicenna, which were commented and studied at the new-born Universities. In Europe, universities were born as corporations of teachers and students (Prodi, 2013); the first one in 1088 was the University of Bologna and soon after, there were the Sorbonne University in Paris, the University of Salamanca in Spain and the Oxford University in England.

For centuries, schoolmasters and students, moving from own town to the other, from Bologna to Paris, from Paris to Oxford, from Oxford to Salamanca, have produced and spread knowledge, promoted the development of new ideas, keeping Europe's spiritual unity always alive; they developed a culture without boundaries. In the Middle Ages each University was a separated entity and all together they made up a European supranational network of students, teachers and knowledge.

In the Middle Ages all universities were open to people of any nationality and students, in the various sites, gathered into corporations. Young people felt that, in order to get a valuable intellectual and scientific education, they needed to attend several universities and, for this reason, they moved from one institution to another, facing exhausting journeys on foot or on horseback. Students who aimed at acquiring a good training in law attended the University of Bologna, for theology and philosophy they went to Paris and to attend courses on sciences and mathematics they moved to Oxford. Besides their interest in the discipline, what attracted the students most was the scholars' reputation. There were the most famous scholars such as Saint Thomas Aquinas, who taught philosophy and theology at the University of Paris where he was considered as a kind of "guru", a university "star" and for this reason his courses were requested also by other universities. Saint Thomas moved from Paris to Salamanca to deliver his lectures on Aristotle's theories, followed by a lot of students, animating the intellectual life of the time with his ideas on the relationship between faith and reason as well as on the question of free or paying access to the university studies which inspired debate between Dominicans and Franciscans (Garito, 1983). The relatively few universities of the medieval era were sufficient to weave the plot of a unitary, strong and coherent culture that soon became a common heritage of Europe.

Between the 15th and the 16th century, with the Renaissance, universities changed their juridical and administrative model: from corporations they became foundations, from private organizations public institutions, from supranational bodies they changed into national structures, from expression of pluralism of different classes they became expression of selected social groups. The universities changed their roles and functions. Princes who gave them prestigious premises and material assets funded them but, in change, Universities bowed to the needs of power and, therefore, partly lost their autonomy and freedom, fast surrendering to public powers in juridical as well as in economic terms (see Hammerstein, 1995).

The universities' international character began to fade away and give way to their nationalization and regionalization. Universities had the well-defined task to train officers, magistrates, diplomats, as well as the whole staff that would make up the ruling class of the States (Boehm & Raimondi, 1981).

It would take many years before significant internationalization models of the universities emerge.

Nowadays, the 21st century is actually emerging as the century in which new models of university internationalization become real, thanks to the use of the new technologies. Exploiting the potential of the Internet, in fact, it is easy to build networks of universities based in different countries of the world, which jointly disseminate knowledge without boundaries of space, time and place.

The Internet: New models of internationalization – Universities without Boundaries

Nowadays a most significant historical turning-point is under way; everyone is the protagonist and spectator of a cultural revolution fuelled, driven by technologies able to affect the processes of our minds and connect them on a global and planetary scale.

In a few years, the Internet has become the most powerful platform across the world; it connects intelligences and allows people, belonging to countries that are different in terms of history, culture, religion and economy, to take part interactively in the development of knowledge.

A true revolution is in progress, based not just on the increase of knowledge and of its applications, but also on the evolution of the processes of knowledge codification, memorization and transfer.

The globalized and interconnected world is part of everyone's life and political, economic, social and cultural spheres.

For millennia, on Earth, people kept on building, destroying and rebuilding separated worlds, frontiers and borders aimed at protecting what they deemed as precious and incorruptible. The Web is the largest public place that humankind has ever had at its disposal; it is the new public arena of the global society.

The new communication technologies accelerated the processes of internationalization of our society and created a new interconnected world that lives locally and acts globally. Global and local are interconnected. The Internet, as a set of interconnections, is at the same time centralized and delocalized. All the institutions that make up society today are mustering the courage to reinvent themselves using the Internet, the most powerful platform in the world that allows accelerating the processes of innovation, distribution, creativity, bringing together people, knowledge and skills at a global level. A new era has truly arisen, slowly changing the hierarchies and powers of a new globalized and interconnected society, enabling the academic institutions to collaborate and together train the younger generations needing the tools to move in the globalized and interconnected world and to create together the future. The technological network is also enabling the creation of an international network of universities and people who transfer and share their knowledge. Technology has become an important connector that allows the realization of international partnerships of universities belonging to both developed and developing nations. The collaborative nature of this technology promotes mutual understanding between peoples, and the benefits for individuals go far beyond the accumulation of knowledge. By means of the new technologies, universities can arrive directly in the homes of students from different countries of the world. They can create competences for global labour markets at distance, can act locally, nationally and internationally, emerging at the same time as important actors facilitating the internationalization of both universities and companies. Globalization, interdependence and communication technologies are now going on together and can give universities the tools to develop new models of collaboration in teaching, in research, in common programs design, in teachers and students exchange also in a virtual way. The existence of the Internet network, external to man, built on memories connected to each other, profoundly changed processes and mechanisms of knowledge production and communication. It has changed the languages with which today we communicate knowledge, has allowed access to knowledge for all the citizens of the world, even outside the traditional educational or training structures; it has really democratized access to the various levels of education. The creation of higher education global network, in which professors from different countries of the world participate in the collaborative construction of knowledge, is no longer a utopia but a concrete reality. The evidence of the great changes brought about by the Internet is the basis for the construction of the teaching and learning model of the International Telematic University UNINETTUNO (Garito, 2016).

The experience of the International Telematic University UNINETTUNO testifies what has been stated. Moreover, if we analyse the results of the international collaborations carried out by UNINETTUNO with universities in different countries, we can see how these collaboration models have brought to the partner universities a new vitality making them become protagonists of the global reticular economy.

UNINETTUNO University's Internationalization Models

UNINETTUNO's psycho-pedagogic-didactic model developed and keeps on developing taking into account the results of several research programs related to the application of computer-based and satellite technologies, to cognitive processes, artificial intelligence linked to the neurosciences, to Big Data etc. Based on the results of these research activities, several Internet-based learning environments were realized. These learning environments, available in UNINETTUNO's didactic cyberspace, allow for directly transmitting, from the university to the student-user, lessons, multimedia products, databases, self-assessment systems, tutoring support, exercise and organizing exam sessions. UNINETTUNO's model has greatly expanded knowledge communication models, created extremely dynamic virtual environments triggering collaborative learning processes between professors and students of different countries of the world. This facilitated the establishment of international relationships and the creation of new real and virtual environments aimed at establishing shared networks of knowledge among the various universities of the world and at supporting institutions' convergence. UNINETTUNO, through its model of internationalization, established a global network of public and private universities sharing their knowledge, their resources and technologies, curricula, research laboratories; easily arranging mobility plans for professors and students, still maintaining the specificities of each institution as a value and enrichment for the network. It built, on the Internet, a network of universities including not just technologies, but also and above all people, intelligences that are able to connect together their knowledge while respecting cultural, political, religious and economic differences. The development of this pattern of international relationships contributes to the establishment of a common area for globalized and interconnected knowledge.

UNINETTUNO University has made of internationalization one of its most important strategic pillars. The internationalization process has been developed and continues to develop according to two profoundly different models.

The First Internationalization Model

The first of these models is characterized by a completely new phenomenon, both in terms of modality and rapidity of diffusion, and is directly related to the Internet. Through the Internet, the citizen of the information society can select the training path that best meets his/her needs. Anybody, without moving from home, can decide whether to follow a distance degree program or training course to acquire competences and professional skills; s/he can customize his/her own study paths in a flexible way for meeting his/her needs in terms of space and time, by adapting them to his/her own cognitive style. Everybody can easily access to multimedia contents and interaction tools even using different mobile devices such as smartphones and tablets.

Web users explore and select information and services available in the Web, making choices that are no longer strictly related to their country of origin, but that are mainly functional to their own interests. The Internet, and social networks in particular, allows these users to play an active role in promoting, suggesting and valorising information, contents and services they directly use. Web users themselves give importance to the *Web nodes* they deem more interesting and worthwhile to be suggested and recommended to their social network. This new model of quality recommendation and promotion at a global scale is possible through social bookmarking, by sharing a link and *likes* on social networks such as Twitter, Facebook, LinkedIn o Google+, as well as through an active participation in discussion groups, thematic forums and social review services.

It is through this spontaneous, networked, global, not supervisioned word-of-mouth mechanism that, in a few years, the International Telematic University UNINETTUNO has succeeded in getting, among its enrolled students, people coming from 167 different countries of the world (the 167 countries of origin of UNINETTUNO' students: Albania, Algeria, Andorra, Angola, Antigua And Barbuda, Argentina, Australia, Austria, Azerbaijan, Bahamas, Bahrain, Bangladesh, Barbados, Belarus, Belgium, Benin, Bolivia, Bosnia And Herzegovina, Botswana, Brazil, British Overseas Territories, Brunei, Bulgaria, Burkina Faso, Burundi, Cambodia, Cameroun, Canada, Cape Verde, Cayman Islands, Chile, Cyprus, Colombia, Costa Rica, Côte d'Ivoire, Croatia, Czech Republic, Denmark, Democratic Republic of the Congo, Dominica, Dominican Republic, Ecuador, Egypt, El Salvador, Estonia, Ethiopia, Fiji, Finland, France, Gambia, Georgia, Germany, Ghana, Great Britain And Northern Ireland, Greece, Grenada, Guatemala, Guyana, Haiti, Honduras, Hong-Kong, Hungary, India, Indonesia, Iran, Iraq, Ireland – Eire, Island, Israel, Italy, Jamaica, Japan, Jordan, Kazakhstan, Kenya, Kyrgyzstan, Kosovo, Kuwait, Latvia, Lebanon, Liberia, Libya, Lithuania, Luxemburg, Macedonia, Madagascar, Malawi, Malaysia, Maldives, Mali, Malta, Martinique, Mauritius, Mexico, Moldova, Monaco, Mongolia, Morocco, Mozambique, Myanmar, Namibia, Nepal, Netherlands, Netherlands Antilles, New Guinea, New Zealand, Nicaragua, Niger, Nigeria, Niue, Norway, Pakistan, Palestine, Panama, Papua New Guinea, People's Republic Of China, Peru, Philippines, Poland, Portugal, Puerto Rico, Qatar, Republic Of South Africa, Romania, Russia, Rwanda, Saint Lucia, Saint Vincent And The Grenadines, San Marino, Saudi Arabia, Senegal, Serbia, Sierra Leone, Singapore, Slovakia, Slovenia, Somalia, South Korea, Spain, Sri Lanka, Sudan, Swaziland, Sweden, Switzerland, Syria, Taiwan, Tajikistan, Tanzania, Thailand, Trinidad And Tobago, Tunisia, Turkey, Uganda, Ukraine, United Arab Emirates, United States Of America, Uruguay, Uzbekistan, Venezuela, Vietnam, Yemen, Zambia and Zimbabwe).

UNINETTUNO is actually an institution without boundaries, as data prove. The data related to internationalization show that, in the latest 5 years, the foreign nationality students increased by 40%. The faculty with the highest number of enrolled students is Engineering and it is followed by Psychology, Economics and Communication Sciences. 95% of the students enrolled in the master's courses live abroad. In addition, the data about USA is very interesting. UNINETTUNO is the only Italian university counting 230 students residing in the United States among its enrolled students. UNINETTUNO fuelled this trend also by democratizing the access to knowledge and to its contents, freely available on manifold media:

- On the satellite television channel, UNINETTUNO University TV; free on air on the Hot-Bird satellite reaching the whole Europe, the Arab World, Asia and Sub-Saharan Africa, broadcasting 24 hours a day academic lectures in Italian, English, French, Arabic, Greek, Chinese and Russian language.
- On UNINETTUNO Web TV, providing on-demand free access to a selection of the best academic lectures and to collections of special lectures in which politicians, intellectuals, international artists, actors, directors, writers and poets address relevant and current topics.
- On UNINETTUNO YouTube Channel, where video-lessons posted autonomously by UNINETTUNO students reach millions of views.
- On OpenUpEd European portal, realized by the EADTU (European Association of Distance Teaching Universities) under the patronage of the European Commission, where UNINETTUNO published its MOOCs (Massive Open Online Courses).

UNINETTUNO's courses (realized in several languages), and specifically courses provided in English language, saw the enrolment of a greater number of foreign students compared to the Italian users enrolled: an unexpected and non-promoted phenomenon, that occurred spontaneously, mainly due to the driving power of the Web.

Of course, having realized an educational platform unique in the world, available in five languages (Italian, English, French, Arabic and Greek) and ready for delivering educational contents in further languages, made international relations much easier. Even the decision of not relying on the mere "translation" of contents produced by Italian Universities' professors, but, on the contrary, to involve the best lecturers coming from various universities of the world – giving them the opportunity of preparing contents of the various courses in their own language – greatly helped internationalization. Students and teachers come from several countries of the world, not just from European and U.S. universities, but also from the universities of the Arab World countries. Several university professors coming from these countries, selected by special scientific committees according to their publications' international relevance, provided and are still providing their courses on UNINETTUNO learning environment. The courses of some faculties, such as engineering, are delivered in Arabic, French, English and Italian; other faculties are developing their contents also in English while all master's courses are already available in English and some of them in Greek. This choice was made both to make linguistic diversity become an element of cultural strength and to respect the different cultures cooperating. Additionally, this linguistic variety allows accessing information and sharing it, building one's own knowledge no longer only according to a local dimension, but also in a global perspective, finding out that some problems can be better overcome by working jointly with people having different cultural backgrounds.

The Second Model of Internationalization

The second model of internationalization is based instead on international agreements with universities and ministries of various countries of the world, aimed at creating, harmonizing and sharing curricula allowing students to acquire a qualification acknowledged both in their country of origin, in Italy and therefore also in Europe.

In the curriculum design process, UNINETTUNO follows the guidelines ensuing form the Bologna and Sorbonne Process related to study levels organization, and the ECTS (European Credit Transfer System) for structuring its curricula.

More specifically, all degree courses are compliant to the European Qualification Standards. For instance, for the design of the Psychology Study Program we took into account the standards of the EuroPsy (European Qualification Standard for Psychologists), as it regards the scientific-disciplinary sectors and university credits to be assigned to each discipline. This process of curricula compliance to international standards enables study courses and study titles acknowledgement at European level. For cooperating with partner Universities based in a country that did not join the Sorbonne/Bologna process, UNINETTUNO developed a model for the design of common curricula already successfully tested. A practical example of application is the conclusion of an agreement aimed at a double title jointly with Helwan University, Cairo. A first phase of analysis and comparison of the structure and contents of the Computer Engineering Curricula provided by the two institutions, both at a general structuring level and at single course contents level, revealed that, in spite of the different timing structure, learning outcomes and contents in the 3 years of UNINETTUNO program were equivalent to the first four-year course delivered in Egypt. Consequently, a common study program was designed according to which the Egyptian students get an Italian (and therefore European) study title in the first three years, and then integrates in their study programs courses envisaged by their fifth year of study for completing the 5-years Egyptian program. This process of analysis, comparison and integration among curricula can be extended to any degree course of any country.

Today UNINETTUNO has more than 257 agreements with traditional universities in different countries of the world such as Argentina, Azerbaijan, China, Columbia, Ghana, Japan, Guatemala, Ethiopia, Mongolia, Mozambique, Nicaragua, Russia, Senegal, Somalia, Singapore, United States of America, Vietnam, in addition to the most important European and Arab world universities.

This model of internationalization based on agreements between UNINETTUNO University and traditional universities of the various countries, allows two University models, distance and on campus, live together. In a natural way, an *intra muros* and *extra muros* educational and training model is being developed globally. All this is made possible by the fact that UNINETTUNO has created, exploiting the results of many research activities, a very innovative psycho-pedagogical-didactic model based on cognitive and connectionist theories, which allowed creating online learning environments characterized by the quality of contents and the constant interaction between students and teachers.

These models of collaboration between distance universities and traditional universities are reinforcing a new model of real and virtual academic community that is enormously expanding the field of educational solutions and is increasingly promoting collaborative learning among students and professors from different countries of the world. The network of traditional universities has offered UNINETTUNO an extremely rich reservoir of human resources and knowledge. In order to produce the digital learning contents for its Didactic Cyberspace, UNINETTUNO involves professors from the best universities in the world who are open to implementing a collegial educational project. This model also helped traditional universities to develop innovation, both in organizational models and in the teaching methods of their universities. The traditional partner universities operate in spaces of collaboration and virtual cooperation but, at the same time, they are able to enrich with new meanings the physical spaces of meeting between students and professors. Socratic interaction models are developed in the face-to-face interaction where the student becomes the protagonist of the whole learning process, replicating the interaction models always applied in UNINETTUNO Interactive Class system, where dialogue is always at the base of a conscious growth of knowledge. In many years of collaborative relationships with traditional universities, exchanges of formative models have taken place between the different institutions, automatically leading to the development of new learning methods and new languages of knowledge communication both in presence and at distance. The international alliances really allowed UNINETTUNO to establish a global network of public and private universities that bring together their knowledge, share resources and equipment, curricula, laboratories, internal mobility of professors and students. All these results are achieved protecting the specificities of the individual universities as a value and enrichment of the network. On the Internet a network of universities has been built, made up of people, of intelligences that know how to connect their knowledge in respect of cultural, political, religious and economic differences.

Using the UNINETTUNO Interactive Class system and UNINETTUNO's Island of Knowledge on Second Life, students have the opportunity to study and think critically with their professors and tutors. They become active builders of new knowledge; together they create a true network of shared knowledge and concretely demonstrate that it is possible and easy to make young people of different cultures coexist with success and dignity.

Dialogue among cultures is not a utopia, but it is really possible. It is through this method that the University engaged in establishing a Euro-Mediterranean Area for Education and Research. The establishment of Euro-Mediterranean Area for Higher Education, deriving from the cooperation among distance universities, traditional universities, vocational training institutions and companies of several European and Mediterranean countries, is essential from a strategic, cultural, political and economic viewpoint.

Establishing cooperation relations among the academic institutions of different countries, aiming at producing educational contents designed for Internet-based virtual spaces and at jointly creating new systems and structures for Distance University, allowed to:

- promote universities' internationalization processes;
- design and develop shared curricula, and create for the attending students the necessary competences needed to live in a globalized and interconnected world;
- realize on the Internet multimedia educational contents also in different languages.

UNINETTUNO's model created new alliances among universities and educational institutions, developed real and virtual spaces, aiming at the creation of shared knowledge networks and a common Euro-Mediterranean Area in order to launch a path of harmonization of educational and training systems and to make them cope with the changes that globalization brought about.

The experience made confirms that it is possible to share curricula and create, jointly with the universities belonging to different political and cultural backgrounds, common paths of reflection and thinking.

Together, the interconnected minds of professors and students from the North and South of the world develop a network of competences and knowledge, based not on imposing one cultural model upon the other, but on comparing cultures and educational models. Together, a true laboratory for intercultural and inter-linguistic cooperation was created, enabling the development of a new virtual space, where all actors produce the contents and new teaching and learning models to make younger generations capable of becoming change leaders (Garito, 2008).

UNINETTUNO's professors and students are well aware of the fact that this internationalization model allows to create new balances between unity and diversity: the unity of values and traditions that memory gives us, and the diversity of cultures and languages. Universities moving under open skies, with no boundaries, build competences for social development and lay the foundations to build the future together.

References

Boehm, L., & Raimondi, E. (1981). *Università, Accademie e Società Scientifiche in Italia e in Germania dal Cinquecento al Settecento.* Bologna: Il Mulino.

Garito, M. A. (1983). *L'Università in Europa.* Torino: ERI.

Garito, M. A. (2008). Universitries in Dialogue in a World Without Distance. In I. Guske & B. C. Swaffield (Eds.), *Education Landscapes in the 21st Century. Cross-cultural Challenges and Multi-Disciplinary Perspectives.* Cambridge Scholars Publishing.

Garito, M. A. (2015). *L'Università nel XXI Secolo tra Tradizione e Innovazione.* Milano: McGraw-Hill Education.

Hammerstein, N. (1995). *Universitaten und Aufklarung.* Gottingen: Wallstein Verlag.

Prodi, P., (2013). *Università dentro e fuori.* Bologna: Il Mulino.

CAPACITY BUILDING FOR VIRTUAL INNOVATIVE TEACHING AND LEARNING IN JORDAN – EXPERIENCES OF THE JOVITAL PROJECT

Katherine Wimpenny, Arinola Adefila, Alun DeWinter, Coventry University, United Kingdom, Valerij Dermol, University of Ljubljana, Slovenia

Introduction

In a world that is increasingly interconnected, interdependent and diverse, engaging in international and intercultural learning and exchange is a key focus for higher education (HE) (Krutky, 2008; Altbach, Reisberg, & Rumbley, 2009). This trend can be considered in relation to several issues. For example, universities are experiencing an increase in their recruitment of international students (Beech, 2018; Borjesson, 2017; Fliegler, 2014); online international learning is increasingly becoming a core pillar of university collaborations for globally networked learning (Villar-Onrubia & Rajpal, 2016; Redden, 2014; Bell, 2016); and open courses such as Massive Open Online Courses (MOOCs) target learners, regardless of their geographic and cultural background (Maringe & Sing, 2014; Brahimi & Sarirete, 2015; Affouneh, Wimpenny, Ra'Fat Ghodieh, et al., 2018).

In countries like Jordan that, due to their demographic and socioeconomic context, are experiencing a massification phenomenon with respect to learners accessing higher education (HE), responsive, effective education processes are required to maintain quality learning experiences (Affouneh & Amin Awad Raba, 2017; Foley & Massingila, 2014; Dian-Fu & Yeh, 2012).

This paper presents the activities and the findings of ongoing the JOVITAL project in its goal of building the capacity of Jordanian educational technologies.

JOVITAL is an international cooperation project co-funded by the Erasmus+ Capacity Building in HE programmes of the European Union during the period October 2017 – 2020 involving four European institutions and five Jordanian universities. The aim of JOVITAL is to foster academic exchange using virtual mobility in order to offer learning opportunities to academic staff, university students and disadvantaged learners in Jordan.

State-of-the-art technologies and the evolution of delivery within Higher Education

There is a growing emphasis on using state-of -art technical infrastructure and design to captivate learners. More applications are being designed exclusively for learning and new technologies are adapted for e-learning relatively quickly in the modern age. Many institutions now view e-learning as a strategic tool which can be used to boost their reach, reputation and finances and there is increased competition to deliver e-learning programmes across the world, which has many implications for HEIs who do not engage. Students can attend many programmes without leaving their country, and this is beneficial for vulnerable and disadvantaged groups who have little access to HE (Affouneh et al., 2018). Nonetheless, there needs to be strategic recognition by governments in regions where there is no strategic oversight over quality, language, development and learner satisfaction for quality provision of online learning. JOVITAL explores the world-wide state of the art in terms of education technologies and this paper outlines how new and emerging technologies are being innovatively used in institutions around the world and how they are being adapted and implemented for use in Jordan. This includes applications of technology for domestic online learning, as well as worldwide partnerships that develop intercultural competences though the use of Online International Learning (OIL).

Challenges in HE and Jordan

Implementing E-learning can be a significant challenge for HE institutions at this paper explores the wider challenges of online learning, particularly, those institutions that have not explored interactive learning pedagogies or engaged in distance learning or other practices which involve engaging students outside the didactic models of classroom teaching. E-learning is dynamic and constantly evolving as new technologies and social processes become available; this means institutions have to be agile, modifying their systems and infrastructure, upskilling the workforce and adequately preparing their staff and their learners (Serdyukov, 2015). This of course can be expensive and requires strong internet connectivity. Institutions are also forced to 'keep up' with current trends and technologies, which may not be practical or affordable.

The paper also examines some of the specific and unique challenges for the region. In Jordan, e-learning has been associated with removing barriers for female learners in remote locations and providing opportunities to upskill the existing workforce (Al-Rashdan 2009). However, the challenges of ensuring high quality training is offered has been discussed by employers leading to restrictions; at present, for example, Jordanian undergraduate degrees cannot contain more cannot contain more than 25% of its total content on online learning.

This limit can also be seen as a rejection of E-learning methodologies as an inferior or lazy option where learning content is simply dumped online with little effort to contextualise the learning or to improve the learner experience. A key challenge is therefore a change in mindset from using technology not as a tool, but as platform for education, something which requires a change of mindsets away from the "teacher at the front" model of learning and a shift in approach to course design and pedagogical implementation.

This paper explores another unique challenge for Jordan; equity of access and inclusion of Syrian refugees in the region. Although Jordanian institutions wish to include refugees in e-learning, a number of barriers exist. In 2017, the Open University attempted to deliver online courses to Syrian Refugees in Jordan, which was not well received due to the lack of interactivity (Bothwell, 2017). This paper explores attitudes towards e-learning within the different learner communities and how the JOVITAL project has come to address them.

Gains and benefits to student experience and changes to pedagogy

One of the most important benefits of e-learning is the choice it affords to students to study at a convenient "pace, place and mode" in order to ensure that the quality of teaching and learning is maintained (Serdyukov, 2015; p.15). This paper argues that the mode of delivery can enhance or inhibit this affordance and properly designed e-learning programmes allow for learner-centred flexible approaches to HE education. As such, a key area for consideration is the role of the academic / facilitator, and their skills and competencies in e-learning, which the next section moves on to discuss.

Buhl, Andreasen, and Pushpanadham (2018) suggests e-learning fragments lecturers' traditional roles. They are no longer the sage responsible for "planning, practice and reflection", rather, such activities may now be "performed by different actors with different areas of responsibility" (p.180) Many institutions have had to introduce support for the technical and design areas of delivering e-learning –and roles have emerged in terms of learning technologists, e-developers, etc. (Veletsiano, 2011).

In addition, lecturers have to adopt new skills and techniques so they can prepare and engage their learners to become reflexive learners in e-learning environments. This is challenging because though modern learners are accustomed to the technology, they are not necessary adept as engaging in transformative learning and lack the kind of digital capital that enables them to be co-creators of their own learning (Warner & Palmer, 2015; Sadeghi, 2018). The JOVITAL project has made training an integral part of the delivery, with methods and approaches to teacher training being discussed as part of the paper.

Institutions have the responsibility to ensure that staff are adequately equipped to perform their role, and equally learners need to be supported to study online, with the necessary skills of autonomy and self-efficacy. The preparation of learners is a considerable task, not least because pre- university education does not typically prepare learners with these skills. E-learning also requires that learners have communicative and networking tactics to engage in such online learning spaces.

Furthermore, institutions need to concern themselves with ensuring that assessment practices are suitable for e-leaning. Assessment needs to align with the evolution of e-learning. Students of the 21st century need to develop requisite skills (problem-solving, team work and communication skills) for the workplace (Warner & Palmer, 2015). As such, assessments should be varied and flexible.

Final thoughts

Through presenting and exploring the activities and findings of JOVITAL, this paper seeks to outline the challenges and benefits of e-learning technologies in Higher Education teaching and learning, and how these can be tailored for use within the unique Jordanian context. This paper argues that online learning, in many forms, is of benefit to students and teachers alike, but utilisation of technologies requires careful planning, tailoring and training in order to see maximum benefit. As such, it is imperative that time is taken to train teaching staff and to prepare student expectations of online learning in order to gain the maximum benefit e-learning technologies have to offer. It is not simply enough to buy into technology and expect it do all of the work – changes to approach and implementation are vital to the success of online approaches to pedagogy.

References

Affouneh, S. J., & Amin Awad Raba, A. (2017). An Emerging Model of E-Learning in Palestine: The Case of An-Najah National University. *Creative Education, 8*, 189-201.

Affouneh, S., Wimpenny. K., Ra'fat Ghodieh, A., Abu Alsaud, L., & Abu Obaid, A. (2018). Reflection on MOOC Design in Palestine: A MOOC as a tool for nationality building. *The International Review of Research in Open and Distributed Learning, 19*(2), 23-36. Retrieved from http://www.irrodl.org/index.php/irrodl/article/view/3469/4610

Al-Rashdan, A.-F. A. (2009). Higher Education in The Arab World: Hopes and Challenges. In M. Elmenshawy (Ed.), *New Chapter of Political Islam. Arab Insight* (Vol. 2, pp. 77–90). ISSN 1936-8984.

Altbach, P. G., Reisberg, L., & Rumbley. L.E. (2009). *Trends in Global Higher Education: Tracking an Academic Revolution.* UNESCO.

Beech, S. (2018). Adapting to change in the higher education system: international student mobility as a migration industry. *Journal of Ethnic and Migration Studies, 44*(4), 610-625.

Bell, S. (2016). Sustainable distance learning for a sustainable world. *Open Learning, 31*(1), 1-8.

Borjesson, M. (2017). The global space of international students in 2010. *Journal of Ethnic and Migration Studies, 43*(8), 1256-1275.

Bothwell, E. (2017). Online higher education 'unappealing' for Syrian refugees. Times Higher Education [Blog post]. Retrieved from https://www.timeshighereducation.com/news/online-higher-education-unappealing-syrian-refugees#survey-answer

Brahimi, T., & Sarirete, A. (2015). Learning Outside the classroom through MOOCS. *Computers in Human Behaviour, 51*, 604-609.

Buhl, M., Andreasen, L. B., & Pushpanadham, K. (2018). Upscaling the number of learners, fragmenting the role of teachers: How do massive open online courses (MOOCs) form new conditions for learning design? *International Review of Education, 64*(2), 179-195.

Dian-Fu, C., & Yeh, C. C. (2012). Teaching Quality after the Massification of Higher Education in Taiwan. *Chinese Education and Society, 45*(5/6), 31-44.

Fleigler, C. M. (2014). Recruiting the World. *University Business, 17*(10), 36-41.

Foley, A., & Masingila, J. (2014). Building capacity: challenges and opportunities in large classes pedagogy in Sub-Saharan Africa. *Higher Education, 67*(6), 797-808.

Krutky, J. (2008). Intercultural competency: Preparing students to be global citizens. *Effective Practices for Academic Leaders, 3*(1), 1-15.

Maringe, F., & Sing, N. (2014). Teaching large classes in an increasingly internationalizing higher education environment: pedagogical, quality and equity issues. *Higher Education, 67*(6), 761-782.

Redden, E. (2014, July 9). Teaching with Tech across Borders. Inside Higher Ed [Blog post]. Retrieved 12 May, 2015, from https://www.insidehighered.com/news/2014/07/09/faculty-use-internet-based-technologies-create-global-learning-opportunities

Sadeghi, S. H. (2018). *E-Learning Practice in Higher Education: A Mixed-Method Comparative Analysis.*

Serdyukov, P. (2015). Does Online Education Need a Special Pedagogy? *Journal of Computing and Information Technology – CIT, 23*(1), 61-74. doi:10.2498/cit.1002511 61

Veletsianos, G. (2011). Designing Opportunities for Transformation with Emerging Technologies. *Educational Technology, 51*(2), 41-46. Retrieved from https://www.jstor.org/stable/44429917

Villar-Onrubia, D., & Rajpal, B. (2016). Online International Learning: Internationalising the Curriculum through Virtual Mobility at Coventry University' Perspectives. *Policy and Practice in Higher Education, 20*(2-3), 75-82.

Warner, T., & Palmer, E. (2015). Personalising learning: Exploring student and teacher perceptions about flexible learning and assessment in a flipped university course. *Computers & Education, 88*, 354-369

Connecting through Educational Technology
Proceedings of the European Distance and E-Learning Network 2019 Annual Conference
Bruges, 16-19 June, 2019

A NETWORKED LEARNING ENVIRONMENT FOR THE EDUCATION OF AN ARCHITECT

Melis Baloğlu Aşut, Yüksel Demir, Istanbul Technical University, Turkey

Abstract

During a design process, a student of architecture learns how to communicate with various tools, understanding the problem and reflect his/her own solution and how to work together with his/her peers. To be able to examine how a student of architecture learn, communicate and act in a networked environment, this study analyses an architectural theory lesson as a case study in consideration of ACAD (Goodyear & Carvalho, 2014) framework. An online assistant acts as an observer of the online platform of the course used as a case study, analyses the 14-week course according to ACAD framework. As a conclusion, students can learn collaboratively by articulating and sharing their ideas while they follow their education if they have a chance to frame their own curriculum, and they also continue to share their experience and expertise through discussion and dialog with the help of online communities after they had graduated.

Introduction

The time spent in a classroom or in an architectural studio is not only part of the learning experience of a student of architecture. It is important to develop and orchestrate learning tools to promote learning for the education of an architect both inside and outside of the classroom since the learning process itself creates the learning space each time. That's why, the boundary of a classroom can be measured by the free sharing of ideas inside and outside of the classroom by its learners, discussions, and the free license for the manipulation to the projects created as a part of the lesson. This requires more than a formal environment to learn but a dynamic network. Horizon Report states that "many experts believe that a blending of formal and informal methods of learning can create an environment that fosters experimentation, curiosity, and above all, creativity" (Johnson et al., 2016; p.22). However, the complexity of orchestrating or navigating the diversity of tools to foster curiosity, tasks to foster experimentation and people required to demonstrate knowledgeable action in the networked learning environment. In an educational setting, orchestrating and navigating are mainly done by the teacher but the teacher is not the one and only authority in the networked learning setting. In other words, the teacher is found variously described as "e-moderator" (Salmon, 2004), "facilitator" (Jones & Steeples, 2002). McConnell et al. (2012) borrowed the terminology "resource person and co-learner" to characterize the teacher's role in the networked learning setting. Teaching is becoming learning by students' active participation. Briefly, we can say that in a networked learning environment:

- Students and teachers construct the learning process actively so that they are all learners.
- Students are envisaged in connectedness by way of strong and weak ties (Jones et al. 2008) actively supporting each other's learning and mutually fostering a learning network (Goodyear & Carvalho, 2014). It means that student A learns through student B's comments, questions, and experience.
- In a networked learning environment, it is not so much about the technologies and the types of connections as it is about the promotion of connections for learning: "between one learner and other learners; between learners and tutors; between the learning community and its learning resources" (Goodyear et al., 2010; p.1).

In architectural design education, the learning process can be seen as a result of reflection-in-action during design process described by Schön (1983). Students build their own repertoire consists of ideas and experiences so that when they come face to face with a design problem, they recall something already situated in their repertoire and see the new one as a variation of old which means there is no knowledge independent from our experiences. During a design process, a student of architecture learns how to communicate with various tools, understanding the problem and reflect his/her own solution and how to work together with his/her peers. To be able to examine how a student of architecture learn, communicate and act in a networked environment, this study analyses an architectural theory lesson as a case study in consideration of ACAD (Goodyear & Carvalho, 2014) framework. In very simple words, according to ACAD framework, design needs to attend to (a) what students are being asked to do, (b) how they should work together to do it, (c) what tools etc. they'll need.

As a conclusion, this study finds potential solutions to support the networked learning environment for the education of an architect. The course named as Architectural Design Theory (ADT) and has been teaching since 2003 by Yüksel Demir and with many participants in the department of Architecture in Istanbul Technical University, Istanbul. There are also other sections who teach the same course with different approaches. The main aim to choose this specific course is related to its dynamic content which is built by its students every semester. Students enrolled the course reflect their own agenda and the course is moderated around students' agenda. ADT is going to be illustrated by ACAD framework to be able to examine:

- What students have been being asked to do and what students should be asked to do?
- How they have been working together to do it and how they should work together to do it?
- What tools, whether digital or analogue, tutors have been using and what tools, whether digital or analogue, they'll need?
- What tools, whether digital or analogue, students have been using and what tools, whether digital or analogue, they'll need?

With such discussions, this work introduces firstly a theoretical background on what is learning in the context of architectural education; secondly, it explains the essence of ACAD framework; thirdly it analyses the case study (ADT) in the light of the ACAD framework and reflects on it. As an online observer of the course, I will reflect my observations with the help of ACAD framework. These online observations based on Skype video calls and FB group discussions. They had been systematically collected for 14 weeks from September 2017 till January 2018, on Thursday mornings between 09.30-12.30 (GMT+3). As a brief conclusion:

- Students have been asked to reflect their ideas with different mediums so that they feel comfortable in one way and continue to use this particular way in their group project.
- The community which can be defined as all the students who took the same course, needs to have a course memory to be able to continue to work together according to their changing interests.
- From 2003 to 2019, they have been using different platforms to communicate but none of them are designed for educational purposes as Facebook.
- Students can learn collaboratively by articulating and sharing their ideas while they are in universities, but they also continue to share their experience and expertise through discussion and dialog with the help of online communities after they had graduated.

Learning, Network and Networked Learning

The focus of networked learning is both learning and the network.

Learning, as Dewey (1900) puts in words by saying that "his activity shall have meaning to himself" (p.23). And, he puts the child/student/learner at the centre of the learning process and emphasizes "reflection in action" which acts as a base for Schön's (1983) work on "reflection in action". Kolb (1984) defines learning as "the process whereby knowledge is created through the transformation of concrete experience. Knowledge results from the combination of grasping and transforming experience" (p.41) Ackermann (2007) adds that knowledge is derived from experience, and actively constructed and reconstructed by subjects in interaction with their worlds. For a designer, knowledge is constructed and reconstructed by herself/himself in interaction with his/her micro world. Both Schön (1983) and Kolb (1984) saw that reflective process is necessary for experiential learning but Schön's ideas of reflection on the problem framing and its relation with the strategies are deeper than Kolb's. During the learning process, designers observing their sketches, seeing them as something else, observing the result and may discover new things. "The student does not just passively take in knowledge, but actively constructs it on the basis of his/her prior knowledge and experiences." (Piaget, 1972; p.26) Students are not passive during the process like they are absorbing all the information given by educators. And also, even designers have something in their minds, when they start to sketch, their aims are reflected in action. The role of the architectural curriculum for design students is to develop an understanding of how they reason in design. It is also based on the creative process of students which is part of their ability of understanding, analysing, questioning, exploring ambiguity and creating relations between different concepts.

Networks have been the subject of research well beyond the impact of the technology alone. The Networked Society is one of the suggested descriptions of the type of social system that is emerging in the late 1990s (Castells, 1996). "Networks constitute the new social morphology of our societies, and the diffusion of networking logic substantially modifies the operation and outcomes in processes of production, experience, power, and culture. While the networking form of social organization has existed in other times and spaces, the new information technology paradigm provides the material basis for its expansion through the entire social structure (Castells, 1996; p.468). Learning is epistemically, physically and socially situated and foreground the social nature of knowledge through the notion of *networks* (Carvalho & Yeoman, 2018). *Networked learning* is learning in which communications and information technology (C&IT) is used to promote connections: between one learner and other learners, between learners and tutors; between a learning community and its learning resources. Such communication can be synchronous and/or asynchronous. It can be text-only or multimedia. It may involve learners who are geographically distributed and/or learners who spend much of their time at a common location. In networked learning (NL) practice, the emphasis on human relations for learning beyond engagement with learning materials using information and communication technologies (ICT) is a significant shift from the prevalent classroom-based lecture which students are used to. Teachers are assumed to take a less prominent position permitting students to experience learning through active participation in cooperative and collaborative activities with others (McConnell et al., 2012).

To sum up, learning is based on experience which means activity centred. Activity is best understood as situated. It unfolds in ways that are shaped, subtly and powerfully, by the physical/digital tools and resources that come to hand, and by the social arrangements obtaining (divisions of labour, roles, etc.) And, the activity cannot be designed. It has emerged. Tasks, the physical/digital setting, and divisions of labour can be designed (Carvalho & Goodyear, 2014). The next section opens up the framework.

ACAD Framework

In very simple words, according to ACAD (Activity Centered Analysis and Design) framework (Goodyear & Carvalho, 2014), design needs to attend to (a) what students are being asked to do, (b) how they should work together to do it, (c) what tools etc. they'll need (with some careful thought about what can be digital, what should be in material form and so on). ACAD can then be seen as a way of helping participants in a learning network converge on methods of representing important aspects of how the network is functioning, such that discussion informed by the representations they construct stands a chance of leading to beneficial action. It can be applied in broad brush ways to create a holistic picture of epistemic, physical and social design components, emergent activity, co-configuration and outcomes (see Figure 1. by Carvalho & Goodyear, 2014).

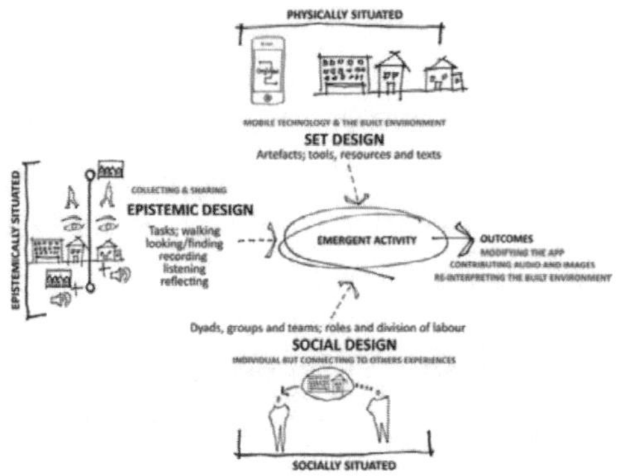

Figure 1. ACAD Framework (Carvalho & Goodyear, 2014)

The framework acknowledges that design elements are likely to influence people's activity, the activity cannot be entirely predicted. The four structural elements are:

- Set design – the material and/or digital elements that are brought together to compose a learning situation. The setting for networked learning includes places, material and digital tools and artifacts, designed tasks, and associated divisions of labour. These physical architectures need to provide human-to-human, things-to-human, and things-to-things connections to allow activities to emerge. Blackboard, the chairs and tables in a classroom, "built forms" were not especially "brought" to the learning situation by the educational designer, albeit they are still part of the set design.
- Epistemic design – the "plan" for what people will do including the proposed learning tasks, along with their structuring, sequencing and pacing of how information is to be communicated to learners.
- Social design – social arrangements and roles, divisions of labour and who is expected to do what.
- Co-creation and co-configuration activity – relates the above designable components to people's activity, acknowledging that they may rearrange and reconfigure the designed learning situation (Carvalho & Yeoman, 2018).

	Set design	Epistemic design	Social design
High-level philosophy	Learning is...	Learning is...	Learning is...
Macro—global Level I patterns	Buildings and technology	Stakeholder intentions	Organisational forms
Meso—structure Level II patterns	Allocation and use of space	Curriculum	Community
Micro—details Level III patterns	Artefacts, tools and texts	Selection, sequence and pace	Roles and divisions of labour

Figure 2. ACAD wireframe (Carvalho & Yeoman, 2018)

ACAD framework is also adopted with multiple dimensions as macro, meso and micro. (Carvalho & Yeoman, 2018) The first three dimensions of design (as per the ACAD framework) are represented from left to right (set, epistemic, and social) and the scale levels across which they operate (macro, meso, and micro) from top to bottom. The shorthand used for the scale levels (macro, meso, micro) is useful, but for a deeper understanding of the distinctions between these levels, it is recommended to see Alexander et al.'s (1977) notation: region (macro), shape (meso) and detail (micro) (see in Figure 2.).

Framing a Course: The Case Study, Architectural Design Theory, Istanbul Technical University

Architectural Design Theory is a theoretical course taught by Yüksel Demir since 2003. The structure of the course makes it unique. The content of the course has been building by its students' agenda in an organized structure for 16 years now. In other words, the curriculum is not designed by a teacher but by students. The tutor acts as a moderator, editor, and learner. I am the online observer of the course for two semesters now. As an online observer of the course, observations are reflected with the help of ACAD framework to be able to see how the course has been processing and how networked learning environment occurs. These online observations based on Skype video calls and FB group discussions. They had been systematically collected for 14 weeks from September 2017 till January 2018, on Thursday mornings between 09.30-12.30 (GMT+3) (see in Figure 3.).

	Set Design	Epistemic Design	Social Design
High Level Philosophy	**Learning is** physically situated	**Learning is** supported through knowledg-oriented activity	**Learning is** socially situated
Macro	**Buildings and technology**	**Stakeholder intentions**	**Organisational forms**
	The classroom designed to accommodate max. 15 students and a tutor, supported by access to a closed group on a social media platform	There is a mix of individual and group project work driven by interest and curiosity.	Each student is responsible for a project that is of particular interest to them. Students enjoy similar interest-based opportunities.
Meso	**Allocation and use of space**	**Curriculum**	**Community**
	The classroom is shared by 16 people. The place has chairs, one board, one desk for teacher and a projection to make a presentation.	Each semester, the curriculum of ADT is designed by students'. From very beginning till end, their works are available online.	The team of 3 people shares their responsabilities and roles while making their final project. They meet at their spare time and also they have opportunity to discuss in class and online.
Micro	**Artefacts, tools and texts**	**Selection, sequence and pace**	**Roles and divisions of labour**
	Students who attend ADT, are also a part of a closed Facebook group of the course where they share their response papers, presentations,GIFs, texts, books, articles,thoughts, and ideas. They also encouraged to comment each others posts.	Students revise their weekly presentations. At the end, they formed groups according their shared interests and write a final paper on it.	Students are experiencing difficulty with academic writing. The tutor works with them during last 3-4 weeks to revise their final project. Each week, the feedback is given both online and offline.

Figure 3. ACAD wireframe applied to ADT (adopted from Carvalho & Yeoman, 2018)

The following subsections reflect the analysis of ADT based on ACAD framework.

Set design in the context of the course Theories of Architectural Design

At the macro level, the interactions in networked learning environments can, in principle, be through text, voice, graphics, video, shared workspaces or combinations of these forms. However, in mainstream higher education practice, a text is still the dominant medium and much of the time that students and tutors spend in networked learning consists of composing, reading and reflecting on electronic texts, such as email messages or entries in text-based computer conferences.

At the meso level, the layout of the classroom is promoting a hierarchical relationship. The tutor has his/her on a place with a big desk compared to students. On the contrary to its layout, the structure of the course makes everybody as learners.

At the micro level, in this case, Facebook supports the constructivist approach to learning through the features as the familiarity of the tool, the interaction of the tool; instructor to student and student to student, connectivity of the tool and opportunity of collaborative learning. There was no length limitation on comment posts. The structure of FB supports good communication in this case since it has the features like tagging people, using hash tags and pinning the important post to the top of the page.

Epistemic design in the context of the course Theories of Architectural Design

At the macro level, students solved their own problems. If there is an ethical problem, the tutor can also contribute to the discussion.

At the meso level, the tutor acts as a moderator, an editor and a learner. He sometimes linked the ideas of other students from literature or his own background, practice, and expertise to raise the awareness. The content of the course is timeless since it has been building according to students' agendas. This way of orchestrating contribute to learning process and increase curiosity.

At the micro level, from very first day till the end, students started to discuss their interest and they formed a group according to their shared interest. They feel motivated enough to work with their peers and learn how to organize a team according to their expertise.

Social design in the context of the course Theories of Architectural Design

At macro level, students who took the similar courses rather than ADT, built up similar agendas. That shows institutional power has a visible part on students' agendas.

At meso level, since the students follow their peers' comments on FB, they easily found the one who shared the same interest. They also saw how one had acted until now so that they formed a group according to their values. Monitoring behaviours were set by the students and the tutor.

At micro level, students learn by experiencing by means doing it, seeing the others work, commenting on it and analysing it. Students also learn from the other students' comments, works, and behaviours.

Conclusion

As it is mentioned in the introduction, ADT is going to be illustrated by ACAD framework to be able to examine:

1. what students have been being asked to do and *what students should be asked to do;*
2. how they have been working together to do it and *how they should work together to do it;*
3. what tools, whether digital or analogue, tutors have been using and *what tools, whether digital or analogue, they'll need;*
4. what tools, whether digital or analogue, students have been using and *what tools, whether digital or analogue, they'll need.*

- As an answer to (1), students have been asked to reflect their ideas with different mediums so that they feel comfortable in one way and continue to use this particular way in their group project.
- As an answer to (2), the community which can be defined as all the students who took the same course, needs to have a course memory to be able to continue to work together according to their changing interests. In that way, after graduation, students of architecture can remember the theory while heavily practicing.
- As an answer to (3), from 2003 to 2019, they have been using different platforms to communicate but none of them are designed for educational purposes as Facebook. During architectural education, students share their design ideas in various forms. Current learning management systems fail in collecting files, storing them and sharing them. And also, in that tools, there is no room for custom design which can be another topic to study as a user interface design for educational purposes.
- As an answer to (4), students can learn collaboratively by articulating and sharing their ideas while they are in universities, but they also continue to share their experience and expertise through discussion and dialog with the help of online communities after they had graduated. Lifelong learning communities can be constituted with the communities formed during the formal education based on shared interest and continue to grow.

As a final word, the networked learning environment shaped itself. Even there is an online community to support or a tutor who gives all the answers all the time, it is not possible to create a community. The only way to create it, to let people join with their own agenda and form a group according to their shared interest. One can influence the community to hold as one, but if there is a solid structure defined without community's voice, that will be failed. In today's world, curriculums should be designed according learners needs. This is almost impossible because of the crowd of the learners, and everybody is unique, there can be no one who can design a curriculum each time according to changing needs. The proposed way could be a collaborative act of design of the curriculum with the help of the learners and experts together. Tools, both digital and analogue can support to design a dynamic curriculum in a networked environment. ACAD framework helps to see the relations between tools, organization, curriculum and so on.

Further discussions can be done on vicarious learning and see/measure the relevance of the dialog generated by other learners.

References

Ackermann, E. K. (2007). Experiences of artifacts: people's appropriations / objects' affordances. In M. Larochelle (Ed.), *Ernst von Glasersfeld, Key Works on Radical Constructivism.* Sense Publishers.

Alexander, C., Ishikawa, S., Silverstein, M., Jacobson, M., Fiksdahl-King, I.. & Angel, S. (1977). *A pattern language: Towns, buildings, construction.* Oxford: Oxford University Press.

Carvalho, L., & Yeoman, P. (2018). Framing learning entanglement in innovative learning spaces: Connecting theory, design and practice. *British Educational Research Journal, 44*(6), 1120–1137.

Carvalho, L., & Goodyear, P. (Eds.) (2014). *The architecture of productive learning networks.* New York: Routledge.

Castells, M. (1996). *The Rise of the Network Society: The Information Age: Economy, Society, and Culture.* Oxford: Blackwell Publishers.

Dewey, J. (1900). *The School and Society, The Child and the Curriculum.* Chicago: University of Chicago Press.

Goodyear, P., & Carvalho, L. (2014). Framing the analysis of learning network architectures. In L. Carvalho & P. Goodyear (Eds.), *The architecture of productive learning networks.* New York: Routledge.

Goodyear, P. (1999). Pedagogical frameworks and action research in open and distance learning. *European Journal of Open and Distance Learning.* Retrieved from http://www.eurodl.org/?p=archives&year=1999&article=35

Jones, C. R., & Steeples, C. (2002). Perspectives and issues in networked learning. In C. Steeples & C. R. Jones (Eds.), *Networked learning: perspectives and issues* (pp. 1-14). London: Springer.

Kolb, D. (1984). *Experiential Learning, Experience as the Source of Learning and Development.* Englewood Cliffs, NJ: Prentice Hall.

Papert, S. (1980). *Mindstorms: Children, computers, and powerful ideas.* Basic Books, Inc

Schön, D. (1983). *The Reflective Practitioner: How Professionals Think in Action.* Basic Books.

Connecting through Educational Technology
Proceedings of the European Distance and E-Learning Network 2019 Annual Conference
Bruges, 16-19 June, 2019

THE CO-EVOLUTION OF EQUITABLE TERTIARY EDUCATION IN A GLOBAL NETWORKED SOCIETY: THE CASE OF THE OERU

Daniele Dubien, Niki Davis, University of Canterbury, Wayne Mackintosh, OERu, New Zealand

Introduction

The continuing evolution of ubiquitous learning technologies and networks is reshaping models of learning with increasing potential for underserved populations of learners who cannot afford tertiary education. This paper presents a case study of innovative highly networked organisation called the "Open Education Resource universitas" (OERu).

As the theme of EDEN 2019 conference has recognised, "Technology is with us everywhere which validates the horizontal-holistic approach for imperative questions of the period. For the transforming education landscape, challenges come increasingly from the socio-cultural-economic, structural and policy fields. Education has to be visionary to reach efficiency gains, new sources – and to offer sustainable services, reflecting the complexity of modern societies." The OERu is on the far left of such visionary developments with a radically open approach to its equitable mission to expand higher education to come within the reach of all of students who are likely to remain underserved.

Established in 2011, the OERu as an educational organisation is co-evolving with cutting edge technologies such as, micro-learning, alternative digital credentials, and implementation of an open source Next Generation Digital Learning Environment (NGDLE) (Brown, 2017). Its strategy is to evolve by scaling up with partners worldwide. Innovations already documented include a successful small mOOC (Davis & Mackintosh, 2013). This case study plots the OERu in Niki Davis' (2018) Arena Framework to clarify the complexity of the evolution of this organisation. The findings aim to support the OERu and its partners to fulfil their vision of providing affordable access to education.

Background

According to UNESCO, demand for higher education increases globally by approximately 1% each year (Marginson, 2016). This demand will stimulate further coevolution of educational organizations and educational technologies. Along with the increasing demand for higher education is a desire for equality, which can be partially attained through access to higher education (Marginson, 2016). One option for helping to fill this demand is to use open educational resources (OERs) (William and Flora Hewlett Foundation, 2019). OERs are widely available, as are guides for their adoption (e.g. UNESCO & COL, 2015).

Theoretical Framework

Since 2005, drawing on the increasing knowledge of change with technology in education and human ecology, Davis (2018) has developed her Arena Framework to clarify the worldwide scope of the complexity of the co-evolution of education and digital technologies. Concepts and terminology used in ecology are used extensively within this framework. For example, many Arenas have as their central ecosystem inhabited by a class of learners, their teacher and their learning resources, including physical and digital spaces as shown in the generic Arena in Figure 1. In order to clarify the influences on the learning ecosystem, the systems in considered in five sectors: resource, professional, community, bureaucratic and political (see Figure 1).

The whole Arena Framework depicts the interaction of education systems worldwide as being contained within a sphere, the global ecosphere of education. Within that global ecosphere layers of ecosystems can be mapped; the nationwide ecozones contain the national educational systems of each country, such as the USA and New Zealand. Embedded within each of those nationwide ecozones are many millions of ecosystems inhabited by students and their teachers. Many, but not all, of the ecosystems nest in layers, one completely within the other. However, ecosystems in which digital applications evolve are unlikely to be embedded; instead they spread across many ecosystems and often globally. One Arena inhabited by the OERu centred on the ecosystem inhabited by an OERu course development team is illustrated later in this article.

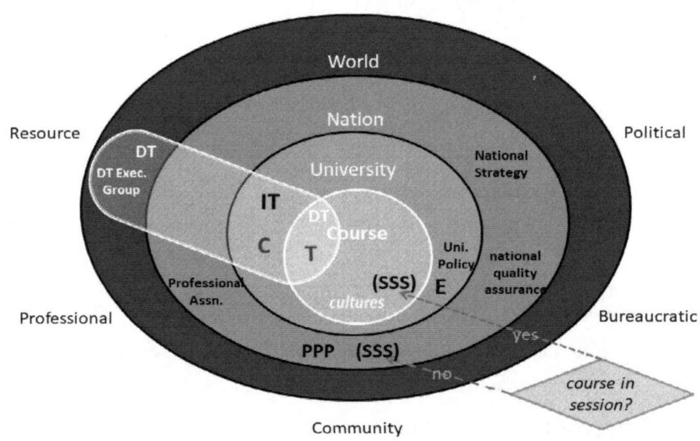

Figure 1. An Arena with one teacher and her course ecosystem in a university at the centre of the global ecosphere. It also includes the ecosystem of an organisation that provides Digital Tools (DT). The course has two phases, in session with students in the ecosystem and out of session without students.
Key: Teachers (T), Parents (P), Students (SSS), Executive managers (E), technical support staff (IT), Colleagues including Educational Technologist (C), Digital Tool or service (DT).

The Arena Framework goes beyond human ecology to recognise that behaviour of the various roles of the people in each ecosystem evolve in a similar way to the human ecologist's conception of species. The most common roles in education are teacher, learner, educational technologist, librarian, technician, and last but not least executive, so these are the common species in Arena ecosystems. There is also non-living matter in ecosystems, which includes books, furniture, and mobile devices that connect the species through Cloud-based ecosystems. Thus educational ecosystems are often a blend of the physical and digital world; one percolates the other (Gillen et al, 2018). The teacher is recognized as the 'keystone species' in a learning ecosystem inhabited by students in a traditional university because of the dominance of that role on behaviour in that ecosystem; the learning ecosystem is disrupted when a teacher leaves (unless there has been collaborative preparation for the transition), but the same is not true for a learner or a technician. Other keystone species can be identified in different types of ecosystems: the parental role is a keystone species in a family ecosystem. Similarly, the executive is a keystone species in a business organisation, whereas a technician is not. However, the inhabitants of an ecosystem change with its phases and these roles evolve over time (as do educational technologies) and, as they do, they influence one another. Thus co-evolution of education and technology deserves more research, and the Arena Framework is useful to frame such research.

Methodology

Data about organizational culture and processes were collected through interviews with OER developers, analysis of literature pertaining to the OERu and its partners, online planning documents, course content, and observations of meetings (synchronous and asynchronous). The data set includes 12 interviews with 8 people plus more than 50 documents and over five observations including online meetings. The data collection period was two years from October 2016, particularly 2017 when the course was under development for the first time. The analysis consisted of identifying patterns of different behaviour and identifying all living and non-living matter. In addition to other analyses the data was mapped within the global Arena Framework (Davis, 2018). A few of the behaviours most pertinent were selected to illustrate the behaviour in the ecosystems, especially the behaviour of keystone species.

Findings: The Case of the OERu

The OERu is mapped in an Arena Framework in 2017 (see Figure 2) was developed to encompass all the ecosystems in the ecosphere within which the selected "Learning in a Digital Age" (LiDA) course was being developed. It should be noted that the radically open processes of the OERu design process lead us to estimate some of the actors and behaviour where it cannot be "seen" such as when a participant may have decided not to take action in response to an OERu communication. We begin with the central course ecosystem and work outwards to the global ecosphere.

The LiDA Course Ecosystem During the Design Phase

"Learning in a Digital Age" (LiDA) (OERu, n.d.) aims to help students develop technological and critical thinking skills and to prepare students for subsequent online studies to enable higher achievement while also reducing attrition. This course is part of the Certificate in General Studies and the Certificate of Higher Education (Business); certificates that equate to a first year of study in a general Bachelor of Arts and Business degree respectively. The modular design of the course and the programme supports open education. It is interesting to note that by January 2019 OERu partner universities in four countries offer graduates of this course credit in one of their programmes.

The living species in this course design ecosystem included both employees of the OERu, the director (acting in the roles of subject matter expert, educational technologist and course leader) and the open source technologist (on request). Another expert educational technologist also supported this course development for a time. Periodically the course leader invited OERu supporters to contribute through calls on open online forums and social media. The course was developed openly in WikiEducator and other non-living matter included content and curriculum ideas from two OERu partners (OERu, 2017). The behaviour in this ecosystem was very "agile" (the term here is used in the sense of agile design (Brown, 2017). For example, the development team used an online Kanban software tool (WeKan) to brainstorm the curriculum outline and then progressed course design and development using an open wiki (WikiEducator) The approach had been described by the course leader in the earlier planning curriculum phase during an online meeting in June 2016 when he said:

> *"What I'm proposing we do […] anybody who wants to be involved in this process, we'll develop those micro-course outlines […] We will be doing that in the wiki. Anybody will be able to see and comment and add and tweak, but I'm aiming to get to the point where we can have a curriculum outline within 7 to 10 working days. We will of course take in any feedback we receive. But I should also just add… It's a very open source approach that we use. We work on a model of rough consensus and running code. What that means - you would have seen that in action here – we try and achieve a rough consensus and then we implement things and get things done. We don't go into eighteen months of deliberation around a particular point. If you aren't at the table to make a decision, you've got to accept the decision that the folk around the table are taking. The people that are actively involved are the folk that determine how this thing goes forward. So, if you do want to shape the future of this development, I strongly advise that you be involved because in ten days' time, there's going to be an outline and we're going to implement it. So, at the risk of sounding like a benevolent dictator, I just want to open it to the floor and just make sure we are comfortable with that approach: rough consensus and running code. This is not a democracy. We don't work with 50% + 1. If there are three people at the table those are the people who are going to take the decision (57:54 – 59:55)" (OERu, 2016b).*

The course design process also helped to focus OERu's crowd sourcing innovations. For example, the OERu launched a crowdsourcing activity using a WikiEducator page (OERu, 2016c), a discussion forum (OERu, 2016a), and Twitter (OERu, 2016d). Based on similar courses from partner institutions, the course leader selectively integrated the crowdsourced suggestions into the LiDA curriculum. He presented the resulting course curriculum in an online meeting and requested feedback from the participants, making changes instantly on the online Kanban board hosted by OERu (2016b).

This OERu course is one of the courses that are called 'open boundary' courses because they include two types of student: (a) credited learners who register, pay for assessment, and earn credit upon successful completion of course requirements; and (b) non-credited learners who participate informally without seeking assessment. Both can participate in the course and communicate with one another. This tends to increase in student-student interactions which can increase both technical and subject-matter support, plus an enriching experience given the variety of student perspectives. This flow of communication was designed to be controlled so that the students would not become overwhelmed. The ecosystem changed into its course phase 14/3/18 – 14/6/18 for its first successful offering. The OERu's 2018 mid-year report indicated the reach of this offering,

> *"Of the 703 registered participants from 60 different countries, the top thirteen countries according to the number of registrations were: India, United States, Canada, Fiji, Nigeria, New Zealand, Papua New Guinea, South Africa, Uganda, Australia, Egypt and Kenya. Site analytics recorded 1,362 users visiting the course websites during the active cohort period, indicating that 48% of visitors chose not to register for course announcements. The course sites generated 19,839 page views with 9,083 being unique for the active cohort periods" (OERu, 2018; p.5).*

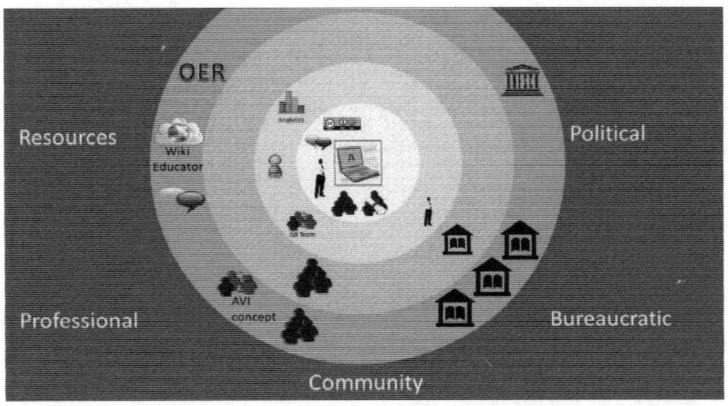

Figure 2. The OERu in Davis' Arena Framework, with the ecosystem of a course under development at the centre of the global ecosphere

The OERu Technical Ecosystem

As shown in Figure 2 the OERu technical system shown surrounding the course ecosystem has adopted and adapted a range of open source software tools in its platform (Technology Stack). The first tool was WikiEducator used for collaborative authoring, and in 2016 and 2017, the OERu used Kanban boards to structure the LiDA curriculum in an agile fashion. The course site was published in WordPress which contained links to tools for student-student interaction such as discussion forums on the Discourse platform, hypothes.is which is an application for social annotation of web pages, bookmarks.oeru.org which uses Semantic

Scuttle - a social bookmarking tool, Mastodon which is for microblogging, and WENotes (WikiEducator Notes) which aggregates all the posts that contain specific tags mentioned in the course and emails to the students. In addition to these tools that are linked throughout the course, students are recommended to use open source blogs such as WordPress which is used as the course platform, or Medium and Blogger. This practice allows the students to maintain control over their course contributions during and after the course session. The OERu would normally invite students to send in their blog URLs and aggregate them into a blog feed. However, this practice was not used in this offering of LiDA.

The keystone species in this ecosystem is the open source technologist employed by the OERu who ensures orderly behaviour in this evolving system, adapting tools on request and updating their fit as they evolve. The range of tools in the OERu Technology Stack has greatly expanded since the first OERu mini course was piloted by Davis and Mackintosh (2013). The OERu both adopted and adapted these tools to work together coherently (OERu Technology, 2018). Further analysis would be needed to identify if that has impacted the evolution of these tools in other contexts, which is to say whether this co-evolution of education and technology has spread beyond the OERu.

The OERu ecosystem

The OERu aims to cover much of the global ecosphere, rather than be limited to one ecozone. However, it is notable that is domiciled in New Zealand and therefore subject to the laws of that country as well as international law. By 2017 it had over 25 partners in 8 countries. The OERu uses an open business model with transparent planning processes aimed at sustainability. It is "[a]n international network of recognised partner institutions from five continents – providing top-quality tertiary courses to students everywhere" (OERu, n.d., para. 1). In 2017 the OERu employed only two staff, the OERu director is the chief executive and therefore the only the member of keystone species. However, it is important to note that many other people acting in a number of roles contributed to the behaviour in this ecosystem and the director reports to the OER Foundation Board.

As described earlier the OERu has "radically open" behaviour in which staff from partner institutions attend OERu consultations and participate in informing and making decisions. One instructional designer employed in a partner institution and regularly involved in OERu activities including this course design was interviewed. He also saw the intended culture as one that is "fully open and allows for shared learning". However, he believed that the intended culture was somewhat different from the actual culture where a core group of people drive the OERu's activities. This aligned with the chief executive's view of the encompassing OER Foundation's (OERF) approach to leadership, which he described in this way:

> *"Meritocracy is a guiding principle of the OERF. Leadership roles in our community projects are 'earned' through sustained performance. Individuals who have gained respect from their community peers through engagement*

> *have a greater influence on decision-making. Transparent planning promotes trust in our open decision-making practices" (Mackintosh, 2017; p.104).*

Other species in the OERu were organised into working groups. For example, marketing working group prepared a case study of the LiDA course to market it and also to explain the OERu's approach to course design, and fit with OERu's first year of study (see https://oeru.org/news/learning-in-a-digital-age/).

Discussion

Davis' Arena Framework was applied successfully to map the actors and networks of this highly networked global organisation that aims to evolve agile equitable higher education. The ecosystems briefly described here showed various ways in which the various living and non-living species influence the activities of the OERu, for example by inviting people to contribute ideas using specific digital tools. OERu courses have instructional designers as one of the keystone species during the design and development phases, and this species is unusually dominant when compared with traditional universities. For courses that are not facilitated by a teacher the course delivery phase, the keystone species has yet to be identified.

The analysis has also identified that students have two subspecies. Open boundary courses are designed to include credited and non-credited students who interact for an enriching experience and for support. The two types of students will behave in different ways, depending on their goal to earn credit, or not. Davis and Mackintosh (2013) describe an early OERu open boundary course module that was identified as a community approach micro Open Online Course (mOOC). The course designer and most influential educational technologist (Mackintosh) was the same person as in this LiDA course. It provided evidence that including the two subspecies of students could enrich the course ecosystem during its delivery phase to enhance learning as well as intensive professional development for a teacher who had much to learn about open course design.

These findings demonstrate some of the possibilities and realities of open processes and in this way our findings may help to manage expectations. Staff who are aiming to develop courses as OER may be able to better grasp the additional potential and challenges of working with radically open course design, development, and delivery. Current and prospective members of the OERu may be able to consider the species and matter that can become involved when starting to design and offer innovative open courses. The extraordinary openness of the OERu enables new partners to offer credit for open courses before they engage in designing one.

We plan to continue this research into LiDA and the OERu, including the co-evolution of the digital tools that have been deployed. Possibilities for future research and development include analysis of ecosystems for a variety of OERu courses plotted on an Arena and compared to find trends and changes over time as courses are designed, launched and revised.

References

Brown, M. (2017). THE NGDLE: We are the architects. *EDUCAUSE Review, 52*(4), 11. Retrieved from https://library.educause.edu/topics/teaching-and-learning/next-generation-digital-learning-environment-ngdle

Davis, N. E. (2018). *Digital technologies and change in education: The arena framework.* London & New York: Routledge.

Davis, N. E., & Mackintosh, W. (2013, November). A mOOC prepared to make a difference. *DEANZ Magazine*, 1-7.

Mackintosh, W. (2017). Open course development at the OERu. In R. Jhangiani & R. Biswas-Diener (Eds.), *Open: The philosophy and practices that are revolutionizing education and science* (pp. 101-114). London: Ubiquity Press.

Marginson, S. (2016). The worldwide trend to high participation higher education: Dynamics of social stratification in inclusive systems. *Higher Education, 72*(4), 413-434. Retrieved December 1, 2018, from https://link.springer.com/article/10.1007/s10734-016-0016-x

OERu (n.d.). OERu partners. Retrieved December 1, 2018, from http://oeru.org/oeru-partners

OERu (n.d.). Learning in a digital age. Retrieved February 2, 2019, from https://oeru.org/learning-in-a-digital-age/

OERu (2016a). Crowdsourcing topics for inclusion in the Learning in a Digital Age (LiDA) course. Retrieved January 15, 2019, from http://groups.oeru.org/groups/lida-course-team/messages/topic/7dmqEphNaBlF8hyi34DuA2/

OERu (2016b). Learning in a digital age/1st Meeting. Retrieved January 15, 2019, from http://wikieducator.org/Learning_in_a_digital_age/1st_Meeting

OERu (2016c). Learning in a digital age/Crowdsourcing topics for LiDA. Retrieved January 15, 2019, from http://wikieducator.org/Learning_in_a_digital_age/Crowdsourcing_topics_for_LiDA

OERu (2016d). #oerulida. Retrieved January 15, 2019, from https://twitter.com/hashtag/oerulida

OERu (2017). Learning in a digital age/Curriculum planning. Retrieved February 4, 2019, from http://wikieducator.org/Learning_in_a_digital_age/Curriculum_planning

OERu Technology (2018, October 31). 2018 update on the OERu Technology Stack [blog post]. Retrieved February 4, 2019, from https://tech.oeru.org/2018-update-oeru-technology-stack

UNESCO, Commonwealth of Learning (2015). *Guidelines for open educational resources (OER) in higher education.* Vancouver: COL & UNESCO. Retrieved December 1, 2018, from http://oasis.col.org/handle/11599/60

William and Flora Hewlett Foundation (2019). Open Educational Resources. Retrieved February 4, 2019, from https://hewlett.org/strategy/open-educational-resources/

Acknowledgements

Thanks to all of those who have contributed to the LiDA course and the establishment of the OERu. This article retains the Creative Commons licence adopted by OERu. The University of Canterbury membership of OERu was a project of the e-Learning Lab from 2012-2104. We also acknowledge Danielle Dubien's Commonwealth Scholarship and Fellowship Plan (CSFP) PhD scholarship.

Connecting through Educational Technology
Proceedings of the European Distance and E-Learning Network 2019 Annual Conference
Bruges, 16-19 June, 2019

THE PRESTO PROJECT RELAY: OPEN, ASYNCHRONOUS LEARNING IN VIRTUAL PEER GROUPS

Pieter W. G. Bots, C. Els van Daalen, Sofia M. Dopper, Delft University of Technology, The Netherlands

Abstract

Academic education entails that students engage in open-ended assignments. Global education entails that students interact in projects with peers world-wide. The logistic challenge of offering academic project work to a large, heterogeneous student body, while keeping instructor workload manageable, is daunting. Project relays on the PRESTO software platform meet this challenge. In a project relay, students work in a virtual peer group on assignments that are organized in successive steps, where each step is peer reviewed. Unlike a regular peer review, the reviewing students revise the work they have reviewed. They then add the next step to it, and pass the improved-and-extended work on to another student. The PRESTO software fully automates the relay workflow, facilitates defining, monitoring, and grading projects, and has been adapted for use in LTI-compliant MOOCs. Since 2013, over 20 project relays have run in several courses at Delft University of Technology. Evaluations show that a project relay realizes the intended learning outcomes, but can at times be stressful for students. This prompts ideas for further pedagogical and technical improvements.

Introduction

Courses that aim at attaining Bloom's application level of learning typically require repeated practice from students. For some subjects, exercises can be devised that have a single correct result, but to achieve deep learning, students must work on open-ended assignments (Ke & Xie, 2013). Providing feedback on, and assessing, open-ended assignments (e.g., writing an essay or reporting on a problem analysis) requires interpretation and judgement, which makes courses very teacher-intensive. Reducing teacher load by conducting the work in project groups introduces other problems, such as free rider behaviour (Brooks & Ammons, 2003). Faced with the challenge to provide students with sufficient individual practice and feedback, while at the same time keeping the teaching burden manageable, we have developed the project relay method and its supporting software (PRESTO).

The project relay was originally developed for teaching first-year students the basics of constructing quantitative models. Since then, it has been adapted to support any type of project work that can be partitioned into consecutive steps, e.g., writing an essay (literature review → thesis statement → introduction → body of information → conclusion) or conducting a life cycle analysis (goal and scope → inventory analysis → impact assessment →

interpretation). The higher level skills required for these activities cannot be learned by only studying a textbook, but require learning by doing.

The objective of this paper is to explain how the relay system can be used by students and instructors. In order to do this, we first introduce the relay method and present the key features of the PRESTO software. We then briefly report some of our experiences using project relays in several courses, argue that it affords open, asynchronous learning in virtual groups across educational institutions, and outline our plans for future development.

The project relay method

The assignments students carry out in a relay are divided up into a number of consecutive steps. In all but the first step, students receive – similar to the relay baton in athletics – completed preceding steps from an anonymous predecessor. As each step will concern a different case or topic, students cannot continue their own work on the previous step. Knowing that they have to perform their primary task on this new case gives students a natural incentive to immerse themselves in their predecessor's work. Having to review and – if necessary – improve their predecessor's work before extending it with their "own" step makes that students gain a deeper understanding of their predecessor's work, allowing them to provide more substantive feedback to their predecessor. Moreover, having to "take ownership" of their predecessor's work makes that students receive additional practice in conducting the previous steps.

Figure 1 shows an example of a relay process in which students are asked to develop a quantitative model, given a written description of a system. The assignment is divided into 6 steps that follow on from each other, starting with a research question and ending in conclusions that can be drawn from running the computational model with different input values. In Step 1, students start from scratch, and submit work that is strictly their own. In each following step, students have to perform four tasks:

1. study the work which has been submitted by the predecessor,
2. provide constructive feedback and assess the work of the predecessor on a 5-point scale,
3. improve the work,
4. extend the work by adding their "own" step (primary task).

The result of the final step is then reviewed and assessed by two different successors.

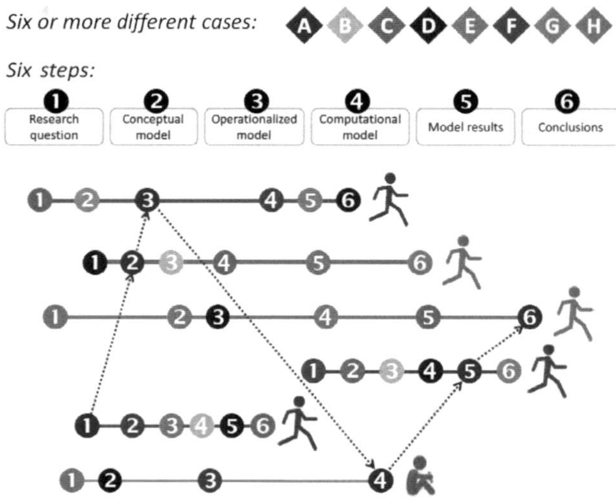

Figure 1. Schematic diagram of students going through the steps of a project relay

When starting with the first step, a student is assigned a randomly selected case. The result of the first step then goes to another student who has done Step 1 on another case. This student reviews and improves the work, and adds Step 2 to it. This work then goes to another student who just did Step 2 – also on another case. This student then reviews and improves the work, and adds Step 3. In Figure 1, the dotted arrows show how, in this process, an instance of case A is passed on from student to student. The horizontal lines reflect students performing – asynchronously and at their own pace – consecutive steps on different cases. At the end of the relay, a student has worked on all steps for 6 different cases, and will have iterated several times through earlier steps because giving feedback and improving the work always relates to *all* previous steps. For a video explanation of the procedure, see https://youtu.be/SGm-DstdElk.

It does not matter if a student drops out after a step, as this student will then not receive a case for the next step. Moreover, the relay system does not require a fixed schedule of who evaluates which work, since the work will be sent to the next person who is ready for an assessment. This allows students to do the steps of the relay at their own pace, as long as they finish the whole relay before the end date.

A downside of the asynchronous process is that students receive feedback on a step relatively late, because successors can still modify their review and assessment until they upload their own work. Their predecessor then gets to see the feedback (typically structured according to a rubric), and is invited to respond and appraise the feedback. In addition to the feedback, students can also view the work submitted by their successor to see how their own work has been modified and extended.

To ensure that students put in serious effort, we have introduced some specific incentives. The students know that after every step their work is assessed on a 5-point scale by peers, and – more importantly – that it will count towards their final grade following a *differential* scoring system. This means that students earn points if they score higher than (or maintain the high score of) their predecessor, and lose points if they score lower (or fail to improve on a low score). Although this motivates students to do their work well, it has as a perverse effect that it may lead students to underrate their predecessor's work. The PRESTO system therefore invites students to appeal if they feel that they have been unfairly assessed. When they appeal, a referee (typically an instructor or a qualified student) will judge the peer assessment, change it if needed, and impose penalty points on students rating too harshly or raising unfounded appeals.

Even with these incentives, it may happen that students receive work from a predecessor that is below par and would require a disproportionate amount of time to improve. For these situations, we allow students to reject such work. They then immediately receive the work of a new predecessor. Since the students must justify rejection with a thorough review, to which their predecessor can still appeal, this effectively prohibits rejection merely to get better work to build on.

The PRESTO software

The PRESTO software manages the workflow of a project relay, and facilitates defining, monitoring, and grading projects. It has been programmed in Python on the open source platforms Django and Semantic UI, and will be available under an open source license. The software discerns four user roles: student, instructor, developer and administrator. Students can enrol in courses, are led through relay steps and invited to respond to reviews for ongoing relays, and can view past relays in their personal history. Instructors can develop and share case sets (for use in different relays), create and operate relays for their courses, monitor progress, and grade students. Developers can design and share templates that define step sequences and specify what a student has to do within every step. Administrators can create courses, and assign instructor and developer roles.

Student interface

The student interface leads students through the tasks that have to be performed in each of the different steps: commit to "the rules of the game", read first assignment and case, upload own work, proceed to next step, download predecessor's work, review and assess predecessor's work, and upload own (new) work again. These tasks are "colour-coded" (e.g., green = proceed, blue = download, orange = review), and are always carried out in the same sequence. Students first see information about the task for their current step, possibly followed by other tasks (responding to reviews of prior steps, and to referee decisions).

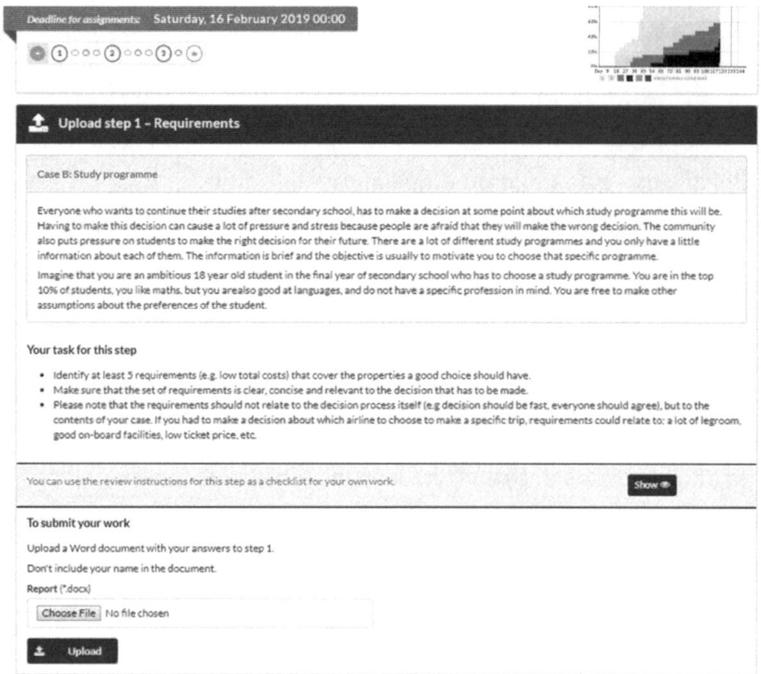

Figure 2. Screenshot of the student interface (upload task for Step 1)

Figure 2 shows what students see for an upload task: a case description, instructions on the primary task for this step, and a button to view the (itemized) review and assessment guidelines that their successor will apply. The progress bar at the top shows how far students have progressed in the relay: the large, numbered circles denote upload tasks (and hence completed steps) and final review tasks, the smaller circles denote the other tasks (start, download, and review). As the student progresses, the circles for completed tasks are filled in with their colour, and when the cursor is moved over, a balloon with the completion time pops up. The chart on the right shows the progress of all participants in the relay: time on the horizontal axis, the percentage of participants having completed a step on the vertical axis.

To improve the work and to add their own step, students edit and expand the document(s) submitted by their predecessor. These files are anonymised (stripped of metadata) each time they are downloaded. Students can enter their (itemized) reviews using a rich text editor. At the end of the review activity, students are asked to assess their predecessor's work with a star rating on a 5-point scale. Predecessors will see the review and assessment they received, and can respond, appraise the feedback on a 3-point scale (☺ - 😐 - ☹), and can click the appeal button and write a rebuttal, which the instructor will then review.

Developer interface

Project relay templates define the number of steps for a relay, and for each step the specific instructions for the primary task, uploading the work, and reviewing work. Figure 3 gives an impression of how PRESTO enables developers to design templates. For each step, developers can specify the number and type of files that must be uploaded, add constraints (e.g., mandatory key words and titles to protect students against uploading the wrong document), and define specific review items with (optionally) partial assessments. The instructions for each of the steps should be generic so as to apply to different case sets.

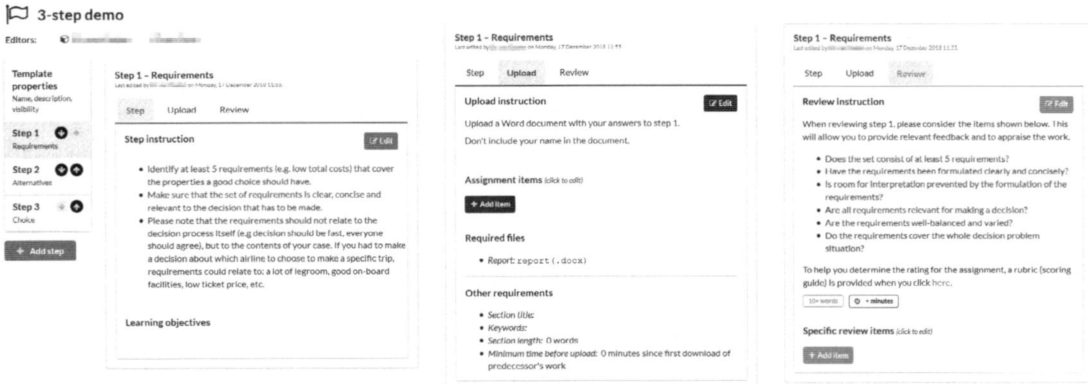

Figure 3. Partial screenshots illustrating how relay templates can be defined

Instructor interface

Figure 4 shows how PRESTO enables instructors to define case sets and create project relays.

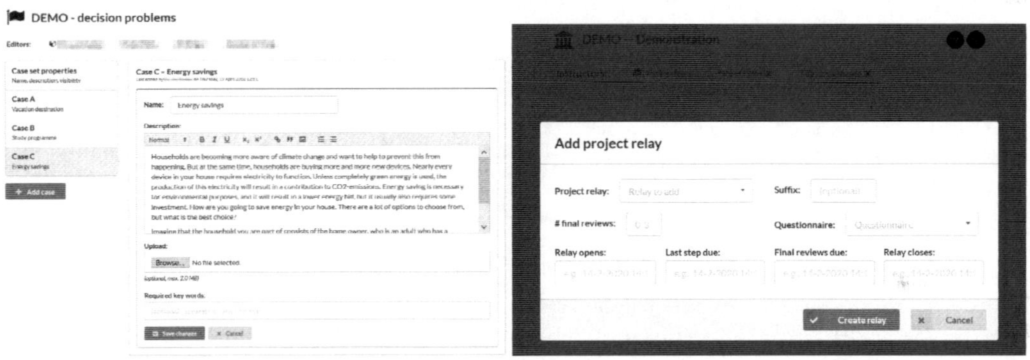

Figure 4. Partial screenshots illustrating how case sets are developed (left) and project relays created for a course (right)

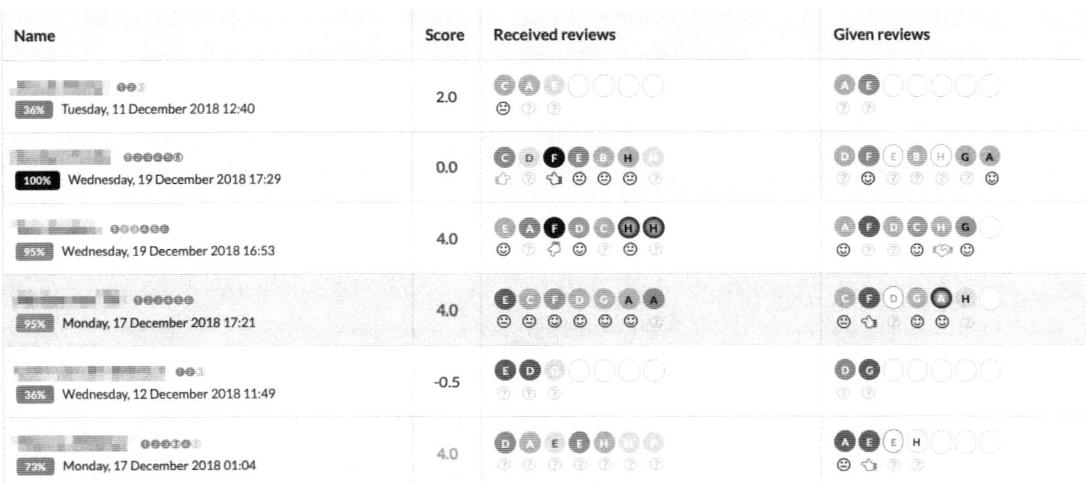

Figure 5. Partial screenshot of the instructor dashboard for a project relay

From the set starting time on, students enrolled in the course can carry out the project relay. Figure 5 gives an impression of the dashboard that allows instructors to monitor a relay. The first column in the overview shows the names of participating students, their overall progress rate, and the time of their most recent activity. The small circles indicate the completed steps, their colour reflects the similarity score computed by PRESTO's plagiarism scanner. When clicking on the name of the student, the instructor can see this student's history (uploaded work and associated interactions with predecessors, successors, and referees). The second column shows the total score of the students. When a project relay has finished, these scores can be scaled to grades once the instructors have benchmarked the work with the lowest and highest scores (cf. Figure 6). The third and fourth column show, for each completed step, the reviews received and given. The letters indicate the case worked on, while colours correspond to the rating of the step (red = ★, dark green = ★★★★★, black = rejection). The icon underneath a circle reflects the reviewed student's appraisal of the feedback and rating. A hand icon indicates that the student appealed, its colour the referee's rating. Pointing hands indicate the student incurring a penalty. Moving the cursor over a circle (icon) will reveal the time of the event and the identity of the other student.

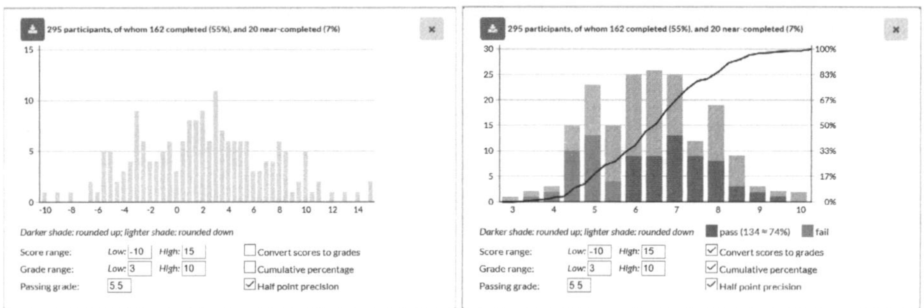

Figure 6. Scaling total scores to grades

Experiences with the project relay

We first applied the relay in the quantitative modelling course in 2013. In this course we now have run more than 15 relays with cohorts of over 200 first-year BSc students. Since 2017, the relay has also been used in a first-year MSc course on methods and tools for policy analysis with for some 40 students from 10-15 different countries. In 2018, we ran pilot relays in three different online courses (Creative Problem Solving, Next Generation Infrastructures, and Responsible Innovation) on the edX platform. This confirmed that project relays can be tailored to the subject matter and academic level of a wide range of courses, and that the PRESTO software performs well for relays with up to 350 students (the highest enrolment to date). In addition, we have also used the software in support of courses with "regular" peer review, as this corresponds with a relay comprising only a single step.

We have evaluated the project relay based on data stored in the system, such as time spent on a step, and also by means of student surveys. Students indicate that they learn a lot from the relay, and that this way of working is a good way to practice. Students also state that the workload of the relay is high. This follows in part from the effort of first improving one's predecessor's work before one can perform the primary task of a step. A secondary explanation of the experienced workload is that students tend to procrastinate: facing a deadline only for the final step, many students do not spread their work over the available time period (typically 2-3 weeks). This behaviour is consistent across level (BSc – MSc) and cohort (2013 – 2018).

Students find a project relay quite stressful. Although stress is inherent to project work, and can be functional (Pope, 2015), many students resent the differential scoring mechanism makes that students can gain more points by being more critical towards their predecessor. Despite the protection offered by the opportunity to appeal, we observe much stronger emotions than those observed for absolute scoring (Vickerman, 2009). Although incentives to be critical are important for good quality work, we think we can make it less stressful by enhancing the students' capacity for evaluative judgement (Tai et al., 2017) by providing better instruction/guidelines for formulating constructive feedback (Landry et al., 2015).

Conclusions and further developments

Faced with the challenge to provide students with sufficient individual practice and feedback, while at the same time keeping the teaching burden manageable, we developed the *project relay*: a way of working in which students evaluate, improve, and then build on work of fellow students. The associated PRESTO software that manages the workflow of a relay will be available under an open source license.

We have used project relays in our education since 2013 in courses with large numbers of students (BSc and MSc level) with a variety of nationalities. The substantive flexibility offered by templates and case sets makes the project relay a feasible option for a broad range of courses. The open, asynchronous, double-blind relay process and the web-based, LTI-compliant PRESTO software show good potential for implementing "virtual mobility", as students enrolled in courses at different educational institutions could participate in jointly offered relays to develop generic academic skills by working in international virtual teams on case sets developed by staff from these different institutions.

The learning outcomes of the relay are quite good, but the relay can be stressful for students. We are planning to better prepare students for the review and assessment tasks with instruction and guidance, and by including formative tests at the beginning of each step to better prepare students for the substantive work. We will also explore incentives for students to write constructive reviews by making their predecessors' appreciation of the reviews (relative to the received rating) count towards the final grade in a relay.

References

Brooks, C. M., & Ammons, J. L. (2003). Free riding in group projects and the effects of timing, frequency, and specificity of criteria in peer assessments. *Journal of Education for Business, 78*(5), 268-272. doi: 10.1080/08832320309598613

Ke, F., & Xie, K. (2009). Toward deep learning for adult students in online courses. *The Internet and Higher Education, 12*(3-4), 136-145. doi: 10.1016/j.iheduc.2009.08.001

Landry, A., Jacobs, S., & Newton, G. (2015). Effective use of peer assessment in a graduate level writing assignment: a case study. *International Journal of Higher Education, 4*(1), 38-51. doi: 10.5430/ijhe.v4n1p38

Pope, N. K. L. (2005). The impact of stress in self- and peer assessment. *Assessment & Evaluation in Higher Education, 30*(1), 51-63. doi:10.1080/0260293042003243896

Tai, J., Ajjawi, R., Boud, D., Dawson, P., & Panadero, E. (2018). Developing evaluative judgement: enabling students to make decisions about the quality of work. *Higher Education, 76(*3), 467-481. doi:10.1007/s10734-017-0220-3

Van Hattum-Janssen, N., & Lourenço, J. M. (2008). Peer and self-assessment for first-year students as a tool to improve learning. *Journal of Professional Issues in Engineering Education and Practice, 134*(4), 346-352. doi: 10.1061/(ASCE)1052-3928(2008)134:4(346)

Vickerman, P. (2009). Student perspectives on formative peer assessment: an attempt to deepen learning? *Assessment & Evaluation in Higher Education, 34*(2), 221-230. doi: 10.1080/02602930801955986

Connecting through Educational Technology
Proceedings of the European Distance and E-Learning Network 2019 Annual Conference
Bruges, 16-19 June, 2019

VIRTUAL LEARNING ENVIRONMENT FOR OPEN ONLINE LEARNING

Estela Daukšienė, Margarita Teresevičienė, Airina Volungevičienė, Vytautas Magnus University, Lithuania

Summary

Digital networked society is learning in various platforms, in different ways and at selected time and pace. What are the preferences of members of digital and networked society for the learning platforms? What resources should be used to better fulfil nowadays learner expectations? And how higher education institutions are preparing for that? These are the main research questions of this research. In order to answer the research questions, the theory analysis and quantitative research were performed. The results of the research findings of the preferred learning ways and requirements for virtual learning platform of the online learners who speak Lithuanian are discussed in the paper.

Introduction

Open educational resources and open online courses and already not a new practice in higher education institutions. However, opening online courses for the society is more common in open universities, while traditional face-to-face learning universities focus more on bended learning approach and usually stay closed, mainly due to limited offer of open online courses. The use of virtual learning environment in university studies is also a common practice, but what features characterize open online learning environment – the virtual environment of 21st century learning of digital and networked society?

As Newman and Scurry (2001) say, learning environment, based on online technologies helps society to be more educated, because students can gain access to a huge amount of information, including schemes, graphics, pictures and videos. Virtual learning environment for open learning first of all has to be open to ensure the easy way to reach the curriculum.

> *"Many of today's online learning environments are private. This privacy is the consequence of institutional decisions that have resulted in the closing of learning environments to all but those who have officially enrolled in an institution or course. While many of these decisions are logical from an administrative standpoint, educators interested in making learning opportunities available to the masses may have a different perspective." (Mentor; 2007; p.1)*

Grant (2007) has indicated 10 dimensions of online life learning environment which may be grouped to 2 broad ones – Administration and Pedagogical dimensions where the later includes knowledge discovery, analysis, application, management; communication, collaboration, content delivery and evaluation of learner performance.

The use of different tools for learning can be limited if an environment is closed. The use of digital technology various in different learning generations, so the learning environment must be adapted to their needs. Wu, Yu, and Wang (2018) suggest that different interests of learners should be noted and analysed for the platform to better respond to learner preferences. Andone et al., (2007) suggest learning environment should contain

> *"a blend of Internet and mobile technologies which enhance student-tutor and student-student communication through multiple media channels, providing responsiveness, customizability and flexibility to adapt and be adapted to the students' needs". (Andone et al., 2007; p.41)*

A lot of approaches have been used when discussing and exploring modelling of open learning environment. It could be based on learning style (Fasihuddin, Skinner, & Athauda, 2017), collaboration (Barbosa, Barbosa, & Rabello, 2016; Tissenbaum, Berland, & Lyons, 2017), issues related concepts and skills, collaborative problem-solving opportunities, motivation of learners and context of learning (Lubin & Ge, 2012) or designed to establish personalized learning (Rahimi, van den Berg, & Veen, 2015). When analysing professional learners, it was found necessity to rely on aggregation of theory and practice (Milligan & Littlejohn, 2014) and to create learning environment taking to account learning needs, background, motivations.

Summarizing the theoretical findings on the features of open online learning environment the following categories were noted – easy accessible and stimulating learning, creating a community for communication and collaboration, and pedagogically well organized.

Research methodology

The aim of the research is to characterize open online learning environment in order to meet the digital and networked society needs. The case of Lithuania was selected for the research, focusing on the needs of digital and learning society for open online learning environment. The used survey method was mixed – combining online survey and face-to-face survey.

In order to construct survey questionnaire, the theory analysis was implemented. The questionnaire was developed, approved and used for a statistically representative survey of adult population 18-65 in Lithuania in 2018, by the research team. The research questionnaire involved demographical questions and questions about their preferences for online learning and open resources, use of social networks for learning, their approach to online learning, and features of the virtual learning environment that are important. As the research focus is on the open online learning environment features, this article analyses and focuses only on questions which are related to virtual learning environment.

Data collection and research participants

The quantitative research was performed in two ways: (a) the electronic version of questionnaire survey, which was put into Openstudies portal of Vytautas Magnus University and (b) direct surveying at the respondent's home using multivariate stratified sampling, which was performed with the help of one of the Lithuanian market and opinion research centre. The total number of respondents, who qualitied for the digital and networked society description, was 1241. The main criterion to quality for the digital and networked society was the use of internet.

The research was performed from March to October, 2018. The research participants were Lithuanians, aged 18-74, living in Lithuania or abroad; mainly situated in cities with more than 10,000 residents (68% of respondents). There were 45% men and 55% women out of 1241 respondents. Research participants' distribution by age was fairly even – 19% were of 18-24, 19% were of 25-34, 18% were of 35-44, 20% were of 45-54, 16% were of 55-64, with exception of persons aged over 65, who represented only 8% of all respondents. Therefore, for more even distribution, respondents in the research analysis were grouped into 4 groups: up to 27 years; 28-38 years; 39-52 years and more than 53 years. Research participants were mostly full-time employees (57%), holding a degree of tertiary education (59%), with a wide range of professions, representing social care, police, agriculture, education, administration, maintaining, industry, management, or services, with the largest part (14.5%) of sales managers.

Data analysis

Online survey and face-to-face survey data merged for statistical analyses using MS Excel and SPSS (Statistical Package for Social Sciences) 23 version. The descriptive statistics and crosstabs were used for data analyses in the initial data analysis phase, which results are presented here. The more in-depth factorial analysis and modelling will be performed in the next research phase. The analysis took place from October 2018 to January 2019. The research findings will be presented in research workshop.

Research findings

Digital and networked society representatives are interested in online study programs (78%), and they prefer flexibility in choosing separate courses to study (82%) or studying in courses for professional development (76%). They think that connections to video conferences or viewing lecture recordings would seem engaging too (73%). About 70% of respondents indicated that they prefer the use of mobile devices in learning.

The most preferable ways of learning of survey respondents were indicated- distance learning course with a teacher (their consultations and lectures) and short video tutorials or lectures with interactive tests (see Figure 1)

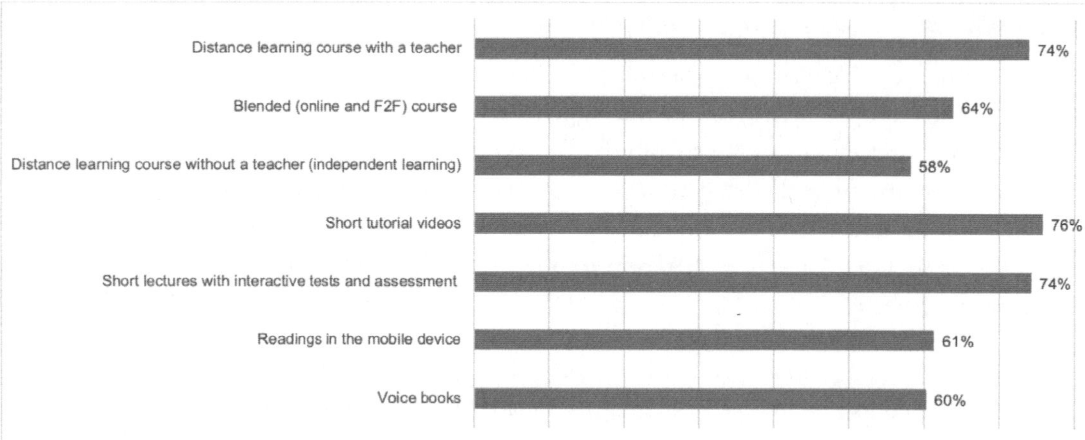

Figure 1. Learner preferences for online learning

The most preferable feature for learning online was studying at a suitable pace and time, which was indicated by 84-87% of the survey respondents. Among the most stimulating factors for online learning were also a possibility to combine learning with the work and family (74%).

The most preferable features of open online learning environment are the possibility to plan the time, to be able to access learning materials, and a possibility to communicate and collaborate with learners and teacher (indicated by 89-79% of respondents, see Figure 2). Among least preferred environment features were the reception of badges, synchronized with virtual learning environment – in total only 38% of all respondents preferred this functionality. However, after the in depth analysis it was noted that 86% of the youngest representatives (18-24 years old) would prefer such a functionality.

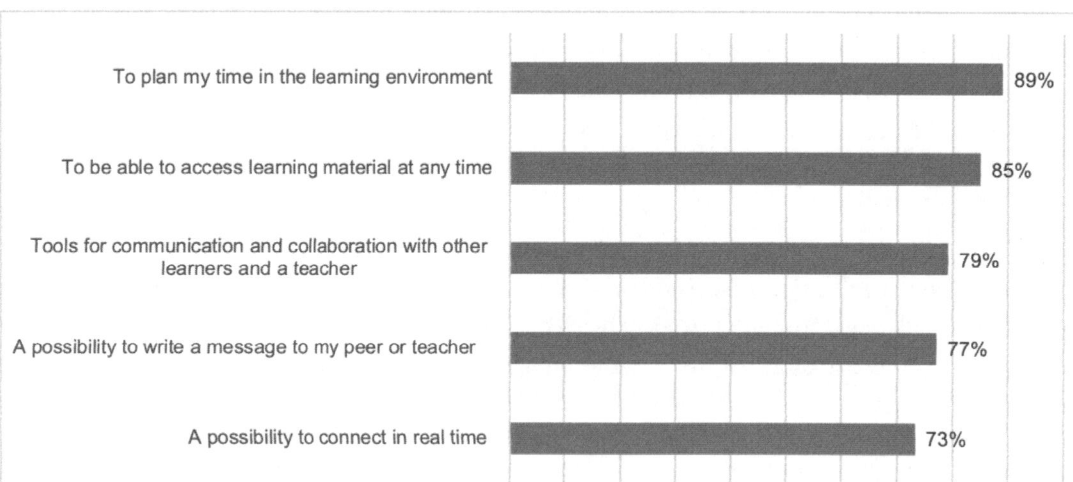

Figure 2. The most preferable open online learning environment features from technical and social perspective

"A possibility to write a message" is more important for younger adult groups – 80% of the 18-52 years old respondents prefer this and 67% of the 53 year and older respondents. This could be explained with the with decreasing senior participation in training and learning activities, less social networking. The importance "to connect in real time" also decreases with age: 79% of young adults would like to do that; 76% in age group 28 -38, 73% in age group 39 - 52 and 65% in the group of more than 53 years old respondents.

From the pedagogical point of view the respondents also indicated some preferences for learning organization and learning content delivery – 84% prefer learning content presented in different forms – written, video and audio; 80% prefer open educational resources (readings and video recordings) to be used, 78% would like learning material to be presented in small chunks and having clear instructions for learning; and 75% would appreciate periodic feedback about the learning progress and achievements.

Practical application of the research findings and insights are integrated in Vytautas Magnus University Open studies platform (openstudies.vdu.lt), which focus on providing the university online courses for the community, not just the university students. The courses are prepared for group learning or learning individually, with teacher consultations.

The theoretical considerations of the paper and further empirical research will be complemented in the further stages of a four-year research project "Open Online Learning for Digital and Networked Society (3.3-LMT-K-712-01-0189)". Project is funded by the European Social Fund according to the activity "Improvement of researchers" qualification by implementing world-class R&D projects' of Measure No. 09.3.3-LMT-K-712.

References

Andone, D., Dron, J., Pemberton, L., & Boyne, C. (2007). E-Learning Environments for Digitally-Minded Students. *Journal of Interactive Learning Research, 18*(1), 41-53.

Barbosa, J., Barbosa, D., & Rabello, S. (2016). A Collaborative Model for Ubiquitous Learning Environments. *International Journal on E-Learning, 15*(1), 5-25.

Fasihuddin, H., Skinner, G., & Athauda, R. (2017). Towards Adaptive Open Learning Environments: Evaluating the Precision of Identifying Learning Styles by Tracking Learners' Behaviours. *Education and Information Technologies, 22*(3), 807-825.

Lubin, I., & Ge, X. (2012). Investigating the influences of a LEAPS model on preservice teachers' problem solving, metacognition, and motivation in an educational technology course. *Educational Technology Research & Development, 60*(2), 239-270. doi:10.1007/s11423-011-9224-3

Mentor, K. (2007). Open Access Learning Environments. *Online Journal of Distance Learning Administration, 10*(1). Retrieved from https://www.westga.edu/~distance/ojdla/spring101/mentor101.htm

Milligan, C., & Littlejohn, A. (2014). Supporting Professional Learning in a Massive Open Online Course. *International Review of Research in Open and Distance Learning, 15*(5), 197-213.

Newman, F., & Scurry, J. (2001, July 13). Online technology pushes pedagogy to the forefront. Chronicle of Higher Education. Chronicle [Blog post]. Retrieved from http://chronicle.com/weekly/v47/i44/44b00701.htm

Rahimi, E., van den Berg, J., & Veen, W. (2015). A Learning Model for Enhancing the Student's Control in Educational Process Using Web 2.0 Personal Learning Environments. *British Journal of Educational Technology, 46*(4), 780-792.

Tissenbaum, M., Berland, M., & Lyons, L. (2017). DCLM Framework: Understanding Collaboration in Open-Ended Tabletop Learning Environments. *International Journal of Computer-Supported Collaborative Learning, 12*(1), 35-64.

Wu, P., Yu, S., & Wang, D. (2018). Using a Learner-Topic Model for Mining Learner Interests in Open Learning Environments. *Educational Technology & Society, 21*(2), 192–204.

Connecting through Educational Technology
Proceedings of the European Distance and E-Learning Network 2019 Annual Conference
Bruges, 16-19 June, 2019

COGNITIVE LOAD DURING ONLINE COMPLEX PROBLEM-SOLVING IN A TEACHER TRAINING CONTEXT

Charlotte Larmuseau, KU Leuven Campus KULAK Kortrijk, Itec-Imec, Hendrik Coucke, Pamela Kerkhove, VIVES University of Applied Sciences, Piet Desmet, Fien Depaepe, KU Leuven Campus KULAK Kortrijk, Itec-Imec, Belgium

Introduction

Online courses are becoming ubiquitous and increasingly tend to use authentic learning tasks as the driving force for teaching and learning. Nevertheless, designing online courses that incorporate real– world tasks is more challenging as these problems require more cognitive processes (van Merriënboer & Sluijsmans, 2009). This phenomenon can be explained by Cognitive Load Theory (CLT) introduced by Sweller (1994). CLT distinguishes three types of cognitive load: intrinsic, extraneous and germane load. The level of intrinsic load is assumed to be determined by the level of element interactivity. An element can be a definition, concept, formula and procedure that needs to be or has been learned. Extraneous load is mainly imposed by instructional procedures that are suboptimal, whereas germane load refers to the learners' working memory resources available to deal with the complexity of the task or learning material (Sweller, 2010). Accordingly, the experienced cognitive load is mainly dependent of students' prior knowledge. Nevertheless, cognitive load can also be determined by students' motivation (Feldon, Franco, Chao, Peugh, & Maahs-Fladung, 2018; Verhoeven, Schnotz, & Paas, 2009). As a consequence, when designing an online course for complex tasks, it is important to understand how the different types of cognitive load are affected by students' cognitive and motivational characteristics. Therefore, in the current study, a high and low complex task was developed relating to the learning and teaching of geometry. The complexity of the task was manipulated by increasing the element interactivity for the high complex task (Sweller, 2010). In the low complex task one element was questioned each time, and consequently students had to apply a single rule, formula or procedure. By contrast, the high complex task was based on a real-life context (e.g., teaching geometry), and had higher element interactivity. Subsequently, the high complex task required learners to engage in a series of cognitive activities such as analysing, decision making, implementing and evaluating, while holding several procedures and rules in mind. Accordingly, we expected the high complex task to induce more cognitive load. The same amount of support containing the same content, was provided during both tasks. Consequently, in this context, students could take initiative in diagnosing their learning needs by identifying appropriate support. Since students could consult different amounts of support, this self-directed learning strategy could also influence the perceived cognitive load (van Merriënboer & Sluijsmans, 2009). Accordingly, the amount of consulted support was also taken into account during the analyses. The aim of the study was twofold. First, as a manipulation check of task complexity, we investigated differences in the experienced cognitive load while solving a high and low complex task. Secondly, we examined whether students' cognitive and motivational characteristics influence the different types of perceived cognitive load, when taking into account the amount of consulted support for both the high and low complex task. A multivariate approach was chosen to assess the degree of interplay that may exist among students' cognitive, motivational characteristics, consultation of support and the different types of perceived cognitive load. By conducting this study, we wanted to gain insight into whether the cognitive, motivational characteristics and consultation of support influence the perceived cognitive load differently for a high and low complex task.

Theoretical framework

CLT is a broadly applied theory within the field of instructional design for complex learning (Sweller, 2010). CLT uses current knowledge about the human cognitive architecture as a baseline. Basically, the human cognitive architecture consists of an effectively unlimited long-term memory, which interacts with a working memory that has limited processing capacity (Sweller, 1994). Long-term memory contains cognitive schemata that are used to store and organize knowledge. Learning occurs when information is successfully processed in working memory and when new schemas are created or incorporated into consisting schemas in long-term memory. As the processing capacity of the working memory is limited, overcoming individual working memory limitations by instructional manipulations has been the main focus of CLT (Sweller, 2010). According to CLT, cognitive load can be defined as a multidimensional construct representing the load that solving a particular problem imposes on the learners' cognitive system (Leppink, Paas, van der Vleuten, van Gog, & van Merriënboer, 2013). Specifically, CLT claims that the cognitive load that learners experience can be intrinsic, extraneous or germane as indicated in Figure 1. For effective learning to occur, the sum of these loads must remain smaller than the capacity of the learner's working memory (Sweller, 1994). *Intrinsic load* involves element activity which is determined by the nature of the task demands in relation to the expertise and motivation of the learner. Instructional design may result in *extraneous load* (which is ineffective for learning) and in germane load (which is effective for learning). Extraneous cognitive load is defined as unnecessary extra load due to poorly designed instruction. *Germane load* is defined as load that contributes to learning (Sweller, 2010).

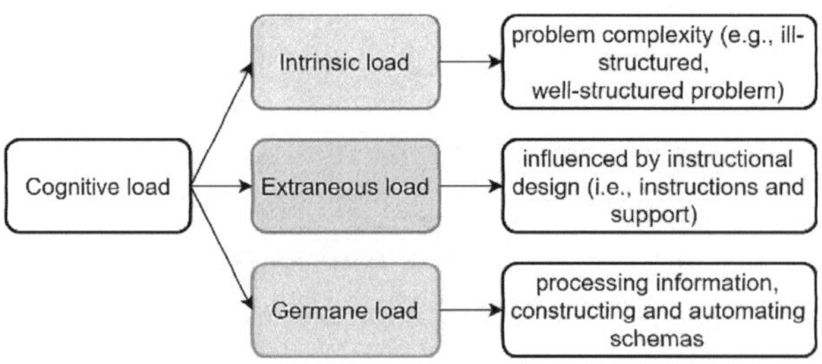

Figure 1. Overview theoretical framework

From the perspective of CLT, the major factor influencing an individual's success in learning from instruction is the limited ability of working memory to assimilate and structure target information (Sweller, 2010). The availability of relevant well-structured *prior knowledge* can increase the functional capacity of working memory relative to the task, such that an individual with greater expertise will experience a lower burden on working memory resources than an individual with less expertise. Research within the CLT framework also engages *motivation* as a necessary precursor to learning (Paas, Tuovinen, van Merriënboer, & Darabi, 2005; Verhoeven et al., 2009). CLT research studies assume that sufficient motivation is required for participants to invest the mental effort necessary to meet the cognitive demands of instruction. Self-efficacious learners believe that they can accomplish a task. There is evidence that self-efficacious learners tend to demonstrate a more strategic approach to learning tasks and direct mental effort toward processes that are more pertinent to learning (Feldon et al., 2018). Task value essentially refers to the reason for doing a task. More specifically, students with high task value pursue enjoyment of learning and understanding of new things. The level of motivation can be particularly important if high complex tasks need to be solved as a higher degree of cognitive demand imposes higher cognitive load and requires greater effort (Paas et al., 2005). CLT furthermore indicates that the cognitive demands within a learning situation are defined by the complexity of the problem (Verhoeven et al., 2009). Nevertheless, in interactive online learning environments, students can often consult additional support that may moderate the level of complexity (van Merriënboer & Sluijsmans, 2009). Van Merriënboer (1997) designed a four-component instructional design model (4C/ID-model) that has proven to be useful to design complex problem-solving instruction. Van Merriënboer (2013) claims that in this model cognitive load can be managed by providing a large amount of support and guidance. Accordingly, learners are more guided into how to solve the complex problem and accordingly spend less time on irrelevant aspects of the task. In the 4C/ID-model two types of support are incorporated, namely procedural and supportive information. *Procedural information* specifies how to solve the routine aspects of the problem. *Supportive information* is basically, the theory and supports the learning and performance of the non-routine problem solving and reasoning aspects. Even though this model is more focused on the instructional design of educational programmes than the design of instructional materials, it offers directions in reducing extraneous as well as intrinsic cognitive load (van Merriënboer & Sluijsmans, 2009). Against this theoretical background, following research questions were formulated.

- *RQ1*: Does the manipulation of the level of complexity of a task based on element interactivity, result in differences in perceived cognitive load between a high and low complex task?
- *RQ2*: Does students' cognitive and motivational characteristics influence the perceived cognitive load of a high and low complex task, when taking into account the amount of consultation of support?

Methodology

Participants were 70 future primary school teachers of which 56 were female and 14 male (age between 18-24). All participants were first year bachelor students (i.e., second semester). The study was highly ecologically valid as the study was orchestrated by the students' lecturer of the teaching mathematics course unit. Moreover, the intervention was integrated into the students' study program (i.e., primary school teacher training). The intervention consisted of a within-subject design and was conducted online in the Moodle learning management system (LMS). The intervention took place in the auditorium of the students' faculty where students could solve the tasks individually on their own computer among their fellow students. This session was supervised by their lecturer and a researcher. Students first received an online questionnaire where students' self-efficacy was measured. Next, all students had to solve a high complex and a low complex task on preparing a lesson in geometry. After each condition, cognitive load was measured. In order to control for order effects, (a) half of the subjects were exposed to the high complex task during the first session and the low complex task during the second session, whereas for (b) the other half, the sequence was vice versa.

High and low complex problem

The high and low complex task were developed in Moodle. The content of both tasks was preparing a lesson on the circumference of a circle. Students had not yet been taught about teaching the circumference of the circle. Both tasks contained six elements where aspects of pedagogical content knowledge (PCK, i.e., inductive teaching strategy, selecting adequate lesson material and using it in a correct manner, aligning the topic of the lesson with the Flemish curriculum and taking into account differentiation in the classroom) and content knowledge (CK; i.e., formula of the circumference of the circle) were addressed. The difference between the high and low complex task was that in the high complex task students had to coordinate and integrate six elements consisting of CK and PCK in order to write a course preparation about the circumference of the circle, whereas the low complex task consisted of six questions where each element was addressed separately. During both problems, the same support consisting of procedural and supportive information was provided. Supportive information is much more extensive (i.e., background theory). Both procedural and supportive information could be consulted by clicking on the words in italics, during the complex problem-solving process. Students spent on average 25.82 min ($SD = 6.82$) on the high complex task and 8.04 min ($SD = 2.57$) on the low complex task. Students were assessed concerning the aforementioned six items (e.g., inductive teaching). Task performance was 56.7% ($SD = 31.2$) for the high complex task and 75.7% ($SD = 22.6$) for the low complex task.

Measurements

For the measurement of *cognitive load,* a validated instrument for intrinsic, extraneous and germane load in complex knowledge domains was used as originally developed by Leppink et al. (2013). *Self-efficacy* (5 items) and *task-value* (3 items) were retrieved from the motivated strategies for learning questionnaire (MSLQ; Duncan & Mckeachie, 2005). Questionnaires consisted of a 7-point Likert scale (i.e., ranging from *totally disagree* to *totally agree*). Construct validity was checked by conducting a confirmatory factor analysis (CFA). The standardized factor loadings from the latent variable constructs were all significant with standardized values ranging from .42 to .93. Internal consistency was investigated by measuring Cronbach's Alpha [Self-efficacy: .88; Task Value: 67; Low complex: intrinsic load: .86; extraneous load: .72 and germane load: .79; High complex: intrinsic load: 75, extraneous load: .73 and germane load: .80], indicating medium/good reliability (Schreiber, Nora, Stage, Barlow, & King, 2006). Sample items are:

- *intrinsic load:* "the topics covered in this problem were very complex";
- *extraneous load:* "the instructions were very unclear";
- *germane load:* "The task really enhanced my understanding of the topics covered";
- *self-efficacy*: "I'm certain I can understand the most difficult material presented in this online course";
- *task value*: "I am very interested in the content of this course".

Information about *students' prior knowledge* was gathered in the first semester during their examination. Students were tested on their knowledge of PCK (*mean* = 57.4%, *SD* = 18) and CK (*mean* = 45%, *SD* = 24). Content was (teaching) mathematics in general and geometry in particular. *The amount of consulted support* was collected by tracking students' activity, namely, the registration of views by the Moodle LMS. Specifically, these are the set of variables that were included: (a) amount of consultation of support during the high complex task (*mean* = 6.33, *SD* = 1.75, *min* = 0, *max* = 27) and (b) the amount of support during the low complex task (mean = 3.84, *SD* = 2.92, *min* = 0, *max* = 13).

Results

RQ1 investigates whether the manipulation of the level of complexity of a problem results in differences in perceived cognitive load. Results reveal that the perceived intrinsic load and extraneous load is significantly higher for the high complex problem. This indicates that students perceived the high complex task as more difficult. Germane load is significantly lower for the high complex task indicating that it was harder for students to learn from the high complex task.

Table 1: Paired Samples Test comparing differences of cognitive load between a high and low complex task

	Mean difference	*SD*	*t*	*p*
Intrinsic load	.59	1.08	4.48	.00
Extraneous load	.54	.97	4.65	.00
Germane load	-.29	1.19	-2.04	.05

RQ2 investigates how students' cognitive and motivational characteristics influence the different types of perceived cognitive load in a high and low complex task. Results of a multivariate regression for the *high complex task* reveal that less self-efficacious students perceive more intrinsic load. Partial $\eta 2$, which is the proportion of variance accounted for by an effect, indicates that 29% of all variance in perceived intrinsic load is attributable to

students' level of self-efficacy. Results furthermore indicate a positive significant influence of the amount of support consulted on perceived intrinsic load. Partial $\eta 2$ indicates that 8% of all variances in perceived intrinsic load is attributable to the consultation of support. Results reveal that students' characteristics have no significant influence on perceived extraneous and germane load. Finally, results reveal that consulting support has a positive influence on germane load. Partial $\eta 2$ indicates that 11% of all variances in perceived germane load is the result of the consultation of support. In the *low complex condition*, results reveal that students' self-efficacy has a significant influence the perceived intrinsic load. Partial $\eta 2$ indicates that 11% of all variances in perceived intrinsic load is due to students' self-efficacy. Students' characteristics had no influence on the perceived extraneous and germane load. Nevertheless, results indicate a positive significant influence of the consultation of procedural information on perceived extraneous load.

Table 2: Influence of students' characteristics on the perceived cognitive load in a high complex condition

High complex		*B*	*SE*	*p*	η_p^2
Intrinsic load	Intercept	4.76	.73	.00	.44
	Prior knowledge	.09	.07	.18	.03
	Self-efficacy	-.75	.16	.00	.29
	Task value	.22	.17	.21	.03
	Amount of support	.06	.03	.03	.08
Extraneous load	Intercept	4.67	.82	.00	.38
	Prior knowledge	-.09	.07	.22	.03
	Self-efficacy	-.27	.18	.15	.00
	Task value	-.04	.19	.85	.04
	Amount of support	.04	.03	.16	.01
Germane load	Intercept	1.13	1.06	.29	.02
	Prior knowledge	-.06	-.60	.55	.01
	Self-efficacy	.30	1.28	.21	.03
	Task value	.31	1.26	.21	.03
	Amount of support	.10	.04	.01	.11

Table 3: Influence of students' characteristics on the perceived cognitive load in a low complex task condition

low complex		*B*	*SE*	*p*	η_p^2
Intrinsic load	Intercept	4.06	.91	.00	.27
	Prior knowledge	-.02	.08	.86	.00
	Self-efficacy	-.61	.21	.01	.14
	Task value	.32	.22	.15	.04
	Amount of support	.03	.05	.52	.01
Extraneous load	Intercept	3.47	.78	.00	.27
	Prior knowledge	-.07	.07	.34	.02
	Self-efficacy	-.20	.18	.26	.00
	Task value	.02	.19	.92	.00
	Amount of support	.10	.04	.02	.09
Germane load	Intercept	3.72	.90	.00	.24
	Prior knowledge	-.02	.08	.84	.00
	Self-efficacy	-.03	.21	.91	.00
	Task value	.07	.22	.76	.00
	Amount of support	.04	.05	.40	.01

Discussion

RQ1 investigated the manipulation of complexity of the conditions based on element interactivity. Results reveal that the students indicate higher perceived intrinsic load for the high complex task when compared with the low complex task. This indicates that the manipulation of complexity based on element interactivity was successful. Additionally, results indicate that extraneous cognitive load was significantly higher for the high complex task. Nevertheless, the instructions for both conditions were of the same level of difficulty. The difference in extraneous load could be the result of differences in students' problem-solving strategies across the high and low complex task. Former studies indicated that problem-solving strategies such as selecting and processing relevant information, can induce extraneous cognitive load (Boekaerts, 2017; Likourezos & Kalyugo, 2017). Finally, results reveal a significant higher germane load for the low complex task, indicating that students found it easier to learn from the low complex task. Findings indicate that a task with higher element interactivity requires more cognitive processes. As a result, there are not always enough cognitive resources available to learn (e.g., process information) from such complex tasks (Sweller, 2010). *RQ2* examined the influence of students' cognitive, motivational and consultation of support on the different types of cognitive load for a high and low complex task. Results of the high complex condition reveal that more self-efficacious students experience less intrinsic cognitive load. These results indicate that students who believe in their capability to solve the complex problem perceive the task as less complex. Moreover, students' self-efficacy seems to exert more influence on perceived intrinsic load when compared with students' prior knowledge and students' task value. These preliminary results therefore emphasize the importance of students' self-efficacy when investigating cognitive load (Paas et al., 2005). Results furthermore indicate that students who consulted more support, perceived higher intrinsic load. From a CLT perspective, we would rather assume that consulting support reduces cognitive load. More specifically, we would assume that students might have tried to compensate for their lack of prior knowledge by consulting support (Larmuseau, Elen, & Depaepe, 2018). In this study, it is not entirely clear whether students have consulted support to compensate for the complexity of the task, or whether the consultation (and maybe the complexity) of the support has increased their cognitive load. Findings reveal that consulting support also had a positive influence on germane cognitive load. This actually means that the support helped the students to learn from the high complex task. When we combine all findings, we can deduce that students consulted the support when they probably lacked the knowledge to solve the high complex task and that, thanks to this support, they were able to learn new things. When investigating the low complex task, results also reveal that more self-efficacious students perceive less intrinsic cognitive load, nevertheless the effect size is smaller when compared with the high complex task, indicating that students' self-efficacy is even more important when task complexity increases (i.e., higher element interactivity). Findings also reveal that consulting support induced perceived extraneous load. Again, the direction of the effect of the consultation of support is not completely clear. Intuitively, we would think that the lack of clarity of instructions caused students to seek more support. On the other hand, we do not immediately see a link between the consulted support and the perceived intrinsic load, which might indicate that the low complex task was easier (i.e., which also became clear from the findings or *RQ1*) and that the extra support induced extraneous load, as this might have been redundant (Boekaerts, 2017).

Conclusions and further research

Results reveal that students' self- efficacy has a major influence on the perceived intrinsic load for both the high and low complex task. Additionally, results of the current study indicate that students' level of self-efficacy is even more important than students' prior knowledge and task value for both the high and low complex task. The consultation of support also influences perceived intrinsic and germane load for the high complex task, and perceived extraneous load for the low complex task. Due to the study design it is not completely clear whether students have consulted support to mediate their experienced cognitive load, or whether the consultation of support induced intrinsic or extraneous cognitive load. To gain insight into that process for both the high and low complex task, it is interesting to perform repeated measurements of self-reported cognitive load in follow-up studies during online complex problem solving. In addition, it would be an added value to incorporate continuous measures of cognitive load and relate differences to actual problem-solving behaviour (Larmuseau, Desmet, Vanneste, & Depaepe, 2019).

References

Boekaerts, M. (2017). Cognitive load and self-regulation: Attempts to build a bridge. *Learning and Instruction, 51*, 90–97. https://doi.org/10.1016/j.learninstruc.2017.07.001

Duncan, T. G., & McKeachie, W. J. (2005). The making of the motivated strategies for learning questionnaire. *Educational Psychologist, 40*, 117-128 https://doi.org/10.1207/s15326985ep4002_6

Feldon, D. F., Franco, J., Chao, J., Peugh, J., & Maahs-Fladung, C. (2018). Self-efficacy change associated with a cognitive load-based intervention in an undergraduate biology course. *Learning and Instruction, 56*, 64-72. https://doi.org/10.1016/j.learninstruc.2018.04.007

Larmuseau, C., Elen, J., & Depaepe, F. (2018). The influence of students' cognitive and motivational characteristics on students' use of a 4C/ID-based online learning environment and their learning gain. *Proceedings of the 8th International Conference on Learning Analytics and Knowledge – LAK '18.* https://doi.org/10.1145/3170358.3170363

Larmuseau, C., Desmet, P., Vanneste, P. & Depaepe, F. (2019). Multichannel data for understanding cognitive affordances during complex problem solving. *Proceedings of the 8th International Conference on Learning Analytics and Knowledge – LAK '19.* https://doi.org/10.1145/3303772.3303778

Leppink, J., Paas, F., van der Vleuten, C. P. M., van Gog, T., & van Merriënboer, J. J. G. (2013). Development of an instrument for measuring different types of cognitive load. *Behavior Research Methods, 45*, 1085-1072. https://doi.org/10.3758/s13428-013-0334-1

Likourezos, V., & Kalyuga, S. (2017). Instruction-first and problem-solving-first approaches: alternative pathways to learning complex tasks. *Instructional Science, 45*, 195-219. https://doi.org/10.1007/s11251-016-9399-4

van Merriënboer, J. J. G. (1997). *Training complex cognitive skills: a four-component instructional design model for technical training.* Englewood Cliffs, NJ: Educational Technology Publications.

van Merriënboer, J. J. G. (2013). Perspectives on problem solving and instruction. *Computers and Education, 64*, 153-160. https://doi.org/10.1016/j.compedu.2012.11.025

van Merriënboer, J. J. G., & Sluijsmans, D. M. A. (2009). Toward a synthesis of cognitive load theory, four-component instructional design, and self-directed learning. *Educational Psychology Review, 21*, 55-66. https://doi.org/10.1007/s10648-008-9092-5

Paas, F., Tuovinen, J. E., van Merriënboer, J. J. G., & Darabi, A. A. (2005). A motivational perspective on the relation between mental effort and performance: Optimizing learner involvement in instruction. *Educational Technology Research and Development, 53*, 25-34. https://doi.org/10.1007/BF02504795

Schreiber, J. B., Nora, A., Stage, F. K., Barlow, E. A., & King, J. (2006). Reporting structural equation modeling and confirmatory factor analysis results: a review. *The Journal of Educational Research, 99*, 323-338. https://doi.org/10.3200/JOER.99.6.323-338

Sweller, J. (1994). Cognitive load theory, learning difficulty, and instructional design. *Learning and Instruction, 4*, 295-312. https://doi.org/10.1016/0959-4752(94)90003-5

Sweller, J. (2010). Element interactivity and intrinsic, extraneous, and germane cognitive load. *Educational Psychology Review, 22*, 123-138. https://doi.org/10.1007/s10648-010-9128-5

Verhoeven, L., Schnotz, W., & Paas, F. (2009). Cognitive load in interactive knowledge construction. *Learning and Instruction, 19*, 369-375. https://doi.org/10.1016/j.learninstruc.2009.02.002

TEACHING THE GENERATION Z

Hristo Chukurliev, New Bulgarian University, Bulgaria

Abstract

The article presents the experience of New Bulgarian University to create a training program for its academic staff to resume bilateral communication with students born after 2000. It examines the alienation of the faculty from the students due to digital technologies and the change in the perception of knowledge as a value and access to information. It presents results of a survey of the professors' opinion and presents a structure of a training program.

Introduction

One of the main characters of the Generation Z is that it has been using the Internet from a very early age and has been working well with technology and social media. Other distinction is that this is the generation for which the internet is given. Thanks to the internet and the smart devices to access it, as well as with the help of search engines and Wikipedia, this is the generation for which information and knowledge are being pushed apart. Have you tried to give your students a task to find information about something and to see how much shorter time they need compared to you?! It's impressive.

I recently had a case with a distance learning student who asked me two and a half days before the deadline for submitting coursework on "Civilizations and Religions" to give her a topic to write about. Annoyed I search what the available materials in Bulgarian were on the theme "Mythology and religion of the Hittites" (I did, as I imagined what the student would have done), finding that they were scarce, sent the topic and asked the usual volume and text requirements. I put a control question – to make a comparison of the religion of the Hittites with that of the Slavs – in order to force student to develop the information gathered and presented in knowledge. I was confident that the student would fail in the task. As you guess, I received the work on time, even a few hours before the deadline. It was in full volume and with impressive and comprehensive information gathered and presented on religious and mythological systems of the Hittites and Slavs. There is no way to find out what happened. Whether it was translated by automatic text from another language and then carefully corrected or a search engine was used to reach a paper that I could not find. There was, however, one thing that was repeated with both this student and almost all of whom I had given a different subject for this semester and directly encouraged to use copy/paste from Internet, Wikipedia, etc. The information was gathered accurately, thoroughly and in detail. However, almost no one was able to answer the control question. The Hittites and Slavs student had read a great deal of facts, but she had not been able to compare them.

The broken communication with the Millennials

There is a distance between us and our students in their favour in terms of using technology and the Internet as means of completing immediate tasks. Learning how to do something, buying something, understanding what is something and what to do with it. However, this "information" does not turn necessarily into knowledge.

I'm far from the idea of blame someone. On the contrary, I want the communication and socialization between me and the students, my colleagues and their students to resume. Our students are more withdrawn than self-sufficient. Unlike us who are set to change, riot, break with the previous generation, they have no sense of such a need. On the contrary, they are willing to share our views, but rather because they do not understand them and intuitively use them to build around their lives.

According to Bernard Toussaint, communication as an element of meta-language is: "Creating encrypted relations between the speaker and the listener, provided that the listener can turn into a speaker". With the Generation Z we seem to have no communication. The rules of communication require the message to be personal, to present facts, to be concrete, to be possible to ask questions, questions to be heard and to monitor body language. We are unable to adapt these rules to the Z Generation and the communication is virtually absent.

Teaching teachers how to teach

The need for action to overcome this gap between us and our students is obvious. For years, the results of the semester surveys for our students' satisfaction with a teacher, course and program have been problematic for use. It is increasingly difficult to motivate students to participate. The poll is in electronic form and students complete it at the end of the semester until the second week of the session. It visualizes to them as a dialog box in the e-learning platform, which they can minimize or just close. As a result, it reaches less than 10% participation. Perhaps we do not ask the right questions or worse, our students do not think that their answers will follow change and action. We are working on this issue, but this is another topic.

We needed to get to the names of those teachers whom the Generation Z liked. We crosschecked the information. We have selected the teachers permanently having high score most of the time. There were about 40 names out of a total of 446 full-time lecturers or 9%. In another survey among all the lecturers, we asked few questions to identify a group of them willing to change. Out of the same group of 446, 124 responded or 28%. We compared the names of the 40 "high ranked" professors with those with willingness to change. As expected, they were in the group. So we came to the conclusion that we can invite these 40 lecturers to a series of interviews. We asked them what were their practices they thought made them successful with the students of the Z Generation. 20 of them responded or 4.5% out of the 446 initial sample.

I believe that this low rate is one of the proofs that we used reliable methodology and we are on the right track.

We divided the 40 high ranked by the students' lecturers into 6 groups. We have separated as groups the lecturers from the fields of Law and Psychology. The other four groups were: Arts; Economics and Administration; Humanities and Social Sciences; Technical Sciences and Architecture. We did this in order not to mix groups of teachers with different profiles and specifics in teaching.

From these interviews, we found two facts that stand out. The teachers were well aware of and clearly shared what in their teaching is more special and appealing to the students. Along with that the teachers needed an environment and a situation where they could share the methods they use to get feedback and support from their colleagues and also to borrow good practices.

The skeleton of the teaching program

From the collected information from the interviews we were able to distinguish 5 specific problems:

1. Motivation for learning

Teachers are finding it increasingly difficult to keep student's attention on the material taught. The reasons for this lack of motivation for learning are different.

Most of the high scored teachers indicated that in their introductory lecture they clarified what would be studied in their course, why and for what purpose. Information is not knowledge, and lecturers explain to their students their role as mediators in this process of turning information into knowledge.

2. Visual information

Classical linear text is increasingly difficult to understand for students as a source of information.

The use of presentations with rich illustrative material is the most commonly used mean to overcome this deficiency. At the same time, lecturers break their lectures by projecting short videos on critical topics of the material. They use mostly documentaries from YouTube and also they produce some by themselves more and more.

3. Theory vs. Practice

Universities are increasingly preparing their students for the labour market rather than teaching pure science.

Teachers have found that practical training in a real work environment is particularly important. As some of our teachers are real life practitioners they integrate their students into their work. The others create simulations and invent games in which students practice their knowledge. Some of the teachers are critical and restrictive about smartphones by limiting their use in class. Others have realized that they can turn the usage of smartphones in class to their advantage for easier transmission of information into knowledge by asking the students, to seek a solution to a problem by the use of their phones.

4. Evaluation

A major problem to overcome in the learning process is the focus of the students on the evaluation and the grade they get rather than the learning itself.

The solutions shared by the teachers range from extreme clarity of the evaluation, as stated in the first lecture, to the diversification of the forms of evaluation. Some of the most interesting interview results follow. The lecturers shared forms of assessment that ranged from self-assessment of students and their choice of how to be evaluated to different forms of project activity in which students were evaluated not only for the achieved outcome but also for the different phases of the project: teamwork, adherence to deadlines, delegation of responsibilities, communication and leadership.

5. Personal attitude

In view of a growing lack of empathy in human relations, keeping the distance and at the same time the integration of students in a community with the teachers was the last important topic shared in the interviews.

The need for tutoring on one hand and on the other hand getting close just like a parent and kids have been pointed out to be especially important for the Generation Z. Building on a strong relationship with students – both hierarchical and supportive – was identified in many of the interviews.

Based on the information gathered and summarized in the above 5 problematic topics, we decided to create a training program for trainers. In the first phase, we relied on the information concerning the students directly received from the lecturers. In parallel, changing the survey system for students' satisfaction will provide us feedback about the effect of this training program over the next three semesters and whether it is in the right direction.

The Teacher Training Program will start in the spring semester of 2019. By the time of submitting the paper, the program is in draft form and at the time of the conference the first edition of the program will have been completed and the report issued. The first phase of the program will take the form of a seminar with six meetings, distributed evenly throughout the semester. A classical structure of a seminar will be used - moderator introducing the subject and one or two presenters and discussion in the end. In the second phase, it is intended to transform the seminars into workshops to accumulate sufficient information for creation of a standard to be adhered to by the lecturers.

The topics for the seminars are as follows:

1. Presentation of a course (curriculum of course in an understandable language) – the subject is related to the need of the students to be explained at the beginning of the course why they study the specific discipline, what they will learn and how they will be able to use it.
2. Presentations, films, images and video lectures – the topic will focus on the student's need to be presented visual rather than textual information.
3. Case Studies, Simulations, Terrain, Games, Learning by Working – the topic will explore possible ways to use practical tasks in the learning process as well as involving the student's personal smart devices in the learning process.
4. Creating a Knowledge Necessity – the topic will look at how to awaken the perceived need to transform information into knowledge and the ability to reproduce what has been learned.
5. Evaluation - freedom and boundary – the subject will focus on innovative ways of evaluation.
6. Attitude, distance, trust, dialogue, empathy – the theme will focus on soft skills and empathy between the teacher and the students; the emphasis will be on how teachers are to be tutoring their students and at the same time bringing them to the academic community while keeping the distance between themselves and their learners.

Conclusion

The Generation Z is a generation that does not know the world before the Internet. This qualitatively different condition made Marc Prenski in 2001 call this generation *digitally born*, and the rest *digital immigrants*. At the same time, Prenski discusses how teachers should not train with *yesterday* and even *today* methods, but with *tomorrows*. The options for this are two, the students to learn our language or the opposite. The answer will predetermine the future of higher and university education. And as if this question has already been answered – we must learn to communicate with Generation Z on its own language.

Universities face a complex and multifaceted situation where they must simultaneously make a number of transformations, often revolutionary, in teaching, appraising, and communicating, while at the same time preserving their mission in places where elite minds are grown and create knowledge. A positive side is that almost everything that needs to be done already exists and happens in one form or another. The challenge is how conservative institutions and minds, such as those of most university people, can accept this externality as their own.

References

Campbell, A. J., Cumming, S. R., & Hughes, I. (2006). Internet use by the socially fearful: Addiction or therapy? *Cyberpsychology and Behavior, 9*(1), 69–81.

Junco, R., & Mastrodicasa, J. (2007). *Connecting to the Net.Generation: What higher education professionals need to know about today's students.* NASPA. ISBN 978-0-931654-48-0.

Prensky, M. (2001). Digital Natives, Digital Immigrants Part 1. *On the Horizon, 9*, 1-6. doi: 10.1108/10748120110424816.

Toussaint, B. (1978). *Qu'est-ce la séminiologie?* Privat.

TECHNOLOGICAL RESOURCES FOR LIFELONG LEARNING OF TEACHERS IN THE DIGITAL ERA: AN ANALYSIS FROM THE LEARNING ECOLOGIES

Alba Souto-Seijo, Iris Estévez, Mercedes González-Sanmamed, Patricia Romero, Universidade da Coruña, Spain

Introduction

Permanent education has become not only a requirement, but an unavoidable necessity to respond to the requirements of the school, as a precise change for the quality of teaching and teacher training (Imbernón, 2014). The need for a permanent education is driven and/or promoted by the changes that society is generating, simultaneously, in the training and education processes, since the incorporation of ICT in these processes has caused a change in the relationship between the didactic components. Therefore, pedagogical practice must adopt new forms of work that adapt to the new training needs. Consequently, it can be said that education does not remain external to changes and incorporates new media in its didactic relationship, which causes a redefinition of the teacher's work and, surely of the teaching profession, of its formation and its development professional (Sangrà & González Sanmamed, 2011).

Assuming the relationship of ICT with training implies admitting some changes in the structures in which such training converges. Thus, for example, educational institutions seek new strategies that facilitate change in the digital era and provide dynamic, creative responses that are commensurate with social demands (Carril, Sanmamed, & Sellés, 2013).In line with previous ideas, the ecological metaphor or, properly, the Learning Ecologies provide an ideal analysis framework for the study of new forms of learning and professional development (Sangrà, González Sanmamed, & Guitert, 2013; González-Sanmamed, Sangrá, Souto-Seijo, & Estévez, 2018). In the words of Siemens (2010; p.63) the Learning Ecologies are "the space in which learning takes place". This author states that ecologies allow adaptation to the needs of agents within a space, so we can say that they are adaptive, dynamic and sensitive. For his part Barron (2006) considers ecology as "a series of contexts, found in physical or virtual spaces, that provide opportunities for learning. Each context is composed of unique activities, resources, relationships and interactions that arise in them" (Barron, 2006; p.195).

The ability to create and use a Learning Ecology to achieve a certain goal, implies a complex set of skills, qualities, elements and attitudes that must refer to the key dimensions of a learning ecology (Eraut, 2009). Within these key elements we can distinguish: activities, motivations, relationships, contexts, processes, and, also, resources. In this study we will focus on the analysis of this last key element of learning ecologies: resources. Understanding these, like those tools, with or without a technological base, that help teachers to develop professionally and stay updated.

For everything previously mentioned, the main purpose of this research is to understand and reflect on how Primary Education teachers carry out their training and professional development, and what is the role of resources (personal and technological) in the configuration of their Learning Ecologies.

Methodology

This research is of a qualitative nature. In addition, we must take into account, that it is launched within a biographical-narrative approach. The tradition of qualitative research relating to narrative is a form of qualitative research that deals with the analysis of human experience, more specifically "it studies the lives of people and asks one or more people to provide stories about their lives. It is then told by the researcher in a narrative chronology" (Clandinin & Connellly, 2000). Other authors such as Creswell (2013) also define it as a research tradition in which narrative is understood as a spoken or written text that explains an event, an action or a series of events and/or actions, connected in chronological order.

Participants

The sample of our study is composed of 5 Primary Education teachers from different public schools in the province of A Coruña (Spain). To preserve the anonymity of the participants and the confidentiality of the data, we have assigned them different names instead of the real ones. The characteristics of our sample are presented in Figure 1.

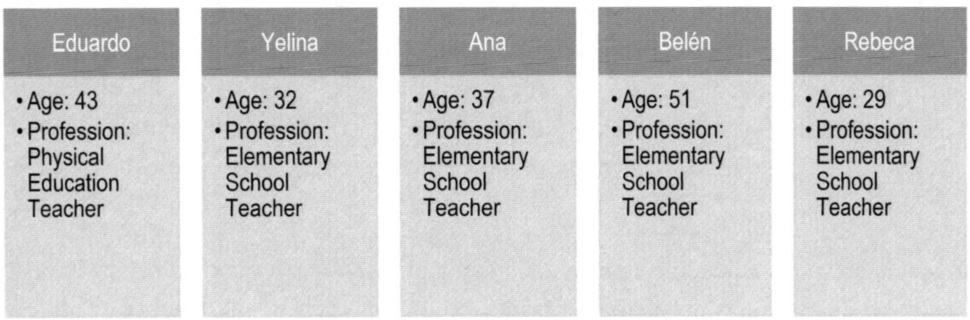

Figure 1. Participant Characteristics

Instruments

The data collection of the study has been carried out through an open-ended interview about learning mechanisms. This was made up of 71 questions, of which 25 related to learning resources used by teachers. Some of the questions that have allowed us to understand the meaning attributed to both technological and personal resources were, for instance, the following:

> *"How does the update of your colleagues influence your own update?";*

"What is your motivation to train yourself using ICT?";

"What technological tools do you use in your professional field?";

"What role do virtual platforms play in your training process?" and

"The aim was to identify the learning ecologies of each of the participants".

Process

First, we contacted with the selected teachers, to invite them to participate in the research, always ensuring confidentiality and anonymity. They were also informed of the importance of the study and its purpose. After that, their doubts were resolved, and the days were set with each of them to carry out the scheduled interview. In order to accurately record the interaction between the interviewer and the interviewee, a tape recorder was used. Then they were transcribed.

Data analysis

As determined by Glaser and Strauss (1967; 1999) and Corbin and Strauss (2014), the interpretation of data is the essence of qualitative research, therefore, we cannot ignore the importance of coding them. Coding refers to the process through which we fragment or segment the data according to the objectives and research questions that we have proposed (Strauss & Corbin, 2002). The method used to classify the data has been content analysis (Bardin, 1986). Once the information was collected, it was distributed according to the units of meaning that were emerging. These units of meaning were labelled by codes that, finally, were grouped into thematic categories, following the recommendations of L'Écuyer (1990), who points out that they are grouped into categories or broader topics under a generic title that brings together all the sentences whose meaning is related (Figure 2). As we can see in this figure the key component of our study is "Learning Resources" which is related to resources that teachers use because they allow them to satisfy a need or achieve what they want. Later, data was divided into two main components: technological resources and personal resources.

On the one hand, personal resources include people and groups of people that have influenced or influence the configuration of the learning ecology of each of the teachers This category was named "The Importance of personal resources". On the other hand, the component of technological resources include resources related to ICT that help each teacher to develop professionally and configure their learning ecology. In this category, we can find three subcategories named:

"How they learned to use technological resources",

"What and how they use the technological resources", and

"How they value the technological resources".

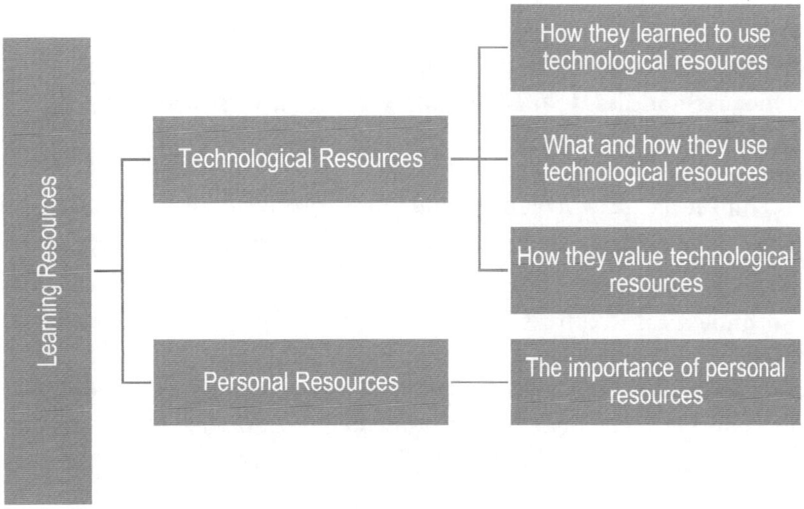

Figure 2. Analysis categories

Results

At this point we are going to present the results of the study organized in the following four categories:

How they learned to use technological resources

The responses of the five participants allow us to differentiate two groups to explain how they learned to use technological resources. On the one hand, there is a first group in which there are two teachers (Eduardo and Yelina) who have been learning to use technology, at first, through courses and, later on, in a more self-taught way:

> *"If there is something that I do not know, I look for tutorials or do courses related to that (...)" (E2-C, 15).*

It is important to point out that Eduardo is passionate and very interested in the ICT world, so he is very involved in updating himself in this area. In addition, he did his thesis on the computerization of schools and that helped him a lot to advance in this subject. On the other hand, there is a second group formed by three teachers (Ana, Belén and Rebeca), who have been discovering the potentialities of ICT through their peers:

> *"Mainly through other colleagues who use ICT to train and through the social networks that allow you to know different groups of teachers or educational websites that advertise or promote learning using technology" (E2-E, 15).*

What and how they use technological resources

All of them, to a greater or lesser extent, use digital tools to facilitate the development of their classes. The difference resides in the possibilities offered by the schools in which they teach and the ability that each one has to manage with these tools with a certain skill.

Thus, both Yelina and Eduardo use collaborative work tools (Dropbox, Google Drive...), applications to communicate with family and other professionals (WhatsApp, Telegram...), applications to work on aspects such as reading and writing, vocabulary, story creation, or applications for the management of blogs and educational web pages. In addition, Yelina uses other types of technological resources:

> *"I also use different videos, documentaries and/or presentations to complement the teaching-learning process. For example, if we are talking about animals and reproduction, I use videos with the reproduction of different types of animals (viviparous and oviparous)" (E2-E, 15).*

In the same way, Eduardo uses Edmodo to work together with his students. In addition, he has several educational blogs, creates activities and develops educational material.

On the other hand, Ana, Belén and Rebeca do not have such a wide knowledge and they limit themselves to using resources such as the Smartphone, the Interactive Digital Whiteboard, the computer and instant messaging applications such as WhatsApp. Only Belén explains that blogs are a resource that is especially useful:

> *"The world of blogs is very interesting because you can find people who have a lot of information" (E2-B, 12).*

How they value technological resources

As we can see in the results, both Eduardo and Yelina are two teachers very committed to new technologies, so they value them in a very positive way. Yelina says that the flexibilization of schools to adapt to the needs of today's society involves the exploitation of ICT in teaching processes. According to her, this would imply changes in the conception of the students, changes in the teachers and administrative changes in relation to the design and distribution of the teaching and with the communication systems that the institution establishes:

> *"ICT, nowadays, are fundamental in the teaching-learning process. On the one hand, we teach children who learn to use a Smartphone before they speak, so the teaching must be adapted to this change. On the other hand, new technologies facilitate visual and participatory teaching, in which students learn by doing, and I consider it fundamental" (E2-E, 12).*

Eduardo is passionate about new technologies. He says:

> *"I really like this world, to be constantly learning as platforms or digital educational resources are advancing because it is a way to update yourself. I have always done many courses on ICT and I have also given them, since I believe it is important and essential that teachers have, at least, a basic command in their use and in their educational use" (E2-C, 11).*

Despite the fact that Rebeca has more limited knowledge of ICT, she considers that these are fundamental in daily life in the classroom, because they allow her to develop new knowledge strategies and new methodologies based on the discovery and research:

> *"They help me to present knowledge and promote greater autonomy in students, developing in them the ability to learn" (E2-D, 12).*

Finally, Ana and Belén highlight both positive and negative aspects of ICT. On the one hand, Ana explains that the benefits of using these types of tools are many, among which she highlights the following:

> *"Create material, search for information, as an evaluation method (recordings of exhibitions), etc." (E2 -A, 8).*

On the other hand, their opinion about virtual networks and platforms is not so positive:

> *"I value them not great because I think they eliminate a lot of direct connection from person to person, which I consider essential within the educational sphere" (E2-A ,11).*

Finally, Belén tells us that ICTs have completely changed the way she teaches classes:

> *"I was aware in my career that a change was necessary for the classroom, and I think that in some way ICTs offer us this "(E2-B, 14).*

However, she believes that they also have negative aspects:

> *"The students, in general, have a serious attention problem. And I think it's related to ICT, because, in addition to the computer, the child has a PlayStation, an Xbox, a Game Boy ... and more games on the computer. In the computer, it is very easy to go from one information to another without going deep. Without having to pay attention to what you are reading until you find what you want. It's very easy, and then you start reading and you say this is not useful, but maybe what you were looking for was in the middle of that" (E2-B, 11).*

The importance of personal resources

Finally, it is convenient to point out that, in addition to the technological resources, all the participants emphasize the importance of the people in their training, from their family or friends to their colleagues. Eduardo, one of the teachers most committed to the use of ICT, says:

> *"I am still in contact with colleagues from the university and colleagues from other schools where I was working. Through social networks, we are always in contact, commenting on doubts or opinions on various topics. We also make casual encounters in which you talk about everything a little "(E2-C, 6).*

In the same way, Ana affirms:

> *"People have always occupied a large place in my continuing education, perhaps I can say that it is the most important aspect because from them you learn unwittingly and totally unconsciously" (E2-A, 12).*

Conclusions

As we have seen throughout this research, one of the most important topics in the configuration of learning ecologies derives from the use of ICT (Sangrà, González Sanmamed, & Guitert, 2013, González-Sanmamed, Sangrá, Souto-Seijo, & Estévez, 2018). The continuous and fast succession of changes has gone beyond the traditional response of teachers' professional training based on courses with a specific beginning and end. Currently, there are multiple resources that can help teachers to develop professionally and stay updated and, therefore, it is so important to know what is the learning of ICT of teachers, what and how they use these resources, how they value them and what others resources they consider fundamental in their training.

In this research, it has been observed that some of the participants learned to use technological resources in a self-taught way and others have introduced into this world with the help of their workmates. It should be noted that all of them use, to a greater or lesser extent, digital tools to facilitate the development of their classes. The difference resides in the possibilities offered by the schools in which they teach and the ability that each one has to manage with these tools with a certain skill. In addition, the five participants found positive the use of ICT, both to teach and to learn, but also reveal some negative aspects, such as the loss of personal treatment with people. Finally, in addition to technological resources, all participants highlight the importance of personal interactions in their training.

Finally, we would like to point out that our study is of an exploratory type and, for this reason, we thought it would be appropriate to expand our research using other types of data collection techniques, such as document analysis or observation. In addition, it could be very interesting to complement this qualitative study, with a quantitative one, to investigate more in depth and from different methodological perspectives the learning ecologies of Primary Education teachers. This would allow us to better understand what resources teachers have in an increasingly uncertain social context.

References

Bardin, L. (1986). *L'analyse de contenu.* Paris: PUF.

Barron, B. (2006). Interest and Self-Sustained Learning as Catalysts of Development: A Learning Ecology Perspective. *Human Development, 49*(4), 193–224.

Carril, P. C. M., Sanmamed, M. G., & Sellés, N. H. (2013). Pedagogical roles and competencies of university teachers practicing in the e-learning environment. *The International Review of Research in Open and Distributed Learning, 14*(3), 462-487.

Clandinin, D. J., & Connelly, F. M. (2000). *Narrative inquiry: Experience and story in qualitative research.*

Corbin, J., & Strauss, A. (2014). *Basics of qualitative research: Techniques and procedures for developing grounded theory.* London: Sage.

Creswell, J. W. (2013). *Research design: Qualitative, quantitative, and mixed methods approaches.* Thousand Oaks: Sage.

Eraut, M. (2009). How Professionals Learn through Work. In N. J. Jackson (Ed.), *Learning to be Professional through a Higher Education* (Chapter 2). Authorhouse: E-book. Retrieved from http://learningtobeprofessional.pbworks.com/How-professionals-learn-through-work

Glaser, B. G., & Strauss, A. L. (1967). *The discovery of grounded theory: strategies for qualitative theory.* New Brunswick: Aldine Transaction.

Glaser, B. G., & Strauss, A. L. (1999). *Discovery of Grounded Theory.* New York: Routledge. https://doi.org/10.4324/9780203793206

González-Sanmamed, M., Sangrà, A., Souto-Seijo, A., & Estévez, I. (2018). Ecologías de aprendizaje en la Era Digital: desafíos para la Educación Superior. *Publicaciones, 48*, 11-38. http://doi.org/10.30827/publicaciones.v48i1.7329

Imbernón, F. (2014). *Calidad de enseñanza y formación del profesorado: un cambio necesario.* Barcelona: Octaedro.

L'Écuyer, R. (1990). *Méthodologie de l´analyse développementale de contenu.* Sillery. Presses de l'Université du Québec, 51-120.

Sangrà, A., & González-Sanmamed, M. (2011). The role of information and communication technologies in improving teaching and learning processes in primary and secondary schools. *Australasian Journal of Educational Technology, 26*(8).

Sangrà, A., Gonzalez-Sanmamed, M., & Guitert, M. (2013). Learning ecologies: Informal professional development opportunities for teachers. *Proceedings of the Educational Media (ICEM), 2013 IEEE 63rd Annual Conference International Council for. IEEE*, 1-2.

Siemens, G. (2010). Conectivismo: Una teoría de aprendizaje para la era digital. *Conectados en el ciberespacio, 20*, 77-140.

Strauss, A., & Corbin, J. (2002). *Bases de la investigación cualitativa: técnicas y procedimientos para desarrollar la teoría fundamentada.* Medellín: Editorial de Antioquia.

Acknowledgments

This study has been conducted in the framework of the research project (ECO4LEARN-HE), funded by the Ministry of Economy and Finance (Reference EDU2015-67907-R), and thanks to the funding received by one of the authors, Iris Estévez, in the FPI programme from the Ministry of Economy and Finance (BES-2016-077330).

Connecting through Educational Technology
Proceedings of the European Distance and E-Learning Network 2019 Annual Conference
Bruges, 16-19 June, 2019

INFORMAL LEARNING: CONTRIBUTIONS OF TECHNOLOGY IN A DIGITAL SOCIETY

Iris Estévez, Alba Souto-Seijo, Mercedes González-Sanmamed, Verónica Iglesias,
University of A Coruña, Spain

Introduction

We live in a complex society, with multiple questions and challenges. Since computers and the Internet invaded our lives, our way of communicating and relating has changed drastically. The digital revolution is causing continuous changes in different contexts, and education is one of them. Nowadays, knowledge has expiration date, for this reason citizens have to assume that training is not a one-time activity that takes place at a certain time, but that life consists of a continuous learning.

This fact, perhaps, in the case of teachers, has a greater importance, because they not only have the need to learn, but also the responsibility to teach in a changing environment. Different educational institutions must respond to the new challenges posed by the information society, but this formal education is not enough. According to González-Sanmamed, Sangrà, Souto-Seijo, Santos, and Estévez (2018), learning does not take place linearly or in specific spaces; nor can it be limited to the closed parameters of the formal training proposals. Nowadays, there are many possibilities to train and learn. For this reason, informal training models are becoming increasingly important, in addition to the classical formal training models.

Now we will explain what is meant by formal, non-formal and informal training. On the one hand, formal training takes place in institutions that are specifically dedicated to training and is intentional (Martín, 2013). On the other hand, non-formal training includes those activities offered by various institutions that are not explicitly educational but contain important components to favour the learning process (Cobo & Moravec, 2011). These activities are characterized by having a more flexible format. Finally, informal training corresponds to the daily learning that occurs spontaneously in everyday situations (González-Sanmamed, Sangrà, Souto-Seijo, & Estévez, 2018). It is important to emphasize that the ideal is to integrate all these training opportunities (Cross, 2007), because it will be what facilitates the complicated task of responding to the training and personal and professional updating needs that are presented to us.

At this point, we will explain what is the current situation of teacher training in Spain. Until recently, teacher training was synonymous with face-to-face training courses, although this reality has been changing thanks to the possibilities offered by technology (Marcelo, 2002).

Thus, on-line training and blended-training have been added, naturally, to the training that traditionally was done face to face (Paniagua, Luengo, Torres Carvalho, & Casas, 2017).

Although some studies highlight the importance of new training modalities and the relevance they have progressively in the day-to-day work of teacher education (Nunes & Meneses, 2014), it is also true that the most classical training is still preferred by them (Paniagua, Luengo, Torres, Carvalho, & Casas, 2017). Therefore, the specific objectives that structure this study are the following:

- Identify which are the activities of lifelong learning, with or without a technological base, more frequent within the informal contexts of learning.
- Study the reasons that cause the involvement of teachers in the informal-training activities.

Methodology

This study, of a quantitative nature, is developed through a non-experimental-descriptive design (McMillan & Schumacher, 2005). Following, the information related to the participants, the instrument used, the procedure followed and the data analysis will be explained in more detail.

Participants

The sample consisted of 73 teachers of Primary Education of 11 public schools located in A Coruña, a city in the north of Spain. This was done by a convenience sampling (Schreier, 2018). A 27.4% of the participants were men and 72.6% were women. In a 16.4% the average age is between 25 and 35 years old, 47.9% are between 36 and 50 years old and 35.6% are over 51 years old.

In relation to their professional experience it should be noted that a 43.8% had between 21 and 35 years of experience as a teacher, the 28.8%, had an experience of between 11 and 20 years, the 13.7% had between 5 and 10 years of experience and, finally, 8.2% had an experience of fewer than 5 years.

Instruments

The instrument used for data collection was a self-created questionnaire. The characteristics of the questionnaire, among which are versatility, efficiency, and generality (McMillan, 2012), have been what led us to select this instrument to collect the information. For its validation, a system based on the judgment of the experts, which consists of an assessment of the instrument, was used (Escobar-Pérez & Cuervo-Martínez, 2008). In addition, the information provided by the expert judgment was complemented by a pilot study. In these study, participated teachers from the Primary Education stage, because we could easily access.

The questionnaire was divided into 6 dimensions, although to carry out this study we focused on two of them. The first of these dimensions refers to the different types of informal activities that teachers carry out to develop themselves professionally, and the second is linked to the different reasons, which are behind the participation of Primary Education teachers, in this type of informal training activities. In the first one, thirty items are differentiated; and in the second, twelve items. Both have a Likert response scale from one to four. First scale response is: 1 – *never*, 2 – *almost never*, 3 – *almost always* and 4 – *always*. In addition, second scale response is: 1 – *totally disagree*, 2 – *disagree*, 3 – *agree*, 4 – *totally agree.*

Process

In the first place, the school management, where the questionnaire was intended to be applied, were informed of the study purpose. Once their consent was obtained, the information was collected. Thus, the questionnaire was delivered in person to the faculty of the different schools. The way their doubts are resolved and the anonymity and confidentiality of the data were guaranteed.

Data analysis

To carry out the statistical analysis, was used the computer program called SPSS. It started with an exploratory analysis, which allows us to evaluate the quality and distribution of the data (asymmetry and kurtosis), determine the summary measures (mode, media, and median), and calculate the dispersion measures (variance and range). In addition, we did descriptive and frequency analysis, in order to know the average score and percentages of each variable.

Results

The first objective was to identify what are the permanent training activities, with or without a technological base, more frequent within the informal learning contexts.

Attending now to this objective, we intend to identify which are the most frequent activities within the informal learning contexts. Some of the activities are based on the use of ICT and others are not, therefore, we differentiate both groups, to see if there are significant differences in the realization of both. For this, we have calculated the means of all the variables corresponding to informal activities, forming a group of activities with a technological base and another group of activities without a technological base.

The means for each variable, of the group of activities without a technological base, are the following: *Self-reflection on the daily experience* ($\bar{x} = 3.19$); *reflection with classmates on the daily experience* ($\bar{x} = 3.16$); *reflection with colleagues from other centres on daily experiences* ($\bar{x} = 2.47$); *informal meetings with other professionals (communities of practice, interest groups, ...)* ($\bar{x} = 2.08$); *visiting to other classrooms and / or other centres* ($\bar{x} = 1.93$); *visiting museums* ($\bar{x} = 2.49$); *visiting exhibitions* ($\bar{x} = 2.49$); *periodic consultations / printed professional journals* ($\bar{x} = 2.27$); *periodic consultations / printed scientific journals* ($\bar{x} = 2.18$); *consulting professional printed books* ($\bar{x} = 2.36$); *consulting printed books of scientific, cultural or literary content* ($\bar{x} = 2.34$), *consult printed academic reports* ($\bar{x} = 2.26$); *informal conversations with relatives* ($\bar{x} = 2.16$); *informal conversations with friends* ($\bar{x} = 2.40$); *informal conversations with colleagues* ($\bar{x} = 2.79$); *elaboration of classroom resources/materials* ($\bar{x} = 3.01$); *use of material resources for the classroom* ($\bar{x}$ = 3.08); *design of specific work plans* ($\bar{x}$ = 2.59); *exchange of experiences* ($\bar{x}$ = 2.60).

The average direct scores for the group of variables with a technological base are shown below: *internet searches* ($\bar{x}$ = 2.51); *internet tutorials* ($\bar{x}$ = 2.60); *digital library consultation* ($\bar{x}$ = 2.53); *work with digital books* ($\bar{x}$ = 2.53); *consult digital materials* ($\bar{x}$ = 2.67); *participation in digital social networks* ($\bar{x}$ = 1.93); *development of blogs* ($\bar{x}$ = 1.96); *search of blogs* ($\bar{x}$ = 2.68); *search in open resource repositories* ($\bar{x}$ = 2.33); *participation in a MOOC (mass open online courses* ($\bar{x}$ = 1.40); *mass media: TV, cinema,…(* $\bar{x}$ = 2.37).

Following, Figure 1 is presented to summarize graphically the aforementioned data:

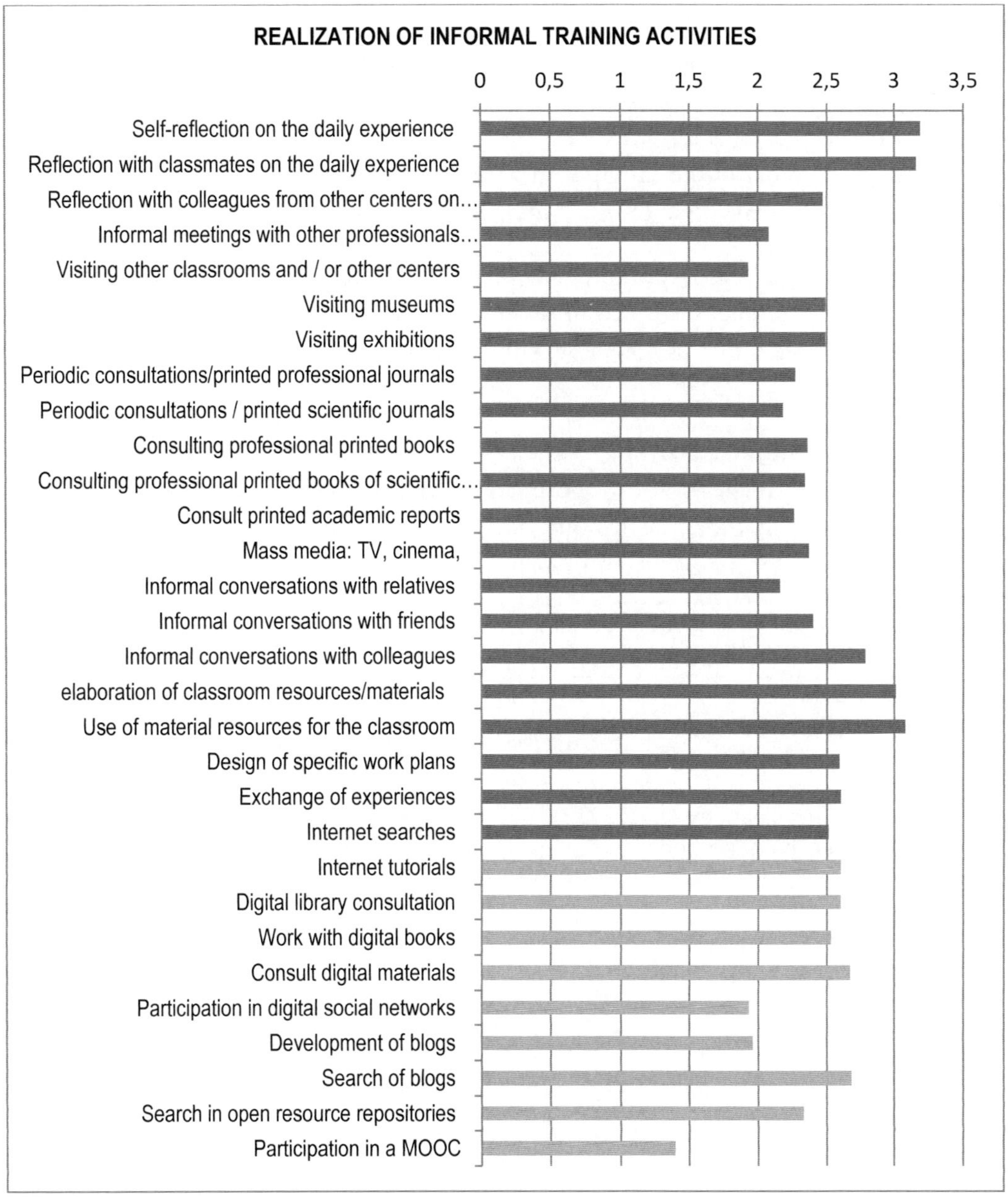

Figure 1. Frequency of realization of informal training activities

As can be seen in Figure 1, the most unusual informal training activity is *participation in Mass Open Online Courses* (MOOC); In fact, if we turn to the frequency analysis of this variable, we can see how 49% of the participants in our study have never attended a MOOC. On the other hand, the most important activity carried out by the Primary Education teachers, in order to improve their professional development, is *the self-reflection on the daily experience* with an average of 3.19. If we resort again to frequency analysis, but this time focusing on this last variable, we observe that 63.17% of the sample very often performs this type of informal training activity.

If we focus on the results, differentiating in activities with a technological base, and without a technological base, we find that the activity with the digital base that is carried out most frequently, among the teachers of Primary Education, is the *Consultation of Blogs* ($\bar{x}$ = 2.68). The one that participates to a lesser extent is in the *realization of MOOC* ($\bar{x}$ = 1.40). It should also be noted that another of the activities in which teachers are involved to a lesser extent to develop professionally is the *Blogs Design and development* ($\bar{x}$ = 1.96).

Among the activities without a technological base, that teachers perform to keep themselves updated, as the most frequent, we can find *self-reflection on daily experience* ($\bar{x}$ = 3.19); and that which is established as less frequent within this group is *the visit to other classrooms and/or other centres* ($\bar{x}$ = 1.93).

In addition, the second objective was related with the reasons behind the performance of informal activities by teachers. We propose twelve general possible reasons that could had teachers to carry out this kind of training. In the following table, we present descriptive statistics of each variable.

Table 1: Reasons for carrying out informal training activities.

	N	R	Min	Max	$\bar{x}$	TD	Asim	Curt.
To be better professionally	73	3	1	4	3.07	1.262	-.900	-.972
Because I have deficiencies in my initial training	73	3	1	4	2.16	1.000	.173	-1.224
To help my students	73	3	1	4	2.92	1.288	-.684	-1.302
To interact with other colleagues	73	3	1	4	2.45	1.236	-.023	-1.628
To innovate in my teaching methods	73	3	1	4	2.90	1.271	-.650	-1.309
To earn points to advance in my career	73	3	1	4	1.45	.943	1.826	1.812
To have many accreditations in my CV	73	3	1	4	1.26	.646	2.555	5.900
To share information and knowledge with my colleagues	73	3	1	4	2.23	1.161	.240	-1.461
To exchange resources with my colleagues	73	3	1	4	2.32	1.165	.111	-1.503
To adapt myself to the new social and education changes	73	3	1	4	2.47	1.226	-.128	-1.614
To learn new educational methodologies	73	3	1	4	2.53	1.365	-.074	-1.845
To be updated	73	3	1	4	2.67	1.334	-.307	-1.713

As we can see in Table 1, the most important reason to carry out informal training for Primary teachers is *to be better professionally* ($\bar{x}$ = 3.07), followed by: *to help students* ($\bar{x}$ = 2.92), *to innovate in teaching methods* ($\bar{x}$ = 2.92), and *to be updated* ($\bar{x}$ = 2.67). Nevertheless, we need to highlight the reasons least valued by teachers to carry out this type of training are *to earn points to advance in professional career* ($\bar{x}$ = 1.45) and *to have many accreditations in the CV* ($\bar{x}$ = 1.26).

Conclusions

From the results previously showed, we can conclude that the participants of our study do not prefer the activities based on technology to continue learning, it is still preferred the face-to-face training, according with Nunes and Meneses (2014). However, in the same way as Paniagua, Luengo, Torres Carvalho, and Casas (2017) said, the ICT became in an important tool to help teachers stay up-to-date. Online and blended training was added to the traditional face-to-face, but they have not taken their place.

The training of teachers as competent subjects for the pedagogical use of ICT has received special attention in recent years. Thus, UNESCO (2008) offers a proposal for teacher training in which it is clear that this should not only be aimed at acquiring the skills to use technological tools, but should prioritize the acquisition of skills and knowledge, both theoretical and procedural, to use them in an innovative and creative way in teaching-learning situations (Area, Borrás, & Sannicolás, 2014). That is to say, the training of teachers should not be reduced to the acquisition of instrumental competences for the use of technology, something that does occur in the Spanish context (Sancho et al., 2008).

It seems that the use of Technology for professional development has a fundamentally instrumental use for Primary Education teachers. In addition, it is assumed that they acquire the role of consumers of information, instead of producers of it. This seems to be reflected when the teachers determine as an activity (with a technological base) the frequency of *the consultation of blogs*, and, nevertheless, as one of the least frequent *the elaboration of blogs*. One of the reasons behind the fact that, almost half of the sample (49%) has never made a MOOC, may be the lack of knowledge of this type of training alternatives.

The conclusion around the second objective of this study, point out the reasons behind performing of informal training by Primary Schools teachers. The results, we have obtained, show that teachers decide to involve in this type of training in order to be better professionals, therefore, to help their students, to innovate their pedagogical methods and to be updated. All this reasons are related to intrinsic motivation. Thus, it seems that informal training, as conversations with colleagues or friends, meetings with other professionals, participating in social networks, self-training, consult digital materials, etc. are more related with intrinsic motivation. Although, on the other hand, the reasons least valued by teachers for carrying out informal activities are related to the acquisition of certificates, or any kind of external rewards. Due to this fact, we deduce that, carrying out informal training is more associated with intrinsic motivation than to extrinsic one. It has sense in the way that, teachers maybe prefer getting involved in other types of training, like formal or non-formal, in order to get external rewards. For instance, a teacher who wants to get a French language certificate, he will probably opt for a formal French language-training course, instead of doing practice sessions with a friend who knows the language.

Finally, it is necessary to comment on the limitations of this study. Fundamentally overwhelmed by the number of participants in the study. The self-report instrument can also create biases in the results. On the other hand, we propose some future research lines that could be based on deepening the data and performing correlational or inferential analyses.

References

Area, M., Borrás, J. B., & Sannicolás, B. (2014). La formación del maestro 2.0: el aprendizaje por tareas en entornos b-learning. *Revista Interuniversitaria de Formación del Profesorado, 28*(1), 51-66.

Cobo, C. & Moravec, J. (2011). *Aprendizaje Invisible. Hacia una nueva ecología de la educación.* Barcelona: Publicacions i Edicions de la Universitat de Barcelona. Retrived from: http://www.publicacions.ub.edu/ejecuta_descarga.asp?codart=07458&mp=43L41o31B75I&formato=pdf

Cross, J. (2007). *Informal Learning: Rediscovering the Natural Pathways that Inspire Innovation and Performance.* San Francisco: Pfeiffer.

Escobar-Pérez, J., & Cuervo-Martínez. A. (2008). Validez de contenido y juicio de expertos: una aproximación a su utilización. *Avances en medición, 6*, 27-36.

González-Sanmamed, M., Sangrà, A., Souto-Seijo, A., & Estévez, I. (2018). Ecologías de aprendizaje en la Era Digital: desafíos para la Educación Superior. *Publicaciones, 48*, 11-38. http://doi.org/10.30827/publicaciones.v48i1.7329

González-Sanmamed, M., Sangrà, A., Souto-Seijo, A., Santos, F., & Estévez, I. (2018). Learning Ecologies Oriented to the Professional Development of University Teachers. *Proceedings of the 10th EDEN Research Workshop, Barcelona*, 398-407.

Marcelo, C. (2002). La formación inicial y permanente de los educadores. En Consejo Escolar del Estado (Ed.), *Los educadores en la sociedad del siglo XXI* (pp.161-194). Madrid: MECD.

Martín, R. B. (2013). Contextos de aprendizaje. Formales, no formales e informales. *IKASTORRATZA e-Revista de Didáctica, 12*, 1-14. Retrieved from http://www.ehu.eus/ikastorratza/12_alea/contextos.pdf

McMillan, J. H. (2012). *Educational Research: Fundamentals for the consumer* (6th ed.). Boston: Pearson.

McMillan, J. H., & Schumacher, S. (2005). *Investigación Educativa. Una introducción conceptual* (5th ed.). Madrid: Pearson.

Nunes, R., & Meneses, A. (2014). Facebook's contribution in the process of collaborative learning. *Proceedings of the 3º Congreso Ibero-Americano en Investigación Cualitativa*, 62.

Paniagua, A., Luengo, R., Torres Carvalho, J. L., & Casas, L. M. (2017). Blended learning en la formación permanente del profesorado. Aportaciones de asesores de formación sobre modalidades formativas. RED. *Revista de Educación a Distancia, 52*, a3. http://dx.doi.org/10.6018/red/52/3

Sancho, J. M., Ornellas, A., Sánchez, J. A., Alonso, C., & Bosco, A. (2008). La formación del profesorado en el uso educativo de las TIC: una aproximación desde la política educativa. *Praxis Educativa, 12*(12), 10-22.

Schreier, M. (2018). Sampling and generalization. In U. Flick (Ed.), *The sage handbook of qualitative data collection* (pp. 84-97). London: Sage.

UNESCO (2008). ICT Competency Standards for Teachers. Retrieved from https://unesdoc.unesco.org/ark:/48223/pf0000156207

Acknowledgments

This study has been conducted in the framework of the research project (ECO4LEARN-HE), funded by the Ministry of Economy and Finance (Reference EDU2015-67907-R), and thanks to the funding received by one of the authors, Iris Estévez, in the FPI programme from the Ministry of Economy and Finance (BES-2016-077330).

Connecting through Educational Technology
Proceedings of the European Distance and E-Learning Network 2019 Annual Conference
Bruges, 16-19 June, 2019

FINDING THEIR PLACE IN THE WORLD: USING DIGITAL STORYTELLING TO UNDERSTAND THE INTERSECTIONS BETWEEN STUDENTS TECHNOLOGY USE AND THEIR WORK, LIFE, PLAY AND LEARNING

Peter Bryant, University of Sydney, Australia

Abstract

Understanding how and with your students participate in learning and how technology and social media supports that learning is a key challenge for modern higher education institutions. Learning practices intersect personal, professional and educational lives in complex, inter-connected and personally defined and managed ways. Drawing on the analysis of digital stories told by 100 students at the University of Sydney Business School, this paper will explore the unique methodological approaches of digital storytelling and student-led research to understanding how technology shapes and intersects the learning experience. It will also identify how students use technology (and especially extended forms of social media) to forms connections between their work, life, play and learning.

The challenge of understanding the student experience

How universities use information and data from students to ascertain and improve their experiences is central to most modern higher education institutional and policy frameworks on teaching and learning (Neary, 2016). Depending on the country where the University is located, this data is collected centrally by government authorities (the National Student Survey in the United Kingdom, for example) or at significant points during the student journey (near completion of a unit of study in the case of many student institution-level satisfaction surveys). Much of this data collection is directly related to the teaching activity within a degree program or specific course or unit. The collection of this data is also controversial and divisive in both the literature and in many institutions, in part as it is often used as an academic staff performance management instrument or contribute to the metricisation of education through global ranking tables or government mandated measures like the Teaching Excellence Framework in the UK (Berbegal-Mirabent, Mas-Machuca, & Marimon, 2018).

Student satisfaction surveys specifically can also profligate and sometimes reward reactive decision making by both the academics under scrutiny, the wider institutional management and the government setting the policy agenda (Klemenčič & Chirikov, 2015). Measuring student satisfaction in this way often focuses on the lowest scores and poorest performances and does not provide insights into how to scale and sustain exceptional performance (Burgess, Senior, & Moores, 2018). The information collected by these instruments locates the student in the abstract (to support the necessity of ensuring student anonymity in many cases). The student experience is reduced to measurable and comparable numbers on scales and simple free text associations related only to the delivery of unit at a single point in time (Aldemir & Gülcan, 2004). The student's story and how those experiences are related other learning experiences in different units or their holistic experience of being at University can get lost. The challenge that student satisfaction surveys fail to address is how do we as institutions understand the collective experience of higher education. How do our students engage in learning and teaching, free from the influence of attainment and success in a specific unit taken at snapshot moments?

Defining student learning

How and why our students participate in learning represents a critical challenge for higher education institutions. Learning is not bound by the seats and lecterns of the lecture theatre or the user experience of the Learning Management System. It is more than the combination of series of assessment tasks, consumed content and didactic instruction. Learning practices intersect personal, professional and educational lives in complex, inter-connected and personally defined and managed ways. Learning inhabits conversations, reflections, casual and fleeting connections, ambitions and expectations that are not always located in the classroom or even on campus. The ways in which university students engage in the activity of learning outside of the "classroom" are part determined by how curriculum, assessment and teaching (and the teacher) shape the kinds of social learning practices needed by or enforced on students to successfully complete a unit of study or programme (Huda et al., 2017; Lai, 2015). How students engage in learning has further evolved within the socially constructed environment of social media, exposing intersections between learning and the rest of a student's life and challenging and defining notions of expertise, authority, informality, expediency, immediacy and representation (Ellis & Goodyear, 2016; Greenhow & Lewin, 2016). Learning practices intersect personal, professional and educational lives in complex, inter-connected and personally defined and managed ways affording students the opportunity to make and share identity and to tell the stories of their lives to who they choose (Clark & Rossiter, 2008). Learning inhabits conversations, reflections, casual and fleeting connections, ambitions and expectations that are not always located in the classroom or even on campus (Fried & Harper, 2017; Hare, 2018). The use of technology and social media and the practices that emerge from them is at the nexus of these connections, creating personal ecosystems of engagement and relationships. Students, when engaging in learning through and with their technology and social media presence are challenging and reshaping the sources of authentic and credible knowledge through the messiness of social media mediated practices (McLoughlin & Lee, 2008). This is both as creators and makers of knowledge themselves (through social media making, remixing and repurposing (bricolage and found) and sharing for example) and as aggregators of expertise or credibility from within their own peer networks or more fleeting and searchable links to networked knowledge residing on-line (Bridgstock, 2016; Hamid, Waycott, Kurnia, & Chang, 2015).

Digital storytelling as model of engaging with students and their learning

The University of Sydney Business School (USBS) is a faculty of the University of Sydney, Australia and is one of the leading Business Schools in the Asia-Pacific region. It has over 16000 students, across a range of undergraduate and postgraduate programs. It delivers specialisations in areas such as Accounting and Finance, Management, Human Resources and emerging areas such as Big Data, International Business and Supply Chain Management. The scope and scale of the educational offering have made community development challenging at the School. Students are distributed across a large and sprawling campus, in fractured groups and classes that do not afford many opportunities to connect and build strong links with a cohort. With student experience surveys focusing on specific classes, the capacity to explore and understand the holistic student experience was critical. We needed to expose the impacts of technology, the ways in which students interacted with each other and the engagement they sought and made with the School and the community. Building on the model of student conversations that had been piloted at the London School of Economics since 2015 (Bryant, 2017; Liote & Axe, 2016), the Work. Live. Play. Learn project (WLPL) was started in 2018 to provide an opportunity for students to tell their story and have that shared with colleagues, academics and the wider community. The heart of the project was the recording of conversations with one hundred USBS students over a one-month period in situ around the campus. These conversations were led by a former student (working as a research assistant) and three current students of the School, giving the project an ethnography-like feel, with students from within the community leading the storytelling. The conversations were conducted with individuals or small groups of students and were recorded on video to make the artefacts shareable and lasting. The use of video and high-quality audio changed the dynamic of the conversation, with students knowing that the words they used, and their images would be shared. The result was fifty-five stories featuring one hundred students from across all our programs and over forty-one hours of video.

This application of digital storytelling methodology represented a form of social pedagogy, where interaction, engagement and learning emerged from the telling of asynchronous and sometimes disconnected stories shared widely with participants and the wider community (Benmayor, 2008; Stewart, 2017). Sociality and social constructivism informed how other students located themselves in the institutional community, both through the consumption of the stories of other students but more importantly, through the telling of them to others (Yang & Wu, 2012). These stories represented encounters between students that may never have happened without the intervention of the project. The use of digital stories provided an opportunity to share human insights into learning, a concept often blurred by the metrics of satisfaction and outcomes (Robin, 2016; Stewart & Ivala, 2017). This project created fleeting encounters between students and their stories, which we hoped would provide insights to both themselves and the institution to make education better.

Using the same small group of student researchers and using thematic and content analysis, the conversations were interpreted to expose the lived authentic experiences of our students and show the connections and linkages between their experiences and uses of technology. It was also critical that students who shared their stories were not seen as data or in the abstract, but as active and identifiable members of the community, and that their insights would be used to better their (and others) learning experiences. Four key questions informed both the digital storytelling aspect of the project and the ensuing analysis:

- What are our students lived and authentic experiences of learning?
- How do our students react/respond to the requirements placed upon by us?
- How do they balance the intersections and tensions of work, life and play on learning?
- What role does technology and social media play in all this?

Authentic experiences and the role of technology

The core principle of WLPL was to explore and understand how students lived and authentic experiences of learning and locate those stories within the fuzzy boundaries of what it means to study at USBS. Whilst the School has structured the student experience within the traditional mechanisms of qualifications, majors, specialisations and requirements, learning for our students was described in their stories as a far more complex process. Achieving a degree, passing a unit or completing an assessment placed pressures and expectations on our students, ranging from time and deadlines, to group engagement and problem solving through to competing priorities channelled into single unitary windows of submission or performance. For many students, studying with the School was a multi-year commitment, rent with uncertainty and change; moving homes or countries, finding themselves in new and unfamiliar places, having to study, learn and live adult lives. There was not a single or common purpose or motivation amongst our students for coming to University, or what they wanted to achieve at the end of it. There were no common sets of skills or knowledge that informed practices or behaviours or prepared them for the pressures of living their lives. Expectations of the kinds of support, structures or pastoral care that the University could provide were contested, sometimes contradictory and critical. The types of activity (such as assessment) they were undertaking as students were in equal parts scaffolded and underprepared for. The student's stories revealed varying states of transition, with the impacts of uncertainty, development, growth and reflection often starkly (and critically) described. These states of transition effected how they engaged with their learning and how they interacted with other students, academics and their discipline. Technology played a critical part in shaping and coping with the transition, acting as a both a catalyst for change and the balancing force between two uncertain states. The analysis identified three examples of these transient and uncertain states, aligned with dichotomous perspectives on social engagement and interaction, use of technology, teaching and learning, work and career and identity as a person and professional. What emerged were complex, intersecting narratives describing personal pathways through their work, life, play and learning. Whilst our students shared the experience of being in transition, there were significant differences in how they got here, how they coped with being in transition and how they planned their way out into more defined and stable places. There were also substantive differences in what role they saw for themselves, technology and social media, their academics and the institution in supporting, facilitating or challenging their transition.

Alone/Together

Social interaction, engagement and connections were at the core of many of our student's stories, both in the context of learning and teaching, but equally in how they understood their university experience:

> *"You talk to people in class and stuff, and that's all right. But in between classes, especially if you have long breaks, you don't really know who to talk to. You don't really know where to go. I remember my first semester, just wandering around, not really knowing what to do."*

As their university experience progressed our students acquired new skills, different sets of connections and engagements with people and learn from their experiences. Students were pragmatic about the importance of a social network; some so that they could engage with others, others to do group work and share and for others, the opportunity to discuss thorny or challenging issues or problems in order to find the best or most strategic solutions:

> *"One thing I want after completing my degree is to be able to work independently. And by this, I meant not by myself. But just being able to know what to do in situations that maybe I wouldn't be able to handle, before I came to university. And just knowing how to approach different situations with – what kind of strategies to use and things."*

Social media was an interesting lens through which transition was observed. One student deleted many of their social media accounts when they moved from their home country to Australia, as social media reminded them of all the social contacts and networks they were missing out on. Even though they shared their sense of isolation and loneliness in their story, being connected on social media amplified those feelings rather than abrogating them.

Life/Job

This was an interesting example of the state of transition being described by our students. One of the common conceptions of higher education is that it is designed to deliver job-ready graduates with an agile set of skills as defined (and required) by industry. Whilst many of the students discussed the type of job or career they anticipated having after they graduate, there was significant uncertainty about where their degree would take them. Even though a Business degree by its nature is both generalist and specific, many of the students talked about how the degree would help them live their lives, achieve their hopes and dreams or achieve ambitions that were not specifically related to that important "first job":

> *"Well, I think by doing a commerce degree here, I do want to try and be my own – you know, like an entrepreneur. Create my own business. I mean, that being said, it is quite far into the future. So I'm not entirely sure just yet. But I like to think I can get, given the skills that allow me to pursue that path, should I want to."*

Many of the students described how the degree will make them more mobile, support portfolio careers, facilitate travel and international experiences. Running counter to the notions of job-ready graduates, these students wanted to use their university experiences and technology to be life ready, developing skills that were transferable across contexts and industries:

> *"I think, personally, I want to go and see the world first. And with my degree I feel like I don't want to go through a straight-line career path through business, move up the ladder. I want to do something creative, maybe join a start-up business, maybe do something along those lines. But not necessarily heavy numbers, heavy bookkeeping, heavy work like that."*

Finally, the importance of networks and connections was a prominent theme in many stories. Students were critical of the value of friend or click aggregation on sites like LinkedIn, instead valuing networks that supported their career or life ambitions and supported the development of lasting connections:

> *"I'm (not) like, oh, hey, I added X amount of people on LinkedIn or made X amount of friends. It was more just a different way of viewing where I can see myself long term in both my professional career and personal life as well. Because sometimes at uni, you're kind of stuck in your own little bubble."*

Teaching/Learning

Teaching and learning represented very visible lenses through which to explore transition. The exploration of a student's personal learning journey, with its requisite set of choices and decisions about which teaching and learning resources and activities to access and prioritise was another way in which transition was described. Not necessarily located within solely reflective frames, personal learning choices represented pragmatic decisions often made in relation to the pressures of work, life and play on learning, but also made based on the skills and knowledge they believed they needed for success:

> *"To be honest, I don't think it's (online recording of lectures) helpful to me personally because it's a different interaction when you come to lectures and when you watch them online. Even when I'm trying to retain the information, I feel like I retain better information when I go to the face-to-face lectures*

> *rather than online lectures. Because it's so easy to get distracted when you're online and you have all of these tabs open and everything."*

Conclusions

Writers such as Palmer, O'Kane, and Owens (2009) have described the first-year student experience transition as a betwixt state, where students are in-between spaces without feeling like legitimate members of the University community. Rooted in the imperative to succeed that permeates modern higher education, transition has become a byword for facilitating that success and minimising attrition (and maximising attainment). As Baker and Stirling (2016) note:

> *"'Transition' has become a powerful discourse around the processes of change that are negotiated as students move between different educational spaces (in the cases described here, school and university), which involve many aspects of the individual's experience (physical, social, cultural, economic, emotional, educational, disciplinary, professional." (Baker & Stirling, 2016; pp.46-47)*

The stories told by our students describe their transition within complex constructs of their experiences at our School. They told of their issues with sociality, with integration, with identify, with direction and ambition and with expectation. These were not simply rooted in the classroom or the way they are assessed. Their experiences at our School are technological, cultural, social, economic, disciplinary and pragmatic. But it was equally evident that each of these experiences was part of the journey of the student through their betwixt states, building confidence, leveraging their technology and social media presences and identifying insights and advice for the students to come after them. It is, in the truest definition of liminality, a rite of passage between pre-liminal and post-liminal states that create community in part generated by a shared uncertainty about the journey and destination (Turner, 1977; 1987).

Our students' digital stories described their location within a variety of liminal spaces (personal, professional, cultural, technological and educational) that intersected their common expectations of engaging in higher education. It was clear that for some of our students being in these liminal spaces was disruptive and uncomfortable. It was also clear through the that for the students in the early stages of their experience at the School, the skills required to build and develop connections that might bind them together with other people in similar liminal transition states were nascent. Many of the students told us how they relied on the School to provide the fertile contexts to meet people, develop and understand the connections between places, authorities and knowledge. It was through this that our students learnt how to build and maintain connections and friends, how to break and adjust them when necessary, and where to apply the technology they owned or we provided them with (group work was a good example of this) and ultimately find commonality and difference and form lasting bonds. But equally they rarely relied on us to provide the ways and platforms through which they forged and maintained those connections.

Students with more experience of education and the School demonstrated clearly in their stories a desire to help other students with their transition or to provide them with ways to benefit from their experiences. It was one of the unintended outcomes of this project. The digital storytelling methodology provided a lasting artefact to students that they could use to make their experiences and insights widely shared with emerging colleagues and networks. It could be argued that it was both the experiences of making these broader spans of connections between work, life, play and learning, and the opportunity to reflect and share them that contributed towards their progressions towards a more certain, less transitional post liminal state. Learning in both its transdisciplinary form, as well as the more specific discipline level learning is a part of their transition. The student experience literature can sometimes privilege more traditional first year experience activities such as orientation, clubs and societies, icebreakers and other pre-disciplinary exposures as critical to determining the student experience (often as measured in student experience/satisfaction surveys). From our stories, learning and teaching played an equally critical role in forming and maintaining connections and helping clarify identity, ambition and intention.

This was not a universal experience in our classes or learning experiences. There is significant opportunity to build on how these impactful experiences could help us to better define assessment, shape the kinds of examples or cases we use in class, provide better career development opportunities and interventions, how we plan Welcome Week and Open Day activities and how we better use the human and disciplinary capital extant within our lectures, tutorials, seminars, research outputs and online spaces to minimise dissonance and provide the capabilities for students to move through transitory states. Our learning and teaching can provide the opportunity test connections, experiment with pathways in and through knowledge and skills and the capacity to learn from the uncertainty and liminality. There is no benefit to our students in assuming we can eliminate all the uncertainty before they arrive. But we can create the environment that affords the opportunity to learn through liminality and transition.

References

Aldemir, C., & Gülcan, Y. (2004). Student satisfaction in higher education. *Higher education management and policy, 16*(2), 109-122.

Baker, S., & Stirling, E. (2016). Liminal Spaces, Resources and Networks: Facebook as a Shaping Force for Students' Transitions into Higher Education. *Learning and Teaching: The International Journal of Higher Education in the Social Sciences, 9*(2), 42-65.

Benmayor, R. (2008). Digital storytelling as a signature pedagogy for the new humanities. *Arts and Humanities in Higher Education, 7*(2), 188-204.

Berbegal-Mirabent, J., Mas-Machuca, M., & Marimon, F. (2018). Is research mediating the relationship between teaching experience and student satisfaction? *Studies in Higher Education, 43*(6), 973-988.

Bridgstock, R. (2016). Educating for digital futures: what the learning strategies of digital media professionals can teach higher education. *Innovations in education and teaching international, 53*(3), 306-315.

Bryant, P. (2017). *It doesn't matter what is in their hands: understanding how students use technology to support, enhance, and expand their learning in a complex world.* Paper presented at the Proceedings of the 5th International Conference on Educational Technologies (ICEduTech 2017), Sydney, Australia.

Burgess, A., Senior, C., & Moores, E. (2018). A 10-year case study on the changing determinants of university student satisfaction in the UK. *PloS one, 13*(2), e0192976.

Clark, M. C., & Rossiter, M. (2008). Narrative learning in adulthood. *New directions for adult and continuing education, 2008*(119), 61-70.

Ellis, R. A., & Goodyear, P. (2016). Models of learning space: integrating research on space, place and learning in higher education. *Review of Education, 4*(2), 149-191. doi:10.1002/rev3.3056

Fried, J., & Harper, R. (2017). *Learning Everywhere on Campus: Teaching Strategies for Student Affairs Professionals.* Routledge.

Greenhow, C., & Lewin, C. (2016). Social media and education: reconceptualizing the boundaries of formal and informal learning. *Learning, Media and Technology, 41*(1), 6-30.

Hamid, S., Waycott, J., Kurnia, S., & Chang, S. (2015). Understanding students' perceptions of the benefits of online social networking use for teaching and learning. *The Internet and Higher Education, 26*, 1-9.

Hare, R. (2018, May 2). The importance of weak ties. Hare of the Blog [Blog post]. Retrieved from https://rosiehare.com/2018/05/02/the-importance-of-weak-ties/#more-89

Huda, M., Sabani, N., Shahrill, M., Jasmi, K. A., Basiron, B., & Mustari, M. I. (2017). Empowering Learning Culture as Student Identity Construction in Higher Education. *Student Culture and Identity in Higher Education* (pp. 160-179). IGI Global.

Klemenčič, M., & Chirikov, I. (2015). How do we know how students experience higher education? On the use of student surveys. *The European Higher Education Area* (pp. 361-379). Springer.

Lai, C. (2015). Modeling teachers' influence on learners' self-directed use of technology for language learning outside the classroom. *Computers & Education, 82*, 74-83.

Liote, L., & Axe, H. (2016). *LSE 2020: Capturing the Student Voice On the Future of Educational Technology.* Retrieved from http://lti.lse.ac.uk/wp-content/uploads/2016/08/LSE2020visionReport-FINAL.pdf

McLoughlin, C., & Lee, M. J. (2008). The three p's of pedagogy for the networked society: Personalization, participation, and productivity. *International Journal of Teaching and Learning in Higher Education, 20*(1), 10-27.

Neary, M. (2016). Teaching Excellence Framework: a critical response and an alternative future. *Journal of Contemporary European Research, 12*(3).

Palmer, M., O'Kane, P., & Owens, M. (2009). Betwixt spaces: student accounts of turning point experiences in the first-year transition. *Studies in Higher Education, 34*(1), 37-54. doi:10.1080/03075070802601929

Robin, B. R. (2016). The power of digital storytelling to support teaching and learning. *Digital Education Review, 30*, 17-29.

Stewart, K. D. (2017). Classrooms as 'safe houses'? The ethical and emotional implications of digital storytelling in a university writing classroom. *Critical Studies in Teaching and Learning, 5*(1), 85-102.

Stewart, K. D., & Ivala, E. (2017). Silence, voice, and "other languages": Digital storytelling as a site for resistance and restoration in a South African higher education classroom. *British Journal of Educational Technology, 48*(5), 1164-1175.

Turner, V. (1977). Variations on a Theme of Liminality. In S. F. Moore & B. Myerhoff (Eds.), *Secular Ritual* (pp. 36-52). Amsterdam, NL: Van Gorcum.

Turner, V. (1987). Betwixt and between: The liminal period in rites of passage. In L. C. Mahdi, S. Foster, & M. Little (Eds.), *Betwixt and Between: Patterns of masculine and feminine initiation* (pp. 3-19). La Salle, IL: Open Court.

Yang, Y.-T. C., & Wu, W.-C. I. (2012). Digital storytelling for enhancing student academic achievement, critical thinking, and learning motivation: A year-long experimental study. *Computers & Education, 59*(2), 339-352.

Connecting through Educational Technology
Proceedings of the European Distance and E-Learning Network 2019 Annual Conference
Bruges, 16-19 June, 2019

FIVE YEARS OF KAHOOT! IN THE CLASSROOMS – WHAT DOES RESEARCH TELL US?

Matthias Murawski, Md Tawhid Hasan, Markus Bick, ESCP Europe Business School Berlin, Germany

Introduction

One of the current major trends in education is the integration of innovative technology. In this context, gamification – which encompasses the integration of game elements in non-gaming systems (Licorish, Owen, Daniel, & George, 2018) – plays an important role. In this paper, we consider one specific game-based learning tool: Kahoot! (Existing literature uses both options, Kahoot and Kahoot!. We select the latter as the exclamation mark belongs to the term.), which can be classified as a student response system (Plump & LaRosa, 2017). Although there are similar tools such as Socrative (www.socrative.com), Kahoot! proved to be the most played one. As stated on the company website (https://kahoot.com/company/, accessed January 29, 2019), Kahoot! reached more than 70 million unique monthly active users at the end of 2017. Around 60% of them were from the United States of America but the tool has been played all over the world. There are 60 million games available, and a total of 2 billion players have played on the Kahoot! platform since its launch. Aside from classroom settings, 97% of Fortune 500 companies use Kahoot! as of October 2018. Kahoot! was founded in Norway and published in September 2013. Thus, when preparing this article in late 2018, it has been in the classrooms for around five years.

We also use Kahoot! regularly during our lectures, for example to review the content of previous classes. Our experiences have been very positive in terms of students' motivation and increased interaction. But these are, of course, only our subjective impressions and therefore we searched for insights from academia on questions such as effects of using Kahoot! (e.g., regarding increased performance of students). During this process, we quickly learnt that an overview of academic studies on Kahoot! does not exist, which indicates a clear gap given its above-mentioned importance. In this context, Bawa (2018; p.2) even states: "However, at present, there is no literature on the use of Kahoot". We approach this gap by screening academic literature dealing with Kahoot!. After our literature search, we can decline the quote of Bawa (2018) as there is at least some academic literature, although the number is small. Nevertheless, we think that an overview of existing research on Kahoot! is valuable, particularly to identify gaps and corresponding needs for future research. Therefore, the research question (RQ) of this paper is:

- RQ: What is the current state of research on using Kahoot! in education?

This question is answered by conducting a structured literature review. For structuring the selected papers, we suggest a socio-technical perspective. This approach, which covers the dimensions: *human*, *technology*, and *organization*, is often used in the field of information systems (Laudon & Laudon, 2014) but is also suitable for the topic of this paper. Using Kahoot! in the context of education contains *humans* such as teachers and learners, but also *technology* such as devices and other technical requirements. Finally, educational institutions provide the *organizational* context. We structure our paper as follows: In section "Theoretical background", we present a brief overview of gamification in the learning context and some more details on Kahoot!. Subsequently, we explain the suggested socio-technical system. Section "Methodology" contains the main aspects of our research design. The core of the paper is section "Research findings and discussion" in which we answer our RQ. Finally, the paper ends with the section "Conclusion and outlook" in which future research opportunities are presented.

Theoretical Background

Gamification in Education – The Case of Kahoot!

Gamification describes the integration of game elements in non-gaming systems (Licorish et al., 2018) and has become popular in contexts such as education or health in the past years (e.g., Böckle, Novak, & Bick, 2017). Key elements of gamification are rewards and competition (Turan, Avinc, Kara, & Goktas, 2016). Applied to education, the implementation of gamification is found to be beneficial for academic achievement, motivation and classroom dynamics (Wang, 2015). It is important to note that gamification is different to game-based learning. The latter refers to "a pedagogical approach in which games are used to achieve educational outcomes through incidental learning", while gamification means "an integration of game elements in non-gaming systems […], which engage students and improve the experiential nature of active, intentional learning" Licorish et al. (2018; p.2).

In our study, we consider the case of Kahoot! which turned out to be a very popular game element to enrich learning since its publication in 2013. Wang (2015; p.218) describes it as follows: "Kahoot! is a game-based student response system that transforms temporarily a classroom into a game show." In this show, the teacher becomes the game host and the students become competitors. In its very basics, quiz-like questions, usually with four answer options of which one is correct, appear on the screen, and the students can select one answer using their own devices. Once all answers are submitted or the pre-defined answer time is expired, the correct answer is displayed and can be discussed. The teacher then decides when to proceed, which makes the tool very flexible. Depending on speed and accuracy, a scoreboard is calculated after every question. More details on how to apply Kahoot! in the classroom are presented by, among others, Bicen and Kocakoyun (2018) or Plump and LaRosa (2017).

Wang (2015), who is also mentioned as one of the initial Kahoot! project members, provides some insights on the theoretical background of the tool. He refers to the theory of intrinsically motivating instructions and lists the three categories to make things fun to learn: *challenge* (goals with uncertain outcomes), *fantasy* (captivate through intrinsic or extrinsic fantasy), and *curiosity* (sensor curiosity through graphics and sound, and cognitive curiosity where the player should solve something unsolved). He describes the development of Kahoot! with these categories in mind, "where the challenge is to answer unknown questions and try to beat other players, the fantasy is to be part of a game show, and the curiosity is provided both through inviting graphics and audio as well as solving a cognitive puzzle (finding the correct answer and wait to see if it was correct or not)" (Wang, 2015; p.218).

Using Kahoot! in education as a socio-technical system

We suggest structuring the topic of Kahoot! in education as a socio-technical system as depicted in Figure 1. Socio-technical systems deal with the interactions of *humans* and *technology* while also considering the *organizational* setup (Laudon & Laudon, 2014). It is therefore not about the question *technology or human?* but about the design and optimization of a mutually synchronized system. Transferred to our specific topic, we can identify some sub-categories of the three main dimensions. Regarding *technology*, related aspects are the different *devices* that can be used to play Kahoot!. In addition, there are further *technical requirements* such as a stable internet for all the players and the instructor. These two roles, also called *learners* and *teachers*, represent the sub-categories of the *human* dimension. The dimension *organization* means the *educational institution* in our setting. This dimension covers the *effects* of using Kahoot! such as increased students´ motivation and better achievements, as these belong to the overall objectives of educational institutions. Furthermore, Kahoot! can be used in different *subjects*, and it can have different *purposes* such as reviewing or introducing content.

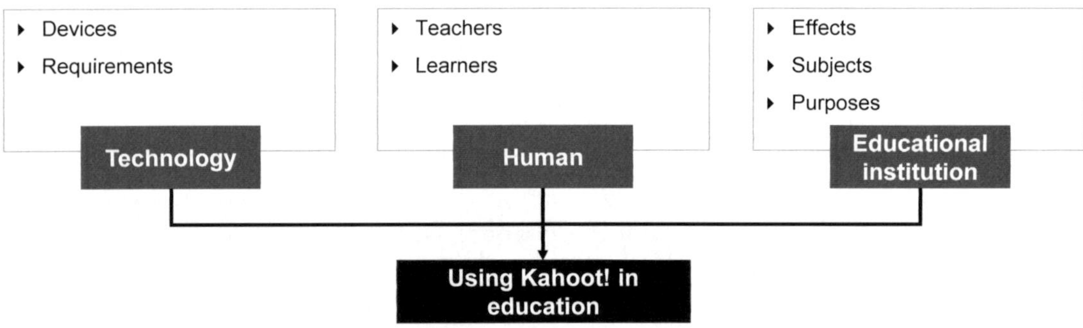

Figure 1. Kahoot! in education - a socio-technical perspective

Methodology

According to our research question, we first conducted a structured literature review (e.g., Webster & Watson, 2002) and subsequently applied a content analysis (e.g., Mayring, 2014). Table 1 provides an overview of the main parameters of the literature review.

Table 1: Overview of literature review parameters

Data bases	EBSCO, JSTOR, Google Scholar
Search terms	"Kahoot" and "Education"
Time frame	2013 – 2019 (Kahoot! started in 2013)

Language	English
Type	Academic journal articles or conference proceedings

The described search strategy initially resulted in 23 papers which indicates the very early stage of research of the topic at hand. After reading the abstracts, we excluded seven of the 23 papers because they were not relevant to our analysis. We furthermore applied a backward search (a forward search was not useful as all selected papers are very new) which yielded one additional paper that has been included in our sample. Thus, our final sample contains 17 academic publications about Kahoot! in the context of education. For the content analysis, we used the dimensions and sub-categories of the socio-technical model (see Figure 1) to assign the selected articles. We furthermore distinguished between *conceptual* and *empirical* papers. Thus, we conducted a deductive category assignment (Mayring, 2014).

Research findings and discussion

The findings of our analysis are summarized in this section and in the corresponding Table 2. We briefly mention the key aspects of each paper in an alphabetical order. Akbar (2016) generally places the focus on recent innovative technological solutions which are used in higher education. She clearly emphasizes the perspective of the educators. Pointing on Kahoot!, she particularly describes its use as an assessment tool but mentions interacting and engaging students as well: "Systems, such as […] Kahoot, […] allow educators to share interactive lessons, engage students, and view student responses in real time" (Akbar, 2016; p.3). Ares, Bernal, Nozal, Sánchez, and Bernal (2018) present an empirical study conducted with chemistry students in Spain. They found that the application of Kahoot! "has proven to be positive for the students' academic performance in a Chemistry course" (Ares et al., 2018; p.1221). They furthermore mention different devices such as smartphones, tablets, or laptops. Bawa (2018) can find similar evidence regarding the positive effects of Kahoot! in student's performance. He applied a mixed-methods analysis considering 96 American undergraduate students from introduction to business courses. He states that "additional limitations are that this study focused on learners and did not include the teachers' perceptions" (Bawa, 2018; p.11), which confirms our choice to consider the holistic socio-technical system as the framework of our study.

Bicen and Kocakoyun (2018) also consider mainly the student's perspective and present the results of their analysis of 65 undergraduates who were studying Preschool Teaching at a Turkish university. They found, amongst others, a positive impact of using Kahoot! on the motivation of the students. Interestingly, they also describe typical issues such as internet connection problems. Gonen, Sharon, and Lev-Ari (2016) discuss how innovative technology can be used to improve education of nurses in Israel and mention Kahoot! as an example for encouraging students. They integrate the perspectives of both educators and students for suggesting improvements of the nursing curriculum. By conducting a questionnaire study with 113 medical students in Malaysia, Ismail and Mohammad (2017) find that Kahoot! supports in making learning fun and enjoyable, and that it fosters motivation of the students.

They however elaborate that "Kahoot was unable to simplify complex subject matters" (Ismail & Mohammad, 2017; p.21), thereby indicating potential barriers of the game.

Aside from a very detailed and deep introduction to Kahoot! and gamification in education in general, Licorish et al. (2018) select a qualitative research design and conducted 14 interviews with students of an information systems strategy and governance course at a university in New Zealand. They find "that Kahoot!, and the use of games and gamification in general, have a positive influence on classroom dynamics, students' engagement and motivation, and ultimately, their learning" (Licorish et al., 2018; p.21). They furthermore emphasize that "challenges are still likely to remain in terms of the time needed to learn and setup these technologies, creating appropriate content, and providing students with useful and timely feedback" (Licorish et al., 2018; pp.21–22). Mehring (2016) provides a conceptual analysis of the flipped classroom and places the focus on the subject English as a foreign language. He considers both human perspectives, educator and learner, and briefly discusses Kahoot! as a "clicker" (Mehring, 2016; p.8), which is just another term for student response system. Mu and Paparas (2015) start with discussing the positive effects of using clickers in higher education (e.g., regarding performance, attention, or attendance) and the role of devices (i.e., bring your own device, byod) before presenting the findings of a study conducted with undergraduate students of economic and business environment at Harper Adams University, UK. The respondents state that they are satisfied with using Kahoot! and most of them would like to use it in other modules. Olofsson, Lindberg, and Fransson (2017) put the teacher in the centre of their study. Pointing on Kahoot!, they find a "teachers' lack of preparation for the uptake and use of ICT in the classroom and the emergence of new technological applications over time" (Olofsson et al., 2017; p.2910).

Table 2: Summary of paper analysis

	Human		Technology		Educational institution			Research type	
Paper	Teachers	Learners	Devices	Requirements	Effects	Subjects	Purposes	Conceptual	Empirical
Akbar (2016)	✓				✓			✓	
Ares et al. (2018)		✓	✓		✓	✓			✓
Bawa (2018)		✓			✓	✓	✓		✓
Bicen and Kocakoyun (2018)		✓		✓	✓	✓			✓
Gonen et al. (2016)	✓	✓				✓			✓
Ismail and Mohammad (2017)		✓			✓	✓			✓
Licorish et al. (2018)		✓			✓	✓			✓
Mehring (2016)	✓	✓				✓		✓	
Mu and Paparas (2015)		✓	✓		✓	✓			✓
Olofsson et al. (2017)	✓								✓

Plump and LaRosa (2017)	✓	✓	✓	✓	✓	✓			✓
Røkenes and Krumsvik (2016)	✓	✓							✓
Turan et al. (2016)		✓			✓	✓			✓
Veljković Michos (2017)	✓	✓	✓	✓	✓	✓	✓	✓	
Wang (2015)		✓			✓	✓			✓
Wang and Lieberoth (2016)		✓			✓	✓			✓
Yapıcı and Karakoyun (2017)	✓				✓	✓			✓
Total	8	14	4	3	13	14	2	3	14

The paper of Plump and LaRosa (2017) is probably the most-cited one in the fairly new research field around Kahoot!. They provide both a comprehensive overview of the tool and corresponding advantages and disadvantages (such as limited characters for questions). Their empirical study is focused on students (undergraduate and graduate students in two different business courses), but they also make useful suggestions for instructors. Aside from increased comprehension and motivation of the learners, they find, amongst others, that Kahoot! increases the engagement from "even the most introverted" (Plump & LaRosa, 2017; p.157) students. Røkenes and Krumsvik (2016) investigate digital competencies of Norwegian teachers. Interestingly, they combine the human perspectives teacher and learner as their case study considers "four cohorts of postgraduate student teachers taking an ESL (English as a second language) didactics course". Kahoot! is mentioned as an example that is often shown as a valuable tool during the study programme, but the teachers criticize the missing reasoning and background information. Turan et al. (2016) analyse the answers of Turkish students of an information technologies and software course. Kahoot! is applied as the gamification element. They, amongst others, elaborate that Kahoot! users reach higher achievements.

Veljković Michos (2017) covers most of the dimensions of the socio-technical system. She presents different purposes of using Kahoot!, i.e., "flipped classroom", "icebreaker activity", and "review activity" (Veljković Michos, 2017; p.514). Furthermore, both teachers and learners and different technical aspects are briefly mentioned. The main added value of the paper of Wang (2015) is the comparison of results from students using Kahoot! for the first time in a single motivational lecture versus using Kahoot! in every lecture in a class for five months. Through applying quasi-experiments with 252 Norwegian students, he elaborates a decrease in classroom dynamics while engagement, motivation, and learning remain high after using Kahoot! repeatedly which underscores the high value of this tool for keeping students' attention. Wang and Lieberoth (2016) conduct a study on 593 Norwegian software engineering students to investigate the impact of points and audio when applying Kahoot! in class. They find statistically significant differences for concentration, engagement, enjoyment, and motivation. Furthermore, they observed in the classroom that "audio and music affects the classroom dynamics in a significant positive way, and points also contribute to improve the classroom dynamics but to a more limited extend" (Wang & Lieberoth, 2016; p.746). Yapıcı and Karakoyun (2017) investigate the effects of using Kahoot! on Turkish Biology teachers and find an increased motivation of the teachers. However, they also discuss some negative aspects such as "students' insufficient technological skills" (Yapıcı & Karakoyun, 2017; p.397).

Looking at the total counts per dimensions (see Table 2) enables us to better understand the current state of research. On the meta level, the focus is placed on the dimensions: *human* and *educational institution* while, so far, less research efforts are put on *technical* aspects. Most of the articles put the *learner* in the centre of interest while only three out of 14 exclusively analyse the *teachers*' perspective. Also, *effects* of using Kahoot! are part of most of the papers (13 out of 17). Most studies are furthermore very context-specific, meaning that a concrete *subject* is considered. The *purpose* of using Kahoot! is hardly investigated. Regarding the research type, 14 out of 17 papers are of *empirical* nature. However, it must be noted that in most cases relatively small samples were collected and analysed. Exceptions are particularly Wang (2015) as well as Wang and Lieberoth (2016), who work with larger samples.

Conclusion and Outlook

The overall objective of this paper was to elaborate the current state of research on using Kahoot! in education. This objective has been reached by conducting a structured literature review and a subsequent content analysis. The main findings are summarized in Table 2. Despite its practical importance and dispersion, our analysis reveals that research around Kahoot! is still in an early stage. This is firstly indicated by the very small number of academic articles dealing with Kahoot!. Secondly, existing articles place the focus on specific aspects of the socio-technical system while other also important aspects are neglected, which, in turn, paves the way for further research opportunities. This is especially true for *technical* questions around Kahoot!. For example, does the *type of device* (i.e., mobile, tablet, laptop) have an influence on the mostly positive effects of using Kahoot!? Or could a change of device even increase attention in specific settings? Also, *technical requirements* such as a sound internet connection even for large student groups or the availability of sound systems are hardly picked out as a central theme. Regarding the *educational institutions*, there seems to be a kind of agreement on the *effects* of the use of Kahoot! which are generally found to be positive. However, except for Wang (2015), differences between short-, medium-, and long-term effects are not researched yet. Thus, future research could be focused on longitudinal studies to fill this gap. Also, the *purpose* of using Kahoot! is associated to interesting questions, but rarely exists in current research. For example, how could Kahoot! be applied or – if required – modified in the context of distance learning? What is furthermore completely neglected in research so far is the use of Kahoot! in companies, e.g., for training purposes. This topic seems to be highly relevant, given that almost all Fortune 500 companies use Kahoot!. Future research could start with case studies to explore related questions. Finally, considering the *human* dimension, we believe that more efforts are necessary to better equip the *teachers* with, for example, competencies to apply Kahoot! appropriately which is linked to the topic of digital competencies in general (Murawski & Bick, 2017). In addition, scholars should try to generate more generalizable results, for instance, through studies with larger samples or cross-subject analyses. This would contribute to a better overall understanding of Kahoot!.

References

Akbar, M. (2016). Digital Technology Shaping Teaching Practices in Higher Education. *Frontiers in ICT, 3*, 1–5. https://doi.org/10.3389/fict.2016.00001

Ares, A. M., Bernal, J., Nozal, M. J., Sánchez, F. J., & Bernal, J. (2018). Results of the use of Kahoot! gamification tool in a course of Chemistry. *Proceedings of the 4th International Conference on Higher Education Advances (HEAd'18). Valencia: Universitat Politècnica València.* https://doi.org/10.4995/HEAd18.2018.8179

Bawa, P. (2018). Using Kahoot to Inspire. *Journal of Educational Technology Systems, 47*(3), 1-18. https://doi.org/10.1177/0047239518804173

Bicen, H., & Kocakoyun, S. (2018). Perceptions of Students for Gamification Approach: Kahoot as a Case Study. *International Journal of Emerging Technologies in Learning, 13*, 72. https://doi.org/10.3991/ijet.v13i02.7467

Böckle, M., Novak, J., & Bick, M. (2017). Towards adaptive gamification: a synthesis of current developments. *Proceedings of the 25th European Conference on Information Systems (ECIS), Guimarães, Portugal, 2017*, 158–174.

Gonen, A., Sharon, D., & Lev-Ari, L. (2016). Integrating Information Technology's competencies into academic nursing education – An action study. *Cogent Education, 3*, 686. https://doi.org/10.1080/2331186X.2016.1193109

Ismail, M. A.-A., & Mohammad, J. A.-M. (2017). Kahoot: A Promising Tool for Formative Assessment in Medical Education. *Education in Medicine Journal, 9*, 19–26. https://doi.org/10.21315/eimj2017.9.2.2

Laudon, K. C., & Laudon, J. P. (2014). *Management Information Systems: Managing the Digital Firm* (13th ed., Global edition). Boston: Pearson.

Licorish, S. A., Owen, H. E., Daniel, B., & George, J. L. (2018). Students' perception of Kahoot!'s influence on teaching and learning. *Research and Practice in Technology Enhanced Learning, 13*, 1–23. https://doi.org/10.1186/s41039-018-0078-8

Mayring, P. (2014). *Qualitative content analysis: theoretical foundation, basic procedures and software solution.* Retrieved from http://www.ssoar.info/ssoar/handle/document/39517

Mehring, J. (2016). Present Research on the Flipped Classroom and Potential Tools for the EFL Classroom. *Computers in the Schools, 33*, 1–10. https://doi.org/10.1080/07380569.2016.1139912

Mu, H., & Paparas, D. (2015). Incorporating the advantages of clickers and mobile devices to teach Economics to non-economists. *Cogent Economics & Finance, 3*, 233. https://doi.org/10.1080/23322039.2015.1099802

Murawski, M., & Bick, M. (2017). Digital competences of the workforce – a research topic? *Business Process Management Journal, 23*, 721–734. https://doi.org/10.1108/BPMJ-06-2016-0126

Olofsson, A. D., Lindberg, J. O., & Fransson, G. (2017). What do upper secondary school teachers want to know from research on the use of ICT and how does this inform a research design? *Education and Information Technologies, 22*, 2897–2914. https://doi.org/10.1007/s10639-017-9590-5

Plump, C. M., & LaRosa, J. (2017). Using Kahoot! in the Classroom to Create Engagement and Active Learning: A Game-Based Technology Solution for eLearning Novices. *Management Teaching Review, 2*, 151–158. https://doi.org/10.1177/2379298116689783

Røkenes, F. M., & Krumsvik, R. J. (2016). Prepared to teach ESL with ICT? A study of digital competence in Norwegian teacher education. *Computers & Education, 97*, 1–20. https://doi.org/10.1016/j.compedu.2016.02.014

Turan, Z., Avinc, Z., Kara, K., & Goktas, Y. (2016). Gamification and Education: Achievements, Cognitive Loads, and Views of Students. *International Journal of Emerging Technologies in Learning, 11*, 64. https://doi.org/10.3991/ijet.v11i07.5455

Veljković Michos, M. (2017). Gamification in Foreign Language Teaching: Do You Kahoot? In A. Milenković, M. Veinović, Z. Konjović, D. Cvetković, M. Šarac, A. Jevremović, . . . V. Miškovic (Eds.), *Proceedings of the International Scientific Conference - Sinteza 2017* (pp. 511–516). Belgrade, Serbia: Singidunum University. https://doi.org/10.15308/Sinteza-2017-511-516

Wang, A. I. (2015). The wear out effect of a game-based student response system. *Computers & Education, 82*, 217–227. https://doi.org/10.1016/j.compedu.2014.11.004

Wang, A. I., & Lieberoth, A. (2016). The effect of points and audio on concentration, enagagement, enjoyment, learning, motivation, and classroom dynamics using Kahoot! *Proceedings from the 10th European Conference of Game Based Learning, Reading, UK*, 737–748.

Webster, J., & Watson, R. T. (2002). Analyzing the past to prepare for the future: Writing a literature review. *MIS Quarterly, 26*, xiii–xxiii.

Yapıcı, İ.Ü., & Karakoyun, F. (2017). Gamification in Biology Teaching: A Sample of Kahoot Application. *Turkish Online Journal of Qualitative Inquiry, 8*, 396–414. https://doi.org/10.17569/tojqi.335956

Connecting through Educational Technology
Proceedings of the European Distance and E-Learning Network 2019 Annual Conference
Bruges, 16-19 June, 2019

VIRTUAL REALITY TRAINING FOR AVIATION MAINTENANCE, REPAIR AND OVERHAUL (VI-MRO 1.0)

Joke Van Vooren, VIVES University of Applied Sciences, Belgium

MRO aviation is struggling

The economic crisis of 2008–2013 had a huge impact on the industry and this was no different within aviation. During this period the number of recruitments within the industry was kept on a bare minimum, resulting in an ageing workforce today. According to the Q4 2017 Educavia survey on the employment by age and sector over 46% of the staff in the Aviation Maintenance, Repair and Overhaul (MRO) sector in Belgium and the Netherlands is over 50 years old. The sector indicates to be looking for extra and "younger" aviation mechanics to guarantee the continuity of the sector, but is announcing at the same time that there simply aren't enough suitable candidates.

In the meanwhile, the future within aviation is looking brighter. The European aviation industry is expected to grow by 5% a year. As a result, more and newer aircraft are being put into service. This next generation of aircrafts are quieter, have the latest technologies on board, are made of lightweight materials and emit less CO_2 than other units of the same size. The introduction of these innovative technologies changes the landscape for aviation mechanics and the nature of their job.

Consequently, the MRO sector is sounding the alarm as they aren't able to optimise their workforce, not in number not in knowledge and experience in terms of approaching innovative technologies.

To make matters worse, the fierce competition within the aviation industry to keep flying affordable puts the operational costs under constant pressure. As the Maintenance, Repair and Overhaul (MRO) usually amounts to 10-15% of the operational costs, the MRO sector is constantly looking for new opportunities to be more time- and cost-efficient, in addition to existing challenges.

The solution for this wide range of challenges within the MRO sector lies in the application of virtual technology.

Virtual Reality Training as a solution

The use of Virtual Reality (VR) as a training tool is well known and various studies have already shown its added value in numerous areas. This has not gone unnoticed within the aviation industry.

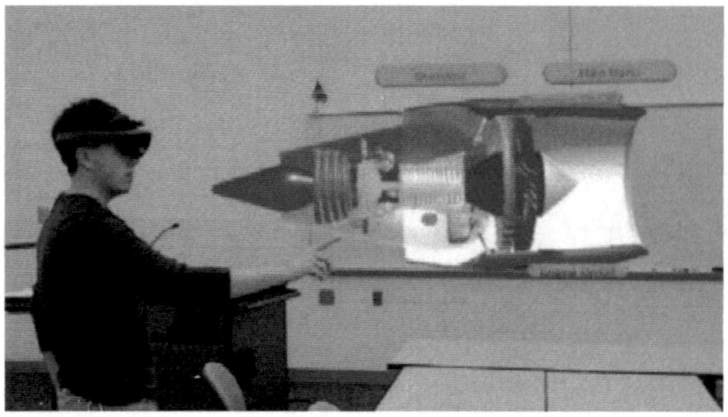

Figure 1.

Various aircraft manufacturers and world-class airlines have started test projects and, based on the results, have introduced VR within their organisation to improve training efficiency, reduce risks, speed up maintenance processes, etc.

Figure 2.

Boeing, for example, is of the opinion that VR training reduces training time by 75% per person by literally getting to grips with the procedure, thanks to the so-called *learning by doing* principle.

VR training benefits for Aviation Maintenance Repair and Overhaul (MRO) in specific:

- *Increase in effectiveness.* The key selling point of VR training is its ability to create highly immersive environments. Greater immersion increases the retention rate and since the trainees can practice their skills as many times as needed, the knowledge becomes part of their muscle memory too.
- *Elimination of risk for people and material.* As novices are the most likely to make mistakes, they need a safe place to practice their skills until they are confident in them and VR training provides just that. This way the unexperienced aviation mechanic can't lose his/her fingers, but also the 8-million-euro aircraft engine can't get damaged.
- *Endless repeatability.* Trainees can repeat exercises as often as required or desired. This way the "young" aircraft mechanic can get to grips with the procedure. But also the more experienced aircraft mechanic can refresh the specific procedure before having to perform it in real-life under time pressure.

- *Increased flexibility.* VR training is an on-the-job-training for which the aircraft does not even be on the ground. In this way, trainees can already gain knowledge and experience with new technologies that – as a matter of speak – are still on the drawing board.
- *More affordable training.* Official multi-day MRO training courses in official training centres abroad go hand in hand with a considerable loss in time and money. Also the in-house on-the-job-training requires large modular spaces for large and expensive equipment, needing constant renewal. Taking all this in consideration, makes VR training very affordable.

Figure 3.

These are a few of the features that make VR training so much better than regular old instructional based training. As the technology evolves, more immersive training solutions will emerge allowing people to train faster, better and cheaper than ever before.

Despite the fact that many aviation companies have put VR training into use, experienced and confirmed the benefits of it, none of them offers it to their customers.

Figure 4.

In response to the needs within the Flemish-Dutch MRO sector, the research group Aviation of VIVES campus VLOC in Ostend has taken up the challenge and started this Vi-MRO project within the Interregions project Educavia. Together with potential end-users, MRO companies within the Educavia project group, bachelor students, VR and aviation experts the optimal VR MRO training will be developed.

Virtual Reality Training: Set-up

In order to result in an effective VR MRO training the most immersive implementation of virtual reality technology is needed. In such a fully-immersive simulation, hardware such as head-mounted displays and motion detecting devices are used to stimulate all of a trainees' senses. As only if it looks real and feels real, the human brain accepts the artificial, virtual environment as real.

Next to this it should be created to maximize intuitiveness as this VR MRO training will be used as on-the-job training tool for young inexperienced aviation mechanics but also for older aviation mechanics needing additional training. This was achieved by the construction of the different modules and the realisation of each module separately, as explained below.

Onboarding tutorial

The story of dealing with an innovative VR training starts from the first impression through the decision on trying and up to the actual interaction. All this process usually takes a little time but it's often crucial to set the bonds between the user and the product.

This onboarding tutorial is the first interaction with the product, the first module of the VR MRO training. It is created to smoothen the transition of the trainee from the real into the virtual world. It will help newcomers to adapt to the new environment and the use of its controllers. It is crucial that the unboarding tutorial is fun and easy to understand, so that trainees are well-informed but more importantly also triggered and interested in what is yet to come.

Tutorial

The creation of the tutorial and testing module starts with the selection of the most suitable MRO task. On the one hand, the selected MRO task must be suitable for a development in VR. On the other hand, this task must be an answer to the existing needs within the sector.

The selected maintenance task is specified to its smallest detail and translated into a VR MRO training.

In the tutorial module the level of interactivity of the trainee is kept at a minimum to allow the trainee to get acquainted with the new environment and grow into the new experience. It is crucial that even in this tutorial module, the training approaches reality as closely as possible with attention to the importance of intuitiveness. Therefore, at each step the work card with the relevant part of the procedure must remain visible while every detail is explained and demonstrated. It is also essential to emphasise the signing off of the work card after each well executed intermediate step.

Testing module

The testing module is the heart of the VR MRO training. Through immersive VR scenes and extensive interactivity, the human senses reach a sufficient belief that the digital environment is real. As of that moment the trainee will be able to interact with the environment in a natural, intuitive manner and feel part of the simulated "universe".

Figure 5.

In the testing module interactivity is key. Based upon the previous 2 modules the trainee can now demonstrate his/her knowledge of each step of the working procedure. Again it is important that the work card with the relevant part of the procedure remains visualized, as in real-life. Each step must be carried out completely and correctly by the trainee. After execution, the trainee should also have the reflex to sign off the finished part of the task.

Along the way, each action is evaluated by the system. Each mistake is identified and the correct way of working is demonstrated so that the trainee can repeat his/her action and learn from it.

Archive

In order for the trainer to get an overview of overall and individual training results a wide range of training parameters will be archived, such as trainee data, number of training sessions, time needed, problems etc. These data will also be used to evaluate possible issues within the VR MRO training.

Virtual Reality Training: Optimization

A differentiated test panel of potential end users – namely Flemish, Dutch, young, older aircraft mechanics with different knowledge levels – will be selected amongst the partner MRO companies and VIVES aviation bachelor students. These potential end-users will participate in test trainings to evaluate the (interim) result from concept to end product. Based on their iterative feedback, possible product modifications will be investigated to achieve the most optimal VR MRO training for the end user.

Continuation

The technological and operational knowledge developed will be included in the curriculum of VIVES Aviation Bachelor in the field of Industrial Sciences and Technology. This will give the course "MRO Aircraft Maintenance" more practical added value through the availability of digital tools. This is an important preparation for the moment that EASA, the European regulator, allows VR/AR as a recognised training tool.

The Vi-MRO project will be completed by the end of the 2018-2019 academic year, so intermediate and final results shall be available at the 28th Eden Conference in Bruges 16-19 June 2019.

References

Airbus' Training (Oct 2017). Maintenance Training – Reaching new horizons together

Boeing (n.d.). Introducing the 737 MAX 10. Retrieved from http://www.boeing.com/commercial/737max10/index.page#/videos/employees-use-virtual-reality-for-737-max-10-preparations

Educavia (n.d.). https://educavia.eu/about-educavia

European Commission (2012). *Transport: New horizons for EU aviation.* Retrieved from http://europa.eu/rapid/press-release_IP-12-1027_en.htm

Farra, S., Miller, E., Timm, N., & Schafer, J. (2013). Improved training for disasters using 3-D virtual reality simulation. *Western Journal of Nursing Research, 35*(5), 655-671.

Houtkamp, J. M., & Bos, F.A. (2007). Evaluation of a virtual scenario training for leading firefighters. *Proceedings of the 4th International ISCRAM Conference*, 565-570. Delft, the Netherlands.

IATA's Maintenance Cost Task Force (Nov 2018). IATA Airline Maintenance Cost – Executive commentary. Chapter 1.3

Kishore, A. (2017, June 6). Boeing: Productive VR Cuts Training Time by 75%. LightReading [Blog post]. Retrieved from https://www.lightreading.com/video/video-services/boeing-productive-vr-cuts-training-time-by-75-/d/d-id/733756

Reality (n.d.). The Ultimate Guide to Understanding Virtual Reality (VR) Technology. Retrieved from https://www.realitytechnologies.com/virtual-reality/

Connecting through Educational Technology
Proceedings of the European Distance and E-Learning Network 2019 Annual Conference
Bruges, 16-19 June, 2019

TEACHERS' AND STUDENTS' VIEWS ON THE EFFECTIVENESS OF TECHNOLOGY INTEGRATION INTO TEACHING AND LEARNING IN MUSCAT, OMAN

Adenike Adeyemi, Evdokia Pittas, Unicaf University, Cyprus

Abstract

This cross-sectional study examined primary and secondary teachers' and students' views regarding the effectiveness of technology integration into teaching and learning in Muscat, Oman. The target group consisted of teachers (N = 44) and students (N = 219) from two bilingual and two international schools in Oman. Results showed that both teachers and students enjoy the use of technology in teaching and learning and they similarly evaluate the appropriateness and effectiveness of available technologies. The majority of teachers agreed that teaching has become easier and faster with technology and that students' academic performance is enhanced. Although most of the teachers are positive about the role of technology in Education, only a small percentage integrate technology into teaching and very few teachers have ever been trained to use technology in classroom. Factors hindering technology integration among others concern curriculum design, network issues, time constraint and other. A great number of students use technology to complete school work and they agree that technology tools are inadequate in their school. This study makes theoretical and practical educational implications. In theory, the study contributes to our understanding of the reasons why teachers' and students' find it challenging to use technological innovations in the educational setting. In practice, the study provides educational authorities with suggestions on how technology can be used to support, enhance and extend the curriculum.

Introduction

The aim of this paper is to discuss the impact of technology integration in education. More specific, the aim of this study was to examine the type of technologies the primary and secondary school students perceive as effective for teaching and learning and the teachers'-students' perception of effective teaching and learning with technology in Oman.

Numerous works have been done by a lot of researchers on teaching and learning effectively in the past decades. For teaching to be effective, strategies must be put in place. Methods of teaching are constantly changing and ways to improve learning and teaching are in high demand. For instance, Ansari and Malik's (2013) discussed the effective attributes a 21st century teacher/classroom should have and the need to keep "abreast with the advancement, expansion and growth" of the technologies that are introduced (Ansari & Malik, 2013; p.67). Kivunja (2014) discussed the attributes teachers need to teach effectively in other to equip students with the right skills that can sustain them in life after school. Another paper discussing teachers' effectiveness is Education Development Trust (2016).

Alemu's (2014) mixed methods research that used two population groups (students & instructors) shed lights on the qualities that improves the importance and qualities of education through various teaching practices. Similarly, another study that employed a multiple case study approach by Gebre, Saroyan, and Aulls (2015) discusses professors' perception of technology use (computer in an active learning classroom) in relation to conceptions of effective teaching. In a like manner, Scott (2015) advocates that for transferability to occur between teachers and students, technology should be integrated into learning through the application of skills and learning practices in multiple situations and context. For instance, Raymond (2016; p.73) views teaching as an outcome of learning, she defines teaching as "... the process of carrying out those activities that experience has shown to be effective in getting students to learn".

Andrew and Jones (2015) affirm that mobile phone is universally accepted (by the university students) and it facilitates collaborative learning. This qualitative study investigated students' use of the mobile devices through a seminar. The students' participants of the study are 68 composing of 18 studying BA (Hons) in Primary Initial Teacher Education and 50 studying BA (Hons) in Education Studies). The researchers asked the participants if they use their mobile devices only for academic purpose or other activities. The study participants showed they know the "proper" use of the devices and appreciate the collaborative learning environment mobile has allowed them. Such as making videos and taking photos of group. A finding worth noting is the participants have different ways of managing the use of their devices to meet their academic needs. However, the authors suggested the use of personal mobile devise for learning be revisited for further research due to mixed perceptions of mobile use.

Various studies have enumerated the role technologies play in education. The Office of Educational Technology (2017) discuss that technology integration in education motivates learners, encourage personised learning, help learners to learn beyond the classroom and inspires learners to pursue their passion and interest. It closes the digital divide between the teachers and the learners. Also, it is used to engage learners that find learning difficult or boring. It aids collaboration between learners and their peers and teachers and their colleagues. These views are similarly discussed by Ahmad and Nisa (2016) and Learning Forward (2014). In addition to the similarity of these studies, Li et al. (2015) research participants state that technology integration encourages students' participation in class activities and it makes lessons more exciting and comprehensible.

While there have been extensive researches on the roles of technology in the classroom, there are arguments that education is a continuing process that goes beyond the classroom. Suleman (2011) conducted a survey to investigate the role of educational technology in primary schools. The author enumerates five roles educational technology plays. The research states educational technology provides continuing education, gives equal opportunity in education, solves the problem of mass education by easily providing access to a large number of students at a time, improves the standard of teaching by providing rich instructional materials and media accessibility for learning. Additionally, it allows personalised instructions.

Arguments favouring technology integration in education confirms it is very fast and easily accessible when compared to a paper textbook. Katz and Gandel (2008) as cited in Okoro, Hausman, and Washington (2012; p.295) state that "...Often the most practical and freshest information now resides online, rather than in textbooks or libraries.". However, technology is difficult to use if the teachers do not properly plan before the class. Advocates for technology as an instrument that makes both teachers' and students' work easier are Mac Callum et al. (2014) and Ghavifekr et al. (2016). Ghavifekr et al. (2016) in particular, asserts that technology in education improves work performance and work productivity. Also, it is more effective than paper-based learning since it helps to do the work faster. The ease of access it provides gives the users and teachers positive perceptions of its usefulness.

As important as students' participation is in a class so is learners' willingness to work in teams. Peer work may come as an in-class activity or home-based project that requires learners work hand in hand when they are given a task. For example, Okoro et al. (2012) discuss that educational technology like Web 2.0 is used to support collaborative learning among students. More so, teachers use it to keep track of students' discussions. At the same time, it expands teachers' capability of merging ideas, course contents and concepts in the class. In another study, Li et al. (2015) consider the integration of technologies in a classroom to be advantageous because it produces *rich resources* and *visual effects*. While this is true, students may be distracted by it (Andrew & Jones, 2015).

This section showed that education has benefited a lot from the use of technology. Nevertheless, a lot of barriers still hinder technology efficacy in education. Lisenbee (2016; p.115) asserts that the only way to change how teachers and learners feel about technology is to give them adequate training which increases their self-confidence. However, UNESCO (2015; p.8) warns that although educational technologies provide new remarkable opportunities in learning, still, technology alone does not guarantee successful learning participation. In view of the need for more cross-sectional studies to investigate students' and teachers' perceptions regarding the use of technology in Education in order to interpret their attitudes towards technology, the present study sets to investigate the impact of technologies in teaching and learning as perceived by the teachers and the students and what technological tools are useful for teaching and learning.

Methodology

Participants were 44 teachers and 219 students of grade 6 to 12. The data were drawn from two bilingual and two international schools in Muscat, Oman. The schools that integrate technology into teaching in Muscat, Oman were chosen based on the non-probability purposive sampling method. Fraenkel et al. (2015; p.139) assert that researchers use "…personal judgment to select a sample" which is why purposive sampling is the appropriate research sampling method for this thesis. Purposive sampling helps select the schools that participated in the research intentionally. Despite the popularity of technology, some schools in the areas where the selected participants are located still do not maximise the use of technology. The reason for the lack of technology integration in some of these schools is unknown. The second sampling strategy used to collate the data was Probability cluster sample. The data were organised into groups which are schools, teachers and students. Cluster sampling was used to ensure internal validity and external validity of the data. Identifying schools that integrate technology out of many is not possible if this research used only cluster sample to gather its data. Therefore, purposive sampling was used to identify schools with similar characteristics.

For this cross-sectional study, self-administered questionnaires with open-ended questions were administered. The research design provided the researcher with the opportunity to examine the interaction between independent variables and their influence on dependent variables, that is, the relation between the teachers' and the students' data result. The research aims if teachers' perception of technology efficacy in education is the same or different from the students' was examined. Additionally, this design is used to gather information regarding the problem being researched (investigating the effectiveness of teaching and learning with technology and the technologies most used in Oman international and bilingual schools), to identify the characteristics of the participants and to explore the similarities between the variables.

Typed/printed questionnaires were distributed to the students and teachers. An added consent and anonymity form was attached to the bottom of each questionnaire that was distributed to the participants. Questionnaires were given to the participants with enough time to fill it out. Further explanation without bias was provided by the researcher to any participant who was confused when filling out the questionnaire. The questionnaires were of three sections; section one included the details or neutral information of the participants, section two was directed to answer the research questions and the third part was an additional consent to participate. The open and closed-ended questionnaire which were two pages each, entailed questions with definite answers and some required other suggestions or opinion of the participants.

The questionnaire was disseminated in the participants' natural environment (school) for authentication of data findings and external/ internal validity. The participants needed 15-20 minutes to complete it. It was distributed during morning school hours at break-time. Teachers helped distribute the students' questionnaire in cases where the researcher was unable to go round the whole school and verbally informed the students. The first author was always available on the school premises to answer any question the participants had. The questionnaires were piloted with a group of three teachers and three students in order to correct any question that could be ambiguous. All the teachers who attempted the pilot study confirmed that there were not any ambiguous items.

Conclusions and discussions

The study examined that teachers and students who participated in the present research (Effective Learning and Teaching with Technology in Oman Primary and Secondary schools) have technologies such as Google, internet, whiteboard, Laptop, Projector and PowerPoint. Projector in particular is most used by both teachers and students. Corroborating this finding is Khodabandelou et al. (2016); and Gebre et al. (2015), these authors confirm the findings that projector is widely used in formal education. The three most helpful technologies according to the teachers were PowerPoint, Laptop and Google, this correlates with students finding. These findings confirm Hastür and Doğan (2016) discussion on the benefits of internet web-based learning.

Other important findings were the presence of newer technological applications such as ManageBac, Quizlet and Kognity which were available to students of the international schools. On the other hand, Social Medias (WhatsApp and Blogs) were not widely used by the teachers and students participants as they were among the least indicated. This finding is in contrast with Okoro, Hausman, and Washington (2012), Khodabandelou et al. (2016), Mac Callum et al. (2014), Andrew and Jones (2015) claim that social media facilitates learning.

This research found that both students and teacher participants are competent in technology use. However, finding shows that teachers of international schools are advanced users of technology compared to bilingual teachers with the majority being average users of technology. Furthermore, there is no evidence in this study that indicates teachers' self-efficacy of technology is a motivating factor for the teachers that integrated technology into teaching as discuss in Mager (1992) as cited in Li, Worch, Zhou, and Aguiton (2015) and Admiraal et al. (2017). In addition, it can be generalised that participants believe technology is effective for learning and teaching. Hence, as explained by Kent and Giles (2017), technology self-efficacy equals effective teacher.

The majority of the teacher participants do not regularly but sometimes get professional training. On the other hand, the lack of regular professional training did not hinder technology integration by the teachers. As with previous research discussed (Wahsheh & Alhawamdeh, 2015; Sabzian & Gilakjani, 2013; Reinsfield, 2016; Davies & West, 2014; Mac Callumm et al., 2014), the lack of professional training as a barrier to teaching effectively is lacking in this findings. Results also show that teachers are given more access to technology than students in the schools. The majority of the international students indicated 'yes' to having adequate technology and the bilingual students do not have adequate access to technologies in the school. Over one-third of the teachers indicated that their access to technology was adequate. Although, some students in the bilingual schools have limited access to technology use, there is no evidence it discourages technology use as asserted by Buabeng-Andoh (2012) and Ghavifekr et al. (2016).

The majority of students' use technology to do projects, read/do research and do homework. Surprisingly, a limited number of respondents talk to their teachers and check their scores with technology. Some respondents from the international schools in the open question state that technology is used to write exams, do short tests and play educational games (grade six students). Similarly, respondents from bilingual schools state technology is used to watch educational videos (science) and translate unknown words. These findings reinforce Li et al. (2015) discussion of technology as a tool that provides *rich resources* and *visual effects*. Teacher respondents commented they use technology to easily get faster access to teaching resources, motivate and interest students, make learning easier, help students visualise subjects, give detail instruction and make students learn better. Over half of the teachers indicated that they use technology to plan lessons and monitor activity. These were similarly discussed in Wahsheh and Alhawamdeh (2015) and Davies and West (2014).

All teacher and student participants believe technology is an effective tool in education. The reasons teachers' gave are, technology is effective because it enhances teaching, it keeps teachers updated, it provides a better understanding for students, it makes learning easier, it motivates students and it provides quick access to information. Similarly, students responses as to why technologies are effective for learning are; it is easy to get fast access to information, technologies help them to learn and search for new things, it gives them better understanding, it is easy to use, they use technologies to confirm answers to questions or task, technologies improve their academic performance, they also use it monitor class activities and it motivates them to complete given tasks and some participants sees technology as an effective tool because learning has become fun. As earlier discussed (Tunmibi, Aregbesola, Adejobi, & Ibrahim, 2015; Mac Callum et al., 2014; Ghavifekr et al., 2016) affirm these findings.

The main limitation of this study is that some of the schools were reluctant to participate because they were afraid of bad or negative results. Secondly, this quantitative research is cross-sectional. For gathering stronger evidence, a longitudinal study will complement this cross-sectional study in other to confirm if more technologies have been provided to the bilingual schools with limited technologies. Lastly, questionnaires were filled at school during break-time. A few students who did not finish filling out their questionnaire before the bell rang for classes were allowed to take it home and the questionnaires were collected two days later. Hence, the researcher has no way of knowing if such students' responses could have been influenced by the change of environment or the people around them at home.

This study contributes not only to theory but also to policy and practice. The study shows that the implementation of technology into education is successful as the impact that technologies have on teachers and students are positive. Policy and practice needs to take into account that limited availability of technology and bad network limits technology use. Educational authorities need to implement a flexible but qualitative curriculum that enables teachers to integrate more technologies to prevent its limited usage. This research shows a homogenous indication in the technologies that both teachers and students participants found effective.

Nonetheless, teachers have better access to technologies than students. Therefore, it is important that school authorities take note of this pressing issue and provide equal access.

References

Abuid, B. A. (2014). A student participation assessment scheme for effective teaching and learning. *Learning and Teaching in Higher Education: Gulf Perspectives, 11*(1). Retrieved April 14, 2017, from http://lthe.zu.ac.ae/index.php/lthehome/article/view/109

Admiraal, W. F.; Louws, M. L., Lockhorst, D., Paas, T., Buynsters, M., Cviko, A., Janssen, C., Jonge, M. de. Nouwens, S., Post, L. S., Ven, F. van der., & Kester, L. (2017). Teachers in school-based technology innovations: a typology of their beliefs on teaching and technology. *Computers and Education, 114*, 57-68.

Ahmad, S., & Nisa, M. (2016). The Significance of Educational Technology in Teaching Learning process. *The International Journal of Indian Psychology, 4*(1). 163-170. Retrieved November 10, 2017, from http://www.ijip.in/Archive/v4i1/18.01.097.20160401.pdf

Alemu, M. B. (2014). Enhancing the Quality and Relevance of Higher Education Through Effective Teaching Practices and Instructors' Characteristics. *Universal Journal of Educational Research, 2*(9), 632-647. Retrieved June 4, 2017, from https://eric.ed.gov/?q=effective+teaching&pg=2&id=EJ1053951

Andrews, J., & Jones, M. (2015). What's happening in 'their space? exploring the borders of formal and informal learning with undergraduate students of education in the age of mobile technologies. *Journal of Interactive Media in Education, 1*(16), 1-10. Retrieved June 4, 2017, from http://files.eric.ed.gov/fulltext/EJ1085223.pdf

Ansari, U., & Malik, K. S. (2013) Image of an effective teacher in 21st century classroom. *Journal of Educational and Instructional Studies in the World, 3*(4), 61-68. WJEIS. Retrieved April 15, 2017, from http://www.wjeis.org/FileUpload/ds217232/File/08.ansari.pdf

Buabeng-Andoh, C. (2012). Factors influencing teachers' adoption and integration of information and communication technology into teaching: A review of the literature. *International Journal of Education and Development using Information and Communication Technology (IJEDIC), 8*(1), 136-155. Retrieved November 10, 2017, from http://files.eric.ed.gov/fulltext/EJ1084227.pdf

Davies, R. S., & West, E. R. (2014). Technology Integration in Schools (4th ed.). ResearchGate.

Education Development Trust (2016). Effective teaching, Education Development Trust media report. Retrieved June 4, 2017, from https://www.educationdevelopmenttrust.com/~/media/EDT/Reports/Research/2015/r-effective-teaching.pdf

Fraenkel, R. J., Wallen, E. N., & Hyun, H. H. (2015). How to design and evaluate research in education (9th ed.). United States of America: McGraw-Hill Education.

Gebre, E., Saroyan, A., & Aulls, W. A. (2015). Conceptions of effective teaching and perceived use of computer technologies in active Learning classrooms. *International Journal of Teaching and Learning in Higher Education, 27*(2), 204-220. Retrieved June 5, 2017, from http://files.eric.ed.gov/fulltext/EJ1082880.pdf

Ghavifekr, S., Kunjappan, T., Ramasamy, L., & Anthony, A. (2016). Teaching and learning with ICT tools: issues and challenges from teachers' perceptions. *Malaysian Online Journal of Educational Technology, 4*(2), 38-57. Retrieved June 4, 2017, from http://files.eric.ed.gov/fulltext/EJ1096028.pdf

Hastür, G., & Doğan, A. (2016). Effect of triadic teaching approach in some environmental subjects: prospective science teachers practice. *International Journal of Environmental & Science Education, 11*(5), 893-905. Retrieved June 4, 2017, from http://files.eric.ed.gov/fulltext/EJ1114262.pdf

Kent, M. A., & Giles, M. R. (2017). Preservice teachers' technology self-efficacy. *SRATE Journal, 26*(1), 9-20. Retrieved June 4, 2017, from http://files.eric.ed.gov/fulltext/EJ1134392.pdf

Khodabandelou, R., That, E. M. J., Selvaraju, A. M., Ken, Y. T., Kewen, Z., Yan, Z., & Ning, Y. T. (2016). Exploring the main barriers of technology integration in the English language teaching classroom: a qualitative study. *International Journal of Education & Literacy; Australian International Academic Centre, Australia Studies, 4*(1), 53-58.

Kivunja, C. (2014). Innovative Pedagogies in Higher Education to Become Effective Teachers of 21st Century Skills: Unpacking the Learning and Innovations Skills Domain of the New Learning Paradigm. *International Journal of Higher Education, 3*(4). Retrieved April 15, 2017, from http://www.sciedu.ca/journal/index.php/ijhe/article/viewFile/5513/3263

Learning Forward (2013). Meet the promise of content standards: The role of technology for teacher and student learning. Oxford, OH: Learning Forward. Retrieved November 10, 2017, from https://learningforward.org/docs/default-source/commoncore/the-role-of-technology-for-teacher-and-student-learning.pdf

Li, L., Worch, E., Zhou, Y., & Aguiton, R. (2015). How and why digital generation teachers use technology in the classroom: an explanatory sequential mixed methods study. *International Journal for the Scholarship of Teaching and Learning, 9*(2), Article 9, 1-9. Retrieved June 4, 2017, from http://files.eric.ed.gov/fulltext/EJ1134641.pdf

Lisenbee, S. P. (2016). Generation Gap Between Students' Needs and Teachers' Use of Technology in Classrooms. *Journal of Literacy and Technology, 17*(3), 100-125. Retrieved November 10, 2017, from https://www.researchgate.net/profile/Peggy_Lisenbee/publication/311426801_Generation_gap_between_students%27_needs_and_teachers%27_use_of_technology_in_classrooms/links/5845ba7208ae61f75dd7cb4e/Generation-gap-between-students-needs-and-teachers-use-of-technology-in-classrooms.pdf

Mac Callum, K., Jeffrey, L., & Kinshuk (2014). Factors impacting teachers' adoption of mobile learning. *Journal of Information Technology Education: Research, 13*, 141-162. Retrieved November 10, 2017, from http://www.jite.org/documents/Vol13/JITEv13ResearchP141-162MacCallum0455.pdf

Office of Educational Technology (2017). Reimagining the Role of Technology in Education: 2017 National Education Technology Plan Update U.S. department of education. Retrieved November 10, 2017, from https://tech.ed.gov/files/2017/01/NETP17.pdf

Okoro, A. E., Hausman, A., & Washington, C. M. (2012). Social media and networking technologies: an analysis of collaborative work and team communication. *Contemporary Issues in Education Research, 5*(4), 295-300. Retrieved June 4, 2017, from http://files.eric.ed.gov/fulltext/EJ1073130.pdf

Raymond, A. B. (2016). Investigating psychological parameters of effective Teaching in a diverse classroom situation: the case of the higher teachers' training college Maroua, Cameroon. *Journal of Education and Practice, 7*(23), 72-80. Retrieved June 4, 2017, from http://files.eric.ed.gov/fulltext/EJ1112928.pdf

Reinsfield, E. (2016). A future-focus for teaching and learning: technology education in two New Zealand secondary schools. *Teachers and Curriculum, 16*(1), 67-76. Retrieved November 8, 2017, from http://files.eric.ed.gov/fulltext/EJ1122021.pdf

Sabzian, F., & Gilakjani, A. P. (2013). Teachers' attitudes about computer technology training, professional development, integration, experience, anxiety, and literacy in English language teaching and learning. *International Journal of Applied Science and Technology, 3*(1), 67-75. Retrieved November 10, 2017, from http://www.ijastnet.com/journals/Vol_3_No_1_January_2013/9.pdf

Scott, E. D. (2015). The nebulous, essential dimensions in effective university teaching: the ethic of care and relational acumen. *Journal of University Teaching & Learning Practice, 12*(2), 1-17. Retrieved June 4, 2017, from http://files.eric.ed.gov/fulltext/EJ1072384.pdf

Suleman, Q. (2011). Role of Educational Technology at Primary School Level in District Karak. *International Journal of Academic Research in Business and Social Sciences, 1*(3), 85-95. Retrieved November 10, 2017, from http://www.hrmars.com/admin/pics/332.pdf

Tunmibi, S., Aregbesola, A., Adejobi, P., & Ibrahim, O. (2015). Impact of e-learning and digitalization in primary and secondary schools. *Journal of Education and Practice, 6*(17), 53-59. Retrieved June 4, 2017, from http://files.eric.ed.gov/fulltext/EJ1079751.pdf

UNESCO (2015). The futures of learning 3: what kind of pedagogies for the 21st century? Education research and foresight. Retrieved April 15, 2017, from http://unesdoc.unesco.org/images/0024/002431/243126e.pdf

Wahsheh, R., & Alhawamdeh, H. (2015). The role of female teachers in activating effective teaching skills and methods among High School Students from the teachers' perspective –

Najran, KSA. *Journal of Education and Practice*, *6*(36), 162-174. Retrieved June 6, 2017, from http://files.eric.ed.gov/fulltext/EJ1086477.pdf

HOWEST EDHUB: THE INTERACTION BETWEEN DIDACTICS, LEARNING SPACE AND TECHNOLOGY

Basiel Bonne, Rina Dauwens, Tijs Verbeke, Howest – Hogeschool West-Vlaanderen, Belgium

Introduction

In our teacher training department, we noticed that our students are fearful to teach with the use of ICT and flexible or non-classic learning environments. When microteaching to their peers or when on internship, teachers in training always seem to fall back on the textbooks and a fixed pattern. We noticed some barriers in the mindset of our students regarding the adaptivity of classrooms and the integration of ICT in a classroom. Even in the schools where our students do their internship, the mindset to explore these areas of didactics often falls short.

Our literature survey was aimed at indexing what barriers often appeared and if there were other barriers we had to overcome. Barriers we came across were plenty: financial difficulties (lack of funds to adapt classrooms or the acquire ICT-tools), a lack of knowledge on the subject often combined with the fear to adapt 'new' tools, it could be the mindset of a teacher of a school and so on.

Our research intends to fill the gap between existing technological applications and education practice and thus create room for the work field and the students to explore and experiment. We intend to address two problems we are confronted with and which are also described in literature: the often-high financial threshold and the mindset of (starting) teachers and students in teacher training. We'll look at these barriers on school level (what can schools do or engage in) and on level of the teacher (how can he or she respond to the learning space and/or the technology). What we intend to avoid in this research is to erect a high-tech future classroom which would discourage schools and teachers because this would require a financial investment they can't make.

Methodology

In order to facilitate our investigation on low-tech in-class differentiation strategies, we erected an experimentation space within our own building, close and easily reachable for our students yet also available for teachers and schools in our city (and beyond). In this highly flexible classroom, there's a wide variety of technological tools with which future teachers can experiment and learn. They can experiment with different didactical strategies without being assessed.

Schools and teachers are encouraged to bring their pupils to our learning space. This way, they themselves can experiences the effects of different technologies and adaptations in order to determine which changes have the most impact. Providing this *test drive* allows us to lower the financial barrier that currently holds back a lot of ICT-integration in schools. Alongside our experimentation space, we organize *Teacher Design Teams* to bring the experiences of teachers into our research and into our experimentation space.

We wanted to establish a baseline on first year students' expectations and ideas on ICT and our education at school. Specifically, we looked into how they can be persuaded to adopt a flexible mindset towards ICT and new learning environments. The baseline measurement was conducted in January, the survey was repeated in September 2018 and will be repeated in the last year of these students' teacher training trajectories.

In February of 2019, we will expand the survey scope to teachers in our region. We want to investigate what they already know about computational thinking and what role we can take up to support them in implementing this framework. We are conducting the inquiry together with VIVES University of Applied Sciences and Provincie West-Vlaanderen (Province of Occidental Flanders) in order to maximize our range of schools and teachers.

Starting this research, we explored how pupils thought about the *future classroom*. In a challenge in which more than 500 pupils participated we asked them what a classroom would look like when their children are populating the classrooms. From these results we distilled some common characteristics of a future classroom (according to the pupils) and assessed which elements can be incorporated in our experimentation space.

To meet the challenge of the mindset we are using the *computational thinking* framework. In the new *basic objectives* the Flemish government imposes on the schools; computational thinking is one of the key components. Digital literacy is to be achieved in all courses. As these new 'basic objectives' are not familiar to most teachers, part of our research is supporting schools in implementing a framework for computational thinking in the classroom.

Discussion

On the mindset of teachers

Little investigation has been done into how teachers integrate computational thinking ideas into their teaching practices. In the 2017 study, Bower states that teachers, after a workshop concerning the implementation of computational thinking in their courses, were able to swiftly adopt the basic framework, pedagogy and technology into their teaching practice. This could imply that computational thinking strategies can be encouraged with only a small investment of time if you have well suited workshops. Yet, the same research stipulates that teachers themselves indicate they need more time, resources, peer mentoring and workshops to fully achieve their goals.

Important, alongside of training, is to address the mindset of teachers and students. Teachers who have a negative perception of the topics they teach negatively influence the way in which pupils learn given skills and subjects, influence negatively the way learners adapt the given skills and subjects. This is also addressed in the study by Vongkulluksn et al. (2018) "[...] teachers' value beliefs also predicted how well teachers integrated technology, including how much they used technology to foster student-centered instruction and higher order tasks. These results echoed previous studies of technology integration, which have pointed to the large effect teachers' value beliefs have on classroom practice with technology". Several other studies come to the same conclusion.

This is the field in which our research aims to support teachers. To that end, we do not just put the focus on learning how to work with ICT or on tool-oriented workshops, but on the coherence between a thoroughly elaborated didactic scope, a flexible and inspiring environment/space and approachable technological adjustments to this space and didactical methods. We investigate how we can achieve learning gains by making minimal interventions in the context or the learning process. In our "quest" to change teacher behaviour, especially in the case of technology, not too much consideration can be given to these underlying mindsets. Not in the least because the decisions teachers make are often based on familiar images of what they perceive as working than by frameworks and instructional design. Decisions teachers make are often based on their own estimation of a good teaching approach, rather than by frameworks and instructional designs. The challenge will be to find the most effective way for each individual teacher to modify/change these beliefs. This modification or change can be made if personal and alternate experiences (modelling) with these new technologies and environments are positive. To make the experience as positive as possible, it is important to introduce teachers to all kinds of technology that satisfy their immediate needs. This should, at a minimum level, increase confidence of teachers to interact with the technology and eventually may even lead to a "higher level use".

To respond to these results, we developed a didactical analysis tool that aids us with mapping the needs and desires of teachers. We'll use this tool to answer specific and individual needs of teachers. This way, we can work on a micro level to support them and disseminate the results of our research bottom-up into the schools to change school culture to a more adaptive approach to technology and flexible learning environments

This tool emanates from the Bloom's taxonomy and combines this with the SAMR model. To describe the current ICT practices of a teacher, we can use the Pedagogical Framework of Mobile Learning as described in Kearny and Burden. Looking at the learning process supported by tablets, we are using the conversational Framework by Laurillard (2002) to examine how interactions between learners and teachers as well as between learners among themselves can be supported to make the learning process more effective. The SAMR model helps us describe the integration of ICT into the didactical approach of teachers.

Results

In following paragraphs, we summarized our preliminary results. Please note, this is ongoing research in which we don't want to draw any final conclusions yet. We aim to strengthen in-class differentiation by use of technology and adjustments to the learning space. Our focus is on two barriers we try to overcome: the mindset of teachers who are not willing to use technology or change their environment and financial implications that come with the introduction of technology. Results regarding teachers' mindsets are very preliminary.

Inquiries

Drawing of a future classroom by pupils

Most of the pupils drew impossible classrooms to create with current available technologies but not necessarily impossible in the near future. Examples include teachers popping out of tablets (Holograms), foldable tablets (Samsung and others are creating them at the moment) and mobile furniture. Most important though was, and this came back in nearly every drawing of a classroom, some place to eat and drink within the classroom, preferably with comfortable seating.

Base line measurement of our first-year students

Our first-year students (18 years old) are enthusiastic about the use of technology and are quite fond of flexible classrooms. At the same time, they are suspicious of flexible hours and individual trajectories for pupils. While in most situations, they have not yet experienced these two elements of classroom environments, they will encounter them more often during their higher education. It will be interesting to note whether their perceptions change as they themselves get more familiar with it.

Online survey on computational thinking

This will be launched in February 2019. Conclusions to be made after.

Teacher Design Teams

These will be held in 2019. Conclusion to be made after.

Pedagogical tool

We developed a pedagogical tool which will be tested in the coming months. The tool consists of three steps. The first steps involve the description of the challenge. Teachers are asked to write down the challenges they wish to tackle using technology and flexible space into learning goals and learning activities. In the second part, the teachers can analyse, together with the researchers, how the learning goals and activities fit into Bloom's taxonomy. The second step also deals with how they want their lessons to be enhanced by space or technology. For this second question we are using the SAMR model.

The third step involves devising a solution for the proposed challenge, either by adding technology, adopting an already used technology, by implementing changes to the learning environment, by didactical changes or by any combination of these strategies. These three steps result in a model for analyses which, currently, looks like this (see picture). It's still written in Dutch and the lay-out will be improved. The purple part is step one, the red part step two and the green part step three.

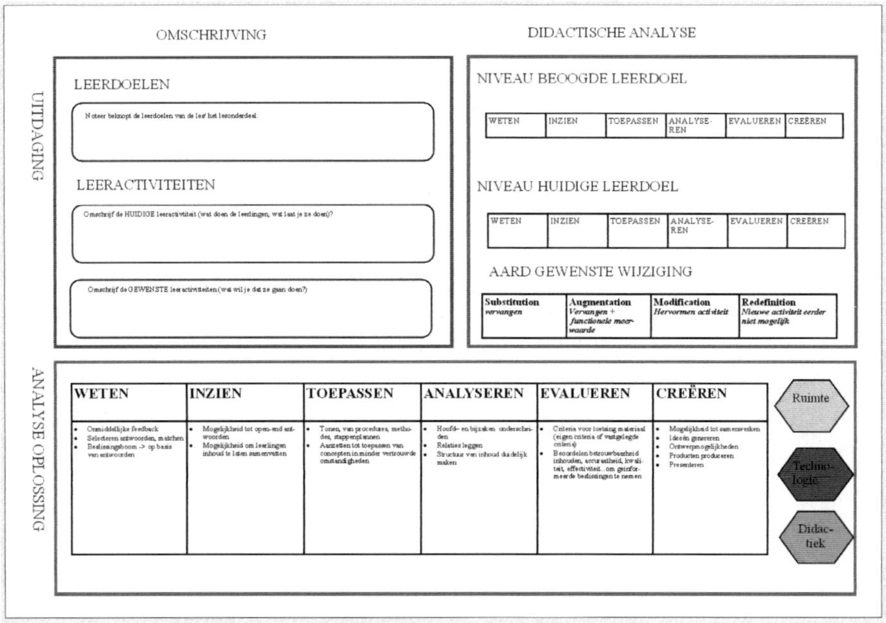

Figure 1. Didactical tool (in progress)

This tool will be tested in coming months to see if it can help teachers redesign their lessons and in-class differentiation.

References

Barr, V., & Stephenson, C. (2011). Bringing computational thinking to K-12: what is Involved and what is the role of the computer science education community? *ACM Inroads, 2*(1), 48-54.

Bower, M. (2017). Improving the computational thinking pedagogical capabilities of school teachers. *Australian Journal of Teacher Education, 42*(3), 53-72.

Ermter, P. A. (2005). Teacher pedagogical beliefs: The final frontier in our Quest for Technology Integration? *Educational Technology Research and Development, 53*(4), 25-39.

Kearney, M. (2012). Viewing mobile learning from a pedagogical perspective. *Research in Learning Technology, 20.*

Laurillard, D. (2002). Rethinking university teaching; A conversational framework for the effective use of learning technologies. Oxon, UK: Routledge Falmer.

Levin, T., & Wadmany, R. (2006). Teachers' beliefs and practices in technology-based classrooms: A developmental view. *Journal of research on technology in education, 39*(2), 157-181.

Paniagua, A., & Instance, D. (2018). Teachers as Designers of Learning Environments: The Importance of Innovative Pedagogies, Educational Research and Innovation. OECD Publishing.

Puentedura, R. (2014, August 22). Building transformation: An introduction to the SAMR model. Hippasus [Blog post]. Retrieved from http://www.hippasus.com/rrpweblog/archives/000130.html

Vongkulluksn, A. W., Xie, K., & Bowman, M. A. (2018). The role of value on teachers' internalization of external barriers and externalization of personal beliefs for classroom technology integration. *Computers & Education, 188*, 70-81.

DESIGNING AND ASSESSING AN OPEN VIRTUAL MOBILITY MOOC: THE CASE STUDY OF THE "MEDIA AND DIGITAL LITERACY" MINIMOOC

Antonella Poce, Francesco Agrusti, Francesca Amenduni, University of Roma Tre, Italy

Introduction

The present paper is related to part of the activities foreseen within the Erasmus + project "openVM: Opening Education for Developing, Assessing and Recognising Virtual Mobility Skills in Higher Education" (https://www.openvirtualmobility.eu). Virtual mobility (VM) stands for ICT supported activities, organized at an institutional level, that realise or facilitate international, collaborative experiences in a context of teaching and/or learning. VM has a great potential to contribute to the internationalisation and opening up of Higher Education by creating international, collaborative experiences for educators and students as well as equal possibilities of participation in exchange programs, including those who are unable to travel for social, financial or other reasons (EuroPACE, 2010).

The project is expected to achieve 7 intellectual outputs related to different aspects of the Open Virtual Mobility ideation and implementation:

- O1 Conceptual Framework and Guidelines: a detailed look at the concept of VM, by defining which skills are necessary for engagement in VM and the skills gained by teachers and students participating in VM actions.
- O2 Virtual Mobility Learning Hub: the VM Learning Hub will be developed as a Personal Learning Environment which will include a responsive interoperable interface, a social software, tools for mobile learning, a common working/collaboration space, a semantic features and learning analytics, self-assessment and validation of open digital credentials (Buchem et al., 2018).
- O3 Competency Directory and Matching Tool: The semantic competency directory will include a number of semantic description of VM skills and the matching tool will be a tool for building learning groups by an algorithmic solution.
- O4 E-assessment concept and tool: A concept for assessing virtual mobility is developed and practical tools will be tested and validated.
- O5 Open credentials and Gamification: a set of open credentials to recognize VM skills and visual design of Gamification for learning.
- O6 OER, MOOC and Pilots: VM OER and the VM MOOC will be designed and integrated with the VM Learning Hub and a piloting phase will be conducted to validate and ensuring the sustainability of the project outcomes.

- O7 Quality and Sustainability: a quality assurance framework for the entire project it is developed with the dissemination, implementation and monitoring plan (Buchem, Tur, & Urbina, 2018).

In this paper the design and the assessment of the pre-pilot phase of the project is described in details.

The Design Based Research (DBR) approach was adopted in order to contribute to innovation and improvement of educational practices in the OpenVirtual Mobility MOOC. According to Easterday and colleagues (2014), the six phases of the DBR should be (a) Focus; (b) Understand; (c) Define; (d) Conceive; (e) Build; (f) Test.

Output 1 of the project was devoted to the first three phases, since skills necessary for engagement in VM were identified and re-defined according to the specific goals of the project. The latter three phases are indeed part of Output 6 concerning OpenVM MOOC construction and pilot phase. The pre-pilot phase has consisted in conceiving, building and testing a miniMOOC named "Media and Digital Literacy". The results of the pre-pilot assessment are presented in this paper. Since DBR is an iterative process, the results of the evaluation of the pre-pilot phase will be used to improve the OpenVirtual Mobility MOOC structure. In addition, the results could provide insights also for institutions, educators and practitioners interested to develop Virtual Mobility at their own institution.

State of the art: from the OPENVM general structure to the realization of the pre-pilot course on Media and Digital Literacy

According to Bates (2015) design features indications, it was chosen to incorporate in the MOOC a Matching Tool (O3), different forms of e-Assessment (O4) and Open Credentials (O5) as well as all the necessary descriptions, explanations of the topics, bibliographical references, introductions to sessions and supplemental material. The Matching Tool (O3) will be used for group formation, i.e. connecting users for joint learning activities including the "Open Learning by Design" process in which user will create OERs and MOOC sessions together. The E-Assessment (O4) will be used to assess students and teachers' VM Skills, and Open Credentials (O5) will be used to provide a formal recognition of VM Skills acquired not only through the MOOC but also elsewhere, following the principles of distributed assessment.

Design

Eight areas have been identified as main content for the OpenVM MOOC (OVMOOC):

1. intercultural skills;
2. collaborative learning;
3. autonomy-driven learning;
4. networked learning;

5. media and digital learning;
6. active self-regulated learning;
7. open mindedness;
8. virtual mobility knowledge.

Three levels are then identified for each area: beginner, intermediate, advanced. Defining the eight areas with the three levels gives the following picture (Figure 1).

MOOC Structure

Mini MOOC 1 **Intercultural skills**
- Sub Mooc. 1.1 Beginner
- Sub Mooc 1.2 Intermediate
- Sub Mooc 1.3 Advanced

Mini MOOC 2 **Collaborative learning**
- Sub Mooc. 2.1 Beginner
- Sub Mooc 2.2 Intermediate
- Sub Mooc 2.3 Advanced

Mini MOOC 3 **Autonomy-driven learning**,
- Sub Mooc. 3.1 Beginner
- Sub Mooc 3.2 Intermediate
- Sub Mooc 3.3 Advanced

Mini MOOC 4 **Networked learning**
- Sub Mooc. 4.1 Beginner
- Sub Mooc 4.2 Intermediate
- Sub Mooc 4.3 Advanced

Mini MOOC 5 **Media and digital learning**
- Sub Mooc. 5.1 Beginner
- Sub Mooc 5.2 Intermediate
- Sub Mooc 5.3 Advanced

Mini MOOC 6 **Active Self-regulated learning**
- Sub Mooc. 6.1 Beginner
- Sub Mooc 6.2 Intermediate
- Sub Mooc 6.3 Advanced

Mini MOOC 7 **Open mindedness**
- Sub Mooc. 7.1 Beginner
- Sub Mooc 7.2 Intermediate
- Sub Mooc 7.3 Advanced

Mini MOOC 8 **VM knowledge**
- Sub Mooc. 8.1 Beginner
- Sub Mooc 8.2 Intermediate
- Sub Mooc 8.3 Advanced

8 Mini Moocs * 3 Levels = 24 Sub Moocs
Each SubMooc contains 1 or 2 videos, assessment and 6 hours of individual study.

Figure 1. OpenVM MOOC general structure

Each combination between content and level has been called SubMOOC. A SubMOOC is a section of the Open VM MOOC and it has the following characteristics:

- It has an entrance test to verify the level of the participant. If the participant has already obtained the Open Badge from the previous level, this test will be omitted.
- It is referring only to a complexity level (beginner, intermediate, advanced).
- It is referring only to one of the area identified;
- It contains 1 or 2 videos (maximum length 9 minutes, minimum length 5 minutes).
- It contains at least 1 presentation and 1 hypertext document.
- The intermediate and advanced SubMOOCs have also online scientific references (online e-book or online articles).
- Once the participant completed it, an Open Badge will be issued.
- It lasts 1 week.
- It contains at least 1 formative assessment quiz composed by closed items (MCQ, FIB, T/F, Matching) with included feedback.
- It contains at least 1 summative assessment quiz composed by MCQ items with included feedback.

- The intermediate and advanced SubMOOCs have a peer assessment based on the Tune Models of Peer Assessment.

Methodology

The first mini-MOOC has been realised to be tested during the pilot phase and it is focused on the 5th skills "Media and Digital Literacy". The main topics of the course are open education, open resources and licenses, the web mechanisms that could affect learning processes, and media languages (multimediality, hypertextuality). The pedagogical approaches used to design the pre-pilot are collaborative and social learning (Andriessen, Baker, & Suthers, 2013), reflective practices (Schön, 2017), and self-regulated learning (Zimmerman, 2010).

Before starting the course, participants are required to fill in a pre-assessment. According to the score obtained, participants could be directed to the basic level, to the intermediate level or to the advance level. For each level students need to read texts, e-books or pdfs, watch videos and participate to forum discussions. When they complete all the tasks, they fill in summative quizzes, write a post on their e-portfolios, make and receive peer-assessment in order to obtain a badge.

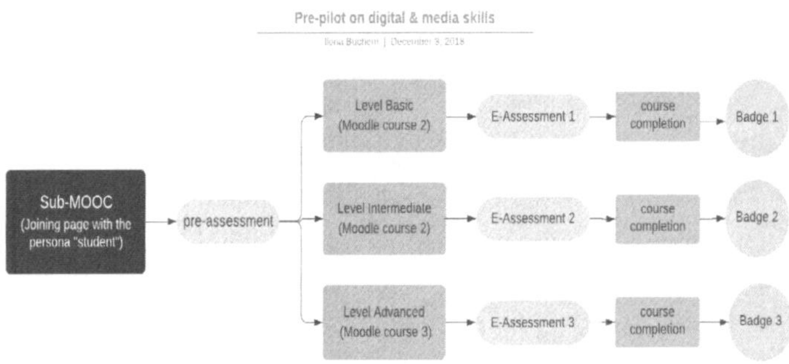

Figure 2. Pre-pilot technical structure

The course has a small narrative, by differentiating personas stories according to the user profile: teacher and student. The joining course includes the narrative (scenario, problem-based) for the two personas, and the pre-assessment. The pilot phase will last 2 weeks, 10 days to complete all the tasks and 4 days to complete the peer-assessment. In the present table an overview of the kinds of content selected for each level is presented.

Table 1: Overview of kinds of OERs selected for each level

Level	Kind of OERs and contents
Basic	1 e-book + 1 pdf + 1 video + 1 discussion forum + summative assessment
Intermediate	2 video + 1 pdf + 1 discussion forum + peer assessment
Advanced	1 video + 2 scientific papers + 1 discussion forum + peer assessment

The learning objectives defined for each level are the following.

Basic level:

- define and describe the basic principles of fact-checking while working with web-based sources;
- define and describe the basics of copyright and creative commons;
- define and describe Council of Europe Common European Framework approach to recognizing the role of culture in language learning.

Intermediate level:

- develop knowledge and awareness about filter bubble and how to avoid its traps;
- develop knowledge and awareness about skills and competences students and teachers need in the 21st century;
- develop knowledge and awareness about the power of advertisement for YouTube users and effect on brain;
- Raise awareness of the term *network* as applied to the digital age and to learning. Understand the relevance of this theory to your own online learning experience and MOOCs.

Advanced level:

- knowledge and deep insights about supertraces and digital footprints;
- knowledge and deep insights about narratives as they have evolved from print to digital media;
- understanding what OERs are, how to collect and use them and have deep insights about the merits and challenge around the use of OER.

The learning outcomes defined for each level are the following:

- basic level: knowledge is demonstrated in short online quizzes;
- intermediate: knowledge is demonstrated in quizzes and awareness can be demonstrated in a blog post, a portfolio post and self-reflection,
- advanced: knowledge is demonstrated in quizzes and deep insight can be demonstrated in a blog post, a portfolio post and self-reflection.

Analyses and Findings: the pre-pilot assessment

At the end of the course, students were invited to fill in an online questionnaire (https://goo.gl/forms/tAcITPIpKn57vSJr2) aimed to investigate (a) participants' general evaluation, (b) participants' specific evaluation, (c) participants' recommendations for improvement and (d) hours spent to complete the course. Qualitative data from 9 participants have been collected until now (at the EDEN presentation the data will be updated with a larger number of participants). 194 sentences and 259 segments were analysed through sentiment analysis by using the software meaningcloud (https://www.meaningcloud.com). The following figure (Figure 3) shows that in the most of the comments participants express positive sentiments related to the mini MOOC media and digital literacy. Positive comments

(Figure 4) are related with the nouns "learning, topics, content, design, visual, videos, community" and the adjectives "simple, clearer".

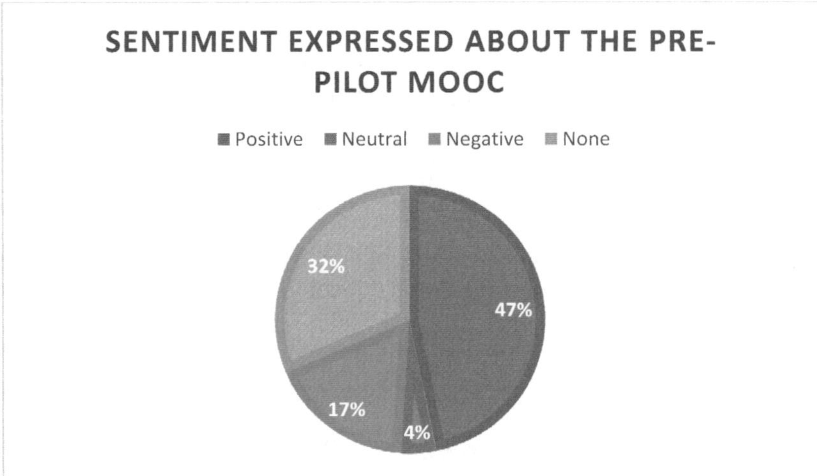

Figure 3. Sentiment expressed in the open answers regarding the pre-pilot MOOC "Media and Digital Literacy"

On the other hand, negative comments are related with the nouns "the structure, e-test, e-portfolios, problems, task" and the adjectives "confusing, much, unattractive".

Figure 4. On the left words related with positive sentiment and on the right words related with negative sentiments

Participants enjoyed the selected contents, especially in form of videos (see the Extract 1). The basic level course (related with Creative Common) was the most endorsed.

> *"The course was a useful introduction to Media Literacy. It contained useful information about important topics in the internet like verifying source in the internet. That might be helpful for students. The videos on TEDx are*

> *fascinating. The instructions were easy to follow. All in all, I liked the course because it is a new way of learning and dispute with a new topic." (E1)*

Although participants appreciated the opportunity to test their skills through of e-assessment and e-portfolios, they also suggest to improve the e-portfolio functionality, as reported in the Extract 2. Participants would need clearer instructions regarding how to fill in the e-portfolios, providing for instance a template.

> *"The E-Assessment was very useful to reflect the stuff I have learned. The small tasks where well. At first creating my E-Portfolio was difficult for me, because I didn't have an example on how to start or write something. I also didn't want to post my tweets publicly e.g. my skills. Students may think my skills are not enough. The E-test are on a good level." (E2)*

Participants have contrasting ideas about sharing publicly their reflections in the discussion forums or e-portfolios. Whilst someone appreciated the opportunity to share their ideas with the communities (E3), other instead did not (E2; E4).

Table 2: Positive and negative attitudes towards sharing public participants' reflections

Positive attitude towards sharing publicly reflections	Negative attitude towards sharing publicly reflections
"I found it very good that one could write a community contribution with the courses to a certain question or problem definition. It also gave me the opportunity to exchange knowledge and give feedback." (E3)	*"I also didn't want to post my tweets publicly e.g. my skills. Students may think my skills are not enough." (E2)* *"I didn't like the fact that we had to answer questions or share tips publicly." (E4)*

Some participants found the text contents in the advanced level were too long and complicated and the instructions related with the exercises not always clear. They did not appreciate to be re-directed to external links, both for e-portfolio and for contents because they lost the track. Participants spent about 4 hours to complete the course. 60 minutes for the basic level, 90 minutes for the intermediate level and 90 minutes for the advanced level in average. Some of them completed the course within a week.

Discussion and conclusion

Virtual mobility implementation needs to follow an iterative process of ideation, design, assessment and re-design to be effective. In the OpenVM Erasmus+ project it was followed the DBR approach to constantly monitor and improve the quality of the OpenVM MOOC. More specifically, a pre-pilot phase was designed to collect data about participants' experience of the miniMOOC named "Media and Digital Literacy". Although the general assessment of the course was positive, there are still rooms for improvement. The results here presented will be used to improve the quality of the OpenVM MOOC and they could be useful insights also for whom who are interested to implement VM at their own institution.

References

Andriessen, J., Baker, M., & Suthers, D. D. (Eds.) (2013). *Arguing to learn: Confronting cognitions in computer-supported collaborative learning environments* (Vol. 1). Springer Science & Business Media.

Bates, T. (2015, February 16). What do we mean by 'open' in education? Online Learning and Distance Education resources [Blog post]. Retrieved from https://www.tonybates.ca/2015/02/16/what-do-we-mean-by-open-in-education/

Buchem, I.; Konert, J.; Carlino, C.; Casanova, G.; Rajagopal, K.; Firssova, O.; Andone, D. (2018). Designing a Collaborative Learning Hub for Virtual Mobility Skills – Insights from the European Project Open Virtual Mobility. In P. Zaphiris & A. Ioannou (Eds.), *Learning and Collaboration Technologies. Design, Development and Technological Innovation, Lecture Notes in Computer Science* (vol. 10924, pp. 350-376). Springer International Publishing AG, ISBN 978-3-319-91742-9. https://doi.org/10.1007/978-3-319-91743-6_27

Buchem, I., Tur, G. & Urbina, S. (2018). Quality assurance for attainment, assessment and recognition of virtual mobility skills in context of open education. QA Framework in the Open Virtual Mobility project. *Proceedings of the Edulearn18 Conference, 2-4 July 2018*, 945-952. Retrieved from https://iated.org/concrete3/view_abstract.php?paper_id=65036

Easterday, M., Rees Lewis, D., & Gerber, E. (2014). Design-based research process: Problems, phases, and applications. *Proceedings of International Conference of Learning Sciences (Vol. 14), 2014 January.*

EuroPACE (2010). Interests – Virtual mobility. Retrieved November 15, 2010, from http://www.europace.org/interest3.php

Schön, D. A. (2017). The reflective practitioner: How professionals think in action. Routledge.

Zimmerman, B. J. (2010). Self-regulated learning and academic achievement: An overview. *Educational Psychologist, 25*(1), 3-17.

Acknowledgement

The paper was edited in the following order: Antonella Poce (Introduction, State of the Art, Discussion); Francesco Agrusti (Design and Methodology); Francesca Amenduni (Analyses and Findings).

Connecting through Educational Technology
Proceedings of the European Distance and E-Learning Network 2019 Annual Conference
Bruges, 16-19 June, 2019

FLEXIBLE TEACHER TRAINING PROGRAM IN DISTANCE LEARNING

Sofie Dossche, Matthias Lefebvre, VIVES University of Applied Sciences, Belgium

Introduction

Our education institution can rely on 30 years of experience in distance learning. Throughout these years we have always considered the work-life balance of the students. One of our main targets is to establish a flexible organisation and an adequate coaching concept for our distance learning students. In this paper we present a number of factors which – in our opinion and based on our experience – can improve the success rate of study combined with work and (family) life.

Historical context

In 1997 University college VIVES (formerly known as KATHO) started providing an extended teacher trainer program for primary school. The program was designed to enable teachers, working in kindergartens, to obtain a certificate in primary school via a shortened study program. The aim was to try to eliminate the lack of primary schools teachers. In the beginning 7 students were registered. As they were working students the lessons were limited to Wednesday afternoons and Saturday mornings and the students had to study the course content autonomously. Back then, that was considered revolutionary. This training concept was often criticised. From 2002 on students could also obtain a degree in preschool teaching. The number of lessons were gradually dismantled and didactics through distance learning were increasingly developed. From 2007 on VIVES chose radically to support the concept of obtaining a bachelor in education through distance learning.

7 factors for a good work-life balance of distance learning students

In what follows, we have listed up 7 factors which enable distance learning students to combine their studies with work and life. Based on our experience, we can determine these factors:

Factor 1: 100% distance learning

Candidate-students can enrol throughout the academic year. The enrolment happens online. Student do not have to come to campus unless they want to for certain reasons. We organise a start day for candidate-students on campus twice a year, once in September and once in February. During that day students can follow a number of sessions: concept of distance learning, planning schedules, digital tools for distance learning, information about teaching practice etc. We advise students to participate, but all information about these sessions is also available on our digital learning environment via documents and instruction videos.

Students buy courses online and study the subjects autonomously. We organise no lessons on campus. There have been experiments with blended learning, in which classes on certain subjects were given, but the turnout on these activities were often very low, because of organisational reasons for students. We have come to the conclusion that flexibility is of key importance to support students in their work-life balance, although we face student drop out and procrastination.

Factor 2: Study program with exemptions

We take the previous studies of candidate-students into account, as much as possible. Bachelor students and Master students get exemption packages when they start with the teacher training studies. They can get accreditations of prior certificated learning (APCL) or accreditations of prior (experiential) learning (AP(E)L). We are aware that other teacher trainer colleges can be generous when it comes to exemption packages, but we try not to participate in such "contest".

Factor 3: Flexible study program

Our students can choose how many credits a year they take on. They have to write a motivation letter to the study coach when they take less than 27 study credits, because we find it crucial that there is some continuity in the study progress of students. If not, we fear that students will lose touch with the study program.

We invest in thorough study coaching. When students struggle with their study schedule because of work or family issues, they can mail, phone or Skype with their study coach. Together with the coach, students try to find a solution that works for everyone. Students can adjust their study program throughout the academic year. We advise students to start with 30-35 study credits. When the studies go well, students can take on extra study credits. After reflecting with their study coach, students can also decrease the number of study credits if they would struggle with the program. When students did not succeed at the end of the academic year because of bad results or because they did not participate at exams nor handed in assignments, they are given binding study advice and they will be watched more closely by the study coach.

In order to help students dealing with the flexibility of the study program, we provide standard programs and model planning schedules. Students are obliged to take on certain subjects before they can start their teaching practice.

Factor 4: Flexible exam schedule

Our exam schedule is very flexible. We provide approximately ten exam weeks on campus throughout the academic year. The first exam week starts already in October. Students get the possibility to take an exam on different moments throughout the exam week, even on

Saturday morning. They can also sit two exams on the same day or they can choose to spread the exams. This flexible exam schedule enables students to plan the exams in consideration with their work and life at home. It helps students to study subject after subject on their own pace while keeping overview on the study progress. Besides that, the feedback given after taking an exam or after dropping an assignment, is a stimulant to do the next exam or assignment even better.

To set up this flexible exam schedule, our teacher training team must provide different versions of exam questions.

Next to a flexible exam schedule on campus, we have designed a system in which students are put under electronic supervision in order to take exams off campus, so at home. If possible, oral exams are organised via Skype.

Factor 5: Flexible teacher training planning

During their study program students have different periods of teaching practice. They are allowed to plan this in half days in accordance to their work and life balance. Within their first periods of teaching practice they can combine two different subjects. They can, for instance, give a lesson mathematics and a language lesson within a half day. Gradually their teaching practise will take on a more integrated focus and students will then plan their teaching periods in one week or more consecutively, because that reflects the reality. Students can choose the school of practice, but their own children should not attend the school and family members should not be working there.

Factor 6: Coaching from a distance

Quality study material

Throughout the years we have improved the quality of our study material. Everything has been written down in detail which enables our students to study autonomously. A template for written courses with standard icons (learning goals, video links etc.) has been provided by the colleagues of the educational policy of VIVES, which enhances the individual study progress of students.

The associates of the campus library put a lot of effort in providing teaching manuals and educational magazines in an online format. In the past the library was accessible on Saturday mornings for students of distance learning, but that was not a great success.

The evaluation of every subject is clearly defined in a study indicator. These study indicators are all designed in a similar way, so students can easily find their way through them. The criteria for evaluation are transparent in every study indicator and students can rely on the given study hints.

They can also find additional learning material on our learning platform Toledo: supplementary information, updates, video examples, tutorials, discussion fora, etc. A number of skills are also taught by online tools and exercises.

Personal approach

Every student needs a personal approach and coaching. We work within a general framework, but for distance learning students we often provide alternatives or deviations. The first communication generally happens by e-mail, because our communication is not bound to place and time. We try to be inviting and open within our online communication to make sure that students feel welcome at our campus and dare to ask questions. Listening to students and helping them with personal questions, is our main focus.

We notice however that coincident contact is only suitable for a number of students. That is why students always have the option to phone/Skype us or to make an appointment on campus. This supports some students in their study process. We have experimented with fixed online appointments by mail and Skype during week nights and weekends, but that did not generate the assumed effects, because those hours did not always correspond with those of the students.

For several years now our campus invests in individual reflection talks with students after a period of teaching practise. Those talks are highly appreciated by our students, based on inquiries.

This way of individual coaching is not always easy for our distance learning team, because of other duties on campus. In order to facilitate the work load of our team, we set up a number of practicalities. Mails need to be answered within three working days, exams need to be examined within 14 days and assignments need to be corrected within a month. Furthermore, we designed a communication policy specific for learning distance students.

Factor 7: Supporting the distance learning team

The concept of distance learning requires a team of motivated lecturers. We therefore invest in sessions of digital learning tools by which our team feels equipped to support our distance learning students. Our director tries to collect the lecturers' needs and take these into account. Sometimes individual coaching of lecturers are necessary. We also stimulate them to co-create or to support each other.

Future challenges

Although we strongly belief that our flexible teacher training program helps students with their work-life balance during the studies, we are not blind for a number of shortcomings. In what follows, we present some challenges for the future.

Dropout students

The dropout of students remains bigger in distance learning than in day learning. When we question students who drop out, they say that changes in work situation or in personal life no longer make it possible to continue. Other students indicate that the program is too heavy. In general, drop out students are pleased with the concept of distance learning.

Procrastination

Because of our flexible concept, we cannot apply temporary deadlines and that leads to procrastination. This leads to brief moments of examination stress in June and August within our team of distance learning. We are currently exploring different ways in order to find solutions.

Collaboration with training schools

Within a distance learning concept, it is not easy to set up an intensive collaboration with training schools. Students are free to choose a school in the vicinity of their home or work place. This generates a great spreading in Flanders. Besides that, our students do not practise their teaching at the same time, so it is difficult to reach out to coaching teachers during a certain time frame.

Collaboration with fellow-students

For a number of subject students need to work together. They can use digital tools to meet up. The individual study programs make it often difficult – if not impossible – for students to find a fellow-student for collaboration assignments. We need to think about ways to facilitate mutual contact between students so they can support each other in their study progress.

Personal follow-up of students

Nowadays our coaching method is partly inquiry-based. When students ask questions, our team gives the support and coaching they need. Students can get detailed feedback after dropping assignments and there are reflection talks as mentioned. And throughout the year they can read encouraging mails by our team. There are however still challenges to measure the individual study progress of distance learning students so that our team can adjust the coaching support in a better, more effective way. One of the ideas we have is tracking the activity of students throughout the academic year, in order to intervene on time. We are currently trying to raise funds to make that happen.

THE INFLUENCE OF HIGH-FIDELITY PATIENT SIMULATION TRAINING ON SELF-CONFIDENCE AND STRESS IN NURSING EDUCATION

Sofie Merlevede, Birgit Vincke, Lisa Kerckhof, VIVES University of Applied Sciences, Belgium

Introduction

Healthcare environments have become more complex and diverse. Interdisciplinary collaboration, teamwork, problem-solving skills, communication, clinical reasoning… are necessary competences for a nurse to meet the increasing complexity of the healthcare system (Jeffries, 2007; Kamge et al., 2010; Lee et al., 2015; Ranjbar, 2015). As a result of this, nursing education and schools are challenged to best prepare students for the complex healthcare system and to produce nurses who are competent in many areas of health care (Labrague et al., 2019; Lee et al., 2015). In order to achieve a certain level of competency, the nursing education and schools provides high fidelity patient simulation (HFPS) within the nursing education. With HFPS it is possible to re-enacting actual clinical situations in a safe and controlled setting (Lee et al., 2015; Weaver, 2011). HFPS mirrors the clinical setting by the use of realistic full body mannequins that provide real physical inputs and real environmental interaction (Weaver, 2011; Weiler et al., 2018). The use of HFPS promotes student competency by giving an opportunity to care in diverse clinical situations in a simulated environment, to practice skills and not harm and endanger real patients. (Lee et al., 2015; Weaver, 2011; Weiler, 2018). Previous studies have shown positive results regarding the use of high fidelity patient simulation (HFPS) within nursing education on several items such as clinical reasoning/judgement/thinking/decision making, teamwork, knowledge, psychomotor skills, value, realism, self-efficacy (Baptista et al., 2016; Lee et al., 2015, Weaver, 2011; Weiler et al., 2018). On the other hand, little is known about the effects of HFPS sessions on the perceived stress and self-confidence level of students during internships (Weaver, 2011). However, students experience often stress during clinical education (Ranjbar, 2015) and stress can affect clinical performance (Ignacio et al., 2015). Therefore, this study examines whether HFPS has an added value on perceived self-confidence and stress levels of first-year nursing students during their internship.

Methods

Participants and context

In the Healthcare department of the VIVES University of Applied Sciences, HFPS is included (obligated) in the curriculum of the four-year bachelor program in Nursing. HFPS (three hours of simulation including debriefing) contains computerized full-body manikins. The simulation occurs in a realistic environment, with actual medical equipment and supplies (Can & Cooper, 2009). The first-year nursing students (n = 287) of the academic year 2018-2019 of 3 nursing schools in West-Flanders (Belgium) were invited to participate in the study.

Pre-Test/Post-Test

The first-year nursing students were assigned, according to the planning of the internship weeks, to an experimental (n = 191) and a control group (n = 51). A pre-test/post-test experiment is designed to compare the control and experimental group.

Questionnaires used to collect data

Questionnaire "Stress and self-confidence during internships"

The questionnaire "Stress and self-confidence during internships" was developed and validated to examine the levels of self-confidence and stress during internships. Various sources were used to build up the questionnaire: State Trait Anxiety Inventory Scale (Spielberger et al., 1983), expert's opinions and the literature/previous studies. The final questionnaire contains 26 questions, from a Likert-type scale, with a variation from one to ten, in which one stands for *totally disagree* and 10 stands for *totally agree.*

To test the self-developed questionnaire, a pilot study occurred in September 2018. Second year nursing students received, at the start of the academic year, the self-developed questionnaire (digital (personal mail), Lime Survey). These second year nursing students completed the questionnaires based on their experiences of HFPS and their internships in their first year. The response rate was 30% (received questionnaires: 51; fully completed questionnaires: 39). Based on the results of the pilot study, a principal component analysis (SPSS version 24) was executed (26 variables (26 questions), Varimax rotation, Kaiser-Meyer-Olkin Test (.798), Barlett's test of spericity (.000)). Two main components could be distinguished after interpretation: "Self-Confidence" (12 questions) and "Stress" (9 questions). The internal consistency of the components "stress" and "self-confidence" is high (Cronbach's Alpha Self-confidence: 0.964 and Stress: 0.949). Five of the 26 questions could not be subdivided in the components "Self-Confidence" and "Stress".

Table 1: Questionnaire "Stress and Self-confidence during internships"

Self-Confidence (Cronbachs α: .949)	Stress (Cronbachs α: .964)	Extra
• I feel competent to apply the acquired technical skills • I feel at ease • I feel content • I feel comfortable • I feel pleasant • I feel joyfull • I feel good about myself • I feel secure • I feel agreeable • I feel steady • I feel self-confident • I feel calm	• I feel stressed • I feel tense • I feel jittery • I feel nervous • I feel worried • I feel unsecure • I feel relaxed • I feel rushed • I feel high strung	• I feel rested • I feel anxious • I feel upset • I feel indecisive • I feel competent to apply the acquired communication skills

Simulation Effectiveness Tool-Modified (SET-M)

The Simulation Effectiveness Tool (SET-M) is used to estimate how students experienced their simulation session (three-point scale: *do not agree, somewhat agree, strongly agree*) (Leighton et al., 2015).

Table 2: Questionnaire: SET-M

SET-M
Prebriefing increased my confidence
Prebriefing was beneficial to my learning
I am better prepared to respond to changes in my patient's condition
I developed a better understanding of the pathophysiology
I am more confident of my nursing assessment skills
I felt empowered to make clinical decisions
I developed a better understanding of medications
I had the opportunity to practice my clinical decision-making skills
I am more confident in my ability to prioritize care and interventions
I am more confident in communicating with my patient
I am more confident in my ability to teach patients about their illness and interventions
I am more confident in my ability to report information to health care team
I am more confident in providing interventions that foster patient safety
I am more confident in using evidence-based practice to provide nursing care
Debriefing contributed to my learning
Debriefing allowed me to verbalize my feelings before focusing on the scenario
Debriefing was valuable in helping me improve my clinical judgment
Debriefing was valuable in helping me improve my clinical judgment
Debriefing was a constructive evaluation of the simulation

Procedure: Planning internships, HFPS and questionnaires

The pre-test occurred after the first internship (duration of the internship 2 weeks; planned: November 2019). The students completed their first internship without HFPS sessions. After this first internship, all these students received an invitation to complete the questionnaire "Stress and Self-Confidence during internship" by their personal mail (link to the Lime survey).

The post-test occurred after the last internship (duration of the internship: 5 weeks; planned for the control group: February 2019; planned for the experimental group: April 2019). The experimental group will have completed HFPS before the start of their last internship, while the control group will not have received HFPS before ending their last internship. After the last internship, both groups receive the questionnaires: "Stress and self-confidence during internships" by their personal mail (link to the Lime survey). This way, it is possible to examine whether HFPS has an impact on the perceived self-confidence and stress level of nursing students during their internship. In addition, after each HFPS session, the Simulation Effectiveness Tool (SET-M) is used to estimate how students experienced their simulation session. The students receive the link to the SET-M by their personal mail.

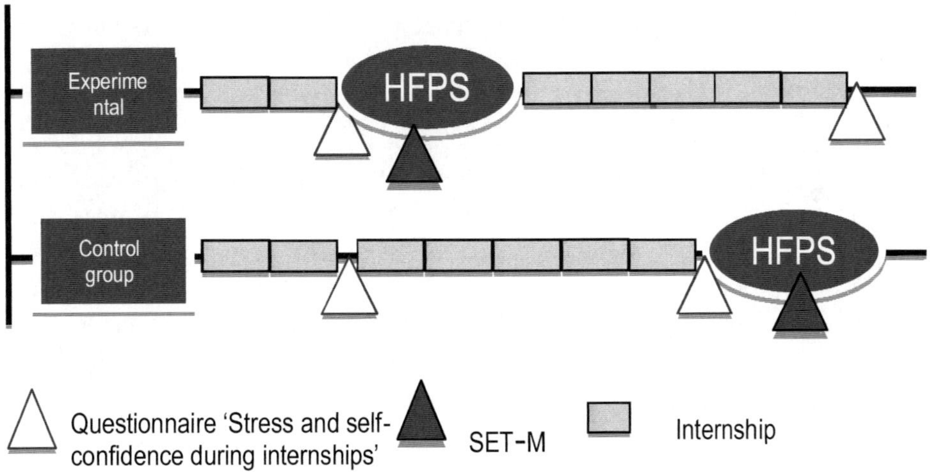

Figure 1. Procedure pre-post test

Data-analysis

For the statistical treatment of the data, the program SPSS version 24 was used. A descriptive analysis is performed (mean, minimum, maximum, frequency and percentages distribution). The comparison between the experimental and the control group, is still in process.

Preliminary results

Baseline/Pre-Test

From a total of 287 nursing students, 114 students completed the questionnaire "Stress and Self-Confidence during internships" (response rate: 39.72%). Of the 114 nursing students who completed the questionnaire, the majority was female (76%). 66% of the students were 18-year our younger.

The average scale score for self-confidence was 6.78/10. "I feel secure" scored the highest (7.28) and "I feel self- confidence" scored the lowest (5.82/10). The average scale score for stress was 4.97/10. "I feel relaxed" scored the highest (6.02/10) and "I feel high strung" scored the lowest (4.10/10).

Post-Test

Control group

Questionnaire "Stress and Self-confidence during internships"

From a total of 51 nursing students, 17 students completed the questionnaire "Stress and Self-Confidence during internships" (response rate: 33.33%). Of the 17 nursing students who completed the questionnaire, the majority was female (88.2%). 52,9% of the students were 18-year our younger.

The average scale score for self-confidence was 6.19/10. "I feel competent to apply the acquired technical skills" scored the highest (7.18/10) and "I feel self-confidence" scored the lowest (5.12/10). The average score scale for stress was 5.25/10. "I feel unsecure" scored the highest (6.06/10) and "I feel high strung" scored the lowest (4.35/10).

SET-M

The HFPS sessions for the control group are planned in April/May 2019. The data collection is in process.

Experimental group

Questionnaire "Stress and Self-confidence during internships"

For the students in the experimental group, the last internship (and the data collection) is in process (from April 2019 until the middle of May 2019).

SET M

The students of the experimental group received HFPS before their last internship (February/March 2018). From a total of 191 nursing students, 76 students completed the questionnaire SET-M (response rate: 39.8%).

The students score mainly between *somewhat agree* and *strongly agree* with an average score of 2.48 (3 – *strongly agree*). The students agreed mostly with the categories regarding "Debriefing". "Debriefing was a constructive evaluation of the simulation" scored the highest (2.86/3).

Conclusion

This study examines whether HFPS has an added value on perceived self-confidence and stress levels of first- year nursing students during their internship. First-year nursing students (n = 287) of 3 nursing schools in West- Flanders (Belgium) were studied. To achieve the purpose of the study, the students were assigned to an experimental and a control group and a pre-test /post-test occurred. The pre-test occurred after the first internship (2 weeks). The students did not receive HFPS on that moment. To examine the self-confidence and stress, the students completed the questionnaire "Stress and self-confidence during internships". The post-test occurred after the last internship (5 weeks). The experimental group will have completed HFPS before the start of their last internship, while the control group will not have received HFPS before ending their last internship. After the internships, both groups receive the questionnaires: "Stress and self-confidence during internships". This way, it is possible to examine whether HFPS has an impact on the perceived self-confidence and stress level of nursing students during their internship. In addition, after each HFPS session, the Simulation Effectiveness Tool (SET-M) is used to estimate how students experienced their simulation session.

Pre-test

The first year nursing students completed their first internship before they received HFPS sessions. The average scale score for self-confidence was 6.78/10. "I feel secure" scored the highest (7.28) and "I feel self-confidence" scored the lowest (5.82/10). The average scale score for stress was 4.97/10. "I feel relaxed" scored the highest (6.02/10) and "I feel high strung" scored the lowest (4.10/10).

Post-test

Control group

The students in the control group finished their last internship before receiving HFPS. The average scale score for self-confidence was 6.19/10. "I feel competent to apply the acquired technical skills" scored the highest (7.18/10) and "I feel self-confidence" scored the lowest (5.12/10). The average score scale for stress was 5.25/10. "I feel unsecure" scored the highest (6.06/10) and "I feel high strung" scored the lowest (4.35/10). The HFPS sessions for the control group are planned in April/May 2019.

Experimental group

For the students in the experimental group, the last internship is not finished yet (from April 2019 until the middle of May 2019). However, the students received HFPS before their internship. The students scored mainly between *somewhat agree* and *strongly agree* on the statements of the SET-M. More concrete, the students agreed mostly with the categories regarding "Debriefing". The statement "Debriefing was a constructive evaluation of the simulation" scored the highest.

References

Baptista, R. C. N., Paiva, L. A. R., Oliveira, L. M. N., Pereira, M. C. R., & Martins, J. C. A. (2016). Satisfaction and gains perceived by nursing students with medium- and high-fidelity simulation: a randomized controlled trial. *Nurse Education Today*, 127-132.

Can, R. P., & Cooper, S. J. (2009). Simulation-based learning in nurse education: systematic review. *Journal of Advanced Nursing*, 3-15.

Ignacio, J., Domans, D., Scherpbier, A., Rethans, J. J., Chan, S., & Ying Liaw, S. (2015). Comparison of standardized patients with high-fidelity simulators for managing stress and improving performance in clinical deterioration: a mixed methods study. *Nurse Education Today, 35*, 1161-1168.

Jeffries, P.R. (2007). Simulation in Nursing Education, from conceptualization to evaluation. New York: National League for Nursing.

Kamge, K., Clonchesy, J., Mitchel, A. M., & Suresky, J. M. (2010). The impact of high fidelity human simulation on self-efficacy of communication skill. *Issues in Mental Health Nursing*, 315-323.

Labrague, L. J., McEnroe-Petitte, D., Bowling, A. A., Nwafor, C. E., & Tsaras, K. (2019). High-fidelity simulation and nursing students' anxiety and self-confidence: A systematic review. *Nursing Forum*, 1-11.

Lee, J., Lee, Y., Lee, S., & Bae, J. (2016). Effects of high-fidelity patient simulation led clinical reasoning course: Focused on nursing core competencies, problem solving, and academic self-efficacy. *Japan Journal of Nursing Sciences, 13*, 20-28.

Leighton, K., Ravert, P., Mudra, V., & Macintosh, C. (2015). Updating the Simulation Effectiveness Tool: Item Modifications and Reevaluation of Psychometric Properties. *Nursing Education Perspectives, 36*, 317-323.

Ranjbar, H. (2015). Stress management: An ignored challenge in clinical nursing education. *Nurse Education Today*, editorial.

Spielberger, C. D., Gorsuch, R. L., Lushene, P. R., Vagg, P. R., & Jacobs, A. G. (1983). *Manual for the State-Trait Anxiety Inventory.* Palo Alto: Consulting Psychologists Press.

Weaver, A. (2011). High-Fidelity Patient Simulation in Nursing Education: An Integrative Review. *Nursing Education Perspectives*, 37-40.

Weiler, D., Gibson, A. L., & Saleem, J. J. (2018). The effect of role assignment in high fidelity patient simulation on nursing students: an experimental research study. *Nurse Education Today, 63*, 29-34.

PONTE EN LÍNEA: A STRATEGY FROM DATA-BASED RESPONSE SYSTEM FOR PERSONALIZED LEARNING

Jorge León Martínez, Edith Tapia Rangel, National Autonomous University of Mexico (UNAM), Mexico

Abstract

The implementation case of "Ponte en Línea" is presented, a data-based response system for personalized learning organized by mobile-based micro-learning structures called UAPA (Learning Support Units). This program was implemented by the Faculty of Accounting and Administration (FCA) and the Coordination of Open University and Distance Education (CUAED), both dependencies of the National Autonomous University of Mexico (UNAM), for the benefit of the student population.

Introduction

Today, students have at their disposal large amounts of information which can support them in their learning processes, institutions of higher education, aware of this, make extraordinary efforts to generate and make available to students, educational resources developed by their teaching staff, either to use they in independent study or as part of their teachers' teaching strategies. Additionally, mobile devices have permeated society irreversibly and they have allowed access to content to be generalized, in such a way that they can be recovered virtually at any time and place where there is an Internet connection.

Considering these situations, the "Ponte en Línea" program was proposed, to bring young students from the National Autonomous University of Mexico (UNAM by its initials in Spanish) closer to them, educational resources developed through a collaborative effort between an academic entity and the Coordination of Open University and Distance Education (CUAED by its initials in Spanish).

"Ponte en línea" is considered a space for learning by presenting resources in a data-based response system for personalized learning. The categorization of the information included in this space is based on the organization and cataloguing of the so-called Support Units for Learning (UAPA by its initials in Spanish), which are mobile-based micro-learning tools that have their origin in academic undergraduate programs. The elements of this proposal will now be presented.

Micro-learning

Hug cited by Sun et al. (2017) defined micro learning "as learning activities that are carried out within fragmented time pieces". While micro learning is a highly accepted resource in the field of job training, Robes cited by Coakley, Garvey, and O'Neill (2017), notes that micro-learning "can even potentially be used to compliment, rather than replace, more formal, time-consuming means of learning, further indicating the flexibility of the approach".

In the case of UNAM, micro learning has been implemented through UAPA, which is a self-contained, interoperable and reusable educational resource that promotes autonomous learning in the student through logical sequencing and interaction between objectives, activities and contents oriented to favour meaningful learning.

The UAPA exposes a theme through a didactic sequence and a structure made up of:

- Introduction. Text that presents in a general way the contents of the UAPA indicating how they are organized, their relevance and suggestions for their study.
- Objective. It establishes the goal that the user will reach when concluding the study of UAPA
- Content. It refers to the presentation in different formats of the disciplinary, procedural or attitudinal knowledge that the user wishes to apprehend.
- Learning activities. Work designed for the user to achieve the learning objective.
- Self-appraisal. Automatic evaluation with positive and negative feedback that measures if the learning objective was reached.
- Information sources. List of documents that served as reference for the construction of UAPA.

Due to its conception and structure, the UAPA can be used, reused or serves as a reference during different moments of the teaching and learning processes.

Mobile-based micro-learning

The Mobile Global Report, published by comScore in 2017, established that mobile devices have the first place among users worldwide. In Mexico alone, 89% of Internet users connect to the Internet through their Smartphone above laptop computers, desktop computers and tablets (Asociación de Internet.mx, 2018). The Mobile Global Report concluded that many of the behaviours driven by mobile consumption align with the human needs established in the famous Maslow's pyramid.

With the above, it is evident that mobile devices have been transformed from communication tools to life instruments for people as they support the satisfaction of practically the entire Maslow's pyramid of needs, and in the case of students, they have become instruments to develop their school and social activities. In other words, students now require learning tools based on mobile devices, that's the reason why these tools must consider some of the aspects that mobile-learning (m-learning) comprises. Kukulska-Hulme and Traxler cited by Latchem (2018) characterize m-learning as "a personal, unobtrusive, spontaneous, "anytime, anywhere" way to learn and access educational tools and material that enlarges access to Education for All [and] reinforces learners sense of ownership of the learning experience, offering them flexibility in how, when and where they learn".

From this perspective and given that mobile devices also allow access to educational materials, it must be guaranteed that UAPAs are fully operable from these devices. In this sense, the UAPAS are considered as mobile-based micro-learning tools, since in addition to the structure that shapes them previously, they are built according to the rules of responsive design. The responsive design implies that the "applications are built to change in response to available screen size. The idea is to build one application that looks good on both large desktop workstations and small tablets or even smartphones" (Vesterli, 2017).

In this way, the UAPA is an example of the so-called mobile-based micro-learning that in the words of Nikou (2018) "combines features of mobile learning and micro-learning to deliver small learning units and short-term learning activities". This is because UAPAs have the potential to support learners' autonomy to facilitate self-directed learning. As Meng and Li (2016) point out "with this learning form, learners' learning activities are not confined by time and place; they can study anytime, anywhere with relatively small learning units for a short time. Combing the two learning forms, mobile micro-learning has the features of convenience, flexibility and interactivity".

Cataloguing

Cataloguing is the process by which metadata is generated for educational resources. Metadata is then "all that descriptive information about the context, quality, condition or characteristics of a resource, data or object that has the purpose of facilitating its recovery, authentication, evaluation, preservation or interoperability" (Senso & de la Rosa, 2003).

Among other things, cataloguing has the following objectives: the identification of resources in different environments; the description of the resources, their location and accessibility; the management of its legal use; and the generation of automatic responses by crossing data. In this sense, the generation and validation of metadata for the UAPA became important, since it allows, among other things, increasing the accessibility to them, facilitating their search and recovery, decrease traffic on the network since the data is retrieved through metadata information, establish the conditions of use and exploitation of the resource, and improve the conditions of reuse of resources for teaching and self-directed learning (Marzal, Calzada, & Cuevas, 2006).

The implementation of the cataloguing for UAPAs required the initial effort of a group of librarians who defined the metadata scheme would be based on the Dublin Core Metadata Initiative, which provides simple and normalized standards levels to facilitate the search, sharing and management of information through the description of resources. Fields related to the academic structure that gave rise to the resource were added to this scheme.

Subsequently, a revision of the syntax of the elements of the metadata schema was carried out, that is, they were established among other things: the elements to be considered by resource, the order of registration and the way in which the information for each element would be encoded. After a pilot implementation was carried out, the need to establish semantics for the scheme was identified, which established the use of specific vocabulary for some elements.

Finally, it was defined that the metadata would be incorporated externally, that is, they would be described in a database that would link to the referenced resource. In this way, it was possible for UAPAs to be organized and catalogued in the data-based response system for personalized learning called "Ponte en Línea".

Data-based response system for personalized learning

Bulger (2016) establishes that personalized learning "describes adaptation to students' unique combination of goals, interests, and competencies and the ongoing process of shifting instruction as these conditions change" and that currently includes a wide spectrum of implementations that go from the interfaces customizable to adaptive tutors, or educational events focused on the student learning management systems.

Nowadays, personalized learning systems can be categorized into two groups mainly: the group of adaptive systems that seek to reflect and support the learning process, which is flexible and is constantly changing; and response systems, which offer an interface with predetermined and hyperlinked contents, such as an interactive textbook or as recommendation systems (Bulger, 2016).

Within the response systems, there are those that are based on data and provide materials appropriate to the level of competence of students based on the collection of information on use and search for them. Through analytical information, these platforms recommend playlists that give a different line of study to each student. An important aspect to consider in these systems is that they favour socialization, in such a way that the student does not feel isolated in the process. To solve this situation, data-based response systems can allow users to share their playlists, so that they share their journey with their peers in case it is useful for someone else.

Implementation of "Ponte en Línea" in the Faculty of Accounting and Administration (FCA by its initials in Spanish)

At the beginning of 2018, CUAED proposed the FCA a program for the creation of UAPA, in order to comply with the Strategic Program 7 "Information and Communication Technologies (ICT) and Learning and Knowledge Technologies (TAC)", Line of action 7.7 "Open access policy of the UNAM", project 7.7.2. "Support the academic entities in the creation of contents for their inclusion in the different repositories of the UNAM" of the Institutional Development Plan of Dr. Enrique Graue Wiechers, rector of UNAM.

The program was approved and during the period from February to December 2018, the planning of activities for the construction of the UAPAs was carried out. The program counted on the participation of more than 50 professors of the FCA of the careers of Accounting, Administration and Informatics. During that period, more than 300 UAPAs were developed.

For the second half of 2018, the FCA got in touch with CUAED to propose that through the UAPA, the hundreds of educational resources (in multiple formats) generated by the FCA itself over the course of 5 years would be organized. It was defined that "Ponte en Línea FCA" (https://ponteenlinea.fca.unam.mx) was a program of the FCA, in collaboration with the CUAED of UNAM, to make available to students various digital educational resources for use and reuse during their learning process. The proposal was accepted and the resources were organized under the categorization and cataloguing generated for the UAPA, so they would be accessed through them on the site "Ponte en Línea FCA". This is how "Ponte en Línea FCA" is organized by UAPAs from where you access other educational resources related to the subject such as digital notes, audiotexts and video lessons.

The site was designed and implemented in Drupal, an open content manager, organized by categories in such a way that it could function as a data-based response system for personalized learning. In this way the student could access the resources through searches for keywords related to the subjects of his degree. "Ponte en línea FCA" is also self-managed, and is available 24 hours a day, 365 days a year.

Conclusions

If mobile-based micro-learning has been a widely accepted option for professional training, it is important to implement it in the higher education educational field, since at the same time that it graduates professionals, it prepares them for educational formats that will be found in his professional training throughout his life.

Another aspect that universities should consider is the personalization of learning, and a strategy to start with this scheme is the implementation of data-based response systems for personalized learning, as in the case of "Ponte en Línea FCA".

References

Asociación de Internet.mx (2018) Estudio sobre los Hábitos de los usuarios de Internet en México 2018. México. Retrieved from https://www.asociaciondeinternet.mx

Bulger, M. (2016, July 22). The conversations we´re not having. Data and Society Working Pape. Retrieved from https://datasociety.net/pubs/ecl/PersonalizedLearning_primer_2016.pdf

Coakley, D., Garvey, R., & O'Neill, Í. (2017). Micro-learning—Adopting Digital Pedagogies to Facilitate Technology-Enhanced Teaching and Learning for CPD. In G. Teh & S. Choy (Eds.), *Empowering 21st Century Learners Through Holistic and Enterprising Learning* (pp. 237-242). Singapore: Springer.

comScore (2017) Mobile Global Report. Comparativa internacional sobre tendencias y comportamientos móviles. México. Retrieved from https://www.comscore.com/lat/Insights/Presentations-and-Whitepapers/2017/The-Global-Mobile-Report

Facultad de Contaduría y Administración (2019). Ponte en línea FCA. Retrieved from https://ponteenlinea.fca.unam.mx

Latchem, C. (2018). Mobile Learning. In C. Latchem (Auth.), *Open and Distance Non-formal Education in Developing Countries.* (pp. 29–35). Singapore: Springer.

Marzal, M., Calzada, J., & Cuevas, A. (2006). Development of a Metadata Scheme to describe Educational Resources: The Mimeta Application Profile. *Revista Española de Documentación Científica, 9*(24), 551-571.

Meng, J., & Li, Z. (2016). *Feasibility of Applying Mobile Micro-learning to College English Learning.* Paper presented at the 2016 International Seminar on Education Innovation and Economic Management (SEIEM 2016), China. Retrieved from https://doi.org/10.2991/seiem-16.2016.123

Nikou, S. A. (2018). Mobile-Based micro-Learning and Assessment: Impact on learning performance and motivation of high school students. *Journal of Computer Assisted Learning, 34*(3), 269-278.

Senso, J. A., & da la Rosa Piñero, A. (2003). El concepto de metadato: algo más que descripción de recursos electrónicos. *Ciência da Informação, 32*(2), 95-106. Retrieved from https://dx.doi.org/10.1590/S0100-19652003000200011

Sun, G., Cui, T., Beydoun, G., Chen, S., Xu, D., & Shen, J. (2017). Organizing Online Computation for Adaptive Micro Open Education Resource Recommendation. In H. Xie, E. Popescu, G. Hancke, & B. Fernández Manjón (Eds.), *Advances in Web-Based Learning – ICWL 2017. ICWL 2017. Lecture Notes in Computer Science* (10473). Cham: Springer.

Vesterli, S. (2017). Layout and Skins. In S. Veterli (Auth.), *Oracle ADF Survival Guide* (pp. 53–76). Berkeley, C.A.: Apress.

Connecting through Educational Technology
Proceedings of the European Distance and E-Learning Network 2019 Annual Conference
Bruges, 16-19 June, 2019

CONNECTING WITH STUDENTS IN AN OPEN DISTANCE LEARNING

Rodney Mabusela, Itumeleng Molefe, University of South Africa, South Africa

Abstract

This paper aims on exploring/expands mechanisms in which universities could utilize to connect with students studying in an open distance learning.

Introduction

The introduction of open distance learning has transformed the image of tertiary education globally. ODL has dealt with many challenges to learning that were experienced with traditional distance education, as it is more, practical, flexible and sometimes effective, particularly in an age of excess to connectivity.

Moore and Kearslely (1996; p.6) defined ODL as the distribution of learning materials to student who are especially distant from their lectures. Moore (1993; p.22) points out that it not merely entails a geographic separation by time. As the grates portion of teaching and learning is realized outside educational institutions, it requires special educational and communication technology.

The implementation of information and communication technologies (ICT) has transformed the ODL university culture. There is a huge transformative in the way we teach and learn. Students are no longer passive listeners, but need to be able to do pro-active reading, encoding and decoding anywhere, anytime. In an online learning environment, students required to take greater responsibility in their leaning paths, and can share their vast of experiences and knowledge with others (Dela Pena-Bandalaria, 2007; p.12). Quality ODL requires interactive communication between student and lectures and other relevant support staff that is realized with the aid of modern ICT.

Effective communication is significant in human life, in education, where two or more individuals share information, knowledge, values, and skills, it is imperatives to communicate in such a way that any misunderstanding is avoided at all cost. with ODL this is the real challenge; to communicate effectively with students at a distance, in the third world countries, it is even more challenge to assist students to understand the expectations of ODL. The problem is that many students do not have access to electronic devices for online communication. Students who do have access to devices, do not always have access to connectivity such as internet access particularly when they should study off campus.

Connecting with students is not an event which means it cannot be achieved over night, however it requires perpetual efforts to achieve it. Connecting with students means one must do the following: caring about the work-life balance of students, attentive to students' needs, expectations and the changing behaviour of diverse student populations including career, other studies, family life.

Method

We were able to use a *Descriptive Design* which helped us to designate the current status of a phenomenon which is effective communication with students. The approach in which we had collected the data, was through our term of office as the SRC (Student Representative Council) by mostly observation the trends of the students' participation in the activities within the institution. And through those years/ period of observation we applied the following as well, Comparative descriptive design; cross-sectional design and longitudinal designs.

Cross-Sectional designs

In our study we would simply record cases which were brought to us by student who were doing walk-ins. We would have a register for them to record or note down their challenges faced in the institution. We therefore chose to measure connection of students in open distance learning between students who interact with the university vs the student who do not interact with the university support system and compare their pass rate. We had classified them in groups of their academic level, for example; 1st level, 2nd level, 3rd level and 4th level of study.

Longitudinal designs

We have over a period of four (4) years observed student who have enrolled in the institution (University of South Africa) in the year 2014 until their completion of their qualification from the onset of their first year of study. We observed their energy/ enthusiasm towards the support which our institution has. Therefore, the effects of all these measure gave us a guidance on what is to be done.

Results

Throughout the study was able to find that the following issues; we found that student (a) were not submitting their assignments, most of them (b) have failed the module more than once and (c) did also not seat for their examination.

Approximately 19% of 18 – 24-year-old South Africans now attend university, Low in comparison to most other countries. Currently only about 27% of students entering university for the first time complete a first degree or diploma in regulation time, with one in four students in contact institutions failing or dropping out before their second year of study (CHE 2016: 145)

We did an overview to try understand if the online connection support is the only factor affecting students, or are there other factors. Therefore, the following table links inability to gain accesses at the institution and their background as a factor.

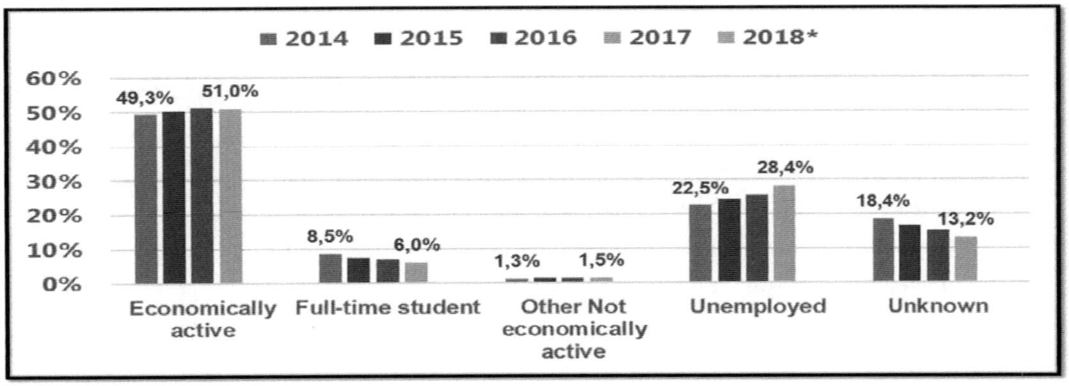

Figure 1.

Discussion

It seems as though many UNISA students involved in the survey were either not comfortable with the use of ICT and the proposed support systems, or they do not have the necessary skills to use them. Access to the various media may be a further problem. Many of the students are still in the first phase of ODL – they want written material and written comments mailed to them through the postal system as was the case with traditional correspondence education. The lecturers are still seen as the main source of knowledge and information, so many opt for one-way communication where the lecturer gives a lecture through which information is distributed. Students prefer postal services or phone contact for communication, because most of them do not have access to internet or even fax machines, or cannot use the internet. They prefer to submit their assignments through the postal system and want feedback from lecturers via tutorial letters.

Although these results cannot be generalised, the outcomes of this survey are not encouraging for any ODL institution and lecturers should be aware of the situation. Although UNISA's ODL is in its transitional stages and is still developing and undergoing change, the requirements of the student population will have to be considered or the target marked will have to change. Students need more resources particularly those in remote rural areas. They need more training in the use of multimedia from the moment they commence their studies and need practise in the use of the various communication media. Lecturers need to incorporate such training possibilities in the tutorial matter and appropriate guidance as to what is expected them. Students need to be gradually introduced to the idea that lecturers should serve more as facilitators than transmitters of information

Further factors the respondents mentioned as barriers to learning are "problems with time management", "poor study techniques and skills", "work obligations", "no contact with other students", "lack of availability of lecturers", "difficulty in getting hold of the right person in the university", and "administration problems". These factors coincide with those mentioned by

Fozdar and Kumar (2007; p.6) and may be possible reasons for student drop-out. Similar problems seem to be experienced in ODL worldwide.

Fozdar and Kumar (2007, p.6) also mention the following common problems of distance learners as proposed by various researchers:

- Lack of personal contact with especially teachers and the immediate feedback from lecturers on work done;
- Sense of isolation;
- Pre-course orientation to help with management of studies;
- Tutor support during course of studies;
- Improved information and formative advices.

References

Carneiro, R. (2007). The big picture: Understanding learning and meta-learning challenges. *European Journal of Education, 42*(2), 151-172.

Creswell, J. W. (2008). Educational research – planning, conducting and evaluating quantitative and qualitative research (3rd ed.). Upper Saddle River, NJ: Merrill Prentice Hall.

Dela Pena-Bandalaria, M. (2007). Impact of ICTs on open and distance learning in a developing country setting: The Philippine experience. *International Review of Research in Open and Distance Learning, 8*(1), 1-15.

Merriam, S. B. (1998). Qualitative research and case study applications in education. San Francisco, CA: Jossey-Bass.

Moore, M. G. (1993). Theory of transactional distance. In D. Keegan (Ed.), *Theoretical principles of distance education* (pp. 22-38.). London: Routledge.

Moore, M. G., & Kearsley, G. (1996). *Distance Education: A systems view.* Belmont: Wadsworth Publishing Company.

Oliver, M., & Trigwell, K. (2005). Can 'blended learning' be redeemed? *E-learning, 2*(1), 17-26.

Orey, M. (2002). One year of online blended learning: lessons learned.

Sethy, S. S. (2008). Distance education in the age of globalization: an overwhelming desire towards blended learning. *Turkish Online Journal of Distance Education, 9*(3) Article 3. Retrieved April 26, 2019, from http://tojde.anadolu.edu.tr/makale_goster.php?id=422

Simpson, O. (2004). The impact on retention of interventions to support distance learning students. *Open Learning, 19*, 79-95.

Singh, H., & Reed, C. (2001). A White paper: Archiving success with blended learning.

Tatkovic, N., Ruzic, M., & Tatkovic, S. (2006). *Open distant learning: Pedagogical terms of reference and dilemmas.* Accessed on 12 April 2010. http://files.eric.ed.gov/fulltext/ED494214.pdf

Unisa (2008). Open distance learning policy.

Acknowledgments

We would like to acknowledge the support we got from the studend support during the times we were in the src there contribution to knowledge and guidance. We would like to also acknowledge the collegues we were working with in the project. Last we would like to put it categorically clear that me (Itumeleng Molefe) and my collegue (Rodney Mabusela) we have agreed on co-authorship becuased we were working hand in hand and we are as well currently in the same project to try to implemant the intendet said project.

VALIDATION OF QUALITY INDICATORS FOR E-LEARNING

Dieter Maes, Marieke Metzger, Heidi Vanden Eeckhoute, VIVES University of Applied Sciences, Belgium

Abstract

This study aims to identify and validate quality indicators for e-learning modules.

Background: E-learning plays an important role in education training for nurses and other healthcare professionals. It has a lot of advantages such as flexibility, high impact learning, cost-effectiveness. In case of quality care and accreditation it can be used as a new way of learning. Recently, a lot of different e-learning modules have been created and are available for care organisations. However, the quality of these modules cannot be guaranteed and care organisations do not know how to create good and qualitative e-learning modules on their own. A tool that screens the current e-learning modules for quality does not exist yet, but could help care organisations on their search for good and qualitative e-learning modules.

Methods: Firstly, a review of the most current e-learning literature was conducted to identify different quality indicators. Secondly, the results were discussed with experts to create a list of important quality indicators. Finally, the list was sent to a second group of experts who made a ranking according the degree of importance so that a final list of quality indicators could be derived.

Results: A list of quality indicators was created and divided into two categories: motivation and pedagogical framework.

Conclusion: This study was important to define qualitative indicators for e-learning. Those indicators can be used to check current e-learning modules for quality so that healthcare professionals can keep on delivering good and qualitative care.

Introduction

For every care provider and every healthcare facility (hospital, home care service, residential care centre, etc.) it is expected to provide good, high-quality care, guarantee patient safety and provide up-to-date professionalization.

Quality healthcare can be defined as "consistently delighting the patient by providing efficacious, effective and efficient healthcare services according to the latest clinical guidelines and standards, which meet the patient's needs and satisfies providers" (Mosadeghrad, 2013). Care providers within care and welfare facilities should strive for quality of care as well as patient safety.

In order to objectively determine quality and patient safety, various hospitals and home care institutions call on international bodies that accredit hospitals worldwide (Joint Commission International (JCI) or the Netherlands Institute for Accreditation in Care (NIAZ)). Accreditation (JCI, NIAZ) is one way of improving care quality and patient safety (Groeninge, 2013) (Joint Commission International, 2015). Up-to-date and evidence-based trained staff is necessary to achieve quality care. Therefore, a regular training is essential.

Health care institutions, knowledge institutions and companies are convinced that e-learning can bring about an optimal learning return if good didactic, content and technological conditions are met. Health care institutions are gradually making the switch to using e-learning. But use remains limited and certainly not all possibilities are used.

E-learning is a way of learning that uses the internet and the associated (communication) technology (Groeninge, 2013; Ruiz, Mintzer, & Leipzig, 2006; Mayer, The Cambridge Handbook of Multimedia Learning, 2005) (Mayer, Learning environments: the case for Evidence-Based Practice and Issue-Driven Research, 2003). E-learning is a powerful didactic tool. It provides standardised content and also makes evaluation possible. E-learning stimulates efficient learning. After all, the learner acquires knowledge, skills and attitudes faster than in traditional lessons. The flexibility exists to choose from an extensive menu of media options that fit the learner's own learning style. In addition, the learner can choose the time and space to process the content. This has a motivating effect. (Liang, Wu, & Tsai, 2011; Meewis, 2009; Tung & Chang, 2008; Mimi, Lisa, & Chan, 2007; Yu & Yang, 2006; Ruiz, Mintzer, & Leipzig, 2006).

A big disadvantage is that there are currently no validated criteria that can check the quality of an e-learning module. Developers use their own system of indicators developed by their own company. Furthermore, there is no recognised accreditation agency for E-learning. Accreditation could be used to assess quality and should be enforced by the government.

Methods

Study design

A review of the most current e-learning literature to identify quality indicators was conducted. This review was followed by an exploration of needs and opinions using semi-structured expert-group discussions. This qualitative approach aided the investigation of attitudes and beliefs and also helped to generate new ideas. Afterwards a survey was sent out to validate the existing results and check the degree of importance for all quality indicators.

Study participants

Two groups of participants were used. The first group consisted of important stakeholders, namely the developer of an LMS (Infolearn), the responsible developer for e-learning (AZ Groeninge), the coordinator of the centre of expertise for care innovation and Tom Madou, e-learning expert and developer (VIVES). It was considered that involving those people would ensure a complete insight in e-learning programs, learning strategies, assessment-methods, and feedback mechanisms. Secondly a survey was sent to a diverse group of experts who are responsible for all learning programs using e-learning within their care organisation

Data analysis

The first step was to look for validated indicators that could be used to monitor the quality of e-modules through a literature review. The result (list of indicators) was verified in the first group of involved participants. As a final step, the list of indicators was sent to the second group by means of a survey. This last step was necessary to validate and approve the list of indicators and the data was analysed using the statistical software package SPSS.

Results

Several indicators that can be used to assess the quality of an e-learning module were found. Based on these indicators, a difference was made between indicators with focus on motivation and indicators with focus on the pedagogical framework. Table one shows the results of the literature study and was examined by the first group.

Table 1: List of indicators as a result of the literature review

Motivation	Pedagogic
Show progress	Learning goals (knowledge, skills, attitude)
Time (20-30'no longer than 2u+break (possibility to stop in between)	Practice tests
User-friendliness (simple, easy to read, clear instructions, attractive)	Differentiation
Summaries + link to sources	On- and offline practice material
Well structured	Variety of educational material
Author is known	Feedback
Help function	New questions if somebody doesn't pass the test
GDPR proof	Interaction
	Learning content adapted to target group

At this moment the survey is still running and the results still have to be processed. This is the final step in the validation process and will lead to a final list of indicators. These indicators will be used to objectively monitor the quality of existing e-learning modules.

HIGHER MOTIVATION AND SUSTAINABILITY OF KNOWLEDGE THROUGH SOCIAL MEDIA FOR TEENS

Nataša Rizman Herga, Andreja Kolar, Primary School Ormož, Dejan Dinevski, University of Maribor, Slovenia

The Use of Technology and Social Media in Natural Science Education

In the process of knowledge acquisition individual personal experiences play an important role. Experiential learning is presented as a recommended didactic strategy which enables an intense mental, emotional and creative implementation of students' activities. In chemistry, this strategy is realized with a laboratory experimental method. Students train their manual skills, develop the ability to describe chemical changes, learn about physical and chemical properties of matter, develop safety at work abilities in the school laboratory, they strengthen and complement knowledge, abilities and skills, develop an experimental approach as a form of research work. Alongside with the experience emotional-motivational aims are achieved which are the basis for achieving cognitive and action aims of a school subject. From a didactic point of view, the experimental work is of the utmost importance because it sometimes discontinues the monotonous teaching of theory with practical work (Rizman Herga & Dinevski, 2014). For the successful implementation of experimental learning, it is important to teach up to date content and connect it to everyday life. This way of teaching enables higher motivation for learning.

In a dynamic social, production and service environment such an environment as today's traditional forms of education and training no longer suffice. ICT opens up a new educational world of creativity for students and teachers. Students (with the use of smart phones, tablets and similar) are sometimes more capable to use the IT then teachers.

Communication landscape has been profoundly changed due to social media tools. It is also leaving a significant impact in education. Students have access to various digital technologies and the use of social media. Technology and social media can be used to promote students' engagement. Students may feel comfortable when express their creativity and voice their opinion on a social media. They can foster student`s collaboration to work together, connectivism and media literacy. Social media platforms can be grouped into three major categories. The first category includes social network sites like Facebook, MySpace, Twitter etc. that serve as online communities via which users connect with friends or colleagues, and share ideas and resources. The second category consists of content sharing and organizing sites like Delicious, Digg, Flickr, YouTube and RSS readers.

Figure 1. Some social network sites used by the student

The third category is composed of content creation and editing websites such as Blogger, Google Docs, Wikipedia and WordPress (Faizi et all, 2013). The most benefit in terms of learning will provide when there is integration of technology and social media use in educational settings and student's everyday lives.

Methodology of teaching chemistry in this Case Study

A conceptual approach to teaching chemistry combines experimental work, problem oriented teaching methods and the use of the information communication technology with the goal to facilitate efficient learning and students' motivation on all levels of the learning and teaching processes. Students can concretely meet up with the teaching contents by actively procedure different practical activities. The aim is teaching from life experiences as a school for life.

Characterisation of problem

The point is that students do the research, which demand experimental work, about real problem and consequently learn from it and use it in a real life. This is important since the problem that is completely understand offer students to use their learned knowledge to inspire peers and preserved it longer in memory.

Collecting the information

Understanding the problem requires studying sources and having prior knowledge about acids, bases and salts. Students are firstly introduced with ionic reactions from everyday life. The challenge is to find interesting experiments that will present ionic reactions.

Experimental work

Students discover the method of researching by firstly making the questions and then with experimenting answer to them. The teacher guide students which are writing the preparation to perform experiments. The preparation includes theoretical basis, the list of requisites, descriptions by steps of work, sketch of experiment or a picture of it and the explanation of experiment. Students must to abide by safety instruction and safe work with chemicals.

AKCIJE I-REAKCIJ

Teoretske osnove

Ionske reakcije so reakcije, ki potekajo med ioni (največkrat v raztopini). Običajno so zelo hitre (Duden, 2004). Ionska reakcija lahko poteče med trdno snovjo in raztopino. Ionske reakcije so kemijske reakcije, ki potečejo med ioni, ki so prosto gibljivi (Wissiak Grm in Devetak,2013). Pri ionskih reakcijah nastanejo topne snovi, slabo ionizirane snovi in v vodi slabo topne snovi - oborine.

Reakcijo pri kateri iz dveh topnih soli dobimo netopno sol – oborino, imenujemo obarjanje (Ryan, 2000). Splošno obarjalno reakcijo lahko zapišemo:

$$AB(aq) + CD(aq) \rightarrow AD(s) + CB(aq)$$

Med ionske reakcije sodi tudi reakcija kisline z bazo oziroma reakcija nevtralizacije. Pri reakciji reagirajo oksonijevi in hidorksilni ioni, nastane voda – nevtralna snov. Pri reakciji nastane tudi sol. Soli so ionske spojine, ki so zgrajene iz kovinskih kationov in anionov kisline (Graunar idr, 2016). Enačbo nevtralizacije lahko poenostavljeno zapišemo z besedno enačbo:

$$baza + kislina \rightarrow sol + voda$$

Potek ionskih reakcij lahko **spremljamo** v naslednjih primerih:

1. **nastanek** slabo topne snovi, ki iz vodnih raztopin izpadejo kot **oborine**,
2. **nastanek plinov**, ki izhajajo iz raztopine ali
3. **nastanek slabo disociirane snovi** (Wissiak Grm in Devetak, 2013)

Potrebščine

Pri vseh eksperimentih (razen prvega kjer delamo s snovmi iz vsakdanjega življenja) uporabljamo zaščitna sredstva: zaščitno haljo, zaščitne rokavice in očala.

Prav tako v primeru, ko gre za nevarne snovi izvajamo poskuse z majhnimi količinami snovi.

Kemikalije:	Inventar:

- $NaHCO_3$ (s)
- 9 % CH_3COOH (aq)
- NaOH (aq)
- NH_4Cl (aq)
- KI (aq)
- $Pb(NO_3)_2$ (aq)
- Indikatorji:
  ○ metiloranž
  ○ fenolftalein
  ○ lakmusova tinktura
  ○ rdeče zelje
- koka kola
- limona
	– 3 pladnji
	– balon
	– steklen kozarec
	– erlenmajerica (250 ml)
	– 4 kapalke
	– 4 čaše (100 ml)
	– stojalo za epruvete
	– 4 epruvete
	– 2 čaše (500 ml)
	– urno steklo
	– žlička
	– čaša (250 ml)

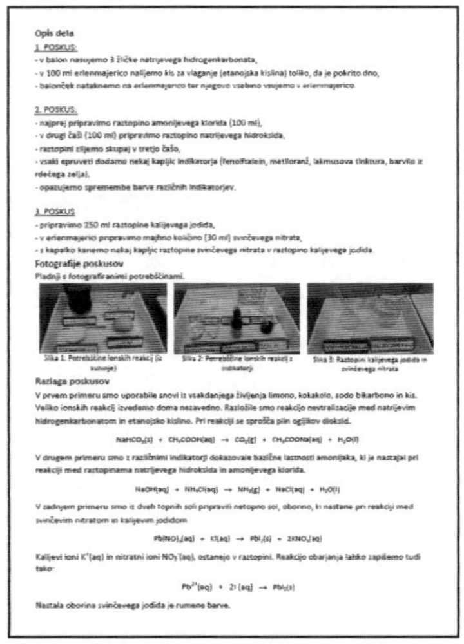

Opis dela

1. POSKUS:

- v balon nasujemo 3 žličke natrijevega hidrogenkarbonata,
- v 100 ml erlenmajerico nalijemo kis za vlaganje (etanojska kislina) toliko, da je pokrito dno,
- balonček nataknemo na erlenmajerico ter njegovo vsebino vsujemo v erlenmajerico.

2. POSKUS:

- najprej pripravimo raztopino amonijevega klorida (100 ml),
- v drugi čaši (100 ml) pripravimo raztopino natrijevega hidroksida,
- raztopini zlijemo skupaj v tretjo čašo,
- vsaki epruveti dodamo nekaj kapljic indikatorja (fenolftalein, metiloranž, lakmusova tinktura, barvilo iz rdečega zelja),
- opazujemo spremembe barve različnih indikatorjev.

3. POSKUS

- pripravimo 250 ml raztopine kalijevega jodida,
- v erlenmajerici pripravimo majhno količino (30 ml) svinčevega nitrata,
- s kapalko kanemo nekaj kapljic raztopine svinčevega nitrata v raztopino kalijevega jodida.

Fotografije poskusov

Pladnji s fotografiranimi potrebščinami.

Slika 1: Potrebščine ionskih reakcij (iz kuhinje) | Slika 2: Potrebščine ionskih reakcij z indikatorji | Slika 3: Raztopini kalijevega jodida in svinčevega nitrata

Razlaga poskusov

V prvem primeru smo uporabile snovi iz vsakdanjega življenja limono, kokakolo, sodo bikarbono in kis. Veliko ionskih reakcij izvedemo doma nezavedno. Razložile smo reakcijo nevtralizacije med natrijevim hidrogenkarbonatom in etanojsko kislino. Pri reakciji se sprošča plin ogljikov dioksid.

$$NaHCO_3(s) + CH_3COOH(aq) \rightarrow CO_2(g) + CH_3COONa(aq) + H_2O(l)$$

V drugem primeru smo z različnimi indikatorji dokazovale bazične lastnosti amonijaka, ki je nastajal pri reakciji med raztopinama natrijevega hidroksida in amonijevega klorida.

$$NaOH(aq) + NH_4Cl(aq) \rightarrow NH_3(g) + NaCl(aq) + H_2O(l)$$

V zadnjem primeru smo iz dveh topnih soli pripravili netopno sol, oborino, ki nastane pri reakciji med svinčevim nitratom in kalijevim jodidom

$$Pb(NO)_3(aq) + KI(aq) \rightarrow PbI_2(s) + 2KNO_3(aq)$$

Kalijevi ioni K^+(aq) in nitratni ioni NO_3^-(aq), ostanejo v raztopini. Reakcijo obarjanja lahko zapišemo tudi tako:

$$Pb^{2+}(aq) + 2I^-(aq) \rightarrow PbI_2(s)$$

Nastala oborina svinčevega jodida je rumene barve.

Figure 2. Preparation to an experiment

Experimental work is incredibly importance from didactically aspect, because sometimes is necessary to interrupt monotonic teaching of theoretic subject matter by practical work. Students are interested by chemistry, because it involves experiments, as the research from Slovenia confirm (Devetak & Glažar, 2010).

Video recording plan

By planning the experiment students simultaneously plan the recording of video. Planning includes writing the script, preparation of chemicals and requisites, division of labour, cover making and music choosing. After-effect is cooperation and team work building.

Recording and film editing

Oppositely of watching experiments on television or computer, are students by filming experiments on their own in the role of actors, cameraman, photographers and so on. Film was record by previously written script for two actors speaking in a dialogue. Students were describing and explaining the experiment and chemical reactions. For optical effects were provided of simultaneously.

Film's cover had been chosen before editing and same the music for its beginning and end. Video recorders that were used for making film were selected. While some video recorders were shortened, were others, since some reactions are gradual, fasten.

The new educational film was made after the film had been edited. The film title is called "Akcije I- reakcij" (Actions of ionic reactions). It enriches and diversion chemistry lessons.

Figure 3. Shooting a movie

Dissemination of video

Media sharing sites enable users to upload and share their multimedia content (photos, videos and audio) on the web. Using social media, teachers are able to improve the involvement of their students in studies and education, improve technological ability, provide a great sense of collaboration in the classroom and make good communication skills; especially if students feel affiliated and accountable to work. When we finished the film installation, we uploaded video on YouTube and added abstract and key words.

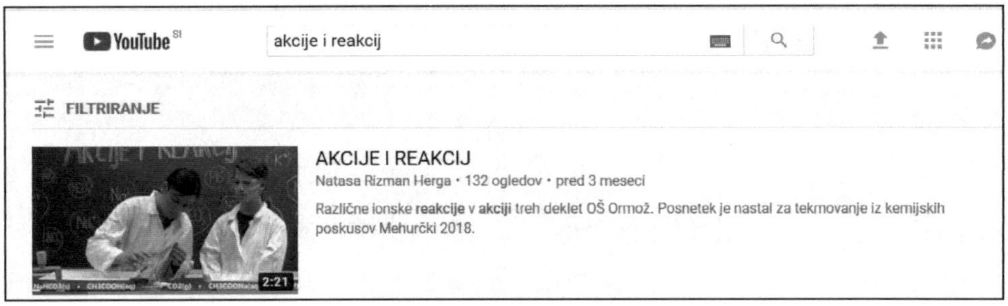

Figure 4. Uploaded video

With great pleasure and pride on the final product, we shared the video through various social media. We did not forget the website of our school and FB profile.

Figure 5. Dissemination of video

Conclusion

The objective of this work is to present the benefits of using technology and social media in science education. Experiences gathered on its own have an important role when gaining knowledge. Through personal experiences emotional motivation aims are reached and are the foundation for attaining cognition and action aims of the subject. Personal research, experimenting, solving simple realistic problems, accustoming to group and cooperative learning are the basis for reaching aims from the valuable and cognition area. In science (chemistry), this strategy is realized with a laboratory experimental method through hand-on experiment. Many researchers have successfully proven that these methods of teaching and learning develops student`s interest in learning science as well as other subjects.

We present a form how to make teaching and learning more effective. Students are already interested and engaged in using technology. "To effectively educate the youth of today teachers must interact using the modes of communication embraced by their students" (van Vooren & Bess, 2013). By filming and editing a video, students are actively involved in the process not only with experimental work but also with technology. Using technology in the classroom improves engagement, knowledge retention, collaboration, creativity, etc. Students can also learn useful skills through technology (recording and film editing). YouTube has become the perfect place to find entertainment or knowledge. The possibilities for augmenting education with the wealth of knowledge available in online video are vast. Students are using Facebook, Pinterest, Instagram and other websites to socialize. We used their inclination by making learning enjoyable and effective (students were filming and directing video). For dissemination of learning-video they used applications they know.

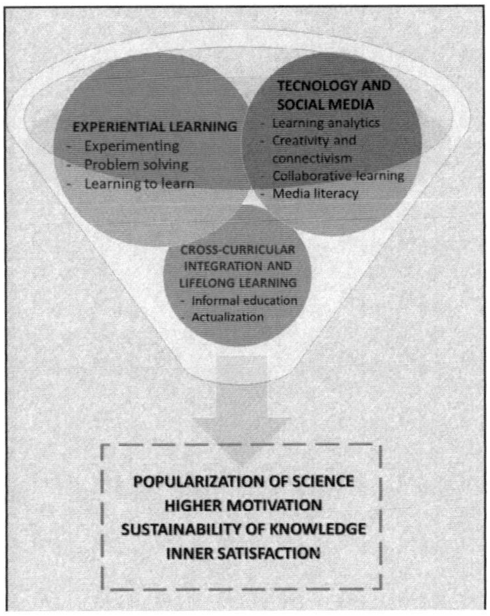

Figure 6. The benefits of using technology and social media in science education

The offered methodology of teaching science (chemistry) illustrates how with different ways actualize the learning content custom learners. We strongly believe that technology and social media could be used as valuable educational tools capable of enriching the learning experience.

References

Faizi, R., El Afia, A., & Chiheb, R. (2013). Exploring the Potential Benefits of Using Social Media in Education. *International Journal of Engineering Pedagogy, 3*(4), 50-53.

Devetak, I.; Glažar, S. A. (2010). The Influence of 16-Year-Old Students' Gender, Mental Abilities, and Motivation on their Reading and Drawing Submicrorepresentations Achievements. *International Journal of Science Education 32*(12), 1561-1593.

Rizman Herga, N., & Dinevski, D. (2014). The use of a virtual laboratory among Slovenian primary school chemistry teachers. *Proceedings of the 2014 Annual Conference of the European Distance and E-Learning Network*, 527-535.

van Vooren, C., & Bess, C. (2013). Teacher tweets improve achievement for eighth grade science students. *Journal of Education, Informatics & Cybernetics, 11*(1), 33-39.

Connecting through Educational Technology
Proceedings of the European Distance and E-Learning Network 2019 Annual Conference
Bruges, 16-19 June, 2019

THE ROLE OF MOTIVATION IN COMPUTER-SUPPORTED COLLABORATIVE LEARNING (CSCL) IN BUSINESS EDUCATION – A FOCUSED, NARRATIVE STATE-OF-THE-ART LITERATURE REVIEW

Carina Aichinger, Mathew Docherty, Sandra Mühlböck, David Kronawettleitner, University of Applied Sciences Upper Austria, Austria

Introduction

Since the 1990s, computer-supported collaborative learning (CSCL) has become a pedagogical approach widely used (Stahl et al., 2006). Digital media are gaining more and more influence in education and, therefore, opening up new possibilities for collaborative learning and communication. Thus, they have the potential to change the way we learn and communicate (CSCL being more text-based, making emotional expression more difficult, see Wang & Hwang, 2012).

In the complex field of CSCL, motivation is one area of particular interest due to its potential influence on learning success (Wang & Hwang, 2012). Research indicates that motivation influences students' contributions in CSCL (Rienties et al., 2009) and that high motivation has a positive effect on cognitive strategies and cognitive quality (Wang & Hwang, 2012) and learners' behaviour and attitude in general (see e.g. Ryan & Deci, 2000).

Despite extensive research in this area, the role of motivation in (computer-supported collaborative) learning is not yet fully understood (Martens, Gulikers, & Bastiaens, 2004) and more research in this field is necessary (Wang & Hwang, 2012).

Therefore, a focused, narrative state-of-the-art literature review was conducted to get a deeper insight into the current state of knowledge in this field. The focus was placed on business courses in tertiary education.

Questions of interest include, but are not limited to: (How) does CSCL influence motivation? More precisely, which (technological, social etc.) factors and measures influence motivation and how?

Definition of key terms

Collaborative Learning and CSCL

The term collaborative learning is based on a constructivist learning approach (see Lee, Long, & Visinescu, 2016) and is often used synonymously for *group learning* (Barkley et al., 2015). However, for some authors, e.g. Barkley et al. (2015), collaborative learning is more specific: An important characteristic is the intentional integration of collaboration in the learning task. *Co-labouring* means that students work together intentionally for a specific collaborative purpose and meaningful learning is essential (Barkley et al., 2015).

Due to the different definitions of the term collaborative learning in the literature, any type of team work for a common goal will be considered as collaborative learning in this article.

Computer-supported collaborative learning, often abbreviated CSCL, means that a computer, often an online solution, is used for learning purposes and create knowledge in collaboration with others (Stahl, 2017). Examples are collaborative online games, wikis, learning forums etc. CSCL can be used in a blended learning context or in a fully digital class.

Motivation

Motivation is often described as the force behind our actions or non-actions; it is what "moves" us (Ryan & Deci, 2000). When we are activated and energised, we are motivated (Ryan & Deci, 2000). Although there are different ways to describe motivation and different theories (e.g. Self-Determination Theory, see Deci & Ryan, 1985), a very common distinction of motivation is between intrinsic, extrinsic motivation and amotivation (Ryan & Deci, 2000).

Intrinsic motivation is motivation that comes from within, without an external reward (Ryan & Deci, 2000). It occurs when something is perceived as desirable, interesting and/or brings pleasure. It is often the desired type of motivation in education (Looy et al., 2016) and an important aspect of flow experience (Buil, Catalán, & Martínez, 2018).

Extrinsic motivation prevails when somebody performs an action in order to get some kind of external reward (Ryan & Deci, 2000), e.g. a good grade or a salary, or to avoid a sanction. Extrinsic motivation can play an important role in educational games, e.g. in rewards like badges (Hanus & Fox, 2015)

Amotivation, on the other hand, "is the lack of intention to act" (Ryan & Deci, 2000) and occurs in an absence of perceived value of the goal or perceived lack of competence (Ryan, 1995).

Methodology

For the literature review, extensive research was conducted, mainly using Google Scholar for a comprehensive/extensive search, as well as the databases Wiley, ScienceDirect, Research Gate as well as accessible articles in the database Springer. The snowball method was used to complement the database research.

The formal inclusion criteria were:

- Published 2014 or later;
- Online full text availability;
- Classified Q1 or Q2 on SCImago;
- Written in English.

SCImago is a public journal ranking portal with data from over 34,100 titles and 5,000 publishers worldwide, (see https://www.scimagojr.com). It also takes different indices (e.g. H-index) into consideration, which make it useful to compare a wide range of journals across disciplines.

Due to ongoing technological advances, CSCL is a rapidly changing field. Therefore, articles published before 2014 were no longer considered state-of-the-art for this literature review. Articles from Q3-Q4 journals and non-listed journals were excluded in order to keep the quality of the selected literature high.

To narrow down the pre-selected articles to the most relevant literature, abstracts were read and only articles relevant in all three areas were included:

- CSCL;
- Tertiary business education;
- Motivation.

The research focus was narrowed down to articles in the field of business studies in higher education. The reason behind this measure is to reach a certain homogeneity of the papers in terms of study participants and learning content in order to improve the comparability of the studies.

Findings

The research showed that, although much literature can be found on the subjects of CSCL and business education, far fewer papers have their focus on motivation. Only 8 articles met the criteria for the final selection.

The 7 articles selected came from 5 different countries:

- Taiwan (2x);
- Spain (2x);
- Finland;
- USA;
- UK.

All articles were empirical studies with sample sizes from 54 to 182. In two papers, no sample size was specified.

Regarding motivational theories used as a research basis, three of the papers (Tsai, Shen, Chiang, & Chen, 2018; Nisula & Pekkola, 2018; Hernández-Lara & Serradell-López, 2018) did not rely on a motivational theory for their study. Two papers (Buil et al, 2018; Kiili et al., 2014) based their research on flow theory. Although flow is not synonymous with motivation, intrinsic motivation is a crucial part of flow experience (Buil et al, 2018). The expectancy-value theory of motivation (see Wigfield & Eccles, 2000) was used as a theoretical background for the study of Lee et al. (2016). Lin, Yen, and Wang (2018) mention intrinsic vs. extrinsic motivation as a theoretical background for their research.

Articles could be roughly divided into two approaches: (a) studies that tested a precondition like a specific teaching strategy, a learning technology or design element and its effects on motivation and (b) motivation as a precondition and its effects on collaboration and/or learning outcomes. The second approach (b) was used less frequently in the selected papers.

Findings regarding the influence of a precondition/variable on motivation

Buil et al. (2018) studied the game design elements challenge, skills, feedback and goal clarity (so-called *flow preconditions*) on flow experience, operationalized as heightened absorption, enjoyment, and intrinsic motivation, in a collaborative setting.

A browser-based business simulation game was used by teams of 4-6 members each. The teams collaborated and competed against each other. The simulation game was accompanied by briefing and debriefing sessions in which students were helped with technical questions and could compare themselves with other teams.

Students filled out a questionnaire related to flow preconditions and flow experience at the end of the semester. The findings show that if students feel that their ability or skill level can meet the challenges in the business simulation, they experience flow in terms of high intrinsic motivation, absorption, and enjoyment. Goal clarity, however, did not seem to have an impact on flow experience.

In a quasi-experiment, Tsai et al. (2018) studied how the (collaborative) teaching methods web-mediated socially-shared regulation of learning (SSRL) and experience-based learning (ExBL) influenced learning performance over one semester. In this collaborative learning process, students work together to regulate their learning activity and make relevant decisions (see also Panadero et al., 2013). Experience-based learning means that knowledge is gained from students' own experiences (Matsuo et al., 2008).

The authors compared four groups:

- C1: SSRL and ExBL (42 students);
- C2: SSRL and non-ExBL (37 students);

- C3: Non-SSRL and ExbL (30 students);
- C4: Non-SSRL and nonExBL (37 students).

The authors also analysed the students' motivation before and after the intervention.

Findings show that the differences in learning motivation between the ExBL and non-ExBL, as well as between the SSRL and non-SSRL groups were not significant. However, group C2 had a significantly higher learning motivation at the end of the semester compared to the beginning. The reasons for these findings remain largely unclear in the article. Therefore, the authors suggest that future research is made to gain more insight into this area.

In a case study, Nisula and Pekkola (2018) tried to develop a holistic, multidisciplinary curriculum model to combine theoretical learning content with practical training. For this purpose, they implemented an open-source ERP (enterprise resource planning)-supported business environment in which students learned to set up and run a business. The content focused on the basics in business management: marketing, sales, logistics, finance, economics and law. Students were assisted by coaches who helped teams with difficult learning situations.

For the evaluation, the course feedback system, a survey and a focus group interview were analysed. Findings regarding motivation indicated that students support and encouragement (by the coaches) throughout the course were crucial to preserve students' motivation. Also, workload needs to be balanced in order to avoid demotivation. Another finding from the evaluation was that the responsibility and ownership that is felt in the simulation game can have a positive effect on motivation in some students. However, the study showed that a collaborative learning environment was not automatically motivating for most of the students.

Hernández-Lara and Serradell-López (2018) look into the effectiveness of business simulation games and try to identify recommendations on instructional design for learner engagement and learning success by examining online forums of different university courses.

A collaborative online simulation game was played by 41 teams of different bachelor's and master's courses and 3681 forum messages were posted at the end. A qualitative analysis (content analysis, inductive approach) was conducted to investigate a possible connection between forum participation and learning outcomes.

The most relevant skills acquired were of general nature (decision-making, team work, dealing with uncertainty etc.). In addition, some management skills (handling competition, evaluating financial information etc.) were gained.

The authors of the study also found out that students could become demotivated if they did not understand the consequences of their decisions, the calculations, the software (especially in the beginning) or when they performed poorly in the game.

To avoid demotivation/increase motivation, the authors suggest that teachers offer support and teach decision-making techniques or help with content questions and uncertainties.

Lee et al. (2016) focused their study on the constructivist practices collaboration, active learning, meaningful learning, and subject integration and their effect on motivating students towards developing business intelligence (BI). For this purpose, business students were using a digital Enterprise Resource Planning (ERPSim-BI) simulation game to apply BI knowledge in 5 rounds over four weeks.

In two surveys, participants were asked about their expectancies, value beliefs and perceptions of the instructional practices in the game environment.

Results showed that collaboration had a positive effect on active learning and subject integration had a positive effect on meaningful learning. Collaboration, active learning and meaningful learning increased motivational behaviour towards business intelligence.

To summarize, the study showed that positive learning experiences, like discovering solutions or gaining a better understanding about real world business, increase the BI motivation.

Findings regarding the influence of students' motivation on collaboration and learning outcomes

Newbery, Lean, and Moizer (2016) studied the impact of a serious business game on entrepreneurial intent (EI), intention to start a business (Newbery et al., 2016), and its moderating factors like the motivational factors personal attitude, perceived social norms and perceived behavioural control.

In a pre-test/post-test quasi-experimental design, first-year undergraduate students played in teams of 4-5 in a business game that simulated 36 "virtual" months (of a business start-up) in three weeks. Students filled out questionnaires at the beginning and at the end of the quasi-experiment.

In this study, the business game seemed to have a negative impact on entrepreneurial intent, and the pre-game motivation had no significant effect on EI. The reasons for the decrease in entrepreneurial intent, however, remain unclear in the paper.

Lin et al., (2018) explored the influence of learning method (individual vs. collaborative) and learning motivation (high vs. low) in a business simulation game on learning achievement. For this purpose, marketing students played a Virtual Business Retailing software where they had to open and run a convenience store over a virtual year.

Students' game scores (= learning performance) as well as answers to a questionnaire about learning motivation were analysed. Findings indicated that highly motivated students did not have significantly better learning results than students with low motivation. However, learning motivation had a moderating effect on the relationship between learning method and performance: highly motivated students show a higher learning performance than those with low motivation in the collaborative mode.

Another surprising finding was that independent of learning motivation, the individual group showed higher learning outcomes than the collaborative group. The authors assume that one of the reasons could be that students in the individual groups could focus more on the learning tasks, whereas the collaborative group members had to perform additional activities (participate in discussions, give explanations etc.), which could have led to cognitive overload. Non-ideal team dynamics due to "mismatched" personalities could have been another reason for the lower performance of the collaborative group.

Discussion & Conclusions

The analysis of the articles shows that a wide variety of different approaches and methods are used in the field of CSCL in tertiary business education, although especially simulation games seemed to be a common instructional tool in the papers analysed. One reason for their popularity could be that they are considered as a holistic and practical approach to teaching (see Nisula & Pekkola, 2018).

Due to the small number of sample articles, no generalisations about the role of motivation in CSCL can be made. However, the selected studies indicate that motivation is an influential factor in CSCL; not only learning tools (e.g. business game) are relevant when it comes to students' motivation, but a wide range of context factors like pedagogical concepts, support from the teacher(s), group dynamics and overall cognitive load (see Lin et al., 2018).

In order for business simulations and similar instructional tools to fulfil their goals, students need to know how to work with the software (computer literacy, software training etc. required) and have a good understanding of what is expected from them (see Buil et al., 2018).

Teachers and facilitators play an important role in supporting students where necessary and providing guidance in order to maintain students' motivation (see Nisula & Pekkola, 2018) or to avoid demotivation (see Hernández-Lara & Serradell-López, 2018). Enough room for exploration and independence, especially as a group, should be given to students (see e.g. Lee et al.,2016).

The findings in the selected articles indicate that collaborative learning does not automatically lead to better learning outcomes or increased motivation, nor does motivation always result in higher learning performance. However, several factors can facilitate effective collaborative learning and/or improve motivation, for example: students' perceived competence and sufficient knowledge to deal with the learning tasks (see Buil et al., 2018), support and encouragement by teachers (Nisula & Pekkola, 2018; Hernández-Lara & Serradell-López; 2018), a sense of ownership (see Nisula & Pekkola, 2018) and a clear understanding of the working task. On the other hand, unequal distribution of workload (Nisula & Pekkola, 2018), cognitive overload (Lin et al., 2018) should be avoided.

Limitations

Despite the interesting insights that could be gained from this literature review, some limitations should be mentioned.

Due to the qualitative approach to this literature review, the results do not mirror a complete picture of the current state-of-the-art, but a careful selection of available, relevant papers. For a more general analysis, it would be interesting to include other disciplines in future literature reviews (e.g. medical education), as well as other educational contexts (e.g. primary or secondary education).

As the research was conducted using Google Scholar, the reproducibility of the results might be limited. Although SCImago is considered as a comprehensive database for journal rankings, the definition of what is a *high quality* paper or journal remains subjective to some extent.

As there is no commonly accepted definition of *collaborative learning*, a choice was made to use a less restrictive approach and include *team work* if the context of the paper stated that collaboration was intentional (see Barkley et al., 2015). Combined with the fact that CSCL itself is a very diverse field of research, findings of other literature reviews might differ, depending on their focus of research. Moreover, the selected papers come from different countries and thus cultural differences might play a role that could not be investigated in this article.

References

Barkley, E. F., Cross, K. P., & Major, C. H. (2014). *Collaborative learning techniques: A handbook for college faculty.* John Wiley & Sons.

Buil, I., Catalán, S., & Martínez, E. (2018). Exploring students' flow experiences in business simulation games. *Journal of Computer Assisted Learning,* (December 2017), 183–192. https://doi.org/10.1111/jcal.12237

Deci, E., & Ryan, R. M. (1985). *Intrinsic motivation and self-determination in human behavior.* Springer Science & Business Media.

Hanus, M. D., & Fox, J. (2015). Assessing the effects of gamification in the classroom: A longitudinal study on intrinsic motivation, social comparison, satisfaction, effort, and academic performance. *Computers & Education, 80*, 152–161. https://doi.org/10.1016/j.compedu.2014.08.019

Hernández-Lara, A. B., & Serradell-López, E. (2018). Student interactions in online discussion forums: their perception on learning with business simulation games with business simulation games. *Behaviour & Information Technology, 37*(4), 419–429. https://doi.org/10.1080/0144929X.2018.1441326

Lee, H., Long, J., & Visinescu, L. L. (2016). The Relationship between a Business Simulator, Constructivist Practices, and Motivation toward Developing Business Intelligence Skills. *Journal of Information Technology Education: Research, 15*, 593–609.

Lin, H., Yen, W., & Wang, Y. (2018). Investigating the effect of learning method and motivation on learning performance in a business simulation system context: An experimental study. *Computers & Education, 127*, 30–40. https://doi.org/10.1016/j.compedu.2018.08.008

Looy, J. Van, All, A., & Patricia, E. (2016). Assessing the effectiveness of digital game-based learning: Best practices. *Computers & Education, 93*, 90–103. https://doi.org/10.1016/j.compedu.2015.10.007

Martens, R. L., Gulikers, J., & Bastiaens, T. (2004). The impact of intrinsic motivation on e-learning in authentic computer tasks. *Journal of Computer Assisted Learning,* (July), 368–376.

Matsuo, M., Wong, C. W. Y., & Lai, K. (2008). Experience-based learning of Japanese IT professionals: A qualitative research. *Journal of Strategic Information Systems, 17*, 202–213. https://doi.org/10.1016/j.jsis.2008.03.001

Newbery, R., Lean, J., & Moizer, J. (2016). Evaluating the impact of serious games: the effect of gaming on entrepreneurial intent. *Information Technology & People Evaluating, 29*(4), 733–749. https://doi.org/10.1108/ITP-05-2015-0111

Nisula, K., & Pekkola, S. (2018). How to move away from the silos of business management education? *Journal of Education for Business, 93*(3), 97–111. https://doi.org/10.1080/08832323.2018.1425283

Panadero, E., Järvelä, S., Malmberg, J., Koivuniemi, M., Phielix, C., Jaspers, J. G., & Kirschner, P. A. (2013). *Enhancing socially shared regulation in working groups using a CSCL regulation tools.* Retrieved from http://ceur-ws.org/Vol-1009/1002.pdf

Rienties, B., Tempelaar, D., Bossche, P. Van Den, Gijselaers, W., & Segers, M. (2009). The role of academic motivation in Computer-Supported Collaborative Learning. *Computers in Human Behavior, 25*, 1195–1206. https://doi.org/10.1016/j.chb.2009.05.012

Rienties, B., Giesbers, B., Tempelaar, D., Lygo-baker, S., Segers, M., & Gijselaers, W. (2012). The role of scaffolding and motivation in CSCL. *Computers & Education, 59*, 893–906. https://doi.org/10.1016/j.compedu.2012.04.010

Ryan, R. M. (1995). Psychological Needs and the Facilitation of Integrative Processes. *Journal of Personality, 63*(3), 397–427. https://doi.org/10.1111/j.1467-6494.1995.tb00501.x

Ryan, R. M., & Deci, E. L. (2000). Intrinsic and Extrinsic Motivations: Classic Definitions and New Directions. *Contemporary Educational Psychology, 25*(1), 54–67. https://doi.org/10.1006/ceps.1999.1020

SCImago, (n.d.). SJR — SCImago Journal & Country Rank. Retrieved January 30, 2019, from http://www.scimagojr.com

Stahl, G. (2017). *Global Introduction to CSCL.* Lulu.com. Retrieved from https://books.google.at/books?id=akOCCwAAQBAJ

Stahl, G., Koschmann, T., & Suthers, D. (2006). Computer-supported collaborative learning: An historical perspective. *Cambridge Handbook of the Learning Sciences*, 409–426.

Tsai, C., Shen, P., Chiang, I., Chen, W., & Chen, Y. (2018). Exploring the effects of web-mediated socially- shared regulation of learning and experience- based learning on improving students' learning. *Interactive Learning Environments, 26*(6), 815–826. https://doi.org/10.1080/10494820.2017.1415940

Wang, S., & Hwang, G. (2012). The role of collective efficacy, cognitive quality, and task cohesion in computer-supported collaborative learning (CSCL). *Computers & Education, 58*, 679–687. https://doi.org/10.1016/j.compedu.2011.09.003

Wigfield, A., & Eccles, J. S. (2000). Expectancy – Value Theory of Achievement Motivation. *Contemporary Educational Psychology, 25*(1), 68–81. https://doi.org/10.1006/ceps.1999.1015

Connecting through Educational Technology
Proceedings of the European Distance and E-Learning Network 2019 Annual Conference
Bruges, 16-19 June, 2019

A SYSTEMIC MODEL FOR PERSISTENCE – A HUMANISTIC THINKING

Tomás Bautista-Godínez, Coordinación de Universidad Abierta y Educación a Distancia – UNAM, México

Abstract

The objective of this paper is to propose a humanistic and systemic model for persistence in Distance Higher Education. In Mexico, as in other parts of the world, from an instrumental perspective, research suggests that socioeconomic level and skin colour have a strong correlation among those who finish their studies (Blanco, 2017). At the same time, persistence models, at least their representations, are generally shaped by variables and deterministic factors. As an alternative to these perspectives, we propose a model of persistence that integrates dimensions such as ethics, utopia, democratic dialogue between opposites, and hospitality for the development of life through knowledge.

Introduction

Low persistence is a phenomenon that faces Distance Higher Education. According to Rovai (2003), "Persistence, that is, the behaviour of continuing action despite the presence of obstacles, is an important measure of higher education program effectiveness".

Understanding of this phenomenon has been approached basically from two approaches. The first of these are models built with a deterministic approach. The other is the systemic approach. The first model that reports the literature in the category we have called deterministic is the Bean and Metzner model (1985). Subsequently, Rovai (2003), Park and Choi (2009) have proposed similar models. In the second category is the model of Glazer and Murphi (2015) and Bautista, Canales, and Bras (2018). In a previous study we showed different approaches to build models of school persistence. These kinds of models are in the trend of deterministic construction (Bautista et al., 2018). Our initial proposal of the persistence model, as we have said above, is systemic.

Together with the aforementioned model, we are currently developing research on social representations of distance higher education from the perspective of its graduates. he results of this study have opened the door to propose an alternative model of school persistence, from a humanist perspective. Findings reveal that those who complete their distance studies created fantasies. Their expectations are associated with the achievement of dreams and their willingness to achieve them. These evidences suggest exploring and building an alternative that encourages persistence beyond the models conformed by variables and deterministic factors.

The model we propose integrates elements of the theory of creative evolution (Bergson, 2007), the systemic approach, and the democratic dialogue exerting the contradiction between opposites (Žižek, 2013) for the development of life.

Firstly, we describe the models developed from an instrumental perspective. Next, we describe the systemic models of school persistence with a humanistic thought.

Traditional model for persistence

The persistence or drop-out in distance higher education has repeatedly been declared a complex phenomenon (Cendeja-Navarro, 2014; Zhang, 2010). The imbricated environments of the work, school and family of non-traditional students alters the learning dynamics.

The understanding of the persistence of this kind of students has been analysed through models such as those formulated by Tinto (1997), Bean and Metzner (1985), Rovai (2003), Park (2009). However, from a systemic perspective, the models have omitted the dynamic dimension resulting mainly from changes in expectations, acquired knowledge and the changing of the environments in which non-traditional learners perform. For these reasons, the aim of this article is to propose a systemic model of persistence, in order to understand the continuous change in the realities of students who at the same time work, have family responsibilities and study.

Psychological models

Psychological approaches analyse the personality traits of students who complete their studies with respect to those who do not. The approach of Fishbein and Ajzen (1975) is pioneer in this field. The authors establish that attitudes and beliefs have a significant influence on the behaviour of students (Hart, 2012) and on their cognitive processes (Simpson, 2015; Rurato & Gouveia, 2014); that is, the decision about to study or leave the school is correlated with the individual's previous behaviours, their attitudes, subjective norms and their achievements, which translate into behavioural intentions to persist during their university life (Rurato & Gouveia, 2014).

Interactionist model

Tinto's model (1986,1987,1975,1997) is the pioneer of interactionist vision in order to understand the scholar retention. The model considers several variables or factors that contribute to reinforce their adaptation to the institution he or she has selected. Family background, such as the family's socioeconomic and cultural level and the values are characteristics that influence the persistence. In addition to this, the personal attributes for interaction (Sung & Mayer, 2012) and self-regulation are important to strengthen academic experience (Sitzmann, 2012).

In the context of Distance Higher Education and from an interactionist perspective, Rovai (2003) and Bean and Metzner (1985) proposed a persistence model. Bean and Metzner (1985) contributed to the characterization of distance students as non-traditional. The Tinto's model incorporated the concepts of "Before and after entering university". At the same time, it suggests adding digital literacy as detonating parts of persistence/abandonment in distance education, among other components.

A Humanistic and Systemic model for persistence

The systemic model of persistence developed by Bautista et al. (2018), now integrates humanistic principles. The humanistic category considers the next dimensions: ethics, hospitality, and democratic dialogue between teachers and students, as opposites. The main axis of our becoming is knowledge. This axis is into two vortices. One of them corresponds to utopia, the other to expectations. All this is immersed in an environment, which is considered an ideology (see Figure 1).

The equidistant points between these vortexes constitute the exercise of introspection; that is to say, it is the own recognition and valuation of the acquired knowledge of the student and of the teaching practice. The environment as an ideology is a core component of the model because it alters our perceptions, of which we must necessarily become viewers and actors. Ideology, in this sense, is understood as a way of thinking that governs society as a whole. It determines social life forms and imposes a direction of life on institutions.

Ethics is associated with the value judgment on the decisions that the student takes to stay in the process of building through knowledge. It is the trace that the student projects and that, in turn, guides to the student. This guide keeps the student away from decisions about the nonsense actions and immediacy or alienation. It is an act for self-care and that of others. In Aristotelian terms, corresponds to the middle term. It is the point where the past, the present and what would have been converge. The imaginary time has been taken from the theory of creative evolution developed by Bergson (2007).

Hospitality, as a way of acting, metaphorically, opens the doors to the Other (Derrida, 1998). Allow the host to become the guest. It is a way of taking care of ourselves. It is the beginning of an emancipatory exercise through the knowledge that builds ourselves and we build it. Through hospitality we show ourselves ethically. It is the form of the relationship established by teachers and students and the community as a whole. Hospitality becomes the condition of democratic dialogue. It allows us to detach ourselves from apathy and enables the exploration of the unknown in search of the resignification of oneself.

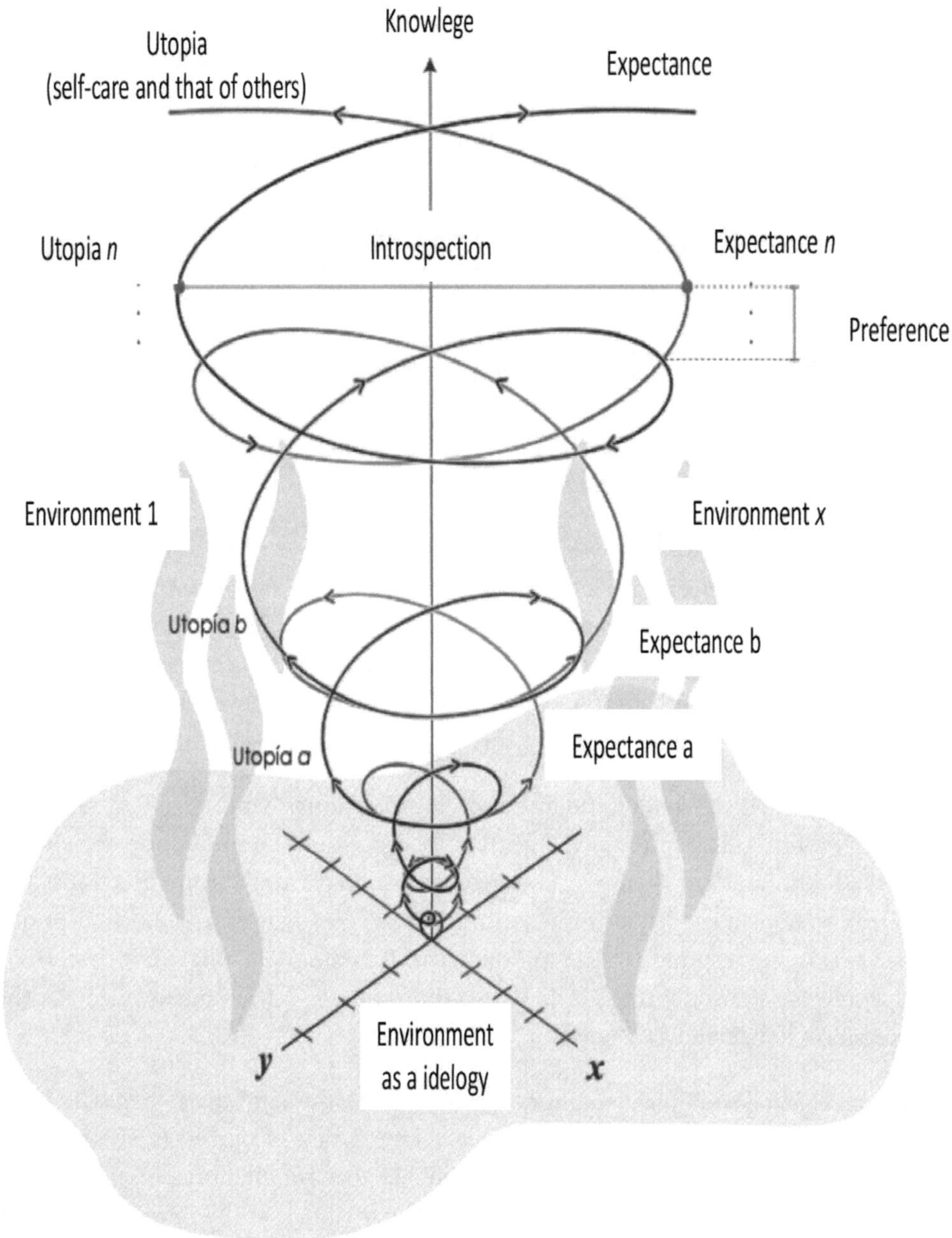

Figure 1. A Humanistic and Systemic Model for Scholar Persistence.

The democratic dialogue between opposites is an idea that we took from Slavo Žižek (2014) and that we integrated the model to strengthen the transforming utopia, in an atmosphere of hospitality (Sánchez, Moreno, Bautista, & Martínez, 2019). In other words, it is the practice of contradiction between those who think differently to build novel ideas based on knowledge. This emancipatory and critical practice needs to be promoted from the school for the progress of society in a just way.

Knowledge

According to Nonaka et al. (2000), the individual acquires knowledge through a continuous process of learning. The process is a spiral that transits from the most elementary situation to transcendence. It covers the individual and the collective. Its conceptual bases are tacit knowledge and explicit knowledge. The stages through which it transits are socialization, externalization, combination and internalization. Knowledge takes meaning in the different environments where students interact. We consider this approach particularly because in general non-traditional students have an active participation in different atmospheres of everyday life.

Expectations

Expectations correspond to the hope of achieving an attainment. They can be classified as short, medium or long term. The student has aspirations, of course, from before entering school, even when he is doing his studies he builds tacitly or explicitly an idealized design of his future after finishing his studies. The knowledge acquired or that which the student is unable to acquire alters any of his or her stated expectations. The acquisition or non-assimilation of knowledge continuously has a direct impact on the decisions that students make during their school career, both to positively and negatively transform their expectations.

Transactional Environments

The appearance of non-traditional students is the result two factors: the increase of social demand of higher education and the rapid massification of higher education systems (Schuetze & Slowey, 2002); these characteristics demonstrate that full-time students are not anymore, the main target of educative systems and the patterns are changing in relation to marketization of universities, occupational structures, rising workers and professionals qualifications, family diversification, gender roles, etc.

In this sense, the non-traditional students have been forgotten from pedagogical studies because of the complexity of their context: adults who enter or re-enter in universities "with a prior major break in their formal involvement in learning" (Schuetze & Slowey, 314), large range of age, enough experiences in life and commitments, and labour and personal expectations for upgrading.

It is important to understand the inter-role that students play to identify the approach context of non-traditional students. Markle (2015; p.4) found a double conflict between family-school and work-school. However, there is a personal and subjective conflict for the student, who has to twine the multiple expectations from familiar, social, labour, and intrapersonal microsystems.

References

Bautista G. T., Canales S. D., & Bras R. I. I. (2018). Three Dimensions of Persistence in Distance Higher Education. The Main Actors: Mexican Non-Traditional Students. *Book abstracts: EDEN 2018. Exploring the Micro, Meso and Macro. Italia. ISBN 978-615-5511-21-9.* Retrieved from: http://www.eden-online.org/wp-content/uploads/2018/06/Annual_2018_Genova_BoA.pdf

Bean, J. P., & Metzner, B. S. (1985). A conceptual model of non-traditional undergraduate student attrition. *Review of educational Research, 55*(4), 485-540. Retrieved from http://rer.sagepub.com/content/55/4/485.short

Blanco, E. (2017, July 19). ¿Cuánto inciden el origen social y el color de piel en la desigualdad educativa? Nexo [Blog post]. Retrieved from https://educacion.nexos.com.mx/?p=605

Bergson, H. (2007). *La Evolución Creadora.* Buenos Aires, Argentina: Cactus.

Derrida, J. (1998). *Adiós a Emmanuel Lévinas. Palabra de Acogida.* Madrid, España: Mínima Trota.

Fishbein, M., & Ajzen, I. (1975). *Belief, attitude, intention and behavior: An introduction to theory and Research.* MA, EE.UU. Addison-Wesley, Reading.

Glazer, H. R., & Murphy, J. A. (2015). Optimizing Success: A Model for Persistence in Online Education. *American Journal of Distance Education, 29*(2), 135-144. doi: 10.1080/08923647.2015.1023093

Markle, G. (2015). Factors influencing persistence among non-traditional university students. *Adult Education Quarterly, 65*(3), 267-285.

Nonaka, I., Toyama, R., & Konno, N. (2000). SECI, Ba, and leadership: a unified model of dynamic knowledge creation. *Long Range Planning, 33*, 5–34.

Park, J. H., & Choi, H. J. (2009). Factors Influencing Adult Learners' Decision to Drop Out or Persist in Online Learning. *Educational Technology & Society, 12*(4), 207-217. Retrieved from http://www.jstor.org/stable/pdf/jeductechsoci.12.4.207.pdf?seq=1#page_scan_tab_contents

Paterson, S. (1993). Career Decision-Making Self-Efficacy and Institutional Integration of Underprepared Students. *Research in Higher Education, 34*(6), 659-686.

Rovai, A. P. (2003). In search of higher persistence rates in distance education online programs. *Internet and Higher Education, 6*, 1-16. Elsevier.

Rovai, A. P., & Downey, J. R. (2010). Why some distance education programs fail while others succeed in a global environment. *Internet and Higher Education, 13*, 141-147. Elsevier. doi:10.1016/j.iheduc.2009.07.001

Rurato, P., & Gouveia, L. B. (2014, June). The importance of the learner's characteristics in distance learning environments: A case study. *Proceedings of the 2014 9th Iberian*

Conference on Information Systems and Technologies (CISTI), 1-6. IEEE. Retrieved from http://ieeexplore.ieee.org/xpl/login.jsp?tp=&arnumber=6876960&url=http%3A%2F%2Fieeexplore.ieee.org%2Fxpls%2Fabs_all.jsp%3Farnumber%3D6876960

Sánchez, M., Moreno, J. G., Bautista, T., & Martínez, A. (2019). *La analítica del aprendizaje en educación médica. ¿Punto de inflexión? Gaceta Medica de México.* En prensa.

Schuetze, H. G., & Slowey, M. (2002). Participation and exclusion: A comparative analysis of non-traditional students and lifelong learners in higher education. *Higher Education, 44*(3-4), 309-327.

Sitzmann, T. (2012). A theoretical model and analysis of the effect of self-regulation on attrition from voluntary online training. *Learning and Individual Differences, 22*(1), 46-54. Retrieved from http://www.sciencedirect.com/science/article/pii/S1041608011001543

Spady, W. (1970). Dropouts from Higher Education: An Interdisciplinary Review and Synthesis. *Interchange, 1*(1), 64-85.

Solís, P. (2013). Desigualdad vertical y horizontal en las transiciones educativas en México. *Estudios Sociológicos, 31*, número extraordinario (2013), 63-95. El Colegio de México. Retrieved from http://www.jstor.org/stable/43202534

Stoessel, K., Ihme, T. A., Barbarino, M. L., Fisseler, B., & Stürmer, S. (2014). Sociodemographic Diversity and Distance Education: Who Drops Out from Academic Programs and Why? *Research in Higher Education, 56*(3), 228-246. Retrieved from http://link.springer.com/article/10.1007/s11162-014-9343-x

Sung, E., & Mayer, R. E. (2012). Five facets of social presence in online distance education. *Computers in Human Behavior, 28*(5), 1738-1747. Retrieved from http://www.sciencedirect.com/science/article/pii/S0747563212001185

Tinto, V. (1975). Dropout from Higher Education: A theoretical synthesis of recent research. *Review of Educational Research, 45*, 89-125.

Tinto, V. (1986). Theories of student departure revisited. In D. Smart (Ed.), *Higher Education Handbook of Theory and Research* (Vol. 2). New York: Agathon Press.

Tinto, V. (1987). *Leaving College.* Chicago: The University of Chicago Press.

Tinto, V. (1997). Classrooms as communities: Exploring the educational character of student experience. *Journal of Higher Education, 68*(6), 599-623.

Žižek, S. (2013). *Introducción in Sobre la Práctica y la Contradicción.* Madrid, España:

FROM IDEA TO IMPACT: A QUALITY ASSURANCE MODEL FOR MOVING DIGITAL INNOVATION TO STANDARD OPERATING PROCEDURE

Deborah Adair, Quality Matters, United States of America

Achieving impact requires turning an innovation into standard operating procedure (SOP)

Innovation disrupts the status quo at significant financial, emotional, cultural and productivity costs

Over the last several years, it has been trendy to talk about innovation in education as a disruption. Digital disruption. While this may have gotten its start with Clayton Christensen's theory of innovative disruption applied to education in the book "Disrupting Class", this idea has taken on a life of its own. We understand disruption comes at a cost, but there is a common understanding that the potential gains will be greater. In fact, we applaud disruption because it requires us to consider new and better ways of doing things. This puts a lot of faith on our ability to move from great idea to significant impact. An innovation, even if "proven" elsewhere, requires significant organizational attention and energy. Learning, customizing, piloting, and refining all take time and money. What comes next however – dissemination, institutional adoption, and institutional practice – is essentially an organizational change initiative (Adair & Shattuck, 2019). An organization must be implementing the innovation at scale to realize the full potential – to see impact.

In online education, in particular, innovation and change have been and continue to be the reality of most institutions

As a more mature eLearning innovation, online education has grown in reach and application – increasingly broadly embraced by both students and educators. The CHLOE surveys, an annual survey on the changing U.S. landscape of online education conducted by Quality Matters and Eduventures, provides insight on planned changes for online programs (Quality Matters and Eduventures, 2018).

Chief Online Education Officers report that either supplementary or major change happened in their online programs over the past few years and a strong major anticipated the same for the next few years (Figure 1). Those who saw both major and supplementary changes in the past were the most likely to anticipate major change in the future. Institutions operating online programs at scale were most likely to anticipate major change in the future.

Some of this change includes the use of new pedagogies. Those more frequently identified, about 45% of those surveyed, included Badging and Micro-Credentials and Simulations/game-based approaches. Competency-Based Education was anticipated by at 33% of the respondents. The new technologies being considered include adaptive learning and the use of learning analytics and student dashboards, as well as virtual reality.

Recent & Planned Innovation

Over the past few years [over the next few years], to what extent have your institution's fully online programs changed in terms of teaching, learning and assessment technologies and tools?

FUTURE CHANGES → PAST CHANGES ↓	FUTURE Few Changes	FUTURE Supplementary Changes	FUTURE Major Changes
PAST Major Changes 36%	3%	23%	10%
PAST Supplementary Changes 49%	3%	36%	10%
PAST Few Changes 17%	6%	7%	4%
FUTURE TOTALS →	12%	66%	24%

Figure 1. Recent and planned innovation in online programs

SOPs reduce organization stress and open up capacity for new opportunities

An organization can support only so many innovations at one time. They must free up time, energy, and resources by moving innovation into standard practice, so that the innovation becomes just the way we do business. Moving from innovation to S.O.P. makes way for new opportunities by releasing creative energy and organization capacity for the next innovation.

Educational innovations must maintain the benefits for students as we move them to SOPs. Indeed, the Chief Online Education Officers surveyed in the CHLOE reports indicated overwhelmingly that the primary reason for pedagogical and technological innovations plans at their institutions were to increase student success. Innovations in teaching and learning must result in improved student learning and success as we move them to scale through recreating them as standard practice. An effective tool to ensure both aims is to implement a robust quality assurance process.

Robust quality assurance processes drive to SOP

Effective quality assurance processes kill innovation by moving it from exception to standard practice

Subjecting an innovation to a robust quality assurance process will, if done at the point where we can differentiate quality indicators, kill the innovation. But it will do so by providing a structure for replication and enhancement until the innovation is transformed into standard operating procedure – business as usual in the institution.

So how do we begin to structure a robust quality assurance process around an innovation? First, we do need to be able to understand quality in terms of the innovation – to describe it, understand how it is evidenced and practically evaluate it. This is a significant challenge for us today with the growth in educational technologies and innovative approaches to education.

What does quality look like, for example, in the use of any of the tools? What does quality look like in "the integrated use" of the set of tools to form a robust learning experience? The pace at which these tools are developed and introduced – the rate of innovation in tool development – preclude us from developing the critical elements of a QA process.

A quality assurance-focused model for moving innovation to impact

Innovation and quality assurance

For any educational innovation, we need to understand how we can replicate and implement in ways that assure quality and achieve the desired outcome. If we are able to clearly define quality in its relationship to the desired outcome, we can put in place a structured quality assurance process that will eventually turn the innovation into a standard operating procedure at our institutions. In the software development field, models such as Carnegie Mellon University's "Capability Maturity Model Integration" or CMMI are widely accepted ways for defining the quality of an organization's processes for designing, delivering, and implementing software and other technology related solutions (Paulk, Weber, Curtis, & Chrissis, 1995). There are similar sets of concerns for implementation of educational innovation.

Innovations in educational technology can be arrayed along a continuum of excellence in quality assurance (see Figure 2). Of the large and growing number of eLearning and educational technology innovations, most are new enough that we don't have established research or good data about quality in implementation. We just don't have research to guide us about relationship between implementation and student learning outcomes. For many of these, we are still piloting and innovating. It would be a mistake to try to "kill off" the innovation with a rigorous quality assurance process because we can't yet define quality criteria for them. For those further along, for which quality criteria can be identified, they may struggle with limited adoption. That is not the case, however, for online learning. Online learning is one of the most mature, and we know quite a lot about quality in online education. For online learning, we know what standards to follow in creating and delivering online education.

Using a quality assurance process to move from innovation to standard operating procedure a common starting place is with an Ad Hoc implementation of the innovation – with the goal of reducing resistance to adoption and other implementation barriers through a period of introduction and familiarization with quality expectations in the use of the innovation. Disseminating quality criteria through persuasion and incentive bur rarely mandating use.

The Quality Evaluation phase requires training on the quality criteria and putting in place an internal, structured, and periodic process to evaluate against the criteria. This is typically used only to evaluate what is/is not meeting criteria. This is often used in a gatekeeping manner –

allowing only implementations meeting criteria to move forward. The continuous improvement phase is a more robust way to modify and improve the implementation of the innovation – by analysing data, making changes based on it, and re-evaluating in a continuous process.

The benchmarking phase requires an unbiased, third-party assessment and validation – ensuring inter-institutional comparison. This step supports broader scalability and dissemination of the innovation as it is a peer-referenced outcome. Finally, at the top of the QA continuum of excellence, the implementation of the innovation is embedded in the institution's strategic plan, policies, practices, incentive structures, budgets, etc. It becomes "hard-wired" as the operational norm.

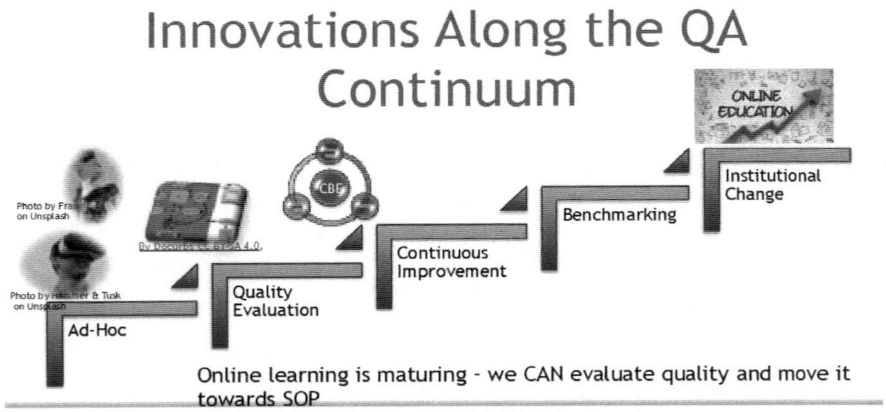

Figure 2. Innovations along the quality assurance continuum

Online education: A case in point

Quality Matters (QM) has been providing research-centred standards for the design of online courses and programs since 2004. The development of the quality criteria starts by focusing on the research on student learning – in the F2F classroom as well as online. After more than fifteen years of studying the application of this quality assurance process to online learning, QM has been able to create a widely shared understanding of online course quality with abundant supporting research and validated by application and practice. The continuum of excellence in quality assurance model was developed from observation of this work as applied in the QM context based on the efforts of approximately 1100 academic institutions in applying the QM Standards to their eLearning initiatives. (see Figure 3). This model has been shared though conference presentations and focus-group style data collected – at events and through targeted interviews. Research on this model is continuing, revealing key barriers in moving the innovation of online learning from an ad hoc implementation to standard operating procedure.

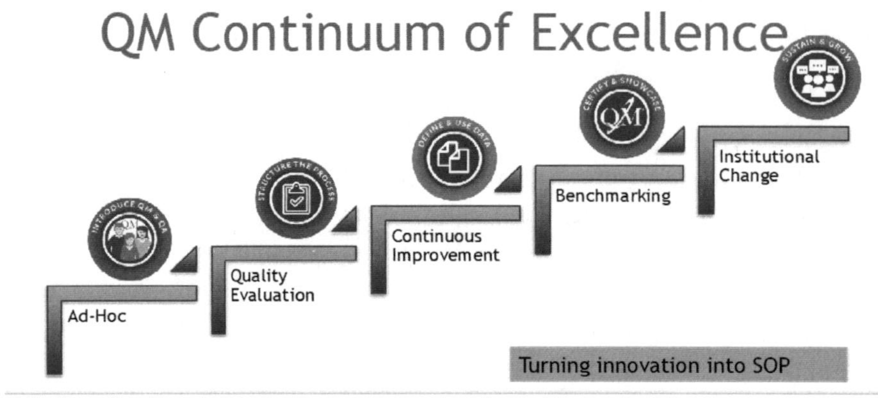

Figure 3. QM Continuum of Excellence

References

Adair, D., & Shattuck, K. (2019). Innovating Online: Assuring Quality While Creating and Innovating. In K.E. Linder (Ed.), *The business of innovation online: Practical tips and advice from e-Learning leaders.* Virginia: Stylus.

Paulk, M., Weber, C., Curtis, B., & Chrissis, M. B. (1995). *The Capability Maturity Model.* Reading, MA: Addison Wesley.

Quality Matters and Eduventures (2018). CHLOE 2 Report. Retrieved from https://www.qualitymatters.org/qa-resources/resource-center/articles-resources/CHLOE-2-report-2018

EDUCATION TO ALL CORNERS OF THE COUNTRY!

May Tove Dalbakk, Tynset Studie- og høgskolesenter, Norway

Vision of Norwegian Education Centres Association

> *"Our vision is to give the whole country's population the same opportunity to get education regardless of residence, life situation and economy."*

Regional and local education centres are our members.

An education centre is a *generator* in local and regional competence development having knowledge of local business life, knowledge of educational opportunities and providing and facilitating study programmes.

Goals of Norwegian Education Centres Association

- Contribute to cooperation and networking, locally, regionally and nationally;
- Increase the amount of flexible study programs;
- Be a consultative body of flexible education;
- Improve the framework of local education centres;
- Become part of the ordinary Norwegian education system;
- Develop a common standard of quality.

What do the educational centres offer?

- Higher education (university/university college);
- Vocational and higher vocational education;
- Secondary education;
- Formal and informal courses;
- Competency mapping;
- Career guidance and consulting;
- Incorporation and approval of education;
- Practical guidance and follow-up of students;
- Recruitment adapted to local and regional needs.

Benefits for students

- Local opportunities; education along with work, family and leisure;
- No need of travelling;
- Inspiration and motivation by educational peers;
- Participation in learning environment;

- Local exams and lower study expenses.

Benefits for local, regional and central authorities having education centres all over the country

- A national distribution network;
- Lifelong learning to the whole population;
- Cost -effective lifelong learning;
- Optimism and attractiveness in all regions of the country;
- Increased digitalization of education;
- Environmentally friendly.

Figure 1. Local students at Kongsvinger Education Centre eager to achieve competence!

Our conclusion

Local and regional education centres are "a win-win situation for everyone"!

Connecting through Educational Technology
Proceedings of the European Distance and E-Learning Network 2019 Annual Conference
Bruges, 16-19 June, 2019

THE CHALLENGES OF LIFELONG EDUCATION IN INFORMATION SOCIETY – TOWARDS A DIGITAL TURN

Anikó Kálmán, Zoltán Szűts, Budapest University of Technology and Economics, Hungary

Introduction

It is evident that lifelong education calls out for making teaching to be both learner and learning centred. This is still regarded as a topical issue. Furthermore, it is essential to restore learning and the organic unity of life (either vertical or horizontal). However, it is just a partial objective and it is neither a new claim. The new factor in education policy today is that the modern state guarantees every citizen's right of access to learning. This means that adults also have the right to study during any stage of their life. This means that the inequality inherent in the system – that legitimizes the reproduction of social inequalities as "natural selection" – can be removed. (Jackson, 2012).

Regardless, learning couldn't at all occur in "certificate giving" schools. "Natural curiosity and inquiry" – giving the internal inspiration to learning – is sadly still rebuffed by the "educational factory" as it is taken as problematic conduct. Normal learning does not happen in the school but rather in a ceaseless connection between the individual and the environment. This process of interaction will be structured as a set of repeated actions of the individual. In every-day life, however, learning means actions initiated with the aim of learning, such as school work, studies, formal and non-formal learning. As a consequence, there is a classification of activities in everyday usage, namely: "learning activities" and "non-learning activities". This is what is reflected in certain purposeful publicity interchanges and slogans, for example "from learning into the universe of work". This means that an unnaturally high achievement is expected from the learning activities in school, which is an area unnaturally designated and excluded from the quotidian reality. In school, higher learning benefit is expected from an artificially separated and constructed system of activities instead of the various learning activities as a natural basis of learning (Kálmán, 2018).

The role of cultural pedagogy

The so called trend of cultural pedagogy constructed this artificial system of activities by examining and imitating cultural activities that are far cry from everyday life, such as reading-writing, foreign languages, arts, sciences and philosophy. In contrary to cultural pedagogy, the "romantic pedagogy" took sides with children and gives preference to the self-state of "natural child" instead of "adaptive child" or "little professor" (Field, 2001).

"Development education" is superior to the conflicts of unilateral viewpoints, because it replaces the contrast (dualism) of the individual and the environment; the subjective and objective with the adoption of such dualities as external-inner, subjective-objective, physical-mental, personal-collective etc. and with taking their interaction into the focus. Certainly, it does not narrow down the environment either to libraries or to forests loud by twittering birds. Furthermore, as for in the interactions between the individual and environment it regards the personal behaviour as a driving motor for the development taking place during human actions. In the simple sense that the one who does not do anything will grow old as well, but more active the person's life is the more the process of growing old or ageing will become the process of lifelong continuous development.

Natural (informal) learning is viewed with suspicion from the schools separated from real life. It may have numerous reasons, but the most important is that by definition one can learn only good things in schools while in real life one can learn both good and bad things, too – or according to the more pessimistic ones only bad things can be acquired. There can be several interpretations of good in the sense of pedagogy and andragogy, but the most fundamental is the relation of learning to the individual development and social development. Learning that serves the individual and social development is considered to be good, or at least does not spoil the future perspectives. Oliver Twist was taught to steal in a perfect way, although herewith his future opportunities and chances for development were drastically limited. The one who makes himself master of cheating in the university in the short-term or from time to time can be more successful than his fellows, but the chance for lifelong development and its soundness is very small.

The education policy of Lifelong Education (UNESCO) primarily focuses on the widening of the meaning of education which has been unnaturally narrowed down to formal (school) learning, together with all its practical consequences. As opposed to the rapidly widespread misunderstanding it is not about that society should transform into being a school, however its reverse is also not valid, i.e. deschooling of the society. It essentially means an amendment, that is the broadening of the horizon of education, which in this way will include non-formal as well as informal learning in addition to formal learning. The concept of new, broader horizon based learning also includes extracurricular knowledge acquisition. As a result of the broadening of the definition all the support activities of education (counselling, development, assessment and evaluation, as well as organisation, management and financing, among others) should also include all types of learning. This, on the one hand will lead to the transformation of the traditional roles in the school.

On the other hand, all other life activities should be organised in a way that they could enable and inspire everybody to learn and develop, or at least not to eliminate learning or make it superfluous. The main function of adult education is not individual therapy but to enhance the transformation and development of the human being's relationships, activities and practices as the "informal" reproduction of the individual takes place through these everyday activities. It does make a difference whether this reproduction – even of themselves and each other - occurs "in a simple way" or "in a tightened way", let it be "in an enhanced way".

It is not an easy task for the reform policy even in the case of formal learning to launch a comprehensive change in the institution system. To increase the developmental effect of both work and life seemed to be impossible or utopistic even a few decades ago regarding the activities outside the school. Since educational policy had no impact at all on the decision makers of economic life, political arena, cultural life and media, etc. Yet, today the practical everyday vocabulary consists of words like informational society, e-Europe, knowledge-based society, human resource development, knowledge management, family-friendly workplace, human and social capital, emotional intelligence, learning organisation as well as reflective practitioner, common actions and communities of practice, partnerships and the learning society and so on. These signal the actual need for learning and development being constantly present in the world of labour as well as other areas of society. Leaders of prosperous multinational companies explain with ease in the media that the ground of their stable competitiveness is their considerable and continuous investment into their human and social resources. Beside the quality improvement logo, many companies proudly wear the logo of being a human investor, too.

"Non-learning" activities

Lifelong Education aimed at widening the scope of social support and recognition to all types of learning activities regardless of organisation, age and place or institution. Since formal (and non-formal) learning is just the top of the iceberg whose predominating part consists of the invisible natural (informal) learning. In reality, "non-learning activities" are activities with "non-learning purpose" at their best or they considered to be "simply" indirect learning activities since learning is an inevitable concomitant of every human activity and every natural, social and historical interaction. Learning is inseparable from human activities. Intended learning and its determined organisation, management, formalization just improves or enhances the frequency, intensity, efficiency, quality of learning, and so on. However, means-end rational kind of management and formalization of learning can be just indirectly aimed at learning as such, because learning itself is an inner process of changing. (In itself, the external behavioural change of the individual can be interpreted as a temporarily applied tactics.). The education directly can be aimed at the activity. In the case of schools, it aims at activities with learning purposes. Learning is just an indirect objective, though it is to be realized in all probabilities. The indirect management of learning takes place by selecting and forming environments, contexts, activities and system of activities with presumably great learning yield.

From this point of view, the origin of higher education and moreover of the top-down system of education is the university itself which can be considered as an archetype for the academic practice. In fact, at the outset, it was rather a knowledge-producing institution than a knowledge-applying one. The English connotation – i.e. academic- still preserves this feature. In general, instructors of a new "subject" are taught by no one but they clarify the teachable knowledge and transfer it on the bases of their own practice or research. "Taught teachers" succeeding this first generation are not more than simple multiplicators. Scientific disciplines, fields of education and subjects developed parallel with each other.

Nowadays, at the same time, the bottom up education system – developing from the practical educational needs – has also reached the level of higher education. In fact, the number of the years spent studying in these colleges belonging to this range is almost five years, which is an established fact in the case of universities. Therefore, neither the lines of traditional academic (scientific nature) nor of the college (practical nature) should be merged – as it started on the secondary level by "bridging the cap" of vocational secondary schools to secondary grammar schools – but they both should be organized according to 3+2 division of education. This would contribute to the end of the mass-like, but at the same time illusive demand for the academic (scientific) education. However, the only motivation for this is the different level of compensation categories related to the university or college degree and the demand for earning the necessary certificates for this. On the condition that they would consider the difference between the university and college education not as a qualitative one but only as a functional difference – as it historically developed – then the universities should not be feared of the "massification" and should not compel students – who never have inclination and aptitude - for academic (theoretical) pseudo accomplishment. It is also a superstition that just the "better ones" apply for universities and the less talented attend colleges. This is just an illusion that can exist as long as the measuring criteria are academically biased. So the majority of students enter a competition that is unfamiliar from their interest and aptitude. This is akin to if allegedly all sportsmen and not just the swimmers should compete with each other at the Olympic Games.

Against the labels

Certainly the labels of either the "university" or "college" should not be necessarily attached to institutions – or not at all – but rather to programmes. As universities may have college faculties then colleges may offer academic programmes as well, since the research of various fields of study and the advanced stage and development of the different disciplines are similarly at different levels. Moreover, the European or global division of labour makes it unnecessary to have a department of every discipline in every small country.

As a consequence of these and other reasons, the ambitions – whether they are ruled by everyday market demands or narrow-minded individual interests withdrawn behind the shield of institutional anatomy – leaving the nearly thousand years old history of higher education out of consideration cannot be dominant in defining the functions of higher education (university, college). To analyse the functions of higher education primarily in relation to the market demands is not just profane but also simply ridiculous. It is at least ridiculous as for example a blindfolded player who is trying to solve a jigsaw puzzle of an elephant. Nevertheless, to merchandise the free capacities seems to be logical from the side of the writing desk. However, in the real world it occurs every time that more capacity is made available then necessary in order to expand the directly profitable (well-paid) services. This only can be supported if the government subsidies are divided in a quasi-market form among the citizens, thus state-funded students appear as quasi consumers. But the task of comparative researches is to verify scientifically the actual realization of the so-called best practices. Anyone can elaborate on the functions of higher education, and then it would result in undervaluing the research made on higher education or – if it is more understandable nowadays – it would result in falling short of the profits of investments invested into the research of higher education provided the decisions are made without the scientific conversation of the researchers of higher education. Defining the institutional function of the university being widespread in time and space is not a matter of voluntary decision, but it requires scientific analysis. Even the Parliament has the right to make decisions of certain universities but it has no right to question what can be considered to be a university.

Before arriving at an academic definition of the functions of higher education we cannot define the adult educational functions of higher education either. We can only outline certain objectives and tasks. However, these are arguable if it is needed. Even the label of target group is equally arguable, because it is not justified by any of the rational arguments that students can be divided as adults taking the adult education act into effect while others are not considered to be adults although members of both groups are of full age. To enhance further the scope of target group or rather the stakeholders, today all higher education institutions keep their would-be or potential students in their horizon besides present ones. Open University defines the scope of potential students in a broadened way in relation to the traditional definition. It does not define requirements for admission but within the Open University everybody can reach the desired level.

If we want to define the target group of higher education in the spirit of LLL, we can say: higher education for everyone. Why? Because it is a basic human right. Or more specifically: to give sense to the twelve years spent in public education. The top-down system of education will only make sense at the lowest level if it provides access to the highest one and finally the degree and the activity whose thorough grounding is justified by the degree. The following diagram demonstrates this concept as a reminder of the conversations held about the functions of higher education and adult education:

The broad arrows signal the fairly independent activities, interaction is shown by rectangular arrows, while mutual interaction is shown by two-way arrows. Learning (may) last lifelong, although it is not a unified process especially if we think of LLL. Learning is attached to two merely different groups of activity. On the one hand, it is divided into formal and non-formal activities with learning purposes and on the other hand, to activities with non-learning purpose and to activities with no means-end rational purpose. This second kind of learning is summarized by informal learning that also can be called as natural learning, as, in case of sufficient conditions, it is an inevitable concomitant of every activity. The activities that are being analysed as learning are either formal activities or non-formal ones. Unfortunately, if we talk about learning, teaching, and education we repeatedly realize that the vocabulary is developed with regard to the school. As for formal education we register for and participate in learning activities. Whereas informal learning take place while we – according to our intentions - take part in activities organized by different objectives. Lifelong formal learning can occur, that is we can return to the educational system more than once during our life, while informal learning begins with our birth (or perhaps even earlier) and only ends with our death, while it takes place with very inconstant intensity or it is just undetected.

The figure shows that teaching covers learning in its full length. To be more precise the variant and supplement of teaching within schools is befitting with supporting informal learning: counselling, training, facilitating, mentorship, learning development, learning support, management, evaluation, recognition, rewarding and so on. University education extracts from the process of accumulation (retrieval, communications, informatics etc.). New knowledge is accumulated onto the input of storage by research. However, looking back at the history of universities it is evident that research derived from university professions (theology, medical treatment, jurisprudence etc.). Doctors and nurses even nowadays can think of both research and education that would serve the therapeutic and preventing work.

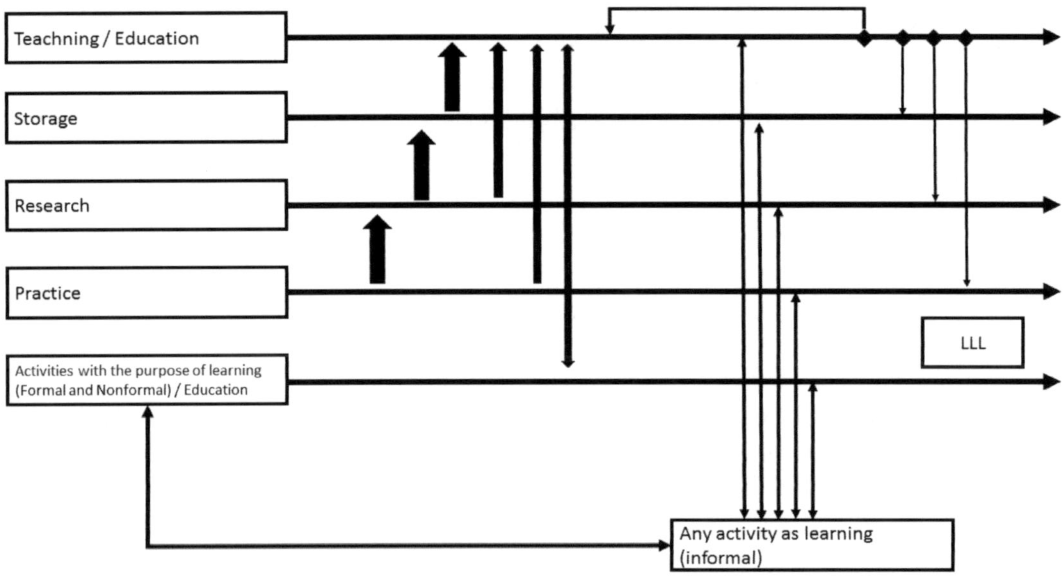

Figure 1.

The main flow in the figure indicates how knowledge gradually flows from practice towards teaching and from teaching towards learning. The narrower lines signal all other influences, which sometimes are more effective than the mainstream influence. As for an example, everybody who teaches knows well that the teaching material is acquired the best during teaching. Many of the teachers frequently apply this as a deliberate method by the means of reviews done by students or "peer-tutoring" or "peer-review" etc.

University traditionally is a knowledge accumulative and knowledge disseminative practice. The students are our future colleagues who will take over and pass on the knowledge through generations and centuries. This is the essential meaning of university. However, there will only be a few who turn towards research, while others will be disseminators of knowledge, and others again will "only" put their knowledge into practice but at the meantime are not engaged with the enhancement and dissemination of knowledge. These three groups – bailing out from the same resource, but with different fields of interest – require three different types of adult education. In addition to these groups there are several others with different interests who turn to universities for what they can offer. They, however, do not need special treatment.

The nature of information society

Due to the nature of the information age, lifelong learners want to acquire knowledge on a broader horizon, and the internet is already used as common ground for quick and convenient access to information that is free to everyone. In this enterprise, many of the learners need to get help but for the time being, the current institutions only largely support institutionalized formal learning.

One of the characteristics of the information society is that it requires digital literacy. Digital literacy as a basic requirement of lifelong learning and is the ability to use the value of digital culture, which means not only the efficient use of a wide range of digital devices but the smart use and selection of digital content. Those learners who lack digital literacy are already suffering consequences, for example at the labour market. In the current state, the older – roughly the X – generation suffers a disadvantage that is no longer involved in the formal acquisition of digital competences. At the same time, the traditional patterns of acquiring knowledge have changed: lifelong learning becomes prevalent, the conceptual gape between the child and the adulthood fades again, and formal school institutions are increasingly being replaced by virtual environments of learning (Benedek, 2008). The growing amount of information surrounding us has radically changed the roles of teachers. Thus, teachers do not only function as a source of information, but they are called upon to provide methodological assistance to the learners and serve as moderators.

The proliferation of information used in lifelong learning is not a new phenomenon. By the middle of the 20th century, it had reached a level where storing knowledge become a problem. Vannevar Bush had described a machine called Memex, which was intended to navigate through the ever-increasing amount of knowledge. The table-sized Memex would have stored the information on a microfilms (texts and pictures), and their linking would have been done by "trailblazers". This way, the paths to knowledge would have been paved (Bush, 1945).

The nature of 21st century technologies, assumes living in the age of digital devices and content. It also transforms the way how we learn. Computing and digital devices are built into our everyday processes that remain undetected (Kálmán et al., 2018; Szűts, 2018)

According to László Z. Karvalics, "postmodern scenarios related to knowledge point out that our brains have become unsuitable for navigating the millennium's information flood" (Karvalics, 2003; pp.178-179).

The use of social media in lifelong learning

Today previously unprecedented opportunities non-formal and lifelong learning can be enumerated. The popular platforms of social media (Facebook, YouTube, Twitter, etc.) have become the field of educational experimentation. Facebook's news feed for example provides access to information independently of space and time, while students are organized in groups related to classes and subjects. Typically, these groups and their communication are less organized than in traditional education and depend on the individual ambition of the members.

In Facebook groups without educators, the focus is much more on communication and sharing opinions, and typically discussions can heat up relatively fast, and often, in the absence of supervision, the information shared is incorrect. On the other hand, the groups in which the instructors are active, generally show less communication activity and weaker cooperation between the members, but the information shared is correct. These groups are also characterized by far fewer questions and weaker interactions, so the personal motivation for learning is important.

In addition to Facebook Twitter also plays a role in lifelong education. The tweets provide a relevant communication form, where 140-character message limit expects good writing skills and the ability so summarize information. For example, learners who share information about their learning related topics this way will learn to make summaries. YouTube can also play a part in lifelong learning. The video content available in the YouTube EDU project is very rich. From writings on literature to atomic physics, from popular culture to know how on digital competencies, learning materials are available across a wide horizon, creating the world's largest free multimedia library. The largest video sharing site provides a feature that TV channels do not. Thanks to interactivity on YouTube channels, learners can comment on any topic and initiate a dialogue. Discussions using comments under the videos are more intensive than those of university seminars, but in most cases the role of the moderators is missing.

There is a clear turn towards the transformation of the educational power centres that seems to have been permanent for centuries because of online communication and social media. All the rituals associated with the phenomenon of learning are reinterpreted. Class attendance (linked to space and time), personal consultation (interpersonal communication with an instructor), teacher-disciple relations (significance of the teacher's personality), taking notes (recording knowledge), will be placed on new, digital foundations. As a consequence of this recognition, since 2012, as a collaboration of the world's leading universities, massive open online courses (MOOCs) were launched. Learning has thus become even more independent of space and time. The personal consultation with the teacher was replaced by chat and forum discussions among the students. Learning has thus become horizontal, and learners can learn from their instructors and peers the same time. They do not need to take notes (but digital dementia is getting stronger), free online courses include notes, and the knowledge base wiki databases or the Google search engine is at the forefront. The most well-known enterprises offering online courses (edX, Coursera) have millions of registered students, a huge number of the being lifelong learners. However, in the case of MOOCs there are also several challenges, the biggest being that only 10% of finish them, so there is a huge dropout rate due to lack of motivation.

Conclusion

Teaching-learning and lifelong learning have become an inevitable issue of the changed teacher-student relationship (besides the omniscient teacher, the knowledge that can be found on the network), the question of authentic sources and the way of gaining knowledge independent of space and time and educational institutions. The incorporation of digital devices, content and networks into the everyday life have radically changed the mechanism of obtaining information, reading and learning. There is a need for lifelong learning and immediate knowledge acquisition. In the midst of the information society, the nature of knowledge is changing: it becomes practical, multi-media and transdisciplinary.

References

Benedek, A. (Ed.) (2008). *Digitális pedagógia. Tanulás IKT környezetben* [Digital Pedagogy. Learning in ICT environment]. Budapest: Typotex.

Bush, V. (1945). As We May Think. *Atlantic Monthly, July*, 101–108.

Field, J. (2001). Lifelong education. *International Journal of Lifelong Education, 20*(1/2), 3-15.

Jackson, N. (2012). Lifewide learning: History of an idea. Lifewide Learning, Education and Personal Development EBook, (February), 1–30. Retrieved from http://www.lifewideebook.co.uk/conceptual.html

Kálmán, A. (2016). The meaning and importance of Thomas Kuhn's concept of 'paradigm shift'. How does it apply in Education? *Opus et Educatio: Munka és Nevelés, 3*(2) 96-107.

Kálmán A. (2018). Changing Lifelong Learning Paradigm and the Digital Learning Age. In A. Volungeviciene & A. Szűcs (Eds.), *EDEN 2018 ANNUAL Conference: Exploring the Micro, Meso and Macro. Genova, Italy, European Distance and E-Learning Network (EDEN)*, 288-295.

Kálmán, A., Balomenou, C., & Kolovos, K. (2018). Comparative analysis if the implementation of Triple Helix Theory in Greece and Hungary, its impact on the local entrepreneurship and lessons learned from both cases'. Retrieved from http://www-sre.wu.ac.at/ersa/ersaconfs/ersa14/e140826aFinal00954.pdf

Kálmán, A., Molnár Gy., & Szűts, Z. (2018). Issues of Lifelong Learning – Behavioral ends of teaching and learning through ICT. In Gy. Sallai (Ed.), *9th IEEE International Conference on Cognitive Infocommunications: CogInfoCom 2018 Proceedings. Budapest, Hungary, IEEE Computational Intelligence Society, 2018* (pp. 395-398).

Szűts, Z. (2018). *Online.* Budapest: Wolters Kluwer.

Z. Karvalics, L. (2003). *Információ, társadalom, történelem* [Information, Society, History]. Budapest: Typotex.

Z. Karvalics, L. (2005). Információ, tudás, társadalom, gazdaság, technológia: egy egységes terminológia felé. [Information, Knowledge, Society, Economy, Technology. Towards a unified terminology]. *Információs társadalom, 5*(4), 7-17.

European Distance and E-Learning Network (EDEN)
Budapest University of Technology & Economics
H-1111 Budapest, Egry J. u.1.
Hungary

CURRAN ASSOCIATES INC.
proceedings.com

ISBN 978-1-7138-2382-7